Bank Politics

Bank Politics

Structural Reform in Comparative Perspective

DAVID HOWARTH
SCOTT JAMES

OXFORD
UNIVERSITY PRESS

Great Clarendon Street, Oxford, OX2 6DP,
United Kingdom

Oxford University Press is a department of the University of Oxford.
It furthers the University's objective of excellence in research, scholarship,
and education by publishing worldwide. Oxford is a registered trade mark of
Oxford University Press in the UK and in certain other countries

© David Howarth and Scott James 2023

The moral rights of the authors have been asserted

Impression: 1

All rights reserved. No part of this publication may be reproduced, stored in
a retrieval system, or transmitted, in any form or by any means, without the
prior permission in writing of Oxford University Press, or as expressly permitted
by law, by licence or under terms agreed with the appropriate reprographics
rights organization. Enquiries concerning reproduction outside the scope of the
above should be sent to the Rights Department, Oxford University Press, at the
address above

You must not circulate this work in any other form
and you must impose this same condition on any acquirer

Published in the United States of America by Oxford University Press
198 Madison Avenue, New York, NY 10016, United States of America

British Library Cataloguing in Publication Data
Data available

Library of Congress Control Number: 2022942794

ISBN 978–0–19–289860–9

DOI: 10.1093/oso/9780192898609.001.0001

Printed and bound by
CPI Group (UK) Ltd, Croydon, CR0 4YY

Links to third party websites are provided by Oxford in good faith and
for information only. Oxford disclaims any responsibility for the materials
contained in any third party website referenced in this work.

Preface

As we write, it is over thirteen years since the collapse of Lehman Brothers, the fourth largest investment bank in the United States. The international financial system is beginning to re-emerge from another bout of instability, this time triggered by the economic shutdown necessitated by the Covid-19 pandemic. The fact that the banking systems in advanced economies appear to have emerged in significantly better shape than they did following the collapse of the United States (US) sub-prime mortgage market in 2007 is arguably testament to the effectiveness of the raft of new regulation imposed on the banking sector over the past decade. These new rules have taken a variety of forms, from higher capital and liquidity requirements, and new rules on bank recovery and resolution, through to bonus caps, bank levies, and strengthened criminal sanctions. The authors of a number of these new regulations claimed to have addressed one of the fundamental challenges posed by the 2008 crisis: the fact that the largest banks had become 'too-big-to-fail' (TBTF)—shorthand for the argument that some banks had simply become so systemically important that no government could ever permit them to fail. As critics pointed out, this meant that TBTF banks posed a threat to financial stability by incentivizing greater risk-taking and speculative activity, enjoyed an implicit state subsidy in the form of lower external funding costs, and would impose an intolerable burden on taxpayers through the guarantee of a bail-out in the event of failure.

As political economists with a longstanding interest in the power and politics of banking, and the political economy of financial regulation more broadly, we were drawn inexorably to the topic of TBTF banks. Our curiosity was piqued by the fact that one of the most important regulatory innovations designed to address directly the issue of TBTF—namely, bank structural reform—proved to be one of the most divisive. Structural reform refers to financial regulations that restrict the ability of retail banks to engage in higher-risk speculative trading and 'market making', either through statutory bans or the structural separation of these activities from deposit taking. We were particularly fascinated by the extent of divergence between different countries with regard to the stringency, scope, and breadth of these reforms. This divergence stood in stark contrast to the trend towards greater financial regulatory coordination and harmonization, through the development of common European Union (EU) rules or global standards, that characterizes most other areas of post-crisis banking regulation. The empirical record therefore presented us with an intellectual puzzle that was simply too tempting to ignore.

We were therefore somewhat surprised to discover that scholarship on bank structural reform since the global financial crisis is rather limited. Despite the existence of several single case and small comparative studies on the subject, we believed that a more in-depth, book-length comparative analysis of the topic was urgently needed. Our motivation was to see if the comparative method could shed important new light on the surprising variation in regulatory outcomes—from stringent reform through to no reform at all—on bank structural reform in major economies. This variation was all the more puzzling given that many of the countries that interested us in Europe and North America were host to numerous TBTF banks that had suffered large losses after 2007, necessitating huge government bail-outs and fanning the flames of public anger towards the banking industry. We were also keen to understand the starkly divergent outcomes of the world's two largest financial jurisdictions—the US and the EU—which appeared to confound widely held perceptions about their respective proclivity for tough financial rules.

In writing this book we have drawn on research undertaken for a number of journal articles that we have published in recent years. Indeed, what sparked our initial interest in this topic was the immensely rewarding experience of editing (with Huw Macartney) a special issue in the journal *Business and Politics* on 'Bank Power and Public Policy since the Financial Crisis', published in January 2020 (Vol. 22, SI. 1). Furthermore, the article that we wrote for this special issue (see Howarth and James 2020) provided a valuable testing ground for the early theoretical development and empirical analysis that we develop and extend in the book. Chapter 5 also draws on research conducted for James (2018). The authors acknowledge the generous financial support of the Economic and Social Research Council, which helped to fund part of the early research on the chapter on the United Kingdom (UK) (grant reference ES/K001019/1), and the Luxembourg Fonds National de la Recherche, which funded part of the research on the EU, French and German chapters (grant reference C19/IS/13712846).

Almost certainly our book would never have been written without the immeasurable help, support, and advice of fellow scholars. We would like to thank a range of academic colleagues for their helpful feedback on our analytical approach and the empirical details of our case studies. The authors tested their analytical framework at a number of academic conferences and with a range of financial sector actors in London, Luxembourg, and elsewhere. The intellectual journey for the book began with the organization of a workshop by David Howarth and Huw Macartney on 'The Politics and Political Economy of Bank Reform: Ten Years after the Financial Crisis' for the 46th European Consortium of Political Research (ECPR) Joint Sessions of Workshops at the University of Nicosia, Cyprus, in April 2018. The lively discussion and constructive feedback that this workshop fostered subsequently formed the basis for the *Business and Politics* special issue mentioned above. A revised version of our comparative paper was also presented at the ECPR General Conference at the University of Hamburg in August 2018 and at the Luxembourg Monthly Finance Lunch organized by the Institute for Global Financial Integrity in June 2018. The main arguments made in this book were later presented at a Leiden University summer school in June 2021, at a research seminar at the Sheffield Political Economy Research Institute, University of Sheffield, in September 2021, at the European Consortium of Political Research Standing Group on the EU biennial conference, Luiss University, Rome, and at the Council for European Studies biennial conference, University Institute of Lisbon, both in June 2022.

Although the participants at the numerous conferences and workshops at which earlier iterations of our research were presented are too numerous to mention, we would like to single out the following for special thanks for stimulating discussions, productive exchanges, and collaboration over many years: Huw Macartney, Lucia Quaglia, Aneta Spendzharova, Manuela Moschella, Elsa Massoc, Joseph Ganderson, Jasper Blom, Shawn Donnelly, Iain Hardie, Clément Fontan, Dora Piroska, Stefano Pagliari, and Kevin Young. We also wish to thank the anonymous reviewers for the feedback and comments on our initial book proposal, as well as the fifty policy makers, financial regulators, and financial industry practitioners that selflessly gave up their time so that we could interview them for our book. Finally, we are immensely grateful to the series editor at Oxford University Press, Dominic Byatt, for his prompt interest in and unstinting commitment to our project.

Scott James is indebted to the Department of Political Economy at King's College London for providing a thriving intellectual space and welcoming environment within which the book could develop. Scott is also grateful to the Sheffield Political Economy Research Institute at the University of Sheffield where he was based as a visiting researcher between July and December 2021. The institute provided a wonderful academic 'second home' for completing the book—as such, special thanks must go to Colin Hay and Tom Hunt for making this possible, and to Andrew Hindmoor, Simon Bulmer, and Scott Lavery for their incisive comments and feedback. David Howarth would like to extend his thanks the Institute of Political Science at the University of Luxembourg for its generous financial assistance, which made possible several trips to conduct interviews and graduate student research and editorial assistance. David is also grateful to the Department of Political Science at Leiden University where he was a visiting professor between March and July 2021.

Our book also benefited greatly from the work of five graduate student helpers. Margot Bouchez, a University of Luxembourg Master's student, and Sean Domberg, a former Master's student at the University of Maastricht, located and translated Dutch-language material. Moritz Rehm, a doctoral student at the University of Luxembourg, located and translated German-language material. Sébastian Commain, also a doctoral student at the University of Luxembourg, undertook a number of interviews in Brussels and Paris. Mia Dzepina, another

University of Luxembourg Master's student, assisted with proof reading the text and the preparation of references. Harpal Hungin, a former Ph.D. student at the European University Institute and co-author with Scott James, was also a great source of assistance on regulatory developments in the US, and we are indebted to him for granting us permission to quote several interviews that he conducted with US policy makers as part of his doctoral thesis.

Lastly, but surely not least, we also thank our families and friends for their unwavering support and patience over the past few years.

David Howarth
Scott James

Luxembourg and London
August 2022

Contents

List of Tables	x
List of Abbreviations	xi
1. Introduction: The Puzzle of Bank Structural Reform	1
2. A Comparative Financial Power Approach	31
3. Failing to Tame Too-Big-To-Fail Banks	65
4. From Obama to Trump: Contested Reform in the United States	108
5. The Importance of Being Vickers: Venue Shifting in the United Kingdom	142
6. Germany: Defending Deutsche Bank AG	170
7. France: Defending the National Champions	191
8. The Netherlands: Shifting Structural Reform Off the Agenda	215
9. Liikanen's Legacy: Financial Power and Political Stalemate in the European Union	240
10. Conclusion: Contribution and Future Research	274
References	292
Index	344

List of Tables

1.1.	Overview of adopted bank structural reforms in the UK, US, France, and Germany	4
1.2.	Bank Funding Gap, case study countries, per cent, 2000–7	9
1.3.	Largest universal banks, total assets and as a percentage of national GDP (case study countries; total assets, national currency, billions), end 2000, 2007, 2011, 2014	11
1.4.	Banking system assets as a percentage of GDP, 2002–16	13
1.5.	Banking system assets as a percentage of total financial institution assets (case study countries), 2002–16	13
1.6.	Banking system concentration (percentage of total assets held by largest three/five banks), 2002–16	14
1.7.	Number of systemically important banks by country at end 2018	14
2.1.	Outcomes of bank structural reform	61
3.1.	National rescues/protection of TBTF banks, 2007–10	71
3.2.	Revenue-raising measures to diminish bank risk and cover bail-out costs	73
3.3.	Regulatory measures to diminish TBTF bank risk	78
3.4.	Bank tier-1 capital ratio (as a percentage of risk-weighted assets, recall Basel III target of 6% with at least 4.5% of RWA; 10.5–13% with buffers; case study countries), 2008–18	86
3.5.	Bank leverage: simple tier-1 unweighted capital ratio (recall Basel III target of at least 3%; case study countries), 2008–16	87
3.6.	Bank liquid assets as a percentage of total assets (case study countries), 2002–16	93
3.7.	Share of deposits in total funding (as a percentage of total funding; case study countries), 2002–16	94
3.8.	Share of borrowing in total bank funding (as a percentage of total funding; case study countries), 2006–16	94
3.9.	Bank financial liabilities held for trading as a percentage of total assets (France, Germany, and the Netherlands), 2008–18	95
3.10.	Bank governance measures to diminish TBTF bank risk	100
3.11.	Reinforced supervision to diminish TBTF bank risk	103

List of Abbreviations

ABA	American Banking Association
ABCP	Asset-Backed Commercial Paper
ABI	Association of British Insurers; Italian Banking Association
ABN AMRO	Algemene Bank Nederland-Amsterdam Rotterdam Bank
ABS	Asset Backed Securities
ADAM	Association for the Defence of Small Shareholders (Association de défense des petits actionnaires)
AFEP	French Association of Private Enterprises (Association française des entreprises privées)
AFG	French Society of Financial Analysts (Association française de la gestion financière)
AFME	Association for Financial Markets in Europe
AFR	Americans for Financial Reform
ALDE	Alliance of Liberals and Democrats for Europe
AMF	Financial Markets Authority (Netherlands) (Autoriteit Financiële Markten) / Financial Markets Authority (France) (Autorité des marches financiers)
ANP	Netherlands News Agency (Algemeen Nederlands Persbureau)
ATTAC	Anti-capitalism/anti-globalization movement
BaFin	German Federal Financial Supervisory Authority (Bundesanstalt für Finanzdienstleistungsaufsicht)
BBA	British Bankers' Association
BBVA	Banco Bilbao Vizcaya Argentaria
BCBS	Basel Committee on Banking Supervision
BCC	British Chambers of Commerce
BCCI	Bank of Credit and Commerce International
BDA	Confederation of German Employers' Associations (Bundesvereinigung der Deutschen Arbeitgeberverbände)
BDB	German Banking Association (Bundesverband deutscher Banken)
BDI	Federation of German Industries (Bundesverband der Deutschen Industrie)
BEUC	European Consumer Organization
BFI	Bureau of Financial Institutions
BIS	Bank for International Settlements
BRRD	Bank Recovery and Resolution Directive
BNP	Banque Nationale de Paris
BPCE	Banques Populaires, Caisses d'Epargne

BVR	Federal Association of German Cooperative Banks (Bundesverband der Deutschen Volksbanken und Raiffeisenbanken)
CBI	Confederation of British Industry
CCAR	Comprehensive Capital Analysis and Review
CCPs	Central counterparties
CCSF	Financial Sector Advisory Committee (Comité consultatif du secteur financier)
CDA	Dutch Christian Democratic Party
CDU	German Christian Democratic Union
CEBS	Committee of European Banking Supervisors
CEOs	Chief executive officers
CET	Common Equity Tier
CFPB	Consumer Financial Protection Bureau
CFTC	Commodity Futures Trading Commission
CGT	General Confederation of Labour (Confédération Générale du Travail)
CMOC	Commodity Markets Oversight Coalition
COREFRIS	Council of Financial Regulation and Systemic Risk (Conseil de régulation financière et du risque systémique)
CPE	Comparative political economy
CRAs	Credit rating agencies
CRDs	Capital Requirements Directives
CRR	Capital Requirements Regulation
CSU	Christian Social Union
CU	Dutch Christian Union
D66	Dutch Liberal Democrats
DFAST	Dodd–Frank Act stress tests
DGB	German Federation of Trade Unions (Deutscher Gewerkschaftsbund)
DGS	Deposit Guarantee Scheme
DIF	Deposit Insurance Fund
DIHK	German Chamber of Commerce and Industry (Deutscher Industrie und Handelskammertag)
DK	German Banking Industry Committee (Deutsche Kreditwirtschaft)
DNB	Dutch central bank (De Nederlandsche Bank)
DSGV	German Savings Banks and Giro Association (Deutscher Sparkassen und Giroverband)
EACB	European Association of Cooperative Banks
EAPB	European Association of Public Banks
EBA	European Banking Authority
EBRD	European Bank for Reconstruction and Development
EBF	European Banking Federation
ECB	European Central Bank
ECOFIN	Council of Economic and Finance Ministers
EEA	European Economic Area
EELV	Europe Écologie Les Verts (French Green Party)
EFA	European Free Alliance

EFR	European Financial Services Round Table
EMU	Economic and Monetary Union
ENA	National Administration School (Ecole Nationale d'Administration, France)
EPP	European People's Party
ESA(s)	European Supervisory Agency(ies)
ESBG	European Savings Banks Group
ESM	European Stability Mechanism
ESRB	European Systemic Risk Board
EU	European Union
FBC	Future of Banking Commission
FBF	French Banking Federation (Fédération bancaire française)
FCA	Financial Conduct Authority
FDIC	Federal Deposit Insurance Corporation
FDP	Free Democratic Party
FHFA	Federal Housing Finance Agency
FO	Force Ouvrière (French Trade Union)
FPC	Financial Policy Committee
FSA	Financial Services Authority
FSB	Federation of Small Businesses; Financial Stability Board
FSF	Financial Stability Forum
FSOC	Financial Stability Oversight Council
FSR	Financial Services Roundtable
FTT	Financial Transactions Tax
G7	Group of Seven
G20	Group of Twenty
GAO	Government Accountability Office
GDP	Gross domestic product
G-SIBs	Global systemically important banks
G-SIFIs	Global systemically important financial institutions
HBOS	Halifax Bank of Scotland
HQLAs	High-quality liquid assets
HRE	Hypo Real Estate
ICB	Independent Commission on Banking
ICBA	Independent Community Bankers of America
ICFR	International Centre for Financial Regulation
IDIs	Insured depository institutions
IFLR	*International Financial Law Review*
IIF	International Institute of Finance
IMF	International Monetary Fund
ING	International Nederlanden Groep
IPE	International political economy
IRSG	International Regulatory Strategy Group
ISDA	International Swaps and Derivatives Association
LAC	Loss Absorbing Capacity
LCR	Liquidity Coverage Ratio

Libor	London interbank offered rate
LTO	Dutch Federation of Agriculture and Horticulture (Land- en Tuinbouworganisatie)
MEDEF	French employers' association (Mouvement des entreprises de France)
MEP	Member of the European Parliament
MKB	Dutch Federation of Small and Medium-Sized Enterprises (Midden- en kleinbedrijf)
MREL	Minimum requirements for eligible liabilities
NCUA	National Credit Union Administration
NGOs	Non-governmental organizations
NSFR	Net Stable Funding Ratio
NVB	Dutch Banking Association (Nederlandse Vereniging van Banken)
OBR	Office for Budget Responsibility
OCC	Office of the Comptroller of the Currency
OFR	Office of Financial Research
OFT	Office of Fair Trading
OLA	Orderly Liquidation Authority
OTCDs	Over-the-counter derivatives
OTS	Office of Thrift Supervision
PACs	Political Action Committees
PCBS	Parliamentary Commission on Banking Standards
PCGD	Postcheque and Giro Service
PIRG	Public Interest Research Group
PRA	Prudential Regulatory Authority
PRC	Prudential Regulation Committee
PRG	Parti radical de gauche (French centre-left party)
PvdA	Dutch Labour Party
PVV	Dutch Party for Freedom
PwC	Pricewaterhouse Coopers
RBS	Royal Bank of Scotland
RCO	Council of Central Business Organization
RPS	Rijkspostspaarbank
RWAs	Risk-weighted assets
SEC	Securities and Exchange Commission
SER	Social and Economic Council
SIFIs	Systematically important financial institutions
SIFMA	Securities Industry and Financial Markets Association
SMEs	Small and medium-sized enterprises
SNS	Samenwerkende Nederlandse Spaarbanken (Co-operating Dutch Savings Banks)
SOMO	Stichting Onderzoek Multinationale Ondernemingen (Dutch Foundation for Research on Multinational Enterprises)
SP	Dutch Socialist Party
SPD	German Social Democratic Party
SPOE	Single Point of Entry

SRF	Single Resolution Fund
SRM	Single Resolution Mechanism
SRMR	Single Resolution Mechanism Regulation
SSM	Single Supervisory Mechanism
TARP	Troubled Asset Relief Program
TBTF	Too-big-to-fail
UK	United Kingdom
UKFI	UK Financial Investments
UMP	Union pour un mouvement populaire (French centre-right party)
US	United States
VNO-NCW	Confederation of Dutch Industry and Employers (Verbond van Nederlandse Ondernemingen (VNO) – Nederlands Christelijk Werkgeversverbond (NCW))
VÖB	Federal Association of German Public Sector Banks (Bundesverband Öffentlicher Banken Deutschland)
VoC	Varieties of Capitalism
VoFC	Varieties of Financial Capitalism
VVD	People's Party for Freedom and Democracy
WEED	World Economy, Ecology and Development
WRR	Scientific Council for Government Policy (Wetenschappelijke Raad voor het Regeringsbeleid)
WSBI	World Savings Banks Institute
ZDH	German Confederation of Skilled Crafts (Zentralverband des Deutschen Handwerks)
ZKA	Central Credit Committee (Zentraler Kreditausshuss)

1
Introduction
The Puzzle of Bank Structural Reform

1. From bail-outs to banking reform

The international financial crisis that began in 2007 imposed an unprecedented burden on taxpayers. It is estimated that bailing out the banking sector collectively cost EU member state governments €1.6tn (EU Parliament 2013, p. 4), while the US government faced a bill for $426.4bn. In response to mounting public anger and political pressure for reform, governments imposed a variety of new regulatory instruments designed to strengthen the stability of banking and wider financial systems: from higher capital requirements and new rules on bank resolution, to strengthened criminal sanctions and banking standards. Yet the most persistent issue, and arguably the most difficult to solve, has been how to address the problem of too-big-to-fail (TBTF): shorthand for the notion that some banks are simply so significant in economic terms that no government could ever permit them to fail. This, it is frequently argued, in effect amounts to an implicit state subsidy and exacerbates risk-taking behaviour through the creation of moral hazard (Alessandri and Haldane 2009; Haldane 2012; Hardie and Howarth 2013a; Bell and Hindmor 2015a). The need to protect taxpayers from future bail-outs by restricting the ability of retail banks to engage in higher-risk trading activities was a major theme of the 2009 G20 Pittsburgh Summit (G20 2009). Yet efforts to develop a coordinated approach at the international level have been limited, with the result that countries have pursued their own distinct reform trajectories (Spendzharova 2016). The central aim of this book is to understand why six jurisdictions with banking systems that are among the world's largest pursued such divergent approaches to banking reform.

The book addresses this puzzle by analysing the politics of bank structural reform in the US, EU, and four European countries with large economies and banking systems: the UK, France, Germany, and the Netherlands. In the decades prior to the financial crisis, the banking systems of all six jurisdictions shared a number of important features (Hardie and Howarth 2013a). All the cases we examine had seen the growth of large, universal banks. In the case of Europe, these banks were either explicitly or implicitly supported by governments and regulators as national champions. In the UK, France, and the Netherlands, these large banks also dominated lending to the real economy. More importantly, the large universal

Bank Politics. David Howarth and Scott James, Oxford University Press.
© David Howarth and Scott James (2023). DOI: 10.1093/oso/9780192898609.003.0001

banks in all six jurisdictions engaged in 'market-based banking', characterized by the rapid expansion of trading assets on bank balance sheets and increased dependence of banks on short-term wholesale financial markets to fund lending (Hardie and Howarth 2013a). These common trends brought risks, however. While hugely profitable, market-based banking brought greater vulnerability and weakness to disruption in financial markets, meaning that relatively small losses were amplified by the banks' large trading books (Bell and Hindmoor 2015a, p. 9). As a result, all five of our case study country banking systems were hit hard by the financial crisis—significantly in the US, the UK, the Netherlands, and Germany, albeit less in France—resulting in plummeting share prices and credit rating downgrades for the largest banks, and debt write-downs for several. Moreover, governments were forced to rescue their banks by providing unprecedented state support in the form of liquidity injections, government bail-outs, and credit guarantees (Woll 2014).

In the years that followed, politicians in all six jurisdictions came under political pressure to deal with the perception that banks had become TBTF. In particular, attention focused on excessive risk-taking and speculative activities within large banks, and how to eliminate the implicit subsidy they enjoyed from taxpayers. The impetus for structural reform frequently came from electoral dynamics: including the US presidential election in 2008 and mid-term elections in 2010, and national legislative elections in the UK in 2010, France in 2012 (legislative and presidential), the Netherlands in 2010 and 2012, and Germany in 2013. These dynamics led prominent political figures to make early commitments to pursue bank structural reform: in the US, President Obama made the surprise decision to support tough new restrictions on banks' speculative activities as part of his administration's flagship financial reform bill; in the UK, Prime Minister Cameron established an Independent Commission on Banking (ICB) to make recommendations on banking reform, under pressure from his coalition government partners; in France, President Hollande was elected in 2012 following a campaign that included a pledge to implement a full split between retail and investment banks; in Germany, Chancellor Merkel responded to pressure from the opposition Social Democratic Party for tough new bank 'ringfencing' rules by encouraging her government to develop its own proposals; and in the Netherlands, Finance Minister Wouter Bos spoke positively about the need for new restrictions on proprietary trading at the height of the crisis. In parallel to these developments, the EU Internal Market Commissioner, Michel Barnier, announced the creation of a High-Level Expert Group in 2011 to consider EU regulation on structural reform.

Despite these similarities, the outcome of reform in our six cases differs substantially. In the US, the Obama administration succeeded in mobilizing sufficient political support in Congress to secure legislative approval for a ban on proprietary trading (the 'Volcker Rule'). Likewise, in the UK, the Conservative–Liberal

Democrat coalition government moved quickly to endorse the recommendations of the Vickers Commission which set out to 'ringfence' banks' retail activities in legally separate entities, prohibiting them from trading in a range of financial instruments and subject to much higher capital requirements. In contrast, the French government soon backtracked on its earlier commitment to structural reform, while the German government never showed much enthusiasm. As a result, both governments implemented much weaker measures requiring banks to ringfence only a narrow set of proprietary trading activities, which did not significantly constrain their largest banks (Hardie and Macartney 2016; Spendzharova 2016; Massoc 2020). In the Netherlands, early support for structural reform—from the finance minister and left-wing opposition parties—was challenged by the conclusions of three separate commissions. As a result, the government opted to focus its reform efforts on enhancing bank supervision and curbing banker behaviour through bonus caps and codes of conduct. Finally, in an effort to foster the greater coordination of banking reform across Europe, the EU Commission developed its own ringfencing proposals, based on the recommendations of the expert group chaired by the Governor of the Bank of Finland, Erkki Liikanen. Yet despite Commission consultations attracting over 500 responses, and major debates in the European Parliament, structural reform stalled due to opposition in the Parliament to the weak version of reform accepted by member state governments, and the draft legislation was finally abandoned in October 2017.

The starting point of our analysis is that in all six jurisdictions, the issue of TBTF banking became a salient political issue from 2008, generating significant political pressure on policy makers—from legislators, opposition parties, financial regulators, civil society, and/or voters—to introduce reforms to bank structure. The puzzle we set out to address is why there was such wide divergence in regulatory outcomes in the US and Europe, as summarized in Table 1.1. In other words: *Why did some jurisdictions pursue significant bank structural reforms after the financial crisis, while other jurisdictions introduced only minimal or no reform at all?*

2. The limits of existing scholarship

There are strong empirical and theoretical grounds for writing a book on bank structural reform. The global financial crisis spawned a vast academic literature on the transformation of financial governance and financial regulation. Much of this has been devoted to analysing and explaining the raft of new international standards and EU-level rules introduced over the past decade (for example, see Lall 2012; Young 2012; Baker 2013a, 2013b; Rixen 2013, 2015; Helleiner 2014; Mügge 2014; Pagliari and Young 2014; Quaglia 2014a, 2014b; Goldbach 2015a, 2015b; Knaack 2015; Mügge and Stellinga 2015; Tsingou 2015; Ban, Seabrooke,

Table 1.1 Overview of adopted bank structural reforms in the UK, US, France, and Germany

	UK	US	France	Germany
Structural separation	The UK Financial Services (Banking Reform) Act stipulates that UK banks' retail activities—defined as deposits, small business lending, and payment systems—should be placed in a ringfenced subsidiary. These are no longer permitted to engage in the trading of derivatives and securities, provide services to other financial companies, or services to customers outside the European Economic Area (EEA). The ringfenced entity should also have independent governance and be legally separate and operationally separable.	The 'Volcker Rule' refers to section 619 of the Dodd-Frank Wall Street Reform and Consumer Protection Act. The rule prohibits banks from using their own accounts for short-term proprietary trading of securities, derivatives, and commodity futures, as well as options on any of these instruments, with exemptions for hedging purposes (i.e., interest rate and foreign currency swaps). The rule also bars depository institutions, banks, or insured depository institutions, from acquiring or retaining ownership interests in hedge funds or private equity funds, beyond a *de minimis* exemption (up to 3% of Common Equity Tier (CET) 1 capital / 3% ownership of fund capital).	French law (Law on the Separation and Regulation of Banking Activities—*la loi de séparation et de régulation des activités bancaires*, 2013) requires French banks and subsidiaries of foreign banks (by 2015) to separate certain trading and investment activities (purely speculative activities—few in number) into dedicated subsidiaries that are separately funded from the rest of the bank. The banks can keep the bulk of trading activities, such as market making, with the deposit-taking part of the bank (contrary to recommendations of the Liikanen Report). The ringfenced unit is banned from high-frequency trading and commodity derivatives trading. Retail deposits can thus continue to fund the bulk of speculative activities. A precise definition of whether trading is proprietary or for third parties is lacking.	German law (*Trennbankengesetz*, 2014) requires German banks and subsidiaries of foreign banks to spin off their proprietary trading activities into a company that is legally, economically, and organizationally separate. The law applies to banks with 'risky' activities (including proprietary trading, high-frequency trading or hedge fund financing, and other highly leveraged alternative investment fund operations) that either surpass €100bn in value or amounts to 20% or more of their balance sheets. Deposit-taking credit institutions will still be able to carry out proprietary trading on behalf of clients, including market making, but the German regulator will be empowered to demand the separation of market making in individual cases. Banks have until 1 July 2015 to establish a separate financial trading institution. A precise definition of whether trading is proprietary or for third parties is lacking.

Capital requirements for ringfenced entities	The Banking Reform Act imposes an additional CET1 'ringfence buffer' of up to 3% of risk-weighted assets (RWAs) for ringfenced banks (total 10%), and a leverage ratio (equity to assets) of 4.06% for ringfenced banks. No additional capital requirements beyond international standards are required for non-ringfenced banks.	Dodd–Frank sets a minimum CET1 ratio of 6%, a total capital ratio of 10%, and a minimum leverage ratio of 5% for the largest banks. The 'Collins Amendment' also mandates that capital requirements for bank holding companies be no less stringent than those for depositories.	No distinct capital rules for ringfenced activities. No additional CET1 'ringfence buffer'. Opposition to obligatory leverage ratio (for any banks).	No distinct capital rules for ringfenced activities. No additional CET1 'ringfence buffer'. Opposition to obligatory leverage ratio (for any banks).

and Freitas 2016; Gabor 2016; Howarth and Quaglia 2016b; Newman and Posner 2016a, 2016b, 2018; Quaglia and Spendzharova 2017a, 2019; Stellinga and Mügge 2017; Helleiner, Pagliari, and Spagna 2018). There is also a growing corpus of studies examining financial regulatory reforms adopted in key national jurisdictions (see Pagliari 2013a, 2013b; Kastner 2014; Thiemann 2014, 2018): first and foremost, the US (Carpenter 2010; Pagliari and Young 2014; Ziegler and Woolley 2016; Young and Pagliari 2017), the EU (Pagliari 2011, 2013b; Quaglia 2011, 2012, 2014a; Mügge 2012, 2014; Quaglia and Spendzharova 2017b); the UK (Baker 2013a, 2013b; Bell and Hindmoor 2015a, 2015b, 2016; James 2016, 2018; James and Quaglia 2019, 2020); France and Germany (Hardie and Macartney 2016; Howarth and James 2020; Howarth and Quaglia 2013a; Massoc 2020); and the Netherlands (Ganderson 2020a, 2020b).

Despite this, we argue that there exists a significant gap in the literature with respect to the empirical analysis of bank structural reform. This is not to deny that there have been a number of excellent studies analysing the development of new regulatory rules on the speculative activities of banks and the structural separation of retail and investment banking. Importantly, however, these studies tend to be either single case studies (e.g., Zeigler and Woolley 2016; James 2018; Massoc 2020) or typically only compare a few European countries (Bell and Hindmoor 2015a, 2015b; Hardie and Macartney 2016; Spendzharova 2016; Quaglia and Spendzharova 2017b; Ganderson 2020a, 2020b; Howarth and James 2020). To date, we are unaware of any attempt to conduct a wider comparison of more than three countries *or* to compare banking reform in the US with the European national and EU level experience.

Our book addresses this gap by undertaking a comprehensive comparative analysis of bank structural reform across six jurisdictions. Doing so enables us to address a series of academically and politically important questions. Why did the US and the UK respond robustly by introducing tough new ringfencing rules, while France and Germany were slow to respond and implemented much weaker structural reforms? In the Netherlands, why did structural reform fail to gain traction in the political debate, even though three high-profile commissions were created to discuss regulatory reform? To put it differently, why did the French, German, and Dutch governments choose to defend the interests of industry, while the US administration and the UK government pushed ahead with changes in the face of fierce opposition from their largest banks? Why did the EU Commission create a committee of 'wise men' to examine structural reform—the Liikanen Group—only to dilute significantly the group's proposals in its draft legislation, before scrapping EU-level reform altogether? Comparing cases of significant, limited, and no reform promises to shed new light on the political drivers of post-crisis regulatory divergence.

In Chapter 2, we review the explanatory power of prevailing theories in financial regulatory scholarship. For reasons that we outline at length, we argue that analytical approaches from the sub-disciplines of international political economy (IPE) and comparative political economy (CPE) are not well placed to explain post-crisis patterns of banking reform. For example, IPE explanations rooted in market power (Drezner 2007) and regulatory capacity (Bach and Newman 2007; Posner 2009, 2010) fail to explain why the US (and to a lesser extent, the UK) did not seek to exploit its first-mover position by pushing for greater international coordination of structural reform, modelled around the Volcker Rule. These theories also do a poor job of accounting for the limited role of transnational coalitions of public and private actors—both financial regulators and large banking institutions—in promoting greater international or EU-level harmonization in this area to minimize opportunities for regulatory arbitrage. Traditional CPE explanations, which assume that national regulators will always try to defend the economic interests of their domestic financial sector, are equally problematic. It is self-evident that these theories cannot explain why the two countries embodying a model of 'liberal market' capitalism, and long-standing cheerleaders for financial market deregulation, would move unilaterally to impose much tougher restrictions on their own banks. Similarly, alternative CPE-based accounts—which highlight either the importance of defending universal banks in Europe from US competitors, or variation in the international scope of national banking systems—do not map neatly onto government preferences on structural reform.

Recent studies on banking reform have opened up important new avenues of theoretical inquiry by seeking to 'bring the politics back in'. For example, Bell and Hindmoor (2015a) build on business power approaches by arguing that the politicization of financial regulation, strengthened state capacity, and ideational shifts among policy makers have all served to constrain the influence of financial sector lobbying. To explain the puzzle of financial reform in the US, Zeigler and Woolley (2016) point to the emergence of a highly vocal pro-reform coalition, composed of consumer groups, activists and think tanks, which kept banking reform in the spotlight and maintained pressure on Congress to act. Massoc (2020) develops this argument by examining the critical role of domestic political institutions in shaping the government preferences on bank regulatory reform in the UK, France, and Germany. In particular, she explains how these institutional structures determined the capacity of pro-reform 'factions'—often led by actors within the state—to resist industry lobbying and push for more stringent rules. By contrast, Ganderson (2020a) draws on the comparative democracy literature to contrast the effects produced by majoritarian and consensual party systems in shaping banking reform. His important contribution is to suggest that, while adversarial politics and executive power incentivized the adoption of tough new bank ringfencing rules in the UK, power sharing and coalition formation in the Netherlands reduced contestation between parties and led to political inaction from policy makers.

Nonetheless, we identify a number of limitations with these accounts. For example, while it is impossible to deny that heightened politicization, state capacity and changing ideas have served to constrain the power of banks since the crisis, these accounts fail to explain variation between countries on bank structural reform. In other words, there needs to be some basis for explaining why the politicization of and the relative influence of ideas on banking reform vary between countries. Similarly, focusing on the role of anti-finance coalitions and factions in mobilizing political support for banking reform offers essential new insights, but we would suggest that the precise causal mechanisms by which these societal forces emerge in some countries, but not others, remain under-specified.

Finally, we believe that explanations highlighting the role of political and party systems have been most effective in advancing our understanding. Yet even here, empirical puzzles remain when the framework is applied to a wider set of cases. In particular, while adversarial political culture most likely contributes to the scope of banking reform in the US and UK, and consensual politics potentially accounts for the timidity of reforms in Germany, and the lack of reform in the Netherlands and the EU, the example of France (which combines an adversarial party system with limited structural reform) is obviously more problematic. In addition, how can we explain the fact that bank structural reform *was* a highly salient and politically contested issue following the crisis in France, Germany, and the Netherlands, but was subsequently downplayed by policy makers? We suggest that trying to reduce explanations of structural reform to the institutional features of political systems risks falling into the same trap of structural determinism as CPE-based explanations: namely, that it tends to downplay the role of agency, uncertainty, and contingency in shaping policy outcomes.

3. Case selection and alternative explanations

To address these limitations in the literature, we undertake a comparative analysis of banking reform across multiple jurisdictions. This provides important methodological advantages. First and foremost, the examination of six cases considered in the book maximizes variation with respect to the dependent variable—bank structural reform. Hence, our case selection includes examples of both significant reform (the US and the UK), limited reform (France and Germany), and no reform (Netherlands and the EU) (see Table 1.1). This variation is important because it includes not only 'easy' examples of regulatory reform, but also 'harder' cases of failed or stalled reform. Comparing and contrasting the experiences of policy makers in these jurisdictions promises to reveal how shared policy challenges interact with complex and unpredictable political dynamics to produce a wide spectrum of outcomes.

In this section we detail key political and economic characteristics of our case studies and explain how these logically cannot explain the nature of variation in regulatory outcomes. We begin with important similarities in the development of national banking systems in the decade prior to the crisis. The most important relates to the growth of 'market-based banking' in all of our country cases, characterized by the rapid expansion of trading assets on bank balance sheets and increased dependence of banks on wholesale finance to fund lending (Hardie and Howarth 2013a). The increase in market-based activities was particularly striking in a number of EU member states as governments sought to promote the development of national banking 'champions' to compete with the long-standing financial behemoths of Wall Street. As a result, trading assets increasing from 20 per cent of total bank assets in 2000 to 45 per cent by 2007 in the UK, 13 per cent to 37 per cent in France, and 23 per cent to 50 per cent in the Netherlands (Chang and Jones 2013; Hardie et al. 2013; Howarth 2013). The rise of market-based banking also meant that large universal banks in all five countries became highly leveraged. Over time this seriously depleted their liquidity reserves, increasing the dependence of large universal banks on short-term wholesale funding and leaving them vulnerable to shocks in financial markets. One measure for this increased dependence is the bank funding gap, which is the extent to which bank lending must be financed in financial markets, through either direct sale or securitization, rather than through deposits (see Table 1.2). This gap was particularly high in the UK, the Netherlands, and France.[1] While this figure was lower in Germany—reflecting the relative importance of savings and cooperative banks—and low or negative in the US—reflecting the relative importance of smaller community banks in the country—it was much higher for the largest universal and investment banks in those two countries.

Table 1.2 Bank Funding Gap,* case study countries, per cent, 2000–7

	France	Germany	Netherlands	UK	US
2000	18.70	18.80	18.90	18.10	0.50
2001	16.60	30.39	38.14	4.45	−1.00
2002	19.70	31.60	48.89	13.57	−1.55
2003	14.25	28.01	51.51	25.39	−1.74
2004	15.26	22.79	59.85	32.07	−1.48
2005	16.53	16.53	48.69	34.55	−0.27
2006	25.77	12.6	46.58	43.45	1.26
2007	34.45	6.21	40.53	47.30	2.97

* Bank funding gap defined as percentage of lending not funded by deposits.
Source: ECB 2008; ECB data warehouse; supervisory and prudential statistics, bank sector variables, liquidity, and funding.

[1] The relatively high gap in Germany was covered largely by *Pfandbrief*, long-term bank debt.

Another feature common to the banking systems in all five of our country case studies was the significant increase in the size of the largest banks during the decade leading up to the financial crisis (see Table 1.3). In our European case studies, the assets held by a number of banks came close to the size of their home national economies. In the Netherlands, the three largest banks held assets exceeding the size of the national economy, while the value of International Nederlanden Groep (ING) assets in 2007 doubled national gross domestic product (GDP). While several of the largest banks decreased both in size and relative to the national economy over the decade following the financial crisis—notably in the UK, Germany and the Netherlands—several banks continued to grow in real and/or relative terms, notably in France. In all four of our European country cases, most of the banks that could be described as TBTF in 2007 remained so in 2011 and 2014.

Beyond this, however, the banking systems we analyse also differed in fundamental ways. Crucially, we find little evidence that these systematic differences correlate with the nature of banking reform. For example, the size of the financial, and specifically banking, sectors we examine varied significantly across our cases (see Table 1.4). Particularly noteworthy is the fact that the US and UK represent opposite extremes in terms of the relative size of their respective banking systems (as a proportion of GDP), and yet the two countries adopted similar bank structural reforms. Hence, there is little support for the claim that the stringency of post-crisis measures is related to the relative strategic importance of banking in the national economy, or a country's vulnerability to financial instability.

The relative position of banking within national financial systems also varied considerably among our case study countries (see Table 1.5).[2] The relative importance of banks in both the French and German financial systems might help to explain French and German government caution with regard to structural reform. However, the two countries in which banks had the smallest share of overall financial assets—the US and the Netherlands—adopted radically different policies on structural reform.

Levels of bank concentration may also plausibly provide an alternative explanation. On the one hand, a banking system dominated by a few, very large banks might be construed as a proxy indicator for institutions being TBTF. On the other hand, we might expect the banking industry in highly concentrated sectors to be more effective at wielding influence in the policy process on account of facing fewer barriers to collective action (Olson 1965). The evidence supports neither hypothesis, however. For example, two of our cases were characterized

[2] In addition to variation in banking system size, stock market capitalization as a percentage of GDP in 2017 reached only 50.1 per cent of GDP in Germany, but 86.6 per cent in France, 101.6 per cent in the Netherlands, 111.7 per cent in the UK, and 145.2 per cent in the US (IMF database).

Table 1.3 Largest universal banks, total assets and as a percentage of national GDP (case study countries; total assets, national currency, billions), end 2000, 2007, 2011, 2014*

	2000	% of GDP (2000)	2007	% of GDP (2007)	2011	% of GDP (2011)	2014	% of GDP (2014)
United States								
JPMorgan Chase & Co.	715.0	7.0	1562.1	10.8	2274.4	14.6	2573.1	15.2
Bank of America Corp.	642.2	6.3	1715.7	11.9	2219.6	14.3	2104.5	12.4
Citigroup Inc.	902.2	8.8	2187.6	15.1	1936.6	12.5	1842.5	10.9
Wells Fargo & Co.	272.4	2.7	575.4	4.0	1313.9	8.5	1593.3	9.4
US Bancorp (USB)	164.9	1.6	237.6	1.6	330.1	2.1	402.5	2.4
United Kingdom								
HSBC	451.9	28.6	1172.8	61.9	1649.8	88.1	1689.9	84.6
Barclays (Group)	316.2	20.0	1227.6	64.8	1563.4	83.5	1269.5	63.6
RBS (Royal Bank of Scotland) Group	320.0	20.3	1900.5	100.3	1432.8	76.5	1045.4	52.4
Lloyds-TSB**	218.0	13.8	353.3	18.6	970.5	51.8	854.9	42.8
Standard Chartered	102.4	6.5	329.2	17.4	599.1	32.0	725.9	36.4
Germany								
Deutsche Bank	929.0	44.0	2020.3	80.8	2164.0	80.3	1708.7	58.4
Commerzbank	460.0	21.8	617.0	24.7	527.0	19.6	557.6	19.0
DZ Bank	364.6 (2001)	17.3	431.3	17.3	405.9	15.1	402.5	13.7

Continued

Table 1.3 Continued

	2000	% of GDP (2000)	2007	% of GDP (2007)	2011	% of GDP (2011)	2014	% of GDP (2014)
France								
BNP-Paribas	694.0	46.9	1694.5	87.3	1965.3	95.5	2077.8	96.7
Crédit Agricole	480.7	32.5	1414.2	72.8	1880.0	91.3	1589.1	73.9
Société Générale	455.9	30.8	1071.8	55.2	1181.4	57.4	1308.2	60.9
BPCE***	—	—	—	—	1138.0	55.3	1223.3	56.9
Natixis (BPCE investment bank)	116.2	7.9	520.0	26.8	507.7	24.7	736.0	34.2
Crédit Mutuel	—	—	395.9	20.4	382.3	18.6	428.2	19.9
Netherlands								
ING	650.2	143.8	1312.5	212.0	1279.2	196.7	992.9	147.8
Rabobank Group	342.9	75.9	570.5	92.1	731.7	112.5	681.1	101.4
ABN-AMRO Group	543.2	120.2	892.2	144.1	404.7	62.2	386.9	57.6

* The banks listed were, in order, the largest in their respective home country at the end 2014. A number of the largest banks in 2000 no longer existed in 2011 (e.g., Dresdner Bank in Germany, HBOS in the UK).

** Halifax Bank of Scotland (HBOS) was merged into Lloyds-TSB from 2009.

*** BPCE consisted of two separate banking groups (Banques Populaires and Caisses d'Epargne) prior to 2009.

Source: Author's calculations based on bank annual reports/bank financial statements.

Table 1.4 Banking system assets as a percentage of GDP, 2002–16*

	2002	2004	2006	2008	2010	2012	2014	2016
France	238	257	326	384	392	402	395	388
Germany	292	294	300	311	324	301	268	250
Netherlands	239	289	300	345	358	386	375	368
UK	327	380	451	531	502	466	384	392
US	74	78	83	94	86	87	92	91

* Banking system assets on a domestic or resident basis.
Source: BIS (2018, p. 78); national data, for further details see https://www.bis.org/publ/cgfs60/cgfs60_metadata.xlsx.

Table 1.5 Banking system assets as a percentage of total financial institution assets (case study countries), 2002–16*

	2002	2004	2006	2008	2010	2012	2014	2016
France	69	69	73	72	70	70	66	65
Germany	66	63	62	60	68	65	61	59
Netherlands	35	38	32	33	29	28	26	25
UK	58	50	49	36	38	36	34	36
US	19	19	18	21	19	19	20	20

* As a share of assets of financial corporations, excluding the central bank. Financial assets when available, otherwise total assets.
Source: BIS (2018, p. 80); FSB, Global Shadow Banking Monitoring Report 2016, May 2017; national data, for further details see https://www.bis.org/publ/cgfs60/cgfs60_metadata.xlsx.

by highly concentrated banking systems prior to 2008: in each of France and the Netherlands, the largest five banks accounted for approximately 80 per cent of all bank assets. By contrast, the US and Germany—which adopted very different bank structural reforms—were the least concentrated (with five banks holding 30–40 per cent of bank assets), while the UK appears as an intermediate case (about 50 per cent of bank assets) (see Table 1.6). There is a similar absence of correlation between the stringency of post-crisis reform and the number of systemically important banks (SIBs): with the US and France hosting the most global SIBs, while the US and Germany had the largest total number of banks (see Table 1.7).

Finally, the size and scale of the banking crisis also does a poor job of explaining variation in regulatory outcomes. In the US, total bank losses (including write-downs) in 2008–9 reached at least $1.1tn or 7.6 per cent of 2009 GDP; while in the UK, losses reached 6.3 per cent of GDP in 2008–9; followed closely by the Netherlands (5.4 per cent), Germany (2.4 per cent) and France (1.8 per cent) (Hardie and Howarth 2013a; IMF 2014; ECB 2015). Nor do the size of the subsequent bail-outs correlate with the extent of restrictions subsequently placed on banking activities.

Table 1.6 Banking system concentration (percentage of total assets held by largest three/five banks), 2002–16*

	2002	2004	2006	2008	2010	2012	2014	2016
France				54/77	58/81	58/81	58/81	56/82
Germany	18/26	21/29	21/29	20/27	33/40	31/38	31/37	28/35
Netherlands	71/82	71/84	71/84	72/84	69/82	73/82	76/86	75/89
UK	28/41	32/47	34/50	33/45	42/53	41/54	37/51	33/48
US	21/25	25/31	30/35	32/38	33/44	33/45	33/44	32/43

* For information on the consolidation basis and coverage of these data, see https://www.bis.org/publ/cgfs60/cgfs60_metadata.xlsx.
Source: BIS (2018, p. 85); national data, for further details see https://www.bis.org/publ/cgfs60/cgfs60_metadata.xlsx.

Table 1.7 Number of systemically important banks by country at end 2018

	Global SIBs	Domestic SIBs	Total number of banks
France	4	2	424
Germany	1	12	1623
Netherlands	1	4	94
UK	3	12	347
US	8	N/A	5415

* The total number of banks in each country is shown in parenthesis below the country label. The US has not designated domestic SIBs. A bank that is a domestic SIB in one country may be a subsidiary of a global SIB in another country.
Source: FSB (2020).

Figure 1.1, which shows the fiscal cost of support for the financial sector as a proportion of GDP, tells a similar story. The Netherlands and Germany stand out for requiring the highest initial support (at 17.6 and 12.5 per cent of GDP) followed by the UK and US (at 6.6 and 4.6 per cent of GDP), and finally France at 1.3 per cent. Moreover, the scale of the bailouts across the EU as a whole might lead us to expect strong support for EU-level action against TBTF banks—yet this is not what transpired.

The adoption of banking reforms other than structural reform in the six jurisdictions that we examine only provides limited guidance to explain the varying adoption of ringfencing. In Chapter 3, we discuss the range of regulatory reforms and other measures adopted by governments with the explicit or indirect aim of making TBTF banks safer and/or to enable governments to avoid having to bail them out. With regard to some of these reforms and measures, there appears to be a correlation with the structural reform adopted. There are two main examples: bank capital and liquidity rules, and bank resolution rules and bank-provided funding to facilitate resolution. On the first, national governments that

CASE SELECTION AND ALTERNATIVE EXPLANATIONS   15

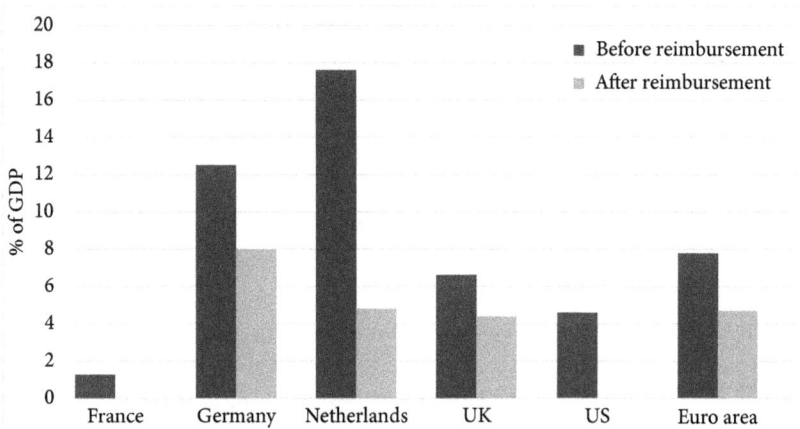

Figure 1.1 The fiscal cost of public support to the financial sector (before and after reimbursement by banks, case study countries and euro area total, as a percentage of GDP in 2014), 2008–14
Source: ECB (2015, p. 81); figures for the UK and US are from IMF (2014, p. 16).

were reluctant to adopt higher and more stringent capital requirements on their banks—notably France and Germany—were also reluctant to adopt major structural reform. The EU significantly diluted international guidelines on bank capital and liquidity, then failed to adopt legislation on structural reform. The US administration and the UK government, on the contrary, demonstrated ambition on both the reinforcement of bank capital and liquidity rules and structural reform. This limited correlation suggests that the political dynamics driving structural reform (or not) in the four country cases are closely related to those shaping financial regulatory change more broadly in these jurisdictions. More problematically, however, the case of the Netherlands does not quite fit this pattern as the Dutch government was more willing to accept constraining capital and liquidity rules than it was to accept structural reform. Similarly, on the adoption of reinforced or new resolution rules and funding, there is no clear correlation. The US already had a long-established process for resolving failing banks, but looked to strengthen the regime after 2008. EU member states moved collectively to construct a European bank resolution regime designed explicitly to make it easier for banks to be resolved without recourse to government bail-out funds. In 2014, they adopted the Bank Recovery and Resolution Directive and the Single Resolution Mechanism Regulation to construct national and then EU-level resolution funds. That the UK, French, German, and Dutch governments adopted very similar resolution regimes during the same period provides little guidance as to their varying preferences on bank structural reform.

Further evidence suggests that policy makers within jurisdictions did not always hold consistent views as to whether structural reform was necessary to complement tougher capital/liquidity requirements and strengthened resolution rules in dealing with TBTF banks. For example, the US Treasury Secretary, Tim Geithner, was initially reluctant to endorse structural reform in part because he believed that the best way to make TBTF safer was to reinforce capital rules (Alter 2010; Cassidy 2010; Heilemann 2010). Similarly, while the Bank of England Governor, Mervyn King, strongly endorsed structural separation of large banks, the head of the Financial Services Authority (FSA), Adair Turner, believed that capital was a more effective tool for making banks safer (Turner 2009). When the EU Commission shelved legislation on structural reform in October 2017, it did so explicitly noting that the European resolution regime that was being put into place was a more than adequate measure to contain TBTF risks (EU Commission 2017). However, the reliability of such claims as an indication of preferences is open to question. The Commission had previously claimed that bank structural reform was a necessary complement to the European resolution regime (EU Commission 2014a). Moreover, analyses demonstrate the ineffectiveness of EU resolution rules and the insufficiency of national and EU resolution funds (see, for example, Asimakopoulos and Howarth 2021). Thus, the relationship between the adoption of structural reform and the adoption of other rules and measures to make TBTF safer—either in terms of official justification or objectively—is far from clear.

Turning to the politics of banking reform, we find that mounting public anger against the banks, and calls for tougher regulation of banking activities, were broadly common to all the cases we examine. For example, Ganderson (2020b) uses an analysis of newspaper coverage to reveal a similarly dramatic increase in the salience of the financial crisis, peaking in 2009, across three countries in our study (UK, Germany, and the Netherlands). This was fuelled in large part by the timing of key national elections held at important points during the crisis: the US presidential election in 2008 and mid-term elections in 2010, and national legislative elections in the UK in 2010, France in 2012 (legislative and presidential), the Netherlands in 2010 and 2012, and Germany in 2009 and 2013. Similarly, at the EU level, European Parliamentary elections took place in late May 2014, less than four months after the Commission had launched its draft legislation on bank structural reform. We would therefore expect TBTF to be an important issue during all these election campaigns, with opposition parties having a particular incentive to exploit voter hostility towards the banks and/or incumbent parties' handling of the issue.

The five countries we investigate also differ significantly in terms of political and institutional structures. Again, however, we find little evidence that these institutional differences help us to explain the variation of regulatory reform across different jurisdictions. For example, we might hypothesize that countries with fewer veto points in the policy-making process (i.e., typically, 'majoritarian' political systems) would introduce tougher restrictions on banks given that their governments face fewer legislative obstacles to doing so. At first glance, the type of political system does appear to have some explanatory relevance with regard to bank structural reform. On a standard continuum of consensual versus majoritarian political systems (Lijphart 2012), the UK is traditionally conceptualized as an archetypal example of a majoritarian system, features of which are also found in the US. By contrast, Germany, the Netherlands, and the EU exhibit institutional characteristics more typical of consensual systems. Problematically, however, France (as an adversarial system) does not fit this explanation.

A further possibility is that political partisanship and/or changes of government could be causally significant. Specifically, it might be expected that the election of a left-of-centre government in the aftermath of the financial crisis would lead to a more stringent regulatory response; while the election of a right-of-centre government would lead to less or even no reform. Yet we find little support for this. In the US and France, for example, incumbent presidents from the main centre-right party (Bush in the US, Sarkozy in France) were replaced by presidents from the centre-left (Obama and Hollande, respectively), yet the outcome of banking reform was very different. By contrast, the incumbent centre-left Labour government in the UK lost power to the centre-right Conservatives, in coalition with the centrist Liberal Democrats, which nonetheless paved the way for stringent new measures. Our other two cases provide further variation. Germany was governed by a coalition of centre-right and liberal-right (composed of the Christian Democratic Union (CDU)/Christian Social Union (CSU) and Free Democratic Party (FDP) led by Chancellor Merkel for most of the period of our analysis (2009–13). In the Netherlands, a centrist grand coalition (composed of the centre-right Christian Democratic Party (CDA), centre-left Labour Party (PvdA) and centrist Christian Union (CU) parties) was replaced by a right-wing coalition (People's Party for Freedom and Democracy (VVD) and CDA) in 2010, and then by a new centrist coalition (VVD and PvdA) in 2012. In sum, our comparative analysis enables us to rule out several potential explanations for the outcome of bank structural reform linked to political and institutional factors.

In the following chapter, we develop our own theoretical framework for explaining bank structural reform. To test this, our book uses a structured comparison and 'within case' analysis. For each case study, we employ process tracing to assess the explanatory power of our theoretical propositions against the empirical material. The book draws on a rich corpus of interview material conducted over several years, beginning in 2013 and continuing through to 2020. This includes over fifty in-depth interviews with senior policy makers, financial regulators, financial industry practitioners, and civil society groups at the national and transnational (EU) levels. All the interviews were conducted under strict confidentiality and thus interviewees are only listed in general terms by position, institution, and/or nationality to ensure anonymity. A full list of interviews can be found at the end of the book. Findings from these interviews have been triangulated with information gathered from publicly available policy documents from public authorities and private organizations in all six jurisdictions, as well as a systematic survey of financial and other quality press coverage from this period.

4. Summary of our argument

Our book develops a *comparative financial power* framework to explain variation in bank structural reform across different jurisdictions since the financial crisis. It integrates insights from political economy and public policy scholarship to provide a fine-grained analysis of how financial power is mediated by the relational and institutional context within which it is located. The development of the framework proceeds in two steps.

The first step draws on the interest group literature to capture how business influence is embedded in a web of inter-organizational relationships through which firms and associations leverage their individual resources (Sabatier 1988; Heinz et al. 1993; Fuchs 2007; Spillman 2012; Klüver 2013). Studies suggest that the financial industry wields a formidable capacity to engage in collective action (Clapp and Helleiner 2012; Kastner 2014, 2018; Pagliari and Young 2014, 2016; Winecoff 2015), and that 'financial unity'—namely, the ability to present a united front when engaging with policy makers—is key to its lobbying success (McKeen-Edwards and Porter 2013; Chalmers 2015, 2017, 2020; Young and Pagliari 2017; James et al. 2021). This leads us to predict that, under conditions of heightened political salience about TBTF banks, the financial industry will be more influential in shaping regulatory outcomes when it is unified. We refer to this as *cooperative financial power*. This unity of voice will be reflected in the financial industry's ability to leverage broad alliances, across both the sector and the wider business community, to articulate its regulatory preferences. These alliances not only serve to strengthen and legitimize the concerns of financial firms, but also ensure that they are less likely to be challenged or contradicted by the mobilization of countervailing groups.

Conversely, we expect the financial industry to be less influential when it is divided because the fragmentation of its voice will inevitably inhibit the articulation of a coherent set of regulatory preferences. We label this *competitive financial power*. Firms will be reliant on lobbying individually, or through (sub-)sectoral associations, and thus less able to draw on broader business alliances to legitimate their grievances. Furthermore, financial actors are more likely to face a greater challenge from countervailing groups with whom they are forced to compete for access and influence in the policy process. Our first hypothesis is therefore that *the financial industry will be more influential in shaping bank structural reform when financial power is cooperative; and less influential when financial power is competitive (H1).*

To provide a firmer grounding for our empirical expectations, we turn to the literature on interest intermediation (Katzenstein 1978; Hall 1986; Lehmbruch 1991; Hall and Soskice 2001; Schmidt 2002; Eising 2009). Specifically, we predict that the legacy of long-standing organizational features or 'modes' of interest representation—namely, *pluralism, neo-corporatism*, and *statism*—continue to structure the capacity of the financial sector to coordinate and centralize lobbying with other economic actors. In other words, these modes will be a key determinant of whether financial power is predominantly competitive or cooperative in different national contexts.

Hence, we expect countries associated with pluralist modes of interest representation—typified by the US and UK—to be characterized by competitive financial power. That is, financial industry lobbying will tend to be fragmented with minimal coordination; industry preferences will be more heterogeneous; and the sector will face significant competition from countervailing groups. By contrast, we argue that cooperative financial power is more characteristic of countries with a legacy of either neo-corporatist arrangements, as in Germany and the Netherlands, or statist intermediation, such as France. Here financial interest representation is traditionally more hierarchical and centralized; lobbying activity will be more tightly coordinated; and industry preferences will tend to be more homogeneous. Finally, we expect that as a hybrid case of 'elite pluralism' (Coen 1997, pp. 98–9; Broscheid and Coen 2007; Grossman 2004; Mahoney 2008; Coen et al. 2021), the EU combines important features of both competitive financial power—reflecting the fragmented and multi-level institutional landscape—and cooperative financial power—due to the access and influence granted to powerful national and European business groups.

The second step in our framework focuses on how the power of the financial industry is mediated by key institutional features of the policy process. We begin by drawing on the agenda-setting literature to highlight the importance of 'conflict expansion', referring to the increased attention and mobilization of policy actors around an issue (Baumgartner and Jones 1993; Rochefort and Cobb 1994; Kingdon 1995; Jones and Baumgartner 2005), but also to 'conflict contraction', in which actors are demobilized, policy conflict is reduced, and issues disappear from the policy agenda. Relatedly, we apply the concept of 'venue shifting' (Princen 2007, 2011) to explain why policy makers delegate salient and contentious issues to ad hoc specialist groups. This is because it provides a powerful tool of depoliticization: encouraging deliberative decision making by drawing on external knowledge and technical expertise; signalling credibility and legitimacy about policy choices to voters; and building consensus and securing agreement from relevant stakeholders. Importantly, reducing political pressures through venue shifting can take the form of either conflict contraction—i.e., deliberately limiting the number and diversity of actors involved in the process in order to facilitate agreement—or conflict expansion—i.e., expanding the number and diversity of participants involved in order to secure 'buy in' from a broader range of societal interests.

By contrast, regulatory reform in the absence of venue shifting—and thus managed through conventional policy processes—will be more politicized and contingent. That is, it is more likely to reflect the particular balance of power that exists between competing political and economic interests. This leads us to formulate our second hypothesis: *Bank structural reform will be less politicized when policy makers deploy venue shifting; and more politicized when policy makers do not deploy venue shifting (H2).*

Combining these two variables—interest group lobbying and venue shifting—generates a typology of bank structural reform, the cells of which provide a theoretically grounded basis for differentiating between four different regulatory outcomes:

1. *Durable reform* is likely where venue shifting occurs in a context of competitive financial power. Here the fragmentation of bank lobbying, heterogeneous industry preferences, and competition from countervailing groups will limit the capacity of the banking sector to 'capture' the process. Consequently, delegating decision making to an ad hoc, specialist group in this context is likely to facilitate depoliticization by mobilizing and engaging a wide range of societal stakeholders (i.e., conflict expansion). We therefore expect both substantive policy reform and durable change as policy makers use venue shifting to leverage both external expertise and build broad public support.

Evidence for this claim comes from the UK case. First, we show how the government's decision to delegate the issue of structural reform to ad hoc specialist groups—the Independent Commission on Banking in 2010, and the Parliamentary Commission on Banking Standards in 2012—provided a high-profile platform for a number of authoritative voices, and expanded engagement with a wide range of societal interests. Venue shifting was therefore pivotal in facilitating depoliticization—in this case, by leveraging conflict expansion to consult with and secure greater 'buy in' from policy stakeholders. Second, we argue that the lobbying power of UK banks was severely curtailed by the competitive nature of financial power. On the one hand, industry was characterized by important internal divisions, encouraging banks to compete with one another rather than forge a common position. On the other hand, UK banks were weakened by the emergence of a disparate coalition of actors in favour of structural reform. The most prominent voices calling for stringent new rules came from 'insider' actors—key government ministers, financial regulators, and members of parliament—who leveraged their political influence and technical expertise through new institutional venues. As a consequence, the UK was able to make credible commitments to bank ringfencing that have remained largely uncontested over the past decade.

2. *No reform* is likely where venue shifting takes place in a context of cooperative financial power. Here the banking industry will be characterized by centralized

lobbying, homogeneous preferences, and the ability to wield broad business alliances. In this instance, delegating decision making to an ad hoc, specialist group is more likely to result in the process being 'captured' by powerful organized interests. Rather than consulting widely, this exercise in depoliticization will facilitate agreement by limiting engagement to a narrow range of technical 'experts' (i.e., conflict contraction). We expect this to lead to no reform as venue shifting serves to legitimize non-decision making.

We explain the surprising absence of banking reform in the Netherlands as a result of the confluence of venue shifting in a context of cooperative financial power. Dutch banks sought to leverage their unity through the powerful Dutch Banking Association (NVB) by establishing an industry-dominated commission in November 2008 (the Maas Commission). By recommending a series of self-regulatory measures related to governance, remuneration, and risk management, this commission successfully deflected blame away from TBTF banks and set the agenda for subsequent government proposals. Subsequently, Dutch policy makers depoliticized the issue of banking reform through conflict contraction by delegating the issue to two ad hoc groups. The De Wit Commission, established in 2009 and composed of parliamentarians with little expertise on financial regulation, focused instead on strengthening supervision and capital requirements. The Wijffels Commission, convened in 2012, headed by a former senior bank executive and composed of a narrow 'expert' membership, only gave lukewarm support for EU ringfencing proposals. This enabled the Dutch government repeatedly to dismiss the need for immediate structural reform, arguing that it should be coordinated at the EU level, and instead it echoed industry's calls for a new code of conduct to change bank culture.

3. *Contested reform* is expected to be the outcome where venue shifting is not possible and financial power is competitive. Structural reform will be more politicized because it is channelled through conventional political processes. It will thus reflect the outcome of competition between different groups—including political parties, organized interests, regulators, and civil society. Substantial reform is possible because bank lobbying is fragmented and subject to challenge by multiple countervailing groups (i.e., conflict expansion). But changes will be more contingent as they will be vulnerable to ongoing politicization and the shifting balance of power between competing interests.

We show that the US experience of banking reform fits well with this type of regulatory outcome. On the one hand, large Wall Street banks could not leverage the unity of the financial sector to block structural reform. On the contrary, the sector was deeply divided as small community banks, with powerful supporters in Congress, became cheerleaders for restricting the speculative activities of TBTF banks. The 'big five' US banks also faced the mobilization of a highly vocal coalition of pro-reform actors—composed of consumer groups, activists, and progressive think tanks—which was cultivated by the White House. On the other hand, the Obama administration was unable to build broad, bipartisan agreement around banking reform through the use of venue shifting. Hence, the issue remained subject to the vagaries of a deeply polarized Congress, with the majority of Democrats and Republicans holding diametrically opposing views and the two parties battling to steer the legislative process. In the end, the Obama administration was able to leverage sufficient support from regulators, congressional Democrats, community banks, and pro-reform groups to secure agreement on imposing tough new restrictions on proprietary trading. But this process contributed to heightened levels of conflict expansion, with the result that the Volcker Rule remained subject to ongoing politicization and the shifting balance of power between competing groups. Hence, implementation was seriously disrupted by disagreements between regulatory agencies, and Republican attempts to block or dilute the reforms—culminating in the attempted repeal by the Trump administration.

4. *Symbolic reform* will occur where venue shifting is not possible in a context of cooperative financial power. In the absence of delegation to ad hoc specialist groups, structural reform will be more politicized and policy makers are likely to face significant political pressures on reform. But the banking industry will also be highly effective at lobbying given its ability to leverage broad sectoral and business alliances, thus facilitating conflict contraction through conventional political processes. To reconcile these contradictory pressures, we predict that policy makers will introduce symbolic structural reforms designed to appease political demands to act, whilst minimizing the economic impact on industry.

Germany provides our first example of symbolic reform which fell significantly short of the proposals recommended by Liikanen's EU High Level Group. How do we explain this? First, the German banking industry—despite its fragmented, three-tier structure—was surprisingly unified around the issue and capable of wielding significant cooperative financial power through powerful industry associations. Hence, the large German banks were strongly supported by both the politically influential savings, cooperative, and regional banks, but also by Germany's powerful export-oriented small and medium-sized enterprises (SME) sector, giving the large bank-led coalition a strong unified voice in relation to government. Despite this unity, the issue of banking reform was (at least initially) highly politicized within the German parliament, and the government faced significant political pressure from all parties on the left to legislate for major structural reform. In the absence of venue shifting, the government attempted to facilitate conflict contraction by steering the process through a series of government-led and parliamentary committees, but it could not be entirely insulated from political pressures. To contain opposition from the Social Democratic Party (SPD), which had campaigned actively in favour of reform prior to the 2013 elections, the government accepted largely symbolic changes to the German Banking Act which introduced a weak form of ringfencing, with little impact on most German banks' trading activities.

France provides our second example of symbolic structural reform. The French case is particularly striking given the politically polarizing nature of the issue in the run-up to the 2012 presidential and parliamentary elections. Notably, the victorious presidential candidate, Socialist François Hollande, was outspoken in his criticism of the financial sector and campaigned on a clear commitment to tackle TBTF banks by introducing stringent new rules on structural separation. In government, however, Hollande's pledges came up against a powerful and unified banking industry. Importantly, the cooperative financial power wielded by French banks also reflected long-standing interconnections between bank executives and senior government officials. We argue that *pantouflage*—here the positioning of elite bureaucratic officials in top banking jobs—was critical in deflecting the Socialist Party's pledge to push ahead with reform. As in Germany, the government did not delegate the issue to a specialist group, but instead engaged in conflict contraction by exploiting a number of government-controlled and parliamentary committees to marginalize supporters of structural separation. Although some political pressure came from parliament to adopt a far-reaching reform, the Socialist government echoed the industry's call to defend national bank 'champions' in order to deflect criticism and facilitate backtracking on previous electoral commitments. The outcome was a limited set of restrictions on proprietary and high-frequency trading adopted in July 2013.

Finally, our analysis of EU developments provides further confirmation of our theoretical claims: namely, the importance of financial interest representation and venue shifting as key determinants of regulatory reform. The early phase of the process in 2012 represents a clear case of venue shifting by the European Commission to an independent 'High Level Expert Group', headed by Erkki Liikanen. This delegation helped to insulate the process from financial industry capture, and contributed to the mobilization of a range of pro-reform groups—notably, Finance Watch—during the Commission's subsequent consultation process. The Liikanen Group therefore adopted a stringent approach, recommending that large EU banks be mandated to separate trading activities from other banking operations. A less ambitious version of this reform proposal formed the basis for the Commission's draft regulation in 2014. However, the multi-level character of the EU polity, and the polarized nature of the legislative debate, ultimately contributed to the delay and eventual defeat of the proposal in two ways. First, we argue that the EU financial industry leveraged cooperative financial power at the legislative stage to reduce momentum for reform: through powerful national bank associations working closely with reform-sceptic governments—including the French, German, and Dutch—in the Council; and through influential European banking associations with close ties to both the European Commission and Parliament. Second, industry influence was counter-balanced by substantial political pressure for reform in the Parliament and, specifically, the opposition from a number of left and Green members of the European Parliament (MEPs) to the repeated dilution of the Liikanen Group's recommendations, resulting in a stalemate. The outcome was that the Commission's efforts to agree EU legislation on bank structural reform were eventually abandoned in 2017.

5. Rationale for the book

Our book focuses on structural reforms which aimed to curb the speculative activities of systemically important banks and reduce the need for government bail-outs in the event of crisis, specifically through the structural separation of investment-related activities from the deposit-taking retail bank. We recognize that this focus necessarily means that we do not analyse in detail a range of other post-crisis regulatory reforms also aimed—at least in part—at addressing the problem of TBTF banks: including higher capital and liquidity requirements, bank recovery and resolution plans, and measures to reform internal bank governance and culture. Nonetheless, we do provide a review of these other important regulatory changes, and their potential impact upon the activities of TBTF banks and their stability in Chapter 3. Our decision to engage in a detailed analysis of bank structural reform is based on four main arguments.

First, structural reform is arguably the most innovative financial regulatory development adopted since 2008. Whereas new capital and liquidity rules were adopted to strengthen pre-existing standards, structural separation marks a substantial departure from existing regulatory practice, and challenged prevailing pre-crisis norms about the benefits of universal banking. As the Bank for International Settlements has argued, structural reform represents a 'paradigm shift' that 'breaks with the conventional wisdom that the banking sector's efficiency and stability stands only to gain from the increased diversification of banks' activities' (Gambacorta and van Rixtel 2013). For this reason, structural reform was fiercely contested by banks and bank associations to a far greater extent than other areas of post-crisis reform. In the UK, for instance, three global banks (HSBC, Barclays, and Standard Chartered) threatened to relocate significant parts of their business outside the UK in response to bank ringfencing (Jenkins et al. 2011c). This in itself tells us something about the potential costs that large banks and their political allies perceived to be at stake. Not only did structural reform threaten to impose substantial new regulatory and capital costs, it also challenged the business models of many large globally present banks.

Note, however, that we are not directly concerned with assessing the *effectiveness* of bank structural reform in addressing TBTF. On the contrary, the focus of our explanation is to understand the politics of reform—that is, why demands for these important policy innovations emerged in the first place, and how political and policy processes help to explain why some countries introduced them while others did not. Critics may argue that the declining international exposure or trading activities of large banks after 2008 ultimately rendered structural separation a moot point. But this fails to address the puzzle of why the governments of certain countries nonetheless proceeded with major reform in the face of substantial industry lobbying, while the governments of other countries adopted weak or no reform. Furthermore, the measurement, analysis, and evaluation of the efficacy of structural reform remains highly contested, among both financial economists and regulators. To interrogate these wider debates is beyond the scope of this book.

Second, structural reform has had a huge impact on the internal structure, operation, and behaviour of large banks, regardless of its implications for TBTF. This is most notable in the two countries where it progressed the furthest—the US and UK. Higher capital and liquidity requirements were viewed by senior regulators in these two countries as important, but woefully inadequate: in their view, only the structural separation of retail from investment banking could address the moral hazard generated by TBTF banks (Jenkins et al. 2011a). For UK banks, the *Financial Times* newspaper described the reforms that came into effect at the start of 2019 as 'the biggest sectoral overhaul in a generation' (Binham 2019). For the head of financial services at KPMG, ringfencing was one of the 'biggest pieces of post-crisis regulation to hit the UK banking industry ... and supersedes Brexit in cost, complexity and resource' (Jon Holt, quoted in Binham 2019). Although the economic costs of reform were notoriously difficult to calculate, a UK Treasury impact assessment at the time estimated that ringfencing would cost banks up to £4.4bn a year, with a one-off transitional cost of up to £2.5bn (HM Treasury 2013).

In the US, Zeigler and Woolley (2016, p. 250) describe the Volcker Rule as 'the most far-reaching overhaul of the country's financial structure since the Great Depression'. Ten years on from the crisis, it was still viewed by financial commentators as 'one of the most significant actions by the federal government to prevent a repeat of the financial crisis', and 'wrought sweeping changes on Wall Street' (Flitter and Rappeport 2018). By forcing banks to shut down their proprietary trading desks, the Volcker Rule constituted a substantial hit to bank profitability, leading to an exodus of senior traders to the hedge fund sector (Touryalai 2012). Leading US regulators at the time were forced to acknowledge that implementation could cost the industry a one-time charge of up to $4.3bn (Miedema 2014), while subsequent academic studies showed that it imposed a significant constraint on market liquidity (see Bao et al. 2016).

Third, bank structural reform is interesting analytically because it is the single most important source of financial regulatory divergence in the world's largest banking systems since the crisis. Regulatory reforms aimed at strengthening bank capital, liquidity, and resolution rules were coordinated, to a greater or lesser extent, from the 'top down' by international fora (notably, the Basel Committee of Banking Supervision (BCBS)) and EU-level bodies. This transnational effort reflects the perceived importance of retaining a level playing field among large global banks, and the need to address cross-border externalities arising from bank failures (James and Quaglia 2020). The outcome of regulatory reform in these areas was therefore greater regulatory convergence. For example, for the first time ever, the EU made use of a regulation, in addition to a directive, on capital rules—thus ensuring direct effect and more limited national margin of manoeuvre.

However, bank structural reform tended to operate according to entirely different dynamics, driven in four of our cases from the 'bottom up' by governments in response to public criticism of bank bail-outs, and/or political pressure from legislatures to break up the largest banks. These pressures were mediated by electoral cycles—*inter alia*, the timing of national elections and changes of government—generating divergent dynamics of timing and sequencing. Hence, the US moved first to introduce structural reform—the Volcker Rule—following the election of President Obama, thereby ruling out the possibility of meaningful international coordination on the issue. The UK moved shortly afterwards, driven by political pressures arising from the formation of the new coalition government in 2010; while French and German governments implemented minimal reforms in part to direct efforts at the EU level, which subsequently failed; while the Dutch government side-lined the issue of structural reform altogether. The outcome was therefore significant regulatory divergence, fragmentation, and opportunities for regulatory arbitrage for national jurisdictions, in direct contradiction to the lofty objectives of senior financial regulators and supervisors at the height of the crisis. The central puzzle of the book is therefore to explain how and why this divergence came about.

Fourth, there are important methodological grounds for the focus of our book. Specifically, we argue that a comparative study of post-crisis regulatory reform to address TBTF must focus on structural reform as the pre-eminent example of post-crisis regulatory divergence. In other words, we aim to explain divergence on the dependent variable. Explaining the adoption of a number of similar post-crisis reforms to address TBTF—*inter alia*, bank capital and resolution rules—is possible, but this would be less well suited to the comparative method. Rather, it would be a study focused principally on regulatory developments at the international and EU levels, the preferences of different national governments and banks, and/or implementation at the national level. While fascinating, we believe that this transnational part of the post-crisis regulation story has already been expertly covered by many scholars, as noted above. Rather, our ambition is to shed new light on how and why elected officials and regulators at the national level have pursued their own policy agendas when it comes to bank structural reform, an area that has received relatively little scholarly attention from either a political economy or a political science perspective.

Our book is therefore structured to locate a detailed analysis of structural reform within the broader context of international and EU-level initiatives on TBTF. But, for methodological reasons, it is essential to separate these analytically in the book. Chapter 3 therefore includes an overview of the full spectrum of post-crisis regulatory reforms adopted at the international and EU levels which have promoted regulatory convergence across our five national cases. The primary focus of the chapters that follow, however, is to explore bottom-up political pressures for bank structural reform at the national level, and how these pressures interact with the top-down regulatory architecture agreed at the international and/or EU levels.

6. Structure of the book

The book is structured as follows. Chapter 2 develops our theoretical framework. It begins by reviewing explanations in international and comparative political economy, and theories of business power, to explain why they offer an inadequate account of patterns of bank structural reform across advanced economies. To address these limitations, we turn to the literature on interest group lobbying which points to the importance of the relational context and 'financial unity' as a key determinant of financial power, and from which we derive our first hypothesis about variation in the stringency of structural reform. This section also draws on theories of interest representation to specify our empirical expectations about cross-national variation, differentiating between 'competitive' and 'cooperative' forms of financial power. Next, the chapter considers the institutional context of financial power, reviewing theories of agenda setting and venue shifting to derive our second hypothesis about the (de)politicization of banking reform. The final section pulls these insights together by presenting our *comparative financial power* framework: combining the two explanatory variables—interest group lobbying and venue shifting—to produce a two-by-two typology of different banking reform outcomes: durable, contested, symbolic, and no reform.

Chapter 3 places bank structural reform into the wider context of bank regulatory reform since the crisis. We analyse how a range of regulatory responses have or might have impacted on TBTF banks principally by reducing their size and higher-risk activities. We group these responses into five categories: 1) conditions attached to government financial support, notably related to deleveraging; 2) revenue-raising regulation and fiscal policy, including bank levies, transactions taxes, and resolution funds; 3) the reinforcement of bank regulations concerning credit rating agencies, remuneration practices, capital and liquidity requirements, and bank resolution; 4) bank governance and transparency, including internal risk management, stress testing, and reporting requirements; and 5) strengthened bank supervision through new macroprudential policy instruments. Our main argument is that the majority of these measures had only a limited effect in addressing the TBTF problem. We therefore devote the rest of the book to analysing the one set of measures designed explicitly to address the issue: bank structural reform.

Chapter 4 presents our first case study, analysing the Obama administration's late conversion to the cause of bank structural reform in the US. This policy shift culminated in the surprisingly stringent ban on proprietary trading by banks (the 'Volcker Rule') in July 2010, but also led to a lengthy and often tortuous process of implementation. We argue that this significant but highly *contested* outcome was a consequence of two key features of the process. First, financial industry lobbying was highly fragmented and frequently divided, giving rise to powerful dissenting voices from within the industry (i.e., competitive financial power). Large Wall Street banks also faced concerted opposition from a powerful pro-reform coalition of consumer and activist groups that maintained pressure on Congress. Second, in the absence of venue shifting through which to build a bipartisan consensus, structural reform remained subject to the balance of power in a deeply polarized Congress. Hence, we show that the Volcker Rule came under sustained attack as Republicans, supported by the largest Wall Street banks, sought to delay and disrupt the rule-writing process using a variety of political, bureaucratic, and legal channels. This culminated in the Trump administration's attempted repeal of the proprietary trading ban in 2017 which succeeded in relaxing some provisions for smaller banks.

The UK's decision to introduce a mandatary ringfence for retail bank activities is the subject of Chapter 5. Despite the UK hosting one of the largest global financial centres, the so-called 'Vickers' reforms introduced some of the toughest rules regarding structural separation and capital requirements in the world. The *durable* nature of banking reform is all the more puzzling given that neither of the two main parties expressed much enthusiasm for ringfencing at the height of the crisis. We explain this durability as the outcome of institutional venue shifting—to the ICB in 2010, and to the Parliamentary Commission on Banking Standards (PCBS) in 2012—which was critical in depoliticizing the process, and curtailing the influence of bank lobbyists, by expanding engagement with a range of societal stakeholders. The collective influence of the sizeable UK financial industry was also weakened by the competitive nature of financial power: internal divisions between the largest banks limited lobbying coordination, and they faced significant opposition from countervailing groups—notably prominent ministers, parliamentarians, and senior regulators. The result was that ringfencing came to enjoy strong cross-party support that served to 'lock in' the reforms over time.

Chapter 6 considers the structural reform introduced in Germany through the *Trennbankengesetz* (Bank Separation Law) in 2013 which had little impact on most German banks' trading activities. This was in spite of commitments made by Chancellor Angela Merkel to tackle the issue of TBTF in the wake of the crisis, and sustained political pressure from the main opposition SPD in the run-up to the September 2013 legislative elections. Our central argument is that the limited ringfencing reforms introduced by the German government can be attributed to cooperative financial power and the absence of venue shifting. Despite the fragmented, multi-tiered structure of the German banking industry, it was nonetheless capable of wielding significant unified collective influence within the policy process. This influence was channelled through multiple centralized associations representing the commercial, cooperative, savings, and public banking sectors. These associations formed a powerful alliance in opposition to structural reform, bolstered by the support of the politically influential SME sector. Although the government sought to manage the reform agenda through existing parliamentary committee structures, structural reform could not be entirely insulated from political pressures—hence, the largely *symbolic* reform designed to appease public anger while inflicting minimal economic costs on the sector.

Our analysis of the French case in Chapter 7 displays important similarities with Germany, despite different party-political dynamics. During the 2012 presidential and parliamentary elections, Socialist candidate François Hollande made bold pledges to introduce stringent new rules to force banks to separate risky speculative activities from retail banking. As president, Hollande faced a ferocious backlash from France's tightly integrated and highly concentrated banking sector. One important difference between the German and French cases is that cooperative financial power reflected not only centralized representation and alliance building with the wider business community, but also tight inter-organizational and interpersonal connections between the French state and the large banks. Steering the process through an *in camera* government committee with close ties to industry, as well as two parliamentary committees dominated by opponents of major structural reform, the Socialist government was able to backtrack on its campaign commitments. The limited set of restrictions on proprietary and high-frequency trading eventually adopted in July 2013 therefore represented a *symbolic* response to waning parliamentary and public pressure, justified on the grounds that protecting large French banks against US competition was in the 'national interest'.

The curious case of *no reform* in the Netherlands is explored in Chapter 8. Conditions appeared ripe for change, not least because of the size of the Dutch banking sector and the scale of the bank bail-outs, but also because of the early support from several political parties and prominent political figures—including the Finance Minister during the crisis, Wouter Bos. We argue that the Dutch case represents a clear example of depoliticization through conflict contraction, resulting from two factors. First, the unified and disciplined Dutch banking industry was able to leverage its cooperative financial power successfully to shape the bank reform agenda more generally, and to marginalize discussions on structural reform in particular. For example, the sector established its own commission in November 2008, chaired by senior bank executive Cees Maas, which recommended a voluntary 'code' to change internal bank culture. Second, the Dutch government used venue shifting to two ad hoc commissions to examine a range of bank reforms—the De Wit Commission in 2009, and the Wijffels Commission in 2012—which narrowed engagement and largely echoed industry's concerns about ringfencing. The outcome was that the government was able successfully to deflect blame away from the phenomenon of TBTF banks.

Chapter 9 places our country-level analysis into the context of EU initiatives on banking reform. This examination provides further corroboration for our explanatory framework in two respects. First, in 2012 the European Commission sought to mobilize support for reform by delegating the issue to an independent 'High Level Expert Group', headed by then Finnish central bank governor, Erkki Liikanen. This exercise in venue shifting led the Commission to adopt a less ambitious version of the group's recommendation for bank trading activities to be located in a separate legal entity as the basis for its own draft regulation. Second, the EU financial industry was able to leverage substantial cooperative financial power to reduce momentum for reform: through powerful national bank associations working closely with reform-sceptic governments in the Council; and through influential European banking associations with well-established ties to the Commission and European Parliament. Where the EU differs from our country cases, however, is in the uniquely fragmented nature of the polity, which generated additional obstacles to reform. In particular, opposition from left and Green MEPs to the repeated dilution of the Liikanen Group's proposals in response to pressure from the Council and industry contributed to stalemate, and the eventual abandonment of the draft regulation on structural reform in 2017.

The concluding chapter begins by recalling the main puzzle and research questions of the book. The second section summarizes the limitations of existing scholarship on bank structural reform, and details the book's wider empirical and theoretical contribution to the relevant fields of academic research. We focus on four literatures: international and comparative political economy, theories of business power, and financial interest lobbying. The final section provides a guide to future research by considering the wider application of the comparative financial power framework to other regulatory issues and economic sectors. In particular, we end with an appeal for future scholarship to extend our analytical horizon, and to contribute to the further refinement of our theoretical framework, through its application to case study countries beyond the narrow confines of Europe and North America.

2
A Comparative Financial Power Approach

1. Introduction

An important aim of this book is to contribute to a wider research agenda which calls for the closer integration of political economy and public policy approaches (see John 2017). Our claim to theoretical originality rests on our ambition to develop a *comparative financial power* framework which is better placed to explain how and why business (or financial) power varies across different jurisdictions. In particular, this chapter sets out to integrate insights from the literature on interest group lobbying with theories of agenda setting and 'venue shifting' in order to present a more fine-grained analysis of how financial power is mediated by the relational and institutional context within which it is located.

We begin by reviewing explanations in international and comparative political economy, as well as theories of business power, to explain why they provide an inadequate account of patterns of bank structural reform across advanced economies. To address these limitations, we turn to the literature on interest group lobbying which points to the importance of the relational context and 'financial unity' as key determinants of financial power, and from which we derive our first hypothesis about the stringency of banking reform. This section also draws on theories of interest representation to specify our empirical expectations about cross-national variation, differentiating between 'competitive' and 'cooperative' forms of financial power. The chapter then considers the institutional context of financial power, reviewing theories of agenda setting and 'venue shifting' to derive our second hypothesis about the (de)politicization of banking reform. The final section pulls these insights together by presenting our *comparative financial power* framework: combining the two explanatory variables (interest group lobbying + venue shifting) to produce a 2 × 2 typology of different banking reform outcomes (durable, contested, symbolic, and no reform). We end with a brief note about the rationale for our case study selection.

2. The political economy of financial regulation

We first assess existing and potential explanations of bank structural reform rooted in the sub-disciplines of international and comparative political economy, before turning to theories of business power.

International political economy

There is an abundant scholarship within IPE devoted to explaining financial regulation. Typically, this focuses on the preferences and power of different countries, and the harmonization of financial rules at the international level over recent decades. This literature assumes that international regulatory cooperation has important redistributive implications, and thus benefits some more than others (Oatley and Nabors 1998). Moreover, international standards in finance will only be agreed when these reflect the interests of the largest 'hegemonic' country—typically, the US (Simmons 2001). Similarly, Drezner (2007) examines the role of the 'great powers', defined as those with large internal markets, in shaping financial regulation. Since the late 1990s, this has enabled the EU to challenge the US as international regulatory pace-setter on the basis of its expanding 'market power' (Damro 2012). Other IPE scholars emphasize the importance of 'regulatory capacity'—defined as 'a jurisdiction's ability to formulate, monitor, and enforce a set of market rules'—as a key determinant of regulatory power and preferences in finance (Bach and Newman 2007; Posner 2009; Büthe and Mattli 2011). This gives large jurisdictions first-mover advantage in rule setting at the international level (Posner 2010).

Bank structural reform poses a profound puzzle for this IPE scholarship. At the height of the global financial crisis, several countries—notably the US and the UK—moved quickly to introduce reforms aimed at curbing the speculative activities of their largest banks. Yet despite constituting amongst the largest financial jurisdictions, with considerable market power and regulatory capacity, and the potential to exploit first-mover advantage, there was almost no serious attempt to coordinate these important regulatory initiatives at the international level. A similar pattern characterizes developments in the EU. Although a small number of member states (including France and Germany) implemented minimal structural reforms at an early stage, the EU authorities were ultimately unable to forge an agreement to harmonize these at the supranational level.

An alternative IPE perspective suggests that the key drivers in regulatory politics are no longer domestic forces, but actors capable of coordinating their activities across national borders (Cerny 2010). This work highlights the importance of powerful transnational 'communities' (Djelic and Quack 2010) and alliances of international firms (Graz and Nölke 2008; McKeen-Edwards and Porter 2013) in the formation of a new 'transnational pluralism' (Cerny 2010). Similarly, the 'new interdependence' approach (Farrell and Newman 2014, 2016; Newman and Posner 2016a, 2016b) examines the formation of cross-border coalitions brought together by mutual interdependence. The reconfiguration of transnational governance also features prominently in work on the growth of transgovernmental networks of regulators (Porter 2014; Tsingou 2015) and professional networks

(Seabrooke 2014; Seabrooke and Nilsson 2015; Henriksen and Seabrooke 2016) as channels of regulatory norm diffusion and convergence.

What these IPE perspectives have in common is the assumption that the mobilization of transnational coalitions of private and public actors serve as a powerful force in defence of cross-border economic activity and the promotion of transnational regulation. In the realm of financial services, studies suggest that cross-border alliances were pivotal in driving financial market integration and liberalization prior to the crisis, particularly within the EU (Mügge 2010; Macartney 2010). Lobbying by transnational associations and firms has also played a critical role in shaping financial regulatory reform since the crisis (Tsingou 2008; Underhill and Zhang 2008; Baker 2010; Young 2012). For example, evidence suggests that transnational finance was instrumental in shaping the development of new global standards on bank capital and liquidity requirements (Lall 2012) and hedge funds (Woll 2013; James and Quaglia 2019). Similarly, transnational regulatory networks played an important part in facilitating the coordination of new international guidelines on the resolution of banks (Quaglia and Spendzharova 2019) and the central clearing of derivatives (Quaglia and Spendzharova 2020). Cross-border alliances also facilitated the resolution of transatlantic regulatory disputes, notably in accounting standards (Farrell and Newman 2015) and derivatives (Newman and Posner 2018).

We argue that IPE explanations perform poorly in explaining bank structural reform, or the lack thereof, since the financial crisis. It is self-evident that accounts focused on the causal role of powerful transnational alliances are not well placed to explain fine-grained variation in banking reforms across different national jurisdictions. Nonetheless, it is possible to construct an IPE-based explanation of post-crisis regulatory divergence based on the economic size and significance of globally active financial firms in different jurisdictions. For example, a transnational perspective would lead us to assume that countries with highly internationalized banking systems should be more vulnerable to lobbying by transnational financial alliances. In other words, governments in these jurisdictions would be expected to come under significant pressure to maintain favourable tax and regulatory regimes, and to push for similar international and EU-level standards. By contrast, countries with domestically oriented banking systems should seek to maintain greater autonomy to impose tougher restrictions on their financial system.

However, these expectations are not borne out by the empirical evidence from our cases. Hence, those countries that were home to the largest number of global systemically important banks (G-SIBs) at the height of the crisis—the US (8) and the UK (5)—implemented the most far-reaching bank structural reforms since the crisis. By contrast, the other three countries we examine hosted fewer G-SIBs—France (4), Germany (2), and the Netherlands (1)—but rowed back on their commitment to tougher regulation. This is not to deny that transnational financial interests devoted substantial resources to lobbying against the structural separation of banks. But it is a recognition that careful comparative analysis of structural reform demands greater attention to country-level factors that have shaped the post-crisis policy response.

Comparative political economy

CPE approaches start from the assumption that national economic systems are characterized by distinct institutional configurations. Rooted in historical institutionalism, these configurations are viewed as highly path dependent because they generate comparative institutional advantages for particular economic sectors (Fioretos 2010, 2011; Howarth and Quaglia 2013a, 2016a, 2016b). Importantly, national governments will seek to preserve these advantages by resisting external initiatives—such as the establishment of common international or EU-level regulatory standards—that threaten the economic interests of these powerful domestic sectors. Applying this to the financial sector, policy makers will therefore engage in a 'battle of the systems' (Story and Walter 1997) by pursuing international and EU regulation that reflects the prevailing economic interests of the national financial industry. From this perspective, several studies have analysed the politics of EU financial services regulation (Quaglia 2010a) and, later, of Banking Union (Howarth and Quaglia 2016a), by looking at the configuration of the financial sector. Other works have adopted historical institutionalism (Fioretos 2010, 2011), or constructivism (Busch 2004, 2008), in order to investigate competition between national financial systems. Applying a CPE framework to bank structural reform, we would expect to find that government preferences should derive from key institutional features of the national financial system, and the particular distributive implications of structural separation on the largest national banks.

A related literature on Varieties of Financial Capitalism (VoFC) differentiates between two main types of financial system (Zysman 1983; Hardie and Howarth 2013): 'bank-based' financial systems, common to coordinated market economies in continental Europe, in which banks provide the bulk of lending to non-financial corporations; and 'capital markets-based' financial systems, typical of liberal market economies like the US and UK, in which securities markets provide an equally important source of external funding to non-financial companies. These distinct financial systems rest on and inform different systems of regulatory governance. The US and UK are typically viewed as neoliberal regimes which favour light-touch 'market making' regulation, based on a benign view of efficient markets (Hodson and Mabbett 2009; Mügge 2011). By contrast, France and Germany are frequently seen as having a 'market shaping' approach, which assumes that financial markets are prone to instability and advocates greater constraints on the activities of banks (Quaglia 2010; Zimmerman 2010).

From this perspective, one would expect the US and UK to resist substantive structural reforms to banking in order to preserve the competitiveness of their lightly regulated banking systems; by contrast, France and Germany should support the imposition of tighter restrictions on the sort of speculative financial activities associated with 'Anglo-Saxon' capitalism in order to create a more level playing field. It is difficult to reconcile these expectations, however, with national patterns of post-crisis reform. Paradoxically, it is the US and UK that intervened decisively to restrict the trading activities of their largest banks, while France and Germany sought to defend the traditional model of universal banking. Moreover, it is unclear from a VoC perspective what position to expect the Netherlands—which combines features of coordinated markets with liberal financial regulation—to take on structural reform.

Later iterations of the CPE approach, examining the existence of Varieties of Financial Capitalism (VoFC) (Zysman 1983), offer a partial answer to this puzzle by highlighting the growth of 'market-based banking' (Hardie and Howarth 2013a). In the four European countries that we investigate in this book, traditional banks remain dominant sources of lending in the economy. But in the decades prior to the crisis, they had become increasingly reliant on wholesale funding markets and the use of securitization, leading to a rapid expansion of banks' trading assets (see Hardie and Howarth 2013a, pp. 39–41). This trend went furthest in the US and the UK, while large banks in all five countries also purchased huge quantities of high-yield securitized assets. In France, Germany, and the Netherlands, these recent developments were actively supported by national governments as a way of building national bank champions capable of competing with Wall Street and the City of London as global financial players (Howarth and Quaglia 2016a).

The rise of market-based banking in Europe offers a potential explanation as to why many countries proved so reluctant to introduce major structural reforms. As Hardie and Macartney (2016) argue, the French and German governments actively sought to protect the investment activities of their largest universal banks in an effort to compete with US investment banks. The Dutch government acted similarly. This meant diluting proposed EU-level ringfencing rules, and legislation on capital requirements proposed by the Liikanen Group, which threatened to prevent the reconstruction of market-making banking following the financial crisis (Hardie and Macartney 2016). While this revisionist CPE analysis helps to explain French and German preferences, it leaves two fundamental questions unanswered. First, why did President Hollande in France initially make firm political commitments to introduce structural separation, only to perform a sudden u-turn in government later on? Second, this perspective offers no explanation for the actions of the US and the UK, as the originators of market-based banking and home to several global systemically important financial institutions (G-SIFIs) with huge investment banking operations. Why did the Obama administration and the

UK coalition government act in such a way as to put US- and UK-headquartered banks at a potential competitive disadvantage?

A final CPE-based explanation would highlight the international scope of banking activities as a key driver of banking reform in different countries (on the growth of cross-border banking, see Mügge 2006; Engelen and Konings 2010; Epstein 2017). Contrary to the IPE account outlined above, a comparative perspective might lead us to expect that higher levels of internationalization—in terms of both assets held abroad by domestically headquartered banks and the presence of foreign bank assets as a percentage of the total—should increase government support for structural reform to minimize exposure to international instability. In the UK case, however, these assumptions generate different expectations about policy preferences. On the one hand, three of the largest UK-headquartered banks—HSBC, Barclays, and Royal Bank of Scotland (RBS)—had both substantial overseas assets and a strong presence in domestic retail lending, leading us to expect tougher rules. On the other hand, with only one exception—Santander—the subsidiaries of large foreign banks in the UK lacked a significant retail presence. Consequently, structural separation would have a negligible impact on foreign bank operations in the UK, while potentially placing three of the largest UK-headquartered banks at a significant competitive disadvantage. UK preferences are therefore not reducible to the international exposure of its banking system.

In the other four country cases, patterns of internationalization do not neatly correlate with industry or government preferences on structural reform. Although foreign bank assets as a proportion of total bank assets in the US were high prior to 2007, they dropped sharply below UK levels (around 15 per cent) in the years that followed (Hardie and Maxfield 2013). Moreover, while foreign bank presence in France and the Netherlands was consistently lower (below 10 per cent), levels in Germany were significantly higher and similar to those in the UK and US by 2013 (14 per cent). Many European banks also had significant exposure to non-domestic holdings. For example, a large percentage of the assets of the three big Dutch banks—which dominated the domestic retail market—were held outside the country. The four biggest universal banks in France—which also dominated the domestic retail market—also had a significant international presence (albeit lower than the UK banks). However, this did not translate into Dutch and French government support for stringent structural reforms.

In Germany, several features of the banking system would lead us to expect diverging preferences on reform: the large internationally focused universal banks—notably Deutsche Bank—would be expected to oppose structural reform; but the smaller, domestically focused savings and cooperative banks would be expected to support restrictions on the speculative activities of large banks on the grounds that this would reduce their competitive advantage. In addition, the substantial political influence of the smaller banks, and their relative importance in the retail market, lead to the expectation of German government support for tougher rules. Yet this is not what happened: in fact, the small banks joined their bigger commercial rivals in opposing structural separation, while the German government quietly abandoned its early pledge to address the problem of TBTF banks.

We argue that existing CPE explanations of bank structural reform perform poorly because of their underlying economic structural determinism. The analytical focus upon distinct national banking systems leads to the assumption that the preferences of policy makers are relatively fixed, rooted in the economic interests of powerful industrial sectors and national firms. In reality, preferences are constantly in flux, contested and ill-defined due to disagreement or uncertainty about the impact of proposed regulations. Second, accounts of change in national banking systems tend to rely on exogenous factors, such as external economic shocks, to which policy makers respond in order to establish a new institutional equilibrium. Yet this downplays the endogeneity of institutional change: namely, how banking systems can be reconfigured from within.

Finally, CPE accounts leave little room for the role of political agency or policy choice. In designing banking regulation, governments do not automatically privilege economic interests. Instead, they confront a dilemma between international competitiveness (prioritized by industry) and domestic stability (demanded by voters) (Singer 2004, 2007)—or, indeed, a trilemma that includes real economy funding concerns (Howarth and Quaglia 2016a). According to Kapstein (1989), the resolution of these trade-offs will ultimately reflect the ideological beliefs, cultural norms, and individual values of policy makers. Similarly, Young (2012) argues that the variability of regulatory outcomes reflects the heterogeneity of industry preferences, divisions amongst interest groups, and the discretion, autonomy, and resources wielded by national regulators and elected officials.

In short, there remains a gap in CPE accounts of financial regulation with respect to explaining when, why, and how politics matters. To explain national divergence and shifting preferences on bank structural reform, we therefore need to incorporate a theoretical account of the political process through which economic interests are mediated. To be precise, this requires a framework that captures how the interests of the financial sector are interpreted by political and bureaucratic actors, and mediated by institutional structures and processes. The following section contributes to this task by reviewing another literature—theories of business power—that have made an important contribution to understanding post-crisis financial regulation.

Theories of business power

With its origins in the work of Lindblom (1977) and (Block 1980), theories of business power suggest that the influence of firms derives from two main sources.

The first, instrumental power, is concerned with the observable qualities of power relations, unrelated to the core functions of the firm, through which business influences politics: this includes the capacity to access and influence policy makers through lobbying, campaigning, and political contributions. The second, structural power, relates to the idea that firms can shape the structural conditions under which governments make decisions (see Quinn and Shapiro 1991; Swank 1992; Przeworski and Wallerstein 1998). Business wields exceptional power because governments are dependent on their investment decisions to sustain economic growth and fund public services. In anticipation of negative inducement effects, and their electoral and fiscal consequences, policy makers tend to avoid any policy that threatens to undermine business confidence. As a result, business interests enjoy an over-proportionate consideration in the formulation of policy, even if they abstain from direct political activity.

Hacker and Pierson (2002, p. 281) criticize these deterministic accounts for assuming that the pressure to protect business interests is generated independently and 'systematically' by an 'investment veto weapon'. They raise three objections. First, structural accounts fail to explain the ubiquitous nature of business lobbying. If policy makers automatically adjust policies in anticipation of the reaction of business, why do they devote so many resources to lobbying policy makers (Smith 2000)? Second, business does not always win in battles with government. Hence policy change has been found frequently to override the preferences of business across a wide spectrum of policies (Bernhagen 2007). Third, these explanations ignore the extent of divisions within the business community (Hacker and Pierson 2002, p. 280). In reality, policies often bestow advantages on some firms or sectors at the expense of others, forcing them to compete against one another for influence (Smith 2000, pp. 13–17).

More recent contributions highlight how business power is mediated by ideational processes. Bell (2012) views business power as inter-subjectively constructed by government actors that use ideational lenses to confront, interpret, and react to business pressures. These ideas can include the appropriateness of particular policies, the value of particular forms of business investment, and perceptions of 'globalization' (Hay and Rosamond 2002). Applying this framework to UK banking reform, Bell and Hindmoor (2015b) show how institutions and ideas have constrained bank power since the crisis. First, the capacity of the state has been significantly enhanced through supervisory reform, strengthening the role and powers of key regulatory agencies and insulating them from external pressures. Second, ideational shifts have contributed to the decline in the perception of threat amongst policy makers, leading them to discount bank warnings of potential disinvestment. Third, financial power has been weakened by the increasingly politicized environment in which regulatory decisions are made (Bell and Hindmoor 2016). This implies that state actors have considerable agency to pursue strategies aimed at interpreting, channelling, and filtering business power.

Culpepper's (2011, 2016) important insight is that the political power of business varies according to two dimensions: the political salience of the issue (high or low); and the nature of institutional governance (formal or informal). The intersection of these dimensions enables us to categorize the type of politics which is likely to characterize government–business interaction (2011, p. 181). Under low salience, business power is likely to be disproportionately greater as policy making is less visible and 'outsider' interests are unlikely to be mobilized, so government is more likely to defer to the expertise of industry. Where institutions are informal, policy making will be characterized by private interest governance as firms can exploit the 'quiet politics' of access, interpersonal networks, and technical knowledge. Where institutional governance is more formal, however, bureaucratic actors play a greater role and so business influence will need to be exercised through networks of regulators (bureaucratic network negotiation). As an issue becomes increasingly salient, the value of industry expertise is undermined as interaction with government becomes more conflictual. In this situation, non-business groups, political parties, and legislatures will increasingly mobilize to challenge industry lobbying (see Mitchell 1997; Dür and Mateo 2014; Rasmussen 2015). Where governance remains informal, business power is constrained by the role of organized labour in social partner bargaining, typically under the possibility or threat of government intervention. Alternatively, issues may be deliberately escalated to formal political settings characterized by partisan contestation. Here, business power is likely to be at its weakest as non-business groups are highly vocal and well organized, and political parties prioritize electoral considerations by responding or appealing to public opinion. The mode of interaction between government and industry is therefore a key determinant of the players involved, their resources, and the rules of decision making.

The traditional business power literature struggles to explain important aspects of post-crisis banking reform. It is self-evident that structural and instrumental power alone cannot explain patterns of cross-national variation. The capacity of large banks to threaten disinvestment (structural power) or to mobilize lobbying resources (instrumental power) has remained largely constant over time, and so cannot explain the sudden shift to more stringent regulation since the crisis in certain jurisdictions but not in others. In particular, those countries with either the largest financial sector (i.e., the UK, as a proportion of GDP), or which have the greatest lobbying capabilities (Wall Street in the US), are—paradoxically—those that have gone the furthest in cracking down on the activities of their own banks. Even if we follow Culpepper and Reinke (2014) in discounting the structural power of US banks on account of their dependency on the US internal market, business power still fails to explain the tough response of the UK authorities— even in the face of explicit threats to leave by the UK's largest global banks (see Chapter 5).

Analysing the mediating role of ideas and institutions, as more recent studies of business power have done, goes a long way to addressing these limitations. Indeed, it is a central contention of this book that these variables are critical to any cross-national comparative analysis of bank structural reform. Despite these theoretical innovations, however, we argue that important aspects of business power remain under-specified. First, most accounts have a relatively limited view of public and private agency. On the one hand, the state is commonly portrayed as a single, unified actor. Yet this ignores the extent of political competition within government, rooted in contestation over the desirability of different policy outcomes and uncertainty over the impact of policy change. On the other hand, business tends to be treated as a 'black box' with unified preferences for less government interference. Yet regulation creates winners as well as losers amongst firms and sectors, creating the conditions for businesses to compete for influence in an effort to gain competitive advantage over others (for example, see Farrell and Newman 2015; Young 2015).

Second, political salience is commonly conceptualized as an exogenous independent variable which constrains business power. Culpepper (2016, p. 462) reminds us that heightened political salience is a necessary, but not sufficient, condition: it must be transformed into political effect by the mobilization of non-business groups and/or through the action of policy makers. But this tells us little about the factors that cause salience to increase or decrease. Put differently, salience may be endogenous to explanations of business power in at least two respects. On the one hand, firms actively seek to affect the salience of issues by shaping public awareness and political attention. Most commonly, this involves (re)shaping their relational environment through mobilization and alliance building with like-minded firms and associations. As Keller (2018) shows, for example, business groups often assert influence through 'noisy' politics: by actively raising the salience of an issue and expanding the conflict. On the other hand, policy makers can also manipulate political salience by changing the institutional context for decision making. This reflects the fact that some institutional venues are more visible, accessible, and (viewed as) legitimate than others. A better understanding of the endogeneity of political salience is therefore needed.

Finally, business power accounts are valuable for explaining how and why policy change is possible in the face of determined business opposition. Typically, as policy issues become increasingly salient, non-business groups are organized, and decision making is escalated to highly visible political arenas. Yet there have been few accounts of the reverse process: how opportunities which appear ripe for policy change may be deliberately closed down. Specifically, we know little about how issues become less salient over time, when non-business groups demobilize, or why issues are moved from 'noisy' public to 'quiet' informal institutional venues. Here the influence of business may be more pernicious as it relates to the second face of power and 'non-decision making' (Bachrach and Baratz 1962). Likewise, we know relatively little about the ability of business to keep issues off the policy agenda or—more intriguingly—to have them downplayed or removed.

To gain a better understanding of how and why financial power—and the salience of financial regulatory reform—varies across national contexts, we therefore need a richer account of the relational and institutional context within which they operate. To address the first of these, we turn to the growing body of scholarship on financial interest lobbying.

3. Financial interest lobbying

The analysis of lobbying has become increasingly popular in the political economy of finance (Oatley et al. 2013; Winecoff 2015; Young 2015; Young and Pagliari 2017), and in comparative studies of financial regulation (see Reinicke 1995; Busch 2008). Studies commonly emphasize the superior resources available to the financial sector when lobbying, enabling them to secure superior access to policy makers and resist new regulatory burdens (Igan et al. 2009; Johnson and Kwak 2010). These resources are not just financial, but also consist of valuable private information and technical expertise which are essential for developing complex regulation (Broscheid and Coen 2007; Rasmussen and Carroll 2013). The resulting 'information asymmetries' give financial lobbyists significant leverage in shaping the (re)distributional effects of new regulation by hindering the participation of non-financial stakeholders (Cerny 1994; Underhill and Zhang 2008; Lall 2015). The institutional environment also plays an important role in mediating the role of finance. Some scholars highlight the formal mandate of regulatory agencies, their internal governance structures, and the transparency of industry–regulator interaction as determinants of financial power (Underhill and Zhang 2008; Barth et al. 2012). Others emphasize how the movement of individuals between the public and private sectors ('revolving doors') fosters dense interpersonal and interorganizational ties (Seabrooke and Tsingou 2009; Baker 2010; Selmier 2013) and 'club-like' policy communities (Tsingou 2008, 2014; Braun and Raddatz 2010).

A recurring theme in the interest group literature is that business power does not simply reflect the attributes and resources of individual organizations, but is embedded in the wider relational context within which they operate. The degree to which the business community is united or divided has long been understood as a critical factor in shaping regulatory outcomes (Sabatier 1988; Heinz et al. 1993; Fuchs 2007; Spillman 2012; Klüver 2013). Hence, lobbying success has been shown to be a function of the capacity of firms to coordinate lobbying activities closely, and to present a unified front in their engagement with policy makers (Hojnacki 1997; Hula 1999; Beyers and Braun 2014; Bunea 2015; Mahoney and Baumgartner 2015). This is facilitated by the presence of 'peak' business associations (Spillman 2012), interlocking directorates (Mizruchi 2013), and shared professional backgrounds (Seabrooke and Tsingou 2009). Interest group unity matters because it constitutes a heuristic for policy makers about the level of support for a policy (Esterling 2005), and helps justify decisions to external audiences, such as elected officials and voters (Greenwood 2017).

Empirical evidence shows that the financial sector wields a formidable capacity to engage in collective action, both within and beyond the industry (Clapp and Helleiner 2012; Kastner 2014, 2018; Pagliari and Young 2014, 2016; Winecoff 2015). For example, empirical evidence confirms that lobbying success is a function of how well finance is able to 'speak with one voice' through centralized associations (McKeen-Edwards and Porter 2013; Chalmers 2015, 2017, 2020). Similarly, other studies suggest that the financial sector is more unified, and enjoys greater support from other business groups, than other economic sectors (Young and Pagliari 2017). This 'finance capital unity' thesis is important because it renders the financial industry uniquely placed to leverage its influence through alliance building with groups that share the same preferences (Pagliari and Young 2014, p. 584).

Related to this, the 'population ecology' approach stresses the structural advantages provided by membership of wider interest group networks—such as the ability to pool scarce resources, coordinate political activity, and develop common positions (Gray and Lowery 1996, p. 40; Hojnacki 1997; Holmes 2009). Collaboration with non-financial groups also serves to legitimize the financial sector's demands by signalling alignment with the wider business community, and allows it to exploit the political and reputational capital that 'real' economy groups wield (Young and Pagliari 2017). Evidence suggests that the financial sector is therefore instrumental in mobilizing a plurality of interest groups around their policy goals (Hula 1999; James and Christopoulous 2018), and that financial industry associations play a critical role in coalition building by facilitating information exchange, supporting consensus building, and acting as a single interlocutor for policy makers (Klüver 2013; Hollman 2018).

The centrality of finance in interest group ecologies is commonly attributed to its critical infrastructural role in modern economies, generating and managing goods and services which other businesses rely on—such as the supply of credit, management of capital, insurance services, and the ability to 'hedge' for the future through derivatives and securities (Broz 1999; Krippner 2011). The financialization literature also highlights the increasing holdings of financial assets (Stockhammer 2004), the spread of 'mark to market' accounting practices (Perry and Nölke 2006), and the importance of 'shareholder value' (Lazonick and O'Sullivan 2000) among non-financial corporates. The result is that financial regulation generates significant externalities for other economic sectors and firms, giving them a powerful incentive to mobilize and ally with the financial sector in response to new policy interventions (Fligstein and Shin 2007; Witko 2016).

Yet other important scholarship points to the limits of business unity. Numerous studies have demonstrated how conflict between economic interests remains a common feature across a range of sectors (Clapp 2003; Falkner 2007; Young 2012; Roemer-Mahler 2013). Cleavages can form within a sector, typically between domestic and internationally oriented firms (Frieden 1988), and across sectors, due to firms' divergent factor endowments (Rogowski 1990) or location in global supply chains (Falkner 2007). Modern regulatory governance also challenges business unity as policy interventions have become increasingly particularistic and discriminatory, thereby undermining the perception of shared interests and incentives to form cross-sectoral alliances (Majone 1997). In addition, interest group scholarship suggests that diffuse interests are less inhibited by collective action problems than standard economic theories assume (Baumgartner et al. 2009; Godwin et al. 2012; Trumbull 2012). The resulting mobilization of 'countervailing groups' can diminish the credibility of business (Lindblom 1997; Falkner 2007), and mitigates the risk of 'groupthink' and intellectual capture in the policy process (Carpenter and Moss 2014).

It is well documented that the 2008 crisis challenged the position of organized financial interests (Helleiner and Thistlethwaite 2013; Kastner 2014; Pagliari and Young 2014). Crises facilitate the mobilization of societal actors by producing a 'demonstration effect', revealing the (re)distributional implications of regulatory policies and opening new channels of access to policy makers (Mattli and Woods 2009). Hence the emergence of coalitions of diffuse interests—including taxpayer and consumer associations, labour unions, think tanks, and civil society groups— around the call for tougher financial regulation (Clapp and Helleiner 2012; Scholte 2013; Pagliari and Young 2016). Regulators have facilitated these trends by deliberately engaging with a wider plurality of voices, and finding new ways to integrate them more effectively into regulatory consultation processes (Helleiner 2010). Nor is the mobilization of corporate interests around post-crisis regulation a guarantee of business unity. Although reliant on private goods like credit, business groups also want public goods like financial stability—which may lead them to support tougher rules to reduce the likelihood of future crises and bank bail-outs (Mügge 2006; Clapp and Helleiner 2012).

We predict that 'financial unity' is a key determinant of the stringency of regulatory reform. Specifically, we hypothesize that—under conditions of heightened political salience and public anger about TBTF banks—the financial industry will be more influential in shaping bank structural reform when it is unified. This unity of voice and purpose will be reflected in the financial industry's ability to leverage broad alliances both across the sector and with the wider business community, to articulate its regulatory preferences. The capacity to draw on a wider interest group ecology not only serves to strengthen and legitimize the concerns of financial firms targeted by new regulation; it also ensures that they are less likely to be challenged or contradicted by the mobilization of countervailing groups—either from inside or outside the industry. Relating this capacity back to the business power literature outlined earlier, we label this *cooperative financial power* to reflect the extent to which a broad range of economic interests engage in cooperation and collaboration in the lobbying process.

By contrast, the financial industry will be less influential in shaping regulatory outcomes when it is divided.[1] In a context of heightened political salience and anger towards TBTF banks, fragmentation of the financial sector's voice will inevitably inhibit the articulation of a coherent set of regulatory preferences. In the absence of a supportive interest group ecology, firms will be dependent on lobbying individually, or through (sub-)sectoral associations, and thus less able to draw on broader business alliances to legitimize their concerns in the policy process. Impacted firms are also likely to face a greater challenge from countervailing groups, from either inside or outside the industry, with whom they are forced to compete for access and influence in the policy process. We label this *competitive financial power* to reflect how fragmented lobbying resembles a conflictual struggle between competing economic and political interests.

To summarize, our first hypothesis is as follows:

H1. The financial industry will be more influential in shaping bank structural reform when financial power is cooperative; and less influential when financial power is competitive.

The literature on financial interest lobbying and 'financial unity' provides an important potential source of variation in financial power. By itself, however, this literature tells us little about how or why the financial industry is more or less influential in particular countries. To provide greater specificity with regard to our empirical expectations of cross-national variation, the following section draws on comparative politics and theories of interest intermediation.

4. Modes of interest representation

Theories of interest intermediation refer to key features of political and economic institutions, and established ideas about state–society relations, which structure

---

[1] Importantly, we make no claims about the effectiveness of competitive financial power under non-crisis economic conditions. In a context of low salience, or 'quiet politics', divided and fragmented financial lobbying may be less of a hindrance to industry influence. Instead, policy makers and regulators may simply internalize the preferences of the financial sector, thereby minimizing the number of countervailing voices, and thus reducing the perceived need for centralized lobbying—as in the US and UK prior to 2008 (see Moran 2009; Johal et al. 2014; James et al. 2021).

engagement between policy makers and business in different national contexts (Katzenstein 1978; Hall 1986; Lehmbruch 1991; Hall and Soskice 2001; Schmidt 2002). The character of interest intermediation shapes—and is shaped by—the organization and representation of business. In other words, it is mutually constitutive of the incentives that individual firms have to organize collectively, the number and resource capacity of business associations, and the extent to which these organizations seek to influence the policy process.

Classically, the literature differentiates between three main 'modes' of interest intermediation (Eising and Kohler-Koch 1999; Schmidt 2002; Eising 2009). In *pluralism*, traditionally associated with the UK and US, state and society are separate: the state's role is that of a referee mediating between narrow, fluid, and fragmented organized interests which compete to influence policy makers (Siaroff 1999). In *neo-corporatism*, characteristic of a number of continental European countries—notably, Austria and Germany—the boundaries between the state and society are blurred. Business interests are centralized within functional peak associations which are integrated into the policy process and given rule-making powers in particular sectors (Schmitter and Lehmbruch 1979; Lehmbruch and Schmitter 1982; Lehmbruch 1984). The *statist* mode refers to the role of the central state in wielding political authority above society and directing economic activity from the top down, traditionally associated with post-war France. Consequently, the most powerful organized interests are co-opted by the state to shape policy decisions and facilitate implementation (Schmidt 1996; Clift 2012).

We recognize that these historically rooted modes of interest intermediation have been fundamentally challenged over the past four decades. In particular, a large body of work suggests that neo-corporatist and statist structures of state–business interaction have been progressively eroded since the 1980s, as tripartite institutions and state intervention have given way to demands for liberalization and deregulation (see Deeg 1999, 2001; Eising 2009; Streeck 2009; Jabko and Massoc 2012; Clift 2014; Andeweg et al. 2020). Nonetheless, we argue that an important legacy of these historic modes can still be found with respect to contemporary features of interest representation: namely, the extent to which business interests are represented collectively through centralized peak/trade associations—traditionally found in neo-corporatist systems—and rely on strong elite interconnections—as in statist systems; or, conversely, the extent to which business interests are decentralized and tend to be represented by individual firms and (sub-)sectoral associations—characteristic of pluralist systems.

We argue that long-standing institutional features of interest representation play a critical role in mediating the power of finance at the national level. Specifically, modes of interest representation structure the capacity of financial firms to leverage their influence in the policy process by building alliances with other financial firms, different economic sectors, and the wider business community. Applying these 'ideal' modes as heuristic devices, we hypothesize that the extent to which financial industry lobbying around banking reform is unified or divided differs significantly between systems traditionally characterized by pluralism and those with a legacy of neo-corporatism or statism.[2] This provides a firmer empirical grounding for our conceptual distinction between *competitive* and *cooperative* financial power, as we detail below.

Competitive financial power

We expect countries traditionally associated with pluralist modes of interest representation to be characterized by competitive financial power. That is, financial industry lobbying will tend to be fragmented between individual firms and relatively weak (sub-)sectoral trade associations, and financial interests will face significant competition for access and influence from countervailing groups. The result is that financial industry preferences are often heterogenous, there is minimal coordination of lobbying activity, and policy makers face multiple organizational interlocutors in the policy process.

Evidence for competitive financial power comes from the US and the UK. In the US, a divided, dispersed, and decentralized system of government historically produced a densely organized but highly fragmented pattern of interest representation—characterized by overlapping, multi-sectoral, and multi-level forms of intermediation (Moran 2009, p. 51). The prevalence of lobbying is also attributable to the development of a distinctive regulatory state since the New Deal of the 1930s. This generated a regulatory culture dominated by legal arguments and juridical reasoning, fostering a highly adversarial contest between firms and regulators (Moran 2009, p. 170). It also produced a byzantine regulatory architecture: in financial services, for instance, the ad hoc proliferation of new bodies in response to the expansion and diversification of the sector produced no fewer than six separate agencies (Carpenter 2010; Jacobs and King 2016). This fragmentation created multiple points of access for organized interests, encouraging business to devote vast resources to lobbying. Recent decades witnessed a massive expansion of corporate advocacy, with the number of lobbyists registered in Washington increasing from an estimated 3000 in the 1960s to over 35,000 by 2005 (Heinz et al. 1993, p. 10; Bimbaum 2005; Drutman 2015)—with a further 40,000 lobbyists

---

[2] We do not claim that our cases perfectly fit any of the modes of interest representation. The literature makes clear that these modes are 'ideal' types, key features of which have undergone considerable change in recent decades. Nonetheless, we would argue that the modes do provide explanatory leverage by pointing to distinct and persistent institutional characteristics of interest group organization and engagement in the policy process in different countries. As such, we employ them here as heuristic devices: i.e., necessary simplifications for the purpose of generating testable hypotheses and empirical expectations about the nature and extent of financial power in different national contexts.

registered at state level (Rush 2007). This produced a system of 'organized combat' (Hacker and Pierson 2010) in which competitive industry associations coexisted with an equally competitive, and hugely diverse, world of more specialized interest representation, where a very large number of interests were organized at industry and sectoral level.

The literature on US corporate lobbying identifies three related trends since the 1980s. First, lobbying became increasingly competitive. Prior to this, lobbying in Washington relied overwhelmingly on being well connected and developing interpersonal relationships with key policy makers in Congress, government departments, and the myriad of regulatory agencies. But with the onset of financial liberalization in the 1980s and 1990s, these informal ties were increasingly overlaid by a more institutionally complex system of business representation as the number and diversity of lobby groups expanded (McGrath 2005, p. 89). Second, lobbying was increasingly organized and professionalized, with associations and firms devoting huge sums to building up their own 'in house' lobbying capabilities inside the Washington 'beltway' (Baumgartner and Leech 1998; Martin 2000). Third, lobbying became increasingly 'particularistic' (Drutman 2015, p. 13). Where once individual corporations and CEOs tended to stay out of politics, firms accounted for an increasing proportion of lobbying activity and spending in Washington as they sought to defend their particular corporate interests.

Wall Street constituted a formidable special interest group at the start of the financial crisis. The collective interests of the US financial industry were represented by several large industry associations, notably the American Banking Association (ABA), the Financial Services Roundtable (FSR) and the Securities Industry and Financial Markets Association (SIFMA), while business interests more broadly were represented by the powerful US Chambers of Commerce. Finance constituted one of the largest campaign contributors through Political Action Committees (PACs) prior to the crisis (Hacker and Pierson 2010). Of the hundred largest contributing firms, the financial sector donated more than the contributions of the energy, health care, defence, and telecoms sectors combined (Schouten et al. 2008). Numerous studies also document how Wall Street devoted increasingly vast sums of money to lobbying and forging stronger ties to the Washington policy community (Bebchuk and Fried 2004; Bartels 2010; Hacker and Pierson 2010; Johnson and Kwak 2010; Drutman 2015).

Yet Wall Street did not constitute a single, monolithic interest group. Despite decades of steady consolidation of local 'unit' banks into large nationwide banks (Calomiris and Haber 2014), the US banking sector remained one of the most diverse and fragmented in the world. Cumulatively, it included over 5000 individual banks—ranging from the handful of global investment banks clustered around Wall Street, to the thousands of local community banks that characterize 'Main Street'—chartered at both federal and state level (McLannahan 2018a). An important barrier to more centralized interest representation was the fact that

US banks were in fierce competition with one another for market share (Drutman 2015). Since the 1990s, the largest financial industry associations had struggled to reconcile the increasingly heterogeneous interests of the sector, with the result that they tended to articulate the views of their largest members on Wall Street (Kaiser 2013). Importantly, these intra-industry divisions created an opportunity for smaller, sectoral associations—such as the Independent Community Bankers of America (ICBA)—to assert themselves in Washington (see Chapter 4). This financial interest fragmentation was reinforced by the tendency of Wall Street firms to scale up their in-house public affairs departments and lobbying capabilities at the height of the crisis in anticipation of a wave of new regulations (Kaiser 2013).

The pre-crisis period also witnessed increased activism amongst diffuse interest groups, including consumers and taxpayers (Trumbull 2012; Kastner 2014, 2018). This development led to the emergence of increasingly vocal and well-organized ad hoc coalitions of societal groups, think tanks and activists in opposition to Wall Street, such as Americans for Financial Reform (AFR). Despite their wielding far fewer resources than business, Trumbull (2012) showed that diffuse interests can be highly effective in shaping policy outcomes when they forged broader 'legitimacy coalitions' with other societal groups—such as activists, think tanks, industry, and regulators—which claim to represent the broader public interest. A number of high-profile victories for consumer-led alliances in recent years— notably in relation to pharmaceutical regulation—led Trumbull to conclude that the US was undergoing a 'return to pluralism' (2012, p. 207). Similarly, Kastner (2014) details how an alliance of elected officials and civil society groups in the US successfully pushed consumer protection onto the banking reform agenda during the financial crisis. Supported by a wider transnational network of consumer and non-governmental organizations (NGOs), this alliance was able to overcome its collective action disadvantage by raising public attention, reframing the issue, and transforming the discourse about consumer regulation. Hence, the pervasive nature of financial lobbying in US politics in the wake of the crisis therefore guaranteed neither influence nor privilege.

Bank lobbying in the UK was not traditionally characterized by competitive financial power. In fact, for most of the post-war period, the relationship between the financial industry and the British state was quasi-corporatist. The City of London's influence was embedded in the 'Bank–Treasury–City nexus' (Moran 1991; Baker 1999): namely, the informal and closed institutional networks that existed between the City of London, the Treasury, and the Bank of England which ensured that the financial sector's interests were directly represented within government (Hopkin and Shaw 2016). Until the mid-1980s, this nexus underpinned a system of 'club governance' in which the activities of the financial sector were largely self-regulated, and the interests of the City were represented within the British state by the Bank of England and the Corporation of London (Moran 1991).

The system was challenged in two ways by the 'Big Bang' deregulation of 1986 (see Johal et al. 2014; James et al. 2021). First, it led to an influx of foreign firms, particularly US investment banks, lacking institutional ties to the British state, and placed financial regulation on a statutory footing for the first time (Moran 1991, 2009; Baker 1999). Second, financial liberalization led to the transformation of interest representation in the City. In particular, power increasingly shifted away from 'peak' business associations (like the Confederation of British Industry (CBI)), and older institutional trade associations (including the British Bankers' Association (BBA)—later UK Finance—and the Association of British Insurers (ABI)), to new specialist groups representing products and markets (such as the International Swaps and Derivatives Association (ISDA) and the Association for Financial Markets in Europe (AFME)). This produced a highly fragmented pattern of financial interest representation. A City of London report in 2002 described the 'spontaneous order' of associations as a 'jumble', with the sector represented by over fifty separate trade associations (Lascelles and Boleat 2002). The proliferation of groups generated significant potential for overlap, duplication of resources, and fierce competition for members, funds, and access to policy makers, giving the trade association 'industry' a total turnover of around £125m a year and employing around 1,000 people (Lascelles and Boleat 2002).

Mirroring developments in the US, financial interest fragmentation reflected two broader trends in UK business organization from the 1980s onwards: a shift away from the collective representation of business interests to more lobbying by individual firms; and to more formal and professionally organized business lobbying (Moran 2009, p. 44). Structural changes in the economy—the decline of manufacturing and the growth of finance—together with the abandonment of quasi-corporatist institutions by the Thatcher government, eroded the role and influence of business associations, both at the macro and sectoral levels (Moran 2009). Associations no longer had a formal role in the policy process and public officials increasingly sought to maintain an arm's-length relationship with industry, interacting with firms and associations on an infrequent and ad hoc basis around specific regulatory issues. Hence, by the late 1990s, empirical studies found the majority of trade associations to be both poorly resourced and poorly organized (May et al. 1998; Macdonald 2001).

Like Wall Street, the City of London continued to wield tremendous influence in the 1990s and 2000s within government, despite the increasingly fragmented and competitive nature of financial power. Crucially, however, this came to rely less on institutionalized intermediation, and more on a form of government patronage (James et al. 2021). Financial liberalization was first and foremost an ideological project driven by key ministers in the Thatcher government, and senior officials in the Bank of England and Department of Trade and Industry (Hopkin and Shaw 2016, p. 354). Important political support also came from groups closely associated with, and funded by, the City: such as the Institute of Directors and neoliberal think tanks, notably the Adam Smith Institute, the Centre for Policy Studies, and the Institute for Economic Affairs. Financial services were henceforth viewed as integral to the development of the UK's new post-industrial political economy (Johal et al. 2014, p. 412), necessitating a 'light touch' regulatory regime capable of attracting global (but particularly US) financial firms to use London as their European base (Coates and Hay 2001). With the internalization of these policies by successive governments prior to the 2008 crisis, there was consequently little need for the City to 'play politics' by engaging in the sort of 'organized combat' commonplace to Wall Street (Hopkin and Shaw 2016; Baker and Wigan 2017).

Institutionalized representation of the City's interests therefore remained surprisingly limited. The Big Bang reforms eroded the status of older institutions—such as the main municipal authority, the City of London Corporation—which lacked the specialist knowledge to engage with increasingly complex financial markets and regulation. Its role was gradually usurped by a series of ad hoc industry-funded and government-backed promotional bodies, including: International Financial Services London, created in 2001 to strengthen the City's voice in Europe; a new Financial Services Global Competitiveness Group, bringing together representatives from both industry and government; a High-Level Group of senior financial executives, chaired by Chancellor Gordon Brown in 2006; and a think tank, the International Centre for Financial Regulation (ICFR), created to study global and EU regulatory developments. In an attempt to restore the financial sector's reputation following the bail-out of several major UK banks in 2007–8, two new bodies were established: The CityUK, a pan-industry group to promote financial services at home; and the International Regulatory Strategy Group (IRSG) focused on responding to new regulatory developments. Yet these did little to enhance the City's capacity for collective representation. In addition to facing an increasingly hostile environment within government, the new bodies struggled to reconcile the heterogenous interests of the City, while most large non-UK financial firms—particularly US investment banks—preferred to undertake their own lobbying (James and Quaglia 2020).

Cooperative financial power

We argue that cooperative financial power is more characteristic of systems with a legacy of either neo-corporatism or statism. Here financial interest representation is traditionally more hierarchical and centralized—organized around powerful peak and industry trade associations, and (in the case of statism) elite interconnections between state officials and bank executives. Here banks are capable of leveraging broad alliances across the financial sector and the wider business community. This capacity facilitates the formation of a single homogeneous set of industry preferences on major policy issues and regulation, increases the degree to which industry lobbying is closely coordinated, and minimizes the number of industry interlocutors for policy makers.

Germany provides an important example of cooperative financial power. This power was underpinned by the post-war social market economy, a key pillar of which was economic tripartism: that is, negotiated agreements between the 'social partners'—business and trade unions—around key economic objectives, particularly related to employee rights and wage bargaining (Eising 2009). In practice, this involved granting a formal policy-making role to centralized peak associations, such as the Confederation of German Employers' Associations (BDA), the Federation of German Industries (BDI), the German Chamber of Commerce and Industry (DIHK), and the German Confederation of Skilled Crafts (ZDH). These powerful bodies enjoyed the status of public institutions with the state, implicitly committing them to act in the public interest, and codifying into law collectively negotiated settlements among private actors (Lutz 2000, pp. 152–5). The German model also granted banks a central role in mediating access to external funding for firms. The system was underpinned by a strong tradition of cross-shareholdings between SMEs (the *Mittelstand*) and local and regional banks (Crouch and Streeck 1997; Deeg 1999; Streeck 2009). By facilitating the provision of 'patient capital' to the *Mittelstand*, this *Hausbank* relationship was the backbone of Germany's export-led growth model.

A critical feature of the German banking system—which continued to differentiate it from the other European cases examined in this book—was its diffuse and decentralized structure. This was defined by three tiers or 'pillars': hundreds of private banks, dominated by the 'big four' (later, two) universal banks; cooperative banks, the *Volks-* and *Raiffeisenbanken*, with over 1000 in 2008; and approximately 400 public law savings banks, the *Sparkassen*, and the regional public law *Landesbanken*. From the 1990s onwards, German governments partially liberalized the three-tier system by encouraging the unwinding of cross-shareholdings and facilitating the expansion of banks' investment activities (Deeg 2001, p. 23). This was accompanied by the centralization of regulatory authority and the internationalization of the sector, through takeovers or mergers with foreign firms (Woll 2014, p. 114). The *Allfinanz* approach also encouraged large private banks to provide the full range of banking, investment, and insurance services to SMEs, prompting regional banks to retaliate through expansion into market-based banking (Hardie and Howarth 2013; Hellwig 2018). Nonetheless, Germany's distinctive three-tier banking system proved surprisingly resilient in the face of internal regulatory reform and external (EU) liberalizing pressures (Deeg 1999; Hackethal et al. 2005).

Although important features of Germany's neo-corporatist model had been eroded, a key legacy remained the powerful role of trade associations. The tripartite banking system gave this feature a unique quality, however, with power dispersed between multiple associations representing the commercial banks (the German Banking Association, BDB), the cooperative banks (the Federal

Association of German Cooperative Banks, BVR), the savings banks (the German Savings Banks and Giro Association, DSGV), and the Federal Association of German Public Sector Banks (VÖB). While arguably no longer as powerful as they once were, Germany's banking associations continued to enjoy a close relationship with regulators, and privileged access to officials and legislators (Clift 2014, p. 251). This gave the otherwise fragmented financial sector a powerful incentive to coordinate shared policy demands and channel their collective voice through pan-industry groups—and notably, the German Banking Industry Committee (DK),[3] which attempted to build consensus among the sectoral associations on major policy and regulatory issues (Ganderson 2020b). Importantly, the increasingly close ties that developed in the 1990s between the federal state and 'national champions', such as Deutsche Bank, served to reinforce rather than challenge these older institutional relationships (Admati and Hellwig 2014).

Neo-corporatism was also a characteristic feature of post-war Netherlands, which from the 1990s was widely known as the 'Polder model'. The main social partners—business and trade unions—were highly organized, and the myriad of different groups and associations tended to be complementary rather than rivalrous: namely, they represented their own constituency and did not try to compete for members (Andeweg et al. 2020, p. 172). For example, the three main business associations—the Confederation of Dutch Industry and Employers (VNO-NCW), the Dutch Federation of Small and Medium-Sized Enterprises (MKB), and the Dutch Federation of Agriculture and Horticulture (LTO)—established a joint Council of Central Business Organization (RCO) through which to cooperate and present a united front. For most of the post-war period, the social partners were closely integrated into the policy process as a matter of routine (Visser and Hemerijck 1997, p. 73). The incorporation of these groups was facilitated by the creation of advisory boards, tripartite councils, and quangos. At the centre was the Social and Economic Council (SER), an advisory body to government composed of representatives of employers, employees, 'Crown members' appointed by the government, and frequently members from the central bank, universities, and retired politicians (Magone 2011). This structure sat atop a conglomerate of hundreds of advisory bodies covering individual policy sectors.

By the early 1980s, however, this model came under increasing strain as the Dutch economy faltered, and the centre-right CDA-led government pursued a programme of fiscal cutbacks and supply-side reforms to boost competitiveness. The 'Wassenaar agreement', negotiated by government and the social partners in 1982, transformed the centralized neo-corporatist system characterized by tripartite negotiations and heavy state intervention. In its place, a more flexible and decentralized system of bipartite bargaining between the social partners, with less

---

[3] Until August 2011, the German Banking Industry Committee (Deutsche Kreditwirtschaft) was known as the Central Credit Committee (or Zentraler Kreditausshuss, ZKA).

role for the state, was introduced (see Woldendorp and Delsen 2008). The number of advisory councils was drastically reduced, from a peak of over 700 in the late 1970s to just twenty-one by 1997 (roughly, one per government department) (Visser and Hemerijck 1997). Moreover, the role of these councils in shaping policy declined, not least because their policy recommendations became more non-committal: instead, successive Dutch governments made greater use of ad hoc committees of experts in relevant policy areas (Andeweg et al. 2020, 173).

As in Germany, an important legacy of the dismantling of the post-war tripartite architecture is centralized interest representation. In financial services, this feature was reinforced by the gradual liberalization of the Dutch banking sector since the late 1980s, through the opening up of cross-border credit markets and the removal of restrictions on combining banking and insurance activities (Chang and Jones 2013). Rather than leading to an influx of foreign bank competitors, as in the UK, the reforms encouraged domestic financial institutions to scale up rapidly and hastened the consolidation of the sector, which came to be dominated by three large universal banks from the early 1990s (Beck et al. 2018). This increased concentration served to strengthen the existing system of centralized representation and collective lobbying through the influential Dutch Banking Association (NVB) (SOMO 2013, 5). These older industry associations were also complemented by new informal groupings, such as the Holland Financial Group formed in 1988, which brought together the Dutch Ministry of Finance, the Dutch central bank, and the NVB to promote Amsterdam as a global financial centre (Ganderson 2020b). This group relied on informal but dense state–bank networks, institutionalized through regular meetings between financial ministry officials and bank executives (Vander Stichele 2016, p. 29), and the 'revolving door' between industry and the supervisory authorities (Veltrop and de Haan 2014, p. 10). Empirical studies indicate that this collective voice gave the banking sector significant access and leverage within the state (Kosterman 2010), and a continued capacity to shape financial regulation (SOMO 2013).

France provides further evidence of how cooperative financial power was embedded in centralized representation. Unlike Germany and the Netherlands, however, the French model of financial interest representation was not rooted in neo-corporatist structures, but instead rested on the durability of dense inter-organizational and inter-personal networks between banks and the state. The French business elite was typically socially homogeneous, highly selective, and interconnected, and traditionally enjoyed a close relationship with the state (Shonfield 1965; Maclean et al. 2006; Harvey and Maclean 2008). A small number of educational institutions provided entrants to the *grandes écoles*, from which much of France's business and governing elite was drawn. This concentration was underpinned by a tightly interlocking system of directorships at the top of French corporations, and the persistence of business control by powerful family dynasties. France was also characterized by a high level of inter-penetration of business and governing elites through a 'revolving door' between government and industry. Typically, top graduates from the *grandes écoles* moved into elite networks—*grands corps*—of the state and established strong interpersonal networks based on their common educational background. Mid-career, they then engaged in *pantouflage*, leaving the public sector for senior positions within business—and later moved back and forth between state and business positions (Moran 2009, p. 49). These factors produced a uniquely high level of social integration within the French business community, and between French business and the state.

Financial interest intermediation in France was traditionally characterized by a vertically integrated, hierarchical form of dirigisme, in which the state directed finance through its substantial shareholdings in major banks (Clift 2014, p. 247). However, from the 1980s this statist model underwent a fundamental transformation. During the 1990s, the government actively facilitated the selective liberalization of the financial system to enable French banks to expand and compete more effectively with the largest internationally present US banks. French government efforts produced a more concentrated banking system dominated by a few large 'national champions', consisting of two commercial banks and four mutual banks. Crucially, the collective interests of these institutions was highly centralized and represented through the powerful French Banking Federation (FBF), as well as the French employers' association (MEDEF).

Unlike the UK, France's model of financial liberalization therefore produced a more horizontally integrated, oligarchic form of state–bank interaction. Paradoxically, this served to strengthen the interconnectedness of political power and private banks (Clift 2012). Financial power therefore remained 'insider dominated', whereby key bank executives retained privileged access to, and influence over, state officials based on dense interpersonal networks (Jabko and Massoc 2012, pp. 565–6). These durable features generated a powerful mutual dependence and *esprit de corps* whereby the public interests of the state and the private interests of French banks were fused as part of the collective 'national interest' (Schmidt 1996; Offerle 2009; Clift 2012). Financial regulation was therefore the product of consensus decision making amongst an 'informal consortium' of state officials and bankers, governed by powerful norms of cooperation, reciprocity, and trust, and largely insulated from external political or societal pressures (Scharpf 1997; Jabko and Massoc 2012, p. 567).

Support for our claims about modes of interest representation comes from the comparative capitalism literature. Empirical studies that measure and rank countries based on key characteristics of interest intermediation echo the categorization of our five cases (Lijphart and Crepaz 1991; Hicks and Kenworthy 1998; Siaroff 1999; Huber and Stephens 2001). In particular, Jahn's (2016) time-invariant corporatism index, which covers forty-two countries over several decades, ranks the Netherlands and Germany amongst the highest for corporatism (ranking fourth and sixth, respectively); France, ranking twenty-two out of forty-two, appears as an intermediate case; while the UK (ranked fortieth) and US rank (forty-second) are the lowest. Several qualitative studies also point to the importance of key political-institutional features of the state in shaping the influence of sectoral interests (for example, Rogowski and Kayser 2002; Cusack et al. 2010). For example, Trumbull (2006, 2012) argues that the interaction of majoritarian elections with liberal market economies (Hall and Soskice 2001) creates—all else being equal—greater opportunities for highly diffuse interests to prevail over narrow sectoral interests. By contrast, coordinated market economies with proportional electoral systems tend to favour sectoral over universal interests—in part because they are institutionalized through intermediate associations (Trumbull 2012, p. 31). Finally, empirical work on financial lobbying networks points to the durability of distinctive national patterns of financial interest coordination which broadly align with historic modes of interest intermediation (see Young and Pagliari 2017; James et al. 2020).

Finally, we recognize that the sixth case that we examine in the book—the European Union (EU)—does not fit neatly into these national-level modes of interest representation, for at least two reasons. The first is because the EU as a site for business lobbying is particularly dynamic. The gradual transfer of economic and regulatory functions from member states to the EU institutions, together with the introduction of qualified majority voting in the Council of Ministers, encouraged the rapid expansion of lobbying activity in Brussels over recent decades (Coen and Richardson 2009; Eising 2009; Greenwood 2017; Coen et al. 2021). Today the EU boasts nearly 13,000 registered lobbying groups, of which around 7000 are in-house corporate lobbyists and trade, business, and professional associations. All major European firms and associations now have a presence in Brussels, with lobbying split evenly between individual firms/groups and trade/business associations (Coen et al. 2021, p. 61).

The second reason why the EU is distinct from national patterns relates to the hybridity of the EU as a system of 'multi-level governance' (Marks and Hooghe 2001). Much of the attraction of the EU as a target for lobbying reflects the relatively open and institutionally fragmented nature of the polity, creating multiple points of access for interest groups and opportunities for venue shopping (Grossman 2004; Beyers and Kerremans 2007; Schneider et al. 2007; Mahoney 2008). As the EU evolved into a quintessential 'regulatory state' (Majone 1997), the Commission, as agenda setter, and Parliament, as co-legislator, and a raft of new EU regulatory agencies, became the primary focus for most lobbying activity (Cram 2001). As relatively new and comparatively under-resourced institutions, the key to lobbying success at the EU level was the provision of policy-relevant information, rather than political patronage or campaign contributions (Broscheid and Coen 2003, p. 170). Business interests therefore came to dominate the process, constituting over half of accredited interest groups (Greenwood 2017), prompting the Commission to try to redress the imbalance by actively supporting a range of civil society organizations (Mahoney and Beckstrand 2011). This led scholars to label the EU a system of 'elite pluralism', whereby EU policy makers traditionally grant privileged access to a small coterie of 'insider' interest groups capable of supplying technical and timely information (Coen 1997, pp. 98–9).

EU financial lobbying has spurned a large empirical scholarship (Quaglia 2008, 2010; Klüver 2013; Pagliari and Young 2014, 2016; Chalmers 2015, 2020; Coen and Salter 2020). Prior to the financial crisis, the banking industry had considerable influence shaping EU-level regulation aimed at facilitating financial market integration, with EU regulators in the Commission and newly established 'Lamfalussy' committees—including the Committee of European Banking Supervisors (CEBS)—relying heavily on industry expertise (Quaglia 2010). Although reputationally damaged by the crisis, the wave of post-crisis EU regulation ensured that the input and involvement of the bank lobby remained essential (Coen and Salter 2020). Moreover, the substantial strengthening of EU regulatory and supervisory capabilities since 2008—with the creation of the new European Supervisory Agencies (ESAs), including the European Banking Authority (EBA), as well as the European Banking Union and Single Supervisory Mechanism—provided powerful incentives for the banking industry to bolster and centralize its EU lobbying activity (Howarth and Quaglia 2016a; Coen et al. 2021). EU banks therefore maintain substantial influence through long-standing but increasingly powerful pan-European associations, notably the European Banking Federation (EBF), the European Association of Cooperative Banks (EACB), and the AFME. We therefore expect the EU to combine features of both competitive financial power (reflecting the fragmented institutional landscape) and cooperative financial power (due to the power and access of pan-EU groups).

Having specified our expectations with regard to how the relational context impacts upon financial power, we turn next to the institutional context.

5. Agenda setting and venue shifting

This section shifts the focus of our explanation from the power and resources of the financial industry to the way in which these are mediated by key features of the policy process. In particular, we seek to provide a more agent-centered account of financial power by explaining how policy makers can manipulate institutional structures and processes to further their policy goals. We begin by reviewing the public policy literature on agenda setting.

Agenda setting is concerned with understanding the dynamics of policy change (Baumgartner and Jones 1993; Rochefort and Cobb 1994; Kingdon 1995; Jones and Baumgartner 2005). To be precise, it examines the mechanisms though which policy issues rise and fall, and the conditions under which this produces policy stability and change. This perspective challenges traditional assumptions that change in policy sectors is incremental, suggesting instead that long periods of policy continuity can be interrupted by sudden policy shifts or punctuations (Baumgartner et al. 2006). New issues often meet resistance as a result of status quo biases in political institutions and entrenched vested interests. Yet substantive policy change can result from heightened public attention which leads to the 'alarmed discovery' of an issue by government (Jones and Baumgartner 2005). Agenda setting has received most attention in the context of US politics, where it originated as a separate object of study (Schattschneider 1960; Cobb and Elder 1972; Baumgartner and Jones 1993). Recently, authors have extended this research agenda to other states (Considine 1998; Soroka 2002; Albæk et al. 2007; Green-Pedersen 2007) and to the EU (Pollack 1997; Peters 2001; Tallberg 2003; Rhinard 2010).

Conflict expansion is central to agenda-setting processes. It refers to the increased mobilization of policy actors around an issue, beyond the range of participants that normally occupy a policy subsystem (Baumgartner and Jones 1993). As Schattschneider (1960, p. 2) argues, the outcome of policy conflict is ultimately determined by the scope of its contagion: 'The number of people involved in any conflict determines what happens; every change in the number of participants, every increase or reduction in the number of participants affects the result.' By involving participants who support their cause and excluding participants who oppose it, political actors can change the agenda. In order to do so, they need to convince their (potential) supporters that they should devote time and effort to their cause while, ideally, they should also discourage (potential) opponents from becoming involved.

Conflict expansion (re)shapes policy agendas by challenging the prevailing balance of power and resources that exists between vested interests and coalitions, the stability of which underpins predominant issue understandings and sustains particular policy outcomes. In other words, conflict expansion serves to open up and extend 'windows of opportunity' for policy reform (Kingdon 1995). Conversely, conflict contraction refers to the demobilization of participants around a policy issue. By narrowing the scope of actors engaged around an issue, policy conflict and public attention can be reduced. This enables existing coalitions of interests and issue understandings to be (re)asserted, and allows political actors to (re)establish control over the process and steer policy decisions in a particular way. Hence, conflict contraction has the effect of narrowing and potentially closing windows of opportunity for policy change.

The institutional arenas or 'venues' where policy is made are central to dynamics of conflict expansion and contraction (Princen 2007, 2011). This is for at least three reasons. First, institutional venues embody a particular set of internal decision-making rules, procedures, and norms. These constitute opportunity structures that determine the visibility and accessibility of the policy process to outside interests. In this way, internal rules directly shape the level of participation, mobilization of interests, and public attention around an issue (Baumgartner and Jones 1993). Institutional rules also determine the internal threshold for agreement. Where this is high—for example, due to the existence of multiple veto points—the influence of outside interests is likely to be constrained, and the likelihood of policy change limited.

Second, institutions embody distinct epistemic and normative lenses which structure how political actors understand, interpret, and respond to policy issues (Rochefort and Cobb 1994). Institutions are therefore not 'neutral', but will tend to be receptive to certain arguments, narratives, ideas, and interests over others (Baumgartner et al. 2006, p. 968). Institutional venues also influence policy choices by shaping how issues are defined or 'framed': that is, the process of selecting, emphasizing, and organizing aspects of complex issues according to an overriding evaluative or analytical criterion (Daviter 2007, p. 654). By (re)framing the link between policy problems and solutions, the boundaries between opponents and supporters of a policy can be reconfigured, and 'windows of opportunity' for policy change can be opened up or closed down (Kingdon 1995).

Finally, institutional venues can be manipulated to manage the policy agenda. When policy makers are confronted by a new policy issue, they often have substantial discretion over which institutional venues to activate. The concept of venue 'shifting' suggests that political actors can steer policy by shifting debates and decision making on a certain issue to new venues which are susceptible to particular kinds of argument (Baumgartner and Jones 1993). On the one hand, policy makers may seek to challenge prevailing coalitions of interests and policy frames deliberately by shifting policy issues to open and transparent venues (Princen 2007, 2011). This exercise in conflict expansion involves reconfiguring existing institutions, or establishing new ones, in order to mobilize and empower new sets of actors, and provide enhanced sources of access for 'outsider' interests. On the other hand, venue shifting can also be used to close new issues down. In this case, policy makers can facilitate conflict contraction by channelling issues through new or existing venues that are dominated by 'insider' interests, and relatively closed to outsider groups. This is likely to reinforce—rather than challenge—prevailing policy frames, and produce greater policy continuity.

Venue shifting is central to our framework because it can also be used as an instrument for insulating contested policy issues from day-to-day political pressures. Drawing on theories of delegation (McCubbins and Schwartz 1984; Miller and Whitford 2016) and depoliticization (Flinders and Buller 2006; Flinders 2009), we focus on why policy makers choose to delegate policy decisions to ad hoc, specialist groups or committees. These bodies are usually established for a time-limited period, and are given a specific mandate to make policy recommendations on a relatively narrow policy issue. Typically, they operate through a logic of technocratic deliberation, systematically gathering and evaluating evidence, drawing on the authoritative knowledge of technical experts, and consulting a range of societal stakeholders (Haas 1992; Radaelli 1995; Majone 2001, 2005; Dunlop 2010). We argue that delegation to technocratic venues serves to depoliticize difficult policy issues in three ways.

First, delegation to specialist groups can enhance the efficiency of decision making (McCubbins and Schwartz 1984; Miller and Whitford 2016). Policy makers are often unclear about their own policy preferences, particularly with respect to issues characterized by high technical complexity, distributional questions, or political uncertainty. Establishing new deliberative decision-making venues can help to define issues, clarify interests, and facilitate learning by drawing on the technical expertise of a limited number of authoritative participants (conflict contraction); and/or by expanding the range of knowledge through engagement with a broad spectrum of societal groups (conflict expansion) (Dunlop and Radaelli 2013, 2018).

Second, delegation can insulate policy decisions from short-term party-political demands and help to build broader public support for policy choices (Flinders and Buller 2006; Flinders 2009). Handing responsibility to notionally 'independent' experts enables policy makers to convince voters of the benefits and legitimacy of particular policy choices. Moreover, widening the scope of consultation can be used to secure 'buy in' from a range of economic and societal interests. In both cases—conflict contraction or conflict expansion—new institutional venues contribute to consensus building.

Third, decision making by specialist groups can reduce political pressures by making credible commitments over the long term (Kydland and Prescott 1977; Pollack 2002). By removing direct control from elected politicians and insulating decisions from day-to-day politics, there is less scope to manipulate policy recommendations or decisions for electoral reasons. In doing so, policy makers can anchor expectations, reduce contestation about future policy trajectories, and thus potentially bind their successors.

There is an abundant scholarship on the role of delegation and expertise in financial regulation. Multiple studies point to the importance of technical knowledge (Lindblom 1977; Lindvall 2009) and specialist agencies (Mattli and Woods 2009; Büthe and Mattli 2011) in the governance of complex financial markets. For example, recent work details the prominence of professional knowledge and policy experts in financial reform (Tsingou 2003, 2008; Seabrooke and Tsingou 2009, 2014; Seabrooke 2014; Ban et al. 2016), and the development of 'club governance' through powerful transgovernmental communities of regulators (Baker 2006; Newman and Posner 2011; Tsingou 2015; Broome and Seabrooke 2015; Henriksen and Seabrooke 2016). Others warn of the dangers of regulatory 'capture' by industry arising from delegation to private actors and self-regulatory bodies (Pauly 1997; Abdelal 2007; Mügge 2011; Lall 2012; Helleiner 2014).

It is our contention that venue shifting to ad hoc, specialist groups highlights important agenda-setting dynamics with respect to bank structural reform. Specifically, we hypothesize that venue shifting is a key determinant of the extent to which regulatory reform is (de)politicized. This is because delegation to external 'experts' encourages deliberative decision making by drawing on external knowledge and technical expertise; signals credibility and legitimacy about policy choices to voters; and facilitates consensus building and securing 'buy in' from relevant stakeholders. Importantly, and somewhat paradoxically, depoliticization through venue shifting can take the form of either conflict contraction (i.e., deliberately limiting the number and range of actors involved in the process in order to facilitate agreement) *or* conflict expansion (i.e., expanding the scope of participants involved in order to secure 'buy in' from a broader range of societal interests). By contrast, regulatory reform in the absence of venue shifting—and thus managed through conventional policy processes—will be more politicized and contingent. That is, it is more likely to reflect the particular balance of power that exists between competing political and economic interests.

Our second hypothesis is therefore as follows:

H2. Bank structural reform will be less politicized when policy makers deploy venue shifting; and more politicized when policy makers do not deploy venue shifting.

6. A comparative financial power approach

This section proposes a new comparative financial power approach, the aim of which is to explain how and why financial industry power varies across different national contexts. In particular, we suggest that integrating insights from the interest group and agenda-setting literatures enables us to present a more fine-grained analysis of how financial power is mediated by the relational and institutional context within which it is located. Here we combine the two hypotheses outlined above in order to derive empirical expectations about the form of bank structural reform in different jurisdictions.

1. *Interest group lobbying.* We argue that the capacity of the banking industry to remain unified when lobbying is an important determinant of the stringency of structural reform. Under conditions of heightened mistrust and public anger against TBTF banks, financial actors capable of wielding cooperative financial power—i.e., where lobbying involves leveraging broad industry alliances across the financial sector and wider business community—will be more effective at resisting the imposition of new regulatory rules. By contrast, banks operating in a context of competitive financial power—i.e., where lobbying is fragmented among individual firms/sub-sectoral groups

Table 2.1 Outcomes of bank structural reform

		Interest group lobbying	
		Competitive financial power	Cooperative financial power
Venue shifting	Yes	1. Durable reform	2. No reform
	No	3. Contested reform	4. Symbolic reform

which compete with countervailing groups for access and influence—will be less effective at resisting regulatory reform.

2. *Venue shifting.* We hypothesize that the use of venue shifting is an important determinant of the extent to which structural reform is (de)politicized. Delegating contentious policy issues to ad hoc, specialist groups reduces politicization by leveraging external knowledge, legitimizing policy choices, and facilitating consensus building. This can be achieved through mechanisms of either conflict contraction (by limiting the number of actors involved to facilitate agreement) or conflict expansion (by expanding the scope of participants involved to secure broad support). By contrast, structural reform in the absence of venue shifting will be less insulated from political pressures and subject to greater political contingency. The outcome will therefore reflect the balance of power between different political and economic actors.

Combining these two variables—interest group lobbying and venue shifting—produces a 2 × 2 typology (Table 2.1). Constructing typologies can serve as a valuable heuristic device and analytical tool in explaining complex regulatory processes. Distinguishing different outcomes of banking reform helps to clarify and refine our concepts, delineates the underlying causal processes, and creates categories for classification and measurement (Bennett and Elman 2006). Our multidimensional typology is explanatory (rather than descriptive) in the sense that the cells are the outcomes to be explained, and the rows and columns are the explanatory variables. It therefore provides a theoretically grounded basis for categorizing distinct regulatory reforms in conceptual terms, and for generating empirical expectations about the outcome of regulatory processes in different national contexts. We define the four outcomes of banking reform as follows:

1. *Durable reform* is likely where venue shifting occurs in a context of competitive financial power. Here the fragmentation of bank lobbying, heterogeneous industry preferences, and competition from countervailing groups will limit the capacity of the banking sector to 'capture' the process. Consequently, delegating decision making to an ad hoc, specialist group in

this context is likely to facilitate depoliticization by mobilizing and engaging a wide range of societal stakeholders (i.e., conflict expansion). We therefore expect both substantive policy reform and durable change as policy makers use venue shifting both to leverage external expertise and to build broad public support.

2. *No reform* is likely where venue shifting takes place in a context of cooperative financial power. Here the banking industry will be characterized by centralized lobbying, homogeneous preferences, and the ability to wield broad business alliances. In this instance, delegating decision making to an ad hoc, specialist group is more likely to result in the process being 'captured' by powerful organized interests. Rather than consulting widely, this exercise in depoliticization will facilitate agreement by limiting engagement to a narrow range of technical 'experts' (i.e., conflict contraction). We expect this to lead to no reform as venue shifting serves to legitimize non-decision making.

3. *Contested reform* is expected to be the outcome where venue shifting does not occur and financial power is competitive. Structural reform will be more politicized because it is channelled through conventional political processes. It will thus reflect the outcome of competition between different groups—including political parties, organized interests, regulators, and civil society. Substantial reform is possible because bank lobbying is fragmented and subject to challenge by multiple countervailing groups (i.e., conflict expansion). But changes will be more contingent as they will be vulnerable to ongoing politicization and the shifting balance of power between competing interests.

4. *Symbolic reform* is likely when there is no venue shifting in a context of cooperative financial power. In the absence of delegation to ad hoc specialist groups, structural reform will be more politicized and policy makers are likely to face significant political pressures on reform. But the banking industry will also be highly effective at lobbying given its ability to leverage broad sectoral and business alliances, thus facilitating conflict contraction through conventional political processes. To reconcile these contradictory pressures, we predict that policy makers will introduce symbolic structural reforms designed to appease political demands to act, whilst minimizing the economic impact on industry.

7. Case study selection

The case studies selected for the book enable us to test the empirical expectations derived from all four quadrants of the explanatory framework. Hence, we examine structural reform in the US and UK as countries characterized by competitive financial power. These two cases also provide contrasting examples of venue shifting: in the UK, responsibility for developing policy recommendations on banking reform was delegated to ad hoc, specialist groups (the ICB and the PCBS); by contrast, in the US, the issue was shaped by the conventional policy process—with reform proposals produced by the Treasury and Federal Reserve under the Obama administration and debated in the appropriate congressional committees. Similarly, we study three countries (France, Germany, and the Netherlands) which retain important features of cooperative financial power. However, whereas banking reform in France and Germany was largely managed through pre-existing political channels, in the Netherlands policy recommendations were developed by several specialist groups (notably the Maas, De Wit, and Wijffels commissions).

To provide a more complete account of structural reform in the European context, we also analyse policy developments at the EU level. As detailed above, the EU case does not fit the explanatory typology as closely as the individual country cases. At first glance, we might expect the outcome of EU banking reform to be durable change, reflecting important features of competitive financial power (given the challenge of aligning regulatory preferences and coordinating lobbying across the entire EU financial industry) and venue shifting (by the European Commission to the 'High Level Expert Group', headed by former Finnish central bank governor, Erkki Liikanen). As we explain, however, the nature of the EU as a non-sovereign, multi-level polity introduced substantial additional barriers to reform. In particular, the EU's ability to leverage the credibility and legitimacy of policy recommendations developed by an 'expert' group arguably counts for less in a context where policy makers (in the Commission) are not directly accountable to voters, and where agreement is subject to a greater number of powerful political veto players.

We recognize that venue shifting (or not) to some extent reflects established patterns of governance in the case study countries we examine. However, this in no way detracts from our analytical focus: on the contrary, it highlights the importance of thinking more systematically about the way in which business (financial) power is mediated by domestic political institutions and policy processes. Moreover, as we go on to detail in the following chapters, the particular institutional venues that were activated with regard to bank structural reform in our six cases were not always typical of established patterns of governance. For example, while the use of specialist committees of industry experts is certainly a more typical feature of governance in some countries (e.g., the Netherlands) than in others (e.g., the US), the particular form that these institutional venues took was not typical in certain cases (e.g., the ICB in the UK). We reflect further on this point in the concluding chapter.

8. Conclusion

In the empirical chapters that follow, we set out to apply the comparative financial power framework outlined above in the six cases. In doing so, we aim to analyse the key explanatory variables in the framework as systematically as possible. Hence, we try to structure each chapter consistently around the framework: namely, by examining the nature of financial power and evidence of venue shifting. Inevitably, however, each case is distinct and there is some variation in the sub-sections that we deploy in order to provide a richer account of policy developments. Before turning to our case studies, the following chapter places bank structural reform into the wider context of the full range of regulatory reforms and other measures adopted since the global financial crisis to make banking 'safer' and, more specifically, to tackle the issue of TBTF.

3
Failing to Tame Too-Big-To-Fail Banks

1. Introduction

TBTF universal banks engaging in higher-risk investment banking activities was the principal cause of the international financial crisis that hit severely the US and a number of European countries, including the four examined in this volume (Hardie and Howarth 2013a). These activities included the creation, sale, and purchase of securitized assets and involved increased bank reliance on short term interbank funding on wholesale markets. Various governments sought to respond to the financial crisis by introducing reforms that both discouraged TBTF universal banks from excessive risk taking and ensured that, if they did engage in higher-risk investment banking activities, they would not have to rely on the public purse to cover their losses during market downturns. The principal goal of bank structural reform was to shield governments from the perceived need to bail out large banks, the failure of which could result in major losses imposed on depositors and other retail clients, a deleterious impact on the real economy—notably via a credit crunch—contagion to other banks, and the potential collapse of national banking systems. More specifically, structural reform was to protect the depositors, borrowers, and other non-financial company clients of large universal banks from suffering losses caused by their riskier investment banking activities.

In this chapter, we investigate national government responses to the financial crisis in terms of their contribution to decreasing the risk of TBTF. While some government responses to the crisis—such as government-provided loans to and credit guarantees for banks—appear to have had little bearing on TBTF and even contributed to it, they were frequently presented by governments as having an impact on bank activities in terms of hard conditionality or softer expectations. We consider the full range of policy and regulatory responses that were adopted in addition to, or in place of, bank structural reform and the ringfencing of specific banking activities. In this chapter, we examine government responses in terms of their impact and likely impact on the problem of TBTF. We lack the space in this chapter to apply the analytical framework of our broader study—focused on comparative financial power and venue shifting—to regulatory, supervisory, and other relevant policy decisions adopted since the international financial crisis in our five case study countries and at the EU level. We argue that only a few of the reforms adopted during the decade following the financial crisis—apart from the US and

UK structural reforms—made a significant contribution to tackling the problem of TBTF.

Tackling TBTF was not, per se, the explicit target of many government responses to the international financial crisis. The regulatory clarion call of most governments was focused principally on 'stability'—preventing another financial crisis on the scale of the last one. However, in a number of cases, regulatory reform was targeted specifically at minimizing the pressure on governments to bail out TBTF banks with public funds; minimizing the systemic impact of failing banks; ensuring continued lending to the real economy; and either discouraging the highest risk investment banking activities or at least containing these activities. One of the most important and potentially constraining responses—focused on reinforced bank capital requirements—was adopted in late 2010 by the BCBS of the Bank for International Settlements (BIS) which consisted of representatives from the bank supervisory bodies of twenty-five of the world's largest economies, including the five examined in this study, and the EU (represented by the European Central Bank, ECB). If large universal banks possessed sufficient loss-absorbing capital, they were less likely to rely on government funds in the context of future crises. The Basel III provisions were adopted into US, EU, and then EU member state law. EU legislation both significantly watered down Basel III guidelines and also allowed governments margin of manoeuvre in their transposition and implementation of EU capital requirements legislation. In the meantime, the EU member states collectively adopted a range of additional regulatory changes designed to make banks safer. Moreover, all five national governments adopted a number of unilateral changes to domestic bank regulation and supervision. However, in most cases, national governments sought to wait for international guidelines or EU legislation so as to diminish the implications of new regulation for the international competitiveness of national banks.

The Germans and French had a long track record of pushing in favour of tougher domestic, European, and global financial market regulation, while—until the financial crisis—the US, UK, and Dutch governments were in favour of 'light touch' national regulation and supervision and were hostile to almost all international regulatory developments (Zimmerman 2010). On financial regulation more generally, prior to the international financial crisis, the EU Commission tended to align with those governments in favour of less constraining regulation (Quaglia 2010a). German and French governments argued in various international and European settings for a range of reforms to make international finance safer: *inter alia*, constraints on the operation of credit rating agencies (CRAs), stricter reporting requirements for off-balance sheet activities, tighter rules on hedge funds and private equity investors, and tougher rules on the pay—notably bonuses—of chief executive officers (CEOs) and other highly paid executives in the financial sector.

These German and French government efforts usually encountered the resistance of the UK, and, less vocally, the US and Dutch governments. The US failed to adopt earlier BCBS capital guidelines (Basel I and II) into national legislation.

These guidelines, adopted in 1988 and 2004 respectively, were widely criticized as inadequate to ensure the ability of many banks to cover their losses during crises. Before the international financial crisis, their national versions of 'light touch' regulation were seen by the UK and Dutch governments as clearly superior to German and French conceptions and even to the relatively heavy-handed approach in the US after Sarbanes-Oxley (*Financieel Management* 2004, quoting the ex-secretary of the Dutch Commission for Corporate Governance, R. Amba; Blitz 2005, quoting Tony Blair). Not surprisingly, German and French government proposals to reinforce international and EU-level regulation and supervisory standards met with little success. The debate in the EU about financial regulation and supervision after the crisis opened the same cleavage (Posner and Véron 2010; Quaglia 2010a).

While the differences in national positions are important, the argument in this chapter is that in terms of the impact upon the problem of TBTF banks, most of the post-2007 policies adopted by the five national governments were surprisingly similar. The most important exception—as we demonstrate elsewhere in this book—was on bank structural reform and ringfencing—thus a major impetus for our study. In particular, the post-crisis approaches of all five national governments on a range of bank-related regulatory and supervisory matters tended towards caution. For Germany, this caution reflected both the high levels of exposure of a range of German banks to the financial crisis and the massive write-downs on assets in the publicly owned *Landesbanken* (Hardie and Howarth 2013b). Moreover, the new German caution on domestic, European-level, and international regulation reflected the increased reliance of a range of German banks on investment banking for revenues. Similarly, French discourse on challenging the perceived excesses of 'Anglo-Saxon' finance—adopted by both centre-right and centre-left presidents and governments—was rarely met with decisive action at either the national or EU level. At the same time, in most areas of bank-related regulation and supervision, the shift in the US, UK, and Dutch positions should not be exaggerated. In none of the five countries examined in this study was there much appetite to embrace significantly restrictive regulatory and supervisory practices. Notable exceptions were the US administration and UK government positions on bank structural reform and, to a lesser extent, bank capital. If the balance sheets of many of the largest US- and EU-headquartered banks shrank in the years following 2008 in relative and/or real terms, this had less to do with regulatory and supervisory changes than with post-crisis efforts by the banks themselves to clean up their balance sheets, a more cautious approach to short-term wholesale market funding, and a more cautious approach to domestic lending.

2. The continued dominance of TBTF banks

Over the decade prior to the international financial crisis, banking systems had significantly expanded in most advanced industrialized economies. Large universal banks in all our case study countries grew significantly in size up to 2008 (Table 1.3). Over the decade following the crisis, in the majority of these economies—and four of our five country cases—the banking system either shrank or stagnated in size as a percentage of GDP and even in real terms, as in Germany and the UK (Table 1.4). Similarly, the relative position of banks in national financial systems declined or stagnated over the decade following the financial crisis (Table 1.5). However, the relative position of the largest national banks—measured in terms of assets held as a percentage of total bank assets—was maintained or increased (Table 1.6). Thus, while many banking systems decreased in size relative to national economies and many of the largest banks shrank their balance sheets (Table 1.3), notably by reducing their trading activities and foreign operations, TBTF banks largely maintained their relative size and dominance. Given a decade of regulation designed in part to decrease the systemic importance of TBTF banks and make their failure less potentially devastating for national banking systems and economies, it might be surprising to some readers that these banks retained, and in some cases increased, their relative importance—even in the UK where there was considerable shrinkage of bank balance sheets.

High risk investment banking and TBTF

During the decade prior to the international financial crisis, all the large universal banks in our five case study countries engaged increasingly in high-risk trading activities (Hardie and Howarth 2013a; on the US, see Crotty 2008). There was an increasing importance of 'market' relative to 'credit' portfolios for all universal banks with a growing range of investment banking activities and notably derivatives trading and investment in complex securities. Large universal banks came to rely increasingly on short-term borrowing on wholesale markets to finance the asset side of the banks' balance sheets. Furthermore, in the US, a number of investment banks became universal banks as they extended their activities into retail banking.

While much has been written on the increased reliance of the UK upon the financial sector to drive economic growth, growth in all five of our case study countries during the decade leading up to the international financial crisis relied increasingly on the financial sector. The rapid increase in short-term wholesale market bank funding in all five countries during the decade prior to the financial crisis demonstrates the degree to which bank-provided capital came to be, in fact, market provided (Hardie and Howarth 2009, 2013a). This increase in short-term wholesale market funding enabled banks to offer loans at favourable rates (Mullineux and Terberger 2006).

The governments of all five countries facilitated the development of higher-risk investment banking activities and short-term wholesale market funding prior to the international financial crisis. The securitization of bank lending not only reshaped the financing of non-financial firms in the US, UK, and the Netherlands but also resulted in mortgage booms in these three countries. Schwartz and Seabrooke (2008) point to the manner in which easy securitization of mortgages via a deregulated and flexible domestic financial system expanded the scope of potential homeowners, transformed home ownership into a kind of social security net through rising prices, and contributed significantly to rapid economic growth in these and other countries (see also Schwartz 2009; Watson 2009). This strong reliance on investment banking and short-term wholesale market funding for economic growth and a particular form of development in capitalism in these three countries explains their governments' reluctance to adopt any regulation that might restrain these activities. In addition to the potential impact upon banks, in the UK any significant reinforcement of restrictive financial regulation during the years following the financial crisis risked scaring away the private overseas investors who helped to finance the credit expansion in the UK, and created a large current account deficit (Turner Review 2009, p. 32). Dutch, German, and French government support for higher-risk investment banking activities also reflected the saturation of the domestic retail banking market in these three countries and the significant contribution of investment banking to bank profits (see, respectively, Chang and Jones 2013; Hardie and Howarth 2013b; Howarth 2013).

Over the decade after the international financial crisis, the relative importance of high-risk investment banking for the majority of large banks in our five country cases decreased or stagnated—at least initially—and most of these banks shrank their balance sheets. However, most of these banks also remained TBTF. We argue that the bulk of the regulatory and other policy developments adopted by the five national governments had limited impact upon the level of high-risk investment banking and reliance on short-term wholesale market funding, and thus limited impact on making TBTF banks more risk averse. The failure of regulation in this regard reflects the preferences of the banking sector in the five countries, which continued to rely on investment banking activities for profits, particularly in the context of low domestic economic growth and limited domestic market opportunities.

We divide government responses that targeted directly or indirectly TBTF banks into five main categories: 1) government financial support with the aim of immediate systemic stabilization; 2) revenue-raising regulation and fiscal policy; 3) regulation to constrain bank activities; 4) reinforced bank governance; and 5) reinforced supervision. These responses undertaken by the governments of our five case study countries are summarized in Tables 3.1, 3.2, 3.3, 3.10 and 3.11, respectively. National policy making in all these areas is directly shaped by international guidelines and/or EU policy or by the direction of discussions at the international and/or EU level. Thus, national responses cannot be considered in isolation. However, there were major variations in the national policies and legislation adopted which need to be highlighted. At the same time, our overview of these policies and legislation points to their limited efficacity in terms of decreasing the problem of TBTF and the relative importance of far-reaching structural reform.

3. Government financial support

The rescue plans by governments resulted in only limited effective constraints on TBTF banks, with two important exceptions. Where part-nationalized banks—such as RBS and Lloyds-HBOS in the UK, and Fortis in the Netherlands—were encouraged by governments to shrink their balance sheets, much of this shrinkage was in terms of higher-risk investment banking activities. At the same time, bank profits were previously greatest in these activities and, notably, in the trading of complex financial products. Furthermore, it is likely that some shrinking of the balance sheets of all three banks would have occurred as a result of market pressure—as banks sought to boost their share price after the collapse of 2008-9. UK governments in particular were caught by the contradictions of trying to constrain higher-risk investment banking activities and reliance on short-term wholesale market funding, on the one hand, and to expand bank lending to support corporate activity and the housing market and to maximize the eventual resale value of the UK state's large bank shareholdings, on the other.

Table 3.1 summarizes the government support measures for banks (EU Commission 2009). The creation of credit guarantee schemes in all five countries potentially gave more scope for higher-risk investment banking activities, because by insuring a certain percentage of losses on assets, the schemes freed up bank balance sheets. The UK government's requirements that RBS and Lloyds-HBOS increase business lending were not met, and there is little evidence of the government going beyond rhetorical challenges to the banks' explanation of a lack of loan demand—despite widespread evidence to support such a challenge (Macartney 2014a). Government financial support for banks in both the UK and the Netherlands was linked to demands on restricting bonuses but this only resulted in legislation in the Netherlands in 2012, 2014, and 2015 once voluntary constraints were shown to be ineffective. In the US, a variety of conditions and fees were attached to the Troubled Asset Relief Program (TARP), including the issuing of equity warrants to the US Treasury and new curbs on executive compensation (Woll 2014, p. 90). Recipient banks were required to submit a specific business plan detailing how they intended to deploy the capital, and $45.6bn of TARP funds were set aside to provide homeowner foreclosure assistance. But the programme was widely criticized in Congress for doing too little to support lending.

The rescue plans adopted in Germany and France were ostensibly more constraining on bank activities, with governments linking share purchases and capital

Table 3.1 National rescues/protection of TBTF banks, 2007–10

Regulatory response	US	UK	France	Germany	Netherlands
Equity purchases	Mandatory participation of all nine major banks: $250bn programme of preferred stock purchases in return for warrants.	Reluctant but massive purchase of shares; non-intervention: 78% RBS/23% Lloyds-HBOS/100% Northern Rock.	Limited: BNP; forced merger of Caisse d'Epargne/Banques Populaires.	Reluctant: 100% Hypo; 25% stake in Commerzbank.	Reluctant: ABN-AMRO, 70% stake; SNS Bank 100%; Dutch part of Fortis (€16.8bn).
Capital guarantees (with/without conditions)	FDIC guarantees 100% of banks' senior unsecured debt, and all deposits in non-interest-bearing transaction accounts, paid for by a bank fee.	Yes: voluntary asset protection programme. Lloyds-HBOS and Barclays do not use.	Voluntary asset protection scheme. Not used. Government set lending targets/constraints on bonuses.	Voluntary asset protection scheme. Little used.	Yes (€200bn): limited conditions, not imposed.
Regulation/policies to force banks to lend	Informal pressure from White House to increase lending.	Project Merlin: not enforced. Lending conditions not met by RBS/Lloyds-HBOS.	Yes for 2009 (but not enforced); strong public threats.	No regulation but strong public threats: including legislation if necessary.	None.
Asset purchases	Voluntary $700bn TARP to buy toxic debt, but only $431bn used.	Some asset relief. Voluntary asset protection scheme. Lloyds and Barclays did not use.	Limit to boost share price.	€480bn stabilization fund (bad bank). Highest level of asset relief in EU.	Yes: €20bn fund created: €10bn for ING, €3bn for AEGON; limited conditions, not imposed. Rapid repayment (ING by 2012).

Source: authors' own compilation.

guarantees to demands that banks continue lending and curtail bonuses. However, tough government discourse in both countries was not matched by imposed obligations. In France, banks bought back government held shares with impressive speed. A number of governments even forced the merger of two large TBTF banks as a means to stabilize weaker banks and in exchange for financial support—thus working against other efforts to decrease the size of the largest banks. The UK, French, and German governments, respectively, forced through the mergers of six of the largest European banks—HBOS and Lloyds TSB, Banques Populaires and the Caisses d'Epargne, and Commerzbank and Dresdner Bank. The US Treasury also oversaw several mergers and acquisitions early in the crisis in an effort to find private sector solutions to bank failure, including Bank of America's takeover of investment bank Merrill Lynch, JP Morgan's purchase of Bear Stearns, and Wells Fargo's rescue of Wachovia.

4. Revenue-raising regulation and fiscal policy

Revenue-raising regulation and fiscal policy is of potential significance to constraining bank activities. However, the measures adopted at the national level over the decade following the international financial crisis had, at most, only a marginal impact on the TBTF problem. Revenue-raising regulation and fiscal policy adopted to constrain bank activities in the five countries is summarized in Table 3.2. The one-off bonus taxes of 50 per cent announced by the UK and then French governments were designed to raise money for national treasuries, reimburse loans provided and (as emphasized particularly by the British) encourage banks to increase their capital rather than pay bonuses. The impact upon trading activities is questionable, especially because it was always unlikely that the tax would be repeated. The US administration and German and Dutch governments avoided following the UK lead on the bonus tax. Following public outrage at bonuses paid out at the height of the crisis, the US House of Representatives and Senate adopted separate bills that taxed bonuses at very high rates—with the House version calling for a 90 per cent levy on firms that accepted at least $5bn of federal bail-out funds (Hulse and Herszenhorn 2009). Although President Obama initially signalled his support for such a measure, his administration ultimately refused to endorse the legislation (Herszenhorn 2009).

The adoption of an international tax on short-term financial transactions (such as the proposed Tobin Tax) had some potential to contribute to tackling the TBTF problem. Such a tax could contribute to a stabilization fund to assist struggling banks in future crises, thus decreasing pressure on governments to offer bail-out funds. With a surprise announcement by Prime Minister Gordon Brown in favour of a transactions tax on 21 September 2008, the positions of the governments of the four European case study countries on the matter appeared largely aligned.

Table 3.2 Revenue-raising measures to diminish bank risk and cover bail-out costs

Regulatory response	US	UK	France	Germany	Netherlands
Permanent international/ European taxes	Obama administration opposed to Tobin Tax.	PM Gordon Brown supported tax on financial transactions but no details provided; Conservative–Liberal Democrat government opposed. No to EU FTT.	Tobin Tax: strong and consistent supporter. No to one-off levy. Use of EU closer cooperation provisions to adopt FTT.	Neutral on Tobin Tax but open minded (willing to be directed by IMF report, April 2010). Pro-EU tax. Use of EU closer cooperation provisions to adopt FTT.	Opposed to Tobin Tax and to the EU's FTT tax.
Multiannual national bank levy	No: Obama administration proposed a Financial Crisis Responsibility Fee in 2010 at 0.15% rate for financial firms with at least $50bn consolidated assets, but never enacted.	Yes (from 2011): 0.075% for 2011, rising to 0.078% from 1 January 2012. Funding liabilities of greater than one-year maturity and certain other liabilities will be charged at half the rate otherwise applicable. Total equity and liabilities shown on a relevant balance sheet, except for tier-1 capital (*not* tier-2 capital) and other items such as insured deposits, certain tax and pension fund liabilities, sovereign repos, and	Yes: 0.25% on the amount of minimum regulatory capital as determined based on risk-weighted assets. Applied to nationally headquartered banks and subsidiaries of foreign banks and non-EEA branches.	Yes: (i) Rate for relevant liabilities is progressive and cumulative: relevant liabilities of up to €10bn are chargeable at 0.02% annually, relevant liabilities of €10bn or more up to €100bn are chargeable at 0.03% annually, and relevant liabilities in excess of €100bn are chargeable at 0.04%. Relevant derivatives are chargeable at 0.00015% on the nominal value of the derivatives. Two bases for levy: (i) relevant liabilities	Yes: (from 2012) larger banks (>€20bn) to pay quarterly levy of 2.5 bps of deposits; additional premium to be levied based on risk, ranging from 0% for the least-risky banks to 100% of the basic contribution for the riskiest. The riskiness of a bank is based on the ratio of risk-weighted assets to total assets, leverage, and its liquidity ratio, defined as liquid assets divided by total assets. Riskier banks are

Continued

Table 3.2 Continued

Regulatory response	US	UK	France	Germany	Netherlands
		sovereign stock-lending liabilities. Adjustments to balance sheets may be required in order to net certain assets and liabilities, e.g. cash-collateralized derivatives. Credit is given for 'high quality liquid assets'. Applied to nationally headquartered banks and subsidiaries and branches of foreign banks.		equal total liabilities less liabilities to customers less profit participation right capital less funds for general banking risks (*Fonds für allgemeine Bankrisiken*) less equity (*Eigenkapital*); (ii) relevant derivatives equal value of all off-balance-sheet derivatives. Applied to nationally headquartered banks and subsidiaries of foreign banks and non-EEA bank branches.	punished because the risk premium has to be paid until the fund reaches a size equivalent to 2.5% of all banks' deposits, whereas the basic premium of 2.5 basis points has to be paid until a bank's total payments equal 1% of its deposits.
Temporary bonus tax	None. House of Representatives passed a bill to impose a 90% tax on bonuses in bailout companies, but not supported by Obama adminisration.	50% bonus tax adopted.	50% bonus tax proposed but never adopted.	No bonus tax.	No bonus tax.

Source: authors' own compilation.

French governments had long supported a Tobin Tax. The German and Dutch government positions were broadly in favour and 'willing to be directed' by the IMF position on the matter. Despite this surprising apparent convergence of views, an international agreement on a transactions tax never materialized. There was considerable opposition in the UK—including from Bank of England Governor Mervyn King, who explicitly did not see a transactions tax as a valid solution to the TBTF problem despite his support for 'radical reform' (Castle 2010).

The Obama administration was opposed to a transactions tax and instead proposed a backwards-looking levy of 0.15 per cent on any bank balance sheet larger than $50bn (€36bn, £31bn), aimed at recouping $90bn used to bail out banks during the financial crisis. Such a levy would have worked as less of a constraint on bank activities because it failed to distinguish between different activities, but it could have encouraged some TBTF banks to shrink their balance sheets—given that it would be directed at only the largest institutions. The French and German governments argued that such a fee should be levied not just once, but as a matter of course on all systemically important banks (Le Guernigou 2010). At its Iqaluit meeting in February 2010, Group of Seven (G7) finance ministers appeared to coalesce around the idea of imposing forward-looking levies on banks principally as a way to insure the global economy against future financial crises (Fifield 2010). Still, an agreement on whether this would be a transactions tax or a levy on deposits remained elusive. A levy on deposits, rather than the overall balance sheet, would have been an even more marked contrast to a transactions tax, and would have represented little more than an imposed increase in bank payments to deposit guarantee schemes. Such a levy would even have provided an incentive to make greater use of wholesale markets by encouraging more non-deposit funding. The risk of moral hazard created by a future international stabilization fund could also have had, at least in theory, a mitigating effect on any decline in higher-risk investment banking activities caused by the creation of a tax or levy.

Despite the failure to reach an agreement at the international level on a bank levy, several national governments adopted levies unilaterally and, by 2016, sixteen European countries had a bank levy in place (Lauermann and Struve 2015), although half of these were tax deductible. The purpose and design of the levies varied. For example, the UK levy funded the general budget, while the German levy fed a separate fund to pay down toxic bank assets. The scope of levies varied massively in terms of: base (bank deposits, capital assets, risk-weighted assets, and other calculations with respect to a bank's balance sheet); tax-deductible contributions; implementation date (from 2011 onwards and some with phased-in time periods for different components); and varying application of the levy to the branches and subsidiaries of foreign banks. The level of the levies also varied considerably as did the amounts raised. The anticipated yearly yields for the UK, French, German, and Dutch levies were, respectively, £2.5bn, €800m from 2012, up to €1.3bn from 2012, and a total of approximately €4bn. The German government set a target size of its bank restructuring fund at €70bn but had only raised €1.28bn in the first two years (Lauermann and Struve 2015). The UK government raised more than £18bn from its bank levy between its introduction in 2011 and 2018, increasing significantly the effective tax rate of the country's largest banks (OBR 2019). The Dutch levy adopted in 2011 was focused entirely upon *ex ante* funds for bank deposit guarantees and would have been necessary given the adoption of the revised EU Deposit Guarantee Scheme in 2014 (PwC 2011). The Netherlands was one of the EU member states which previously had no *ex ante* funds to pay for guaranteed deposits. Banks in the US were not subject to a similar levy. All the levies were structured to attract higher tax revenues from higher-risk investment banking activities. Thus, given their design, the levies should have worked to discourage the engagement of large universal and other banks in these activities. All the national-level European bank levies were ostensibly and officially adopted to punish riskier bank activities. However, almost a decade after their launch, the actual impact of bank levies on bank size and activities remained far from clear, while some studies point to the increased risk caused notably on the asset side of balance sheets (Devereux et al. 2019).

The failure to reach an agreement at the international level on a bank levy led the European Commission to propose EU legislation on a Financial Transactions Tax (FTT) in September 2011. The Commission proposed a harmonized minimum tax rate for all trading activities in the financial market if at least one of the financial institutions was based in an EU member state (EU Commission 2011). After threats by the UK government to veto draft legislation, it was suggested that the tax only apply to euro area member states (Torello and Horobin 2011). However, several euro area member state governments were also opposed, including the Netherlands. In May 2014, using the Enhanced Cooperation procedure, ten EU member states agreed to introduce an FTT by the start of 2016. With the aim of reducing the risk of tax evasion, the European Commission added the 'issuance principle' to its draft regulation, which would have imposed the FTT upon financial institutions based outside the member states having adopted the FTT but trading in these member states (EU Commission 2013a). The EU member states that did not want to join the FTT thus had an extra incentive to block the implementation of the tax. The UK government issued a formal complaint against the use of the Enhanced Cooperation procedure which the Council's legal service supported (Council of the EU 2013). Final adoption of the FTT by national governments was thus postponed indefinitely.

EU member states did, though, agree upon two forms of revenue raising that were designed to facilitate the resolution of failing banks, eliminate reliance on government bail-out, and prevent contagion to other banks: resolution funds and increased deposit guarantee funds. These mechanisms were intended as part of national and EU-wide resolution regimes that were similar to what already existed in the US. The Bank Recovery and Resolution Directive, adopted in 2013, required member states to create bank resolution funds from a levy on banks (Howarth and Quaglia 2014). An intergovernmental side agreement to the Single Resolution Mechanism Regulation (SRMR 2014), also adopted in 2014, provided for the gradual mutualization of the national resolution funds of Banking Union member states, starting in 2016, into a European-level Single Resolution Fund (SRF) to reach a target size of 1 per cent of covered deposits or roughly €55bn. Member state governments agreed for bank contributions to national resolution funds to consist of a flat contribution based on the amount of each bank's liabilities excluding own funds and covered deposits and a risk-adjusted contribution—thus in effect increasing the relative contribution of larger universal banks engaged in higher-risk investment banking activities. There were widespread concerns that the (estimated) €55bn European fund was not sufficient to ensure financial stability because the balance sheets of at least fifty euro area member state headquartered banks were larger than the amount in the fund. If the SRF was not sufficiently large to cover a bank resolution, the intergovernmental side agreement to the SRMR allowed for *ex post* contributions to be raised, imposing an additional levy on covered banks. These *ex post* contributions per year could not exceed three times the amount of annual contributions.

The revised Common Deposit Guarantee Scheme (DGS) Directive, adopted in 2014, set €100,000 as the minimum deposit to be protected in the event of bank resolution. Banks were also required to increase up-front (*ex ante*) national deposit guarantee funds to cover 0.8 per cent of covered deposits. In order to ensure consistent application of the DGS Directive in member states, the EBA issued guidelines in May 2015 to specify methods for calculating the contributions to deposit guarantee schemes (EBA 2015; Howarth and Quaglia 2018a). The contributions to these schemes were to be based on the amount of covered deposits and the degree of risk incurred by the respective bank, thus in effect increasing the contribution of large universal banks engaged in higher-risk investment banking activities and of investment banks. Member states could also set lower contributions for low-risk sectors governed by national law.

5. The limited and varying reinforcement of bank regulation

Regulatory change that was designed to discourage excessive risk-taking activities and reinforce the stability of large financial institutions had considerable potential to tackle the problem of TBTF. Here we consider regulatory change on CRAs, remuneration, capital requirements, liquidity, resolution rules, and obligatory resolution planning. In addition to the structural reform adopted in the US and UK, we argue that only one regulatory change was potentially significant in terms of diminishing the problem of TBTF: Basel III capital requirements, although these were watered down significantly in the EU context. Other changes were of limited likely impact on TBTF. Table 3.3 summarizes the regulatory reforms adopted in the five countries.

Table 3.3 Regulatory measures to diminish TBTF bank risk

Regulatory response	US	UK	France	Germany	Netherlands
Credit rating agencies	Dodd–Frank sought to strengthen rules governing CRA conflicts of interest, transparency, and disclosure, but SEC enacted minimal changes.	UK supported modest reforms to 2009 EU CRA regulation to address registration, transparency, and conflicts of interest.	Reduce conflict of interest/increase transparency. Create a European credit rating agency—little detail/not created.	Reduce conflict of interest/increase transparency. Create a European credit rating agency—little detail/not created.	Reduce conflict of interest/increase transparency.
Remuneration rules*	Limits for recapitalized banks: prohibition of 'golden parachute' contracts; $500,000 limit on annual tax deductibility; elimination of compensation structures that encourage 'unnecessary and excessive' risk taking; bonus clawback procedures.	Initial discouragement of bonuses on short-term gains. EU rules adopted in CRD IV (2013) and EBA guidelines (quantitative and qualitative) with a bonus cap of 100% of fixed remuneration; 200% with shareholder approval.	Ban on bonuses for more than a year. Half the bonus paid out over three years or cancelled if performance and profits turn bad. Then EU rules adopted (see UK).	Strong government focus on bonuses. Initial voluntary commitment of eight biggest German banks not to pay bonuses. 2010 law: BaFin can forbid high bonuses if: a) institution violated other regulations; b) if performance does not justify bonuses. Finance Ministry given more powers to supervise bonuses. Then EU rules adopted (see UK).	Voluntary Banking Code, then 100% rule/EU rules (see UK) and then, 2015, more restrictive cap on bonuses to maximum of 20% of fixed remuneration, with some exceptions for key staff.

Capital strengthening: definition of capital	Tougher capital requirements and elimination of hybrid capital.	Tougher capital requirements and elimination of hybrid capital.	Keep hybrids.	Keep hybrids.	Tougher capital requirements.
Capital Strengthening: figure	Significant reinforcement beyond Basel III.	Significant reinforcement beyond Basel III/CRD IV.	Very limited reinforcement. Delayed implementation of Basel III.	Very limited reinforcement. Long delay to implementation of Basel III.	Reinforcement in accordance with Basel III.
Double counting of insurance subsidiary capital	Elimination of double counting.	Elimination of double counting.	Allow double counting.	Allow double counting.	Allow double counting.
Liquidity	Supported new international rules on liquidity in Basel III. Introduced LCR in 2013—imposes minimum requirement for liquidity to allow a bank to survive a supervisory 30-day stress scenario—and NSFR in 2016 for large banks.	Regulatory change in 2009 to increase liquidity so that all bank subsidiaries can stand alone unsupported by their parent or other parts of the group; up to 8% of banks' assets could be tied up in cash and gilts that banks are forced to hold. In favour of binding Basel III rules.	Regulation seeks to limit the ability to use wholesale financing to increase the size of banks' balance sheets. Reduction in the assumed percentage of sight deposits that might be withdrawn in a crisis situation. Opposed to binding Basel III rules. Then preference for delayed implementation (to 2018).	Regulatory change but only general requirements established. Law opens way for domestic imposition of tighter BIS guidelines. Opposed to binding Basel III rules. Then preference for delayed implementation (to 2018).	Supported new international rules on liquidity in Basel III.

Continued

Table 3.3 Continued

Regulatory response	US	UK	France	Germany	Netherlands
Leverage	Yes: introduced leverage ratio of 4% in 2013, and a supplementary leverage ratio of 5% for G-SIFIs in 2014.	Yes: to be included in CRD IV. Easiest measurement.	No.	No.	No.
'Living wills'/resolution plans	Dodd–Frank mandated 'Living Wills' and statutory bail-in rules for SIFIs; and Fed to introduce minimum standards for Total Loss Absorbency Capacity (TLAC).	'Living wills' recommended in the Taylor Report; delay to introduction of national reforms; greater international cooperation. Support for less margin of manoeuvre in resolution plans required by EU's BRRD (2013).	Law adopted but limited constraint. Reinforcement of international monitoring groups for major cross-border French banks. Support for more margin of manoeuvre in resolution plans required in EU's BRRD (2013).	Law requiring 'resolution regime' adopted but limited constraint. Greater international cooperation. Support for more margin of manoeuvre in resolution plans required in EU's BRRD (2013).	Intervention Act of 2012 required 'living wills'; EU's BRRD (2013) requires resolution plans.
Off-balance-sheet activities	Dodd–Frank included strengthened risk retention, disclosure and reporting requirements for Asset Backed Securities (ABS).	Securitization to be encouraged but subject to reporting requirements and increased monitoring.	Securitization to be encouraged but subject to reporting requirement and increased monitoring.	Reporting requirements and increased monitoring.	To be encouraged but subject to reporting requirements and increased monitoring.

* Remuneration rules listed include voluntary commitments and government legislation restricting salaries and bonuses.
Source: authors' own compilation

Constraining credit rating agencies

In the aftermath of the international financial crisis, loose international commitments in the Group of Twenty (G20)—the recently created gathering of the political leaders of the world's twenty largest economies—and the BIS focused upon the reduction of CRA conflict of interest with the banks and other firms being rated and the danger of inaccurate credit ratings shaping investment decisions. The Obama administration tightened up US rules on CRAs to reduce the conflict of interest. However, the EU member states agreed legislation that went even further (Quaglia 2014a). The Dodd–Frank Act (Title IX, Subtitle C, 'Improvements to the Regulation of Credit Rating Agencies') reinforced US regulation of CRAs that already included elements of direct public oversight. However, the CRAs maintained discretion over ratings methodologies and content (Pagliari 2013b). The new provisions assigned to the Securities and Exchange Commission (SEC) the power to suspend or revoke a rating agency's now mandatory registration, or to penalize individual agency employees for misconduct. It also created at the SEC an Office of Credit Ratings to administer regulations and conduct annual examinations. The Dodd–Frank Act also required the SEC to adopt a range of rules on CRAs concerning, *inter alia*, internal controls, conflicts of interest, and transparency (see Acharya et al. 2011).

These US efforts to tighten the regulation of CRAs aligned largely with EU collective efforts. EU member states adopted a new regulation focused on CRAs in April 2009 (European Parliament and the Council 2009; Wittenberg 2015). The regulation required the regulation of all CRAs, the ratings of which were used in the EU, the need to comply with conflict of interest rules, and quality controls on rating methodology and the ratings (García Alcubilla and Ruiz del Pozo 2012). Many new CRAs established globally were closely connected to the existing three main US-headquartered CRAs—Fitch, Standard & Poor's (renamed S&P Global Ratings) and Moody's Investors Services (Sinclair 2005, p. 123), the so-called 'Big Three'. Given their dominance of the European credit rating market, the EU regulation in effect specified the terms by which foreign CRAs could continue servicing European customers. Regarding banks specifically, the regulation specified how credit ratings issued outside the EU could be used in the EU for the regulatory purposes of calculating bank capital requirements. Either the European Commission had to confirm the equivalence of third country rules to enable a third country CRA to apply for certification, or the ratings of third country agencies had to be endorsed by a European subsidiary (Pagliari 2013b; Quaglia 2014a). Subsequent amendment of the EU regulation in 2013 added more rigorous requirements than those mandated in the US and recommended by IOSCO (Wittenberg 2015). These included a double and independent rating for structured finance (i.e., securitization) instruments, disclosure requirements for sovereign country ratings, and a mandatory four-year rotation of CRAs in the case of re-securitization transactions

(Faure-Dauphin and Atthenout 2013). The German government unsuccessfully proposed the creation of a more tightly regulated European CRA as a possible solution to CRA conflict of interest (Issing et al. 2009).

Limited restrictions of bank remuneration practices

German and French governments argued that bank remuneration practices, inspired by Anglo-American practices, were one of the principal causes of the crisis (Hardie and Howarth 2009). However, on bank remuneration, the distinction between populist government discourse and real policy preference was frequently far from certain and there is no robust evidence of a link between financial crises and remuneration policy (de Andrés et al. 2019). The G20 endorsed the 2009 recommendations of the newly created Financial Stability Board (FSB) that governments and banks should adopt guidelines and/or rules aimed at aligning compensation with long-term value creation, rather than excessive risk taking.[1] The recommendations included the remuneration of bank staff through bank shares with tie-ins rather than through cash.

The French government's action on bonuses was very newsworthy—with meetings at the Elysée Palace between President Nicolas Sarkozy and top bankers—but the real impact of this action was of limited significance (Hardie and Howarth 2009). As a stop-gap measure, the government reached an agreement with the chief executives of the country's six largest banks on a ban on bonuses for more than a year and then half the bonus paid out over three years or cancelled if performance and profits declined. The German government had a well-publicized focus on bonuses. A 2010 law—the Regulation on the Regulatory Requirements for Compensation Systems in Financial Institutions—allowed the Federal Financial Supervisory Authority (BaFin) to forbid high bonuses if an institution violated other regulations or if performance did not justify bonuses (Haag and Steffen 2020). The law gave the finance ministry more powers to supervise bonuses. The de facto emphasis, though, remained on voluntary action. The UK government also publicly discouraged banks from giving bonuses that encouraged excessive risk taking, instead encouraging banks to adopt alternative remuneration schemes to

---

[1] The G20 policy on compensation—the FSB's 'Principles for Sound Compensation Practices'—adopted in 2009 in the aftermath of the international financial crisis, encouraged countries/banks to avoid multi-year guaranteed bonuses; required a significant portion of variable compensation to be deferred, tied to performance, and subject to appropriate clawback; ensured that compensation for senior executives and other employees having a material impact on the firm's risk exposure aligns with performance and risk; made firms' compensation policies and structures transparent through disclosure requirements; limited variable compensation as a percentage of total net revenues when it is inconsistent with the maintenance of a sound capital base; and ensured that compensation committees overseeing compensation policies are able to act independently. The G20 assigned the FSB the tasks of monitoring the implementation of FSB standards and of proposing additional measures as required by March 2010.

reward long-term value creation. However, UK government policy on the matter remained entirely voluntary.

In the UK, France, and Germany—as in most EU member states—the principal legislative restrictions on bank bonuses came via the EU's Capital Requirements Directive (CRD) IV, adopted in 2013 (Directive 2013/36/EU; European Parliament and the Council 2013). This directive set 100 per cent of salary as the normal maximum allowed bonus, while shareholders were given the power to increase this level to 200 per cent of salary. The rest of the EU regulatory effort on bonuses came via EBA guidelines on sound remuneration practices designed to avoid excessive risk taking by bankers. These guidelines involved a risk alignment process between variable remuneration and the manager's risk profile. The guidelines establish a range of mechanisms in order to make this alignment easier, such as payments in instruments and notably shares, deferrals, retention periods, and clawbacks. The mix of quantitative and qualitative measures has been criticized as excessively complex by some observers (de Andrés et al. 2019). The bonus cap was also controversial, with many arguing that it could produce perverse incentives (de Andrés et al. 2019). Furthermore, it was later feared that Brexit would help avoid the implementation of this regulation for those UK bankers who were likely to be most affected by the remuneration cap.

The Dutch government initially shied away from legislation on bonuses. It supported the 2009 Banking Code which included voluntary bonus caps. When it became clear that no banks were imposing particularly restrictive bonus caps, the Dutch government intervened with legislation in 2012 that limited bank bonuses paid in the Netherlands to 100 per cent of salary—thus anticipating the forthcoming EU provisions in CRD IV. However, the Dutch legislation allowed banks considerable wiggle room and notably the possibility of paying higher bonuses outwith the country. The 2012 legislation also prohibited state-supported companies from granting their directors a variable remuneration. In 2014, following EBA guidelines, the Dutch government introduced a clawback rule allowing banks to recover or adjust excessive remunerations. In 2015, the Dutch government adopted new legislation that was far more restrictive than EU rules, limiting bonuses to 20 per cent of salary while shareholders could increase this to 200 per cent for Dutch bank subsidiaries outside the EU. The degree to which this Dutch legislation on bonuses or EU legislation constrained bank risk taking remains the subject of debate (Price Waterhouse Coopers 2017; Colonnello et al. 2018).

In the US, the 2008 TARP included curbs on executive compensation, clawbacks for past compensation, the prohibition of golden parachutes to senior executives, and a $500,000 limit on annual tax deductions for executive payments (Woll 2014, p. 90). Scandals surrounding the payment of bank bonuses—notably including Goldman Sachs and AIG—prompted Obama to tighten the rules in February 2009 by announcing a $500,000 annual pay cap for executives at banks receiving exceptional levels of federal aid. But the restrictions were not retrospective, and banks were incentivized to pay TARP funds back as quickly as possible to get around the pay cap. Public anger over bank bonuses led to a raft of new rules in the 2010 Dodd–Frank Act intended to strengthen disclosure requirements on executive pay; safeguard the independence of corporate compensation committees; link compensation more explicitly to financial performance; and provide for clawback of compensation. The Act also empowered shareholders by giving them a non-binding 'say on pay' vote on executive compensation and 'golden parachutes'. Nonetheless, many of the changes in Dodd–Frank were largely cosmetic and the impact on bankers' pay was very limited.

(Inadequately) reinforced capital requirements

Capital represents the portion of a bank's assets which has no associated contractual commitment for repayment. It is, therefore, available as a cushion in case the value of the bank's assets declines or its liabilities rise. International guidelines and EU and national legislation to strengthen the capital of European banks may have made large banks less reliant on government bail-outs come the next financial crisis, notably by increasing the loss-absorbing capital that all banks were expected to hold and imposing higher risk-weights on investment banking assets. Capital requirements for banks have traditionally been regarded as one of the main instruments to ensure the stability of the banking sector and hence financial stability *tout court*. Capital requirements are regulations limiting the amount of leverage that financial firms can assume. As the US Treasury Secretary Timothy Geithner put it in the wake of the financial crisis: 'The top three things to get done are capital, capital and capital' (Leonhardt 2010). In 1988, the BCBS issued the Basel I Accord on 'International convergence of capital measurement and capital standards', which was updated by the Basel II Accord in 2004 (revised in 2005). Over time, these 'soft' international rules were incorporated into (legally binding) national legislation. In the EU this was done through the CRDs (see Quaglia 2010a), which allowed significant margin of manoeuvre to national governments in their transposition of the directives into national legislation and implementation. Prior to the 2007–9 financial crisis, US administrations failed to implement Basel guidelines.

In the aftermath of the financial crisis, the Obama administration took the lead internationally on capital adequacy by calling for the strengthening of the capital that banks were required to keep—and specifically a ban on 'hybrid' capital, which was considered loss absorbing during non-crisis periods—and an increase in the amount of this capital through leverage rules. The FSB embraced a similar but vaguer position on capital quality and quantity—a commitment to an agreement by the end of 2010—with support for the introduction of a leverage ratio as a supplementary measure to the Basel II risk-based framework. In December 2009, the BCBS took a surprisingly hard-line approach on capital requirements, pushing for a higher adequacy threshold and a restriction on hybrids with minimum capital to be composed of predominantly equity capital.

In December 2010, the BCBS agreed upon the Basel III Accord. The new rules: provided a more restrictive definition of what counts as bank capital; increased the risk weight of several assets in the banking book and introduced capital buffers; set up a recommended and potentially obligatory leverage ratio; and outlined international rules on liquidity management. All in all, the new rules increased the proportion of capital that must be of proven loss-absorbing capacity—i.e., core tier-1 (equity) capital—over Basel II requirements, and were to be phased in gradually from January 2013 until 2019. The Basel III Accord also recommended the eventual adoption of a simple leverage ratio of 3 per cent for SIBs (BCBS 2010a). The Basel III Accord is an agreement between national regulators gathered in the BCBS; hence it had to be implemented into national (and/or EU) legislation in order to become legally binding.

Although the US had been reluctant to implement the Basel II Accord prior to 2008, the political fallout from the crisis brought a renewed vigour to strengthening the resilience of US financial institutions. In December 2011, the Federal Reserve announced its intention to comply substantially with all the Basel III requirements, making clear that they would apply to all banks and non-banks with more than $50bn in assets. Unlike Europe, however, the Basel III Final Rule—issued by the Federal Reserve, the Office of the Comptroller of the Currency (OCC), and the Federal Deposit Insurance Corporation (FDIC) in July 2013—adopted a differentiated approach designed to impose more stringent requirements on the largest banks. Hence, on top of the minimum CET1 ratio of 4.5 per cent stipulated in Basel III, US regulations introduced an additional capital conservation buffer of 2.5 per cent, raised the minimum ratio of tier-1 capital to RWAs from 4 per cent to 6 per cent, and introduced an additional G-SIB surcharge for the most internationally active US banks from January 2016. US regulators also went significantly beyond the 3 per cent leverage ratio proposed in Basel by imposing a supplementary leverage ratio requiring the largest bank holding companies to have a ratio of 5 per cent. Importantly, the US maintained bank capital levels above those required by global standards, even as the Trump administration sought to unwind many of the Dodd–Frank regulations after 2017, reflecting the fact that this was a rare area of (relative) bipartisan consensus.

By contrast, the implementation of the Basel III rules in the EU proved far more politically controversial and potentially challenging for many EU-headquartered banks, which would have to raise equity or other forms of capital, or reduce lending and higher-risk investment banking activities sharply (BCBS 2010b). In 2013, the EU member states adopted the fourth version of the CRD which set minimum capital rules but allowed national governments margin of manoeuvre on implementation and introduced two capital buffers: the capital conservation buffer identical for all banks in the EU and the countercyclical capital buffer to be determined at national level. The EU member states also adopted the Capital Requirements Regulation, which set a maximum capital level to be applied to all EU-headquartered banks; contained prudential requirements for credit institutions and investment firms; and covered the definition of capital, increasing the amount of own funds that banks needed to hold as well as the quality of those funds (Howarth and Quaglia 2013a).

A decade after the Basel III agreement, the FSB (2020) concluded that four of our case study countries had failed to implement key elements of the capital requirement guidelines. Only the US was largely compliant, or compliant in all the categories, with the exception of the Net Stable Funding Ratio (NSFR) which is considered in the section on liabilities below. France, Germany, the Netherlands, and the UK were all evaluated as materially non-compliant on risk-based capital rules and only largely compliant on the Liquidity Coverage Ratio (LCR). All four countries failed to implement Basel III guidelines on large exposures (deadline of 2019), the leverage ratio (deadline of 2018), and the NSFR (deadline of 2018). The EU-wide implementation problem reflects efforts from 2011 to water down Basel III guidelines in EU legislation. Over the decade following the international financial crisis, banks on average in all five countries improved their capital position (Tables 3.4 and 3.5). However, the headline figures for many European banks disguised significant problems facing these banks and the flawed implementation of Basel III rules in the EU (Goldstein 2012; Howarth and Quaglia 2013a).

Following the agreement on Basel III and during the intra-EU negotiations on CRD IV, some of the compromises reached in the BCBS unravelled. Several EU member states—notably the German and French governments—the European Parliament, and even the Commission itself called for the need to take into

Table 3.4 Bank tier-1 capital ratio (as a percentage of risk-weighted assets, recall Basel III target of 6% with at least 4.5% of RWA; 10.5–13% with buffers; case study countries), 2008–2018)[*]

	2008	2010	2012	2014	2016	2018
France	11.3	13.7	15.6	13.1	14.5	15.5
Germany	9.7	11.9	13.9	15.3	16.3	16.1
Netherlands	10.0	12.2	12.7	15.4	17.9	18.8
UK				12.2	15.1	17.8
US	9.8	12.6	13.0	13.0	12.9	

[*] Weighted averages for groups of countries, based on total assets. For information on the consolidation basis and coverage of these data, see https://www.bis.org/publ/cgfs60/cgfs60_metadata.xlsx.
Source: BIS (2018, p. 97), national data. For further details, see https://www.bis.org/publ/cgfs60/cgfs60_metadata.xlsx. Figures for 2018 come from the ECB Data warehouse: https://sdw.ecb.europa.eu

Table 3.5 Bank leverage: simple tier-1 unweighted capital ratio (recall Basel III target of at least 3%; case study countries), 2008–16[*]

	2008	2010	2012	2014	2016
France	3.8	4.9	4.6	4.2	4.9
Germany	3.8	4.4	4.2	5.3	5.6
Netherlands	3.7	4.5	4.6	4.6	5.3
UK				4.3	4.8
US	7.2	8.7	8.7	9.1	9.3

[*] Weighted averages for groups of banks, based on total assets. For information on the consolidation basis and coverage of these data, see https://www.bis.org/publ/cgfs60/cgfs60_metadata.xlsx. In July 2013, the US Federal Reserve announced that the minimum Basel III leverage ratio would be 6% for SIFIs and 5% for their insured bank holding companies.
Source: BIS (2018, p. 97), national data. For further details, see https://www.bis.org/publ/cgfs60/cgfs60_metadata.xlsx.

account 'European specificities' in incorporating the Basel III rules into CRD IV, reopening some of the issues that had already caused friction within the BCBS. Basel III applied to internationally active banks, whereas EU legislation was to apply to all banks, making some Basel III provisions—notably the calculation of tier 1—impossible to apply in EU member states without a massive shift in the structure of a large range of banks and banking systems. The Commission justified its decision to apply Basel III rules, as with Basel I and Basel II, to all EU banks on both stability grounds and reasons linked to the application of EU competition policy and the need to ensure an 'international level playing field' (Paulis 2012). Of particular concern to several EU member state governments and banks was that in the US, the Basel III Accord would be applied only to financial institutions with over (US)$50bn in assets (EU Parliament 2010, 2011). The former Governor of the Bank of France, Jacques de Larosière, argued that Basel rules risk punishing the wrong banks—that is, the 'diversified' and safer continental European universal banks—rather than specifically those banks including both universal and investment banks which, he claimed, engaged in riskier investment banking activities (de Larosière 2010, 2011).

CRD IV was criticized by many regulators and by the IMF for significantly watering down key Basel III elements (IMF 2011; Barker and Masters 2012). Speaking at a meeting of EU economic and finance ministers held to discuss CRD IV, the UK Chancellor complained that 'We are not implementing the Basel agreement, as anyone who will look at this text will be able to tell you' (Barker 2012). The UK government was one of the leading European cheerleaders for closely aligning CRD IV with Basel III (IMF 2011). The UK Conservative–Liberal Democrat government (joined by several other member state governments, including the Swedish) criticized the European Commission's CRD IV draft on the grounds that it did not go far enough (see, for example, Djankov et al. 2011). In particular, UK regulators opposed the move under CRD IV to embrace a leverage ratio for guidance purposes only and sought to keep open the possibility of imposing capital requirements higher than those eventually set by EU legislation. Many UK policy makers, including the Governor of the Bank of England, were critical of the European Commission's position on a maximum capital ratio, arguing that the new level of required capital should have been 'much higher'—and even 'many times higher'—than the levels set out in the Basel III proposals (Guerrera and Pimlott 2010). The UK's ICB recommended that large retail banks be required to have a minimum core tier-1 ratio of 10 per cent of risk-weighted assets, which would significantly exceed the Basel III minimum of 7 per cent (core tier-1 at 4.5 per cent plus the 2.5 per cent capital conservation buffer and the proposed surcharge for G-SIBs—possibly up to 2.5 per cent.

The governments of France and Germany were aligned in their opposition to Basel III's exclusion of hybrid capital—which has some features of both debt and equity and notably 'silent participations' (long-term loans) (*Financial Times* 2010). Many European banks made use of hybrids to count towards their tier-1 capital base, right up to the 15 per cent maximum allowed under Basel II. These banks would be disadvantaged if hybrid rules were enacted and they were forced to reduce lending. The implications of the new capital rules were potentially greatest for the many non-listed savings and cooperative banks—a much more significant element of the German and French banking systems than in the UK and the Netherlands—which did not use equity, relying on other forms of capital to meet capital requirements in the past, including hybrids. Basel III threatened to impose a significant overhaul of the capital structure and legal status of internationally active, publicly owned/public-law banks and mutuals. Proportionately, the ban on hybrids would hit the German banking system the most, particularly the *Landesbanken*. However, Germany's largest private commercial banks also relied on hybrid capital to meet capital targets. Thus, the German government made certain that CRD IV explicitly allowed for 'silent participations' to count towards core tier-1.

The French, German, and a number of other EU member state governments were also opposed to the adoption of a simple leverage ratio to determine the quantity of capital to be held by banks. Basel III called for a leverage ratio of 3 per cent—an assets to tier-1 capital ratio of approximately 33. The position reflected the much higher leverage ratios of most large French- and German-headquartered banks. Basel II rules on bank capital had allowed banks to amass assets with high credit ratings without setting capital aside to cover potential losses. This allowed many banks in Europe to become highly leveraged despite meeting international rules on capital cushions. A range of governments and central banks, including the ECB, pushed for a leverage ratio as a simple mechanism to curb excessive risk taking (Masters 2012). The US administration favoured a uniform and mandatory leverage rule, while the UK and Dutch governments were moderately supportive. In large part, this reflected the capital position of nationally headquartered banks in the aftermath of the crisis. Broadly speaking, while the leverage ratio of US and UK banks increased significantly in the years prior to 2008, these fell quickly after the crisis, whereas the leverage ratios of French, German, and Dutch banks generally remained much higher. By 2015, for example, the largest US banks had an average asset to equity ratio of 9.5 : 1 by 2015, compared to 19.5 : 1 in the euro area, and 14.4 : 1 in the UK (Bell and Hindmoor 2018).

German and French government policy on capital requirements directly contradicted their otherwise strong push for tighter EU and international financial regulation. In early July 2009, just prior to the adoption of its own ostensibly restrictive national legislation, the German government lobbied for a temporary loosening of existing EU bank capital and accounting rules. Officially, this was motivated by the German government's push to give banks more leeway to make additional loans. Observers (Tett 2009) noted, however, that the move appeared to be driven by a desire to avoid too much transparency on bad loans. The German government's request was rebuffed by the other EU member states but the debate on the matter reinforced a growing impression that Germany was intent on pursuing a policy of forbearance towards its troubled banks—on capital rules, accounting, and much else.

Given the growth and competition effects of capital strengthening, it is not surprising that most national governments refused to tighten national rules unilaterally (Howarth and Quaglia 2016c). In March 2009, the German federal cabinet approved a draft bill on regulatory reform (the *Gesetz zur Verstärkung der Finanzmarkt- und Versicherungsaufsicht*), which was passed in the federal parliament on 10 July 2009. The law included enhanced capital requirements for securitization and increasing capital reserves above Basel II requirements. However, the devil is in the detail and the German federal government did not move to clarify new German rules unilaterally. Rather the law permitted the government to implement the BCBS guidelines once adopted at the EU level.

Reinforcing liquidity rules and the focus on stable bank funding

At the peak of the crisis the interbank markets froze, highlighting the importance of banks holding liquid assets[2] in order to meet short-term obligations (*The Economist* 2010). Hence, in addition to capital requirements, liquidity rules became the focus of international, European, and national efforts to tackle the TBTF problem and make banks more resilient in the context of future crises. Basel III liquidity rules effectively discouraged reliance on short-term funding (less than

---

[2] Liquid assets are cash or any other negotiable assets that can be quickly converted into cash.

a year) on wholesale markets. Overall, UK bank reliance on short-term funding was the highest of the five countries in 2007, and much of this was short-term funding of less than three months. The boom in UK bank lending over the decade preceding the crisis was due in part to this short-term funding. But by 2010 this reliance had dropped dramatically, moving from above 60 per cent of GDP in 2007 to 30 per cent (own calculations on the basis of central bank data), contributing to the UK's massive credit crunch following the financial crisis. UK banks went the furthest, and by a significant margin, to reduce their reliance on short-term funding and increase the resilience of their funding positions. Thus, UK authorities were more comfortable with the Basel III liquidity rules and ambitious phase-in dates than authorities in the other four case study countries. This improved position of UK-headquartered banks was due in large part to the early introduction in 2009 of restrictive liquidity rules in the UK, on which the Basel III and CRD IV rules were largely modelled. UK banks thus had a head start on liquidity.

New UK liquidity rules adopted in 2009 had clear potential to limit bank reliance on short-term wholesale market funding (see Financial Services Authority 2009), and the FSA expected such an impact:

> We fully expect our new requirements to have a significant further impact on firms' business models over the coming years—for example, by further discouraging reliance on short-term wholesale funding; increasing the quality and quantity of liquid asset buffers; and putting a higher cost on unsustainable bank lending during favourable economic times. (Financial Services Authority 2009, p. 6)

Most noteworthy was the tightening on the kinds of assets that could be held as part of the liquid assets buffer to mainly government bonds. The holding of higher-yielding asset-backed securities as liquid assets, which then proved harder either to sell or to use as collateral for borrowing, was highlighted as a particular source of losses by HBOS (HBOS 2009). It was argued that this could result in banks holding a larger percentage of their assets in government bonds (Brandão de Brito 2009; BBA official cited in *The Economist*, 11 February 2010).

In several respects the Basel Committee liquidity guidelines were less restrictive than the rules already adopted in the UK in 2009. The Basel III liquidity regime consisted of two components: the LCR, designed to ensure that banks had a big enough pool of high-quality liquid assets to weather an 'acute stress scenario' lasting for one month, including such inconveniences as a sharp ratio downgrade and a wave of collateral calls; and the NSFR, aimed at promoting longer-term financing of assets and thus limiting maturity mismatches. The NSFR required a certain level of funding to be for a year or more. The UK government had already gone further than Basel III in its legislation: it required all domestic entities to have enough liquidity to stand alone, unsupported by their parent or other parts of the group. Also controversial was the composition of the proposed liquidity cushions.

Some national governments wanted to restrict these to government debt, deposits with central banks, and the like. The Basel proposals allowed high-grade corporate bonds too, but UK legislation did not.

As one of the cheerleaders for higher liquidity requirements, US regulators moved swiftly to implement Basel III rules which they had played a lead role in designing. In October 2013, the Federal Reserve proposed a version of the LCR which was significantly tougher than the BCBS's version. Importantly, US regulators made clear their intention to apply all Basel requirements to all financial institutions with more than $50bn in assets, if designated as such by the new Financial Stability Oversight Council (FSOC)—established in 2010—and not just banks (Hamilton 2013). For example, the LCR required large bank holding companies (with over $250bn in consolidated assets) and systemically important non-banks to hold sufficient high-quality liquid assets (HQLAs) to cover thirty days of net cash outflow; while smaller institutions (with between $50bn and $250bn in assets) would need HQLAs to cover twenty-one days. US regulators also adopted a more conservative stance towards the treatment of corporate debt by removing references to credit ratings, as in Basel III. The proposal also included a multiyear transition period, necessitating full compliance by 1 January 2017, two years earlier than required.

By contrast, the implementation of the NSFR in the US proved more controversial, thereby delaying implementation. In May 2016, US regulatory agencies proposed a rule applying the NSFR to US bank holding companies and depository institutions with $250bn or more in consolidated assets, or $10bn or more in on-balance sheet foreign exposure; and to depository institutions with at least $10bn in assets that are consolidated subsidiaries of holding companies. A modified NSFR would also apply to certain depository institutions (including foreign bank intermediate holding companies) with consolidated assets of between $50bn and $250bn, and less than $10bn in on-balance sheet foreign exposure (Forrester et al. 2020). In 2019, the LCR and NSFR were both recalibrated so as to comply with the new 'tailoring rule', designed to reduce regulatory compliance for those institutions deemed to pose less risk. The scope of both rules was subsequently narrowed so as to apply to domestic and foreign financial institutions with at least £100bn in total assets. These were now placed into four categories—based on asset size, cross-jurisdictional activity, reliance on short-term wholesale funding, non-bank assets, and off-balance sheet exposures—around which liquidity rules would be tailored. As such, implementation of the NSFR was delayed and only entered force on 1 July 2021.

As with capital requirements, a number of EU member state governments—led by the French and Dutch governments—sought to water down Basel III guidelines on liquidity in EU legislation (Masters 2012). French and Dutch bank reliance on short-term funding of less than a year was greater than most other EU member states. In France, this reliance reached 45 per cent of GDP in 2007, remaining high after the financial crisis and at 40 per cent by 2010. Basel III guidelines included a prolonged phase-in period for the LCR to 2015 and the NSFR to 2018, while CRD IV watered down the first ratio and delayed introduction of the second. The Capital Requirements Regulation (CRR) introduced the LCR—the exact composition and calibration of which was to be determined after an observation and review period in 2015. The EU member states also adopted a less prescriptive definition of liquid assets than had been agreed by the BCBS: for the LCR to include transferable assets that are of both 'extremely high' and 'high' liquidity and credit quality. This preference for gradualism and flexibility can be explained by the concerns of a number of member state governments—and notably the French and Dutch—about the potential impact of these liquidity measures on bank lending.

The German government was less preoccupied about Basel III liquidity rules given that German bank debt was issued principally in the form of longer-maturity covered bonds—*Pfandbriefe*—itself a reflection of the 'patient capital' that had long characterized the German financial system. For German banks, reliance on short-term funding was low, dropping from slightly above 10 per cent in 2007 to slightly below 10 per cent of GDP in 2010 (Bundesbank data). The German Finance Market law from July 2009 had included broad provisions on liquidity, comprising increased liquidity reserves above existing Basel II requirements and binding limits on interbank exposures—a relatively significant source of financing for German banks. On 14 August, the German government clarified rules on liabilities in a circular on 'Minimum requirements for risk management' (Rundschreiben 15/2009) (Bafin 2009). The German circular was less proscriptive than new UK rules. The requirements imposed were general: banks were required to guarantee that they could meet their liabilities at any time, which would involve a sufficient diversification of their asset and capital structure. Banks were also required to define their risk tolerance for their liability risks and make sure that they acted accordingly; undertake stress tests for liability risks; make emergency plans for liquidity bottlenecks; and produce a risk strategy and emergency plan. The circular did not mention sight deposits.

Prior to Basel III, the French Banking Commission had also reformed national liquidity rules in ways that were, on balance, likely to limit further bank reliance on short-term wholesale market funding by reducing the ability of banks to use this funding to increase the size of bank balance sheets (French Government 2009). The French working group considering the proposals was established at the end of 2007 in response to problems in wholesale bank funding markets. The reduction in the assumed percentage of sight deposits that could be withdrawn in a crisis situation (from 20–30 per cent to 10 per cent but over a week rather than a month) increased the attraction of deposits relative to wholesale funding, and was combined with a distinction between individual and company deposits that recognizes the greater stability of the former (French Government 2009, p. 148). Overall, however, this was a move aimed at reflecting the reality of a crisis situation in France rather than at constraining activity. More significantly, changes in the treatment of off-balance sheet commitments—including liquidity commitments to special-purpose entities such as Asset-Backed Commercial Paper (ABCP) programmes—were more in line with previously under-recognized liquidity risks inherent in these structures (French Government 2009). The requirement that banks diversify their funding sources, rather than concentrating on the cheapest, also potentially raised the cost of short-term wholesale market funding (French Government 2009, p. 152). New French liquidity rules, however, did not result in French acceptance of Basel III liquidity rules.

Overall then, the new Basel III liquidity guidelines had the potential to limit bank reliance on short-term wholesale market funding. Their US implementation was significant, although the US failed to meet the NSFR deadline of 2018. Reinforced UK liquidity rules from 2009 went further than the Basel guidelines. Reinforced French and German rules from 2009 and Dutch rules from 2011 did not. The French and German governments in particular were in favour of watering down Basel III guidelines in their EU and national transposition and implementation. In terms of reliance on short-term funding on wholesale markets, the UK liquidity rules went the furthest, followed by the Basel III guidelines in those jurisdictions where they were implemented in full. While the EU rules adopted were restrictive for many of the large universal banks in EU member states, they were more flexible in their definition of liquidity and in the timescale of their implementation. In all five countries, the liquidity position of banks improved significantly from 2008. However, a decade after the crisis UK banks held far more liquid assets, on average, than banks in the other case study countries, while Dutch and German banks, on average, held the least (Table 3.6).

A range of figures demonstrate that large universal banks in the five countries came to rely less on short- and very-short-term funding on wholesale markets. Table 3.7 shows increased bank reliance on deposits as a source of bank funding

Table 3.6 Bank liquid assets as a percentage of total assets (case study countries), 2002–16*

	2002	2004	2006	2008	2010	2012	2014	2016
France			10	10	10	11	13	13
Germany	6	6	5	4	6	7	8	9
Netherlands		7	6	4	6	8	7	11
UK			8	8	15	18	17	19
US	6	5	4	8	9	11	15	14

* Liquid assets calculated as cash and balances with central banks plus government securities; weighted averages for groups of countries, based on total assets. For information on the consolidation basis and coverage of these data, see https://www.bis.org/publ/cgfs60/cgfs60_metadata.xlsx.
Source: BIS (2018, p. 89), national data. For further details, see https://www.bis.org/publ/cgfs60/cgfs60_metadata.xlsx.

Table 3.7 Share of deposits in total funding (as a percentage of total funding; case study countries), 2002–16*

	2002	2004	2006	2008	2010	2012	2014	2016
France	40	37	33	31	34	37	38	41
Germany	13	14	13	12	15	16	17	17
Netherlands		33	39	40	36	36	42	42
UK			48	48	52	56	62	63
US	65	65	65	65	70	74	75	76

* Domestic banks only. Excludes deposits with banks. Total funding is measured as a sum of deposit funding, other borrowings and equity. Weighted averages for groups of countries, based on total funding. For information on the consolidation basis and coverage of these data, see https://www.bis.org/publ/cgfs60/cgfs60_metadata.xlsx.
Source: BIS (2018, p. 94), national data. For further details, see https://www.bis.org/publ/cgfs60/cgfs60_metadata.xlsx.

Table 3.8 Share of borrowing in total bank funding (as a percentage of total funding; case study countries), 2006–16)*

	2006	2008	2010	2012	2014	2016
France	48	39	32	26	23	24
Germany	81	81	78	76	73	73
Netherlands	43	43	45	43	38	39
UK	46	47	41	37	29	28
US	24	26	19	15	14	13

* All borrowings excluding deposits with non-banks. Total funding is measured as a sum of deposit funding, other borrowings, and equity. For information on the consolidation basis and coverage of these data, see https://www.bis.org/publ/cgfs60/cgfs60_metadata.xlsx.
Source: BIS (2018, p. 95), national data. For further details, see https://www.bis.org/publ/cgfs60/cgfs60_metadata.xlsx.

in all five case study countries since the financial crisis, and notably in the UK, but least in the Netherlands. However, a focus on deposits alone does not clarify relative reliance on short-term wholesale market funding. Notably, low German figures point to ongoing heavy German bank reliance on secure long-term wholesale market funding—*Pfandbriefe*. Table 3.8 points to the significant drop in borrowing as a share of total bank funding in all five countries and again most significantly in the UK and least in the Netherlands. Table 3.9 shows the significant drop in bank financial liabilities held for trading as a percentage of total French, German, and Dutch bank assets. None of our case study national governments had implemented the NSFR by 2018 (FSB 2018, 2020). EU member states chose not to include a set NSFR deadline in the CRD IV directive (Howarth and Quaglia 2013a).

Table 3.9 Bank financial liabilities held for trading as a percentage of total assets (France, Germany, and the Netherlands), 2008–18[*]

	2008	2010	2012	2014	2016	2018	Change (%)
France	33.2	24.0	25.5	22.6	18.3	16.8	−49.4
Germany	29.6	22.6	24.7	23.6	20.4	9.9	−66.6
Netherlands	15.6	7.7	7.2	7.5	5.9	2.6	−83.3

[*] Domestic banking groups and stand-alone banks only.
Source: ECB Data Warehouse: https://sdw.ecb.europa.eu.

Bank resolution rules

In the aftermath of the financial crisis, at the September 2009 G20 summit in Pittsburgh, government leaders committed themselves to improve the rules to ensure effective bank resolution and work towards a common resolution regime. However, the resolution rules reformed or adopted over the next decade in the G20 were distinct and resulted in very different resolution processes.

In the US, a long-established resolution regime for insured national and state banks—following provision set in the Federal Deposit Insurance Act of 1950—ensured that most failing or likely-to-fail banks could be resolved without resort to government funds. The FDIC was created to manage the process, determining in conjunction with the bank's primary regulator whether an institution had failed. Rather than being placed in bankruptcy, a failed bank would be taken over by the FDIC, the first responsibility of which was to protect depositors (insured up to $250,000) and then to manage the rest of the bank's assets to minimize costs to taxpayers and maximize returns to depositors. To pay for resolution, the FDIC collected fees from banks that were pooled into a pre-funded Deposit Insurance Fund (DIF) and it was also given access to borrow from the US Treasury, to be reimbursed subsequently by other banks. No EU member state had an equivalent regime in place. Yet despite the relative frequency of bank resolution in the US, the regime failed to shield taxpayers from the huge bail-outs in 2008. Indeed, the financial crisis also exposed the FDIC's mandate—which extended only to commercial banks and not investment banks, insurance companies or other very large financial institutions—as woefully inadequate in a systemic crisis. Hence, ineligible for FDIC financial assistance, the Lehman Brothers investment bank was forced to declare bankruptcy, while Bear Stearns and AIG received emergency support from the Federal Reserve (Klein 2017).

The 2010 Dodd–Frank Act extended the FDIC's authority to resolve failed institutions to include all bank holding companies and all firms—including non-banks—designated as systemically important. It also contained several important reforms designed to strengthen the US resolution regime (Crabb 2018). The most important was the creation of an Orderly Liquidation Authority (OLA), giving regulators special powers to wind down a complex financial institution in an orderly manner, including the temporary use of taxpayer funds (with the agreement of the Federal Reserve Board and the Treasury Secretary) to provide emergency liquidity. Although Dodd–Frank explicitly prohibited any federal government bail-out of covered entities, the OLA required all resolution funds spent to be recouped by imposing a fee on the surviving institution. In 2013, the FDIC issued a joint paper with the Bank of England endorsing the Single Point of Entry (SPOE) method for resolving complex banking groups. This involved funneling losses to the top holding or parent company, which was then to be placed into bankruptcy. The SPOE method was designed explicitly to address the problem of TBTF by ensuring that in the event of a bank failure, senior managers would be replaced, shareholders would be 'wiped out', and creditors—rather than taxpayers—would bear the losses. As in Europe, the FDIC also issued regulations requiring large financial institutions to issue convertible long-term debt that could be 'bailed in' in the event of failure, which was designed to facilitate resolution where bankruptcy was not viable.

As with other regulatory provisions contained in Dodd–Frank, resolution rules were amended in 2019 following the passage of the Economic Growth, Regulatory Relief, and Consumer Protection Act (2018), driven by congressional Republicans and the Trump administration. It was claimed that the changes were necessary to reflect resolvability improvements over the previous eight years, and to comply with the new 'tailoring rule' outlined by the Federal Reserve. Henceforth, covered companies were subject to resolution requirements depending on which of the three new categories for enhanced prudential standards they fell into—the purpose being to reduce compliance costs for all but the largest US financial institutions.

In 2014, EU member state governments agreed upon the main elements of the EU's bank resolution rules—the Bank Recovery and Resolution Directive (BRRD)—and the main element of the resolution regime that applied only to Banking Union countries—the Single Resolution Mechanism Regulation (SRMR) (European Parliament and the Council 2014; SRMR 2014). The member state governments agreed that these new rules were to be applied to nearly all—with few exceptions—of the EU's banks, both 'significant' and 'less significant' (SRMR, Article 4). It was hoped that 'public interest' (BRRD, Article 32(5); SRMR, Article 18(5)) would be sufficient to justify the use of the bail-in tool through which private share- and debt-holders were expected to assume some losses before resolution funds and the public sector provided financial support.

Thus, four of our case study countries accepted a new EU resolution regime which involved unprecedented rules and funds to make it easier to resolve banks with less government support and ideally none. None of these countries had national resolution regimes in place previously, which explains why bank resolution was seen as both economically and politically problematic. Governments used public funds either to bail out banks or to force their liquidation. Governments also encouraged bank mergers, normally with other national banks.

In the euro area, it was hoped that new EU-wide resolution rules would break the sovereign-bank debt loop, which was particularly worrying in the euro area periphery where government debt loads were very high. Effective bank resolution rules serve a dual purpose: first, they enhance financial stability and, second, they reduce pressure on governments to bail out banks—and especially TBTF banks (Asimakopoulos and Howarth 2022). On the first purpose, the internalization of losses in resolution instead of relying on bail-outs by governments was seen as leading to a fairer risk pricing of bank liabilities and ultimately as enhancing market discipline and financial stability. On the second, minimizing the need for bail-outs would decrease the likelihood of host member states suffering from a debt crisis because of the need to rescue banks.

However, EU resolution rules have not been applied with much success by either European or national authorities. More generally, the FSB concluded in 2020 that 'substantial work remains to operationalise resolution plans for systemically important banks' in the G20 (FSB 2020). The FSB concluded that the implementation of its effective resolution regime guidelines was 'still incomplete' in some jurisdictions. In the EU, only one out of six banks under the Single Resolution Board's remit facing solvency problems ended up in resolution, namely Banco Popular Español (Popular). Popular was sold to Santander for one euro, while part of the losses were covered through a bail-in of shareholders and junior subordinated debt-holders (Mesnard et al. 2017). The Popular resolution was highly exceptional and due to Santander intervention. The banks in the other five cases—Monte Paschi di Siena, Veneto Banca and Banca Popolare di Vicenza, ABLV Luxembourg, and the German NordLB—avoided resolution (Asimakopoulos and Howarth 2022).

The implementation of EU bank resolution rules was hampered by national political pressures but also because of the inadequate own funds and eligible liabilities held by many EU banks. On the former, the failure to apply EU rules to the resolution of a number of Italian banks (to date) demonstrated that at least some EU national governments would rather use public funds to bail out banks or force their merger than force national bond-holders to incur losses through bail-in (Donnelly and Asimakopoulos 2020). The political dangers of imposing losses on voters thus repeatedly trumped broader financial stability concerns.

EU bank resolution rules were ineffective especially vis-à-vis retail banks that relied on deposit funding (Ayadi 2019), which comprised the very large majority of banks headquartered in the EU. This created a particular problem for those banks that were too small to liquidate under corporate insolvency rules and too large to have bail-inable buffers of high quantity and quality for resolution purposes—approximately 120 banks out of the EU's largest 200 banks in terms of assets

(Asimakopoulos 2019). This ineffectiveness is due in large part to the difficulty of accessing and the insufficient availability of resolution and deposit guarantee scheme funds in most EU member states, in conjunction with the relatively high minimum requirements for own funds and eligible liabilities (MREL) for many EU banks (Asimakopoulos and Howarth 2022). These requirements are unlikely ever to be met by many banks—particularly by those banks most likely to require resolution in the euro area periphery (Asimakopoulos 2019). However, German, French, and Dutch preferences on bank capital requirements, MREL, resolution financing, and national deposit guarantee schemes ensured that EU bank resolution rules could not be applied to most banks, which simply lacked sufficient bail-inable capital and were not required to have this by other EU rules. Many of the largest EU-headquartered universal banks were in a better capital position to ensure the bail-in of bank losses. However, the non-application of the rules to other banks would make it very difficult politically to apply them to the largest TBTF banks.

Thus, the antecedents of under-capitalized banks, combined with the absence of credible resolution financing, resulted in a European bank resolution regime that was bound to fail. Market fragmentation and the inadequate development of an EU Capital Markets Union resulted in many banks—especially in those member states lacking deep financial markets—being unable to increase the amount or improve the quality of their MREL to ensure successful resolution according to EU rules. The inadequacy of MREL levels undermined the efficacy of the European bank resolution regime because, for bail-in to be enforceable, banks needed to have a sufficient level of capital, as well as a sufficient amount of 'eligible' liabilities to absorb losses. Without this capital and liabilities buffer (MREL) there was a greater risk of imposing losses on depositors and of placing governments in a position in which they had to pay to save or liquidate the bank. Large bail-ins affecting retail investors and depositors could be politically difficult for governments, while bail-outs contributed to government debt and ultimately imposed the costs of either saving or liquidating banks on taxpayers.

Obligatory resolution planning

All of the governments in our five case study countries adopted legislation requiring banks to draw up contingency plans—also known as 'living wills'—to be put into effect if they were evaluated by supervisors to be failing or likely to fail. Resolution plans were to facilitate the resolution of the largest banks, thus preventing or limiting government bail-outs and contagion to other institutions. In the US, Section 165(d) of the Dodd–Frank Act mandated that all bank holding companies and foreign banks with total consolidated assets of $50bn or more, as well as any non-bank financial institution designated as systemically important, had to prepare and submit detailed resolution plans to the Federal Reserve each year. Separately, the FDIC required all US insured depository institutions (IDIs) with assets of $50bn or more to submit a resolution plan. Although Dodd–Frank did not require institutions to develop recovery plans, the Federal Reserve later required several of the largest US bank holding companies and non-bank systematically important financial institutions (SIFIs) to prepare and submit detailed recovery plans. Significantly, in April 2016, US agencies issued joint determinations in which they 'failed' the living wills of five of the country's eight largest banks. They were granted until 1 October to modify their wills sufficiently or face sanctions, including higher capital requirements or limits on business activities (Lambert 2016).

In 2013, EU member states agreed the BRRD which imposed the adoption of resolution plans upon all systemically important banks. Previously, all four of our case study country governments in the EU either recommended that banks adopt 'living wills' or, in the case of the Dutch Intervention Act of 2012, adopted legislation that required this. In terms of the wills' impact upon higher-risk investment banking activities and reliance on short-term wholesale market funding, this was at best limited and indirect. However, failure to demonstrate an ability to allocate sufficient resources to wind down derivatives potentially encouraged the shrinkage of certain activities and an increase of bank liquidity.

6. Reinforcing bank governance and transparency

The regulatory authorities in all five case study countries examined in this volume called for tighter internal bank risk management in order to crack down on poor bank management and decrease the TBTF problem. Table 3.10 summarizes the reforms adopted to reinforce bank governance and transparency in the five countries. The UK's Walker Review on bank governance published in November 2009 recommended this, as did the French government's Lagarde Report of February 2008. However, both were limited to 'tweaking' and considered disappointing to observers who sought tighter controls (Finch 2009). In the Netherlands, the Dutch government largely accepted the findings of the Maas Commission—consisting of bankers or former bank officials—and the voluntary measures on internal bank governance adopted in the Banking Code that the Commission designed. Germany lacked a national commission—government or bank-led—that focused specifically on internal bank governance. In his wide-ranging study of banking culture in the US and the UK, Macartney (2019) concludes that none of the voluntary collective or unilateral measures adopted by banks following the financial crisis to improve the governance and transparency of their operations had a significant impact on shifting bank culture away from higher-risk activities.

Table 3.10 Bank governance measures to diminish TBTF bank risk

Regulatory response	US	UK	France	Germany	Netherlands
Tighter internal controls (risk management)	Dodd–Frank included 'enhanced prudential standards' for risk management, including governance reforms.	Walker Report (2010): recommendations, no obligations.	Lagarde Report (2010): regulation with limited constraint.	None.	Banking Code (2009): voluntary measures.
Transparency—stress testing, etc.	Dodd–Frank mandated stress testing of the largest banks, expanded to mid-sized firms from 2014, with full disclosure of results.	Yes, plus moderate increase in reporting requirements. Accepts need for EU-wide coordinated stress tests with full disclosure of results.	National controls good enough. Reluctant acceptance of EU-wide coordinated stress tests with full disclosure of results for largest banks.	Greater reporting requirements (off balance sheet and leverage)—yet to be clarified. But strong opposition to full transparency on stress testing. Reluctant acceptance of EU-wide coordinated stress tests with full disclosure of results for largest banks.	Dutch stress tests in 2009 and 2010 to assess both micro- and macroprudential stability with publication of results. Then discontinuation at the national level and reliance on EBA stress tests from 2011.
Accounting rules	Greater international harmonization. Mark to market.	Greater international harmonization. Mark to market.	Greater international harmonization. Mark to market.	No greater harmonization. Opposed to mark to market.	Greater international harmonization. Mark to market.

Source: authors' own compilation.

Government policy in our five case study countries remained limited to—at best—recommendations on desirable bank governance reforms, although the threat of regulation remained. In the UK, the FSA moved to 'strongly encourage' banks to appoint board-level risk officers and establish board-level risk committees, as recommended in the Walker Review (quoted in Robinson 2010; see also Walker 2009). Board members would also have to seek regulatory approval if they were to head risk, audit, and remuneration committees under the proposals in the FSA's consultation paper, in a move that was intended to make it easier for the FSA to hold individual directors to account. The FSA appointed a panel of senior City figures to help interview would-be bank board members, as recommended by the Walker Review. In France, regulatory change on internal bank management focused specifically on rogue trading—a reflection of the political importance of the Jérôme Kerviel/Société Générale scandal that broke out in early 2008. These controls (whether obligatory or recommended) had, at best, only a marginal effect on trading activities.

On transparency, the governments of all five countries accepted the need for more regular bank stress testing to focus on the quantity and quality of capital needed, with results made publicly available. Such stress testing was also seen as an important mechanism to tackle the TBTF problem. The Dodd–Frank Act authorized the Federal Reserve to conduct forward-looking tests on bank holding companies, US intermediate holding companies, and non-bank financial institutions, as determined by the FSOC. Banks with consolidated assets of at least $50bn were to undergo an annual Comprehensive Capital Analysis and Review (CCAR); while separate Dodd–Frank Act stress tests (DFAST) were to assess an institution's ability to cope with adverse economic conditions—in 2018, defined as a 65 per cent decline in equity prices, 30 per cent and 40 per cent drops in residential and commercial real estate, and 10 per cent unemployment (Crabb 2017). Biannual stress tests were also to be run by financial institutions with total assets of $10bn or more. Several banks failed key aspects of the new stress tests—including Citigroup in 2012 and 2014, and the US subsidiaries of Deutsche Bank and Santander in 2015 and 2016—while conditions were regularly imposed on major banks at risk of failing, including Bank of America in 2014, and JP Morgan and Goldman Sachs in 2013 (Heltman 2017). In 2017, all thirty-four of the largest US banks passed the stress tests for the first time.

In the UK, the stress tests were to be managed jointly by the Bank of England's Financial Policy Committee (FPC), and the Prudential Regulation Committee (PRC) of the Prudential Regulation Authority (PRA). The Bank conducted annual concurrent stress tests on the largest UK banks and building societies (seven in 2015), while other financial firms carried out their own stress testing following PRA guidance. Biennial tests were also used to probe the resilience of the banking system to risks not linked to the financial cycle—the 'biennial exploratory scenario'. The most notable stress test failure was RBS in 2016, forcing it to raise capital and reduce exposure to risky assets, while other banks—including Barclays,

Standard Chartered, and Lloyds TSB—received repeated warnings after failing aspects of the tests. All eligible institutions passed the tests from 2017 onward.

French, Dutch, and German governments pushed rather for EU-wide coordinated stress tests, as well as the coordinated publication of the stress test results. The first EU-wide tests by the EBA were noteworthy for their ineffectiveness (Gren et al. 2015). Most famously, Dexia—the Dutch–Belgian–Luxembourg bank—collapsed less than three months after the publication of its favourable score in the EBA's first stress test in 2010 (Pignal and Jenkins 2011). The EBA's tests were subsequently strengthened but many criticisms remained (*Financial Times* 2016).

At the national level, the increased push by governments in the three countries in favour of transparency in bank governance had little effect on banking practice. The German government's position on bank transparency initially appeared to move in a different direction. The July 2009 finance law increased the reporting requirement of banks' 'off balance sheet' exposure; and reporting requirements on bank leverage ratios (including off-balance-sheet assets) (IMF 2009). However, there were clear limits to the German government's push for greater transparency due to the extent to which the financial crisis hit its publicly owned regional banks. Most German banks, particularly the public *Landesbanken*, continued to record the value of their credit assets at book, not market prices, even though banks in the four other case study countries were required to mark these down. In the immediate aftermath of the financial crisis, the IMF informally reckoned that German banks sat on hundreds of billions of euros of losses, much of which banks failed to report (Tett 2009). The German government's position on accounting contradicted most of the western world, which embraced the ideal of mark-to-market accounting—together with a goal of promoting more, not less, harmonization of international accounting rules. But the German government's position was bolstered by the US stance, which also opposed harmonization. In 2009, the US Financial Accounting Standards Board, under strong pressure from the Obama administration, announced that it would give banks more leeway over how they valued illiquid assets. The move was made without any prior consultation with the International Accounting Standards Board (*Financial Times*, 8 July 2009). The option to move away from marking some assets to market was enthusiastically exploited by banks in all five countries.

7. Reinforcing bank supervision

The ostensible reinforcement of bank supervision was one of the principal responses to the financial crisis in a number of jurisdictions. Significant reforms to national supervision were adopted in the UK, Germany, and the Netherlands. Table 3.11 provides a summary of national reforms to reinforce bank supervision. At the national level, the French government made no proposals for change to its model of supervision, which was largely but not entirely vindicated by the

Table 3.11 Reinforced supervision to diminish TBTF bank risk

Regulatory response	US	UK	France	Germany	Netherlands
Reinforced macroprudential supervision (monitoring of systemic risks)	New FSOC to provide prudential oversight; identify systemic risks; and designate individual firms as systemically-important.	Yes at national level: strengthening Bank of England and its Court of Directors. Creation of Financial Stability Committee in Bank of England. Yes to reinforced macroprudential supervision at EU level (ESRB) but no power to force changes in government policy.	Kept present domestic model of supervision. Reinforced EU and international monitoring. Pro-ESRB but no power to force changes in government policy.	More monitoring powers to Bundesbank. Pro-ESRB but no power to force changes in government policy.	More monitoring powers to the Dutch National Bank. Pro-ESRB but no power to force changes in government policy.
Reinforced microprudential supervision	Federal Reserve given enhanced powers to supervise all bank/non-bank financial institutions designated as systemically important.	Yes (transferred to Bank of England). Pro-SSM (Banking Union) but not for the UK.	Already strong/no change in domestic supervisory framework. Pro-SSM but decentralized to allow national control.	Yes: transfer of some supervisory powers back to Bundesbank. Reluctant on SSM.	Yes, with reinforced central bank supervisory powers. Pro-SSM.

Source: authors' own compilation.

comparatively limited impact of the crisis. EU member states and, specifically, euro area countries also agreed to reinforce supranational bank supervision. In 2010, all EU member states agreed the creation of the EBA, the mandate of which was to improve supervisory standards in the EU through the adoption of binding technical standards and to conduct stress tests of the EU's largest banks. In 2013, euro area national governments agreed the transfer of the supervision of the euro area's largest banks—over a hundred institutions—to the ECB, the main supervisor of the new Single Supervisory Mechanism (SSM) that began operation in November 2014 (Howarth and Quaglia 2013b). The actual impact of these changes in supervision upon higher-risk investment banking activities remained uncertain. However, the transfer of supervisory powers to the ECB almost certainly limited opportunities for supervisory arbitrage by national authorities and their willingness to turn a blind eye to more problematic bank operations (Howarth and Quaglia 2016a). Furthermore, the ECB moved quickly to encourage the harmonization of national supervision of less significant banks.

In the UK, the 2009 Turner Review recommended a substantial reinforcement of bank supervision through the adoption of wide-ranging macroprudential tools. The Labour government's response, published in its July 2009 White Paper, fell short of these proposals, but did moderately strengthen the FSA by granting it new powers to intervene in a firm or limit its business; the ability to suspend individuals or firms for misconduct; and powers to take emergency action in relation to short selling independent of the market abuse regime. The FSA also sought to enhance its scrutiny of bank executives at overseas holding companies with 'significant influence' over UK banks and brokers. The Conservative–Liberal Democrat coalition government formed in May 2010 went significantly further, abolishing the FSA and transferring bank supervisory powers to the new PRA located within the Bank of England. A separate Financial Conduct Authority (FCA) was also created to regulate financial products and consumer services, and, in effect, was responsible for the day-to-day supervision of non-SIFIs (Hungin and James 2018). In this way, the UK's pre-crisis 'light touch', principles-based approach to bank supervision was comprehensively transformed into a more interventionist, rules-based regime (McPhilemy 2013).

The Obama administration entered office with ambitious plans to bolster macroprudential policy making, proposing to grant sweeping new prudential powers to the Federal Reserve. It also planned to reduce agency fragmentation by centralizing bank supervision into a single national regulator for depository institutions (consolidating the OCC, FDIC, and Office of Thrift Supervision (OTS)); bringing the Commodity Futures Trading Commission (CFTC) and SEC under the Federal Reserve's authority; and establishing a powerful new Consumer Financial Protection Bureau (CFPB). Unsurprisingly, the plan met with fierce opposition from both sides of Congress critical of the Federal Reserve's handling of the crisis, together with bureaucratic opposition from those US agencies which were under threat (Hungin and James 2017). Although the plan for agency consolidation was eventually abandoned, the Federal Reserve was granted far-reaching supervisory powers over all FSOC-designated SIFIs with assets over $50bn, while Obama's flagship institutional reform—the CFPB—was founded in 2011.

The Germans also moved to redesignate supervisory responsibilities. In August 2007, when the impact of US subprime took its toll on the first German banks, the federal government launched an inquiry into BaFin, the German financial services regulator, amid accusations that the watchdog took too long to address crises at IKB and Sachsen Landesbank that had to be bailed out. Both banks had to provide support to ABCP programmes that far exceeded their capacity. The ABCP programmes were designed legally to be off balance sheet, and thus avoid regulatory limits on credit exposures. The supervisor was criticized for not acting soon enough over the banks' exposure. The Bundesbank had explicit responsibilities for assessing bank capital and risk management procedures, although on-site inspections had to be ordered by BaFin, and both refused to comment on when the Bundesbank last assessed the capital of the two banks, citing privacy clauses in German banking law (Hardie and Howarth 2009). The German Grand Coalition government agreed to a clearer separation of the regulatory and supervisory responsibilities of BaFin and the Bundesbank, which was incorporated into the July 2009 financial market law. BaFin was to remain responsible for supervisory arrangements, such as the granting of banking licences, while the Bundesbank would be charged with the actual supervision of financial institutions. The July 2009 law also assigned supervisory authorities greater intervention powers beyond the previously limited powers that allowed them to intervene only in strictly defined circumstances, where a bank's finances were already precarious. The aim was to enable regulators to act pre-emptively to see off dangers. The new CDU–FDP government elected in September 2009 was less sensitive to BaFin and moved rapidly to transfer full supervisory powers to the Bundesbank. It is doubtful that any of these developments had a significant impact on higher-risk investment banking activities. The Bundesbank's (2007, p. 8) conclusion as late as November 2007 that '[n]ot least thanks to a marked improvement in their risk-bearing capacity over the past few years, the German banks have coped well on the whole' does not suggest greater central bank prescience. In March 2012, the Dutch government (2012) adopted the Intervention Act, giving the central bank greater powers to intervene in banks and even split them up if they ran into irreversible problems.

The governments in all five case study countries moved to reinforce the monitoring of systemic financial—macroprudential—stability and all five governments supported the reinforcement of international-level (notably the FSB) and European bodies to monitor systemic stability, although the UK and Germany were more reluctant to transfer additional powers to the EU level (Buckley and Howarth 2010). Less directly affected by the financial crisis, the French pursued no change in the domestic system to monitor systemic stability, despite longstanding criticism of the division of supervisory authority in the financial sector.

Following the recommendations of the De Larosière Group (2009), the EU established the European Systemic Risk Board (ESRB) in 2010, with responsibility for macroprudential oversight. It was assigned the power to collect and analyse information on the EU's financial system, identify and prioritize systemic risks, and issue warnings and recommendations to national and European authorities on a 'comply or explain' basis. The ESRB's decision-making body, the General Board, consists of thirty-eight voting members, including all twenty-eight national central bank governors, the President and Vice-President of the ECB, a member of the European Commission, the chairs of the three ESAs, the chair and the two vice-chairs of the Advisory Scientific Committee, and the chair of the Advisory Technical Committee. Several non-voting members also represented the relevant financial supervisory authorities of the member states.

The UK government moved to reinforce the systemic monitoring capacity of the Bank of England and created the FPC, chaired by the Governor, with thirteen members, including six from the Bank, five external to the Bank, the FCA's chief executive, and a non-voting representative from the Treasury. The FPC's formal mandate was to contribute to achieving the central bank's financial stability objective, and it was granted broad oversight and responsibility for identifying, monitoring, and addressing systemic risks to the financial system (Lombardi and Moschella 2017). The FPC was granted two main powers to do so: it could issue recommendations to micro-prudential regulators (the FCA and PRA) on a 'comply or explain' basis, and also recommendations to the Bank of England and Treasury; and could give direction to regulators concerning the implementation of macroprudential measures—although it lacked powers of enforcement.

In the US, the Obama administration's initial plan for a powerful new macroprudential agency housed in the Federal Reserve was soon abandoned in the face of congressional opposition. The impasse was eventually broken by a proposal from the House of Representatives for an inter-agency council, the FSOC. Chaired by the Treasury Secretary, the FSOC henceforth brought together ten voting members, including the heads of the Federal Reserve, OCC, CFPB, SEC, FDIC, CFTC, Federal Housing Finance Agency (FHFA), and the National Credit Union Administration Board (NCUA), plus an independent member with insurance expertise. The FSOC was charged with three statutory missions: monitoring the US financial system, identifying risks that threatened the system's stability, and promoting market discipline to mitigate excessive risk taking in financial markets (Lombardi and Moschella 2018). To these ends, the FSOC facilitated information sharing between agencies, could request data and analysis from the Treasury's Office of Financial Research (OFR) and, most importantly, could designate bank and non-bank financial institutions as 'systemically significant'—and thereby subject to consolidated supervision and tougher prudential requirements. The FSOC could also make recommendations to the lead regulatory agency about the need for heightened standards regarding practices or activities on a 'comply or explain' basis.

8. Conclusion

An analysis of their responses to the financial crisis demonstrates that, with very few exceptions, the governments of our five case study countries were unwilling to adopt regulatory changes that would significantly reduce the TBTF problem. Apart from the bank structural reforms adopted in the US and the UK, the only other potentially efficacious set of reforms focused on reinforcing bank capital requirements and liquidity. However, the qualifications to the Basel III guidelines adopted in EU legislation decreased the potential impact of these reforms on the TBTF problem. Notably, the EU member states agreed that banks could continue to count hybrids as tier-1 capital and continue to double count the capital of their insurance subsidiaries. By discouraging reliance on short-term funding, new rules adopted on bank liquidity—especially the reform adopted in the UK in 2009—were designed to create a buffer for banks to cover losses in the event of a crisis and without reliance on government funds. The Basel III agreement included similar rules. However, EU member states watered down Basel III guidelines on liquidity and none of our case study national governments respected the recommended NSFR target date set in the Basel III agreement. The actual impact of the new capital and liquidity rules on the higher-risk investment activities of banks and their ability to withstand a major future bank crisis remained to be seen.

Limited national government enthusiasm for both unilateral domestic regulatory responses to the financial crisis and constraining international action that did not have universal application demonstrates that governments sought to avoid undermining the competitiveness of their own banking sectors. This chapter demonstrates the limited extent to which national and EU regulatory and policy responses to the international financial crisis diminished the TBTF problem in the five case study countries examined in this volume. US and UK bank structural reforms were among the few reforms adopted by any governments that worked effectively to constrain banking activities—by restricting how they could be funded—and to protect the retail banking customers of large universal banks from losses incurred from these activities. These reforms decreased the systemic threat of TBTF banks and thus reduced the expectation that national governments would have to bail them out. The analysis in the following six chapters explains why US and UK policy makers were able to adopt far-reaching reforms, why French and German policy makers implemented minimal changes, while Dutch and EU policy makers failed to agree any new restrictions.

4

From Obama to Trump

Contested Reform in the United States

1. Introduction

Of all the cases of bank structural reform that we explore in the book, the United States stands out for the degree to which the issue was—and remains—highly contested. It is tempting to attribute the political furore about how to tame TBTF banks in the wake of the crisis to the paralysis in the US financial system caused by the collapse of the subprime mortgage market, and the sheer scope and scale of US federal government intervention to rescue some of the largest and most high-profile institutions on Wall Street. As the origin of the global financial crisis, the US was thus a 'first-mover' in regulatory terms (Interview 1), forcing policy makers to act quickly to restore financial stability and address public anger. It also meant that US regulators had to act unilaterally as there was little prospect of leveraging their influence through international regulatory fora, such as the Basel Committee, by coordinating their efforts with other countries. The political timing of the financial crisis was also critical in shaping the US response, as it took place against the backdrop of a particularly fraught presidential election in late 2008. The victory of Democrat presidential candidate Barack Obama, and large Democrat Party gains in Congress, opened up an important window of opportunity for banking reform.

We argue that the uniquely *contested* nature of structural reform in the US can be attributed to two key features of the policy process. First, the US is characterized by competitive financial power. Financial industry lobbying was therefore highly fragmented, characterized by hundreds of individual firms and associations competing for influence—and frequently divided, giving rise to powerful dissenting voices from within the industry. In addition, Wall Street banks faced concerted opposition from a vocal and highly mobilized pro-reform coalition of consumer and activist groups that maintained pressure on Congress to take action against TBTF banks. Second, the Obama administration was unable to depoliticize the process or forge a broad, bipartisan agreement through venue shifting to an ad hoc, specialist group. On the contrary, the banking reform agenda remained firmly in the hands of a deeply polarized Congress, with Democrats and Republicans holding diametrically opposing views and each battling to steer the legislative process.

We show how the Obama administration successfully leveraged anti-bank sentiment, both within and outside Congress, to secure passage of the ambitious Wall Street Reform and Consumer Protection Act (or 'Dodd–Frank' Act) in July 2010, albeit along highly partisan lines. Section 619 of the Dodd–Frank Act, known as the 'Volcker Rule', did two things (H.R. 4173). First, it prohibited banks from engaging in proprietary trading, which relied heavily on high-risk trades including derivatives, for their own account. Second, it stipulated that banks could no longer acquire or retain any equity, partnership or other ownership interest in or sponsoring an alternative investment vehicle—including hedge funds, private equity funds, and certain other covered funds. Systematically important non-banks could continue to engage in these activities, but they were required to carry additional capital and comply with other restrictions. The Rule became effective on 21 July 2011, two years after enactment, while covered entities were granted a further two years to comply. However, the legislation left a great deal of detail on implementation to be determined by the rule-writing agencies.

As our framework would predict, however, the highly contested process of bank structural reform in the US left it subject to heightened politicization and vulnerable to the shifting balance of power between competing groups—including legislators, regulators, industry lobbyists, and pro-reform campaigners. In addition, the same dynamics of conflict expansion which facilitated the passage of the Dodd–Frank Act at the height of the crisis also served seriously to delay and undermine its subsequent implementation. For instance, the partisan nature of the bill's passage through Congress encouraged Republicans to attack Dodd–Frank continually, with the Volcker Rule becoming the focus of their opposition. Following repeated gains in Congress, the Republicans sought the partial repeal of the Volcker Rule with the Financial CHOICE Act of 2017.

Structural reform was further weakened by the election of Republican President Donald Trump in November 2016. Within months of taking office, Trump issued an Executive Order directing regulators to review Dodd–Frank and replaced the heads of the main US regulatory agencies with officials favouring a less stringent approach. Hence, unlike the other cases in the book, structural reform in the US remained uniquely vulnerable to the febrile political context over the next decade: subject to continued contestation, repeated attacks, and attempted repeal by political opponents. The result is that, while the Obama-era structural reforms broadly survived this decade-long onslaught, important boundaries, definitions, and details contained in the Volcker Rule were relaxed or eroded.

2. The US banking crisis

The collapse of Lehman Brothers on 15 September 2008 sent shockwaves through the US financial system, serving as a catalyst for a string of further bank failures and paralysing international financial markets. It also provided a wake-up call to senior US regulators—including Treasury Secretary Hank Paulson, Federal Reserve Chair Ben Bernanke, and New York Fed Chair Timothy Geithner—who recognized that allowing prominent financial institutions to fail only served to exacerbate, rather than contain, financial contagion. In the weeks and months that followed, US regulators worked closely with Wall Street executives to manage the fallout from Lehman through a package of hastily arranged private sector rescues, publicly funded bail-outs, and/or the orderly resolution of institutions (see Johnson and Kwak 2010).

In the process, the face of Wall Street changed for ever. Bank of America took over the investment bank Merrill Lynch, Bear Stearns was bought by JP Morgan, and regulators closed down Washington Mutual, the largest savings and loan association in the US. The fourth largest bank holding company in the US, Wachovia, was eventually taken over by Wells Fargo, while investment banks Goldman Sachs and Morgan Stanley sought legal conversion into conventional bank holding companies to qualify for federal support. All of the 'big five' Wall Street banks received unprecedented government bail-outs through a mix of capital injections and loan guarantees—the largest sums going to Citigroup, JP Morgan, and Bank of America—while the insurance giant AIG received the largest bail-out in US history (Woll 2014). Finally, the giant government-sponsored enterprises with responsibility for mortgage finance—Fannie May and Freddie Mac—were placed under government conservatorship.

The keystone of the US federal response was a massive financial rescue package, which the Bush administration persuaded a reluctant Congress to approve in October 2008. The TARP authorized the US Treasury to spend up to $700bn in purchasing assets tainted by the collapse of mortgage-backed securities. Losses (including write-downs) at US financial institutions totalled $1.1tn, and funds equal to 30 per cent of US GDP were committed to supporting the financial sector. In total, $125bn of capital was injected into the largest nine banks. Paulson drove a hard bargain, however, and was determined that all US banks should be forced to accept government capital, even in the face of fierce protestations. This was to avoid bank rescues being stigmatizing, and to ensure a better return for taxpayers by cross-subsidizing the costs of the bail-out. The US Treasury charged all banks a standard low fee for debt guarantees and capital injections, and demanded warrants requiring banks to extend it a ten-year option to buy shares at 2008 prices. The warrants generated over $4bn, with $3bn paid by just three banks: Wells Fargo, JP Morgan, and Goldman Sachs (US Treasury Department 2012). This enabled the government to reap a $100bn profit on its initial investment by buying further shares when the banks returned to profit (Culpepper and Reinke 2014). The US government's TARP therefore generated an overall net benefit to the economy of between $86bn and $109bn (Veronesi and Zingales 2010).

The politics of US structural reform

Despite the eventual financial windfall for the US Treasury, the tumultuous events of late 2008 were a profound shock to the US political system, challenging the bipartisan consensus that had encouraged financial innovation and credit expansion to fund increased home ownership (McCarty, Poole, and Rosenthal 2015). They also provided the backdrop to the US presidential election which took place in November 2008. The framing of the crisis became increasingly polarized during the campaign, with the two main candidates, Republican John McCain and Democrat Barack Obama, adopting highly partisan rhetoric. John McCain was a long-term proponent of financial deregulation. Although he vowed to crack down on Wall Street 'greed', McCain defended the Republicans' record in office and offered no detailed proposals on how banking regulation or supervision should be strengthened. By contrast, Obama had no financial legislative record to defend and he sought to tie the incumbent Republican administration's policy mistakes to the worsening economic situation. He advocated strengthening the supervisory role of the Federal Reserve, and streamlining the existing framework of competing regulatory agencies (Obama 2008). Obama's election to the White House opened a window of opportunity for banking reform, bolstered by Democratic gains which saw the party increasing its majority in the House of Representatives and taking control of the Senate. The new administration had an ambitious policy agenda, but its main legislative priority upon taking office was economic stimulus and healthcare reform.

During the first half of 2009, however, the new administration's attention increasingly shifted to developing a comprehensive financial regulatory reform package. This was a direct response to growing public anger and resentment about the high-profile failures and taxpayer-funded rescue of Wall Street (Woolley and Zeigler 2011). The President made it clear that he wanted to push strongly ahead with financial reform at the beginning of his administration, rather than wait until the crisis had subsided, to increase the chances of success. Responding to this newfound urgency, the US Treasury published a White Paper in June 2009 setting out an ambitious plan for financial regulatory reform (US Treasury Department 2009).

The White Paper envisioned a strengthened architecture for financial supervision, with greater powers for the Federal Reserve and the creation of new centralized agencies (Hungin and James 2017). The first of these envisaged a new body, the FSOC, responsible for macroprudential oversight. Chaired by the Treasury Secretary, this was an attempt to overcome the fragmented supervisory architecture by bringing together the heads of all the relevant federal agencies: including the Chairs of the Federal Reserve, SEC, FDIC, CFTC, the Director of the Federal Housing Finance Agency, the Chair of the National Credit Union Administration (NCUA) Board, the Director of the (new) CFPB, and one independent member with insurance expertise appointed by the President and approved by the Senate. Its key role would be to designate firms as 'systemically important' and henceforth subject to heightened regulatory standards, a rule that would automatically apply to all banks with over $50bn in assets.

The second main institutional innovation was the establishment of the new CFPB, with a Director appointed by the President and funded by the Federal Reserve. The bureau, modelled on that proposed by former Harvard law professor Elizabeth Warren in 2008, was granted powers over consumer protection that would be transferred from several existing agencies. This transfer was intended to form part of a broader consolidation of financial supervision around a single national regulator for depository institutions, and to combine the CFTC and SEC under the Federal Reserve's authority (Hungin and James 2017).

The White Paper also contained far reaching changes on financial regulation, particularly with respect to securitized markets (US Treasury Department 2009). It identified over-the-counter derivatives (OTCDs) as a major source of contagion in the run-up to the financial crisis, and sought to empower the SEC and CFTC to regulate them for the first time. Specifically, the White Paper recommended that henceforth OTCDs should be traded through verifiable transactions guaranteed by central counterparties (CCPs), and that these trades should be separated from other banking activities.

The idea of bank structural reform originated from a Group of Thirty report published in January 2009. This private policy advisory group was headed by former Federal Reserve Chair Paul Volcker, who was appointed the following month to chair Obama's new Economic Recovery Advisory Board, an ad hoc panel of experts from business, labour, and academia. The group found that losses in proprietary trading, bank sponsorship of hedge funds, and exposure to structured credit products had undermined financial stability and hindered effective regulation (Group of Thirty 2009). It concluded that the complexities and lack of transparency in the proprietary capital market gave some firms a competitive advantage by enabling them to exploit implicit federal subsidies to engage in speculative transactions. The report recommended limiting the proprietary activities of 'systemically important banking institutions' that 'present particularly high risks and serious conflicts of interest'. The report also advocated prohibiting bank sponsorship or management of alternative investment funds—including private equity, hedge funds, and certain other covered funds—and that in packaging and sale of 'collective debt instruments', banks should be required to keep a 'meaningful part of the credit risk' (Group of Thirty 2009).

Volcker pushed strongly for these restrictions, believing that they would at least partially restore the 1930s Glass–Steagall legal divide between commercial and investment banking (Cassidy 2010). Testifying to the Senate Banking Committee on 2 February 2009, he argued that they would address TBTF and moral hazard by changing bank expectations about the prospect of government bail-outs. Specifically, he argued that banks would henceforth expect 'euthanasia, not a rescue', as the government's job would be to facilitate the orderly liquidation of failing institutions, not to rescue them (US Senate 2010).

Throughout 2009, the Obama administration showed little enthusiasm for Volcker's idea of a wholesale ban on proprietary trading. The Treasury's June 2009 White Paper contained only a single sentence on proprietary trading in eighty-nine pages: 'The Federal Reserve and the federal banking agencies should tighten the supervision and regulation of potential conflicts of interest generated by the affiliation of banks and other financial firms, such as proprietary trading units and hedge funds' (Krawiec 2013, p. 60). The idea was also entirely absent from both Obama's accompanying statement (Obama 2009a) and a major speech he gave on financial reform in September 2009 (Obama 2009b). The administration insisted that its proposal to increase oversight of systemically important institutions, and to tighten regulation of derivatives markets, was sufficient to protect against future bank bail-outs (Skeel 2010, pp. 44–52). As a result, commentators even began to speculate that Volcker had become increasingly isolated from the Obama administration (Uchitelle 2009).

The Treasury White Paper divided opinion on both the left and right of the political spectrum. Republicans argued that the recommended reforms would entrench the administration's TBTF policies from 2008, and sought to link them to healthcare reform as further evidence of Obama's 'Big Government'. Critics from the left of the Democratic Party complained that it favoured Wall Street and did little to protect consumers, advocating instead a complete break-up of the largest institutions (Skeel 2010, pp. 49–50). The administration's reforms also received mixed reviews from the wider academic community, with notable critics claiming that a ban on proprietary trading would have done little to prevent the crisis, and that banks would find different ways of taking risks (Cassidy 2010). By contrast, several high-profile figures, including Simon Johnson, Joseph Stiglitz, and Nouriel Roubini, advocated either the creation of strict new internal firewalls or that the largest banks should be broken up altogether (Johnson and Kwak 2010).

The Obama administration was acutely aware that political timing would be key to getting wholesale financial reform through Congress. Strengthening supervision through new institutions (the FSOC and CFPB) remained central to the reform agenda, but wider plans to consolidate the myriad of regulatory agencies was quietly abandoned in late 2009 in the face of concerted bureaucratic and congressional opposition. Instead, the administration decided to concentrate its energies on legislating for much tougher financial regulation of large banks, principally through higher capital and liquidity requirements, and new resolution rules. This meant making a series of choices about what was politically possible whilst having the biggest impact on the financial system. Crucially, according to a former New York Fed official, even at this late stage the Volcker Rule was widely viewed as a potential disruption, which 'no one wanted' (quoted in Hungin 2016a; see

Hungin 2020), to the finely balanced legislative package making its way through Congress.

The President's announcement that he would support a ban on proprietary trading in early 2010 therefore came as a huge shock in Washington. We argue that the decision was a response to sudden conflict expansion, triggered by mounting public anger about the level of executive bonuses and compensation packages being awarded by large US banks, notably Goldman Sachs, in late 2009 (Skeel 2010, p. 55). Reacting to White House polling showing that the President was perceived to be too close to Wall Street, Obama declared, 'I did not run for office to be helping out a bunch of, you know, fat-cat bankers on Wall Street' (Obama 2009c). As a former New York Fed official noted, 'Volcker pushed for it, the politics supported it, and the principals very reluctantly embraced. That's the one piece of outside agency' (quoted in Hungin 2016a). The President's reappraisal of Volcker's proposal was given added impetus by the surprise victory of Republican Scott Brown in a special election in Massachusetts on 19 January 2010 to fill the seat of the late Senator Edward Kennedy. In response, Obama announced that he favoured 'common sense' restrictions on banks' speculative activities, and proposed a 'Financial Crisis Responsibility Fee' to recoup the cost of the bail-outs from the industry.

Obama's decision was also unexpected because the idea was known to be opposed by several senior administration figures—including Director of the National Economic Council, Larry Summers, and Treasury Secretary, Tim Geithner (Alter 2010). Summers was reported to regard the Volcker Rule as 'unrealistic and unworkable' (Wolffe 2011, p. 170), while Geithner believed that capital requirements were a more effective mechanism for preventing bank failures (Cassidy 2010). The Federal Reserve quietly argued that attempting to ban proprietary trading was highly problematic. A former Federal Reserve official argued that the Volcker Rule at the time was viewed as 'complex ... and very contentious', a 'bad law ... like swiss cheese', 'impossible to define', and that it risked 'impeding safety and soundness' (quoted in Hungin 2016d). Similarly, from the perspective of a congressional advisor at the time, 'no one wanted' or 'thought we needed' the ban on proprietary trading included because it made it harder to pass the bill, but the White House insisted that it created a 'political opportunity' to look like they were being 'tough' with the banks (quoted in Hungin 2016b).

With the administration now backing the Volcker Rule, attention shifted to the legislative process and the passage of what became the Wall Street Reform and Consumer Protection Act. Despite the Democrats controlling Congress, and the growing public backlash against TBTF banks, the legislative path to banning proprietary trading was far from assured. Congress was acutely polarized around the issue along strict partisan lines (Carpenter 2010). Moreover, President Obama was determined to secure bipartisan support for regulatory reform for two reasons: in order to get a filibuster-proof majority in the Senate (i.e., sixty votes, of which the Democrats were short by three); but also to send a credible signal to the financial markets about the durability of the changes. This task was made more difficult by Scott Brown's victory in Massachusetts, further reducing the Democrats' Senate vote share. The highly partisan nature of the debate also reflected the polarized nature of public opinion, with support for structural reform split along party lines (CNN 2010).

This strength of opposition forced the Treasury and Federal Reserve to bury their initial reservations. Instead, they worked closely together to build political support for reform, seconding staff members to each other to ensure close coordination, and liaising closely with the Act's main sponsors to guide the legislation—which, henceforth, became known as the Dodd–Frank Bill—through Congress.

3. Competitive financial power in the US

The highly contested nature of US banking reform derives from two key features of the process: competitive financial power and the absence of venue shifting. We begin by analysing the first of these—competitive financial power—characterized by the fragmented character of financial industry lobbying, and the mobilization of a powerful coalition of pro-banking reform interest groups.

The large Wall Street banks did not hesitate to deploy their substantial lobbying machine against the Obama administration's plans for financial reform (Interview 1). Collectively, the US financial industry spent more than $750m on lobbying government during 2009–10, and hired more than 2700 lobbyists in Washington, to defend its varied interests (Kaiser 2013, p. 152). Importantly, as we detail below, the US financial industry was not represented by a single, centralized group capable of bringing the collective pressure of industry to bear on policy makers. Nor was the sector unified in its opposition to either the Dodd–Frank Bill in its entirety, or the Volcker Rule specifically. On the contrary, financial lobbying was characterized by a dizzying array of organized interests, including trade and sectoral associations, individual financial firms, and organizations representing other sectors of business. Although most were broadly hostile to more stringent financial regulation, the sheer breadth of the Dodd–Frank proposals meant that different groups had diverse economic interests and heterogeneous preferences with respect to specific reforms. The result was that hundreds of financial industry groups were frequently in competition with one another in Washington to access and influence regulators and legislators, preventing the sector as whole from projecting a clear, consistent, and coherent voice.

Financial lobbying against the Volcker Rule was spearheaded by the 'big five' Wall Street banks, namely Goldman Sachs, JP Morgan, Citigroup, Morgan Stanley, and Bank of America. A leading financial reform advocate described this effort as 'relentless, nonstop, day and night lobbying. ... It is absolute total nuclear war that

Wall Street is engaged in' (Eichelberger 2012). The ferocity of the response underlay the importance of proprietary trading to their business models: it was estimated to be worth $40–50bn to the largest US banks, with the Volcker Rule threatening to reduce combined profits for the largest eight banks by up to $10bn (Moore and Campbell 2013). The lobbying also reflected the oligopolistic character of the market, with the largest five banks accounting for 95 per cent of all derivatives trading in the US (Rivlin 2013). Bank lobbyists were instructed to resist the administration's entire regulatory agenda, including those reforms that enjoyed some degree of bipartisan consensus, like higher capital and liquidity standards, so as to warn legislators away from more contentious proposals, such as limits on bonuses. On the Volcker Rule specifically, industry lobbyists continued to defend the role of the largest banks on the grounds that they were essential to meet the demands of a globalized economy and the 'real' economy. In particular, it was claimed that stronger prudential regulations would impair their ability to compete with foreign universal banks, and that reform would reduce the availability of credit for business and consumers (Interview 1).

The banks were supported by the largest financial interest organizations—including the ABA, the FSR, SIFMA, and the International Institute of Finance (IIF). The largest of these groups—the ABA—spent more on lobbying in 2010–11 than any other single organization ($17.2m), while the FSR and SIFMA spent $14.4m and $10.5m respectively (OpenSecrets), figures that are broadly comparable to spending by each of the largest banks (see below). Importantly, these figures capture an important aspect of the fragmentation of US financial lobbying: while collective industry lobbying through the three main financial associations was undoubtedly formidable—totalling $42.1m—it was less than the amount spent by the big five banks on lobbying individually ($45.2m). Major US financial institutions therefore continued to rely more on their individual relationships with the public authorities than on collective initiatives in responding to Obama's regulatory reform agenda (Woll 2014, p. 99).

In addition, a number of separate associations representing the main market-makers and dealers in derivatives also mobilized around the Dodd–Frank proposals—the largest being the ISDA—warning against the costs of restricting banks' ability to trade in these financial contracts. As the legislative process reached a critical point in mid-2009, the number and breadth of financial groups competing to shape the final drafting of the bill in Congress continued to proliferate. For example, representatives from the asset management, investment fund, and alternative investment fund industries increased their lobbying activities, claiming that the Volcker Rule would impinge on their economic interests in different ways (Woolley and Zeigler 2011, p. 35).

Many of these arguments were echoed by the largest business groups, led by the US Chamber of Commerce through its Center for Capital Markets Competitiveness, which opposed any attempt to ban banks from proprietary trading

(Johnson and Kwak 2010). Major non-banking firms—including Caterpillar, IBM, and Boeing Aerospace (Scannell 2009)—also mobilized against the new restrictions, arguing that it would constrain their ability to use derivatives to offset specific risks in their business activities. From August 2009, the US Chamber of Commerce joined with the Business Roundtable and National Association of Manufacturers to organize a new lobbying group, the Coalition for Derivatives End-Users, composed of over 170 firms and associations, which enabled them better to distinguish themselves from the traditional Wall Street banks.

The barrage of bank lobbying against Dodd–Frank nonetheless masked important differences in the preferences and strategy of the largest institutions. Lobbying statistics compiled by public interest groups capture some of this variation. For example, JP Morgan significantly outspent its Wall Street rivals on lobbying in 2009–10 with $13.58m, followed by Citigroup ($10.9m), Bank of America ($7.7m), Goldman Sachs ($7.4m), and Morgan Stanley ($5.6m) (OpenSecrets). Similar variation is revealed by figures for the total number of meetings held with federal regulators: Goldman Sachs held no fewer than 97 meetings between June 2010 and June 2011, followed by JP Morgan (75), Morgan Stanley (73), Bank of America (61), and Citigroup (42) (Biegelsen 2011).

Evidence of the competitive character of US bank lobbying also comes from first-hand testimonies of those involved at the time. For example, the CEO of Goldman Sachs, Lloyd Blankfein, initially struck a conciliatory tone in early 2010, suggesting that he could support some limitations on proprietary trading, depending on the details: 'The Volcker Rule's best application is if it stopped banks from doing things that were specifically dangerous for them to do' (Reuters 2010). But as it became clear that the rule could cost the bank $1.5bn in profits a year, Goldman Sachs became one of the most vociferous critics. According to one lobbyist, 'they were totally freaked out about Volcker' because, as an investment bank, their business model was highly dependent on trading (quoted in LaCapra 2011). In response, the bank hired an 'all-star team' of lobbyists, consisting largely of former government and congressional officials, whose 'single focus, more than any other bank, is the Volcker Rule' with the aim of getting it abolished altogether (Jopson 2017b). Others confirmed that Goldman was an 'aggressive' institution and 'incredibly powerful at the time' given its ability to leverage contacts within government (LaCapra 2011).

JP Morgan and Citigroup also lobbied hard against the new proprietary trading provisions, but in a less aggressive manner (LaCapra 2011). This was attributed, at least in part, to the fact that as universal banks their business model was less dependent (in relative terms) on speculative trading (Jopson 2017b). JP Morgan CEO, Jamie Dimon, was initially highly critical of the Obama administration's ambitious plans for regulatory reform, warning of 'huge negative unintended consequences' and scornful of Paul Volcker for not understanding capital markets (quoted in Patterson and McGrane 2012). But the bank was later forced to row back its opposition following the reputational damage inflicted by the exposure of the multi-billion dollar ('London Whale') trading scandal in early 2012. JP Morgan found itself increasingly isolated from both Congress and the rest of the industry, according to a former lobbyist: 'I don't care how many [lobbyists] you have. When you have a situation like this, it's going to put you on the defence and it's going to be a while before they can get back on offense ... This is going to be a significant distraction for them for a long time' (quoted in Palmer 2012). Another confirmed that the bank's ability to shape the banking reform agenda was significantly diminished, forcing it to shift position for fear of antagonizing regulators even more (Rathee 2012). Hence, Dimon was forced to admit in a Senate hearing that the Volcker Rule would probably have prevented the London Whale trades from taking place, and later claimed that 'part of the Volcker Rule I agreed with ... is no prop trading. We did very little, so I have no problem' (quoted in Fox Business 2012).

Citigroup broadly aligned with the rest of Wall Street in opposing the Volcker Rule, but its voice was necessarily diminished by the huge bail-out it received in 2008. This led it to channel much of its lobbying activities through third-party organizations—such as the Bipartisan Policy Center—to which it was a leading donor (Williams 2013). Similarly, the investment bank Morgan Stanley—which might have been expected to be a natural ally of Goldman Sachs—was also less forthright in its public advocacy. This was largely related to early decisions to reconfigure its business model: the bank was quick to start closing down its proprietary trading desks in 2008 in response to mounting losses, and in late 2010 decided to spin off its last remaining operations in favour of a shift into wealth management (Baer 2011a).

We argue that the big five banks therefore did not always constitute the united front against the Volcker Rule that is commonly assumed. For example, Goldman Sachs was concerned that its highly visible lobbying strategy risked looking like it was on a 'lone crusade' and that it would be 'a kiss of death for any proposal to be branded the "Goldman Sachs amendment"' (quoted in Jopson 2017b). Consequently, Goldman Sachs sought to corral the other Wall Street banks behind its position on the Volcker Rule and was 'relentless' in pushing its position for full repeal through one of the main trade associations: 'What SIFMA came out with on Volcker is what Goldman wanted. That's where they did their fighting' (quoted in Jopson 2017b). However, the price of this effort to unify the banks was to strain relations with those banks that sought to revise (rather than repeal) the Volcker Rule, on the grounds that this strategy stood a greater chance of success. According to one senior lobbyist, the different approaches revealed cracks in the Wall Street banks' façade of unity: 'Goldman don't play well with others. Unless there's something they want and feel collectively they can do ... Whatever the industry view is, it has to be their view' (quoted in Jopson 2017b).

The influence of the large banks was also muddied by a number of dissenting voices from within the sector. The most prominent of these was former Citigroup CEO, John Reed, who became one of the leading industry exponents of structural reform. As early as October 2009, Reed publicly endorsed Volcker's call for a partial return to Glass–Steagall era restrictions on the explicit grounds that Wall Street banks had become TBTF (The New York Times 2009). Providing a significant boost to Obama's plan to ban proprietary trading, Reed famously testified before the Senate Banking Committee in February 2010 that the risk-seeking culture thriving in capital markets should not be permitted in depository institutions, and later called the universal banking model 'inherently unstable and unworkable' (Better Markets 2021). These arguments were also echoed by former Merrill Lynch senior executive, Roger Vasey, who penned a *Wall Street Journal* op-ed arguing that the Volcker Rule 'is necessary to correct a mistake that poses a danger to our economy' (Eichler 2012).

The wider business community was also characterized by internal divisions over the Dodd–Frank Bill, particularly with respect to the ability of banks to engage in derivatives trading. The Commodity Markets Oversight Coalition (CMOC)— whose membership included household oil delivery firms, trucking associations, airlines, farmers, and other retailers—backed new restrictions on the grounds that derivatives markets had been infiltrated by speculators since 2000. Moreover, they allied with congressional agriculture panels and the CFTC in opposing end user exemptions from clearing requirements and attacked the rival Coalition for Derivatives End Users for not representing the genuine interests of commercial end users (CMOC 2010). Furthermore, while hedge and private equity funds pushed for limited restrictions on the ability of banks to invest in their activities, powerful institutional investors with prominent backers in Congress were broadly supportive of the changes to reduce the potential conflict of interest between banks and their customers caused by proprietary trading (Krawiec 2013, p. 81).

A serious obstacle to the efforts of the large banks to corral the wider US financial industry against structural reform was the simple fact that the Volcker Rule disproportionately impacted on just a handful of very large global banks (Elayan et al. 2018). As the Federal Reserve was at pains to point out, the vast majority of US banks did not have an ownership interest in or relationship with hedge funds or private equity funds, and very few owned collateralized loans or debt obligations (McKenna 2017). As a senior banker acknowledged: 'There are 800 banks [in the US], and my guess is that 795 of them don't do private equity or have an internal hedge fund' (quoted in Frontline 2012). For this reason, the proposed proprietary trading ban was widely interpreted by many smaller banks as an opportunity to level the playing field with multinational investment banks that enjoyed a hidden subsidy owing to their TBTF status. This heterogeneity of preferences made the task of forging a collective industry position on banking reform by the ABA and SIFMA all the more difficult. As Camden Fine, head of the community banks' association remarked, 'Ed Yingling [then President and CEO of the ABA] had a very, very difficult time. ... Ed had to satisfy the behemoths on Wall Street at the same time he was trying to please the community banks. That was a very awkward position' (quoted in Kaiser 2013, p. 138).

US community banks proved to be a formidable force in shaping the Obama administration's post-crisis regulatory agenda. It is important not to underestimate the scale and importance of this part of the financial sector. In terms of assets, large Wall Street banks dominated the sector, with the largest four banks holding approximately 50 per cent of total bank assets. But in terms of numbers, the 4800 community banks constituted around 97 per cent of banks operating in the US (Banking Strategist 2021). Moreover, the geographical spread of community banks, chartered across all fifty states, gave the sector significant sway in Congress—but particularly in the Senate, in which smaller states enjoyed disproportionate influence. Moreover, the relative homogeneity of the sector gave its main industry association—the powerful ICBA—a more coherent voice than the larger and better resourced ABA.

Since the financial crisis, community banks had waged a relentless public relations campaign to distance themselves from the largest US banks and to build support in Congress (Price and Schroeder 2018). As Camden Fine, CEO and President of the ICBA later testified, 'Washington saw banks as all pretty much alike. But I realized this was a Wall Street-centered crisis. ... Our goal was to differentiate community banks from—the term we used was the Wall Street megabanks. We made this about Main Street versus Wall Street' (quoted in Kaiser 2013, p. 138). As another anonymous lobbyist remarked, 'Goldman Sachs was on the verge of collapse ... and they got TARP money. Small banks throughout the country had their applications rejected because they weren't healthy. ... Imagine how this played in the mind of 8000 small bankers and everyone they had lunch with' (quoted in Woll 2014, p. 102). As Obama's reform agenda became clear, the ICBA viewed an opportunity to take a 'calculated risk' by quietly supporting the administration with the intention of steering legislation towards targeting Wall Street banks. As Fine later explained: 'The gut reaction of the entire industry was, of course, we have to oppose, oppose, oppose, because it means more regulatory burden', but doing so would be 'the death of our industry' (quoted in Kaiser 2013, p. 138). 'If we just joined up, our voice would be lost, and the community banks would just be road kill on the financial highway. Because we would have played right into the hands of Wall Street, and there were genuine issues that divided us' (p. 138). The resulting split in the US financial industry led JP Morgan's Jamie Dimon publicly to admonish Fine in an interview (quoted in Price and Schroeder 2018).

The White House, and its supporters in Congress, were quick to exploit these intra-industry tensions. In January 2009, for example, Tim Geithner's very first meeting as newly appointed Treasury Secretary was with Camden Fine to discuss the administration's banking reform plans (Kaiser 2013, pp. 139–40). Similarly, in

July 2009, Barney Frank, Chairman of the House Financial Services Committee, sought to woo the community banks in a speech by arguing that 'They were not the perpetrators of the abuses, they will not be the subjects of the corrections, and they need to work with us ... But they have to be careful not to allow themselves to be used by some of their big brothers who would like to have them shelter them' (quoted in Kaiser 2013, p. 140). In private meetings, Frank also appealed directly for the ICBA's tacit support—or at least 'to just stay silent and keep neutral' (quoted in Kaiser 2013, p. 163). This extended courtship eventually paid off as the ICBA broadly supported the full gamut of proposed reforms in the Treasury's White Paper, most of which targeted systemically important institutions (Interview 3). The ICBA's backing was also decisive in securing congressional support for a new Consumer Financial Protection Bureau, on the proviso that small banks would be excluded from its purview, and would pay less into the FDIC bail-out fund (Puzzanghera 2010). This led Fine to boast that 'ICBA is the player on the House financial reform legislation and the other financial trades [associations] are not ... We are on the inside, and the other guys are wondering what is happening' (quoted in Kaiser 2013, p. 163).

The decision of the ICBA to endorse the Volcker Rule in February 2010, just weeks after the President's own announcement, was a huge victory for the White House (Interview 3; CNBC 2010). During the legislative and rule-writing process that followed, the ICBA became an outspoken critic of TBTF banks and a vocal supporter of the administration's legislative efforts to tackle these. Justifying their position, Camden Fine explained: 'These institutions enjoy a privileged position because their size and interconnectedness make them systemically dangerous. ... Not only has their too-big-to-fail status led to riskier [behaviour] and distorted financial markets, it has a real impact on community banks and their customers on Main Street' (quoted in Pike 2013). In particular, the ICBA blamed the over-regulation of community banks since the crisis on the 'repeated policy responses to the abuses of "too-big-to-regulate" financial institutions' (quoted in Pike 2013). This had contributed to the closure of hundreds of local banks over the past decade, with the ICBA adding that 'too-big-to-fail is still with us in all its government supported glory, and too small to save is painfully re-enacted' (quoted in American Banker 2012). In a particularly outspoken attack on TBTF banks in 2013, Fine repeated his assertion that:

> Not only have these institutions received billions of dollars in taxpayer support because of the systemic risks they pose; they are also apparently immune from criminal prosecution. Meanwhile, community banks have been left to pick up the pieces under the weight of crushing laws and regulations enacted to halt Wall Street's unscrupulous behaviour. ... Only after ensuring that all financial institutions operate on a level playing field can we begin to restore our financial system to proper health. (quoted in Pike 2013)

According to the ICBA's legislative counsel, Chris Cole, 'the only way to resolve [TBTF] is to limit the size of big banks. Really, the way to do that is legislatively'—failing that, the Federal Reserve should forcibly break up TBTF banks if they threaten financial instability (quoted in Pike 2013).

Despite the huge lobbying effort, solid evidence of Wall Street bank influence in shaping bank structural reform—at least prior to the rule-writing stage—is difficult to find. A senior Federal Reserve official argued that the large banks were simply in a greatly weakened position: '[The banks] weren't asked too much about what they wanted. They just hoped the reforms wouldn't be too onerous, but they didn't have the political power to stop it' (Hungin and James 2017, p. 31). By contrast, a senior Treasury official admitted that community banks had been important in shaping the Dodd–Frank Bill: 'I think community banks—through the ICBA—had quite a bit of influence in changing how the legislation would impact the smaller institutions' (Hungin and James 2017, p. 32).

The final factor that proved decisive in advancing the Democrats' banking reform agenda was the mobilization of a broad coalition of public interest and campaigning groups against the large Wall Street banks. This included over 250 labour, housing, and consumer organizations brought together under the banner of the AFR, allied with several existing and influential groups—notably, the Consumer Federation of America and the US Public Interest Research Group (Kastner 2014). Although the AFR tended to focus on consumer protection and executive compensation, it also mobilized around the full spectrum of issues contained in Dodd–Frank. Importantly, it provided strong support for banning proprietary trading and forcing all derivatives trading onto fully public exchanges (Gensler 2009; Johnson 2009).

The AFR's annual budget of $1.5m was dwarfed by traditional business groups, such as the Chamber of Commerce which spent over $700m on lobbying in 2010 (Woolley and Zeigler 2011). But what it lacked in financial resources it compensated to some degree by drawing on a wider epistemic community of like-minded campaign groups, think tanks, and prominent figures from government and academia. Important intellectual support came from several leading economic and legal commentators who openly advocated the break-up of TBTF banks (Johnson and Kwak 2010; Skeel 2010), as well as progressive think tanks, such as the Roosevelt Institute and the Bipartisan Policy Center. The coalition was later widened to include the think tank Better Markets, the public interest group Demos, the non-profit Systemic Risk Council (headed by the former FDIC chair, Sheila Bair), and the Pew Memorial Trust (which included senior regulators and industry figures like Paul Volcker, Bill Bradley, John Reed, and Simon Johnson). This support network enabled pro-reform campaigners to wield significant political credibility in regular meetings with members of Congress and Obama administration officials, and to harness considerable technical expertise in the submission of regular comment letters to financial regulators.

Crucially, the mobilization of a broad pro-reform coalition challenged the influence of large US banks by keeping banking reform in the public eye, maintaining pressure on Congress to act, and forcing banks to compete for the 'ear' of legislators (Kastner 2014). Indeed, to this end, the Obama administration deliberately cultivated relations with many of these groups. The AFR had important allies within the administration, notably Michael Barr, a law professor who had been appointed by Obama as Assistant Secretary to the Treasury for Financial Institutions. Barr was known to have strong views on financial regulation and in 2009 was made the designated chief drafter of the consumer section of the administration's regulatory reform package (Kaiser 2013, p. 134). According to Barney Frank, the AFR was 'very helpful' in providing 'good information' and in keeping 'grassroots pressure on the [House] committee' (quoted in Zeigler and Woolley 2016, p. 260). Similarly, a US Treasury official at the time confirmed that consumer groups were particularly influential in 'making the broad cause and creating some momentum to demonstrate how valuable the idea of regulation is' (quoted in Hungin 2016c).

To spearhead the campaign for regulatory reform and build political support within Congress, the White House relied on prominent proponents—notably Paul Volcker and Elizabeth Warren (then a Harvard law professor and special advisor to the President)—to act as policy entrepreneurs and 'thought-leaders' (Kastner 2014). Volcker himself carried enormous gravitas and earned huge respect on both sides of the partisan divide, with Senator Warner referring to him as 'the 101st senator' (quoted in Kaiser 2013, p. 167). Within Congress, Senators Jeff Merkley (D-Oregon) and Carl Levin (D-Michigan) acted as the bill's sponsors, while Senators Sherrod Brown (D-Ohio) and Maria Cantwell (D-Washington) also served as cheerleaders for the legislation. Leading regulators appointed by Obama, notably CFTC Chair Gary Gensler, also became powerful advocates for Dodd–Frank, working closely with pro-reform legislators in Congress, and regularly delivering speeches and publishing articles to make the public case for banking reform. For example, Gensler played an important role during the final stages, and was reported to have 'hovered just behind lawmakers, and could be seen whispering to staff and negotiators as the House and Senate sought to iron out the 2,300 plus page bill' (Crittenden and McGrane 2010).

The resulting alliance between the White House, financial regulators, congressional Democrats, and pro-reform advocacy groups was able to mobilize considerable expertise and political clout with which to challenge the lobbying power of Wall Street banks. The scale of interest group mobilization around banking reform is revealed by the figures on lobbying. According to the Center for Responsive Politics, 788 organizations registered to lobby on the Dodd–Frank Bill, and only 36 per cent of these were identified as mainstream financial sector groups (cited in Woolley and Zeigler 2011). According to Johnson and Kwak (2010, p. 227), the pro-reform coalition proved instrumental in not only defending but strengthening the Dodd–Frank Bill during the legislative phase, putting the administration in the 'prized' position of seeking a 'middle ground' which was closer to its original proposals. But the breadth of the coalition mobilized around banking reform also came at a price for the Obama administration. It encompassed a wide spectrum of societal interests and generated a cacophony of niche policy demands, many of which had to be catered to in the final bill. The result was one of the most lengthy and complex pieces of legislation ever passed, running to over 2300 pages.

4. Institutional venues

The second factor that explains the contested character of US banking reform is the absence of institutional venue shifting. The Obama administration was unable to depoliticize the process, or forge a broad bipartisan agreement, by delegating the issue of structural reform to an ad hoc specialist group. We argue that this was because the political timescale in Washington precluded this option. On the contrary, the administration wanted to pass wholesale financial regulatory reform as soon as possible while public anger and political mobilization against the banks was high. Moreover, Obama was keen to see the Dodd–Frank Bill passed swiftly so that he could move on to tackling the urgent issue of healthcare reform. Consequently, consideration of whether to ban proprietary trading was tagged on to the administration's legislative plans at a late stage in the process, and channelled through conventional institutional venues in Congress.

Attempts were made to forge a bipartisan consensus during the early stages of the financial crisis. The most prominent initiative was the establishment of the Financial Crisis Inquiry Commission: a ten-member commission appointed by Congress in May 2009, and headed by the former California State Treasurer Phil Angelides. Its widely televised hearings in January 2010 helped to keep Wall Street executives in the public spotlight, while its final report published in January 2011 maintained pressure on regulators to implement the Dodd–Frank Bill in full (National Commission on the Causes of the Financial and Economic Crisis in the United States 2011). Separately, the US Senate Permanent Subcommittee on Investigations, headed by Democrat Carl Levin and Republican Tom Coburn, produced its own report in April 2011 on the failure of Wall Street banks. In language strikingly similar to that of the White House and Treasury, the report concluded that the crisis had been caused by 'high risk, complex financial products; undisclosed conflicts in interests [of big banks]; and the failure of regulators ... to rein in the excesses of Wall Street' (US Senate Permanent Subcommittee on Investigations 2011, p. 1).

Importantly, however, these institutional innovations did not constitute venue shifting for two key reasons. First, the committees were primarily tasked with investigating the causes of the financial crisis and the activities of the banks, not developing policy recommendations regarding banking reform. Second, the timing and sequencing of these congressional investigations was misaligned with the political timetable of the Obama administration. Because the US Treasury issued its own legislative proposals on banking reform prior to the publication of the final reports from Congress, these venues were far less effective in facilitating depoliticization or helping to legitimize the administration's plans.

Consequently, the most important institutional venue in shaping the US banking reform agenda was the traditional congressional committee system. The key venues were the Senate Banking Committee, chaired by Chris Dodd, and the House Financial Services Committee, chaired by Barney Frank. As Democrats, Dodd and Frank forged a close working relationship with the Obama administration. While fiercely independent, Dodd and Frank recognized that they had limited technical resources in Congress. Hence, at the height of the legislative process, the two committees were in daily contact with the Treasury and Federal Reserve, which advised on how to write the bill's provisions and to steer it through Congress. At the same time, the White House was acutely aware that it would not secure agreement on everything, and was entirely reliant on the political skills of Dodd and Frank to get as many of the administration's proposals into the final bill as possible.

Spurred by Democratic gains in the November 2008 elections, Congress moved quickly to develop legislative proposals based on the Treasury's June 2009 White Paper. Hence, the House Committee convened hearings during autumn 2009 and passed a version of the bill by December. At this stage, however, the bill did not contain the Volcker Rule, simply a commitment enabling the Federal Reserve to restrict the ability of a financial firm to trade on its own account if the Board determined that it posed 'an existing or foreseeable threat to the safety and soundness of such company or to the financial stability of the US' (H.R. 4173, 1116).

In January 2010, the White House strengthened this provision to include an outright ban on proprietary trading. Volcker's testimony before the Senate Banking Committee days later ensured that the measure gained maximum publicity, and enabled the administration to build political support by leveraging the authority of the former Federal Reserve Chair. The Senate Committee on Banking took up the bill in March 2010 and debated it through April. Its version directed the appropriate federal agencies to develop rules prohibiting trading and fund investment and sponsorship—albeit subject to the recommendations of the FSOC, which was directed to conduct a study regarding the risks and conflicts associated with proprietary trading.

What followed over the next six months was a fierce legislative battle over banking reform, the outcome of which ultimately reflected the relative balance of power between competing legislative factions and interest groups. But the result was far from pre-ordained. On the contrary, it was both highly politicized and contested, as the momentum and influence of different groups waxed and waned over time. The legislative process was also deeply polarized and finely balanced. Although some congressional Republicans were known to be sympathetic to banking reform, Senate Majority Leader, Mitch McConnell, ruled out the prospect of bipartisan agreement. His political strategy was to deny President Obama a big legislative victory and to cultivate the support of Wall Street banks (Interview 1) by encouraging them to contribute to Republican candidates in the 2010 mid-term elections (Kaiser 2013, p. 312). These partisan divisions were overlaid by a highly fragmented institutional context composed of multiple political and bureaucratic actors, all of which scrambled to shape the final legislation.

The administration's endorsement of the Volcker Rule in January 2010 initially met with a lukewarm response from Congress, and by late February speculation was mounting that the White House's enthusiasm was waning in the face of Treasury and congressional opposition (Kosman 2010). By April 2010, however, political momentum behind the Dodd–Frank Bill was boosted by a further series of high-profile Wall Street bank scandals. The most important was the decision by the SEC in May 2010 to file fraud charges against Goldman Sachs in connection with the design and marketing of credit default swaps. The televised Senate hearings which followed, at which Senator Carl Levin famously confronted Lloyd Blankfein with leaked emails claiming that Goldman traders were knowingly selling financial products which they regarded as 'shitty deals', fatally damaged the reputation of Wall Street banks (Kaiser 2013, p. 282). Eager to exploit this political momentum, President Obama delivered a forceful speech to the Business Council reaffirming his political commitment to tackling TBTF banks through tougher prohibitions on speculative activity. As the bill entered the final stages, political pressure from Congress to further strengthen the legislation increased, while the ability of bank lobbyists to access key legislators declined (Woolley and Zeigler 2011).

In April 2010, Democrat Senators Sherrod Brown (Ohio) and Ted Kaufman (Delaware) proposed the SAFE Banking Amendment which sought to prohibit bank holding companies from holding more than 10 per cent of total US insured deposits, and more than 2 per cent of GDP in liabilities, and would have imposed additional capital requirements and leverage restrictions. The measures would have led to the break-up or downsizing of the country's six largest banks. But the amendment was strenuously opposed by senior administration officials: both Summers and Geithner contended that breaking up the US banks would fatally undermine the sector's competitiveness (Connaughton 2012). Former Treasury Secretary Robert Rubin also weighed in on the side of the largest US banks, claiming that 'too-big-to-fail isn't a problem in the system. It is the system. You can't be a competitive global financial institution serving global corporations of scale without having a certain scale yourself. The bigger multinationals get, the bigger financial institutions will have to get' (quoted in Rothkopf 2012, p. 266). This concerted opposition eventually led to the amendment's defeat in the Senate by 33–61 votes on 6 May 2010.

More successful was a stronger version of the Volcker Rule introduced by Senators Merkley and Levin in late April 2010. The Dodd–Frank Bill incorporated the proposal made by Volcker, but was relatively limited in scope because it only applied to funds and investments that were systemically important. The earlier version of the legislation also left the rule open to considerable interpretation, and thus potential watering down, at the rule-writing stage. The Merkley–Levin Amendment, as it became known, sought to firm up the rule's implementation by prohibiting proprietary trading as a matter of law, not just prospective regulation, and by applying the rule to all 'banking entities', rather than only to insured depositary institutions. It clarified that banks would be able to continue to sell, or securitize, loans; and manage clients' money and make trades on their behalf, as long as no bank capital was involved, within limits on banks bailing out investments that went bad and preventing conflicts of interest (Merkley.senate.gov 2010). The amendment also stipulated that institutions that did not make loans, take deposits or access the Federal Reserve's discount window would be excluded from the rule. The Senate approved its version of the bill with the amendment on 20 May 2010.

In May 2010, the bill's provisions were further strengthened so as to require all banks to put their derivatives-trading desks into separate, independently capitalized subsidiaries. This amendment originated from Senator Blanche Lincoln, Chair of the Agriculture Committee, in response to a challenge from a more left-leaning candidate in the forthcoming Arkansas primary elections. The language in the Volcker Rule was subsequently strengthened from preventing speculation by institutions with federal banking guarantees to the 'push out' of all derivative transactions, whether client linked or part of the bank's own proprietary trading portfolio. The big five banks pushed back hard once the bill reached the Conference Committee—a joint committee of the House and Senate, meeting from 10 to 29 June—not least because derivatives trading had earned them $20bn in profit the previous year (Kaiser 2013, p. 292). Large banks deployed over 150 lobbyists, citing Paul Volcker and Sheila Bair of the FDIC in support of their claim that the adoption of the revised Volcker Rule would force trading into unregulated parts of the sector, and sought to channel their influence in the House through the members of the business-friendly New Democrat Coalition. Despite seeking to amend around thirty items in the original Dodd–Frank Bill, the Wall Street banks succeeded in securing changes in only around half a dozen of these, and none that were very significant (Kaiser 2013, p. 306).

Ultimately the most important factor in determining the final language of the Volcker Rule was the political balance of power in the Senate, where the Democrats had been deprived of their filibuster-proof majority by the victory of Republican Scott Brown from Massachusetts in the special election in January 2010. In return for his support, Brown demanded that the bill should not be funded by any new levies on banks, and sought special protections for the Massachusetts-based financial industry, which included State Street, Fidelity, and MassMutual, and a sizeable mutual funds industry (Brush 2010). Brown was ultimately unsuccessful in demanding that the Volcker Rule be removed from the bill altogether, but did succeed in securing some notable last-minute concessions. Specifically, the Senator secured changes to the Merkley–Levin and Lincoln amendments so that the definition of 'systemically significant' firms would be based on activities, rather than size (which was reportedly a carve-out for Fidelity) (Cassidy 2010). The range of permitted activities was also widened to enable banks to continue trading for hedging purposes—namely, interest rate and foreign currency swaps—while all other derivatives had to go through separate subsidiaries. Finally, and perhaps most importantly, text was also inserted to provide a *de minimis* exemption allowing banks to invest up to 3 per cent of their tier-1 capital in private equity and hedge funds, provided that they did not own more than 3 per cent of the fund's capital—an apparent carve-out for State Street (Dealbook 2010).

Despite these last-minute concessions, the substance of the Dodd–Frank bill, and the Volcker Rule, survived the reconciliation process largely intact. The reconciled bill was passed comfortably by the House on 30 June (237 votes to 192), but only by the minimum filibuster-proof majority in the Senate (60 votes to 39) on 15 July. Signed by the President on 21 July 2010, the 'Wall Street Reform and Consumer Protection Act' was hailed as the most far-reaching financial regulatory overhaul since the Great Depression. Reflecting on the successful passage of the bill, Barney Frank summed up the view that banking reform reflected the triumph of politics over commerce: 'Money is influential [in Congress], but votes will kick money's ass any time they come up against each other. In the Senate, once public opinion got engaged, it blew away the lobbyists, the money, campaign contributions. Public opinion drove that Bill' (quoted in Kaiser 2013, p. 327).

5. Obstacles to implementation

The Dodd–Frank Bill left a great deal of legal and regulatory detail to be thrashed out by the various regulatory agencies, giving them significant discretion to determine its impact. The ambiguities and gaps in the legislation also encouraged the continued mobilization of outside interests seeking to shape the final outcome. This combination of sustained conflict expansion and heightened politicization created a dynamic regulatory process in which banking reform was continuously contested and repeatedly challenged over time. We argue that this process was facilitated by the fragmented character of the US political and regulatory system, which created multiple access points and policy venues through which outside interests could try to shape the rule-writing process. This section focuses on the three key venues of conflict: Republicans in Congress, the regulatory agencies, and financial industry lobbying.

Challenging the Volcker Rule: Republicans and Congress

A major source of contestation regarding the implementation of the Volcker Rule was Congress. The approval of the Dodd–Frank Bill along highly partisan lines—it passed with sixty votes in the Senate, supported by only three Republicans—was a harbinger of the battles to come. In response, the large Wall Street banks shifted the bulk of their campaign contributions to Republican candidates in 2010 and 2012, having backed mainly Democrat candidates in 2008 (Wilmarth 2013, p. 1317). In the run-up to the 2012 elections, Republican leaders pledged to repeal or cut back several key provisions in Dodd–Frank if the party gained control of the White House and both houses of Congress. The largest US banks gave most of their contributions to Republican presidential candidate Mitt Romney, having narrowly supported Obama in 2008 (Drawbaugh 2012). Republican gains in both the 2010 and 2012 congressional elections—which saw a Republican majority returned to the House—emboldened senior party figures. Henceforth, they warned regulatory agencies that they should not act 'rigidly' when enacting the Volcker Rule, and launched a sustained campaign to undo the reforms (Solomon 2010).

The federal agencies responsible for implementing Dodd–Frank became a key target for political pressure. Republicans sought to use Congress's power to defund or underfund agencies that relied on congressional appropriations. The House Financial Services Committee, chaired by Republican Jeb Hensarling (Texas), consistently blocked any increase in budgetary appropriations for the agencies in 2010, 2011, and 2012, well below amounts requested by the White House (Wilmarth 2013, p. 1321). In addition, congressional committees stepped up their scrutiny of the agencies. For example, Senate Republicans prevented the new CFPB from beginning any legally binding work by blocking the confirmation of a Director until July 2013. They also introduced legislation aimed at requiring all financial regulators to perform stringent cost–benefit studies before adopting any new rules (Mattingly 2012).

In the years that followed, Republicans in Congress introduced numerous bills and technical amendments in an attempt to repeal or weaken key provisions in the Dodd–Frank legislation. For example, Representative Spencer Bachus (R-Alabama) urged the FSOC to implement the Volcker Rule 'in such a way as to minimize its substantial and very real costs, given that the gains are likely to be illusory' (Bachus 2010). Similarly, Representative Jim Hines (D-Connecticut) sponsored a bill exempting foreign affiliates of US swaps dealers from Title VII of Dodd–Frank—aimed at exempting more than half of all derivatives activities by the five largest US banks. Other Republican bills sought to repeal the FSOC's ability to designate non-bank financial firms as SIFIs, and to stop the Federal Reserve from regulating them (Wilmarth 2013, p. 1319). A group of congressional representatives led by Michele Bachmann (R-Minnesota) went further, introducing a one-sentence bill to repeal Dodd–Frank altogether.

Supporters of banking reform increasingly blamed the White House and Treasury for failing to sustain public support once the Dodd–Frank Bill had been passed. Distracted by the legislative battle to pass Obama's flagship healthcare reform, and in a context of acute partisan polarization, Dodd–Frank was left open to repeated challenges from congressional opponents. As a congressional advisor later testified: 'The Treasury did nothing. They should have been on CNBC, Bloomberg, giving speeches, taking this thing outside the Beltway. ... They just didn't bother to bring the country along, and neither did the White House. They never got politically motivated to create a campaign' (quoted in Hungin 2016b).

Challenging the Volcker Rule: the regulatory agencies

The multiple regulatory agencies responsible for implementing the Dodd–Frank Bill were a second source of ongoing conflict. The legislation directed the FSOC to complete a study within six months, setting out detailed guidance to the regulatory agencies responsible for its implementation. These agencies were, in turn, required to undertake the necessary rulemaking within a further nine months based on the FSOC's recommendations. It also required clarification of key definitions, such as 'market making' activities, a task that was in part entrusted to a study undertaken by the Government Accountability Office (GAO). Prior to issuing recommendations on the Volcker Rule, the FSOC was also required to solicit public input for a thirty-day period in advance of the study. Commencing on 6 October 2010, this exercise prompted a huge lobbying response, with over 8000 comment letters received (FSOC 2011). Mirroring the response to the EU's High-Level Expert Group on bank structural reform (see Chapter 9), over 80 per cent of these were 'substantially the same letter' calling for strong implementation of the Volcker Rule, reflecting a concerted lobbying campaign by the AFR, Public Citizen, and the Public Interest Research Group (PIRG) (Krawiec 2013, p. 72). Similarly, during the rule-writing phase that followed, the surge of comment letters from pro-reform advocates—including academics, legal scholars, overseas regulators, consumer groups, and grassroots organizations—continued. For five of the most contested rules written by the CFTC to implement Dodd–Frank, 19 per cent of comments received came from non-industry groups, while 33 per cent were submitted by unaffiliated individuals.[1] Across all five rules, only 48

---

[1] The five rules (with abbreviated titles) comprise: Interpretive Guidance and Compliance with Certain Swap Transactions (informally known as the 'Cross-Border Rule'); End-User Exception to

per cent of comments came from the financial industry itself (Zeigler and Woolley 2016, p. 261).

The rule-writing process for Dodd–Frank was greatly complicated by the fragmentation of regulatory agencies. The byzantine institutional architecture for regulating financial institutions in the US has evolved incrementally over many decades. As the financial sector expanded and diversified, new regulatory agencies were added, creating a highly fragmented system (Carpenter 2010; Jacobs and King 2016). Responsibility for regulating and supervising individual banks was shared between the Federal Reserve, the OCC, the FDIC, and the Office of Thrift Supervision (OTS), as well as state banking supervisors. In addition, securities markets are regulated by the SEC, while futures and options markets are regulated by the CFTC. Because the Volcker Rule related to so many different banking activities, the legislation required all five regulatory agencies to agree upon the implementing language.

The problem of translating the Volcker Rule into law was compounded by the need to specify multiple definitional boundaries and which transactions would be exempt. The main challenge was to define 'proprietary trading', described in the legislation as 'engaging as a principal for the trading account of [a] banking entity', with 'trading account' defined as any account used for acquiring or taking positions. The problem was the interpretation of 'trading account', which depended on the trader's intent when purchasing—i.e., as speculative trades or long-term investments (Krawiec 2013, p. 65). In addition, a clear boundary was also needed between proprietary trading and other financial activities, such as buying and inventorying financial instruments in anticipation of client demand, and using derivatives and other instruments for hedging purposes. The Dodd–Frank legislation led to ambiguity by granting nine exceptions to the ban on proprietary trading—for underwriting, market-making activities, risk-mitigating hedging activities, and transactions on behalf of customers—together with granting federal agencies the power to draft further exceptions.

The FSOC's guidance to the regulatory agencies signalled a determination to pursue the robust enforcement of the Volcker Rule, proposing quantitative metrics for monitoring bank investment activities and proprietary trading, and suggesting that additional regulatory requirements would be applied to banks. The five agencies followed suit by setting out their proposed rules for enacting Dodd–Frank between November 2011 and early 2012. Despite the creation of an interagency working group, however, regulators struggled to agree amongst themselves about key aspects of the Volcker Rule. The draft rules therefore included 1300 outstanding queries from regulators on 400 topics, leading both supporters and opponents

---

Mandatory Clearing of Swaps; Governance Requirements for Derivatives Clearing Organizations, Designated Contract Markets, and Swap Execution Facilities ('Clearinghouse Ownership'); Position Limits for Derivatives; and Prohibitions and Restrictions on Proprietary Trading (the 'Volcker Rule').

to claim that they had become almost unintelligible (Stewart 2011). The result was that a rule outlined by Volcker in three pages, and which took up six pages in Dodd–Frank, was turned into regulations reaching 298 pages.

Challenging the Volcker Rule: the financial industry

The mobilization of a vast lobbying exercise by the financial industry, in response to the rule-writing process, provided a third source of contestation. In their submissions to regulators, most Wall Street banks complained about the sheer complexity of the task of attempting to ban proprietary trading. Lobbying was dominated by investment and commercial banks—but mirroring the pattern of financial interest fragmentation that characterized the legislative phase, they were joined by representatives from the asset and capital management industry, as well as energy, commodities, and agricultural companies as end users of derivatives (Drutman and Chartoff 2013). For example, the ABA criticized the proposed implementing regulations for being 'unworkable' due to their 'oversized nature and complexity', while the US Chamber of Commerce condemned the proposal as 'the poster child of regulatory complexity' (US Chamber of Commerce 2011). In particular, lobbyists disputed how broadly the exemption should be interpreted and applied, the extent to which limitations on banks' abilities to make markets would reduce market liquidity, and the likely costs of any such reduction (Krawiec and Liu 2015). The major banks argued that they should be permitted to continue broadly defined activities in market making and investment hedging without cumbersome new compliance requirements (Ryan and Zeigler 2016).

The scale of industry lobbying led many to anticipate that the Volcker Rule would effectively be neutered before it could even be brought into effect. Regulators complained that this had the effect of 'sapping, slowing and stymieing' the rule-writing process (Drutman and Chartoff 2013). For example, CFTC Commissioner Bart Chilton suggested that 'Much of Dodd–Frank is dying on the vine. ... Lobbying, litigation and lawmakers who have tried to defund and defang Dodd–Frank have all brought rule-writing to a crawl. Regulators themselves have become overly concerned about finalizing rules. Over-analysis paralysis, fears of litigation risks, and the lack of people-power have all contributed to the slowdown' (Lyster 2013).

In mid-2012, former CFTC Chairman Brooksley Born spoke out against industry lobbying, claiming that the banks were succeeding in delaying or blocking key Dodd–Frank provisions by 'lobbying for the dismantling of protections in the Act, delay[ing] rulemaking procedures, challenging the rules in the courts, trying to defund regulatory agencies and preventing appointment of key regulators' (quoted in Adler 2012). Others complained that industry's strategy was not to block the Volcker Rule, but to render it increasingly ineffective by adding multiple loopholes and exemptions, thereby producing 530 pages of rules. As one pro-reform lobbyist complained, 'most of the length, complexity and questions are in there because of industry lobbying' (quoted in Eisinger 2012).

As regulators issued increasing numbers of draft rules, evidence of industry influence mounted. In late 2010, regulators proposed a threshold of $100m for the value of derivative contracts held by a firm, above which they would be subject to oversight and scrutiny, and required to hold additional capital and file reports. Capturing around 70 per cent of companies, the figure met with a barrage of criticism from the derivatives industry and banks, and a heavy lobbying effort by energy companies as end users of derivatives. For example, a coalition of energy firms, including BP and Shell, lobbied for a $3.5bn threshold, while the Coalition of Physical Energy Companies proposed a $3bn figure. In April 2012, the SEC and CFTC backed down and raised the threshold to $8bn: an eightyfold increase which now exempted 85 per cent of firms, and discounted swaps used to hedge against risk, as well as forwards and options (Protess 2012). Further evidence came in December 2014 when the Federal Reserve granted banks an extension to July 2017 to confirm ownership interests in, and relationships with, certain 'legacy' covered funds (Board of Governors of the Federal Reserve System 2014). This brought criticism from Paul Volcker that the industry was simply trying to drag implementation out for as long as possible in an attempt to change the law (Eavis 2014).

Wall Street banks also sought to challenge rule issuance in the courts. In October 2011, the CFTC issued a final rule establishing position limits, aimed at limiting speculation by investment banks in commodities markets. Two months later, the SIFMA and ISDA launched a lawsuit against the CFTC, citing that regulators had not demonstrated that establishing position limits was necessary and appropriate, as set out in Dodd–Frank, and that the CFTC had not sufficiently studied the economic impact of the rule (Sweetland-Edwards 2013). In September 2012, the US Court for the District of Colombia Circuit overturned the CFTC's rule, arguing that regulators lacked a 'clear and unambiguous mandate' to set position limits.

The cumulative effect of these delaying tactics was that regulatory agencies repeatedly failed to meet their targets for adopting rules to implement Dodd–Frank. Specifically, regulators had failed to adopt more than three-fifths of the 279 rules whose issuance was required by June 2013 (Pompa and Gainer 2013). The federal agencies also failed to issue final implementing regulations for the Volcker Rule by the statutory deadline of 21 July 2012. Despite this, banks had taken significant steps towards compliance with the Volcker Rule by 2012—either by closing their proprietary trading desks or by reassigning traders to asset management divisions. Hence, Goldman Sachs, Morgan Stanley, and Bank of America all announced plans to wind down their proprietary trading desks before regulators had even released their proposed rules (Baer 2011a, 2011b).

The politicization of the rule-writing process was not only a consequence of financial industry lobbying. To counter the influence of the large US banks, pro-banking reform groups also mobilized widely, seizing on the Volcker Rule as the totemic issue in the process of dealing with TBTF banks. Hence, the financial offshoot of the Occupy movement, known as Occupy the SEC, submitted a 325-page letter in early 2012, calling for exemptions to be limited, and demanding that banks be closely monitored to ensure they could not circumvent the ban on proprietary trading (Occupy the SEC 2012).

Importantly, regulatory agencies actively encouraged the mobilization of pro-reform groups to build supportive coalitions of interests around specific regulatory issues (Zeigler and Woolley 2016, p. 268). For example, in designing new rules for derivatives trading, the CFTC recognized that it needed to mobilize support amongst financial industry beneficiaries—such as clearing houses, hedge funds, asset managers, and some mutual fund advisors—given that centralized clearing would challenge the dominance of the investment banks. In particular, the CFTC forged a close relationship with the think tank, Better Markets, regularly quoting their comment letters to support their position and push back against industry lobbying. As one legal observer commented, 'under former Chairman Gensler, Better Markets served as a device to provide the CFTC with cover for virtually any position' (quoted in Lofchie 2014). Similarly, in carving out a new macroprudential regulatory framework and designating firms as 'systemically important', the new FSOC drew heavily on the expertise of 'near insiders', typified by former FDIC Chair Sheila Bair. Indeed, Bair and a group of former senior government officials and financial experts would later go on to form their own think tank, the Systemic Risk Council.

As during the legislative process, momentum behind implementing the Volcker Rule was periodically boosted by a series of financial industry scandals. MF Global, a large commodities broker, collapsed in late 2011 after suffering heavy trading losses. In July 2012, JP Morgan announced that its London trading desks had incurred a $6bn loss as a result of aggressive trading in derivatives (the 'London Whale' scandal). A Senate investigation subsequently accused its senior executives of hiding losses, deceiving regulators, and misinforming investors. Many global banks—including Barclays, UBS, RBS, Bank of America, Citigroup, JP Morgan, Société Générale, Crédit Agricole, Rabobank, and Deutsche Bank—paid large fines in 2012/13 to settle charges that they had colluded to manipulate the London interbank offered rate (Libor) (Wilmarth 2013, p. 1291). In addition, following revelations contained in a Senate committee report issued in July 2012, HSBC was forced to pay $1.9bn to settle criminal money-laundering charges filed by federal prosecutors. The following month the New York bank regulator also fined Standard Chartered $670m for laundering money for Iranian businesses (see Macartney 2019).

Conflict expansion periodically emboldened regulators to face down industry protests. In early 2013, for example, Federal Reserve Bank of Dallas President Richard Fisher and FDIC Vice Chairman Thomas Hoenig repeated their claim that Dodd–Frank did not go far enough to eliminate large implicit subsidies to

TBTF banks. Instead, they advocated a strict ringfencing of the deposit-taking, payment services, and lending activities of commercial banks, which would be covered by the federal safety net; while other financial activities, including derivatives and capital market operations, should be conducted in a separate non-bank entity without federal protection (Wilmarth 2013, p. 1438). On the all-important hedging exemption, the final agreement reached in December 2013 between the five regulatory agencies included a relatively narrow exemption for hedging activities, requiring banks to show that transactions on their own account were linked to specific, identifiable risks (Ryan and Zeigler 2016, p. 80). Moreover, these were to be recalibrated continuously in time intervals that would allow ongoing proprietary trading between risk assessments.

Later attempts to toughen the Dodd–Frank rules in Congress were notably less successful. For example, Senators Sherrod Brown (D-Ohio) and David Vitter (R-Louisiana) introduced a bill in April 2013 requiring banks with a net worth greater than $50bn to hold equity capital of 8 per cent, with SIFIs valued over $500bn required to hold 15 per cent, and requiring separate capital requirements for non-bank subsidiaries (Douglas 2013). The bill also sought to strengthen the Volcker Rule by prohibiting FDIC-insured banks and regulators from using safety net subsidies to protect non-bank affiliates. Critics argued that the stringent new capital rules would hinder lending and growth, and potentially force the breakup of the largest banks. Without the Obama administration's endorsement, the bipartisan bill failed to garner sufficient support in Congress.

Finally, a brief attempt to re-establish New Deal-era rules requiring the full separation of commercial and investment banking was made in early 2013. In the House, Representative Marcy Kaptur (D-Ohio) along with Representatives Walter Jones (R-North Carolina), Tim Ryan (D-Ohio), and Tulsi Gabbard (D-Hawaii) introduced legislation to reinstate the 1933 Glass–Steagall Act. In July 2013, Senators Elizabeth Warren (D-Massachusetts), John McCain (R-Arizona), Maria Cantwell (D-Washington) and Angus King (Ind-Maine) introduced a bill committed to reintroducing a '21st Century Glass–Steagall Act' (Warren et al. 2017). But with public concern about TBTF banks on the wane, and the White House increasingly focused on congressional attempts to defund Obamacare, both bills soon failed.

6. Repealing the Volcker Rule: the Trump administration

A new chapter in the fate of US banking reform opened in late 2016. The bitterly fought presidential campaign between Donald Trump and Hillary Clinton reopened many of the partisan wounds from the battle over Dodd–Frank. While Trump vowed to dismantle many of the Obama-era reforms to boost economic growth, Clinton vowed to strengthen the legislation by targeting non-banking financial intermediaries—i.e., the so-called 'shadow banking' sector. Against this backdrop, House Republicans proposed new legislation in September 2016 aimed at the repeal of the Dodd–Frank bill: the Financial CHOICE Act. The bill, crafted by Jeb Hensarling (R-Texas), Chair of the House Financial Services Committee, aimed at reducing the regulatory burden on the financial industry. Specifically, it promised to exempt banks from Dodd–Frank rules governing capital and liquidity requirements, and the ban on proprietary trading, if they fell into one of two categories: small and medium-sized banks with assets of less than $50bn; or any bank that agreed to hold capital of at least 10 per cent of its total assets.

The Financial CHOICE Act, as it was later designated, was initially predicated on Clinton winning the White House (Conti-Brown 2017, p. 2), and therefore much of the early language was aimed at limiting the powers of the executive. The original bill's main targets for reform were therefore the two new institutions created by the Obama administration: the FSOC and CFPB. Hence, the bill would strip the FSOC of the power to designate banks and non-banks as 'systemically important' and thus subject to greater regulation, would invalidate all previous designations of non-banks as SIFIs, and would remove its ability to break up large banks on the recommendation of the Federal Reserve. This would relegate the FSOC to the role of market monitoring and information sharing. Similarly, the bill proposed to seriously curtail the supervisory authority and independence of the CFPB, restructuring it as an executive-branch agency, thereby enabling Congress to defund it. Unsurprisingly, opinion on the bill was deeply polarized. House Speaker Paul Ryan argued that the legislation would provide 'regulatory relief' to small banks and local communities. By contrast, House Minority Leader Nancy Pelosi criticized the Republicans' 'dangerous Wall Street-first bill', while Senator Elizabeth Warren called it a 'handout to Wall Street' (quoted in Dexheimer 2018).

Trump's surprise election in November 2016, together with Republican control of the House and Senate, changed the political dynamics and provided a commanding position to repeal Dodd–Frank. But this masked important political divisions within the Republican Party, and particularly between the Trump White House and Republicans in Congress. During the presidential campaign, there appeared to be rare bipartisan agreement about the need to take further action to tackle TBTF banks. In 2016, both the Republican and Democratic Party conventions adopted policies which explicitly supported the reinstatement of the 1933 Glass–Steagall Act. Trump himself sent mixed messages. Although early in the campaign he appeared to favour a simplification of the banking system through a '21st century Glass–Steagall Act', Trump later committed a future administration to the wholesale repeal of Dodd–Frank (*Reuters* 2016).

This ambiguity continued in office. In February 2017, President Trump issued an executive order to begin a review of the Dodd–Frank legislation with the intention of moving to a less stringent regime, a move which triggered an immediate surge in bank shares. Trump now declared that 'we expect to be cutting a lot out of Dodd–Frank' because it had restricted lending to ordinary businesses (*Washington Post* 2017). He also made a series of high-profile appointments to his administration recruited from Wall Street. For example, Treasury Secretary Steve Mnuchin, National Economic Council Director Gary Cohn, chief strategist Steven Bannon, and economic advisor Dina Powell were all former executives at Goldman Sachs. In addition, a number of prominent Wall Street figures were appointed to run the federal agencies, such as Jay Clayton at the SEC (a financial sector attorney), Chris Giancarlo at the CFTC (a former executive at an interdealer broker), Joseph Otting at the OCC (a former banker), and Randy Quarles as vice chair of supervision at the Fed (from the private equity industry).

But senior officials sounded a note of caution on the likelihood or desirability of a wholesale repeal of Dodd–Frank. Having promised to 'kill' parts of the Obama-era bill, Trump's new Treasury Secretary, Steve Mnuchin, indicated to Congress that the new administration favoured the retention of the Volcker Rule, commenting that 'the concept of proprietary trading does not belong in banks with FDIC insurance' (Hamilton 2017). Moreover, a few months later, Mnuchin appeared to signal openness to the idea of replacing the Volcker Rule with a version of the UK ringfencing reforms, as championed by FDIC Vice Chair Thomas Hoenig. Adding to the confusion, the head of Trump's National Economic Council, Gary Cohn, briefly revived the idea of Glass–Steagall legislation to break up the largest banks (Jopson 2017a).

On 8 June 2017, the House passed the Financial CHOICE Act along party lines by 233–186 votes. But its passage in the Senate was far less assured. The Senate bill—the Economic Growth, Regulatory Relief, and Consumer Protection Act—was introduced by the new chair of the Senate Banking Committee, Mike Crapo (R-Idaho), who aimed for a bipartisan approach. This reflected the fact that the Republicans only had a fifty-two-seat majority, significantly short of the sixty needed to avoid a filibuster. As a consequence, the bill was amended so as to preserve both the CFPB and the Volcker Rule. Nonetheless, the Senate bill, passed by 67–31 in March 2018, did achieve the Republicans' primary objective of easing the regulatory burden on smaller financial institutions. Hence, it raised the asset threshold for banks classified as 'systemically important' from $50bn to $250bn, thereby reducing capital and liquidity requirements, and the need for stress tests for a range of relatively large financial institutions. Henceforth, the core provisions contained in the Dodd–Frank legislation would only apply to thirteen financial institutions in the US (Jopson 2018). The bill also exempted firms with less than $10bn from the Volcker Rule. This was comfortably passed by the House by 258–159 votes in May 2018, supported by thirty-three Democrats, and signed into law by President Trump on 24 May 2018 (Financial Choice Act 2017).

Evidence that Trump's partial repeal of Dodd–Frank was not a straightforward victory for the large Wall Street banks comes from the response of prominent financial lobby groups. For example, the ABA responded cautiously by calling the bill 'an important first step' designed to introduce 'targeted, narrow changes and adjustments' to Dodd–Frank (quoted in *Dealbook* 2017). But the big five Wall Street banks were notably less enthusiastic: they had pushed for a $500bn oversight threshold, a loosening of capital and liquidity requirements for 'living wills', and a significant relaxation of rules regarding the ban on proprietary trading—none of which they secured. By contrast, the strongest support for Trump's regulatory reform package came from the powerful community bank sector. The ICBA had lobbied relentlessly over many years for a significant easing of regulations on capital, lending, and trading for small banks, assisted by their numerous Republican sponsors in Congress (Price and Schroeder 2018). Armed with government data showing how the sector had shrunk since 2007, they were able to win over moderate Democrats in states with large numbers of small banks but no major institutions. In a repeat of the industry divisions exposed by the passage of the Dodd–Frank Act eight years earlier, it therefore looked like the large Wall Street banks had once again been outmanoeuvred by the community banks on Capitol Hill.

Pro-reform groups, such as the AFR, were outraged by the bill, claiming that it would 'make it easier for big Wall Street banks to take the kind of risks in pursuit of short-term gains … that led to the financial crisis' (quoted in *Dealbook* 2017). They also revealed that many of the recommendations for reform proposed by the Trump administration echoed those put forward by The Clearing House, a powerful trade association (Americans for Financial Reform 2017). Democratic political organizations like American Bridge also viewed the passage of the Act as an opportunity to attack vulnerable Republicans in the run-up to the 2018 midterm elections.

Regulatory measures to ease the burden of compliance with the Volcker Rule followed Trump's executive order in February 2017. Leveraging regulators' discretion to interpret the application of Dodd–Frank, the Treasury and federal agencies released multiple reports proposing rule changes (Scaggs 2017). For example, in June 2017 the Treasury recommended changing the frequency and the severity of the stress-testing process for banks, scrapping the 'gold-plating' of global capital and liquidity standards for the biggest US banks, and a looser interpretation of the Volcker ban to allow banks to engage in market making, and to hold securities for less than sixty days without needing to prove they are not proprietary.

The Treasury report also raised the possibility that all banks should be able to opt out of all capital and liquidity requirements and most Dodd–Frank regulations, including the Volcker Rule, in return for maintaining substantially higher capital levels—echoing the provisions contained in the Financial CHOICE Act. The Treasury also cited regulatory compliance burdens created by the rule and suggested simplifying the definitions of proprietary trading and covered funds to allow banks to hedge their risks more easily. The report was warmly welcomed by several industry groups, with the Institute of International Bankers commenting that it represented a 'thoughtful, well-reasoned, common sense approach to mitigating some of the unintended adverse consequences' of post-crisis reform (quoted in McLannahan and Fleming 2017).

US regulators proposed further changes aimed at relaxing the Obama-era reforms. In August 2017, the OCC embarked on a consultation aimed at tailoring the Volcker Rule's requirements and to clarify prohibited and permissible activities, claiming that there was a bipartisan consensus to reduce the burden on banks that 'do not present systemic risks' (OCC 2017). Similarly, in May 2018 the Federal Reserve and OCC proposed easing limits on how much the largest banks could borrow. Regulators also proposed relaxing the rules governing market making: quantitative measures prescribed by regulators to identify the activity would be replaced by a requirement for banks to establish 'internal risk limits' to ensure they were catering only to clients (Flitter and Rappeport 2018). New 'bright-line rules' also aimed to simplify the range of permitted and prohibited activities, rather than relying on supervisors' judgement as to traders' motives. In October 2018, the Federal Reserve eased the rules for small and medium-sized banks, allowing some to undergo stress tests once every two years instead of annually, and some to hold fewer liquid assets on their balance sheets. All of these changes were detailed and pushed strongly by the financial industry (McLannahan 2018b).

In August 2019, regulators finalized their plans to relax the application of the Volcker Rule. This involved shifting the burden of proof from banks to supervisors, and reducing banks' requirements to keep records and file reports. Under the original rule, regulators presumed that positions held for less than sixty days counted as proprietary trading unless proven otherwise. But under the changes, there would now be a series of specific tests to determine whether large banks' positions counted as such (Stacey 2019). Positions held by smaller banks would also automatically be regarded as compliant with the Volcker Rule if they were held for longer than sixty days. Regulators also granted further exemptions from what counted as proprietary trading by broadening the range of activities that banks could conduct to ensure they held enough liquidity.

Finally, in January 2020, regulators issued further proposals aimed at relaxing the 'covered funds' rule which prevented banks from holding a stake in investment funds. The rule change would permit investments in funds that own bonds and loans, provided that banks were already permitted to own those assets directly; and allowed banks to provide a small amount of cash or securities to loan securitization funds to provide liquidity. Venture capital investments would also be exempt from the rule altogether, but investing in private equity and hedge funds would remain prohibited (Armstrong 2020). The changes were pushed strongly by the SIFMA, which claimed that they would improve competition and market efficiency, but were condemned by the Better Markets lobby group for creating loopholes for banks to return to risk-taking behaviour. As President Trump approached the end of his first term in office, it looked like the largest US banks had finally restored their influence in Washington by persuading legislators and regulators to relax significantly—but not repeal completely—the Obama-era banking reforms.

7. Conclusion

US banking reform stands out as a deeply divisive and highly contested process. Part of the explanation undoubtedly lies in the scale and depth of the crisis in the subprime mortgage market, and the financial contagion that this triggered throughout the US financial system. It also stems in part from the timing and sequencing of events: the early onset of the crisis in the US necessitated a regulatory response prior to efforts to coordinate measures at the international level; while the 2008 US presidential election, and the leftward shift in US politics that resulted, opened a unique window of opportunity for reform.

Nonetheless, studying banking reform from a comparative perspective reveals that these factors can only provide a partial explanation. After all, political change in France (to the left) and in the UK (to the right) at around the same time provide counter examples. Instead, we point to the importance of two different factors in shaping the uniquely contested nature of US banking reform. First, the competitive nature of financial power meant that Wall Street banks could not lead a unified financial industry campaign to persuade legislators to abandon structural reform. On the contrary, divisions quickly emerged between the big five banks over how to respond to the Volcker Rule and, more importantly, they faced opposition from the sizeable and powerful community bank sector which endorsed Obama's regulatory reforms. In addition, large US banks were forced to fight an increasingly public battle with a broad and highly vocal coalition of pro-reform groups which mobilized around Congress. Second, the Obama administration was unable to depoliticize the process through venue shifting, and thus failed to secure a broad, bipartisan agreement around banking reform. Rather, the issue remained firmly in the hands of a deeply polarized Congress, with Democrats and Republicans holding diametrically opposing views and each battling to take control of the legislative process.

The Obama administration nurtured and leveraged conflict expansion—in the form of vocal support from financial regulators, congressional Democrats, community banks, and pro-reform groups—eventually to secure the passage of the Dodd–Frank Act in July 2010. Yet the nature of this process contributed to heightened levels of politicization around US banking reform, with the result that the outcome—the ban on proprietary trading—was never settled politically. On the contrary, bank structural reform remained vulnerable to ongoing political conflict and the shifting balance of power between competing groups. Hence, the implementation of the Volcker Rule was seriously disrupted by disagreements between regulatory agencies, and Republican attempts to block or dilute the reforms. Donald Trump's election in November 2016 opened a new chapter in the fate of US banking reform, paving the way for legislative and regulatory measures aimed at unwinding much of the Dodd–Frank legislation more generally. The fact that the Volcker Rule survived this onslaught, however, is a testament to the difficulty of achieving wholesale repeal in such a febrile political context.

5
The Importance of Being Vickers
Venue Shifting in the United Kingdom

1. Introduction

The UK government was an important first mover in a number of its policy responses to the financial crisis. At the height of the contagion in the banking system in 2007–9, for example, the UK government was the first in Europe to develop a comprehensive bank rescue scheme. Furthermore, following the formation of a new Conservative–Liberal Democrat coalition government in May 2010, the UK moved swiftly by establishing the Independent Commission on Banking (ICB) to make recommendations on introducing structural reforms to UK banks. To the surprise of many commentators and scholars, for whom the UK was the embodiment of Anglo-Saxon capitalism and 'light touch' financial regulation, the ICB's proposals were immediately endorsed by the government and enacted into law in December 2013, despite fierce opposition from the banking industry.

The UK Banking Reform Bill (HM Government 2013) brought about the biggest shake-up in UK banking in a generation (Goff 2011). It required bank retail activities to be placed in a separate and 'operationally separable' ringfenced subsidiary which was no longer permitted to trade most derivatives and securities (ICB 2011b). The reforms also imposed some of the highest capital requirements in the world, requiring the ringfenced bank to hold an additional ringfence capital buffer (up to 10 per cent common equity tier-1 capital), which is significantly beyond international standards. The changes are therefore notably at odds, and much tougher, than those imposed in the rest of Europe, making the UK something of an outlier on banking reform (Gambacorta and van Rixtel 2013; IMF 2013).

The UK's decision to ringfence its largest banks unilaterally is puzzling for two reasons. First, neither of the two main parties expressed any great enthusiasm for structural reform in the run-up to the 2010 general election. Indeed, the Conservative Party manifesto made no explicit commitment to structural reform, and pledged only to 'pursue international agreement' on the possibility of banning forms of proprietary trading so as to avoid damaging the UK financial sector's competitiveness (Conservative Party 2010). Second, in stark contrast to the structural reforms introduced in the US, bank ringfencing in the UK proved remarkably durable. Although the financial industry continued to lobby hard in order to shape the rules regarding the definition and 'height' of the ringfence, policy implementation after 2013 was largely uncontroversial and the reforms continued to enjoy broad support from all the main UK political parties.

How do we explain the UK's approach to bank structural reform? Our framework points to two key factors in explaining this pattern of *durable reform*. First, we argue that institutional venue shifting was critical to the opening of a policy window on bank structural reform in the UK. The government's decision to delegate responsibility to an ad hoc specialist group re-defined the terms of engagement between policy makers and the financial industry; reshaped the balance of power between competing groups for and against reform; and framed the issue around the threat that TBTF banks posed to financial stability. Importantly, we show that venue shifting took place at two separate stages of the policy process: at the agenda setting stage, in the form of the ICB, convened between 2010 and 2011; and at the legislative scrutiny stage, through the Parliamentary Commission on Banking Standards (PCBS), from 2012 to 2013. We argue that this venue shifting was pivotal in depoliticizing the issue of structural reform. Unlike in the case of the Netherlands, however, it did so by facilitating conflict expansion: providing a high-profile platform for a number of authoritative pro-reform voices, facilitating wider engagement with a range of societal interests, and thus curtailing the access and influence of the banking lobby. As a result, the new venues helped UK policy makers build political support for change and secure greater 'buy in' from policy stakeholders.

Second, we argue that the lobbying power of banks in the UK was constrained by the competitive nature of financial power. On the one hand, the UK financial industry was characterized by important internal divisions, forcing banks to compete with one another and thereby limiting its collective influence. On the other hand, UK banks were weakened by the emergence of a disparate coalition of pro-banking reform actors. Unlike in the US, however, this coalition was not dominated by the mobilization of 'outsider' interests, such as consumer groups or financial reform activists. On the contrary, the most prominent voices in the UK calling for stringent new rules to tackle TBTF banks came from 'insiders' within Westminster and Whitehall: namely, key government ministers, financial regulators, and members of parliament. Moreover, these actors leveraged and channelled their political influence and technical expertise through new institutional venues established to manage the banking reform process: namely, the ICB and PCBS. As a consequence of these two factors, the UK government was able to make credible commitments to structural reform that remained largely uncontested over the following decade.

2. The UK banking crisis

In the decades prior to the financial crisis, the UK financial services sector, predominantly based in the City of London, emerged as one of the world's largest and most important international financial centres. The growth of the City followed a series of legislative measures by the 1979–97 Conservative governments to deregulate the UK banking system and financial markets (dubbed the 'Big Bang' reforms) (see Moran 1991). This gradual transformation of the City into one of the world's leading global financial hubs was also underpinned by a shift towards centralized, statutory financial regulation, albeit one based on a 'light touch', principles-based approach (McPhilemy 2013). Following a series of banking scandals in the early 1990s, including the failures of Barings Bank and the Bank of Credit and Commerce International (BCCI), the newly elected Labour government in 1997 centralized financial regulation in the new FSA, symbolically located at the heart of the new financial district at Canary Wharf. Courted by New Labour politicians who championed the competitiveness of the financial sector, the City was ideally placed to exploit the integration of European financial markets and the economic opportunities provided by the launch of the Economic and Monetary Union (EMU) (Hopkin and Alexander Shaw 2016; Thompson 2017).

The City thrived in this favourable regulatory environment, with the financial sector's contribution to total UK economic output increasing from 5 per cent to 9 per cent between 2000 and 2009, the highest of all the G7 economies. Political support from all the main political parties rested on the substantial financial contribution of the City to the UK state, generating over £27bn in tax revenues for the UK government, and a financial services trade surplus of £51bn (House of Commons 2018). Yet this prosperity was built on fragile foundations. We now know that the City's rapid expansion masked the accumulation of systemic financial risk, at the heart of which was an expansive, concentrated, and leveraged banking sector (Alessandri and Haldane 2009). Consolidation in the decade prior to the crisis meant that retail banking had become dominated by large universal banks, with the 'big four' accounting for 77 per cent of personal current accounts and 85 per cent of small business lending (Competition and Markets Authority 2014). In an effort to secure its status as a serious global player, the sector had expanded its higher-risk, 'market-making' activities, with asset trading increasing from 20 per cent of total bank assets in 2000 to 45 per cent by 2007. In doing so, the banks became highly leveraged, with the average exceeding 35:1 by 2007 (ICB 2011b, p. 128), depleting their liquidity reserves and increasing their dependence on wholesale funding. While hugely profitable, this business strategy also brought greater vulnerability to disruption in financial markets, meaning that relatively small losses were amplified by the banks' large trading books (Bell and Hindmoor 2015a).

The first warning sign that all was not well came in September 2007 when news that the bank Northern Rock, which had aggressively built up a huge mortgage and loan portfolio following demutualization in 1997, was seeking government assistance. The result was the first run on a UK-headquartered bank in 150 years, eventually forcing the government to take the bank into public ownership in February 2008 after two unsuccessful takeover bids from private investors. As financial markets in the US gradually seized up during 2008, so the health of the UK banking system and the supply of credit rapidly deteriorated. At the height of the crisis in September 2008, several major UK banks came close to bankruptcy. After months of speculation regarding its survival, the large banking group HBOS, formed out of the merger of Halifax and Bank of Scotland in 2001, was eventually taken over by Lloyds Bank in a government-brokered deal on 17 September. Weeks later, the bank Bradford and Bingley was nationalized on 29 September after its deposit and branch network was sold to Santander. The UK government also took the extraordinary step of using anti-terrorism legislation to freeze the UK assets of two failing Icelandic banks, Landsbanki and Kaupthing. Ominously, in October 2008 the Bank of England estimated that capital losses for the six largest banks were above £100bn, 'threatening the solvency of individual institutions and the collapse of the entire banking system' (Quaglia 2009, p. 1068). These losses were equivalent to 6.3 per cent of GDP (Hardie and Howarth 2013a).

Recognizing that a comprehensive solution to UK bank failures was needed, the Labour government worked with financial regulators and bank CEOs to develop one of the first bank support schemes in Europe (Woll 2014, pp. 91–2). On 8 October 2008, Labour Prime Minister Gordon Brown and Chancellor of the Exchequer Alistair Darling announced a £500bn bail-out package. The British plan had three pillars: 1) £50bn of direct bank recapitalization through equity purchases; 2) a £250bn credit guarantee scheme to support new loans to companies; and 3) £200bn of liquidity provision to banks through short-term loans, operated by the Bank of England. This support was supplemented in December 2009 by the creation of the Asset Protection Scheme, a £200bn scheme to insure assets on bank balance sheets to increase banks' capital and ability to lend, and a £50bn scheme to guarantee newly issued asset-backed securities to stabilize housing market finance (HM Treasury, 2008).

The Bank Recapitalisation Fund allowed the government to purchase ordinary and preferred shares, and was open to all UK incorporated banks and building societies. In the end, only two banks applied for the rescue package: RBS, which initially received £20bn, eventually giving the government a 68 per cent share in the bank; and Lloyds Bank (which included HBOS), receiving £17bn, giving the government a 41 per cent stake. These stakes were to be managed for the government by a newly created private company, UK Financial Investments (UKFI). Crucially, however, unlike in the US, the bank recapitalization scheme was voluntary. Hence, the government did not require 'solvent' banks—i.e., HSBC, Barclays, and Standard Chartered—to accept capital injections from government. This prevented the government from cross-subsidizing the cost of the bail-outs and meant that UK taxpayers would not benefit from holding equity stakes in profitable banks.

The near collapse of the UK banking system in 2008 was a profound shock to the British political establishment. Once the immediate threat of a meltdown in the banking system had subsided, attention shifted to longer-term changes deemed necessary to restore financial stability. Amongst UK financial regulators, this triggered a fundamental transformation in understanding as to how the financial system worked and how it should be regulated. This macroprudential paradigm 'shift' (Baker 2013a) involved a range of stringent new regulatory measures, including: the imposition of substantially higher capital and liquidity requirements for banks; the development of detailed recovery and resolution regimes to help regulators deal with struggling financial institutions; and a range of new macroprudential tools for regulators to monitor and address the build-up of systemic financial risk. But of all the regulatory reforms introduced in the wake of the crisis, the most contentious was the issue of structural separation as a way to end to financial institutions being TBTF.

3. Venue shifting 1: the Independent Commission on Banking

The turmoil of the financial crisis and the fiscal burden of bailing out two of the UK's largest banks had sent shockwaves through the political establishment and all political parties viewed the protection of taxpayers as an electoral priority. However, in the run-up to the general election in 2010, the two main parties expressed little enthusiasm for the structural separation of banking activities. The incumbent Labour government believed that raising bank capital and liquidity requirements was more important in stabilizing the system and addressing TBTF banks, and that structural reform was therefore unnecessary. Indeed, its flagship legislative response to the crisis, the 2009 Banking Act, explicitly rejected calls to separate retail and investment banking formally (HM Treasury 2009, p. 18). The Conservative Party was more amenable to the idea and pledged to consider introducing a ban on proprietary trading, emulating the measures agreed in the Dodd–Frank Act in the US. Crucially, however, the party's manifesto also made clear that this should only be done if coordinated at the international level (Conservative Party 2010).

The Shadow Chancellor, George Osborne, recognized the need to protect taxpayers from future bank failures, but he also sought to avoid unilateral changes that might damage the international competitiveness of the City. Only the Liberal Democrats openly supported structural reform. Under pressure from activists to take a tough line on the banking industry, structural reform was an issue on which it could clearly differentiate itself from the two larger parties. Business Secretary Vince Cable was a firm supporter of breaking up the largest banks, and regularly intervened to ensure that the issue remained firmly at the top of the agenda (Parker et al. 2013).

During the election campaign, all three parties made protecting taxpayers from future bank failures an electoral priority. This task was complicated by the outcome of the election, which led to the formation of a coalition government between the Conservative and Liberal Democrats with opposing views on banking reform. The solution, brokered as part of the Coalition Agreement between the two parties in June 2010, was to delegate banking reform to a new ICB, tasked with making recommendations on structural and non-structural measures to promote both stability and competition in banking. We argue that this exercise in venue shifting served to depoliticize structural reform in two ways. First, the ICB helped to defuse a sensitive political issue by diminishing a potential source of conflict between the two governing parties. Hence, the Conservatives, sceptical of any change that might threaten the competitiveness of the City, were able to delay reform for as long as possible; while the Liberal Democrats viewed an 'independent' process as more likely to propose radical reforms, which they favoured. Second, delegating banking reform to an ad hoc specialist group facilitated agreement though conflict expansion. Hence, by deliberately widening consultation to a range of societal interests, the ICB was able to build broader political support for change and secure 'buy in' from major policy stakeholders.

Four key features of the ICB widened the policy window for UK banking reform. First, delegation of the agenda-setting stage of the process to an 'independent' commission served better to insulate the process from organized interests. The appointment of the former Director General of the Office for Fair Trading, and Chief Economist at the Bank of England, Sir John Vickers, was critical. Though viewed as 'a safe pair of hands' as a signatory to a public letter endorsing the Conservatives' spending cuts prior to the 2010 election, Vickers' background as a champion for competition and consumer issues signalled a robust response to banks that were perceived as TBTF. The authority of the other four commissioners indicated that the group would be both balanced and highly independent. It included former Barclays Chief Executive, Martin Taylor; former co-head of JP Morgan's investment bank, Bill Winters; Claire Spottiswoode, former Director General of Ofgas (and a member of the Future of Banking Commission, 2009–10); and Martin Wolf, chief economics commentator at the *Financial Times*. According to one bank lobbyist, the 'independent minded' membership of the commission rendered it largely 'immune' to industry pressure (Interview 4).

Second, by extending the consultation and scrutiny processes, the ICB was able to accumulate extensive technical expertise. The commission was well resourced with a fourteen-strong secretariat drawn from the Treasury, Bank of England, FSA, the Department for Business, Innovation and Skills, and the Office of Fair Trading (OFT). To reduce its dependence on private information supplied by the banks, the ICB issued two separate calls for evidence. Compared to a standard regulatory consultation, which typically lasts three months, the year-long ICB process was of a different order of magnitude: 'The key difference was the scale. I mean an average sort of government consultation, we'll have three months. ... But this process was enormous. We're talking literally thousands of man-hours within the Bank [of England], the scale and size of the information we gave them' (Interview 11).

The commission required banks to supply a huge volume of commercially sensitive financial information related to bank business models which could then be used to assess the impact of different reform options. To facilitate this, the largest banks established secure online 'data rooms' so that information could be viewed on a confidential basis. This was a deliberate attempt to frame the process as an academic exercise, rather than as a standard industry consultation exercise, designed to elicit objective analysis from a range of expert sources. The ICB also drew heavily on academic research and empirical evidence to enable it to consider the full spectrum of reform options—from higher capital requirements or banning proprietary trading through to 'narrow' banking, whereby retail deposits are backed entirely by reserves (ICB 2011a). The process began with an evidence-gathering exercise by the secretariat, pulling together existing academic research on structural separation for the commissioners to review. Later, the Bank of England supplied its own detailed analysis, much of it privately, which prevented banks from making misleading claims. The ICB also commissioned its own quantitative analysis on the impact of ringfencing from independent City analysts. This enabled it to directly challenge industry framing about the importance of universal banking, and to directly rebut claims about the costs of structural reform. It also led the ICB to conclude that the possibility of banks leaving the UK in response to ingfencingg was a 'low probability' (Treasury Select Committee 2011).

For example, the exercise enabled officials to estimate the cost of ringfencing to the financial industry to be £4–5bn (ICB 2011a), based primarily on the higher costs banks would incur in capitalizing their investment operations without access to large retail deposits or an implicit state subsidy. Importantly, the figure was a direct rebuttal to the £12–15bn cost put forward by bank lobbyists (Treanor 2011). The industry claimed that this figure represented the true cost of making lending to large businesses more expensive by preventing cross-subsidization in universal banks. It also claimed that further costs would be incurred as a consequence of how uncertainty generated by the ICB process had delayed the sale, and damaged the share price, of the state's holdings in RBS and Lloyds Bank.

Third, the commission reconfigured the rules of the game. The ICB created a structured process of engagement involving closed, private evidence sessions with individual banks, calls for written evidence, public roadshows and 'Question Time'-style debates, and formal hearings with senior bank executives modelled on a Competition Commission inquiry. This process of engagement was deliberately designed to mobilize a broader range of policy actors, including representatives of small businesses, consumer groups, and charities, in order to secure wider public legitimation and push back against industry influence. The mix of formal written submissions and structured hearings constrained the ability of industry to wield influence through pre-existing informal channels, and made it largely impervious to traditional 'political lobbying' (James 2018). The use of commission 'away days' to bank headquarters also encouraged firms to compete against one another for influence, and provided an important source of verification, enabling ICB officials to cross-reference banks' publicly stated positions against information supplied in private meetings.

The expertise and information accumulated by the ICB at the start of the process helped to shift the balance of power in favour of regulators. For example, ICB officials argued that the structured process of engagement with individual banks gave them an important informational advantage:

> All the banks were quite independent in the way they communicated with us. One of the most amusing things was that three different institutions all used the same consultant to come in and present to us three completely conflicting arguments about whether investment banking was less risky than retail banking. (Interview 5)

> [The banks] would say things that would contradict each other. And that was often quite useful because you can go that's rubbish, because I've just heard someone else say the completely opposite thing. (Interview 9)

Fourth, venue shifting generated commitments which were politically binding on government. Sir John Vickers made it clear that he wanted to forge an agreement on structural reform that was politically tenable. As a time-limited, ad hoc commission tasked only with making policy recommendations, the ICB was well placed to act as an honest broker between competing interests. Although its proposals were not legally binding, the credibility of the process, and the political imperative of reconciling the divergent preferences of the two governing parties, meant that policy makers had less room for discretion when it came to implementation. The ICB provided greater autonomy for policy makers because, as a senior regulator noted, it permitted 'politicians to be more robust in the face of lobbying, and less on our backs than would have been the case otherwise' (Interview 2). This was confirmed by a bank lobbyist who complained that 'It became clear quite early that ringfencing was a battle that wasn't going to be won. The conclusion had already been hard wired into the process' (Interview 4).

It is important to note that this exercise in conflict expansion through venue shifting was not necessarily a deliberate strategy on the part of the UK government. The ICB was established as a quick political fix to the issue of banking reform as part of the hastily agreed Coalition Agreement. But it unleashed unanticipated dynamics and had unintended consequences for the structural reform agenda. By shifting the agenda-setting process to new institutional venues, the government (inadvertently or not) provided a high-profile platform for pro-reform actors to build political support, and facilitated the mobilization of a diverse group of stakeholders around the issue of TBTF. Ultimately this served to widen the policy window for change, culminating in structural reform legislation that was fiercely opposed by the UK's most powerful banks.

4. Competitive financial power in the UK

Although venue shifting played a critical role in depoliticizing structural reform and facilitating cross-party agreement, it does not by itself explain the inability of the UK financial industry to block reform. Rather, we argue that it is the interaction of venue shifting with the competitive nature of financial power in the UK that accounts for the scope and durability of structural reform.

During the early stages of the process, the UK banking industry attempted to frame the issue by presenting a united front in opposition to structural reform. The banks had two main lines of attack. First, they argued that increased regulation would threaten the competitiveness of the UK's global banks and the position of the City as a leading international financial centre. Second, the industry claimed that structural separation would raise the cost of credit, thereby reducing the ability of banks to lend to ordinary businesses and households. The largest financial trade association, the BBA, defended the universal banking model on the grounds that there was no evidence that it was an important cause of the financial crisis (Interview 8). It pointed out that many of the UK banks that failed in 2007/8 (notably HBOS, Bradford and Bingley, and Northern Rock) were principally focused on mortgage lending (Bell and Hindmoor 2015b, p. 467). Moreover, the BBA suggested that structural reform risked making the UK an international 'outlier', and urged the government to focus on measures to increase competition instead.

At the start of the ICB process the banks engaged in ad hoc cooperation to try to present a united front. In 2010, for example, the banks worked with the accountancy firm Price Waterhouse Coopers (PwC) on 'Project Oak' to detail the impact of high capital requirements on the industry prior to the launch of the ICB. Although the report was never officially released to the public, it was quietly passed on to policy makers in the Treasury, FSA, and Bank of England, and subsequently leaked to the press. The publication of the 'ICB Issues' Paper in September 2010, which included the option of breaking up large banks, imposing a full split between retail and investment activities, and a ban on proprietary trading, caused consternation in the banking industry and triggered a concerted lobbying effort. Following the ICB Interim Report in January 2011, which expressed a preference for retail bank ringfencing, the industry commissioned a report from Oliver Wyman estimating the cost of ringfencing to be £12–15bn—based on the predicted impact of increased bank funding costs (Treanor 2011). The headline figure was used by industry to reinforce the perceived threat that structural reform posed to lending in the real economy, but was robustly challenged by financial regulators. The banks also worked closely with the large professional services firms, leveraging their analytical skills and perceived 'objectivity' by commissioning them to undertake research on the costs of banking reform.

The banking industry sought to circumvent the ICB process by directing its lobbying efforts towards ministers and senior officials who were known to be more sympathetic to their concerns about competitiveness. Prime Minister David Cameron was viewed as particularly receptive to industry arguments, telling ministers that it was 'time to stop bashing the banks', and believed to favour higher capital requirements over structural reform (James 2018). Following intense lobbying of No. 10, senior officials sought to broker a peace deal between the ICB, government, and industry to forestall a public confrontation, ease tensions within the coalition government, and facilitate early privatization of the banks. Following warnings from a regulatory team seconded from Deloitte to advise Vince Cable, senior Liberal Democrats (including Deputy Prime Minister Nick Clegg) agreed to end their push for swift implementation of banking reform to prevent damaging the fragile economic recovery. Soon afterwards, turmoil in the financial markets linked to the euro area crisis, just prior to the publication of the ICB Final Report in September 2011, led the 'Quad' (of Cameron, Osborne, Clegg, and Cable) to agree to legislate on banking reform, but to delay implementation until after the next election.

The Chancellor, George Osborne, together with senior Treasury officials, were viewed as more open-minded on the question of structural reform and keen to protect the competitiveness of the City of London. But they were primarily concerned to ensure that the ICB's recommendations would be 'workable', and reassured industry that changes would not be implemented if they were too 'extreme' (Interview 5). The Treasury also pushed to delay implementation to 2019 to align with the timetable for the Basel III Accord. On occasion, the Treasury allied with specific banks to try to shape the debate. In the case of Lloyds Bank, for example, it urged the ICB to rethink its initial recommendation that it sell off more than the 600 branches it was required to do under EU rules following its merger with HBOS (see below); while encouraging the bank to demonstrate 'enlightened self-interest' by coming up with a compromise figure (James 2018). On occasion, Treasury officials also allied with industry to push back against pressure from the Bank of England. For example, the Chancellor allied with Business Secretary Vince Cable, a long-time champion of the mutual sector, to resist regulators' efforts to force Nationwide to hold more capital (Parker et al. 2013). During the legislative process, the Treasury also canvassed the support of Standard Chartered to secure safeguards aimed at constraining the power of bank supervisors over the implementation of the ringfencing rules (Interview 12).

As a private company owned solely by the government, UKFI also played an important role in counselling ministers on the impact of banking reform.

With responsibility for managing the government's stake in the banking industry, UKFI acted to protect the interests of the bailed-out banks (Lloyds Bank and RBS). It was critical of the ICB for creating uncertainty and delaying the privatization of the state's holdings in the banks; and strongly cautioned against imposing any further restrictions that would make them less attractive to future investors. The investment fund industry added further pressure, as firms with stakes in UKFI-controlled banks—including Fidelity, Schroders, Investec, Standard Life, Landsdowne, Algebris, and Legal and General—warned government against punitive reforms.

Once the government had made its support for the ICB's recommendations known, however, this strategy was undermined by the emergence of industry divisions. As reform threatened to impact on bank business models in different ways, their ability to speak collectively was undermined as firms had powerful incentives to lobby separately. In short, this meant opposing reforms which threatened their commercial interests, but quietly supporting those that would not in order to try to secure specific concessions. As one bank lobbyist explained, 'structural reform is so closely tied to business models that it's an issue on which individual institutions necessarily have to represent themselves' (Interview 14). Henceforth the banks sought to differentiate themselves as much as possible, staking a claim to being genuinely different from the others and therefore deserving of special treatment.

Broadly speaking, the sector divided into two camps (James 2018). Those banks with large investment operations—HSBC, Barclays, Standard Chartered, and RBS—faced the highest adjustment costs from ringfencing. For Barclays and RBS, the reforms threatened to increase significantly the costs of separately funding their investment banking operations, while for HSBC the prospect of complying with new loss absorbency rules at group level was highly problematic because of its large overseas assets.

Given the large size of the government's shareholding, RBS kept a deliberately low public profile during the ICB process, but made its opposition to structural reform known privately and was the only bank to provide an estimate of the financial benefit it derived from combining retail and investment banking. By contrast, HSBC and Barclays, having avoided direct taxpayer-funded support, could afford to be far more vocal in their defence of universal banking. For example, HSBC argued that the government did not understand the wider value of investment banking in the economy, and warned that splitting banks would exacerbate risk by reducing diversification in the sector, and would stifle growth by reducing the supply of credit. Although the UK's universal banks were unified in their opposition to ringfencing, divisions soon emerged over where the ringfence should be drawn: while Barclays and RBS wanted a 'narrow' ringfence limited to retail deposits, HSBC (and Lloyds Bank) preferred a wider ringfence to include retail deposits, payment systems, and small business lending (Goff and Jenkins 2011).

By contrast, Lloyds Bank and the UK subsidiary of Santander, together with new challenger banks, were relatively relaxed about the prospect of structural reform because most of their business promised to fall within the ringfence. Santander's main priority was to ensure that it could still provide risk management products from within the ringfence to enable it to continue expanding its commercial operations in the UK. Lloyds Bank decided to come out publicly in favour of ringfencing from the start in an effort to restore its reputation with policy makers. The decision was a deliberate attempt to try to ensure that the ICB agenda remained firmly focused on structural reform, rather than competition, so as to avoid being required to sell off a larger portion of its retail business than necessary under EU rules (James 2018). Similarly, the building society sector—led by Nationwide—supported ringfencing because it would potentially level the playing field with the UK's largest universal banks.

The main financial trade association, the BBA, articulated the preferences of its largest members (HSBC and Barclays) and came out strongly against reform, arguing that it risked doing irreparable damage to the international competitiveness of the City. Similarly, the CBI opposed structural reform on the grounds that it risked choking off the economic recovery by imposing new costs on retail banks, forcing them to de-leverage, and reducing lending to firms. Hence, CBI Director John Cridland argued that 'taking action at this moment—this moment of growth peril, which weakens the ability of banks in Britain to provide the finance that businesses need to grow—is just, to me, barking mad' (Curtis 2011). He later added that ringfencing was driven more by politics than by building 'safer banks for a safer economy' (Jenkins et al. 2011b). The CBI also echoed the concerns of large manufacturers about the detrimental impact of ringfencing on the availability of trade finance from UK banks, criticizing the ICB for being out of step with international initiatives and risking driving companies away.

But the wider business community was far from unified. Conversely, the Federation of Small Business (FSB) and the British Chambers of Commerce (BCC) supported structural reform on the grounds that reducing financial speculation and risk taking by banks might increase lending to business. For example, FSB Chairman John Walker wrote to the Prime Minister in 2011 urging the government to push ahead with ringfencing as soon as possible to reorient incentive structures in banks so as to strengthen support for SMEs. Later, a joint letter between the FSB, BCC, and Institute of Directors suggested that the ICB reforms did not go far enough in promoting competition in the financial sector (Moules 2011). In contrast to the CBI, these views represented the more domestically oriented SME sector which was more concerned about economic and financial stability.

We argue that these divisions fatally weakened the capacity of UK industry to prevent the framing of the financial crisis as being caused by TBTF banks, fuelled by the rapid expansion of high-risk market-trading activities in large universal banks. Consequently, this created an opportunity for other policy actors to frame the issue on their own terms.

The pro-banking reform coalition

A second feature of competitive financial power that limited the influence of UK banks was the mobilization of a disparate coalition of elected officials and senior regulators that championed structural reform. At the political level, the Liberal Democrats provided a constant source of political pressure from within the Conservative-led coalition government. The Liberal Democrats were under pressure from their own activists to act tough with the banks, and structural reform was viewed by the party leadership as an issue through which to differentiate themselves clearly from the Conservatives, who dominated the government. Business Secretary Vince Cable, the Liberal Democrats' leading figure on banking reform, was a firm supporter of breaking up the largest banks and separating their retail and investment operations, and regularly intervened to maintain the salience of the TBTF issue.

Following Ed Miliband's election as Labour leader in September 2010, the main opposition party's position on banking reform also gradually hardened. Miliband's attacks on so-called 'predatory capitalism' led the party to call for limits on bankers' bonuses and the introduction of a tough new industry code of conduct, and it played an important role in mobilizing parliamentary support for structural separation. Following a series of banking scandals in 2012, Miliband went further and called for the largest UK banks to be forcibly downsized through the sale of 400 branches, and the imposition of a cap on market size (Parker and Goff 2014).

The most important source of support for banking reform came from financial regulators in the newly strengthened Bank of England. At the start of 2010, however, this support appeared unlikely as senior regulators were as divided on the issue as elected officials. FSA Chairman Adair Turner was cautious about the need for structural reform, warning that it would be difficult in practice for banks to separate commercial from speculative activities (Turner 2009). But scarred from the experience of having to bail out the banking sector, the Bank of England Governor, Mervyn King, became a devout convert to the cause of structural reform, framing it as a solution to the challenge of banks that had become 'too-important-to-fail'. The Bank's shift in preference certainly reflected learning on the part of its senior leadership in international settings, such as the Basel Committee (Baker 2013b). But the Bank's demand for structural reforms beyond anything planned in the US or Europe can only be explained as a result of domestic dynamics.

During 2009, the Bank of England intervened to shape the banking reform debate. For example, the Governor openly criticized the Labour government's proposals to strengthen the role of the FSA, complaining that the Bank would be unable to discharge its statutory responsibility for maintaining financial stability if all it could do was 'issue sermons and organise burials' (King 2009, p. 9). Furthermore, following the Conservatives' strong performance in the 2009 European Parliament elections, senior Bank officials held several meetings with the Shadow Treasury team to discuss how the central bank's role could be overhauled following the election (Hungin and James 2018). The Conservative victory in May 2010 gave the Bank the upper hand as the coalition government confirmed the party's pledge to scrap the FSA. In the months that followed, the Governor played an important role in the decision to establish the ICB, advising the new Chancellor, George Osborne, on the membership of the commission, and recommending that it should be chaired by a former senior Bank of England official, Sir John Vickers.

Emboldened by its strengthened supervisory and regulatory powers, the Bank of England intervened to cultivate wider political support for change and to hold the government to account on banking reform. Adopting a hawkish position on TBTF made sense from the central bank's perspective. For example, it helped the Bank to restore some credibility after the crisis and to show 'a bit of muscle' with respect to its new macroprudential powers (Jenkins et al. 2011a). This led Bank regulators to impose some of the highest bank capital requirements in the world on UK banks. Specifically, they were forced to comply with a higher leverage ratio of 3 per cent, years ahead of the Basel III standards. In a particularly outspoken intervention, this led Business Secretary Vince Cable to refer to the 'capital Taliban' inside the central bank, while a Treasury official referred to 'jihadist' elements for forcing banks to comply early with the leverage ratio (Parker et al. 2013). But King argued that raising capital requirements alone, as advocated by former Labour Chancellor, Alistair Darling, and the outgoing Chairman of the FSA, Lord Adair Turner, was woefully inadequate. Instead, the Governor advocated a return to 'narrow banking' to underpin financial stability, requiring a full split between retail and investment banks based on the 1929 US Glass–Steagall Act (James 2018). Structural reform also reduced the risk and associated costs of future supervisory failure, for which the Bank was now ultimately responsible. It argued that restricting the size and activities of the largest banks would facilitate wider cultural change in banking supervision, making the process much simpler and more robust (PCBS 2013b).

Throughout the ICB process, the Bank of England lobbied publicly and privately to hold the government's 'feet to the fire' on banking reform (Interview 16). It regularly provided advice to the commissioners during private sessions, arguing that the inadequacy of international rules on bank capital (agreed in Basel III) necessitated a return to 'narrow banking'. Research produced by the Director of Financial Stability, Andy Haldane, estimating the implicit subsidy to the banking industry, was also important in strengthening the negotiating hand of policy makers and persuading the banks to adopt a more constructive attitude. In the run-up to the publication of the ICB Interim Report, Governor King and Deputy

Governor Tucker intervened to criticize the pernicious influence of bank lobbying as a warning to government not to cave in to industry pressure. Similarly, Robert Jenkins, an external member of the FPC, attacked industry for being 'intellectually dishonest and potentially damaging' (Masters and Goff 2011). Following the publication of the ICB Final Report, the Bank's new FPC (chaired by King himself) issued its own interim recommendations urging the government to implement the Vickers recommendations in full (Bank of England 2011).

The financial industry was frustrated in its efforts to counter the Bank's influence because it was viewed as highly effective at developing authoritative arguments to counter lobbyists' claims:

> It's very, very frustrating arguing against someone like [Andrew] Haldane because people take anything the Bank says as gospel, even when it's pretty contentious... He's very good at making a popular line of argument that newspapers can pick up, and they will use the same phrases again and again for months. We've dismally failed to counter that. (Interview 13)

By forcefully advocating radical policy change, and by staging a series of public interventions to raise awareness of the issue, financial regulators pressured the government not to cave in to industry lobbying and effectively reduced its room for manoeuvre. Although the ICB stopped well short of adopting the return to 'narrow banking' that King advocated, the Bank was successful in shaping the agenda and anchoring expectations towards meaningful separation. As one senior banker acknowledged, 'the more hawkish he [King] is, the less dovish the other camp has the room to be' (Jenkins et al. 2011a).

Finally, consumer groups also played a significant agenda-setting role in the run-up to the creation of the ICB. In particular, the consumer group *Which?* Convened its own Future of Banking Commission in 2009 which brought together a number of experienced politicians to propose reforms to the industry, enabling it to accumulate a wealth of expertise and credibility on the subject (FBC 2009). Its proposal that the core lending and deposit functions of UK banks should be 'ringfenced' placed the policy option firmly on the agenda and was influential in framing the thinking of the ICB. In January 2011, the ICB Interim Report referred to the subsidiarization or 'ringfencing' of retail banks as the commission's preferred option, justified as a form of *ex ante* separation designed to facilitate bank resolution. Unlike in the US, however, we argue that consumer groups were notably less important during the later stages of the process. Being much smaller and less well-resourced than their counterparts in Washington, consumer advocates complained about a lack of access to both the ICB and the Treasury, and had to fight to make their voice heard (James 2018). They were also hampered by disagreements that emerged between different groups over the benefits to consumers of breaking up the largest banks.

In short, financial power in the UK was constrained by the mobilization of a disparate coalition of pro-banking reform actors at the height of the crisis. This was led principally by senior regulators in the Bank of England, allied with key figures within government, prominent members of parliament, academic experts, and non-business groups (in particular, small businesses and consumers) that advocated the structural separation of retail and investment banking. In doing so, they were able to mount a significant challenge to industry's defence of universal banking and reframe the crisis around TBTF banks.

5. The Banking Reform Bill

The ICB's Final Report in September 2011 called for sweeping changes to the structure of the UK's largest universal banks. Its headline recommendation was that banks' retail activities should henceforth be placed in a separate and 'operationally separable' ringfenced subsidiary. Retail activities were defined as 'the taking of deposits from, and provision of overdrafts to, ordinary individuals and small and medium-sized enterprises (SMEs)' (ICB 2011b, p. 11). The report specified that a wide range of services would not be permitted within the ringfence, including: services to non-EEA customers, services (other than payments services) resulting in exposure to financial customers, 'trading book' activities, services relating to secondary markets activity (including the purchases of loans or securities), and derivatives trading (except as necessary for the retail bank prudently to manage its own risk) (ICB 2011b, p. 11). Subject to limits on wholesale funding of retail operations, other banking services—including taking deposits from customers other than individuals and SMEs, and lending to large companies outside the financial sector—would be permitted (but not required) within the ringfence. The ICB recommended that the ringfenced subsidiary 'should meet regulatory requirements for capital, liquidity, funding and large exposures on a standalone basis', and that the permitted extent of its relationships with the wider banking group 'should be no greater than regulators generally allow with third parties, and should be conducted on an arm's length basis' (ICB 2011b, p. 270). Finally, the ICB report also called for the imposition of stringent new capital rules. It specified that ringfenced banks should hold an additional 'ringfence capital buffer', taking total CET1 capital up to 10 per cent; and that both the ringfenced and non-ringfenced parts of the bank should hold additional loss-absorbing capital of 7–10 per cent, in the form of bail-in bonds or contingent convertible bonds.

Although the ringfencing reforms threatened to impose substantial costs on UK banks, the final report sought to mitigate the impact on the international competitiveness of the City. For example, the ringfencing of all UK retail banking activities included both British and foreign-owned firms, thereby preventing the latter from gaining a competitive advantage and undermining the economic case for large UK banks moving their headquarters abroad. On capital, two factors served to ameliorate the imposition of higher requirements. First, to compensate for the fact that smaller banks were to be disproportionately affected by higher capital rules, the 'ringfence buffer' varied between zero and 3 per cent, depending on the size of the bank. For the largest UK banks, the additional buffer would require them to hold core equity tier-1 capital equal to 10 per cent of RWAs, in line with Swiss banks and the ratio expected to be recommended by international regulators for global SIFIs. Second, the ICB sought to ensure that the UK's non-ringfenced banking activities would remain on a level playing field internationally by not imposing additional capital requirements above and beyond those in Basel III and CRD IV. More controversially, however, it did propose a higher leverage ratio of 4 per cent, above the international/EU minimum.

The ICB recommendations heralded a major shake-up of the industry and promised to introduce one of the toughest bank regulatory regimes in the world (Gambacorta and van Rixtel 2013). Significantly, the ICB considered recommending a version of the Volcker Rule. However, although this had support from some senior Conservative ministers, it was ruled out by Sir John Vickers at an early stage on the grounds that it would impact less on UK banks and was too complex to implement given the problem of trying to differentiate and police the boundary between legitimate market-making activities and speculative proprietary trading. Vickers also cited the risk that banning proprietary trading would simply cause it to move to the less regulated parts of the financial system, such as the shadow banking sector (Mustoe 2013). The commission also considered non-structural alternatives to ringfencing, such as simply imposing a core equity tier-1 ratio of 20 per cent across the board, but favoured lower requirements combined with structural reform to facilitate other objectives, such as bank resolution. Finally, the option of ringfencing investment banking operations, as proposed by the EU Liikanen Expert Group, was ruled out as too costly. More fundamentally, the ICB argued that it would contradict the overarching objective to make it easier for large banks to fail by perversely making investment banks 'safer' (ICB 2011b, p. 308).

Despite fierce opposition from the UK's largest banks, the Chancellor had little choice but to endorse the ringfencing recommendations in his Mansion House Speech in June 2011. In September 2011, the banking reform process was handed back to the Treasury. In drafting the final legislation to implement ringfencing, officials conducted a series of consultations with industry stakeholders. Having lost the broader political argument about structural reform, the banks recognized that their ability to influence policy lay in shaping the final design of the ringfence. The bulk of their lobbying effort—around 80–90 per cent according to one lobbyist—was therefore devoted to targeting Treasury officials during the post-ICB process (James 2018).

The Treasury consultation process differed in three fundamental respects from the ICB. First, engagement with industry was less structured and more informal, allowing the banks to exploit regular contacts and existing relationships to push back against the reforms. Second, the process was less insulated from elected officials. Because the banks enjoyed greater influence in government than with an independent body, they viewed the Treasury process as an opportunity to dilute the ICB recommendations. Third, officials' lack of resources and expertise meant that the Treasury was highly dependent on private information and had little basis for assessing its credibility. As a result, the Treasury process had less capacity to resist industry lobbying, or to assess claims about the costs of structural reform. This shifted the balance of power back to the banks, encouraging them to gear up their lobbying efforts and to push for important policy concessions to roll back the impact of the reforms.

HSBC was able to exert more influence in the Treasury consultation process than any other bank for two reasons. First, the bank launched an internal review on moving its head office to Hong Kong, an exercise designed to signal that its threat to disinvest from the UK was a credible one. Second, the bank invested heavily in undertaking high-quality research to make rigorous submissions, which policy makers recognized as persuasive. Third, HSBC was defiant in substance but far less strident in style, preferring to build quiet alliances in an effort to shape the agenda. As one lobbyist explained, 'HSBC were head and shoulders above everyone else given that they had the most solid business model, so they're taken seriously and listened to' (Interview 10).

HSBC's primary concern was how functional ringfencing in the UK would map onto its business model based on geographical subsidiarization, given the huge importance of East Asian business to the bank. Realizing that their message was not getting through, in January 2011 HSBC and Barclays enlisted the support of a wider range of stakeholders at the World Economic Forum in Davos to bolster the case against full separation. In particular, they sought to exploit the structural power of fund managers and investors whose confidence the government needed in order eventually to privatize RBS and Lloyds Bank (Jenkins et al. 2011b). A senior regulator acknowledged that the UK's two largest banks were particularly influential at the start of the process: 'Amongst the banks, Barclays and HSBC were really leading the charge and were very vocal in defending the universal bank model. ... HSBC are intelligent and Barclays are very professional' (Interview 15).

Once the ICB had disbanded, HSBC joined forces with Barclays, Santander, and the CBI in a concerted effort to persuade regulators to permit the sale of simple derivative products, such as interest rate and currency swaps, from within the ringfence (James 2018). It also sought the exemption of overseas assets from group-level loss absorbency (PLAC) requirements, a carve-out which would specifically benefit global banks like HSBC which generate a large proportion of their revenues from outside the UK (Masters et al. 2011). Their combined efforts paid dividends as both concessions were eventually granted by the Treasury. In the case of capital, for example, the Chancellor conceded that additional requirements would not apply to the non-UK operations of British banks, provided that they could demonstrate that it would not pose a threat to UK taxpayers through detailed resolution plans.

Over time, however, Barclays' influence on structural reform began to wane. In 2010, the bank's CEO, Bob Diamond, was an outspoken critic of ringfencing and claimed that the bank might be forced to relocate its investment operations (BarCap) to New York. Yet, this defiance was undermined when the bank was directly implicated in the manipulation of Libor in 2012. The reputational damage that this inflicted, culminating with the resignation of Diamond, undermined Barclays' credibility in the eyes of policy makers. In a sign of Barclays' waning influence, its attempt to corral industry into supporting 'operational subsidiarization' as an alternative to ringfencing ended in failure due to a lack of cross-industry support (James 2018). With its threat to leave London now widely dismissed, the bank indicated to regulators that it was ready to accept some form of ringfencing.

Lloyds Bank's decision to back ringfencing from the start of the ICB process was an attempt to head off the possibility that the Business Secretary Vince Cable would launch a full-scale competition inquiry, which might lead to the bank being forcibly broken up. To this end, Lloyds Bank sought to develop practical proposals aimed at benefiting consumers by strengthening competition in the sector—such as the seven-day current account switching service. As an official noted, 'Lloyds were quite helpful. They were more open because they basically said, we know all of our skeletons. So that was helpful in the sense that they were a bit more pliable ... and can't misbehave' (Interview 9). These efforts eventually paid off as Treasury officials backed down on the ICB's recommendation to force Lloyds Bank to sell off up to 900 branches in return for reducing its share of current accounts (James 2018).

As the highest-profile bank failure in the UK, RBS's voice was greatly diminished. Although it commissioned independent research detailing the significant costs of ringfencing on its business, RBS struggled to advance a credible position and sought to leverage its influence through the main trade associations. Hence, it was noted that 'RBS and Lloyds have had their wings clipped a little bit in terms of criticizing government policy ... So they were probably less vocal than they perhaps would have been if they were still in completely private hands' (Interview 10). The reputational damage inflicted on the two banks forced them to rely on the political capital wielded by the other banks: 'There were points that HSBC and Standard Chartered could make that would have been unseemly if made by us or Lloyds or Barclays ... We were thrilled that [they] pitched in because we weren't in a position to make strong arguments' (Interview 13).

The other large banks—Santander and Standard Chartered—did not receive direct government support and so their reputations remained largely intact. But the Spain-headquartered Santander was slow to engage in the process owing to its retail-based business model and, as a relatively new entrant to the UK market, the under-developed nature of its connections with UK policy makers. Standard Chartered CEO Peter Sands was initially outspoken in his criticism of banking reform, despite the bank not having much of a retail bank presence in the UK, and briefly threatened to shift his bank's operations to Singapore. Having secured an early exemption for private banking from the ringfence, and later a *de minimis* threshold for UK bank assets that excluded all its operations, Standard Chartered retreated to the sidelines.

The only building society to engage directly in the process—Nationwide—welcomed the prospect of bank ringfencing, but was concerned about the impact of higher capital requirements on the mutual sector. With important cheerleaders in government, the building society proved instrumental in getting the ICB to consider the Building Societies Act as a potential blueprint of how bank ringfencing might work in practice. It was also successful in leading industry efforts to persuade the Treasury and FPC to reduce the proposed new leverage ratio from 4 per cent (as recommended by the ICB) to 3 per cent (in line with international standards) (James 2018).

The credibility of the main industry association, the BBA, was fatally undermined by the Libor rate-rigging scandal, in which it was directly implicated. Most bank lobbyists acknowledged that the BBA had 'zero credibility' and had been 'reputationally damaged', with the result that 'some authorities don't take them very seriously' (Interview 13). Indeed, the impact of the Libor and other rigging scandals was greater in the UK than in France, Germany or the Netherlands, despite the imposition of record fines in each of these countries on banks participating in the rate manipulation. More generally, the influence of all the main UK financial associations (including TheCityUK and the Association for Financial Markets in Europe) was constrained by deep divisions between the banks over ringfencing, commercial sensitivity which prevented the banks sharing information about the impact on business models, and the fact that the ICB process favoured analytical arguments over traditional political lobbying. As one lobbyist noted, the ICB 'demanded a level of technical expertise which the traditional trade associations simply did not have' (Interview 6).

Following the Libor scandal, the BBA (together with Barclays and RBS) sought to keep out of the spotlight and leveraged their influence through the wider business community, notably the CBI. The latter's claim that structural reform might damage the real economy resonated with ministers, and was given added credence by using high-profile manufacturers, such as Rolls-Royce, to front the lobbying effort. For example, one leading bank chose to work closely with the CBI because it was 'a more powerful force' and a more 'credible voice', because of its ability to 'represent what is in the best interests of British industry as a whole, not just a few banks' (Interview 11). Leveraging its influence with sympathetic officials in No. 10 and the Treasury, the CBI was able to secure two important concessions: first, that banks would be able to continue providing trade finance from within the ringfence; and second, delaying implementation of ringfencing until 2019 to minimize the impact on the economic recovery (James 2018).

During the Treasury consultation process, individual banks were therefore able to secure specific policy concessions to lessen the burden of structural reform. These helped to further mitigate the implications of the ICB reforms for the UK's largest global banks and minimized the risk that they would undermine the international competitiveness of the City of London. Nonetheless, there was no substantial rollback of the ringfencing proposals. As we explain below, this was because of political resistance from prominent parliamentarians and senior regulators during the final stages of the legislative process.

6. Venue shifting 2: the Parliamentary Commission on Banking Standards

A second example of venue shifting unexpectedly emerged at the end of the banking reform process. Although the deteriorating global economic outlook dampened the Treasury's enthusiasm for reform, the case for structural reform was boosted in mid-2012 by a series of high-profile financial scandals involving the manipulation of interest and exchange rate swaps, and Libor. European Commission and national investigations into this manipulation resulted eventually in significant fines for a number of EU-headquartered banks. Importantly, the UK-headquartered Barclays bank was at the centre of the rate manipulation scandal which—given both the relatively large size of UK bank losses since the outbreak of the international financial crisis and the level of government assistance—ensured that the British banking sector remained firmly in the public spotlight.

The scandals compounded public hostility towards the banks, and threatened to reopen divisions within the coalition government. The opinion of most MPs on structural reform had now hardened, with polls showing a clear majority of MPs in both main parties backing a full split (Stacey 2012). There was also mounting pressure from senior Liberal Democrats (notably Deputy Prime Minister, Nick Clegg and Business Secretary, Vince Cable) to reopen talks on the Vickers recommendations and to retract recently granted concessions to industry over interest and exchange rate swaps. In an effort to limit politicization at a critical stage in the reform process, the government again resorted to venue shifting. This led to the establishment of the PCBS in September 2012, chaired by Conservative MP Andrew Tyrie, to consider professional standards and culture in the banking industry. The commission, the first such inquiry since 1913, had far-reaching implications for banking regulation. Crucially, under pressure from MPs, the government later delegated the PCBS responsibility for completing pre-legislative scrutiny of the Banking Reform Bill (HM Government 2013).

The PCBS was characterized by many of the same features as the ICB. First, although the commission was composed of parliamentarians rather than outside 'experts', its notional independence and insulation from both industry and government was assisted by the highly respected nature of its membership—which included the former Chancellor Lord Lawson, former Cabinet Secretary Lord Turnbull, and the Archbishop of Canterbury Justin Welby. Second, the PCBS accumulated substantial technical expertise on the banking reform process. It was greatly assisted in this respect by regulators in the Bank of England who supplied it with much-needed analysis about the likely implications of various ringfencing proposals. Indeed, PCBS Chair Andrew Tyrie openly acknowledged the advice of the Bank in how to strengthen the ringfence: 'It's clear that the Bank remains extremely concerned that the effect of the Vickers proposals could be diluted over time and that statutory protection against that is desirable' (Jenkins and Jones 2012). The PCBS was also able to gather testimonies from experts to directly counter bank claims, such as threats to quit the UK (see also Macartney 2014a; Bell and Hindmoor 2015b). As former ICB commissioner Martin Taylor testified:

> I do not believe that we will have wholesale moving of banks' head offices, which is what we were worried about two or three years ago, simply because pretty much the entire world is going in the same direction. I work in Switzerland and spend half my time there. I remember in 2009–10, all the people in the City were saying they wanted to move to Switzerland, and all the Swiss banks wanted to move to London. Each of them was ignorant about the changes taking place on the other side. (PCBS 2012, p. 46)

Further doubt on the credibility of banks' claims was provided by Michael Cohrs, external member of the interim FPC:

> Generally speaking, it is really hard—just as it is really hard to separate a bank — for a bank to move its jurisdiction. That is before you get into the cultural issues, which, for a bank, should be very important. So I am dismissive of bankers when they tell me—I used to be one of them—'If you don't give us a good regime, we will go elsewhere.' It is rubbish. (PCBS 2012, p. 46)

Third, the PCBS engaged in conflict expansion by launching a lengthy consultation exercise with a broad spectrum of policy stakeholders. Like the ICB, it relied on formal select committee-style hearings in which senior bank executives were scrutinized by MPs. This provided a public setting to expose and resist industry lobbying. For example, PCBS member Lord Lawson admonished the banks for trying to water down the ICB proposals: 'They [the banks] are anxious to appear reasonable and good citizens in the eye of public opinion, but that is not uppermost in their mind when they are speaking to ministers' (Parker 2013). The commission also provided a high-profile platform for officials to reopen fundamental questions about the scope and scale of structural reform. For example, Governor King used the hearings to reiterate his support for full separation, arguing that ringfencing would lead to ongoing negotiations between regulators and banks about where lines ought to be drawn, and that 'there is only one winner in that, and that will be a very bad outcome' (PCBS 2012, p. 63). The Executive Director for Prudential Regulation at the Bank of England, Andrew Bailey, also cautioned that the ringfence might be undermined by 'the force of lobbying and other pressures' (PCBS 2012, p. 36). Moreover, the decision of former Chairman of the Federal Reserve, Paul Volcker, to testify before the PCBS also emboldened proponents of structural separation. Notably, Volcker urged UK policy makers to heed the lessons of how the Glass–Steagall restrictions had gradually been eroded, warning that ringfences 'tend to be permeable over time' (PCBS 2012, p. 43).

Fourth, the commission's authority enabled it to issue policy recommendations which the government could not afford to ignore. The PCBS preliminary report issued in December 2012 was stinging in its criticism. It argued that the Banking Reform Bill 'fell far short of what is required', and that the height and depth of the ringfence was inadequately defined in primary legislation (PCBS 2012). To address this, the report called for the ringfence to be fully 'electrified' by giving regulators the power to break up banks for breaching the rules. This contradicted the text of the bill which had instead required a time-consuming system of warnings and reprimands. According to the Commission, tougher rules were justified as necessary to prevent banks from constantly 'gaming the system':

> All history tells us that banks will be at the ringfence like foxes to a chicken coop unless they are incentivized not to do so. On past evidence, they will test it nonstop and try to persuade politicians to alter it in their favour. Electrification is therefore essential to ensure that the banks comply not just with the rules of the ringfence but also with the spirit. (Stacey 2012)

Alluding to the cyclical nature of industry lobbying, the PCBS Chair, Andrew Tyrie, urged the government to 'legislate now for more benign economic circumstances, when banks are under less intense scrutiny ... [and] politicians will be particularly susceptible to lobbying and the integrity of the ringfence will be most at risk' (Tyrie 2013).

The Conservative Prime Minister and Chancellor were highly reluctant to endorse the PCBS's call for ringfence electrification on the grounds that this would cause further uncertainty at a time when they were trying to 'reset' relations with the industry. But with several members of the commission threatening to table amendments in the House of Lords to strengthen the bill, the government reluctantly decided to back down. It therefore agreed to amend the legislation to grant regulators additional 'reserve powers' to break up banks forcibly if they breached the ringfencing rules—albeit on a case-by-case rather than industry-wide basis.

A follow-up report from the PCBS in March 2013 included further measures to police the ringfence and to ensure that ringfenced entities are structured as empowered sister companies, not subsidiaries. Its final report, published in June 2013, contained further recommendations, such as giving the Bank of England's new FPC the power to raise leverage ratios, reforms to corporate governance, changes to remuneration structures, and a new criminal offence for reckless misconduct (PCBS 2013a). While most of these changes were later amended in the Banking Reform Bill, the Treasury successfully resisted pressure from the PCBS (and the Bank of England) to raise the leverage ratio from 3 per cent (in line with international standards) to 4 per cent (as endorsed by the ICB).

Effective implementation

In contrast to the US case, where the issue of banking reform remained bitterly contested, the implementation of bank structural reform in the UK proceeded relatively unencumbered. We argue that this was for two reasons. First, venue shifting to specialist groups in the UK context served to depoliticize structural reform by widening consultation, building political support, and encouraging 'buy in' from stakeholders. Although banks continued to lobby regulators about the technical details of implementation, there was little incentive for policy makers to reopen the issue. Second, key pro-banking reform actors maintained pressure on the government not to backtrack on the ringfencing proposals. In particular, financial regulators in the Bank of England's PRA were empowered with a range of new macroprudential powers, and significantly enhanced regulatory and supervisory resources, giving them substantial autonomy from financial industry interests (Hungin and James 2018). As we outline below, the main features of the legislation were therefore politically and bureaucratically 'locked in'.

As attention shifted to producing the secondary legislation to enact ringfencing during 2014, banks continued to push back against the reforms. Those institutions with the smallest wholesale operations, such as Santander and Lloyds Bank, complained that they would be disproportionately hit by the new rules, while RBS warned that ringfencing would create considerable operational and legal difficulties Douglas Flint, chairman of HSBC, went further and called for a pause in the Vickers process while a Competition and Markets Authority inquiry into bank competition was completed; while former Barclays chairman, Sir David Walker, called ringfencing 'actively harmful to the UK' and urged the government to review the rules. In 2015, HSBC adopted an increasingly strident tone, threatening to sell off its retail bank and to relocate its headquarters outside the UK. These arguments were once again echoed by important voices within the business community—notably the CBI—which claimed that SMEs risked losing access to trade finance and hedging products (Fleming 2014).

The government's response was to try to include as much detail as possible in the statutory instrument to prevent the barrier between retail and investment activities being eroded over time. But the final legislation, passed in June 2014, did contain some concessions to industry. For example, the Treasury expanded the range of financial services provided by ringfenced retail banks to include simple options and trade finance. It also permitted smaller banks to borrow from ringfenced institutions provided they secured special permission from the PRA. The Treasury also published an impact assessment of ringfencing in July 2014, estimating the cost to the industry at £1.8–3.9bn each year, with an additional one-off cost of £0.5–3bn (Treasury 2014).

In October 2014, the PRA published technical details about the operation of the ringfence, which included stringent new rules governing the links permitted between ringfenced entities and other banking group members. Regulators proposed that the chair of a ringfenced bank should not hold a similar position in another group entity board, and that an executive on the board of a ringfenced bank would not be permitted to hold other posts in a bank that conducts activities meant to happen outside the fence. The ringfenced bank should also have its own risk, nomination, audit, and remuneration non-executive board committees. Banks were asked to submit a preliminary plan of how they expected to structure their operations by January 2015.

The banks responded by proposing to adopt different strategies for compliance with ringfencing. For example, Barclays and HSBC planned to place as little activity as possible in the ringfenced entity so as to lower the cost of funding their other operations. In the case of Barclays, around 25 per cent of the bank's RWAs would be placed inside the ringfence, while for HSBC it would be only 9 per cent (Arnold et al. 2015). HSBC also went further and announced plans to separate its retail and investment activities physically by relocating its ringfenced operations from London to Birmingham. By contrast, Lloyds Bank, RBS, and Santander sought to establish the widest ringfenced bank possible: this would hold 93 per cent, 80 per cent, and 90 per cent of each bank's RWAs respectively (Binham and Dunkley 2017). Lloyds Bank also hoped to capitalize on regulators' pledge to pursue a 'proportionate' approach to implementation, requesting an exemption from the rule requiring it to establish a separate board of directors for its ringfenced entity on the grounds that very little business would be conducted outside it. Barclays also sought a waiver from the rules by suggesting that it could structure its ringfenced bank as a wholly owned subsidiary of the rest of the group. Significantly, regulators subsequently rebuffed both requests for special treatment.

In response to increased bank lobbying, prominent figures involved with the Vickers process sought to maintain pressure on the Treasury and Bank of England to defend the new rules. For example, in June 2014, the Archbishop of Canterbury,

Justin Welby, warned that the impetus for reforming the banks was fading in the face of industry lobbying. He added that 'the elephant in the room is that banks are still too-big-to-fail', and repeated the PCBS's recommendation that the leverage ratio should be set at 4 per cent (PCBS 2013b). In a surprising intervention shortly after the passage of the Banking Reform Bill, Sir John Vickers himself suggested that, in a 'blue skies' world, core tier-1 capital ratios should be set at 20 per cent, double the level recommended by the ICB just two years earlier, and that leverage ratios should be closer to 10 per cent (Jenkins 2013a). This echoed the call from Robert Jenkins, FPC member from 2011 to 2013, for equity capital of 20 per cent in return for a moratorium on further regulation. Bank lobbying against ringfencing earned a stinging rebuke from former ICB member, Martin Taylor, who suggested that continued industry resistance showed that the rules were effective. In October 2015, Andrew Tyrie also called on the government to resist 'special pleading' from the banks and for institutions to be broken up if they tried to 'game' the rules (Fedor 2015).

UK regulators were also important in pressuring the government to increase capital requirements for the largest UK banks. In October 2014, the FPC recommended a minimum leverage ratio of 3 per cent for all PRA-regulated financial institutions from 2018, but with immediate effect for all G-SIBS. Although in line with international standards, in practical terms the level would be much higher. For a ringfenced bank, for example, the FPC noted that the additional risk-weighted buffer would increase the minimum leverage ratio to 4.05 per cent. Moreover, the PRA requested the power to impose an additional counter-cyclical leverage ratio, and supplementary leverage ratios for G-SIBs, which would potentially bring the overall ratio for the largest institutions to 4.95 per cent. Importantly, the UK ratio for large banks would therefore be significantly beyond the Basel III requirements, and in line with the level recommended by the ICB (4.06 per cent) and the ratio introduced in the US (5 per cent).

Following the national parliamentary elections in May 2015, which returned a majority Conservative government to parliament, the Chancellor sought to reset relations between regulators and the City. In his annual Mansion House speech a few week later, George Osborne argued that banking reform had established a new regulatory 'settlement', and that it was time to 'draw a line' and end the 'banker bashing' (Osborne 2015). The departure of the Liberal Democrats from government, and Martin Wheatley's unceremonious dismissal as head of the FCA shortly afterwards, emboldened the City. In the hope of persuading the new government to roll back banking reform, the industry ramped up its lobbying operations.

These ambitions were largely thwarted in October 2015 when the PRA published its consultation on final plans to implement ringfencing. These granted banks a number of moderate concessions, including the proposal that ringfenced entities should be able to cross-sell products and lend to other parts of the group (provided it was treated as a third party), and would be able to pass excess capital to their parent company in the form of dividends (Dunkley and Binham 2015). Nonetheless, banks were disappointed that the substance of banking reform was left intact. In January 2016, the Bank of England went further and confirmed that large ringfenced banks would have to hold an additional systemic risk buffer of capital—varying between 1 and 3 per cent of RWAs depending on the size of the bank. It also announced that it was considering introducing a new counter-cyclical buffer which would vary over time. Although Sir John Vickers later claimed that this was weaker than the ICB's capital recommendations—which proposed a single 3 per cent buffer for all six ringfenced banks—Deputy Governor Andrew Bailey insisted that cumulatively the new capital rules were actually tougher.

The increased regulatory burden facing UK banks was compounded by two further developments during 2016. The first was the UK's decision to withdraw from the European Union following a referendum in June 2016. Brexit had the potential to complicate structural reform greatly because it created uncertainty about whether UK banks would be able to continue to 'passport' financial services across the European Union. Without this, UK banks would have to replace branches in the EU27 with fully fledged (and separately capitalized) subsidiaries. Second, in November 2016 the European Commission issued a legislative package aimed at strengthening banking regulation. The most eye-catching proposal was that large non-EU banks—either institutions designated as systematically important by the FSB or those with assets in the EU of at least €30bn—would be required to establish an intermediate holding company for their EU-based subsidiaries. These entities would then be subject to separate capital rules on a consolidated basis, thereby 'trapping' capital in the EU27. The proposal was widely viewed as retaliation for similar measures adopted by the US, but it gained added importance as a result of Brexit (as it would now capture UK banks) and because it threatened to conflict with ringfencing requirements. Both developments potentially had profound implications for the structure and operation of UK banks, compounded by huge uncertainty about what the final shape of the regulation would be. Although banks lobbied for the 2019 deadline for the implementation of ringfencing to be pushed back, UK regulators insisted that there should be no delay.

7. Conclusion

The UK Banking Reform Bill brought about the biggest shake-up in UK banking in a generation, requiring bank retail activities to be placed in a separate and 'operationally separable' ringfenced subsidiary, and imposing some of the highest capital requirements in the world. The changes are notably at odds with the other country cases considered in this book: they are much tougher than those imposed in France, Germany, and the Netherlands; and have proven far more durable than the reform introduced in the US. How do we explain this?

Our framework points to two key factors in explaining this pattern of *durable reform*. First, we argue that institutional venue shifting was critical to the opening of a policy window on bank structural reform in the UK. The government's decision to delegate responsibility to ad hoc specialist groups redefined the terms of engagement between policy makers and the financial industry; reshaped the balance of power between competing groups for and against reform; and framed the issue around the threat that TBTF banks posed to financial stability. Importantly, we show that venue shifting took place at two separate stages of the policy process: at the agenda-setting stage, in the form of the ICB, convened between 2010 and 2011; and at the legislative scrutiny stage, through the PCBS, from 2012 to 2013. We argue that this venue shifting was pivotal in depoliticizing bank structural reform. Unlike in the case of the Netherlands, however, it did so by facilitating conflict expansion: providing a high-profile platform for a range of pro-reform authoritative voices, facilitating wider engagement with a range of societal interests, and thus curtailing the access and influence of the banking lobby. As a result, the new venues helped UK policy makers build political support for change and secure greater 'buy in' from policy stakeholders.

Second, we argue that the lobbying power of banks in the UK was constrained by the competitive nature of financial power. On the one hand, the UK financial industry was characterized by important internal divisions, forcing banks to compete with one another and thereby limiting its collective influence. On the other hand, UK banks were weakened by the emergence of a disparate coalition of pro-banking reform actors. Unlike in the US, however, this coalition was not dominated by the mobilization of 'outsider' interests, such as consumer groups or financial reform activists. On the contrary, the most prominent voices in the UK calling for stringent new rules to tackle TBTF banks came from 'insiders' within Westminster and Whitehall: namely, key government ministers, financial regulators, and members of parliament. Furthermore, these actors channelled their political influence and technical expertise through the new institutional venues established to manage the banking reform process: namely, the ICB and PCBS. As a consequence, the UK was able to make credible commitments to structural reform that remained largely unchallenged over the next decade.

6
Germany
Defending Deutsche Bank AG

1. Introduction

In May 2013, the German federal government published its final version of the Bank Separation Law—*Trennbankengesetz*—which included provisions on bank structural reform. The bank ringfence that was proposed was similar to the ringfence outlined in the draft law then being debated in France. It was considerably weaker than the structural reform adopted in the US and about to be passed in the UK. After minor amendments in the Bundestag (lower house) finance committee, the *Trennbankengesetz*—which involved a reform of the German Banking Act—was adopted in August 2013, just weeks prior to the September federal elections (German Ministry of Finance 2013).

The weakness of German structural reform is surprising for several reasons. First, given the high level of German bank losses in the context of the international financial crisis and the cost to the federal government, we might have expected tougher action to prevent or limit the investment banking activities of the country's largest banks, as in the US and the UK. Second, there was strong long-standing opposition across the German political spectrum to large bank bailouts—which had to be reluctantly pushed aside during the financial crisis (Hardie and Howarth 2009). Ringfencing the riskier trading activities of banks was, in political and academic circles, widely presented as a measure to avoid bail-outs in the future. Third, a range of high-ranking German politicians from most of the parties called explicitly for either major structural reform or other measures to tackle TBTF banking. Fourth, there was a strong ideational bias in Germany, found throughout much of the political class, against both non-bank finance and bank trading activities (Zimmerman 2010; Hardie and Howarth 2013a). Fifth, the German real economy—and notably the country's *Mittelstand* (small and medium-sized industries)—depended far more on small public law savings and cooperative banks than in the UK and France. Thus, it was less likely that the non-financial sector would align with large bank opposition to significant structural reform on the grounds that this would result in a significant cut in lending. Sixth, public law savings and cooperative banks also enjoyed more political support and protection than the largest German universal banks (Cassell 2021), which suggests a political class less receptive to the preoccupations of large banks and thus a less effective bank lobby opposed to structural reform. Finally, the great diversity of bank types in Germany, with very different funding models, balance sheets, and activities, suggests a divided bank lobby on structural reform.

The structural reform eventually adopted in Germany in August 2013 differs from the other cases examined in the book in important ways. On the one hand, the changes fell far short of the reforms adopted in the US and the UK, as well as the EU-level reform proposals of the Liikanen Group. On the other hand, the German government was not able to ignore or deflect the issue, such as by diverting attention towards other reforms, as in the case of the Netherlands. As with the French structural reform adopted in July 2013, the timing of the German reform can be seen as a deliberate attempt to pre-empt the adoption at the EU level of the Liikanen Group's reform proposals (Hardie and Macartney 2016). Also, as in France, there were important domestic political reasons for pushing ahead with structural reform in the final months of the centre-right government led by Angela Merkel prior to the September 2013 federal parliamentary elections.

In this chapter, we argue that the surprisingly weak structural reform adopted in Germany reflects two key institutional features of the German policy process. First, the German banking industry—despite its profound divisions in the three-pillar system and competing interests—was surprisingly united on the issue of structural reform, and thus was able to wield cooperative financial power to resist stringent new restrictions on trading activities. Reflecting the bank-dominated German financial system, non-bank financial interests wielded limited influence on the topic. Germany lacked France's tight interpenetration of high-ranking bureaucratic officials focused on financial issues and top bankers. However, the unified German bank lobby nonetheless maintained a privileged access to the bulk of centre-right politicians in government. Second, the policy-making and legislative process on bank structural reform involved no venue shifting. As a result, the issue of structural reform was subject to higher levels of politicization for much of the period, certainly compared to the Netherlands. Notably, this was a result of concerted political pressure from the opposition SPD.

In response, the government sought to engage in conflict contraction—carefully steering the reform agenda through existing institutional channels in an attempt to limit the ability of pro-reform groups to mobilize, and access and influence the decision-making process. To contain opposition from the three main left-wing parties—which had campaigned actively in favour of major structural reform and transformed the issue into an important element in their forthcoming campaigns for the September 2013 elections—the CDU Finance Minister, Wolfgang Schäuble, and government leadership proposed a weak version of structural reform and then accepted marginal symbolic changes to its draft law. As in France, the commitment of a number of political leaders to some form of structural reform—here in the context of looming federal parliamentary elections—created a political dynamic that encouraged the CDU-led government to adopt a weak and symbolic reform, rather than avoid national-level reform altogether as in the Netherlands. However—unlike France—in Germany a centre-right government was pushed into action on structural reform principally due to the political need to respond to detailed proposals first presented by SPD leader and former Grand Coalition Finance Minister, Peer Steinbrück.

Section 2 of this chapter summarizes both the weakness of German structural reform as well as why many observers expected a more significant reform given the promises of a range of leading politicians in the mainstream centre-right and centre-left parties in the country. Section 3 analyses the cooperative financial power that shaped German bank structural reform. Smaller public law savings and cooperative banks, which might have had a collective interest in breaking up the country's largest banks, in fact supported them on the topics of TBTF and ringfencing. Section 4 examines the absence of venue shifting on bank structural reform and the operation of the government and parliamentary venues in which structural reform was designed and debated. Section 5 examines the political, civil society, and academic mobilization on the topic of structural reform. Despite a series of scandals affecting German banks, and the efforts of left-wing parties and other groups to politicize structural reform, the centre-right government succeeded in significantly narrowing—but not completely closing—the window of opportunity for policy change.

2. The surprisingly weak German structural reform

Unlike France and the US, Germany lacked an explicit tradition of separating banking activities. However, the three-pillar German banking system in effect resulted in significant constraint on the activities of the large majority of German banks. Banks in the second and third pillars, the public law savings banks and cooperative banks, were unable to engage directly in the bulk of investment banking activities. In the first pillar, there were a number of large universal banks that had developed their market-based trading activities. The largest by a considerable margin was Deutsche Bank, which in the early 2010s had more assets linked to its trading activities than lending to corporates and households, and more assets held outwith Germany than within. However, this de facto separation of activities within the banking system had its limits. First, the central financial institutions for the cooperative banks, DZ Bank, and savings banks, Dekabank, were also universal banks that operated a range of trading activities often in the service of their linked smaller banks. Second, the regional government-owned *Landesbanken*—the central financial institutions for savings banks in the same region or regions—also engaged in a range of trading activities.

The German version of bank structural reform deviated significantly from the proposals of the Liikanen Committee (German Ministry of Finance 2013). The

Bank Separation Law applied to all credit institutions and to all companies that belonged to a group of institutions, a financial holding group, a mixed financial holding group or a financial conglomerate to which a credit institution—as defined by the EU CRR of 2013—belonged (*Trennbankengesetz*, Article 3.2; see Möslein (2013a, b) and Oppolzer (2019) for a detailed examination of the provisions of the Act). As for threshold, the German Banking Act set €100bn for the total trading portfolio and liquidity reserves of a firm on the balance sheet of the previous year (*Trennbankengesetz*, Article 3.2; see also Stubbe 2016), and a relative threshold of total trading portfolio and liquidity reserves of more than 20 per cent of the institution's balance sheet, which had to reach at least €90bn over the preceding three years. On threshold, the German law deviated significantly from the proposal of the EU's Liikanen Report. The latter recommended the separation of specific riskier activities regardless their proportion in relation to the total trading activities (Brandi and Gieseler 2013). Furthermore, Liikanen recommended that banking groups that provided significant market-making services and held large liquidity reserves due to regulatory requirements were potentially subject to ringfencing, even if their high-risk activities only accounted for a very small amount of their total trading activities. In 2016, the main German bank supervisory body, BaFin, found that eleven banks fell within the scope of the Bank Separation Law (Stubb 2016). Only one, Deutsche Bank, reached the level of global significance. Also included were: the country's third largest bank, Commerzbank; four public law *Landesbanken*—Bayern, Nord, Helaba, and Baden-Württemberg; the public law Dekabank, the universal banking arm of German savings banks; and the private DZ Bank, the country's second largest bank and the universal banking arm of German cooperative banks.

In terms of the activities that could be undertaken by the banks that met the threshold, the German Banking Act limited activities for both the ringfenced retail bank entity and the non-ringfenced trading entity. First, for banking groups above the threshold, the ringfenced entity—responsible for deposit taking and lending—was banned from conducting a number of activities altogether (*Trennbankengesetz*, Article 3.2) including: proprietary business, a certain form of proprietary trading, and lending and guarantee business with hedge funds and alternative investment funds. Proprietary business included all short-term investment activity that involved purchasing and selling of financial instruments on own account that was not proprietary trading (BaFin 2016). This included the purchase and sale of securities, money market instruments or derivatives on own account without service character, usually to benefit from 'existing or expected short-term differences between purchase and sale prices or movement of market prices, market values or interest rates' (BaFin 2016, p. 7). The German Banking Act defined four different kinds of proprietary trading, including one which was considered so risky that it was excluded altogether from the non-ringfenced entity: high-frequency trading that it was not market making. On business with hedge funds, BaFin's

Interpretive Guidance of the Bank Separation Law allowed fully collateralized lending and guarantee business with hedge funds and alternative investment funds (BaFin 2016, p. 12). This exemption to the ban on business with hedge funds was seen by BaFin to conform with the German Banking Act. However, while popular with the larger universal banks in Germany, allowing this business was politically controversial (Oppolzer 2019, p. 227).

The Bank Separation Law assigned the main German bank supervisory body, BaFin, the power to ban additional activities or to allow them only to be conducted in the non-ringfenced trading entity. BaFin was also assigned the important power of banning additional activities by banks under the size threshold. The Bank Separation Law stipulates a number of important exceptions, especially with regard to the prohibition of proprietary business by the ringfenced entity: hedging transactions (other than those with hedge funds and alternative investment funds); the management of interest rate, foreign exchange, liquidity, and credit risk of the banking group; and transactions connected with long-term investments. These exceptions had been considered problematic in terms of financial stability by a range of observers (see Schelo and Steck 2013 on hedging transactions; see Kumpan 2014 on transactions connected with long-term investments).

The financial trading (non-ringfenced) entity was similarly banned from a number of activities, including payment services and e-money business. However, beyond these activities, the Bank Separation Law was widely criticized for failing to clarify the specific activities that a financial trading entity can and cannot provide (see, for example, Möslein 2013a, b). Unlike the Liikanen Report, the Act does not even explicitly prohibit the financial trading institution from engaging in deposit and credit business. The gap in the legislation would have to be filled by subsequent interpretation (Oppolzer 2019).

The 2013 reform of the German Banking Act also included other measures that had nothing to do with structural reform. The reform introduced criminal penalties for bankers who breached essential risk management obligations, with mismanagement resulting in up to five years' imprisonment. Furthermore, as with the French law introducing structural reform, the revision of the German Banking Act included measures to implement provisions of the EU's Bank Recovery and Resolution Directive adopted in 2013 and notably the requirement that larger banks—global and national systemically important credit institutions—draw up recovery and resolution plans to help them prepare for both a crisis and potential resolution.

Thus, to summarize, the German structural reform overlapped significantly with the French structural reform and fell far short of the proposed Liikanen Group recommendations. The German Banking Act banned deposit-taking banks from engaging in a limited range of speculative transactions but only when these banks exceeded relatively high specified thresholds. Furthermore, the impact of the reform on Germany's largest banks was limited, with the ringfenced retail entity barred from engaging only in a relatively small number of proprietary trading activities. These activities could then be transferred to a legally, economically, and operationally separate entity within the banking group. There were a number of important exemptions to these activities focused on market-making activities, including securitization, which were deemed useful to financing the real economy. The French structural reform made a similar distinction, allowing all the large universal French banks to continue to engage in market-making trading activities. In Germany, as in France, the symbolic nature of the reform should be noted. The ban on proprietary trading created the impression of government action on 'speculation' without having a significant impact on banks' trading activities. Indeed, German bank proprietary trading activities had declined considerably since the international financial crisis, contributing at most 4 per cent of total trading revenues for any German bank and a tiny percentage of total bank revenues in 2013 (EU Commission 2014b; see also Hardie and Macartney 2016). In 2012, the BDB—the peak association for commercial banks—confirmed that its members had 'virtually dropped proprietary trading' (BDB 2012a, p.9, 2012b; see also HypoVereinsbank 2010; Interview 40). By allowing market-making trading activities in the ringfenced retail entity, both the German and French reforms diverged significantly from the proposals made in the Liikanen Report at the EU level and subsequently in the EU Commission's draft regulation, which called for a much more encompassing ringfence (EU Commission 2014a).

The politicization of structural reform

The weakness of the structural reform agreed in Germany can be seen as surprising given the heightened levels of politicization that characterized the issue of bank separation. The centre-left opposition moved strategically to mobilize public opinion on the issue of structural reform in the lead-up to the September 2013 federal parliamentary elections. The centre-right—CDU–CSU–FDP, 'black–yellow'—government was thus likely forced to move more quickly with structural reform than it had otherwise intended. The political dynamics of German reform were both similar to but distinct from the politics of the French reform. As in France, the leader of the centre-left, here Peer Steinbrück, launched structural reform proposals with an eye to upcoming elections (Steinbrück 2012). However, Steinbrück's thirty-page proposal was considerably more detailed than François Hollande's electoral programme promises earlier in the year. In France, a Socialist-led government drafted legislation on very limited structural reform which mollified opposition on the centre-right and contained opposition on the left. In Germany, a centre-right government drafted legislation on very limited structural reform. Thus, there remained potential for considerable political mobilization on the issue of structural reform on the part of the German SPD, Greens and the far left Die Linke, especially given that the government's proposed reform fell far short of Steinbrück's more ambitious reform and given the potential gains to be had by the left in manipulating the issue in the context of the 2013 federal election campaign. Nonetheless, the German centre-right government succeeded in containing conflict on the issue.

German Chancellor Angela Merkel was more cautious on the issue of structural reform than many in her CDU party. In the aftermath of the international finance crisis, she repeatedly announced her preoccupation with TBTF banks: 'One of the tasks that we will dedicate ourselves to and that is also being taken into consideration elsewhere is how to make sure that banks and financial institutions do not become so large that they ultimately pose the potential risk of exerting pressure on countries' (quoted in Franke 2020, p. 220; authors' translation; see also Robinson 2009). However, on structural reform she avoided specific comment. The longstanding CDU Minister of Finance, Wolfgang Schäuble, was similarly cautious and abstained from supporting the Liikanen Group's proposals. The leaders of the CDU's coalition partner from Bavaria, the CSU, came out more forcefully in favour of reform. In early October 2012, Markus Feber, the CSU group leader in the European Parliament, argued that there should be a 'high firewall' between investment and retail banking (Kaiser 2012).

On the political left, support for a strong ringfence was nearly universal, at least in the lead-up to the September 2013 elections. This was driven in part by the large bail-outs during the international financial crisis, but also by political opportunity in the context of public opinion that was very hostile to banks. In one late 2012 global poll on trust in a country's banks and financial institutions, only 38 per cent of Germans confirmed their trust, placing the country in 127th place out of 155 countries (Crabtree 2013). In July 2012, SPD leader Sigmar Gabriel launched a vitriolic attack against banks, saying they should be split up because they were holding countries to ransom and dictating government policy (Jakobs 2012). In late September 2012, Peer Steinbrück—the previous Finance Minister of the Grand Coalition government from 2005 to 2009, and the SPD's candidate for Chancellor in the September 2013 elections—launched the German public debate on structural reform. Steinbrück presented a detailed set of proposals for structural reform in a thirty-page report published on 25 September 2012, entitled 'Regaining Trust: A New Approach to Taming the Financial Markets' (Steinbrück 2012, authors' translation, *Bändigung der Finanzmärkte*), a week prior to the publication of the Liikanen Group's own report and a week prior to his nomination as the SPD candidate for Chancellor. These proposals might be considered Steinbrück's response to François Hollande's promises on bank structural reform earlier in the year and a means to demonstrate his left-wing credentials on financial topics to left-wing elements in the SPD. In his report, Steinbrück stopped short of recommending a full separation akin to Glass–Steagall but went beyond the Vickers Report by proposing the legal separation of traditional retail banking activities from investment banking and a national ban on certain forms of proprietary trading, including high-frequency trading. In Steinbrück's proposal, affected banks would be required to run two separate institutions under the umbrella of a holding company. Should the investment bank fail, it would be wound up independently of retail banking. Lending business and savers' deposits would be protected. The shielded retail bank would receive a state guarantee, while the investment bank would not. Steinbrück's reform also applied to all German banks rather than just the country's largest. Steinbrück argued that his proposed reform was motivated by 'fundamental concerns about justice' (quoted in Janssen 2013, authors' translation). Steinbrück argued that the financial world was out of balance, and liability and risk no longer coincided. Profits were privatized, while 'losses were passed on to the community', which contradicted his idea of a market economy (Steinbrück 2012). Steinbrück was in general terms positive on the Liikanen Group's recommendations. However, he cited the Vickers Report from the UK as the principal source of inspiration for his proposals and the need to ringfence retail banking from investment banking rather than the reverse (Handelsblatt 2012). Steinbrück's proposals were popular in a general sense. In one poll by the Forsa Institute for *Handelsblatt*, a leading economics and financial newspaper, 71 per cent of German business leaders wanted stricter regulation of the banks, including structural reform (*Handelsblatt* 2012). Surprisingly, there was also support for Steinbrück's reform on the centre-right. Notably, Philipp Rösler, Minister of Economics and leader of the economically liberal FDP—part of the coalition government—came out in favour of Steinbrück's proposals. CDU General Secretary Hermann Gröhe proclaimed: 'Welcome to the club!' and 'With his proposals, the SPD would-be Chancellor is in many ways in line with the Christian–liberal coalition' (quoted in Janssen 2013, authors' translation). Gröhe insisted on one important difference: 'Steinbrück demands. We act quickly!'

However, there was also significant criticism of Steinbrück's proposal from the ranks of the government coalition parties. FDP General Secretary Patrick Döring accused Steinbrück of being 'mendacious' in deliberately targeting banks 'as a concession to the left in the SPD', in the context of his bid to be nominated as SPD candidate for the chancellorship (quoted in Janssen 2013, authors' translation). Despite the support in the CSU for structural reform, Bavarian Finance Minister Markus Söder warned against making Deutsche Bank 'an enemy'. Söder noted that the SPD left would take the opportunity to break up Deutsche Bank entirely (quoted in Janssen 2013, authors' translation). The CDU leadership was cautious on Steinbrück's proposal. Finance Minister Schäuble warned, more generally, against 'exaggeration' in regulation.

Many observers interpreted the CDU's reaction as awkward, with Steinbrück's concrete proposals for structural reform effectively putting the centre-right on the defensive. The CDU centre-right had promised tougher regulation on banks in the aftermath of the international financial crisis and had supported a range of initiatives at the international and European levels. On 29 September 2012, an editorial in the financial newspaper *Börsen-Zeitung* commented on the CDU's reaction as follows:

> The CDU in Berlin hyperventilated and tried to counter [Steinbrück's proposal]. The parliamentary group's financial policy spokesman, Klaus Peter Flosbach, announced that Steinbrück's demands had long been on the party's agenda or had already been dealt with by the CDU–FPD government. ... Schäuble ... took his own time in order to comment on a very specific topic approved in the cabinet: the regulation of high-frequency trading. The deputy head of the CDU's parliamentary group, Michael Meister, invited the press to a briefing on 'financial market regulation'. Unlike the SPD's own briefing shortly beforehand, only a handful of journalists attended.
>
> (Wefers 2012, authors' translation)

The Merkel government hoped to limited the ability of the SPD to mobilize the electorate on structural reform and thus moved swiftly to propose the *Trennbankengesetz* at the end of January 2013 (Wilson 2013).

3. Defending Deutschland plc: cooperative financial power in Germany

This section examines the cooperative financial power that shaped German bank structural reform. The relationship between the large German banks and top government and civil service officials was weaker than in France. No top German bank officials had previously served in the civil service. Indeed, in 2012–13, the head of the country's largest bank was foreign—Deutsche Bank's Anshu Jain—which was unheard of in the French context. However, a tight relationship between the bank lobby and a broader pro-bank corporate lobby and the federal government nonetheless worked to contain the reach of Germany's structural reform. Smaller public law savings and cooperative banks did not engage in investment banking activities and might have had a collective interest in breaking up the largest commercial banks. However, these banks supported the largest German universal banks in opposing major structural reform and sought to defend their own central financial institutions, which operated as universal banks—DekaBank and DZ Bank (see also Massoc 2020). Moreover, we might have expected significant divisions between banks and non-financial firms. SMEs were funded largely by savings and cooperative banks while Germany's largest companies were funded by equity and—relatively long-term—corporate debt issuance. However, all the country's business associations opposed both structural reform in Germany and the Liikanen Group's proposals.

Only the large commercial banks undertook a concerted lobbying effort on structural reform. These banks, both individually and collectively in their peak association, the BDB, argued that structural reform menaced lending to the real economy, would result in rising costs for banks, and created great dangers for Germany if it was to proceed with reform prior to other countries doing so and, notably, before EU-level reform (Schmidt 2012; Göhner et al. 2013; Janssen 2013). Michael Kemmer, Managing Director of the BDB from 2010 to 2017, was strongly critical of Peer Steinbrück's September 2012 report calling for structural reform (Janssen 2013). Similarly, Kemmer and the leaders of all the German banking associations were critical of the centre-right government's decision to respond to Steinbrück's proposal with their own draft law at the end of January 2013 (Göhner et al. 2013). Kemmer depicted the draft law as part of a 'rabbit and hedgehog' game: Steinbrück made banking regulation his topic, increasing pressure on the government to act. Thus, the federal government sought to play 'the hedgehog' and shout: 'We're already here!' (quoted in Janssen 2013, authors' translation).

Despite commercial rivalries and significant differences in the level and nature of their trading activities, Germany's major commercial banks presented a common front to oppose structural reform (Schmidt 2012). However, Steinbrück's proposed structural reform was widely seen as directed above all at Deutsche Bank. One of the leading business and finance-focused newspapers in the country, *Handelsblatt*, declared that it was 'clear that Steinbrück's paper is a declaration of war on the major German banks—specifically, against the only world class German financial institution: Deutsche Bank' (*Handelsblatt* 2012, authors' translation).

In terms of likely impact, the German banking industry was clearly divided on structural reform. None of the savings and cooperative banks were affected directly by the government's proposed structural reform due to both their small size and their focus on retail banking activities. However, the associations representing savings banks (DSGV), cooperative banks (BVR), and the regional public *Landesbanken* (VÖB) all came out in favour of German universal banks and against structural reform (Göhner et al. 2013; Schröder et al. 2013). They embraced the same arguments produced by the largest commercial banks that structural reform menaced lending to the real economy. This was despite the fact that, in the aftermath of the international financial crisis, the large commercial banks cut their lending to the real economy and a credit crunch was avoided principally due to increased lending by savings and cooperative banks (Hardie and Howarth 2013b). Public law *Landesbanken* owned by regional governments supported research that argued that structural reform was a 'sideline in the discussion on reducing systemic risk', where the main factors contributing to risk were linked to credit growth, inadequate equity, and reliance on short-term capital market financing—factors addressed in the Basel III capital guidelines (Schröder et al. 2013, authors' translation).

This surprising solidarity is due to two main factors. First, the savings banks and cooperatives sought to defend the investment banking activities operated by their commercial banking arms: DZ Bank for the approximately 800 cooperative banks—the country's second largest bank—and Dekabank for the country's 420 savings banks. These large universal banks engaged in a range of trading activities from which the public law savings and cooperative banks were legally prohibited. Georg Fahrenschon, President of the DSGV from 2012 to 2017, came out strongly against structural reform, arguing that he was 'not a big fan of "black-and-white politics" that encouraged structural reform, noting that commercial banks performed a vital role in helping small and medium-sized businesses with currency hedging transactions' (quoted in Becker 2012, authors' translation; also Interview 39).

Second, savings and cooperative banks sought to encourage the international expansion of Germany's largest universal banks as a mechanism to avoid increased domestic competition (Massoc 2020). The regional principle and a range of other anti-competitive practices protected the market position of savings and cooperative banks. These banks feared that the restriction of trading activities and greater constraint on international expansion would force lead universal banks to focus more on increasing their domestic retail market share. Benefiting from economies of scale, these large banks could then challenge the hitherto protected market position of the savings and cooperative banks. Indeed, commercial banks had long made publicly known their frustration with the protected status of the public law banks and lobbying efforts in favour of legislation at the national level against them (Donges et al. 2001; Köhler 2004; Schulz 2010;Cassell 2021).

German banks were also supported by both big business and organizations representing small and medium-sized companies which came out strongly opposed to structural reform. In part this reflected the export focus of German companies of a range of sizes. German business associations warned that structural separation would hit the 'real' economy by threatening the funding and provision of trade finance. In 2013, the leading German trade associations issued a joint statement with the main banking associations calling for retention of the existing model of universal banking (Göhner et al. 2013). The signatories of this statement included the BDA, BDI, DIHK, and ZDH. The BDI also opposed the proposed structural reform on the grounds that it was a serious interference with both the business of banks and their contractual freedom which could not be justified (Deutscher Bundestag 2013a).

A number of leading conservative business-oriented newspapers, including *Handelsblatt* and *Süddeutsche Zeitung*, came out against Steinbrück's proposed structural reform, as did Georg Mascolo, editor in chief of the country's leading news magazine, *Der Spiegel* (*Handelsblatt* 2012; Jakobs 2012; Janssen 2013), and supported a more cautious approach. Similarly, a significant number of German academic experts spoke out against bank structural reform. Professor Jörg Rocholl of the European School of Management and Technology in Berlin was critical of the separation of banking activities. Rocholl argued that the separation of risky business areas ignored major potential difficulties in the resolution of financial institutions, and 'namely their close interlinking and networking' (Deutscher Bundestag 2013a), with 80 per cent of the investment portfolio of German banks consisting of the securities of other banks.

The management of some non-bank financial companies—and notably the heads of Germany's largest insurance companies—spoke out in favour of bank structural reform. Nikolaus von Bomhard, CEO of the Munich Re reinsurance company, spoke out in favour of bank separation, arguing that there should be no banks that are so important to a country that they have to be bailed out with taxpayers' money (quoted in Becker 2012, authors' translation). However, the dominance of banks within the context of the German financial system limited the weight of these views in political circles.

Much has been written on the close ties between the German political class at the local, regional, and national levels and the public law savings and cooperative banks and the regional *Landesbanken* (Deeg 1999; Cassell 2021). Much less has been written on the links between the country's political class and the largest commercial banks, including Deutsche Bank, which has for a long period been one of Europe's largest banks. Moreover, while much is discussed in the press and academic literature of the efforts of the French political class and elite bureaucrats to create and defend bank national champions, there is less analysis of German federal government efforts to defend bank national champions (one exception is Massoc 2020). Clearly, the political support of savings banks and cooperatives is closely linked to their central role in funding the *Mittelstand* backbone of Germany's export-focused economy. Nonetheless, German politicians from a range of parties were still keen to promote the international expansion of the country's largest banks, and notably Deutsche Bank, as national champions. Admati and Hellwig (2014) show how Deutsche Bank's top executives enjoyed privileged access to German Ministry of Finance officials and ministers of finance, the attitude of which is characterized as deference to bankers' expertise. In early 2019, a number of leading German politicians including the SPD Finance Minister Olaf Scholz sought to encourage a merger to reinforce the country's leading bank national champion. Rather than break up the first and third largest banks, which were suffering major financial difficulties and retreating from global markets, Scholz and others called for a merger between Deutsche Bank and Commerzbank (Ewing and Eddy 2019). Thus, one of the country's leading left-wing politicians was calling for a merger of two of the country's largest banks, even though this would have left Germany with only a single massive publicly traded commercial bank.

4. The absence of venue shifting

In Germany, unlike in the UK and the Netherlands, no committees dedicated specifically to structural reform were created. The absence of delegation to a specialist group, and thus the reliance on existing institutional venues, meant that the issue could not be entirely insulated from political pressures. Nonetheless, we argue that, as in France, the government was able to facilitate conflict contraction by carefully managing the issue of structural reform—principally by ensuring that it was considered as part of a wider range of issues or policy proposals.

The mandate of the non-independent Ministry of Finance expert committee that examined the issue of structural reform was more open and general, and arguably vague. This mandate was to focus upon the lessons to be learned from the international financial crisis and to recommend possible reforms to decrease the likelihood of another crisis. In parliament, the principal venue for discussions on the details of the government's proposed structural reform was the Bundestag's finance committee. As with French legislation, the German government added structural reform to a number of other measures to amend the German Banking Act—unlike the more singular focus of draft legislation in the UK and US reforms. Thus, German parliamentary discussion and debate on the government's draft legislation focused on structural reform but also the transposition of the EU's Recovery and Resolution Directive and the proposal to extend criminal charges on banking malpractice. In Germany, none of the main features of venue shifting applied, while scrutiny was only facilitated—not widened significantly—by the Ministry of Finance expert committee in the aftermath of the international financial crisis and the Bundestag finance committee in the lead up to the 2013 federal parliamentary elections. The absence of a significant shift in venue resulted in a process in which banking reform was shaped by important political and parliamentary pressures, the outcome of which was a series of largely symbolic regulatory changes.

In the context of massive losses faced by a number of commercial banks and *Landesbanken* during the international finance crisis, the Merkel government established an 'Expert Commission' (*Expertenkommission*) which operated officially from 2008 to 2011. It was called the 'Neue Finanzmarktarchitektur' or Issing Commission, named after its chair, the former ECB chief economist and Executive Board member, Ottmar Issing. It consisted of a small number—at most six members, including Issing—of high-level public sector and academic experts on finance. Klaus Regling was former Director-General of Economics and Financial Affairs at the European Commission, the head of the European Financial Stability Facility and then, from 2012, the head of the European Stability Mechanism. Jens Weidmann was economics and financial advisor to Angela Merkel from 2006 to 2011 and then, from 2011, head of the Bundesbank. Jörg Asmussen was financial affairs advisor to the Grand Coalition government from 2000–9, State Secretary at the Ministry of Finance from 2008 to 2011, and then member of the ECB Executive Board from 2012 to 2013. A member of the SPD since 1987, Asmussen resigned from the ECB Executive Board in 2013 to assume a ministerial portfolio in the new Grand Coalition government. Jan Pieter Krahnen, an academic economist at the Goethe University Frankfurt was one of Germany's leading experts on the country's banking system and banking more generally. He was also a member of the Liikanen Group. The sixth member was William White, the Canadian economist and former head of the Monetary and Economics Department at the BIS. Of the committee members, at least three were publicly in favour of structural reform along the lines of the Liikanen Report: Weidmann, Krahnen, and Asmussen. However, only Krahnen publicly criticized the German government's weak structural reform (Deutscher Bundestag 2013a).

The principal focus of the Issing Commission was financial regulatory reform at the international level. Specifically, it sought to make recommendations for a new financial framework and systemic risk control that would be adopted at the G20 level. Its focus was not domestic per se—although a number of recommended international guidelines would have to be introduced in EU and national legislation (Bundesregierung *Neue Globale Finanzmarktarchitektur* 2008-10). The commission dedicated surprisingly little time to discussions on bank structural reform—even though this was a major reform idea circulating in international policy-making circles (Interview 22). Although the commission continued working in an unofficial capacity from 2011 (Lobbypedia.de 2011), it did not contribute in any direct/official way to the Merkel government's 2013 draft law on structural reform.

In parliament, only the small German Green Party called for the creation of an independent commission similar to the British ICB with a remit to focus on the TBTF problem and specifically on structural reform, capital and liquidity surcharges, and competition law changes to break up the largest German banks (Bündnis 90/Die Grünen 2011; Giegold 2011). The Greens called for the independent commission to consist of nine Bundestag members and nine experts from the financial sector, regulatory authorities, and academia, while representatives of the federal government and relevant authorities could participate in commission discussions. Modelling their proposed commission explicitly on the ICB, the Greens called for it to hold hearings, set up a working group, and commission expert reports. The Greens also wanted the independent commission to examine explicitly other national discussions on structural reforms. However, this Green Party proposal was blocked by the governing centre-right coalition. The Bundestag created a special commission to focus upon the management of specific financial institutions that had failed during the financial crisis—notably Hypo Real Estate (HRE) and Dresdner Bank—but this commission did not examine broader banking reform issues.

The German law on structural reform was discussed and debated in the Bundestag and Bundesrat finance committees (the *Finanzausschuss*). The Bundestag committee adopted only minor amendments to the government's draft law—which was largely presented as 'a fait accompli' (Interview 29). Some of the amendments were adopted to meet the concerns of affected banks. Notably, the Bundestag agreed to delay the prohibition of speculative transactions and the corresponding exemptions to 1 July 2015, one year later than previously planned. Moreover, the authority of BaFin to prohibit other high-risk transactions in addition to the legally prohibited transactions or to order their outsourcing was also delayed by a year and would apply only from 1 July 2016. The Bundestag committee agreed to permit transactions that served the interest rate, currency, liquidity, and credit risk control of savings and cooperative banks. This amendment specifically met the demands of the *Landesbanken* that reached the draft law's threshold and the concerns of cooperative banks worried about the impact upon DZ Bank.

Other amendments assuaged some of the demands of left-wing Bundestag members. Notably, the Bundestag committee revised the catalogue of those transactions that were to be exempted from the ban applied to the ringfenced deposit-taking banks and the obligation to outsource to financial trading institutions. For example, the Bundestag committee agreed that transactions serving to hedge transactions with customers should not be permitted if they were carried out with alternative investment funds or their management companies. The aim was to prevent banks indirectly using customer deposits for transactions with alternative investment funds and their management companies as a result of this exemption (Brandi 2013).

A number of observers have argued that the rushed adoption of the Bank Separation Law is demonstrated by the significant number of important issues that the law left unclear (Brandi 2013; Interview 29). The treatment of domination and profit transfer agreements with regard to the shielding of deposit institutions from the risks emanating from trading activities lacked clarity. Furthermore, it remained to be seen how the shielding of the deposit business was to be reconciled with the post-conversion liability that was associated with the outsourcing of prohibited activities.

During the spring and summer of 2013—during the parliamentary committee and plenary sessions debating the draft law—the discourse of government members shifted significantly to downplay the need for a high ringfence. The financial policy spokesman for the FDP parliamentary group, Volker Wissing, argued that structural reform was not the solution to financial instability and that the financial crisis had been triggered not by universal banks, but rather by specialist banks (Tagesschau.de 2013). This represents a significant shift from the positioning of the FDP Minister of Economics, Philipp Rösler, who had spoken positively of Peer Steinbrück's proposals on structural reform a few months earlier.

Given the upcoming September federal parliamentary election, Bundestag finance committee members recognized the importance of rapid examination of the law and modifications to the German Banking Act in order to allow sufficient time in the legislative calendar for the Bundesrat to approve the amendments (Brandi 2013; Kissler 2013; Interview 29).

5. Conflict contraction: from engagement to symbolic reform

Bank structural reform was subject to significant politicization during the early stages of the legislative process. In particular, left-wing opposition politicians pushed for amendments in the Bundestag, the aim of which was to strengthen structural reform. Yet the political balance of power in parliament ultimately favoured the government, and hence these efforts proved to be largely in vain. More generally, efforts by German politicians, academics, and non-financial firms to increase the salience of the TBTF issue were also relatively limited. This was despite the public insistence of the German centre-right coalition government on being tough with the banks that had suffered large losses during the financial crisis.

As in France, but unlike in the UK, no high-ranking bureaucratic actors promoted structural reform. Jens Weidmann, the President of the German Bundesbank, was in favour of structural reform along the lines of the Liikanen Report but also the commission's draft legislation—which Weidmann described as 'sensible' (Weidmann 2014). However, while he did not oppose in any way a more ambitious structural reform—as did the Governor of the Bank of France, Christian Noyer—Weidmann did not assume the kind of activist role pursued by the Bank of England Governor, Mervyn King. Weidmann also focused rather upon the reduction of 'incentives to expand to ever greater size' through systemic risk buffers and higher capital requirements for systemically important institutions (Weidmann 2014). Despite the clear divergence between the Liikanen Group's structural reform proposals and those of the German government, the Bundesbank officially came out in favour of the federal government's draft reform which avoided strict separation (Deutscher Bundestag 2013a). According to the Bundesbank, the government's draft reform would contribute 'to protecting traditional banking business, including payment transactions, carried out in deposit-taking credit institutions from risks that resulted from particularly risky transactions' (quoted in Deutscher Bundestag 2013a, authors' translation).

Similarly, Elke König—then head of the German financial supervisory body, BaFin—refrained from criticizing the German government's draft law, seeing it as 'useful' to tackle the issue of TBTF (Deutscher Bundestag 2013a). Moreover, like Weidmann, König noted her support for the Liikanen Group's proposals (Edinger 2013). Like Weidmann, König also argued that the structural reform proposed by the Liikanen Group 'had its limits' and rather was only one of a number of necessary reforms (Edinger 2013, authors' translation). She expressed concern that trading business would be diverted into weakly regulated or unregulated sectors including the shadow banking sector, which could only be addressed effectively through the adoption of regulation at the international level. The recommendations of the G20's Financial Stability Board were only produced in September 2013, after the adoption of the German structural reforms. Echoes of this concern—that a high ringfence imposed on bank activities would work to push these activities out of banks—were also manipulated by those centre-right politicians and bank lobbyists opposed to ambitious structural reform.

SPD leader, Peer Steinbrück, opposed the government's proposed structural reform as insufficient and falling far short of his own proposal of September 2012 (Janssen 2013; Neuerer 2013;). Steinbrück argued that given the high thresholds in the government's draft law only two or three German banks would be affected, directly contradicting the claims of Finance Minister Schäuble that between ten and twelve banks would be covered (Janssen 2013). Steinbrück argued that the government's draft law came 'too late' and was 'insufficient' because:

> The financing of proprietary trading with deposits is not prevented, it is only made more difficult. The fact that a mandatory separation of banking and proprietary trading should only take effect from 100 billion [euros] or 20 per cent of the balance sheet is far too high a threshold and would affect at most only two or three banks. In addition, there are no clear legal requirements to shield the deposit business from commercial transactions involving customers.
> (quoted in Janssen 2013, authors' translation)

Steinbrück insisted that the scope for speculative business in the government's draft law was far too generous and that it was necessary to restrict the investment banking activities of all banks. However, a number of observers argued that, although Steinbrück's proposed reform would be far more significant than the government's, it was unlikely that the SPD could explain this successfully to the wider public and thus transform the difference into a major element of the left's election campaign (see, for example, Janssen 2013).

Bundestag hearings on the draft law were limited to a single finance committee hearing on 4 April 2013 and two plenary debates on 15 March and 15 May 2013 when the law was adopted by the Bundestag (Deutscher Bundestag 2013a, 2013b, 2013c). Bundesrat (upper house) hearings on the draft law were limited to a single finance committee meeting on 27 May and a single plenary debate on 7 June, at which the law was passed without further amendment. In addition to these hearings and debates, opposition members spoke out against the government's proposed reforms in dozens of newspaper, television, and radio interviews (see, for example, Deutschlandradio.de 2013; Zöllmer quoted in Kissler 2013). At the March plenary debate in the Bundestag, the SPD and the Greens tabled a counter-proposal calling for the full adoption of the Liikanen Group's proposals, entitled 'A new attempt to tame the financial markets: Reduce blackmail potential—separate business and investment banking' (SPD and Bündnis 90/Die Grünen 2013, authors' translation; Deutscher Bundestag 2013c; Kissler 2013). Among a number of recommended amendments, the proposal sought the prohibition of proprietary trading and other risky transactions by all banks that carried out a significant level of commercial transactions; and lowering the size and threshold limited to cover a larger range of banks. For the SPD and Greens, the reform provided the opportunity to ban proprietary trading altogether, regardless of the size of the bank. This counter-proposal was further defended by SPD and Green members during the second plenary debate in the Bundestag on the government's draft law on 15 May 2013 (Deutscher Bundestag 2013d).

In the Bundestag finance committee debates, SPD member Carsten Sieling argued that the Liikanen Report offered a better solution to the problem of TBTF than the law proposed by the centre-right coalition government (Deutscher Bundestag 2013a). In the first of the two Bundestag plenary debates on the draft law, on 15 March 2013, a range of SPD members—including Joachim Poß and Manfred Zöllmer—intervened in terms strongly critical of the government's proposed reform (Deutscher Bundestag 2013b, 2013c). Zöllmer, the head of the SPD members on the Bundestag finance committee, argued that this was a 'placebo law that [bore] the separation of banks title, but failed to separate' (quoted in Kissler 2013, authors' translation). Zöllmer predicted that ongoing bank bail-outs funded by taxpayers were inevitable (Deutscher Bundestag 2013e). He accused the government of a reform that was designed to 'demobilize' the SPD electorate in the upcoming parliamentary elections (Kissler 2013). Zöllmer also noted that he hoped that German regional governments would block the draft law in the Bundesrat. He argued that the SPD and the Greens could also prevent the adoption of legislation by calling on a mediation committee, ensuring that parliament would run out of time prior to the elections. However, the mediation committee was not called and there was no left-wing revolt on the legislation in the upper house—despite the presence of the SPD, Greens, and Die Linke in a majority of *Land* governments—allowing rapid adoption on 7 June (Deutscher Bundesrat 2013).

In the first plenary debate, Thomas Gambke from the Greens also mentioned the views of Mervyn King, Bank of England Governor, who found the proposed German reform inadequate and called for a stronger ringfence (Deutscher Bundestag 2013b). In the final Bundestag plenary debate on the law, Gerhard Schick from the Greens argued that 'The banks and the federal government are satisfied with the law. The banks are satisfied because nothing has changed for them, and the federal government because it gives the impression that something is going to change' (Deutscher Bundestag 2013e). Die Linke members were more polemic and insisted that German citizens were being robbed by banks. Sara Wagenknecht of Die Linke argued that the Deutsche Bank did not need to have a high capital ratio because it was assured that it would be rescued by German taxpayers, as demonstrated in the federal government bail-outs of HRE and Commerzbank (Deutscher Bundestag 2013b). In the second Bundestag plenary debate, Die Linke member Axel Troost called for the prohibition of proprietary trading altogether—'closing the casino'—because separation itself was not enough and the government's proposed separation was far from adequate (Deutscher Bundestag 2013d). Several members, including Gerhard Schick of the Greens, accused the Christian Democrats and FDP of backing a reform that was explicitly designed to operate as a brake on EU-level efforts to achieve more far-reaching reform (Deutscher Bundestag 2013d).

Despite the efforts of Bundestag opposition politicians, the politicization of structural reform beyond the Bundestag was more limited and the adopted modifications to the draft legislation—as noted above—involved principally a delay to implementation by one year. Notably, the political debate in the Bundesrat was less polarized and more cautious on the issue of structural reform compared to the Bundestag (Deutscher Bundesrat 2013; Interview 29). This was demonstrated less than a year later in its position paper on the EU Commission's draft regulation on structural reform (Deutscher Bundesrat 2014). In this paper the Bundesrat criticized both the Liikanen Report and the draft regulation for threatening to undermine the universal banking model fundamentally. The Bundesrat presented the German Bank Separation Act as superior because, rather than banning a range of proprietary trading activities, it allowed banks to outsource these to an independent entity within the banking group.

A number of German academic experts on finance spoke against the German government's proposed reform in the Bundesbank finance committee sessions. Professor Joseph Huber of Martin Luther University, Halle, questioned the effectiveness of the proposed reform in diminishing risk and called it a 'permissive Volcker Rule' (quoted in Deutscher Bundestag 2013a, authors' translation). Professor Rudolf Hickel, from the University of Bremen, argued that the draft law went in the right direction but fell short. Hickel argued that 'the desired reduction in speculative trading volume to defuse systemically relevant business areas is not achieved' and called for a reform closer to the Volcker Rule and the Liikanen Report (quoted in Deutscher Bundestag 2013a, authors' translation). Professor Krahnen (a member of the Liikanen Group) argued that the proposed German structural reform was mostly symbolic (Deutscher Bundestag 2013a). Sir John Vickers also gave testimony on the German draft law, arguing that the adoption of the Liikanen Group's structural reform proposals would be far more effective and result in more robust universal banks (Deutscher Bundestag 2013a).

A number of civil society associations provided testimony to the Bundestag as to the inadequacy of the German government's proposed structural reform. For Thierry Philliponat of Finance Watch, the Brussels-based finance watchdog, the proposed German reform would result in 'hardly any impact on bank practice' and he argued in favour of more far-reaching legislation. Moreover, Philliponat warned that 'German taxpayers will in future be involved in the financing of rescue packages for foreign banks' (quoted in Deutscher Bundestag 2013a, authors' translation). World Economy, Ecology and Development (WEED) described the proposed structural reform as a 'paper tiger', while the Federation of German Consumer Organizations argued in favour of a tougher reform (Deutscher Bundestag 2013a). The German Federation of Trade Unions (DGB) also noted that the proposed structural reform was inadequate, but argued that bank separation alone could not safely shield the real economy from risks in the financial services sector (Deutscher Bundestag 2013a).

In 2012, a number of scandals erupted that seriously damaged the already-weak public reputation of Deutsche Bank, including major tax evasion and involvement with other banks in manipulating the Libor interest rate benchmark (Spiegel International 2012). However, even though in December 2013 the European Commission fined Deutsche Bank €725m for its involvement in rate manipulation—considerably more than any other bank involved in the Libor scandal—conflict expansion was limited. No dedicated commission was established by parliament to deal with the Libor scandal. There was a single day-long hearing in the Bundestag's finance committee on 28 November 2012 (Braun 2012). The head of Deutsche Bank, Anshu Jain, was invited to appear before the committee to answer questions on his bank's involvement in rate manipulation but—infamously—failed to show up and there was no subsequent follow-up (Spiegel.de 2012). Rate manipulation had some political salience in German federal politics but only members of the Greens and Die Linke drew a connection between this scandal and the need for major structural reform going beyond that proposed in the Liikanen Report (Demling 2012).

6. Conclusion

Peer Steinbrück presented a detailed thirty-page proposal on bank structural reform at a well-attended and much-publicized 25 September 2012 press conference (Steinbrück 2012). His proposal aligned largely with the recommendations of the Liikanen Group, which were published shortly afterwards but were already widely known. Senior centre-right government members had expressed support for the work of the Liikanen Group and the need to make banking safer. Thus, the political conditions were set for the adoption of a far-reaching structural reform in Germany. However, the reform eventually adopted in the country in August 2013 fell far short of not only the proposals of the Liikanen Group but also the reform adopted in the US and the reform about to be adopted in the UK. The weakness of the German reform was widely noted in the national and international press. In terms of tackling TBTF banks by enhancing their resolvability, the German structural reform—like the French—was widely seen as ineffective. In its study of the Belgian government's structural reform, the National Bank of Belgium also examined the Liikanen Group's recommendations and other proposed national reforms (National Bank of Belgium 2013). The Belgian central bank states that, in the German and French reforms, the amount of trading book activity left in banking groups failed to improve their resolvability significantly, 'perhaps' because the threshold of assets and activity triggering subsidiarization was too high, or because the definition of proprietary trading requiring subsidiarization was too narrow (National Bank of Belgium 2013, p. 2).

We argue that the weak structural reform adopted in Germany reflects two key features of the German policy process. First, as in France and the Netherlands, the German banking industry was united on the issue of structural reform and was able to wield cooperative financial power to resist a tougher ringfence and a ban on proprietary trading. The united German bank lobby maintained privileged access to the centre-right government. Second, as in France, the policy-making and legislative process on bank structural reform involved no venue shifting. The use of standard parliamentary procedures exposed the issue to higher politicization, forcing the government to manage the agenda carefully and hence try to deflect calls for more stringent rules. Placed on the back foot by Steinbrück's early initiative and a later counter-proposal presented jointly by the SPD and Greens, the centre-right government wielded its majority in parliament to manage the reform agenda and to push through the adoption of the Bank Separation Act prior to the September 2013 elections. Why did the centre-right government not move to avoid national-level reform altogether, as in the Netherlands? In this chapter, we argue that, as in France, the commitment of a number of political leaders to some form of structural reform in the context of looming federal parliamentary elections created a political dynamic that encouraged the CDU-led government to adopt a weak and symbolic reform rather than push reform off the agenda.

7
France

Defending the National Champions

1. Introduction

On 18 July 2013, the French parliament adopted considerably weaker bank structural reform than either the US Volcker Rule or the UK ringfencing proposals. The weakness of the French reform can be seen as puzzling given the strong commitment of leading French Socialists, and notably President François Hollande, to bank structural reform during the 2012 election campaigns and the Socialist victory in both the presidential and legislative elections of May and June 2012. Furthermore, the weakness of the French structural reform holds an unflattering light to the government's explicitly stated objectives in the preamble to its draft legislation on reform (French Government 2012). Officially, the government sought reform to achieve four objectives: first, to put finance to the service of the economy and not to the service of itself; second, to change the sector 'profoundly', to become a point of reference in Europe and rebuild the French financial landscape for the next twenty years, by moving away from speculation and towards financing the real economy; third, to avoid being influenced by the weight of finance and the complexity of its operations so as to accept without question the problems of the financial sector; and fourth, to protect the deposits of savers but also taxpayers, by turning finance firmly towards the real economy.[1]

The major US and UK reforms can be explained in terms of the competitive nature of financial power, characterized by fragmented financial industry lobbying and concerted opposition from pro-reform groups. Venue shifting in the UK then resulted in durable reform by facilitating depoliticization and broad political agreement, while the absence of venue shifting in the US resulted in a highly politicized process and a contested outcome. In this chapter, we argue that the

---

[1] Authors' translation. The original French language text in the draft law's preamble is that the government sought reform to: 1. 'remettre la finance au service de l'économie, et non au service d'elle-même'; 2. 'changer profondément le secteur, faire référence en Europe et refondre notre paysage financier pour les 20 prochaines années, contre la spéculation et pour le financement de l'économie réelle'; 3. sans 'prendre prétexte du poids de la finance et de la complexité de ses enjeux pour nous accommoder des défaillances du secteur'; 4. 'protéger les dépôts des épargnants mais aussi les contribuables, en tournant fermement la finance vers l'économie réelle'.

weakness and symbolic nature of French structural reform reflects two key institutional features of the policy process. First, the French financial industry was able to wield cooperative financial power to resist stringent new restrictions on trading activities, reflected in the unified and centralized character of bank lobbying, and the tight interpenetration of high-ranking bureaucrats focused on financial issues and top bankers. Second, the process was not characterized by any significant venue shifting, but was instead steered through existing institutional channels. As in Germany, this potentially exposed the issue of structural reform to significant politicization, particularly from the ranks of President Hollande's own Socialist Party. This fact, together with Hollande's high-profile and specific election commitments on structural reform, meant that the issue could not be deflected or ignored entirely.

In response, the government therefore proposed a relatively weak, symbolic set of reforms, designed to address political pressure to act, whilst minimizing the economic impact on industry. The resulting draft law on structural reform contained a range of financial reform measures which diluted the singular focus on bank ringfencing. Indeed, at least one academic economist expert who had appeared before the National Assembly and Senate finance committees examining structural reform argued that the name of the draft law was misleading and should have been changed in order not to create false expectations regarding the contents of the law and its likely impact (Laurence Scialom, quoted in Tricornot et al. 2014, p. 106; see also Scialom quoted in Sénat 2013, p. 315; Finance Watch's Thierry Philipponat referenced in Tricornot et al. 2014, p. 97; Interviews 21, 30).

We argue that the version of structural reform adopted in France reflected the government's ability to keep tight control of the reform agenda—limiting the ability of pro-reform groups to mobilize, access, and influence the decision-making process, thereby facilitating conflict contraction. The French government's institutional treatment of structural reform from the election of President Hollande in May 2012 to the adoption of the law creating the reform in July 2013 undermined the influence of the already disparate political and non-political actors arguing in favour of bank structural reform. An *in camera* government committee—involving only a limited number of participants and notably bank representatives—drew up the draft law that included bank structural reform. The hearings of the finance committees in the lower house (National Assembly) and upper house (Senate) which examined the draft law involved a greater number of participants, and thus had the potential increasingly to politicize the legislative debate. Nonetheless, we show that parliamentary pressure for a more stringent approach was contained by the Socialist-led government.

Once the 2012 election campaigns were over, the high-ranking Socialist politicians in favour of major reform either fell silent or moved to defend the symbolic reform proposed and eventually adopted. In addition, the main opposition party in parliament—the centre-right Union pour un mouvement populaire

(UMP)—had little incentive to politicize the issue and therefore did not place pressure on the government to adopt stringent new rules. The remaining political champions of major structural reform lacked the political influence and public profile of their counterparts in the US and the UK. There were a number of left-wing and more moderate politicians, academics and NGOs in favour of major bank structural reform. However, a pervasive theme in government and party-political circles from the centre-left to the far right, which was less present in the UK and US, was the conflation of economic nationalism and the protection of large universal national bank champions in order best to serve the national economy. This line of argument was actively promoted by the largely unified financial lobby, while the Socialist-led government created little opportunity for those seeking to challenge this line of thinking.

Section 2 of this chapter summarizes both the weakness of the French structural reform as well as why many observers expected a more significant reform given the promises of leading Socialist politicians and the range of scandals that had potentially increased the political salience of bank reform. Section 3 analyses the cooperative financial power opposed to major structural reform and the unique interrelationship between the bureaucratic, political, and banking elites in France. Section 4 examines the absence of venue shifting on bank structural reform and the use of existing government and parliamentary venues to facilitate conflict contraction on the issue. Section 5 examines the significant but ultimately insufficient civil society, academic, and political mobilization on the topic of structural reform and, on the contrary, the strong opposition to major structural reform from a range of leading politicians—including those in the Socialist Party.

2. The surprisingly weak French structural reform

The French have their own tradition on the separation of banking activities that dates back to the law of 2 December 1945 (45–15) and, initially at least, ensured a separation akin to the Glass–Steagall Act in the US. The law clarified three categories of banks: deposit banks, investment banks (*banques d'affaires*), and banks focused upon the provision of medium- and long-term credit. Deposit banks were excluded from financing industry and infrastructure. This law was abrogated and the separation of banking activities ended through a 1984 law—adopted under a Socialist-led government—which enshrined the universal bank model. However, the separation of banking activities had been collapsing in effect since the 1960s with the adoption of a number of amendments to the 1945 law. By the early 2010s, there were five very large banking groups that dominated nearly 90 per cent of the domestic retail market. These banks were BNP-Paribas, Société Générale, Crédit Agricole, Banques Populaires, Caisses d'Epargne (BPCE) and

Crédit Mutuel (Moody's 2017). Indeed, in the aftermath of the international financial crisis, in 2009, President Nicolas Sarkozy merged two of the country's largest banking groups—the cooperative banks (*banques populaires*) and the savings banks (*caisses d'épargne*) to create BPCE (Hardie and Howarth 2009).

As outlined in Chapter 3, the large French universal banks suffered significant losses during the international financial crisis. However, government bail-outs were not essential to the survival of any French bank. The government forced banks to issue shares, which it purchased, and issued credit guarantees to banks (Hardie and Howarth 2009). The banks bought back their shares by the end of 2012 and the French government made a profit. By the end of 2010, BNP-Paribas had become, by total assets, the world's largest bank. France avoided both a credit crunch and a recession (Howarth 2013). Thus, despite the significant losses in the French banking system, the crisis cannot be seen as existential for the largest French universal banks.

At the same time, the size of the largest banks and the issue of TBTF persisted as a topic in partisan political debate and was notably mobilized by the centre-left and the far left. During the presidential election campaign, the Socialist Party's candidate, François Hollande, announced that his 'main adversary was finance' (Hollande 2012a). In his campaign platform's seventh group of promises, Hollande insisted upon a 'revolution in banking', and in promise 7.1 he called specifically for the 'separation of banking activities contributing to investment (or employment) and speculative operations' (Hollande 2012a). Challenging the power of the financial sector, in general, and calling for bank structural reform, more specifically, were significant elements in Hollande's Bourget speech, with which he launched his presidential campaign. Hollande promised to start his presidency 'with a vote that will oblige banks to separate their credit activities from their speculative market activities' (Hollande 2012b). During the 2012 presidential and then legislative election campaigns, a range of leading Socialist Party politicians of different ideological stripes came out in favour of major bank structural reform. These included two party moderates: Michel Sapin, twice former Finance Minister, and Jérôme Cahuzac, former head of the National Assembly finance committee. Following his election victory, President Hollande charged the Socialist Minister of Finance, Pierre Moscovici, to examine the feasibility of the bank structural reform proposed in the Liikanen Report (Liikanen 2012). Moscovici had been Hollande's presidential campaign manager and was closely involved in the design of Hollande's campaign platform.

The limited nature of the structural reform in the draft law adopted by the Socialist-led government on 19 December 2012 and the final law adopted in July 2013 (French Government 2013) was widely commented upon and criticized in the French press (Nathan 2012), by the Brussels-based NGO Finance Watch (2013c) and by a number of Socialist and other left-wing politicians, including the *rapporteuse* on the draft law in the finance committee of the National Assembly, the Socialist deputy, Karine Berger. The main architect of the UK reform, Sir John Vickers (2016, p. 22) later described the French (and German) reforms as Volcker-lite because they combined the limited scope of the Volcker Rule with a more lenient form of separation. Even French bankers publicly noted the limited impact of the reform. According to Frédéric Oudéa, the head of Société Générale and then President of the FBF, the French structural reform affected between only 0.5 per cent and 1.5 per cent of the activities of his bank (Assemblée Générale 2013a). Almost a year after the draft law was adopted by the Socialist-led government, on 21 November 2013, Alain Papiasse, of the BNP-Paribas' *banque de financement et d'investissement* (BFI) subsidiary confirmed that the reform would only affect 2 per cent of BFI's activities and only 0.5 per cent of BNP-Paribas' total banking activity (see, for example, Erasmus 2017). For Christophe Nijdam, a bank analyst and Finance Watch official:

> You can't call it a reform as [the ringfencing] only affects 0.5 per cent of BNP Paribas' total net banking income. ... The objective of taking away the implicit French state guarantee from risky activities is not fulfilled.
> (quoted in Daneshkhu and Carnegy 2012)

The Socialist-led government's draft law defended the French universal bank model. No significant market activities of banks would be affected by the proposed ringfence. The draft law called for the separation of highest-risk activities and for them to be placed in a special subsidiary, but limited this requirement only to proprietary trading—that is, when the bank uses its own funds for financial market investments—and high-frequency trading. These activities were only a very small percentage of the total activity of all the French universal banks. Both the draft law and the law adopted in July 2013 allowed all activities that were 'useful to the economy' to remain in the remit of the deposit bank. Apart from proprietary trading and high-frequency trading, nearly all other financial instruments were authorized as long as they were used in relation to a client, including: the creation and sale of financial products and of structured investment products, the sale and purchase of derivatives, the financing of speculation, market-marking activities more generally, and, in particular, the creation of financial products for speculative purposes (Erasmus 2017).

The likely impact of the draft law was widely questioned. One investment banker argued: 'in fact, apart from the Kerviel affair, this law would have prevented none of the losses that French banks suffered during the crisis' (quoted in Nathan 2012, authors' translation). Finance Watch (2013c) among others challenged the inadequate impact study that accompanied the draft law, which noted that it was 'sadly' impossible to calculate the precise effect of the proposed ringfencing on bank activities because of the very small number of banks concerned by the future law, for reasons of confidentiality and for respect for business secrecy. Finance Watch

(2013c, pp. 10–28) also proposed numerous precise amendments to the French draft law, none of which were adopted.

While downplaying the need for structural reform, the draft law's more innovative elements were found in its second part, which assigned the government new instruments to manage future bank crises and notably with regard to bank resolution and the creation of a national resolution fund—as required by the draft of the EU's BRRD, then still being debated and eventually adopted in May 2014 (Directive 2014/59/EU). For Moscovici, the creation of this resolution fund was 'the end of the socialisation of [bank] losses' (quoted in Nathan 2012). As a typical example of Socialist Party hyperbole, Karine Berger proclaimed that the draft law was 'in line with François Hollande's presidential campaign programme' (quoted in Nathan 2012).

3. The financial sector speaks with (nearly) one voice

The first factor explaining the largely symbolic nature of French bank structural reform is the cooperative financial power that ensured marginal financial sector support for a more significant reform. Chapters 4 and 5 have demonstrated that in the US and UK the financial sector was divided and the influence of large banks that were opposed to reform was diluted by the diversity of the financial system. However, in France, large universal banks dominated the financial system and the provision of a range of financial services, including asset management and hedging (Howarth 2013). The largest French banks and their peak association, the FBF, thus dominated public discussions on bank structural reform to a much greater extent than in the US and UK, while alternative voices in the financial sector were almost entirely absent. The French Society of Financial Analysts (*Association française de la gestion financière*, AFG), the peak association of the asset management industry in France—the second largest in the EU—was silent on bank structural reform.

A major difference between US and UK and French bank and non-financial industry efforts to water down structural reform proposal was that industry divisions formed early in the US and the UK but not in France. In France, despite significant differences in bank business models and the relative importance of trading activities in bank balance sheets, all five of the country largest banks—BNP-Paribas, Société Générale, Crédit Agricole, BPCE, and Crédit Mutuel—succeeded in maintaining a united front against the Socialist-led government's proposed reform (Daneshkhu and Barker 2012). The first three had substantial trading assets of 40 per cent or more of total assets, which put them well above the 15–25 per cent threshold suggested by the Liikanen Report for ringfencing activities, were this benchmark to be adopted by the French government (Daneshkhu and Barker 2012). Jean-Paul Chifflet, the head of Crédit Agricole and head of the

FBF in 2012, remonstrated that 'The banking reform proposals currently have no equal anywhere in Europe. ... It is going to become extremely difficult for French banks to lend to the economy' (quoted in Daneshkhu 2012). French banks were joined in their chorus of opposition by the main association representing big business in France, MEDEF, which repeatedly noted the dangers of ringfencing to the French economy (Couppey-Soubeyran 2015). France's largest banks had long played an important policy-making role in MEDEF (Couppey-Soubeyran 2015), and MEDEF positions on all major bank reform matters were determined by the largely uniform positions of the directors of the largest banks.

During the early stages of the domestic negotiating process on structural reform, the French banking industry attempted to frame the issue by presenting a united front in opposition to reform. The FBF was the only group in France that can be said to have organized a concerted campaign on structural reform, publishing a number of documents on the topic including *Réforme Bancaire: Mythe ou Réalité* (Banking Reform: Myth or Reality) (FBF 2013c), which challenged systematically all the main arguments presented in favour of ringfencing and, rather, emphasized the dangers of structural reform both to the successful model of French mixed banking and to bank lending to the real economy. The FBF argued that there was no evidence that the 'unique French universal banking model' was an important cause of the financial crisis (FBF 2013c). On the contrary, the FBF emphasized that this unique model ensured the relative stability of French banks during the crisis, despite their size. Large French banks also argued that universal banking lowered bank funding costs and reduced risk through diversification. They argued that reform would both reduce lending to the real economy and damage the international competitiveness of large French banks (Interview 7). The FBF insisted that investment banking activities were complementary to those of deposit and credit banking:

> ... lending activity needs market financing. In effect, the credits accorded by French banks exceeded by €331.5bn the deposits held by these banks. Fortunately, universal banks, thanks to their diverse model of activities which offer more security for lenders, can turn to market financing to fill this gap.
> (FBF 2013c, p. 2, authors' translation)

In the case of France—where the large universal banks had a weaker capital position than the largest British banks—the FBF also argued that structural reform was particularly dangerous and threatened foreign takeovers and a significant cut to lending to the real economy (FBF 2013c). The FBF pointed to the Savings and Loans crisis—hitherto the worst bank crisis in US history—when 1043 small savings banks which had no market activities failed because of the collapse of the housing market (FBF 2013c). Oudéa (2015), the head of the FBF and head of Société Générale, repeatedly made clear his defence of the large French universal banks. All five of the largest French banks and the FBF denounced both the draft law and the final law adopted as excessively restrictive (Daneshkhu and Carnegy 2012). However, this posturing was almost certainly designed to bolster the credibility of a Socialist-led government which had adopted a largely symbolic reform (Tricornot et al. 2014; Couppey-Soubeyran 2015).

There were only few high-profile sceptical and critical voices elsewhere in the financial sector that called for a stronger ringfence. Pierre-Henri Leroy, founder and President of one investment firm, Proxinvest, which specialized in advising shareholders, was a particularly well-known critic of the Ayrault government's draft law (Nathan 2012) and called for major reforms to the French model of universal banking (Leroy 2012). However, such voices were relatively rare.

Ties that bind: bankers and bureaucrats

Cooperative financial power limited financial sector opposition to the symbolic structural reform proposed and adopted by the Socialist-led government. The interpenetration of bureaucratic and bank elites further undermined efforts to challenge the influence of French banks on structural reform. In France, there was little institutional space for public actors effectively to oppose the public–private consensus reached between state actors (from the Ministry of Finance, the Bank of France, and other financial supervisory authorities) and large banks. The relative weakness of public, political, and bureaucratic efforts to support the structural reform of banks can be explained in part by the power of the large French banks. The inter-relationship of bank, bureaucratic, and political elites has been long known, and widely reported and studied by academics (for example, see Jabko and Massoc 2012; and Massoc 2020). On the specific topic of bank structural reform, it is clear that the bank lobby was very influential in shaping government policy (de Tricornot et al. 2014; Pouzin 2014a, 2014b).

However, it can be difficult to distinguish the positions of the French bank lobby and those of the French civil service elite working in the French Treasury division of the Ministry of Finance, who also normally belong to the financial inspectorate (*inspection des finances*), one of the three elite networks in the French civil service. Despite the strength of the French bank lobby, it would be problematic to describe the relationship between the largest French banks and the French state in terms of 'capture' (Jabko and Massoc 2012). The largest French banks were also all nationalized after the Second World War and played a central role in the state's management of the economy. Despite the privatization of all the French banks from the mid-1980s and the decline in the state-led economy, the legacy of state-led finance remained (Howarth 2013), as did the interrelationship of state and private sector, notably banking, elites (Clift 2004; Philippon 2007; Dudouet and Gremont 2010; Massoc 2020).

Indeed, France was unlike any other country in the Organization of Economic Cooperation and Development (OECD) in terms of elite interpenetration: most of the largest French banks were run by former high-ranking civil servants—often from the financial inspectorate—and many returned to the public sector to work in high-ranking civil service positions, as ministerial support staff or as politicians. Thus, top-level French bankers were more likely to be sensitive to government economic policy concerns than in other countries, while civil servants who had served in top positions in banks or hoped to serve in these positions were particularly alert to the concerns of the banks. To take one of many examples, François Villeroy de Galau, a member of the financial inspectorate, was a civil servant, worked as an economic policy advisor to former Prime Minister Pierre Bérégovoy and as head of cabinet to Minister of Finance Dominique Strauss Kahn, became head of the tax division of the Ministry of Finance, and then served in high-ranking positions at BNP-Paribas for twelve years prior to becoming Governor of the Bank of France from 1 November 2015. Moreover, two French presidents since the start of the Fifth Republic—Georges Pompidou and Emmanuel Macron—had similar careers, serving in government, then in banking, and then back in government. Almost all of the bank presidents during the discussions and debates on bank structural reform (2012–13) were from the financial inspectorate and alumni of the French national administration school (Ecole Nationale d'Administration, ENA), as was the Governor of the Bank of France (Christian Noyer). In late 2012, the heads of three of the country's five largest banks were former Treasury officials, had served as financial advisors to the President or Prime Minister, and were members of the financial inspectorate: Xavier Musca (Crédit Agricole, former head of the French Treasury), Gilles Briatta (Société Générale), Michel Pébereau (BNP-Paribas), and Villeroy de Gallau, then a director at the same bank, who had particularly close ties to the Socialist Party, having worked as advisor to a Socialist Prime Minister and two Socialist ministers.

A number of scholars have pointed to the important influence of bank preferences in shaping French public policy since the international financial crisis (Jabko and Massoc 2012; Woll 2014; Couppey-Soubeyran 2015).[2] On bank structural reform more specifically, the close relations between the Treasury, the Bank of France, and banking elites resulted in the issues of TBTF French banks and structural reform being reconceived in a specific manner which undermined efforts to separate bank activities. Large banks were presented as a vital element of the French economy and the autonomy of the French state. Major structural reform was thus presented as highly dangerous to both. The close relations ensured that the draft law minimized structural reform—despite the high-profile promises of

---

[2] Moreover, the significant influence of France's largest banks in academia, media circles, and civil society more generally can be considered (Couppey-Soubeyran 2015). This influence contributed to the weakness of academic and civil society support for structural reform.

major reform earlier in the year. The close relations between the Treasury, Bank of France, and banking elites also ensured that the banks would have considerable control in designing the draft law (Tricornot et al. 2014). Following the election of François Hollande, Bank of France Governor Christian Noyer declared in a 15 May interview in *Les Echos* newspaper that he had recommended that the government avoid moving too quickly on bank structural reform (Drif 2012). French bank directors were well represented within the Council of Financial Regulation and Systemic Risk (Conseil de régulation financière et du risque systémique, COREFRIS), the body created in 2010 to examine and propose desirable legislation to reinforce macroprudential stability. Although the Council was run by the Ministry of Finance, was chaired by the Minister of Finance, and consisted of high-ranking Bank of France and financial supervisory officials, bank directors played an important role in the preparation of the Socialist-led government's draft legislation on structural reform (see below). Moreover, a number of bank directors made presentations to the National Assembly and Senate finance committee hearings on the draft legislation.

Public officials thus combined with former high-ranking Treasury officials working in private sector banks to form an influential alliance. Despite the official mandate of COREFRIS and the objective of most of its recommendations, this alliance should be understood as focused principally on the political-economy and macroeconomic importance of the large universal banks for the French economy and for the French state. The micro- and macroprudential risks stemming from large universal banks were secondary. The evidence for this claim—which might otherwise appear counter-intuitive—comes from the numerous public statements made by COREFRIS members, those invited to participate in the council's deliberations, and other observers. The elements of this alliance—which significantly undermined objective discussions of the intrinsic merits of significant bank structural reform efforts—are considered later in this chapter.

The consistent position of both the French bank and the financial bureaucratic elite was that structural reform would be detrimental to French national interest by undermining the competitive position of the largest French banks in international markets. Individually and collectively through the FBF, the large French banks presented structural reform as an opportunity for 'Anglo-Saxon finance' to increase its domination of international financial markets and even to take over French banks. During discussions in COREFRIS on the details of structural reform, the bank directors participating felt that they did not have to make a significant effort to convince government officials that structural reform was highly problematic (Interview 19).

There were influential government members who were outsiders to this bureaucratic–industrial clique and some even proposed a more significant separation of banking activities in the aftermath of the international financial crisis. However, none succeeded. One noteworthy example is Pierre Lellouche, a UMP politician and former Secretary of State for Trade during the presidency of Nicolas Sarkozy. In an intervention to the National Assembly finance committee on 12 February 2013 on the subject of bank structural reform, Lellouche noted that, when he was working at the Ministry of Finance during the international financial crisis, he proposed to the government and to President Sarkozy the need to introduce a French version of the Glass–Steagall Act (Assemblée Nationale 2013b). However, Lellouche also claimed that he was immediately opposed by the financial–bureaucratic elite and the banks.

The French financial–bureaucratic elite stood firmly behind the Socialist-led government's draft law. While the Governor of the Bank of England, Mervyn King, called for major structural reform in the UK, his French counterpart, the Governor of the Bank of France, Christian Noyer, defended the French model of universal banking and the need for large national champions that could avoid takeover pressures. Noyer had already made clear his opposition to EU-level bank structural reform by criticizing the reform recommendations of the Liikannen Group and the Commissioner then responsible for financial affairs, fellow Frenchman Michel Barnier (Couppey-Soubeyran 2015). Noyer repeatedly came to the defence of the Socialist-led government, arguing that its reform plans were not 'a minima' and that a stricter separation, as adopted in the UK, would have been 'against the national interest' by weakening French banks (Daneshkhu and Carnegy 2012). Noyer also played upon the economic nationalism that infused the French debate on ringfencing by arguing that a stricter ringfence was dangerous because 'the French government would have found itself with only the big Wall Street banks to place its debt. [French] companies would have found only Wall Street banks to finance their operations' (quoted in Daneshkhu and Carnegy 2012). Noyer was also a former Director of the French Treasury. The head of the Treasury in 2012, Ramon Fernandez, also from the financial inspectorate, took charge of the design of the draft law for Minister Moscovici.

4. The absence of venue shifting and conflict contraction

The second major factor that explains the symbolic nature of French structural reform were the venues in which the draft law was designed and debated. As in Germany, the use of existing institutional venues potentially exposed the issue to higher levels of politicization, not least because President Hollande had deliberately sought to exploit the issue of TBTF banks during the 2012 election campaign. However, we argue that, in office, the Socialist-led government set out to contain political and parliamentary pressure for a more stringent approach by carefully steering the draft law through a series of government and parliamentary committees. Crucially, these venues had close links to France's powerful banking industry and undertook limited engagement with wider societal groups, thereby limiting the scope for serious deliberation. In addition, the Socialist-led government's ability to backtrack on its election commitments was facilitated by the fact that the main opposition party—the centre-right UMP—had little incentive to push for major structural reform.

The main non-parliamentary venues for the consideration of financial reforms more generally were the Consultative Committee on the Financial Sector (Comité consultatif du secteur financier, CCSF) and COREFRIS. Both engaged in discussions on bank structural reform. However, COREFRIS was the more engaged of the two committees because it focused more specifically on new legislation. The CCSF was an independent committee of the Ministry of Finance which involved representatives from the ministry, the financial sector, consumer groups, independent financial experts, and two parliamentarians, one from the National Assembly and one from the Senate (CCSF 2014). This independent committee was created prior to the outbreak of the financial crisis and issued its first annual report in 2007 (for 2006), addressed to the French President and the parliament. The CCSF, which met monthly, considered bank structural reform among dozens of major financial issues, but did not dedicate significant time to examining the issue until 2013, after the proposal of the draft law. The CCSF focused on specific matters, in order to add helpful details to the law. However, it did not engage in any public discussion on structural reform. In its 2013 report, the CCSF focused upon elements of the July 2013 law other than structural reform, notably bank charges, information for clients, consumer protection issues, and banking inclusion (CCSF 2014).

Following the June 2012 parliamentary elections, the newly elected Socialist-led government assigned COREFRIS to examine the possibility of bank structural reform. The council had been created by the UMP government of François Fillon in 2010 to advise the Finance Minister on financial issues and specifically on financial sector risks. It was replaced in July 2013—through the adoption of the law that included bank structural reform—by the Council on Financial Stability (Haut conseil de stabilité financière, HCSF). It consisted of only high-ranking public sector officials from the Bank of France and the Financial Markets Authority (AMF), the bodies responsible respectively for the supervision of banks and other financial services, and a number of top bank officials. Following its creation in 2010, COREFRIS was rapidly rebaptized by the French press as the 'Pebereau Committee' after the head of the country's largest bank, BNP-Paribas (Pouzin 2014b).

The selection of COREFRIS as the main body to analyse the issue of bank structural reform and draft the text of the law demonstrates a deliberate strategy of conflict contraction on the part of the Hollande presidency and the Minister of Finance, which for reasons of intra-party positioning and election campaigning a number of Socialist party leaders had sought to politicize over the preceding year. The work of COREFRIS on bank structural reform was organized in parallel with the Prime Minister's office and notably with Jean-Marc Ayrault's advisor on 'financing the economy', Nicolas Namias, who had just left a high-ranking position at France's third largest bank, the BPCE, which combined savings and cooperative banks but also, though its Natixis subsidiary, engaged in a range of investment banking services. Namias was also an Enarque and a former Treasury official.

During COREFRIS discussions on bank structural reform, two bank lobbyists of particular influence represented the sector: Jean-François Lepetit and Jacques de Larosière. The former was a high-ranking BNP-Paribas official who had been the author of the 2010 report for the French government on systemic risk, which advised strongly against the separation of banking activities in the aftermath of the international financial crisis (Lepetit 2010). Jacques de Larosière had a career of possibly unequalled brilliance in French and international public financial circles. He was a member of the elite financial inspectorate, a former Director of the French Treasury, Governor of the Bank of France, and head of the IMF and the European Bank for Reconstruction and Development (EBRD). Most importantly in terms of our analysis, he had been an official advisor to Michel Pébereau, head of BNP-Paribas, since 1998.

Unlike the Vickers Committee and even the CCSF, COREFRIS did not include independent experts and members of parliament. Unlike the Vickers Committee, all its meetings were *in camera*. COREFRIS focused principally on the potential dangers of structural reform to the competitive position of the large French universal banks, notably in relation to the large US investment banks (Finance Watch 2012; Joanny 2012; Nathan 2012; Erasmus 2017; Interview 20, 48).

A number of observers (Finance Watch 2012; Joanny 2012) were critical of the constraints placed on the COREFRIS mandate and the lack of transparency of its meetings and deliberations, the principal risk being that the draft law would be minimal because the government sought to avoid calling into question the French model of universal banking. There were a limited number of *in camera* consultations with banks, the FBF, bank trade union representatives, consumer association groups, and the peak association for big business, MEDEF. Finance Watch compared this consultation unfavourably with what took place at the EU level, where the preparation of the Liikanen Report had involved a major well-published consultation with numerous public and private sector actors, and the publication of their contributions (Finance Watch 2012; Joanny 2012). Some critical observers have claimed that the design of the draft law on bank structural reform represented a 'mascarade of democracy' (Pouzin 2014b). Jérôme Cazes, the former head of Coface, an insurance and lending company which had been privatized in 1994 and then purchased by the Natixis investment bank in 2002, was similarly scathing of the process: 'In France, we launch a consultation that seeks to ask banks what they think of the organization of banks' (quoted in Tricornot et al. 2014, p. 83, authors' translation).

The result was a significantly different approach to the topic of structural reform than in the US and UK discussions on the topic and a significantly different emphasis on important issues. For COREFRIS members, it made little sense to separate banking activities focused upon the real economy from a range of more speculative activities. Market-making activities, for example, were presented as ensuring liquidity on financial instruments and contributing to more accurate pricing. For Finance Watch and a range of other experts in favour of a strong ringfence, commercial and investment banking activities had to be separated. 'On the one hand, there is the commercial bank which is involved in monetary creation via credit and on the other market activities; if the two are not separated, speculation ends up being financed by monetary creation' (Thierry Philipponnat, quoted in Joanny 2012). For critical observers, COREFRIS failed altogether to consider the systemic risk posed by such large French banks—which was the principal issue driving discussion on TBTF and bank structural reform at the international and European levels and in the US and the UK (Interview 30). Rather, the council agreed that large universal banks were inherently safer than investment banks because of the diversity of their activities and funding. One Force Ouvrière (FO) trade union official interviewed by COREFRIS thought that the council had reached its conclusions early in the process: 'when we were allowed to speak, at the end of October [2012], one had the impression the deal was already concluded and that it was more a matter of verifying that we were not going to oppose the government' (Sébastien Busiris, quoted in Nathan 2012, authors' translation).

Limited parliamentary control over the draft law

Neither the National Assembly nor the Senate finance committees that examined the draft law provided a well-publicized venue for challenges to the government's version of bank structural reform. The role of the French parliament in facilitating conflict contraction can be explained by three factors. First, the government's decision to mix the issue of bank ringfencing into the same law as a number of other bank-related provisions undermined the singular attention that the issue of structural reform attracted in the UK and US and at the EU level. The draft law contained a number of measures in addition to the structural reform proposed by COREFRIS, including the transparency of banks in their use of tax havens, the French financial transactions tax, consumer rights, and the creation of a national bank resolution fund—hence the transposition and implementation of the EU's BRRD. Thus, the limited parliamentary committee time devoted to the examination and debate of the draft law had to cover a range of very different issues.

A second factor was the political configuration of the government and parliamentary assemblies. In the June 2012 elections, the Socialist Party won 280 of the 577 National Assembly seats, and was thus only nine seats shy of a majority. The party opted to govern with a number of small left-wing parties, including two which each held two ministerial portfolios: the centrist Radical Party of the Left (Parti radical de gauche, PRG) with twelve National Assembly seats and the left-wing Greens (Europe Écologie Les Verts, EELV) with seventeen seats. While the former was moderate on major socio-economic questions and had participated in several previous Socialist-led governments, the latter was left-leaning, in favour of increasing progressive taxes, and often aligned on major socio-economic questions with the French anti-capitalist and anti-globalization movement. The Socialist Party itself was a broad church including centrists and left-wingers. The domination of the Socialist Party within the governing coalition combined with the limited likelihood that the UMP centre-right would block the parliamentary adoption of its draft law meant that the Socialist leadership did not need to dedicate much energy to placating potentially hostile coalition partners on the issue of bank structural reform. The EELV supported a tougher separation of banking activities during the 2012 election campaigns and throughout the parliamentary deliberations on the draft law (EELV 2013). However, in government, it had other more important priorities on which it sought concessions from the dominant Socialist Party. Its only member on the National Assembly finance committee made no demands on bank structural reform issues, instead focusing his efforts on the tax haven elements of the draft law. The seventeen EELV National Assembly members all voted with the government on the adoption of the law on 19 July 2013.

A third factor explaining the failure of the parliamentary committees to contribute to conflict expansion on the topic of bank structural reform is that the centre-right was not ideologically and politically predisposed to launch opposition to a reform agreed in advance by the financial–bureaucratic elite of the country and with the de facto acceptance of the country's banking elite. The draft law offered limited opportunity for political point scoring. The UMP (from 2015 the Républicains)—the main party on the centre-right, and the second largest party in both the National Assembly and Senate—had based a significant element of its own presidential and parliamentary election campaigns on criticizing François Hollande and the Socialist Party's irresponsible economic 'radicalism' and was unlikely to challenge the government actively on a reform which was far from radical. Thus, following the presentation of the draft law, senior UMP politicians announced that the Socialists had 'come back down to earth' (Daneshkhu and Carnegy 2012; Interview 18). National Assembly and Senate finance committee minutes confirm that the UMP members were largely silent on the structural reform elements of the draft law and their amendments concerned relatively minor matters of wording (Assemblée Nationale 2013a; Sénat 2013; Interview 17). Later, the UMP centre-right abstained from voting for the agreed version of the draft law in both the National Assembly and Senate.

The National Assembly finance committee consisted of seventy-three deputies at the start of 2013, only a small minority of whom—notably from smaller left-wing parties and the Socialist Party—took a clear public position in favour of a stronger ringfence than had been proposed by the government. The Socialist members responsible for the draft law, Laurent Baumel and the committee's *rapporteur* on the law, Karine Berger, were ironically amongst the most public in their expression of concern that the structural reform provided for in the draft law was insufficient. At the same time, given their position as Socialist members, they were not in a position to push the government too actively on the matter (Interviews 17, 20). While the National Assembly committee proposed a range of amendments, the large majority were focused on specific wording issues and on elements of the draft law other than structural reform. Only two amendments focused on the substance of structural reform with the aim of marginally strengthening the ringfence (Assemblée Nationale 2013a).

Forty-two people appeared before the National Assembly committee to speak on the draft law, including public officials, bank officials from the FBF and individual banks, other financial sector officials (notably from the insurance sector), representatives from NGOs, and economists (Assemblée Nationale 2013a, pp. 251–4). Only a small minority of these people were strongly critical of the government's proposed reform and these were notably the independent economists. Laurence Scialom, a professor in economics at Paris Ouest Nanterre and a member of Finance Watch, sought a clearer separation of 'vital' activities for the financing of the real economy and other activities, including trading activities (see also Couppey-Soubeyran and Scialom 2013). She argued that government support should only be provided for the former. The economist Gael Giraud of the left-leaning Roosevelt 2012 association also appeared before the committee, arguing in favour of much tougher structural reform and claiming that Moscovici's draft law 'buried the separation of banks' (Giraud 2013a, 2013b). Colette Neuville, the head of an association defending small shareholders (Association de défense des petits actionnaires, ADAM), and the President of the DiaCrisis association and blogger Olivier Berruyer were similarly critical. The latter referred to the proposed structural reform in the draft law as a 'réforme a minima' and argued that only a full separation of deposit activities from trading activities could ensure the protection of deposits (Mabille 2012). The committee visited Frankfurt and Brussels, meeting with a number of officials in favour of more significant structural reform, including Erkki Liikanen, Governor of the Bank of Finland and head of the committee examining structural reform at the EU level, and Thierry Philipponnat, the General Secretary of Finance Watch.

The Senate finance committee—with a centrist/centre-right majority—examined the government's draft law following the National Assembly committee's initial report (Sénat 2013). The Senate committee supported the weak version of structural reform. In its hearings, a small number of opponents of the government's symbolic version of reform presented their views on the government's draft law, including Scialom and Couppey-Soubeyran (see also Couppey-Soubeyran 2015). Couppey-Soubeyran noted that there was little point challenging the weakness of the government's recommended structural reform because nothing would be changed, and chose to focus instead on other elements of the draft law (Sénat 2013).

5. The weak pro-structural reform coalition

While a range of civil society groups, politicians and academics in France supported significant bank structural reform, there was only limited mobilization in the country, either individually or collectively, to encourage the Socialist-led government to adopt a far-reaching reform.

Disparate forces in civil society

Despite a significant number of major bank scandals—from the fraudulent trading of the 'Kerviel Scandal' at Société Générale that resulted in record bank losses, to revelations of bank involvement in tax havens, to the news report in 2012 of the involvement of Crédit Agricole and Société Générale in the rate manipulation scandal (of Libor, Euribor, and Tibor) orchestrated by Barclays Bank—there was limited sustained public or political mobilization on bank reform. The well-established anti-capitalism/anti-globalization movement ATTAC was the closest France came to the US Occupy movement, but it was never focused principally on bank reform and lacked the intellectual credibility of the latter. Unlike the US and UK Occupy movement, which was principally focused on bank power, ATTAC was an older movement with a range of policy objectives linked to challenging capitalism. It produced a number of statements on bank structural reform but its influence was marginal. ATTAC is, however, an institutional member of the European organization Finance Watch and joined in the latter's ongoing efforts to reinforce bank structural reform and adopt a more far-reaching reform at the EU level than had been adopted in France. The ATTAC economist Dominique Plihon—also professor of economics at the University of Paris-Nord—later contributed to the *Livre Noir des Banques* (the 'Black Book of Banks'), explaining and criticizing the weakness of French structural reform and how the French approach to structural reform undermined EU level regulation (Attac and Basta 2015).

French consumer rights organizations do not have a history of great lobbying success (Trumbull 2012). On bank structural reform, the main consumer rights associations were broadly in favour of a strong ringfence to protect customer deposits. The president of one association spoke before the National Assembly finance committee responsible for examining the draft law on bank separation. However, the focus was on the customer affairs sections of the draft law. The financial consumers association/website, 'La finance pour tous', was in favour of a strong separation. In 2012, the association offered on its website a lengthy interview with one economist, Pierre-Noël Giraud, in favour of a full separation (Giraud 2012; see also Giraud 2009): the creation of subsidiaries was insufficient because if the subsidiary failed, the mother bank would still be expected to come to the rescue. Giraud insisted that structural reform had to involve the creation of two different companies with different shareholders taking different risks. The site makes reference to Maurice Allais, the only French recipient of the Nobel prize in economics: it was necessary to stop the banks speculating with money that they create, just as it was necessary to stop bank subsidiaries and investment funds speculating with money lent by banks. Speculation could never be stopped but it was necessary that speculators speculated with their own funds and not those of others.

A number of trade unions—notably the General Confederation of Labour (Confédération Générale du Travail, CGT), linked to the Communist Party, and the left-wing FO—came out in favour of a tougher ringfence but did not campaign actively on the topic. The Secretary General of FO Banques, Sébastien Busiris, although in favour of the French universal banking model, argued that to save the model it was necessary to introduce a tougher ringfence (quoted in Nathan 2012).

No public demonstrations specifically in favour of bank structural reform took place in France and there was limited public action on the losses of banks more generally. Didier Chabanet and Arnaud Lacharet (2016) attempt to explain the political insignificance of the French Occupy movement, with not a single demonstration involving more than 3000 people and only one involving between 2000 and 3000 people. Occupations were mostly small and short-lived, with the exception of Bayonne which lasted six weeks.

A number of academic economists with influence in French government were critical of the draft law on structural reform. These included notably Jézabel Couppey-Soubeyran (an academic at the University of Paris 1 Panthéon-Sorbonne), who had been a member of the Prime Minister's Council of Economic Analysis. François Morin was a professor in economics at the University of Toulouse and had been member of the General Council of the Bank of France and of the Council of Economic Analysis. Couppey-Soubeyran was one of a number of academic economists who wrote regularly in favour of bank structural reform, including a number of newspaper articles and a book entitled *Blablabanque: Le discours de l'inaction* (Couppey-Soubeyran 2015), which might be translated as 'Say Whatever Banking: The Discourse of Inactivity'. The book strongly criticized the inadequacy of French bank structural reform and other reforms proposed to make banks safer. Morin (2015) wrote of the dangers of very large banks globally, and complained of banking oligopolies and of states that were hostages to these oligopolies, including the French. Some of the loudest opposition to the French law (both draft and final version) came from outwith the country. The French Secretary-General of the Brussels-based Finance Watch, Thierry Philipponnat, described the reform as 'essentially cosmetic'—'credit and trading will still be mixed, and trading will still be subsidized'—and falling far short of President François Hollande's promises during the presidential campaign (Danesckhu and Carnegy 2012). Finance Watch produced a detailed critical analysis of the draft law presented by the French government to parliament in January 2013 (Finance Watch 2013c). It appealed to the French government's own four objectives as listed in the draft law's preamble, which Finance Watch found to be appropriate. A number of economic journalists were also noteworthy critics of both the Ayrault government's draft law and the law adopted in July 2013. These included the authors of *Mon Ami C'est la Finance: Comment François Hollande a plié devant les banquiers* ('My Friend Finance: How François Hollande bowed down to the bankers'; authors' translation) (Tricornot et al. 2014). The authors, from three of France's leading newspapers, Adrien de Tricornot (*Le Monde*), Mathias Thépot (*La Tribune*) and Franck Dedieu (*L'Expansion/L'Express*), were scathingly critical of what they saw as the Socialist President's hypocrisy on bank structural reform and the weakness of other Socialist financial reform measures.

A number of other leading French economists—often with important involvement in government economic policy making—were more cautious on bank structural reform. They included Jean Pisani-Ferry, who wrote a paper challenging Mario Draghi, the President of the ECB, for coming out in favour of bank structural reform. This paper is published on the website of France Stratégie, the government's economic planning agency (Pisani-Ferry 2015).

The political champions of symbolic reform

No French politicians of any significant influence in parliament, or major figures in French political life more generally, spearheaded a campaign to establish a strong bank ringfence. This is surprising given François Hollande's very loud and unambiguous promises during the presidential election campaign. As noted above, Hollande's close political ally and his primaries and presidential campaign manager, Pierre Moscovici, was appointed by the newly elected President in May 2012 as Minister of Economics, Finance and Trade in the Socialist-led government. A former high-ranking civil servant at the Court of Auditors, Moscovici led the design of the government's bank structural reform and the draft law adopted by the French cabinet on 19 December, and then presented it to the National Assembly in one of his first major acts as minister, thus giving it great symbolic importance. On 23 November, speaking before students at an elite business school, Moscovici announced that the election of the Socialist-led government meant 'the return of politics' and called for the separation of bank activities and the suppression of 'immoral' activities (Nathan 2012). Moscovici himself presented the draft law as 'the founding act' of his activity as minister (Nathan 2012). However, the draft law was labelled 'a capitulation' by the leading news magazine *Marianne* (Nathan 2012) and weak by a large number of banking specialists (see, for example, Finance Watch 2012).

In his defence of the government's draft law, Moscovici argued that national economic interests and the interests of Paris as a financial centre had to be defended. Adopting the phrasing common to both French bankers and central bankers, he maintained that a stricter separation risked 'giving a gift to Anglo-Saxon banks' (*Le Parisien* 2012, authors' translation). This conflation of large bank interests—as national champions—and national interests was considerably less present in the British debate on structural reform. The political salience of playing it tough with the banks was absent in France, given the comparatively limited losses of French banks during the financial crisis, their robust health on a number of measures—despite their weak capital position in comparison to UK-headquartered banks—and the limited nature of public discontent on the issue.

Once in government, the number of national-level politicians actively in favour of tough bank structural reform dwindled. No one at ministerial level came out in favour of a tough ringfence. Karine Berger was the closest that bank structural reform had to a 'champion' (Roger 2013; Triconot et al. 2014). After the 2012 elections, Berger became a member of the National Assembly finance committee and *rapporteuse*, the member responsible for preparing the committee's position on the draft law that included bank structural reform. Berger, a neo-Keynesian, had an impressive academic background in economics and significant economic policy-making experience. She was responsible for the economic policy elements of François Hollande's presidential campaign, including the seventh group of promises and, specifically, promise 7.1 on the need for bank structural reform. She was also from 2012 to 2015 the Socialist Party's national secretary on economic matters. Thus, given her background, she was a reasonable choice as *rapporteuse*. Her leading role in partisan political debates on bank structural reform might have transformed her into the country's leading advocate for major structural reform, of which she was clearly in favour. However, her role in this regard was highly curtailed—a number of informed interviewees have pointed to pressures coming from the Minister of Finance and the Ayrault government (Interviews 20, 43, 49). Berger did not attempt to transform her role into that of a leading campaigner. Her position on the law adopted in July 2013 was supportive but critical. She defended the law as a cease-fire in the Socialist government's battle with '*finance folle* but not the end of the war' (quoted in Lejoux 2013). There was a clear ideological and informed intellectual dimension to Berger's support for structural reform. However, she lacked the intellectual and professional credibility of Sir John Vickers. More importantly, as an elected politician and a loyal member of the

Socialist Party, Berger lacked Vickers' autonomy. As a finance committee member assigned to push through a draft law by a Socialist-led government with a comfortable majority of seats in the National Assembly, Berger also lacked the venue to achieve a thorough-going analysis of the need for structural reform, let alone to attract public attention to the cause. Berger accepted that 'the reform [proposed in the draft law] does not seek to correct the activities of banks by transforming their structure' and noted that the spirit of the law was thus that 'the banks should not be separated but we are preparing a pair of scissors to be able to do so if necessary' (quoted in Nathan 2012, authors' translation).

There was some frustration within Socialist Party ranks with the limited nature of the government's proposed structural reform. One Socialist deputy involved in the discussion of bank structural reform text in the National Assembly deplored the consensus between French banks and the government: 'We understood that banks had started their lobbying as soon as 7 May [2012, the day after the election of François Hollande as President], and that the techno-structure of the Treasury ... shared their point of view more than ours' (Bonnefous 2013, authors' translation). This frustration was, however, largely marginalized (Laurent 2013). There was only a modest reinforcement of the government's draft law through two amendments proposed by Socialist members of the National Assembly finance committee. The Senate finance committee confirmed the National Assembly committee's amendments, while asserting the need to protect the universal banking model (Sénat 2013). For left-wing observers outside the Socialist Party, the Hollande presidency and the Socialist-led government represented a complete 'capitulation' on all major socio-economic issues (Mauduit 2013). Thus, the weakness of structural reform reflected a broader failure to address left-wing concerns.

The Socialist National Assembly and Senate members who would have favoured a tougher structural reform were constrained by party discipline. Massoc (2020, p. 150) quotes a former Socialist deputy who recalled: 'Of course, we were seeing that the mountain was about to give birth to a mouse. But it is difficult, politically, to go against your government. There are retaliations. So we thought: at least we got something.' The Socialist President (speaker) of the National Assembly in 2012–13 noted: 'We called for wisdom [among Socialist Party deputies]. ... Accepted amendments would remain cosmetic. We do not wish to make the life of banks more difficult' (Laurent 2013, authors' translation).

Unlike in Germany, the broad bipartisan support that large French banks enjoyed in the National Assembly limited the politicization of structural reform during the legislative process. The mainstream centre-right (UMP and UDI) in both houses of parliament came out early in favour of the Socialist-led government's draft law (Daneshkhu and Carnegy 2012). Gilles Carrez, the UMP chair of the National Assembly finance committee, a strong opponent of a strict separation of banking activities, described the draft law as 'rather balanced' (Roger 2013) and approved of its limited ambitions (Raymond 2013). Carrez noted to Minister Moscovici that he understood that the minister perhaps needed the support of the centre-right opposition members of the finance committee to pass the law and that this support would be forthcoming (Assemblée Nationale 2013a, p. 57). The previous UMP-led government of François Fillon and President Nicolas Sarkozy had repeatedly denied that TBTF was a problem in France, and Christine Lagarde, former UMP Finance Minister and then IMF President, had actively defended the French banking model. The final text of the law faced opposition from the mainstream right, with the UMP members voting against, officially describing the law as 'dogmatic and militant' (Libération 2013, authors' translation). At the same time, the deputies of the centre-right UDI abstained from voting on the grounds that the 'reform was timid and *frileuse*', while the deputies of the Front de gauche, the far left, also abstained on the grounds of the law's inefficacy and the lack of an effective separation (L'Obs 2013, authors' translation).

6. Conclusion

It can be argued that the failure of significant bank reform in France reflected the widespread view in French policy-making circles that the country's banking sector had—despite significant losses—had a comparatively good financial crisis (Hardie and Howarth 2009). There was no significant overhaul of the national regulatory and supervisory regimes from 2009 (Howarth 2021). The bulk of changes in France came from the transposition and implementation of new international guidelines and EU legislation, much of which French governments sought to dilute—such as on capital requirements. The international financial crisis was repeatedly presented as a problem created by excesses in Anglo-American finance to which the French banking system was exposed principally through unwise purchases of securitized assets (Burns and Thomas 2009; Hardie and Howarth 2009). French governments, the French Treasury, and the Bank of France repeatedly challenged the assumptions behind TBTF concerns (Hollinger et al. 2009; Drif 2012). Some French banks got bigger in the aftermath of the crisis. BNP-Paribas—actively supported by the French government in its takeover of Dexia and Fortis' Belgian and Luxembourg operations (Hardie and Howarth 2009)—briefly became the world's largest bank by assets in the aftermath of the financial crisis, recording an increase of 34 per cent in three years to the end of 2010, and retained its position as the largest or second largest EU-headquartered bank for the next decade. While the financial crisis resulted in the decline of the international activities of British and German banks, the internationalization of French banking, principally retail operations, proceeded apace.[3]

---

[3] The non-French financial assets (loans, securities, shares, and other financial products combined) held by French monetary financial institutions rose from 36.4 per cent of total financial assets at the end

Nonetheless, François Hollande, the Socialist Party's presidential candidate, made an explicit election campaign promise to break up France's largest banks and, more generally, tame the power of the financial sector. This chapter explains how this promise was transformed into the weak and symbolic structural reform adopted in July 2013. Cooperative financial power reinforced by a longstanding interrelationship between elite bureaucrats and top bankers worked to undermine far-reaching legislation. The design of legislation in *in camera* COREFRIS meetings involving principally bureaucrats and top bankers ensured that the draft legislation included weak structural reform, while the operation of the French parliament's two financial committees ensured little modification of the proposed reform. The combination of these standard venues of French financial rule making, and the debate and adoption of a law that combined a range of financial reforms, facilitated the government's efforts to reduce conflict on the weak structural reform it had proposed. Efforts in France by political, bureaucratic, and non-bank financial and non-financial firms to increase the salience of the TBTF issue were modest and marginalized in comparison to efforts in the US and the UK. The efforts of a small number of NGOs, academic economists, and economic journalists to inform the public of the dangers of TBTF banks were no match for the influential coalition of top financial bureaucrats and top bankers which prioritized above all the preservation of French national champions. At the same time, however, the absence of venue shifting meant that senior bureaucrats and bank lobbyists were not able to block reform altogether. This contrasts with the process in the Netherlands where venue shifting enabled the bank lobby and pro-bank politicians to sideline serious discussion of structural reform. As in Germany, the Hollande presidency and Socialist-led government were therefore unable to insulate the issue entirely from political and parliamentary pressure. Moreover, given Hollande's explicit election pledges in 2012, the government had an interest in introducing symbolic reform to appease the left wing of the Socialist Party.

A number of different authors have presented a more cynical analysis of French bank structural reform: that it was driven less by the timing of the 2012 elections and the election campaign promises of François Hollande and the Socialist Party, and more by the desire to pre-empt and then direct forthcoming intergovernmental negotiations at the EU level on the topic (Joanny 2012; Nathan 2012; Finance Watch 2013c; Tricornot et al. 2014; Attac and Basta 2015; Hardie and Macartney 2016). According to these authors, the principal aim of the French government was to avoid a far more significant structural reform imposed from above. In February 2012, the European Commission created a High-Level Expert Group to examine bank structural reform, to be led by the Governor of the Bank of

---

of 2007 to 38.1 per cent at the end of 2010. See Banque de France, 'Statistiques monétaires mensuelles: France, Bilan des Institutions Financières et Monétaires hors Banque de France (encours)'. Available at http://www.banque-france.fr/fr/statistiques/ base/statmon/html/tmf_mens_france_fr_bilifmhbdfe. htm.

Finland, Erkki Liikanen. The group produced its report on 2 October 2012, with its recommendations on structural reform potentially affecting between 'twenty and fifty times more market activity than the proposed French law' according to a number of financial analysts, including Christophe Nijdam of Alpha Value and Finance Watch (quoted in Tricornot et al. 2014, p. 44, authors' translation). If applied in France, the Liikanen Group's version of structural reform would have separated off twenty-six times the amount of market activities of BNP-Paribas than required by the French law (Tricornot et al. 2014, p. 87). Nathan (2012) quotes French Ministry of Finance officials who stressed the advantages to France as the first European country to have legislated on bank structural reform, notably in terms of the weight this would give the French government in intergovernmental negotiations to shape the contents of future EU legislation. Jacques de Larosière, the semi-retired elite bureaucrat working as a BNP-Paribas lobbyist, made full use of his international reputation to campaign against the Liikanen Group's version of structural reform, publishing in the *Financial Times* a statement against the separation of bank activities entitled 'The Seductive Simplicity of Ringfencing' (de Larosière 2012). De Larosière wrote:

> The crisis has shown that bank failures are not related to specific structures, but to excessive risk taking. The institutions that were the hardest hit by the crisis were those that pursued risky operations either in trading or in more traditional activities, be they specialised or not.

8
The Netherlands
Shifting Structural Reform Off the Agenda

1. Introduction

A number of European countries—including Spain, Italy, and Austria—failed to adopt any legislation on structural reform. However, the Dutch failure to adopt structural reform stands out for a number of reasons: the large size of the country's banking sector in real and relative terms; the domination of a small number of systemically important banks; the devastation of the international financial crisis due to bank trading activities; and the relative size of the government bail-out and other support for the country's largest banks. The size of the Dutch government's bail-out measures and other support for the country's banks during and in the aftermath of the financial crisis was one of the highest in the world relative to GDP, reaching 17.6 per cent by 2014 prior to reimbursement. The Balkenende-Bos (CDA–PvdA, centre-right and centre-left) government spent approximately €28bn purchasing the toxic assets and shares of ABN AMRO and the Dutch part of the failed Fortis Bank. The government also purchased approximately €13bn worth of shares of ING, Aegon, and Samenwerkende Nederlandse Spaarbanken (SNS) to boost the capital position of these three banks. The government provided credit guarantees of over €200bn to cover the interruption of interbank lending, while it provided €28bn alone to cover ING's US junk mortgage portfolio. By 2011, official figures stated the total cost to the Dutch government as €30bn (Willems 2011). The broader impact upon the Dutch economy—with a drop of 3.7 per cent in GDP in 2009, a rise in government debt from 43 per cent of GDP in 2007 to 66.3 per cent in 2012, and a significant increase in unemployment—created a febrile political mood in favour of banking sector reform.

The Dutch case is also puzzling because there was some political momentum behind structural reform. The Dutch Finance Minister during the crisis, Wouter Bos, called for bank ringfencing when in office and continued to do so when he left politics to return to the private sector. A number of Dutch political parties were either strongly in favour of structural reform or at least open to it. The Wijffels Commission, which was explicitly mandated to examine structural reform, was chaired by a member of the Liikanen Group that had just proposed a strong ringfence. Opinion polls of the post-crisis period demonstrate clear public backing for structural reform. Most of the Dutch political and media classes were familiar with policy developments in the US and the UK to adopt a strong ringfence—with numerous articles in the press and discussions in parliament on these developments. Furthermore, the adoption of a weak reform—as in France and Germany, if principally to direct or avoid EU-level reform—was also pushed aside by Dutch governments.

The very limited attention given to bank structural reform in the 2012 national parliamentary election campaign is also surprising because it took place just after the May publication of the Liikanen Group's draft report, which called for EU legislation enacting major structural reform. The issue had also assumed political importance in the context of the French presidential and parliamentary elections of that year, and François Hollande explicitly called for structural reform in his election campaign programme. The limited Dutch political debate is also surprising given the intensity of the UK and US debates. By the time the next Dutch national parliamentary election campaign was under way in 2017, versions of structural reform had already been adopted in Germany, France, and Belgium, while it had become clear that EU-level reform was blocked in the Council of Ministers. Thus, the issue had completely fallen off the agenda for all Dutch political parties. The TBTF banks that dominated the Dutch banking sector rode out the storm of national, European, and international debates on regulatory reform.

Despite the move by the governments of several neighbouring countries to adopt national-level structural reform, and although the Dutch government formally considered the possibility of structural reform—encouraged to do so by the parliamentary De Wit Commission—this was not prioritized by any government of the period or any of the three commissions that examined possible reform. The Dutch government announced that it would wait for EU legislation, which it did nothing to promote and was content to see shelved. This position was not reached by default. We argue that non-reform in the Dutch case was the outcome of two key features of policy-making on banking regulation. First, the united Dutch banking sector—like its counterparts in France and Germany—was able to wield substantial cooperative financial power by exploiting alliances across the sector and the wider business community. In particular, the banking industry sought to leverage its collective influence to resist structural reform by opposing national-level regulatory change and diverting attention towards largely voluntary cultural change in banking. Second, non-reform reflects the use of venue shifting to a series of ad hoc specialist committees as a mechanism to depoliticize the issue of TBTF banks. The key difference with the UK, however, is that venue shifting in the Dutch case was aimed at narrowing—and eventually closing—the window of opportunity for reform through conflict contraction. This was achieved by limiting engagement to a relatively 'narrow' set of participants—who were known to be sympathetic to the concerns of industry and/or lacked expertise in financial regulation—but also by widening the mandate of the venues to a broad range of reform proposals. In doing so, the Dutch government was able repeatedly to deflect political pressure in favour of structural reform and steer the agenda away from ringfencing.

The chapter begins by examining the first example of venue shifting—the establishment of the Maas Commission by the banking industry itself—which played a critical role in shaping the government's subsequent legislative agenda. We then assess the potential for conflict expansion on bank ringfencing, given the hostility directed towards TBTF banks. Section 3 considers the government's limited response—the parliamentary De Wit Commission—and the surprising absence of debates on structural reform in Dutch electoral politics. Section 4 explains how the cooperative financial power of the Dutch banking industry played an instrumental role in steering the government's agenda, while section 5 reflects on the failed opportunity to reopen the debate on bank ringfencing during the Wijffels Commission. Section 6 reviews our argument.

2. Venue shifting 1: the Maas Commission

Venue shifting at the height of the financial crisis in 2008 played a critical role in depoliticizing the issue of TBTF banks and contributed to facilitating conflict contraction around structural reform. These ad hoc institutional venues therefore proved to be instrumental in shaping the Dutch government's subsequent regulatory agenda. Crucially, this first example of venue shifting was led by the Dutch banking industry itself in the form of an ad hoc 'expert' commission, established by the NVB in November 2008. The Advisory Commission on the Future of Banks—known as the Maas Commission—was intended to learn lessons from the banking crisis and to consider what reforms were necessary to restore financial stability. Named after its chair, Cees Maas, the commission consisted of just four members—three former directors of the country's three largest banks (Rabobank, ING, and ABN AMRO) and one academic economist, Sylvester Eijffinger. Together with the fact that the commission completed its deliberations within five months, this limited membership was a clear indication that the commission's willingness to reflect critically on the failures of banks was likely to be very limited.

In April 2009, the Maas Commission produced its report on the crisis (Maas et al. 2009). While critical of the banks in relation to the crisis, the report assigned blame broadly. The commission's report stressed that it took into consideration 'as much as possible' the international character of the Dutch banking system. 'This means that Dutch banks must not only remain competitive across national borders, but also that they face competition from foreign banks in the Netherlands' (Maas et al. 2009, p. 8). The commission formulated its seventy-three recommendations in four main areas: governance, risk, remuneration, and shareholder structures. The Maas Commission's recommendations directed to banks were principally focused upon voluntary 'soft' measures to be imposed by the banks themselves rather than new regulation. These measures involved changes to the management culture of banks with the aim of restoring public confidence in the system. They included limiting bonuses, strengthening bank risk management, and mandatory training for bankers.

The principal set of recommendations stemming from the report concerned mandatory deposit insurance protection, a 'Bankers' Oath' and a 'Banking Code' of conduct (*Code Banken*). The oath required individual bankers to promise to behave ethically and to declare risky investments. The code avoided recommendations on any regulatory change. Although it discussed some regulatory issues including capital requirements, ringfencing was not mentioned. The code included a number of soft measures, including a non-obligatory 'comply or explain' principle for banks to respect if they failed to maintain ethical standards and a non-obligatory 100 per cent bonus cap. The code included no recommendations of legal sanctions, let alone punishment for faulty bankers. In effect, it consolidated an earlier non-regulatory agreement between the NVB and the PvdA Finance Minister and Deputy Prime Minister Wouter Bos (Maas et al. 2009). Crucially, the Maas Commission briefly discussed structural reform but dismissed it as 'impractical in the Dutch context' (Interview 42; Kalse and van Lent 2009).

Shortly thereafter, the country's main governing parties—the centre-right CDA and centre-left PvdA—reached a parliamentary agreement on the Banking Code and it entered force on 1 January 2010. This agreement was consolidated by the formation of the centre-right (VVD–CDA) coalition government in June that year, as the new centre-right Finance Minister, Kees-Jan de Jager, moved to legislate on the Bankers' Oath, thus making it mandatory. The Maas Commission report and subsequent parliamentary agreement are notable for what they failed to recommend as mandatory—including additional capital requirements—or even mention—including bank structural reform. The code remained the most significant legislative package on bank reform adopted unilaterally by the Dutch government, excluding the transposition of EU directives, in the aftermath of the financial crisis.

The potential for conflict expansion

Despite the Maas Commission's early dismissal of bank structural reform in 2009, multiple factors had the potential to reignite the debate. These included vocal support for structural reform from both mainstream and less mainstream politicians, and a range of non- or less-partisan voices in academic and journalistic circles, a number of high-profile bank-related scandals, and mounting public anger against the banking system. To understand why sufficient political momentum for more stringent regulatory change did not build in the Netherlands, we begin by examining each factor in turn.

One of the most senior Dutch politicians to support structural reform was Wouter Bos, centre-left, PvdA Finance Minister during the financial crisis, who, following the 2010 elections, left politics to work as a partner at the KPMG audit and consulting firm. Bos placed emphasis on the dangers for the national economy of having such large Dutch banks and on the need to examine structural reform. In early 2010, Bos wrote a letter to the US Treasury Secretary, Timothy Geithner, noting his support for the Volcker Rule and a tough bank ringfence, his concern about ever larger banks and moral hazard, and his hope for international agreements on bank reform that restricted room for national arbitrage (Bos 2010; *Financieele Dagblad* 2010). Bos also requested that structural reform be placed on the agenda of the G20 Summit in Toronto, 26–7 June 2010 (Guebert 2010, p. 70). With this support, Bos presented himself as an outlier on bank reform in relation both to most other EU ministers of finance and to the Dutch central bank (DNB), which was not favourable (*Financieele Dagblad* 2010).

Bos argued that 'activities of financial institutions have to be focused again on providing reliable financial services to citizens and businesses on the basis of acceptable and transparent risks, to prevent costs of excessively risky behaviour from being passed on to the taxpayer' (Bos 2010). He claimed that he received 'with great pleasure' the proposals of the Obama administration on structural reform. In the letter, Bos also wrote that he 'will certainly try to win support for [the Obama administration's] views in Europe' (Bos 2010). In a 14 April 2012 interview published in the *Financieele Dagblad*, Bos—now working as a KPMG partner—again called for the government to launch an official examination of structural reform (de Horde and Willems 2012). In an April 2012 interview, Bos argued:

> You also see banks in the Netherlands that are not only too big to fail, but also too big to save. The attack on the Treasury would be disproportionate. In the Netherlands, too, we must enter into the discussion of whether our banks are too large. I do believe in internationally operating banks. ABN AMRO focuses internationally on logistics financing; Rabobank on green finance. Those are clear niches, and that is fine. However, the pre-crisis model was 'we buy business in Brazil and Asia', not because we know so much about it, but because we think that it is a good investment. Such a business model is risky compared to a relatively small [national] Treasury. ... And when the bill hits the taxpayer, that is a major problem. ... Banks have not yet begun to separate themselves. That is why I say the crisis can repeat itself. Unfortunately, the momentum for radical measures is over. The cause of the crisis has not yet been removed and I find that unacceptable.
> (de Horde and Willems 2012, authors' translation)

Bos' views on structural reform were typical of most politicians in the centre-left PdvA and shared by those in the left-wing populist Socialist Party (SP). Both parties called for major structural reform in their 2010 and 2012 electoral campaign documents.

The limited politicization of structural reform is also surprising given significant public support for tougher action against the banks. There was widespread public sentiment that the voluntary measures adopted by Dutch banks and other Dutch government measures following the Maas Commission were wholly inadequate. In 2011, a Motivaction poll found that 53 per cent of those surveyed were in favour in splitting up the country's largest banks with only 9 per cent of the population opposed (ANP 2011; also cited in Nods 2012). Only 11 per cent thought that bankers had learned the necessary lessons from the crisis and less than a quarter thought that the banking sector was able to engage in adequate self-regulation. More than 60 per cent of those polled believed that bank bonuses should be abolished altogether. Thus, the widespread mistrust of banks and bankers in the UK and US was shared in the Netherlands. The poll was commissioned by the Sustainable Finance Lab, a think tank created by Herman Wijffels and Klaas van Egmond, housed in the Utrecht Sustainability Institute of Utrecht University, to develop ideas for a sustainable, stable, and robust financial sector. Another widely discussed study found that a majority of employees working in banks considered the Bankers' Oath recommended by the Maas Commission to be a 'meaningless gesture' (Loonen and Rutgers 2017).

A number of observers have commented on the weakness of the Dutch counter-lobby to bank influence on bank reform (Vanheste and Oberndorff 2011). Nonetheless, Consumentenbon, the country's largest consumer rights organization, came out in 2009 strongly in favour of major structural reform and a strong ringfencing of investment from retail banking (van Aartrijk 2009). Consumentenbon argued that it was unacceptable that consumers had to pay for the mistakes made by investment banks, notably through mortgage interest rate increases. Consumentenbon argued that stricter guidelines on bank investments had to be imposed by government, similar to existing guidelines that applied to pension funds.

In addition, bank structural reform garnered considerable attention from the media. There was a generally hostile media reaction to the findings of the Maas Commission, with the Bankers' Oath and Banking Code treated with derision by a range of authors writing for mainstream news outlets (see, for example, Daan van Lent 2009; van Harskamp 2009). The reaction to the De Wit Commission's final report (see below) was even more scathing (see, for example, Douwes and Giebels 2010a; Wawoe 2010; Jonker 2012). One article in the *NRC Handelsblad*, the country's fourth leading newspaper by circulation, described the commission's findings as 'Collectively blind, and collectively guilty' (Kalse and van Lent 2010a). The article also insisted upon 'a strict separation between retail and investment banking activities. Savings from private individuals are not to be used to speculate on capital markets' (Kalse and van Lent 2010a).

A number of prominent economic journalists and academic economists also called for bank structural reform and other measures to shrink banks. Wijffels' Sustainable Finance Lab, supported financially by Triodos Bank, promoted research, discussion, and debate on bank reform. The Lab undertook research in favour of bank structural reform and other possible reforms, and commissioned surveys demonstrating public support for these measures. During the autumn of 2011, the Lab organized five evening events involving hundreds of academics, financial sector practitioners, and other informed observers with the aim of shaping the discussions of the De Wit Commission and government policy making. The Lab made a number of recommendations in November 2011 including a ban on proprietary trading along the lines outlined in the US Volcker Rule and the UK Vickers Report (Sustainable Finance Lab 2011).

The large size of the Dutch banking sector—five times the size of the national GDP—was a main preoccupation. By way of example, van der Walle and Wester (2011), writing in the newspaper *NRC Handelsblad*, argued that:

> A fundamental problem is that financial institutions are still too big. As a result, society cannot afford the bankruptcy of large banks. Those banks become saved by definition. ... With such incentives it is no surprise that banks have continued to take too much risk.
>
> (authors' translation)

To take another example, Professor of Public Economics at the Erasmus University, Bas Jacobs, argued that:

> Politicians are blindly focused on bonuses and top pay but are not doing anything about the rot in the foundations of the banking system. Far too little has been done about it in the Netherlands and other banking systems. ... The Netherlands still has to discuss the size of banks, because the too-big-to-fail problem has not been solved.
>
> (authors' translation; see also Degenkamp 2013)

A range of both journalists and academics called for greater diversity in the Dutch banking system, and specifically the re-creation of savings banks that had ceased to exist in the 1990s (see, for example, Roest 2011).

As in our other case study countries, there were several high-profile, bank-related scandals during the years following the crisis, sufficient to keep the issue of banking reform high on the agenda. The Dutch government's takeover of the Dutch part of Fortis Bank involved a series of scandals including the massive undervaluation of losses, known to the Dutch central bank but not included in the official valuation presented to the government (Kreling and van der Walle

2012). At the end of February 2010, another parliamentary commission, led by Michael Scheltema, a former deputy justice minister, published its report on the collapse of DSB Bank in 2010 and the role of the DNB in this (Berkowitz and Ten Wolde 2010). This report led to significant reforms at the DNB. The Burgmans Commission—an expert commission with responsibility for monitoring banks' adoption of the voluntary Banking Code recommended by the Maas Commission—concluded that banks were failing to do so (*Verdieping Trouw* 2010; Couwenbergh 2011). The commission found that a quarter of the forty-three researched banks did not intend to cap the bonuses of directors at 100 per cent of annual salary; and that a majority of banks did not intend to follow the Banking Code share plans and option packages. There were also a number of high-profile scandals concerning individual bankers and their bonuses, including Jan Peter Schmittmann, the former Director of ABN AMRO, who received an exit bonus of €8m—after he had voluntarily renounced half of the bonus that had been previously agreed (van der Walle and Wester 2011).

Finally, there were also high-profile scandals involving the manipulation of interest and exchange rate swaps, the Libor, and Euribor. In 2013, US and European authorities agreed to fine the Dutch Rabobank approximately $1bn (€774m)—the second largest fine of any bank involved in the rate-fixing scandals—and the bank's chief executive also resigned (Webb and Bart 2013). However, discussions about Rabobank failed to spark a new debate on TBTF or other necessary reforms. Aftershocks from the financial crisis, including the bailout of SNS Reaal, ensured that bank reform, more generally, remained a public concern. However, this was less targeted at structural reform. ING distributed several million euros in bonuses in 2010, even though the government had previously announced that banks receiving state aid were not allowed to distribute bonuses during the 2008 and 2009 financial years and could only do so if a profit was made in 2010 (Broekhuizen 2011). These bonuses provoked a minor political explosion in parliament, principally on the left and populist right, with several parties calling for legislation on bonuses. A majority of the Dutch lower house was strongly in favour of transforming the self-regulatory code into law, with the issue of bonuses attracting the greatest attention (Broekhuizen 2011).

To understand why these factors—many of which are shared with the other cases we examine in the book—did not result in greater conflict expansion and political pressure for structural reform, we consider the importance of a second example of venue shifting by the Dutch government.

3. Venue shifting 2: the De Wit Commission

On the face of it, the second example of venue shifting in the Dutch case arguably held much greater potential to foster conflict expansion and serious consideration of bank ringfencing. While the Maas Commission consisted almost entirely of senior bank executives, the De Wit Commission had a larger and more diverse membership, consisting of parliamentarians from eight political parties. It also sought to engage with a wider group of actors and interests, as the UK process (the ICB and PCBS) had done—notably through a series of public hearings involving key public officials and bank executives involved during the crisis. But, as we explain below, the commission's very broad mandate—to examine the government's management of the crisis and possible reforms to banking—together with the limited financial regulatory expertise of the commission's membership, had the effect of marginalizing serious discussion on structural reform.

The Dutch lower house (House of Representatives) voted in June 2009 to create its own commission to examine the causes of the crisis, the lessons learned from the Dutch government's and Dutch central bank's handling of the crisis, and potential reforms. The Financial System Inquiry Commission (widely known as the De Wit Commission, named for its chair) included a member of the House of Representatives from each of the eight largest parties. It was chaired by the Socialist Party member, Jan de Wit, who—despite his membership of a far left party—presented himself as an objective observer on banking matters (Willems 2011). The De Wit Commission met in two distinct series, the first from September 2009, reporting in May 2010, and the second from September 2010, reporting in April 2012 (De Wit 2010, 2012). The first series was dedicated to examining the government's and DNB's handling of the crisis, and the second focused on possible regulatory and other reforms. The commission succeeded in generating considerable political debate and public attention, notably through the thirty-nine public interviews conducted with forty-eight officials, including senior politicians, regulators, bank executives, and academic experts. The hearings had the potential to politicize banking reform given their focus on state aid to the financial sector during the crisis, and the purchase of ABN AMRO by the government (van der Walle 2011). Former Prime Minister Jan Peter Balkenende was principally questioned about his role in the acquisition of Fortis and ABN AMRO. Wouter Bos, then Minister of Finance, and Nout Wellink, President of the DNB, appeared before the commission twice. Its hearings focused on the government's capital support for ING, SNS, and Aegon. The collapse of the Icelandic internet savings bank Icesave—which hit the Netherlands harder than other EU member states—and the government's acquisition of the Dutch parts of the Franco-Belgian-Dutch Fortis Bank were also major topics. Bernard ter Haar, former Financial Markets Director from the Dutch Ministry of Finance, appeared before the commission three times.

The De Wit Commission's ability to engage in serious deliberations on banking reform was severely constrained by two main factors. The first was the fact that focusing on the government's handling of the crisis consumed considerable time and energy. Many observers were critical of the commission for principally 'fighting the previous war', doubting whether the parliamentary inquiry would add anything of value (van der Walle 2011). The commission dedicated considerable attention to whether the actions of the Minister of Finance, Wouter Bos, had been undertaken with sufficient justification given the urgency of the situation. Hence, the commission found that the Dutch parliament was informed too little and/or too late by the government on the crisis measures adopted (Kreling and van der Walle 2012) and that the government, specifically Wouter Bos, had deliberately broken the law in using government funds to bail out banks without the prior consent of parliament (Douwes 2010). Commission members also accused both Bos and DNB President Nout Wellink of inadequate management of the ABN AMRO bank losses and the internet bank Icesave's entry into the Dutch market (Douwes 2010). As a result, the commission dedicated surprisingly little time to reflecting on possible capital and structural reform (Willems 2010).

The second factor was the limited financial experience and knowledge of commission members, and the efficacy of the commission itself (Douwes and Giebels 2010b; Kalse and Wester 2010b; van der Walle and Wester 2011). This undermined discussions on more technical issues of regulatory reform, and directed the parliamentarians to focus on the handling of the crisis. The De Wit Commission members, despite including three current party financial affairs spokespersons, were criticized for being insufficiently versed in banking matters, and insufficiently aggressive with their questioning of the politicians and expert officials who appeared before the commission (Stam 2010; van Tilburg 2011). Eight of the ten commission members were not responsible for financial matters during the crisis—prior to the 2010 elections—and had no background in financial issues (Douwes 2010). Moreover, members changed over the life of the commission, with the replacement of the representatives of no fewer than four of the political parties—the VVD, Green-Left, PvdA, and CDA—following the 2010 election (Willem 2010). The weakness of the investigation and its findings—that all were to blame and thus no one—was widely discussed in the press (Douwe and Giebels 2010a; Wawoe 2010).

These limitations had an important bearing on the twenty recommendations issued by the De Wit Commission, which were instrumental in steering the government's banking reform agenda. Most importantly, the commission's final report largely endorsed the conclusions of the Maas Commission, urging banks to tackle the perverse incentives that lead to risky behaviour and recommending the use of non-mandatory tools to shape banking culture (Wawoe 2010). But de Wit also argued that bankers had a 'lack of critical self-reflection' and that, without adequate measures, they would go back to 'business as usual' (de Wit, quoted in Alberts and Oberndorff 2013, authors' translation). The commission therefore made four proposals that went significantly further than the recommendations of the Maas Commission: the introduction of Dutch banking regulations potentially beyond EU rules; capital requirements above Basel III baselines; greater resources for regulators; and working with regulators to explore the feasibility of breaking up Dutch banks, along either geographical or operational lines. At the same time, however, the De Wit Commission was at pains to stress that European and international-level agreements should lead the way on financial regulatory reform.

The De Wit Commission thus presented, but did not advocate, the option of ringfencing Dutch banks along both geographical and operational lines. The commission's geographical understanding of ringfencing focused on insulating domestic and EU operations from non-EU parts of the group (De Wit 2012, recommendation 16, p. 583). This geographical understanding reflected the soft economic nationalism of many of the commission's members and echoed the focus of Wouter Bos on bank structural reform (Interview 46). This economic nationalism melded with the perception that the operation of Dutch bank subsidiaries outside the EU context involved inherently more risk from which the mother bank—or at least its EU-based operations—should be protected. Both considerations also related to capital requirements and the aim to ringfence capital during crises.

The De Wit Commission presented the possibility that banking conglomerates separately capitalize customer-oriented banking practices and those 'not directly consumer-related commercial activities with a higher risk profile' (De Wit 2012, recommendation 15, p. 583, authors' translation). The presentation of this possibility was the closest that any public body in the Netherlands ever came to recommending structural reform. However, the commission did not go as far as specifying precisely which activities should be given which designation, stating that the Ministry of Finance should work with the two main financial supervisory bodies—the central bank (DNB) and the Financial Market Authority (AFM)—to establish the exact scope of the ringfence. The commission's multiple objectives ensured that bank structural reform never attracted significant focus (Interview 46). Moreover, its recommendations came with no compulsion for any party to adopt them as a reform programme.

The politics of bank structural reform

We argue that the Maas Commission and De Wit Commission exerted a powerful effect in shaping the wider banking reform agenda which no Dutch political party dedicated significant effort to challenging. During the 2010 and the 2012 parliamentary election campaigns, none of the largest eight Dutch political parties dedicated any space in party electoral programmes to structural reform, while two supported it vaguely and without elaboration. Few parties prioritized specific additional financial regulatory reforms. Although the De Wit Commission examined specific bank reforms, and recommended the further consideration of structural reform, it did not galvanize either parliamentarians or public opinion to support bank ringfencing prior to either the 2010 or 2012 election.

The response of most Dutch political parties to the De Wit Commission's recommendations was decidedly lukewarm (Willems 2010). Although the House of Representatives subsequently voted in favour of all of the De Wit Commission recommendations, this came with limited commitment actively to push forward any of the regulatory reforms (Alberts and Oberndorff 2013). At no point did the VVD–CDA government ever seriously consider pursuing the regulatory options raised by the De Wit Commission, let alone the possibility of structural reform. Some observers suggested that, in order to obtain a majority in parliament, it was necessary for the commission's recommendations to be politically neutral (Willems 2011). In this context, major issues of an ideological nature were discussed and debated behind closed doors (Willems 2011), and much of the material examined remained confidential for commercial and state secrecy reasons (Giebels 2011).

The implementation of the De Wit recommendations was similarly mixed. In March 2011, the House of Representatives adopted a motion forcing the Minister of Finance to report on the progress of each of the commission's recommendations. The last report on progress took place in September 2011. After that, the government referred to the De Wit Commission only once more, in 2013, with the Finance Minister Jeroen Dijsselbloem referring to the government's handling of the recommendations 'as resolved' (Alberts and Oberndorff 2013, authors' translation). In terms of resulting achievements, only one piece of legislation adopted—the Intervention Act—corresponded closely to a De Wit Commission recommendation. Some observers also claim that there was a difficult-to-measure 'cultural change' in the DNB, resulting in reinforced supervision over bank risks (Alberts and Oberndorff 2013, authors' translation). But the subsequent changes due to Banking Union and the SSM would have had a more significant impact than the De Wit Commission's recommendations. A range of other commission recommendations were never put into effect—from increasing the transparency of bank lobbying activities, to expanding the application of the Banking Code from top officials alone to all bank personnel. The De Wit Commission also recommended greater transparency on the lobbying activities of Dutch banks, but this was ignored by the banks and not taken up by government (Alberts and Oberndorff 2013). A number of commission compromises disappeared from the final report altogether, including increasing the Dutch bank leverage ratio to 5 per cent (Alberts and Oberndorff 2013).

How can we explain the timidity of the Dutch response? While the timing of the 2010 election potentially helps to explain the near silence on structural reform—given that the elections pre-dated the creation of the Liikanen Group—the limited debate on financial regulation more generally is surprising, especially given the significance of parallel debates in the UK and US at the same time. Ganderson (2020a, 2020b) points to difficult government coalition building in the Netherlands following the 2010 election—127 days of negotiations—and the significant decline of press coverage on the 2008–9 financial crisis from 2010 onwards as factors that discouraged focus upon the need for financial regulatory reform. Specifically, there were over four months of negotiations and debates within the centre-right VVD and CDA on the formation of a coalition potentially to include the populist anti-immigrant Dutch Party for Freedom (PVV). However, this explanation in and of itself does not tell us why only the radical right and left highlighted the need for tougher financial regulation during the 2010 election campaign.

The limited extent of conflict expansion around bank structural reform could be interpreted as reflecting Dutch consensus politics more generally (Lijphart 1999), which contrasts with the more adversarial nature of UK and US majoritarian politics (see Ganderson 2020a, 2020b). In the Dutch consensual political system—where power sharing in broad coalition governments, which included a number of political parties, was the norm—the association of individual political parties with inadequate pre-crisis financial regulation was unlikely. Thus, blaming specific political parties for the failure of existing legislation was limited (Powell 2000). In the Netherlands, the construction of governing coalitions tended to be protracted and involved consensus building. The focus on consensus could result in retrenchment, or inaction, and in turn helps potentially to explain Dutch government preference to wait for EU measures on a range of financial legislation. Furthermore, the Polder model of tripartite cooperation between employers' associations, labour unions, and government contributed to the Dutch consensual political culture and, more specifically, the largely united positioning of bank and other major business associations on financial reform (see below; Andeweg et al. 2020). Hence, it could be argued that consensual politics led Dutch political parties to delegate discussions on banking reform, and to defuse demands for stringent regulation by assigning a broad mandate to specialist committees.

While certainly an important part of the explanation, Dutch consensus politics cannot explain why the limited political debate on bank structural reform was not emulated in other areas where blame could be assigned for the financial crisis. The De Wit Commission, which consisted of parliamentarians, like the Maas Commission consisting principally of bankers, assigned blame broadly, thus taking pressure off governments to adopt legislation that significantly restricted bank activities. There was a lively debate on the failure of bank supervision and significant reforms to bank supervision were adopted (Chang and Jones 2013). The Dutch government was also strongly in favour of transferring control over bank supervision to the European level and specifically to the ECB (Howarth and Quaglia 2016a, 2016b). To the extent that the 2012 election campaign touched upon banking issues, the principal debates focused upon the voluntary terms of the provisions of the Bankers' Oath and the Banking Code.

During the four nation-wide election campaigns that followed the financial crisis—the 2010, 2012, and 2017 Dutch parliamentary elections and the 2014 European parliamentary elections—few Dutch political parties explicitly and repeatedly advocated for bank structural reform. Only two parties—the Green-Left (GroenLinks) Party and the left-wing populist SP—repeatedly noted the need for bank structural reform in their national election programmes and their campaign material for the 2014 European parliamentary elections. In 2010, the Green-Left Party acknowledged that the country needed smaller banks and 'the Netherlands' supported separating trading and retail activities, but it did not explicitly commit to enacting this policy (GroenLinks 2010, p. 11, authors' translation). The Green-Left Party was more explicitly supportive of structural reform in its 2012 and 2017 national campaign programmes (GroenLinks 2012, pp. 5, 19; GroenLinks 2017, p. 17), but vaguer in its campaign material for the 2014 European parliamentary elections, arguing that 'no bank should still be allowed to be "too-big-to-fail" in Europe' (GroenLinks 2014, p. 13, authors' translation). The SP was the strongest proponent of far-reaching bank structural reform and other measures, in its campaign programmes for all four elections (SP 2010, p. 8; 2013, p. 8; SP 2014, p. 11; SP 2017, p. 17).

The main centre-left party, the PvdA, also called for structural reform during election campaigns but was never precise on the details. In its 2010 electoral programme, the PvdA noted that 'the Netherlands supports initiatives to separate more and less risky banking activities' (PvdA 2010, p. 43, authors' translation), while in its 2017 electoral programme the party argued that 'the split between commercial and private banking activities must be completed' (PvdA 2017, p. 62)—even though it had never started. In its campaign material for the 2014 European parliamentary elections, the PvdA argued that 'trading activities must be separated from the activities of the bank for general interest (utility parts). In such a way that it is placed in a separate legal entity' (PvdA 2014, p. 6, authors' translation). The PvdA avoided such recommendations in its 2012 electoral platform (PvdA 2012). In response to the De Wit Commission's report, the financial affairs spokesman of the PvdA—then in opposition—Ronald Plasterk, announced his party's support for the cautious government position. The PvdA also argued that it was unnecessary to ringfence banks at present, but that those parts that might eventually be ringfenced should be identified and then split off during a future crisis (Nods 2012). Similarly, the populist right (PVV) member of the commission, Roland van Vliet, argued that the separation of investment and retail banking should come sooner rather than later (Willems 2010). But the PVV itself had no fixed party policy on structural reform and did not mention it in the party's platform for the 2010 elections.

Support for structural reform on the Dutch centre and centre-right was largely absent. The centrist Liberal Democrats (D66) came out explicitly against structural reform in the 2010 elections (D66 2010, p. 27), they failed to mention the topic in their 2014 and 2017 electoral platforms (D66 2014, 2016), while in their 2012 platform they supported a ban on proprietary trading along the lines of the Volcker Rule (D66 2012, p. 14). The three other centrist and centre-right parties—the

VVD, the CDA, and CU—avoided the topic entirely in their 2010 campaign material (CU 2010; VVD 2010). In its 2012 party platform, the VVD argued that 'in the future it must be possible to separate high-risk activities from so-called utility functions of banks', but this was not much of a commitment and could refer to separation at the time of bank resolution (VVD 2012, p. 13, authors' translation). In the VVD's platforms for the 2014 European parliamentary elections and the 2010 and 2017 national elections, structural reform was not mentioned (VVD 2010, 2014, 2016). The CDA also failed to discuss structural reform in its national campaign platforms in 2012 and 2017 (CDA 2012, 2017) but raised the possibility in its campaign material for the 2014 European parliamentary elections: 'Banks should no longer be allowed to trade for profit and savings using risky trading activities. To achieve this, the possibility of internal separation or division of social and business tasks of a bank is not excluded' (CDA 2014, authors' translation). The small centrist CU avoided the topic in all its campaign material while noting vaguely in its 2017 platform that 'Banks are still always too-big-to-fail' (CU 2017, p. 67, authors' translation; see also CU 2012; CU and SGP 2014). It is perhaps surprising that following years of debate and the publication of the Liikanen Group's report, the positions of most Dutch political parties on bank structural reform remained non-declared or vague.

The centre-right CDA Minister of Finance from 2010 to 2012, Jan Cornelis de Jager—supported by most of the centre-right government—successfully redirected discussion on structural reform in such a way as significantly to diminish, if not entirely to sideline, political pressure for such reform. De Jager argued that the ringfencing of retail banking activities should be an option in the context of *future* bank crises (van Tilburg 2012). De Jager sent a note to parliament that banks should organize their activities in such a way that allows for them to be split during a crisis and draw up 'living wills' to facilitate this (Vanheste and Oberndorff 2011). Furthermore, the government approved new powers to the Dutch central bank to split institutions that were threatened with imminent collapse (de Telegraaf 2011; Vanheste and Oberndorff 2011). In March 2012, the government passed the Intervention Act giving the DNB the option to split up banks if they ran into irreversible problems and sideline bank shareholders. However, legally, the bank was to remain one entity (quoted in Lalkens 2012a).

De Jager presented proposals on necessary future bank separation by claiming direct inspiration from the Volker and Vickers reforms and exaggerating the similarity between his reform and the US and UK reforms. He argued:

> The government seeks to make use of both the British and the American approach to protect the retail element of banks against the risks they run in their investment banking activities. The British Vickers Commission recommends splitting banks, so that the business part can easily be highlighted if the utility function

threatens to get stuck. The American Volcker Rule prohibits banks from trading in securities for their own account and risk. The proposal I am working on is very similar to both. We will introduce and want to be able to intervene to separate banking activities when banks engage in unwanted activities.

(de Jager, quoted in Berensten 2012a)

De Jager was supported by the DNB in his firm opposition to immediate structural reform (Berensten 2012b). De Jager's 6 March memorandum to the House of Representatives was accompanied by an explanation by DNB President Klaas Knot. Both de Jager and Knot argued that a strict separation of banking activities, as proposed by the Vickers Commission in the UK, was not feasible in the Netherlands. De Jager argued that that 'the division of banks is not a holy grail' (Lalkens 2012a). De Jager stressed that the retail activities of Dutch banks, and notably the provision of mortgages and the provision of trade finance and credit to companies, relied heavily on wholesale markets, making the disconnection of retail and investment banking activities particularly problematic in the Dutch case. The creation of investment banks would thus fundamentally undermine domestic funding to the real economy and increase reliance upon foreign banks. Both de Jager and the DNB president argued that it was extremely difficult to make a clear distinction between utility and investment banks. De Jager argued that, if bank separation was to be agreed at all, this should be at the EU level.

De Jager and Knot also insisted that the US proposed reform assumed a narrow definition of investment banking which covered activities in which Dutch banks were only marginally involved (Berensten 2012a). Both de Jager and Knot argued that the ringfencing of bank activities had become less relevant in the Netherlands since the split-up and sale of ABN AMRO, which had decreased the country's investment banking activities significantly (Berensten 2012b). The Volcker Rule would therefore mainly have a preventive effect in the Netherlands. Moreover, Knot insisted that the adoption of the Volcker Rule in the Dutch context would offer no benefit, would only harm Dutch banks and would result in a heavy and expensive burden for supervision (Berensten 2012a). De Jager further argued that structural reform was unnecessary because the capital requirements that the Netherlands imposed on its four systemic banks (ING, Rabobank, ABN AMRO, and SNS Reaal) were as strict if not more stringent than the requirements that Switzerland and the UK applied (Berensten 2012b).

Finally, these arguments were supported by a number of centrist and centre-right Dutch newspapers, and their economics editorialists, who were unambiguously opposed to structural reform. In contrast to the rest of the mainstream media (see above), the *Financieele Dagblad* dismissed ringfencing in favour of recovery and resolution plans for banks—eventually required by the Dutch Intervention Act and the EU's BRRD of 2014—to protect taxpayers from forced bail-outs (see, for example, Boonstra 2011). Similarly, many economics commentators highlighted the efficiency of the largest Dutch banks in terms of economies of scale, and thus lower costs for customers (Visser 2012).

4. Cooperative financial power in the Netherlands

We argue that the Dutch government's ultra-caution on banking reform, and its preference to wait for EU-level initiatives, owed less to the Dutch consensual political system than to the powerful and unified Dutch bank lobby. A number of academic observers and journalists have written of the close relationship between banks and the Dutch finance ministry, the central bank, and the political class more generally (Kosterman 2010; Veltrop and de Haan 2014; Vander Stichele 2016). This close relationship reflects a number of factors which we discuss below. Furthermore, financial institutions—banks and other firms—were largely unified in their opposition to structural reform, and instead actively promoted a range of non-mandatory measures aimed at changing bank culture. While individual banks and other financial firms maintained their own individual lobbying efforts on a range of financial regulatory and other issues, on structural reform the position was harmonized and forwarded by the main bank association, the NVB. In part, this reflected the massive dominance of the country's largest banks in the NVB, with three banks paying 80 per cent of the association's membership fee (Hofs 2013; Interview 47). Moreover, there were structural economic reasons for the influence of the country's two largest banks in the early 2010s—ING and Rabobank. In addition to being two of the country's ten largest companies, these universal banks performed a lynchpin role in the export-driven Dutch economy as the major source of trade finance for large Dutch companies.

The international financial crisis had a differing impact upon Dutch banks and other financial market firms. Most, but not all, of the largest Dutch banks received considerable government support. Rabobank, the country's second largest bank in 2008, suffered only minor losses. The financial sector beyond banking was more developed and diverse in the Netherlands than in any other European country with the exception of the UK, Ireland, and Luxembourg. Despite these two factors—differential impact on banks and financial sector diversity—Dutch banks and other elements of the financial system maintained a broadly strong and consistently harmonious front in their opposition to bank structural reform.

The only director of a Netherlands-headquartered bank that came out in favour of structural reform was Matthijs Bierman, Director of Triodos Bank Nederland (de Graaf 2009). Bierman argued that structural reform was desirable to ensure greater bank diversity, consumer choice, and financial stability: some banks could become 'safe' institutions that took deposits and provided loans, while others could focus on investment banking activities. Bierman, director of a financial institution that did not invest in high-risk products and promoted ethical banking and sustainability—and financially supported the Utrecht University's Sustainable Finance Lab—argued that restructuring the sector would help to decrease the impact of investment banking activities on the broader financial system and economy.

Bierman had, however, an unusual position on bank ringfencing. The directors of all the other Netherlands-headquartered banks, including retail-focused institutions such as ASN Bank, came out strongly against structural reform and focused instead on remuneration and the existing bonus culture. The head of Rabobank, Piet Moerland, argued that banks would not be less likely to fail if investment activities were separated from retail activities (ANP 2013) and insisted that the idea that bank separation contributed to safer banking was based on a misunderstanding, pointing to the inherent dangers of traditional banking: 'where money is lent, credit risk arises' (quoted in Ferschtman 2013, authors' translation). Moerland insisted that bank separation brought even greater dangers because it would be more difficult for banks to obtain capital to enable them to co-finance retail activities. Moerland insisted instead on banks increasing capital buffers along the lines of the Basel III agreement as the best route for making banks safer.

In two reports, Rabobank made clear its opposition to structural reform in terms of the impact both on European banks generally, and on Dutch banks and the Dutch economy more specifically (Smolders 2012; Treur 2012). Its arguments were echoed by ING and most other Dutch banks:

> It is definitely worthwhile to explore whether the policy measures proposed in the UK and US could be relevant to the Dutch situation. In so doing, however, we must not lose sight of the main objective, which is to facilitate a stable financial sector that supports the real economy. However, the separation of banks into retail and investment branches is not the most effective method and could even end up backfiring. Specifically, it could destabilise the banks and result in more expensive, lower-quality services to customers.
>
> (Treur 2012)

> If the [European Union] decides to implement the Liikanen Group's separation proposal, this, combined with other regulations and unlevel playing field, will create a situation where only a handful of major players will be able to conduct trading activities on a profitable basis. This will reduce the accessibility of trading services for European banking customers and will make them more expensive than before. At the same time, it is highly doubtful whether benefits in the form of greater financial stability would outweigh these disadvantages.
>
> (Smolders 2012)

The cooperative financial power of the country's largest banks also reflected a distinctive economic nationalism that—despite a pervasive liberal economic bias—was rivalled by few other European countries. The banks argued and most of the political class perceived that the largest Dutch banks were national champions to be protected and supported (Broekhuizen and Piersma 2011; Jonker 2012; van Tilburg 2012). They played a central role in the promotion of other Dutch national champions, notably through trade finance (van Tilburg 2012). Furthermore, Dutch banks could provide a full package of financial services to large Dutch firms (de Waard 2012). While the explicitly protectionist discourse in defence of large national banks found in France—in both political and bureaucratic elites—was largely absent in the Netherlands, it was rarely far from the surface.

Over the twenty years prior to the financial crisis, the Dutch government—and specifically the Ministry of Finance—provided active assistance to Dutch banks in their efforts to expand internationally. 'The bigger the better' was the leading perspective on banks and on the Dutch financial sector (Broekhuizen and Piersma 2011). The DNB also engaged in de facto lobbying in favour of the Dutch banking sector. As one of several examples, in 2006, ABN AMRO took over Antonveneta, an Italian bank, with the support of both the Ministry of Finance and the DNB President, Nout Wellink (Broekhuizen and Piersma 2011). The Dutch government also actively protected the big Dutch banks and intervened to maintain Dutch ownership (Jonker 2012). The government blocked the foreign takeover of ABN AMRO despite EU Commission opposition and attempts to impose EU competition policy (Jonker 2012). The government also imposed enforced restructuring on ING to avoid its takeover by a foreign bank. Finance Minister Bos and DNB President Wellink actively promoted ING to take over ABN AMRO (Tang and Vendrik 2012).

Intertwined with this economic nationalism were arguments about the economic needs of the Dutch economy. A number of economists, led by those working at the largest Dutch banks, argued that the presence of large universal banks in the country was essential to bank lending because Dutch savings rates were insufficient to cover bank credit and surplus savings were located principally in Dutch retirement funds (Boonstra 2011). Banks then relied on wholesale market funding to offer credit (Chang and Jones 2013). Also, Dutch banks and their supportive economists argued that, if banks engaged in riskier investment banking, it was because there was demand for it from Dutch non-financial companies. Dutch banks and their supportive economists argued that the large size of Dutch banks and comparatively large size of the Dutch banking and financial sector reflected the needs of the Dutch trade-oriented economy (van Tilburg 2012). Another fear was that ringfenced investment banks would fail to attract sufficient capital from the market (Nods 2012).

Dutch banks' opposition to ringfencing was exacerbated by their hostility to higher capital requirements under the Basel III Accord and the EU's revised CRD.

The centre-right VVD–CDA government, in power from 2010 to 2012, proposed a capital buffer of 4 per cent, well above the 3 per cent agreed by the BCBS. Finance Minister de Jager argued that this was the best way to increase bank safety, given the widespread view that bank self-regulation was not being reinforced quickly enough (Willems 2013). Dutch banks were unified in their opposition to increasing the bank buffer which, they argued, would hit bank lending (Willems 2013). The fear was that large companies would be more likely to seek funding from capital markets instead of borrowing from banks because of the higher financing costs at banks. Further, a number of financial economists pointed to the important risks to the financial sector coming from the housing market, which had little to do with investment banking activities (Nods 2012). Finance Minister de Jager (2010–12) and DNB President Knot adopted all these points as part of their argumentation against structural reform.

The cooperative financial power of the largest banks also reflected prevalent economic thinking in the Netherlands, where financial sector self-regulation was a longstanding preference of centrist and centre-right Dutch political parties—notably the VVD, CDA, and D66—the Ministry of Finance, and Dutch central bank supervisory officials, approximately half of whom had previously worked in the financial sector (Veltrop and de Haan 2014). Unsurprisingly, the banks were relieved at the change in government in 2010, with one newspaper declaring: 'Banks thank the government: do not separate, but be separable' (Willems and Hermanides 2011, authors' translation).

The Dutch banks worked to push back against the efforts of Dutch parliamentarians to pursue more significant reforms. Unsurprisingly, the NVB was strongly supportive of the voluntary reforms recommended by the Maas Commission. In its official response to the De Wit Commission's first report in 2010, the NVB (2010) argued that:

> The banks have taken responsibility from the onset of the crisis and have shown self-reflection. They themselves have thoroughly investigated the causes of the crisis and have opted for better risk management, more expertise, more attention for the customer and a responsible remuneration policy with the Banking Code.

For the next two years, Dutch banks lobbied heavily to discourage the De Wit Commission from embracing the idea of bank structural reform. In one meeting of the commission in late January 2012, four high-ranking bank officials—the heads of Rabobank, ING, Van Lanschot, and Triodos—and the head of the promotional body Holland Financial Center, the former head of SNS bank, Sjoerd van Keulen, warned commission members of the negative consequences of bank ringfencing, arguing that the economy would suffer, especially those doing business abroad, bank costs would rise, and risks would not change (*NRC Handelsblad* 2012; Willems 2012). Playing the bank nationalism card, these bank officials insisted that foreign competitors would end up taking over a number of services (Willems 2012). Their influence was amplified by the negligible financial expertise of most Dutch parliamentarians which, according to several academic observers, journalists, and policy experts, left them vulnerable to industry capture (*Het Parool* 2010; Vanheste and Oberndorff 2011).

The NVB was disappointed that the De Wit Commission's final report held open the possibility of bank ringfencing along either geographical or operational lines (De Wit 2012). The association argued that such measures were 'not in line with the nature of the Dutch banking system', and that Dutch banks did not risk customer savings in their trading activities (Kockelmans 2012; also Interview 47). However, the NVB had little difficulty with the bulk of the De Wit Commission's findings, and supported its vague call to 'narrow the gap between the financial sector and politics' (quoted in *Reformatorisch Dagblad* 2012, authors' translation). It also warmly welcomed the commission's endorsement of the industry-led measures to address banking culture supported by the Maas Commission.

5. Venue shifting 3: the Wijffels Commission

The publication of the EU High-Level Expert Group's report on bank structural reform in October 2012 provided an important opportunity for supporters of bank ringfencing in the Netherlands to reopen the debate. On 1 November, the Dutch government, at the request of House of Representatives, created the Commission on the Structure of Dutch Banks (in Dutch, the Commissie Structuur Nederlandse Banken) to investigate the possible implementation of the Liikanen Group's recommendations. The Wijffels Commission, named after its chair, was the first and only Dutch body to examine structural reform in detail. In theory at least, the commission could have facilitated serious deliberation and engagement around structural reform, and therefore widened the window of opportunity for more substantial regulatory restrictions on TBTF banks. As we explain below, its failure to do so was for two reasons. First, the issue of structural reform was gradually displaced by consideration of a wide spectrum of banking reforms, mirroring the problems afflicting the De Wit Commission. Second, the commission's members— notably the chair—were known to be sceptical of the feasibility of ringfencing Dutch banks.

The Wijffels Commission met a total of nine times over a six-month period. Officially, the commission was given a mandate to examine bank structural reform and resolution mechanisms for failing banks. But this narrow mandate was later expanded to cover a broad swathe of topics related to banking reform. On 28 June 2013, the Wijffels Commission issued its final report, entitled 'Towards a Serviceable and Stable Banking Sector' (in Dutch, *Naar een Dienstbaar en Stabiel*

Bankwezen) (Wijffels 2013; see also de Groot 2013). The commission made no fewer than eleven recommendations in its report that were of much wider purport than its official focus (Wijffels 2013). Only one of the eleven recommendations concerns structural reform—to accept the Liikanen Group's recommendation that proprietary trading by deposit banks above a certain level should be ringfenced. The other recommendations focused on: ensuring a stable, diverse, and competitive banking sector; improved bank governance; the diversification of mortgage provision beyond banks; increased capital requirements without reducing the flow of credit; the development of bail-in mechanisms for the resolution of failing banks; bank restructuring to allow, in case of failure, both their resolution and the separation of activities that are systemically relevant; the creation of a European Banking Union; and requiring banks to regain the trust of society by stating their role in society explicitly in a 'public statute'. While the Wijffels Commission supported the recommendations of the Liikanen Group, its broader reform efforts necessarily diluted its initial focus on structural reform, and thus diverted the attention of elected officials and the public.

Unlike the De Wit Commission, the membership of the Wijffels Commission had a far greater claim to technical expertise and political 'independence'. Its thirteen members consisted of some of the leading financial economists and other financial experts in the Netherlands, including Sylvester Eijffinger, who had served on the Maas Commission, and Dirk Schoenmaker, the Dean of the Duisenberg School of Finance.[1] Herman Wijffels himself was a former director at Rabobank, centre-right CDA politician, Chair of the Dutch Social-Economic Council, Dutch representative at the World Bank, Chairman and co-founder of the Sustainable Finance Lab, and until 2016 Professor of Sustainability and Social Change at the Utrecht Sustainability Institute of the University of Utrecht. The commission also included the Director of the country's largest consumer associations, the Consumentenbond, Bart Combée.

How should the remit and operation of the Wijffels Commission be understood in political terms? De Jager claims to have created the commission in response to public opinion polls that questioned the efficacy of the Banking Code and thought that more could be done to control bank activities (Lalkens

---

[1] In addition to Wijffels, the commission consisted of Prof. Dr B. E. Baarsma, Director of SEO Economic Research; J. H. A. S. Biesheuvel, Chairman of MKB-Nederland; Prof. A. W. A. Boot, Professor of Corporate Finance and Financial Markets; Prof. R. G. C. van den Brink, Professor of Financial Institutions; Dr B. R. Combée, General Director of the Consumer Association; Prof. Dr S. C. W. Eijffinger, Professor of Financial Economics and Professor of European Financial and Monetary Integration; Dr W. M. van den Goorbergh, Chairman of the Supervisory Board of the NIBC (*Nationale Investeringsbank Capital*) Bank and member of the Supervisory Board of Bank Nederlandse Municipalities; Prof. A. F. Harmsen, Professor of Knowledge Management; Dr F. Meijs ACA, Accountant and Partner, Banking and Capital Markets at PwC; M. Scheltema, member of the Supervisory Board of Triodos and ASR and external member of the ABP Audit Committee; Prof. D. Schoenmaker, Dean of the Duisenberg School of Finance; and Prof. Dr S. J. G. Baron van Wijnbergen, Professor of Macroeconomics.

2012a; Interview 44). With the government's adoption of rules on bank separation in the event of a future crisis—the Intervention Act—a strong separation of banks was off the table (Lalkens 2012a). De Jager's appointment of fellow CDA party member Wijffels as Chair gave the commission legitimacy on bank reform issues—Wijffels had relevant experience and had been a member of the Liikanen Group. However, Wijffels made his cautious views on structural reform publicly known: first, he noted that the Liikanen Group's recommendation on ringfencing would have very limited impact in the Netherlands and he did not believe that the Netherlands should adopt a tougher ringfence (Samsom 2012). The majority of the commission's thirteen expert members were as cautious as their Chair regarding the application of structural reform to the country's biggest banks and had other bank reform priorities (Samsom 2012; Interviews 41, 45).

Despite the relatively narrow official mandate of the Wijffels Commission—on structural reform and resolution rules—de Jager also called for the commission to consider far more than just ringfencing, including: bank competition, regulatory policy, and the sustainability of the 'bancassurance' model used by the two of the largest Dutch banks, ABN AMRO and ING (Lalkens 2012a). The commission duly responded with its broadened focus and eleven recommendations. As for the commission's membership, some observers have also claimed that de Jager had a deliberate strategy to design a commission with diverse membership including consumer organizations, scientists, and bankers—which would undermine any radical proposals in the search for consensus (Lalkens 2012b; Interview 45). Ultimately, the commission failed to increase the political salience of TBTF and structural reform.

Despite having pushed structural reform largely off the agenda, the Wijffels Commission's final report in June 2013 recommended the pan-European implementation of the Liikanen Group's structural reform proposals. Some commission members and other observers saw this surprising recommendation of major reform as an expedient compromise rather than as a manifestation of real support for the Liikanen Report (Interview 45). Crucially, as Wijffels made clear from the start, the commission noted in its final report the view of the country's largest banks that the Liikanen Group's recommended structural reform would have little impact on the country's banks, given the 'current extent of their trading activities' (Wijffels 2013, p. 25, authors' translation). The Wijffels Commission's final report was, however, explicitly hostile to the Vickers model—of ringfencing retail bank activities—on the grounds that Dutch companies would likely become increasingly reliant on foreign banks, 'which is not of interest to the Dutch economy' (Wijffels 2013, p. 25). The echo of economic nationalist arguments against structural reform that were made in France—another country where the national economy relied heavily on a small number of TBTF banks—is clear.

6. Conclusion

This chapter demonstrates the applicability of our analytical model to the Dutch case. Despite the devastation of the international financial crisis in the Netherlands, cooperative financial power combined with venue shifting contributed to the depoliticization of bank structural reform at the height of the crisis. Unlike in the UK, unified bank lobbying meant that the series of ad hoc commissions that were established were largely sympathetic to the concerns of the largest Dutch banks and/or simply lacked expertise on financial regulatory matters. As a result, they served to narrow the window of opportunity for policy change through conflict contraction—limiting engagement to industry 'insiders' and thus deflecting parliamentary pressure and government attention on the issue.

Dutch banks directed the reform discussion at an early stage towards bank culture and voluntary mechanisms, downplaying the need for structural reform and additional regulation. Calls for structural reform by one centre-left Finance Minister and a number of other politicians failed to create a political dynamic in favour of reform. The government created two commissions with a mandate to consider bank reform—including the Wijffels Commission, which had structural reform as one of two main elements of its mandate. However, neither commission devoted substantial effort to considering structural reform, opting instead to focus on a range of wider banking reforms. Structural reform in the Netherlands also lacked a high-profile cheerleader. Centre-left PvdA Finance Minister Bos called for structural reform towards the end of his time in office. But having been widely blamed for mismanaging the government's response to the crisis, Bos was in no position to lead a campaign in favour of structural reform. Although a member of the Liikanen Group, Wijffels did not recommend unilateral national action on structural reform.

Despite the failure to make progress on structural reform in the early 2010s, the possibility continued to be discussed on occasion in Dutch newspapers and academic circles over the next decade. The topic was often presented in the context of building a more diverse national banking system, one of the recommendations of the Wijffels Commission. In 2019, a decade after the financial crisis—and thus long after structural reform had ceased to be an issue of consideration, let alone debate, in Dutch politics—a government advisory body, the Scientific Council for Government Policy (Wetenschappelijke Raad voor het Regeringsbeleid, WRR) recommended setting up a retail bank, either publicly owned or private, which would be banned from engaging in investment banking activities (WRR 2019; de Rooij 2019). The WRR argued in favour of banking diversity, which was sorely lacking in the highly concentrated Dutch banking system, in order to promote competition and increase consumer choice. The WRR had been created following a citizens' initiative, 'Ons Geld' (Our Money), to increase public control over money creation, which attracted over 120,000 signatures. The WRR called for the creation of a traditional savings and loans bank which had existed in the Netherlands in the recent past, up to the mid-1980s, when the Rijkspostspaarbank (RPS) and the Postcheque and Giro Service (PCGD) were merged in 1986 to form Postbank, which later became part of ING, one of Europe's largest universal banks. The WRR included a number of academic experts, notably monetary and financial economists, who recognized that more risk-averse savers and borrowers should have the option of such a bank—even if the interest rates it could offer on savings would be less attractive than universal banks could offer. While structural reform was clearly off the agenda in Dutch politics, at least until the next major banking crisis, one of the goals that underpinned support for it—safer banking—remained a galvanizing force in Dutch society.

9
Liikanen's Legacy
Financial Power and Political Stalemate in the European Union

1. Introduction

In November 2011, Michel Barnier, the EU Commissioner responsible for the Internal Market, announced the creation of a high-level expert group to look into the need and best design for EU-wide bank structural reform and, specifically, the ringfencing of higher-risk proprietary trading activities from retail activities. The Commission announced its intention to launch a new reform initiative that would complement the development of the EU's bank recovery and resolution framework, to 'reduce the probability and impact of [bank] failure, ensure the continuation of vital economic functions upon failure and better protect vulnerable retail clients' (EU Commission 2012). In agreement with Commission President José-Manuel Barroso, Barnier selected Erkii Liikanen, Governor of the Bank of Finland and former Social Democratic politician, as Chair. The High-Level Expert Group on Reforming the Structure of the EU Banking Sector—widely referred to as the Liikanen Group—began meeting in February 2012. In October 2012, the group produced its final report recommending a strong ringfence (Liikanen 2012). However, as an early indication of the difficult negotiations on EU-level structural reform to come, the Liikanen Report also noted the position of a minority of group members who opposed structural reform. Instead, these members called for a solution based on a combination of a higher non-risk-weighted capital buffer for trading operations, and the possibility of ringfencing retail banking from trading activities on a case-by-case basis as a last-resort resolution tool for the competent authorities (Liikanen 2012, p. ii).

On 29 January 2014, the Commission proposed a regulation on ringfencing that incorporated many of the Liikanen Group's recommendations (EU Commission 2014a; Lehmann and Rehahn 2014). The Commission's draft regulation was passed to the European Parliament, but serious consideration of the legislation was delayed by the May 2014 parliamentary elections. Later in the year, the *rapporteur* of the Parliament's Committee on Economic and Monetary Affairs produced a draft position on the draft regulation which failed to receive the support of a majority of committee members. The Council of Ministers also agreed further

Bank Politics. David Howarth and Scott James, Oxford University Press.
© David Howarth and Scott James (2023). DOI: 10.1093/oso/9780192898609.003.0009

amendments to the Commission's draft with the aim of narrowing the application of the ringfence. Commission efforts in 2016 to encourage the Parliament's Committee on Economic and Monetary Affairs to reach an agreement on a compromise draft text failed. Thus, inter-institutional trilateral negotiations—among the Commission, Parliament, and Council of Ministers—were unable to proceed. The Commission officially shelved its proposed regulation in October 2017.

On the one hand, the failure to adopt EU legislation on bank structural reform reflects the opposition of a number of EU member state governments—including the German, French, and Dutch governments—none of which were willing to accept legislation that was more constraining than the weak structural reform already adopted in France and Germany. The failure to adopt EU legislation also reflected the indifference of most of the other member states on the issue. On the other hand, the failure to adopt any EU legislation remains remarkable, given the majority position of the Liikanen Group in favour of major reform and the initial determination of the European Commission to push ahead—albeit with significantly less ambitious legislation. Furthermore, unlike most EU-level financial regulatory developments, there was considerable mobilization of a pro-banking reform coalition of interest groups—led by the Brussels-based Finance Watch—that strongly supported structural reform. Many left-wing MEPs were strongly opposed to any weakening of the Liikanen Group's recommendations. Thus, intergovernmental politics offers only a partial explanation for the resulting failure, in large part because it ignores important supranational-level dynamics.

Although the EU case represents something of a hybrid model of 'elite pluralism' (Coen 1997) for our explanatory framework, we nonetheless argue that it provides important support for our key theoretical claims. In particular, the outcome of the EU process—the development, repeated watering down, and eventual abandonment of the Liikanen Group's ringfencing proposals—involved a combination of both venue shifting and cooperative financial power. Hence, the European Commission used venue shifting to an ad hoc expert group to depoliticize the issue and facilitate the development of substantive recommendations on structural reform. As in the UK, the creation of an ad hoc expert group had the effect of facilitating conflict expansion: the group wielded sufficient expertise to insulate itself from industry lobbying, and encouraged the mobilization of a wide range of societal interests. But operating at the supranational level in the context of a weak European public sphere, we argue that the Liikanen Group lacked the broader political authority needed to forge a durable cross-party and cross-national consensus on the imposition of tough ringfencing rules for EU banks.

Moreover, the uniquely fragmented character of the EU polity, and the polarized nature of the legislative debate, ultimately contributed to the dilution, delay, and eventual defeat of the Liikanen Group's proposals in two ways. First, the EU financial industry was able to leverage cooperative financial power at the legislative stage to reduce momentum for reform: through powerful national banking associations working closely with reform-sceptic governments in the Council; and through increasingly influential European banking associations with close ties to the Commission and Parliament. Second, although industry influence was counter-balanced by substantial political pressure for reform in the Parliament, opposition from a number of left and Green MEPs to the successive weakening of the Liikanen Report's recommendations contributed to legislative stalemate. In this way, the complexity of the EU process is best conceptualized as two separate processes: an initial agenda-setting stage that resembles venue shifting in the UK, which led to the development of stringent regulatory proposals; and a later legislative phase in which reform was thwarted—as in the Netherlands—by concerted industry pressure channelled through existing institutional venues.

Section 2 of this chapter examines the European Commission's use of venue shifting to depoliticize and develop proposals on bank structural reform. We review the design and operation of the High-Level Expert Group, its contribution to conflict expansion on the issue, and the details of its final report. Section 3 analyses the unusually lengthy consultation process on bank structural reform—by the Liikanen Group and by the Commission. We argue that this simultaneously helped to prolong the mobilization of interests and enabled the Commission to stall for time. The resulting draft regulation, published in January 2014, was notably weaker than the Liikanen Group's original recommendations. Section 4 explains the critical role of cooperative financial power in shaping the draft regulation, and its subsequent revisions during the legislative process, through powerful and highly disciplined national and European-level banking associations. Section 5 explores the legislative process in detail. We argue that the opposition of key member states in the Council of Ministers to stringent reform, and political stalemate in the European Parliament arising from the weakening of the ringfencing proposals, ultimately served as a mechanism of conflict contraction. Hence, over time the attention of policy makers and parliamentarians shifted to other regulatory proposals and the draft regulation was eventually abandoned. Section 6 concludes. The chapter contributes to the small body of political science and political economy literature on the failure of EU structural reform in terms of member state—and notably French and German government—preferences (Hardie and Macartney 2016), interest group mobilization (Montalbano 2021), and Commission efforts to alter the objectives of structural reform (Endrejat and Thiemann 2019).

2. Venue shifting: the Liikanen Group

Unlike policy making in almost all other areas of post-crisis EU financial legislation, the European Commission decided to delegate responsibility for developing detailed policy recommendations on reforming bank structures to a new ad hoc specialist group. This group, announced by Internal Market Commissioner Michel Barnier, in November 2011, together with the appointment of a high-profile and well-respected Chair, the Finnish Central Bank Governor Erkii Liikanen, was modelled explicitly on the Independent Commission on Banking in the UK.

How can we explain the EU's decision to emulate the UK's approach to banking reform? We cannot know for certain, but we can speculate as to the Commission's—and specifically Michel Barnier's—underlying interests. First, the move to adopt EU legislation might have been a way to avoid pressure at the national level and in the European Parliament in favour of more significant reform, including reform that more closely approximated the recommendations of the UK Vickers Commission (Pignal and Barker 2011a). Barnier himself came from France's centre-right, which was largely opposed to any structural reform for French universal banks. However, the launch of the Liikanen Group came prior to François Hollande's election promise to undertake structural reform and it was not obvious during the second half of 2011 that there was concerted political pressure for reform in France, or elsewhere in the EU, apart from the UK. Nonetheless, a weak version of structural reform at the EU level could also work to undermine calls at the national level—in France and elsewhere—and in the European Parliament in favour of a more substantial reform.

Second, Barnier might have moved to create a high-level expert group with the aim of 'increasing the legitimacy of bank structural reform and—even if the proposal was doomed from the start—to force the College of Commissioners and the Council of Ministers, to at least consider structural reform which was inherently difficult given strong opposition in a number of member states' (Interview 50). Third, the creation of the Liikanen Group may have been a delaying tactic. Indeed, the creation of the group, the launch of two lengthy consultations after the publication of the Liikanen Report, and the publication of the Commission's draft regulation in January 2014, pushed possible adoption of legislation to the next European Parliament and Commission, following the June 2014 elections.

Fourth, Barnier and the College of Commissioners might have wanted to be seen as taking the lead without taking responsibility for the proposals on bank structural reform. The expert group's report launched a wider debate at the EU level on structural reform and thereby framed subsequent discussions. The creation of a high-level expert group was thus a way to demonstrate vague support for reform without expending the political capital to push actively for this reform. Thus, the creation of the Liikanen Group allowed Michel Barnier 'to wash his hands of whatever would come out of it: whatever wild proposals would result from the exercise would be the word of people who had no link to the Commission, and especially to DG MARKT [Directorate-General Internal Market]' (Interview 50). Barnier might also have been motivated by the 2014 European Parliament elections and his bid to be the European People's Party's *Spitzenkandidat*—that is, candidate for the Commission presidency. Indeed, Barnier had little interest in promoting major bank structural reform, which had very little support in the European People's Party (EPP) or among national governments (Interviews 27, 37, 50).

The make-up of the Liikanen Group provides further clues as to the Commission's motives. Like most high-level expert groups created by the Commission, the membership included senior officials with considerable pertinent experience in relevant industries and public sector bodies, together with several senior academics. However, unlike most other EU advisory groups established in the aftermath of the financial crisis, the Liikanen Group included a majority—seven of eleven members—from outside the financial sector. It should therefore have been anticipated that the design and operation of the Liikanen Group would contribute to conflict expansion: namely, by attracting considerable political and media attention, raising awareness on and the salience of banking reform at the European level, and facilitating the mobilization of a wide range of societal interest groups, policy stakeholders, and campaigners. Furthermore, the composition of the High-Level Expert Group, and the authority and status of its members, should have created the expectation of potentially far-reaching reform proposals.

The eleven members of the Liikanen Group heralded from ten member states and Switzerland. Most of the eleven members had both private and public sector experience and all but three had direct private sector banking experience. Two group members had careers entirely in the public sector, while one had principally academic and research experience, and one had long worked for consumers' rights organizations. We profile each member briefly below:

1. Erkki Liikanen, the Chair of the eponymously named group, had since 2004 been the serving Governor of the Bank of Finland, which was also the body responsible for bank supervision in Finland. As a euro zone central bank governor, he was thus a member of the Governing Council of the ECB. He had previously been a Social Democratic politician, a Finnish Minister of Finance, a Finnish Ambassador to the EU, and an EU Commissioner from 1995 to 2004. His selection as chair of the group might also have reflected the fact that Finland was home to no TBTF banks—and thus had no national champions to protect—but, rather, had a banking system that was overwhelmingly dominated by Nordea bank, then headquartered in Stockholm.

2. Hugo Bänziger was Swiss and the only group member not from an EU member state. He had been a long-time employee of two TBTF banks, Crédit Suisse and Deutsche Bank. He worked for the latter from 1996 and rose to become Chief Risk Officer for Credit and Operational Risk in 2004 and a member of Deutsche Bank's board of directors. In 2010, Bänziger had been awarded 'Risk Manager of the Year' by the Global Association of Risk Professionals and thus had established credibility in the field. Bänzinger had started his professional life working for the Swiss banking supervisor.

3. José Manuel Campa was Secretary of State for the Economy in the Spanish government when he was appointed to the Liikanen Group. Campa had worked as a consultant at the World Bank, the IMF, the Inter-American Development Bank, the BIS, other international financial bodies, and the Bank of Spain. He was later appointed as Chair of the European Banking Authority in 2019.
4. Louis Gallois was one of France's top business executives and, at the time of his appointment to the Liikanen Group, was head of EADS, the European aeronautics defence and space company which subsequently became the Airbus Group—one of Europe's largest firms. Close to the French Socialist Party, in 2012 he was made the new Socialist government's Commissioner for Investment. Like a good number of top business (and bank) executives, Gallois was a graduate of the elite ENA and had served previously in a number of government ministries.
5. Monique Goyens had been Director General of the European Consumer Organization (Bureau Européen des Unions de Consommateurs, BEUC), from 2007. The BEUC represented forty-two independent national consumers' associations based in thirty-one European countries.
6. Jan Pieter Krahnen was a well-known German academic economist and expert on banking, and had been Chair of the Corporate Finance Department at Goethe University in Frankfurt since 1995 and Director of the Center for Financial Studies, a non-profit research body also in Frankfurt. It is noteworthy that Krahnen was one of the more sceptical voices in the group, questioning the relative importance of bank structural reform and arguing that the 'ultimately untested theory behind [bank separation] is that at least a significant part of the complexity of banking, making dismantling and resolution impossible over a crisis weekend, derives from the interaction of banking and commercial transactions' (Krahnen 2013, p. 8). He later warned that structural reform could add to the complexity of bank supervision, generate conflict with bank recovery and resolution rules, and weaken the focus of policy makers on stress testing, living wills, and bail-in bonds (Verma 2015).
7. Marco Mazzucchelli had been a former Managing Director of the Global Banking and Markets division of RBS and had previously worked for a number of large banks including Crédit Suisse, Sanpaolo, and Morgan Stanley.
8. Carol Sergeant had started her career at the Bank of England and then worked as a Managing Director at the FSA, previously the main UK bank supervisory body. After a stint in the private sector as the Chief Risk Officer of Lloyds Banking Group, from 2004 to 2010, she returned to the Bank of England and served as Chair of the UK Treasury's steering group

responsible for devising 'simple financial products' that could be easily understood by retail consumers.
9. Zdenek Tuma, a former academic economist and Governor of the Czech central bank from 2000 to 2010, was a director in the Prague office of the auditing firm KPMG from 2011.
10. Jan Vanhevel was a retired Belgian banker and former CEO of the Belgian KBC banking and insurance group—then the second largest Belgian bank and one of the country's biggest companies—from 2009 to 2012.
11. Herman Wijffels, the Dutch member, was a former executive board member of Rabobank, from 1981 to 1999 and Chair in 1986. He was also a former Chairman of the Dutch Social Economic Council from 1999 to 2006 and a Dutch representative to the World Bank from 2006 to 2009. From 2009, he kept one foot in academia as a part-time Professor of Sustainability and Societal Change at Utrecht University. Wijffels' scepticism as to the desirability of bank structural reform in the Dutch context is discussed in Chapter 8.

Echoing the experience of venue shifting in the UK, the authoritative membership of the Liikanen Group helped to insulate the examination of desirable structural reform from both finance industry and national government influence, enabling the group to develop substantive policy recommendations. This was reflected in its two main proposals for the largest EU-headquartered banks: the separation of trading business from other banking operations, the 'Separation Proposal'; and the mandatory issuing of subordinated bank debt, the strict 'Bail-in Proposal' (Liikanen Group 2012; Krahnen 2013). Published in October 2012, the Liikanen Report also presented the group's interpretation of the causes of the crisis and three additional proposals: the need for effective and realistic bank recovery and resolution plans; the application of robust risk weights in the determination of minimum capital standards and more consistent treatment of risk in internal models; and the need to augment existing corporate governance reforms by specific measures.

Liikanen Group members noted divisions within the group, with a minority reticent to endorse ringfencing and in favour of the alternative measures proposed (Interviews 36, 38; see also Montalbano 2021). The report emphasized the need for structural reform to facilitate bank resolution and the need for banks to hold sufficient subordinated debt to reduce contagion. The report also presented diverse additional recommendations, including larger capital buffers for trading assets and the strengthening of corporate governance. However, the majority of the Liikanen Report and the press coverage on it focused on bank structural reform, which is explicitly presented in the report as the best way to reduce the interconnectedness between banks and financial markets, together with the structural power and vulnerabilities derived from too-interconnected-to-fail and to-manage institutions.

The Liikanen Report stresses that the insulation of core retail functions would contribute to removing implicit state subsidies for TBTF banks. The report also presents the argument that structural reform would reduce market expectations of public bail-outs, thus enhancing investor scrutiny and pricing of risky trading operations, and ensuring a fairer competitive playing field (Liikanen Group 2012).

Similar to the approach adopted in the UK, the Liikanen Group recommended the ringfencing of essential deposit-taking and lending functions from certain investment banking operations. Nonetheless, the insulated retail banking entities would be permitted to engage in market-related operations deemed less risky, like securities underwriting and hedged trading. The report proposes that the two separated entities could be managed under a single holding company. The capitalization and refinancing of both units would have to be separate, while there would be a guarantee only from the trading bank towards the commercial bank and not the reverse. This would prevent the cross-subsidization of the trading arm of the bank by the commercial arm, which was seen as distorting both investment and risk allocation. This prevention of cross-subsidization was presented in terms of ensuring that the implicit government guarantee that existed for commercial banks, due to their deposits, could not be transferred to the trading bank. The trading and commercial arms of the banks would each have to provide their own funding, with the expectation that the refinancing costs of the trading arm would rise and those of the commercial arm decrease. The increased funding costs for the trading arm would likely result in less trading overall—although the main objective was not to reduce trading activities per se or to call into question the economic benefits of trading. The Liikanen Group further recommended that national resolution authorities could 'request a wider separation than considered mandatory ... if this is deemed necessary to ensure resolvability and operational continuity of critical functions' (Liikanen Group 2012, p. iii). This meant that if regulators considered that a bank's trading operations were particularly risky, they could widen the ringfence to include more investment activities, better to shield deposits in the event of the investment arm of the bank failing (Burgis 2012).

The Liikanen Report sets the bank size threshold at €100bn trading assets or the relative volume of these assets to total assets: 15–25 per cent. The report also does not differentiate between proprietary trading and client-related business or between proprietary trading and market making. The report's recommendations thus go beyond the US Volcker Rule, and the subsequent French and German structural reforms that called for banks fully to separate their proprietary trading activities from their other business, but left market making and client-related business untouched. The Liikanen Group decided that the separation of proprietary trading activities from forms of market-making activity would be too difficult to manage because these activities were difficult to differentiate. Elements of the Liikanen Report attracted criticism, not just from banks—which is examined below—but also from those in favour of a more significant separation of banking activities and a number of financial economists and other bank experts. The group decided that the provision of hedging services to clients—for example, arranging derivatives for an exporter to guard against fluctuations in exchange rates—would remain part of the retail banking arm. Many observers argued that defining the difference between such hedging services and trading on the bank's own account could prove difficult (Burgis 2012).

3. The consultation process and draft regulation

Bank structural reform was atypical of most EU legislation because no fewer than three separate rounds of consultations were conducted. As we detail below, this unusually lengthy consultation process contributed to further conflict expansion—by encouraging the mobilization of, and engagement with, a broad range of economic and societal interests. Importantly, however, it also enabled the Commission to delay the publication of its own draft regulation on structural reform until 2014.

The Liikanen Group launched its own consultation on its draft report 'on reforming the structure of the EU banking sector' on 3 May 2012, and deliberately sought out the views of non-bank organizations and academic experts (Interviews 36, 38). The Commission launched a separate consultation on the recommendations of the Liikanen Report, on 2 October 2012. The Commission received eighty-nine responses, with the largest number, thirty-eight, coming from banks, followed by other financial companies, consumer groups, corporate customers, and national public authorities. On 21 December, the Commission published its summary of these responses, noting that there were diverging positions on the need for and necessary design of structural reform, and support for further elaboration and the need for impact assessment.

On 16 May 2013, the Commission launched an additional consultation on structural reform of the banking sector. The consultation was open for eleven weeks to 11 July. The consultation contained both qualitative and quantitative sections, with the former focusing on questions related to the need for EU action and the different options for legislative reform, and the latter containing a template for banks to provide data on the short- and medium-term implications of different reform scenarios on their balance sheets (EU Commission 2013b, p. 1). In response to this consultation, 538 contributions were received, including 49 from registered organizations, 16 from public authorities, 439 from citizens and 34 from non-registered organizations. The Commission consultation document outlined the problems that continued to affect the EU banking sector and the potential contribution that structural reform could make in addressing them. Respondents were then asked whether structural reform of the largest and most complex banking groups could address and alleviate these problems.

The consultation responses demonstrated considerable support in favour of bank structural reform. The Commission itself noted the unusually high number of responses from consumer associations (eleven) and individuals, reaching 82 per cent of the total responses. Eighteen out of the nineteen consumers' associations that submitted responses saw the relevance of structural reform, and most even recommended going beyond the reforms proposed by Liikanen. Individual responses—many of which came from academic experts—were overwhelmingly in favour of the reform at 433 out of 439 respondents. The consultation document also highlighted the 'on-going reforms within Member States and outlined the potential benefits of action at the EU level, that is, to preserve the integrity of the internal market'. It then asked for 'stakeholders' views on whether they considered an EU proposal in the field of structural reform necessary' (EU Commission 2013b, p. 3). Submitted responses on the need for EU action mirrored the views on the merits of structural reform and a relatively high number of responses supported allowing member state legislation to 'go further' than supranational reform, if possible. All 438 individual responses and all nineteen consumer associations agreed with the need for reform, with over 10 per cent and 30 per cent of these, respectively, in favour of allowing member states to go further.

The remainder of the Commission consultation document 'asked for views of stakeholders on the three different elements of bank structural reform: the scope of banks to be subject to potential separation, the activities to be separated, and the strength of separation' (EU Commission 2013b, p. 3). It also asked for respondents' views on the best combination of activities and strength of separation. Nearly a third of all respondents wanted a separation that went beyond the Liikanen Group recommendations, while seventeen of twenty-four individual respondents supported this. The consumer rights associations responding on the issue of the threshold either accepted the Liikanen Group recommendations or wanted to go beyond them. All 216 individuals responding to the question of supervisory discretion wanted no discretion and *ex ante* separation. All individual respondents (243) and eight out of nine consumers' associations were in favour of separating all wholesale and investment activities from retail banking activities. All 215 individuals responding thought that the deposit entity should not be able to provide risk management products, with some exemptions, while consumers' associations were more divided on the topic. All the individual respondents who expressed an opinion on the subject thought that there was 'a case for' stricter legal and economic separation and even full ownership separation. Fourteen of fifteen consumers' rights associations expressing a view on the subject thought that there was 'a case for' stricter legal separation, while fourteen of seventeen were supportive of a stricter economic separation, and fifteen of sixteen thought there was 'a case for' full ownership separation. On the preferred reform approach, all the individual respondents either accepted the Liikanen Group's recommendation or wanted a more far-reaching reform. In short, the launch of the third consultation on structural reform thus prolonged conflict expansion around the issue, and encouraged an unprecedented mobilization of non-industry voices in favour of far-reaching regulatory change.

The delay of over fifteen months between the publication of the Liikanen Report and the publication of the Commission's draft regulation could be interpreted as a strategic move to stall for time. A number of observers argued that the prolonged delay suggests that the Commission had downgraded the relative importance that it assigned to structural reform in relation to other reforms adopted or proposed since the Liikanen Report—notably, strengthened bank capital requirements, bank recovery and resolution rules, the creation of the Single Supervisory Mechanism (SSM) and the Single Resolution Mechanism (SRM), and a new macroprudential framework with the ESRB (Open Europe 2014a). While very aware of these alternative measures to make TBTF banks safer, the Liikanen Group had nonetheless emphasized structural reform as its key proposal. Moreover, the European Commission failed to clarify how structural reform would fit in with these other reforms—in terms of both schedule and structure (Open Europe 2014a). This failure was despite the draft regulation including a provision in its recitals that structural reform was a necessary initiative to prevent regulatory fragmentation, being anchored in the overall framework of Banking Union, to 'facilitate the supervisory tasks of the SSM and the resolution actions of the SRM', and to prevent regulatory gaps (EU Commission 2014a, p. 52). Thus, having previously been a major regulatory reform proposal, structural reform became an uncomfortable add-on. It is noteworthy that the Commission was at pains to play down the significance of the structural reform proposed in its draft regulation. For example, it highlighted that the impact of the ban on proprietary trading would be limited, given the significant contraction of such activity by the large European banks since the crisis, to the point of representing a marginal business activity (EU Commission 2014b, pp. 56–8). The caution of Michel Barnier on structural reform was made publicly known only a few months after the publication of the Liikanen Report, and prior to its own consultation, attracting the criticism of a number of observers (Jenkins 2013b; Kapoor 2013). Kapoor (2013) criticized the Commission's position on structural reform as a 'U-turn symptomatic of the knee-jerk, too-little too-late approach' of the EU to financial reform. Some observers also saw Barnier's decision to propose a draft regulation at the end of January 2014, only four months prior to the European Parliament elections, as a deliberate delaying tactic (Brunsden 2014; see also Bishop 2014).

The draft EU regulation

On 29 January 2014, the Commission finally published its draft regulation, which significantly watered down the recommendations of the Liikanen Group (EU

Commission 2014a; Gonon et al. 2014; Open Europe 2014a). Several observers found both the contents and the timing of the draft regulation to be controversial and predicted that negotiations on it would be 'tricky' (Open Europe 2014a). Taking into account the European Parliament elections of May 2014 and the appointment of a new College of Commissioners—which was under no obligation to retain the draft regulation—the Commission announced that its draft could be adopted by January 2016, with the proprietary trading ban coming into effect from January 2017 and the necessary separation of bank activities by mid-2018 (Open Europe 2014a).

The Commission claimed that its own version of bank structural reform was inspired by both the Volcker Rule and the Liikanen Report—combining the ban on specific trading activities defined as proprietary, and the requirement that certain trading activities were to be carried out by separated entities (EU Commission 2014a, 2014b). In one respect, the Commission went beyond Liikanen's proposals by introducing a 'Volcker-style prohibition' on proprietary trading and relationships with alternative investment funds, a category that was also to encompass hedge funds (Gonon et al. 2014; Masciandaro and Suardi 2014). However, the draft regulation introduced a relatively narrow definition of proprietary trading, referring to activities specifically dedicated to making a profit for the bank itself (Kern 2015). The Commission also exempted specific trading of commodities and certain sovereign bonds from the ban. The recommended ban on proprietary trading thus did not include underwriting activities, market-making-related activities, or transactions to hedge risks resulting from client activity. In this respect, the draft regulation diverged from both the Volcker Rule and the Liikanen Report (Kern 2015; Endrejat and Thiemann 2019).

At the same time, the draft regulation included a relatively broad range of trading activities that were to be transferred to the ringfenced entity. The Commission defined these activities in negative terms: all activities other than critical retail services, including deposit-taking, lending, and payment services, with the exclusion of trading on sovereign debt instruments (EU Commission 2014a, pp. 27–8). The draft regulation assigned the EBA the power to set the specific metrics to define which bank activities should be ringfenced. However, unlike the Liikanen Group's recommendations, the draft regulation assigned the responsibility of applying these metrics for nationally headquartered banks to national competent authorities, which created the potential of varied application of the metrics. Thus, national authorities would determine which activities had to be transferred to the ringfenced entity. Specific exemptions were created for derivative and hedging instruments for risk management purposes. Moreover, the draft regulation allowed mutual, savings, and cooperative banks to maintain some trading functions in the retail bank on the condition that they took 'sufficient measures in order to appropriately mitigate the relevant risks' (EU Commission 2014a, p. 10).

The draft regulation also contained a series of safeguards. Specifically, it adopted the Liikanen Group's recommendation of entrusting competent authorities with the power to separate certain additional activities if specific conditions were met. If bank metrics exceeded certain limits—to be specified later by the EBA—the competent authorities would need to initiate this further separation (EU Commission 2014a, Art. 9). Once this separation was triggered, the trading activities could only be carried out by a group entity that was legally, economically, and operationally separate from the deposit-taking bank. This trading entity would be prohibited from taking deposit guarantee-eligible deposits or providing retail payment services, except when necessary for the exchange of collateral related to trading activities. Conversely, the deposit-taking bank could then only carry out trading activities for the purpose of prudently managing its capital, liquidity, and funding, and could continue selling derivative instruments only under certain conditions. Furthermore, the Commission sought to grant competent authorities the power to separate trading activities further, even where the relevant limits and conditions were not met, if these activities were deemed to pose a threat to financial stability.

As with the Liikanen Report, the draft regulation applied its restrictions only to very large banks, using the definition of the 2013 Capital Requirement Directive IV (Directive 2013/36/EU121) and the thresholds defined in the Liikanen Report— €30 billion in total assets and trading activities exceeding €70 billion or 10 per cent of the bank's total assets—thus covering approximately thirty of the largest banks headquartered in the EU, holding over 65 per cent of total EU bank assets (EU Commission 2014a, pp. 22–3). The ban applied to EU banks, EU parents, their subsidiaries and branches, and EU-based branches of non-EU banks that met the threshold criteria, which, although exemptions could apply, potentially could have affected the operation of some US banks operating in the EU. This was a larger number of bank groups and covered a broader territorial scope than that captured under the UK ringfence rules. However, if these banks were subject to a legal framework deemed 'equivalent' by the EU Commission—which was certainly the case for the US—both EU branches of foreign banks and foreign subsidiaries of EU parents would fall outside the scope of the regulation, including with regard to the separation requirements (EU Commission 2014a: Art. 4(1)(a)–(b)). The draft regulation also established a handy escape clause for EU banks to shift trading operations to their non-EU subsidiaries. The national competent authority was given the power to exempt non-EU subsidiaries of EU banks from the ringfencing requirements of the draft regulation—even if the host country lacked equivalent ringfencing rules—as long as a sufficiently robust group-level resolution strategy between the host country and the EU was in place (EU Commission 2014a: Art. 4(2)).

To see off potential French, German, and UK government opposition, the draft regulation proposed that the European Commission could approve certain structural reforms previously adopted by EU member states. Should national legislation adopted before 29 January 2014 be deemed equivalent by the Commission, member states could obtain a derogation from the draft regulation's separation requirements for certain deposit-taking banks (EU Commission 2014a: Art. 21, p. 37). The structural reforms adopted by France, Germany, and the UK would likely qualify, thus rendering the EU regulation less directly relevant in those three national jurisdictions. However, other member states could not subsequently adopt their own legislation that diverged from the proposed EU regulation.

Most academic and informed observers saw the Commission's draft as a far less significant form of ringfencing than the recommendations of the Liikanen Group, and the Commission's initial plans. Most importantly, the final draft regulation exempted banks' market-making activities from those to be ringfenced (see, for example, Open Europe 2014a; Jenkins 2013b; Kapoor 2013; Interview 38). Erkki Liikanen for his part welcomed the Commission's draft regulation cautiously, which suggested to some observers that he was not very impressed (see, for example, Bishop 2014; Interview 36). That he specifically reminded observers that the Liikanen Group had recommended that market-making trading activities should also be included in the ringfenced entity suggested criticism of the Commission's draft regulation, which excluded these activities. Liikanen noted that:

> Depending on how it is applied, this regulation could bring about needed structural changes in the largest and most systemically important European banks, as envisaged by our group. ... In October 2012 our group proposed that proprietary trading and certain risky trading activities, including market-making as well as exposures to shadow banking entities such as hedge funds, ought to be separated from deposit-taking and lending activities.
>
> (quoted in Bishop 2014)

Endrejat and Thiemann (2019) argue that the exemption was brought about by the Commission's discursive framing of bank structural reform as a balancing act between stability and growth. They argue that, coupled with the incapacity unambiguously to measure the effects of the reform on market liquidity and on growth, this discursive framing pushed the assessment of market making from the technical to the political realm. As explained below, we argue that the exemption of market-making activities ultimately reflected the effectiveness of cooperative financial power—namely, heavy and highly disciplined bank lobbying channelled through sympathetic national governments and the standard institutional venues of EU policy and law making.

4. Cooperative financial power at the national and supranational level

The power of the banking lobby in EU policy making has been analysed by only a relatively small number of scholars (see Quaglia 2008, 2010a, 2010b;

Quaglia et al. 2016; Howarth and Quaglia 2018b; Montalbano 2020, 2021), although there are a larger number of studies on business interests in the EU that include financial and bank interests (Eising 2007; Dür 2008; Howarth and Sadeh 2008; Dür and Mateo 2012). Prior to the international financial crisis, the financial (and, specifically, large bank) industry had considerable influence shaping EU regulations, with the Commission relying heavily on the expertise of financial companies in its drafting of legislation (Quaglia 2008; 2010a, 2010b). While the influence of the bank lobby likely declined in the immediate aftermath of the financial crisis because of the increased political salience of financial regulation, its influence nevertheless remained important (Quaglia 2010a, 2010b). Although the precise nature of financial power in the EU context is contested (Macartney et al. 2020), banks maintained considerable and unrivalled influence.

The cooperative character of financial power on EU structural reform was demonstrated by both the high level of unity of EU national banking associations in their opposition to EU-wide reform, and the centralized and disciplined lobbying effort—much of it channelled through the powerful EBF—in the face of a sizeable pro-reform coalition (see below). This united position included the main UK banking association, the BBA, despite the adoption of a stringent bank ringfence in the UK. With one notable exception—the UK government—most national governments largely aligned their positions with those of their home banking associations in responding to the Liikanen Report and the Commission's draft regulation. In particular, the banking associations of France, Germany, and the Netherlands were able to leverage their substantial cooperative financial power through their respective national governments into the heart of the EU legislative process. Moreover, there was a high degree of unity between cross-border and smaller savings and cooperative banks, which shared a fundamental opposition to the underpinning rationale of the reform. As a result, the EBF was able to launch a concerted lobbying campaign in strong opposition to both the Liikanen Report and the Commission's draft regulation. As others have argued, this resistance was instrumental in persuading the Commission to remove the Liikanen Group's inclusion of market-making activities in the separated ringfenced entity from the draft regulation (Masciandaro and Suardi 2014; Montalbano 2021). As we detail below, bank lobbying, allied with sympathetic national governments, was pivotal in the further dilution of the draft regulation during the legislative process.

The response to the Liikanen Report from banks and trade associations was overwhelmingly hostile, with no major divisions stemming from divergence in bank size or type. The EBF outlined its opposition in a thirteen-page response (EBF 2012a). The EBF presented the main reasons for opposing structural reform, which were also presented and repeated by banks and national banking associations. The EBF (2012b) argued that structural reform would:

not address the issue of systemic risk identified as a main concern by the HLEG [High-Level Expert Group]; [fail] to identify and target the risk associated with banks' high-risk trading activities; [have] a distortive effect upon vital client-related activities, e.g. market-making; reduce diversification benefits of the universal banking model; reduce banks' lending ability and hence restrict economic growth; reduce the competitiveness of the European financial sector vis-à-vis [third] countries; undermine the benefits of the Single Market by restricting cross-border activities.

A repeated argument was that the trading activities of EU-headquartered banks were not a major cause of the international financial crisis. Banks and banking associations argued that banks with large trading books were no more affected by the crisis than other institutions. It was seen as unacceptable that trading should be singled out in this way, making universal banking, including trading activities, less attractive as a business model. The EBF entered into further detail about the negative impact of the Liikanen Report's proposals on important services to consumers and investors; on competitiveness in the market; and on banks' ability to lend to the real economy. The EBF argued that, rather than introducing structural reform, it would be more effective 'to target high-risk and speculative trading activities (i.e., proprietary trading activities with no link to clients' needs) by other regulatory measures than mandatory separation' (EBF 2012b; Interview 34). The EBF was in favour of strengthening the use of Recovery and Resolution Plans, as recommended by the Liikanen Group, on the grounds that this would fit better with the current banking regulation reform agenda, and would have a less distortive impact upon the sector (EBF 2012b). The EBF argued that '[s]eparation of trading activities conditional on the Recovery and Resolution Plans should be the last resort' and should only be imposed on failing or likely-to-fail banks. The EBF focused on other preferred EU-level developments, including the BRRD, and improved micro- and macro-supervision through the SSM and the ESRB. The EBF (2012a, 2012b) called for an impact assessment of any draft legislation on bank structural reform, arguing that the Liikanen Report failed to 'address the potential economic consequences of implementing mandatory separation, in particular higher costs for customers' (2012b, p. 1).

A range of large universal banks from a number of EU member states defended the importance of the universal bank model for national and EU industrial competitiveness (for example, see Barclays 2013; Crédit Agricole 2013; Deutsche Bank 2013). They also argued that large universal banks performed a crucial role in supporting multinational corporations and their exports, a role that would be severely menaced by ringfencing (UniCredit 2013). Smaller savings and cooperative banks were also opposed to the Liikanen Report and sought greater recognition of bank diversity in the EU (EACB 2012a; Interviews 32, 35, 50). In addition to the concern that structural reform would affect smaller retail banks, there was a more general concern that reform would decrease market liquidity as larger banks would be forced to raise capital for their ringfenced entities. The main European association representing savings banks—the World Savings Banks Institute's European Savings Banks Group—produced a nine-page response to the Liikanen Report in which it labelled the report's recommendations as an 'excess of financial regulation' (WSBI-ESBG 2012). The EACB (2012: 4) called for a full cost–benefit analysis of the Liikanen Report's recommendations and cautioned about the impact of these recommendations for its, mostly smaller, members:

> We appreciate that the Liikanen Group moved away from a strict Vickers or Volcker rule and has made efforts to acknowledge differences in the EU and to find a more suitable approach. However, we have doubts about the main proposal and method used to determine the mandatory ringfence of the trading activities in a separate legal entity. If we depart from the point of reasoning of the Liikanen Group, the cooperative sector would foresee and encounter serious difficulties to continue serving their clients.

In its response to the Commission's consultation of May–July 2013, a number of national and European associations representing savings banks—including the German Savings Banks Finance Group and the European Association of Public Banks (EAPB 2013)—argued that the integrated group structures of a range of savings and cooperative banks would 'become incompatible' with proposed ringfencing rules (Interview 31).

Industry opposition at the national level was widespread, although there were a few noteworthy exceptions. In Germany, the associations representing all three pillars of the banking sector—the private commercial banks, public law savings banks (*Sparkassen* and *Landesbanken*), and cooperative banks—argued that a separation of trading activities would threaten their proven model of universal banking. Each of the groups of banks presented somewhat different reasons for their opposition that could be explained by their own different organization and business models (Krahnen 2013). The BDB, the German association representing all banks—from the largest universal banks to small savings and cooperative banks—issued a press statement in which it evaluated the Liikanen Group's recommendations as 'overregulation, [that] would ruin Germany's reputation as a location for finance and thus could damage the German economy' (BDB 2012c).

The bank and business associations from the member states that had already adopted national structural reform were opposed to an additional layer of regulation at the EU level which would result in added costs (see, for example, BBA 2013; CBI 2013). The French and German associations and individual banks opposed a stricter form of structural reform at the EU level which would be harmful for company financing and the real economy (AFEP 2013; BDI-DA 2013; DK 2013a, 2013b; FBF 2013a, 2013b). In total, seventeen national bank and business associations responded to the Commission's call for contributions on structural reform—all noting their opposition to the Liikanen Group's recommendations (EU Commission 2013c).

The BBA—later integrated into UK Finance—was one of the few European national banking associations that initially presented a relatively neutral position on the Liikanen Report, noting:

> The UK's major banks are already preparing for significant structural changes to their businesses. Today's proposals from the European Commission, along with the UK's Vickers proposals and the USA's Volcker rule, require changes in the way banks structure their activities. More details will emerge of these processes in the coming weeks.
>
> (BBA 2012)

This position might have reflected fears about the relative impact of the Vickers proposals in the UK and the competitive disadvantage potentially faced by UK-headquartered banks in relation to their continental European competitors. The BBA subsequently clarified its opposition to the Commission's draft regulation despite the UK government's support. The Italian Banking Association (ABI, 2013) was also cautiously in favour of EU-level structural reform to the extent that it prevented divergence in national regulation in the EU Single Market, which could lead to a privileged treatment of German and French banks benefiting from light ringfencing models. The ABI argued against structural reform as an effective way to reduce risks, and called for a harmonized narrow separation throughout the EU which excluded market-making and hedging activities.

In their responses to the Commission's May–July 2013 consultation, banks and banking associations rehearsed the range of arguments against structural reform presented previously in their reaction to the Liikanen Report (EU Commission 2013c; AFME-ISDA 2013; EACB 2013; EBF 2013; EFR 2013a, 2013b; ESBG 2013). On the question on the relevance of bank structural reform (EU Commission 2013b, p. 3), 80 per cent of the 'standard' (non-public law) banks responded in the negative (twenty-six in total). Of those responding to the question, two out of the three non-financial company associations and four of seven public authorities also responded in the negative. 'Corporate customers, while acknowledging the need to address TBTF, expressed opposition, based on the potential impact of such reforms on the cost of financing' (EU Commission 2013b, p. 3). Only six of the twenty-seven 'standard' banks responding thought that EU-level reform was needed to protect the European Single Market given the legislation adopted in a small number of member states. Two of the three cooperative/savings banks responding thought that EU-level reform was needed but principally for the same reason. Only one of the eighteen banks responding to the threshold question in the Commission's consultation accepted the Liikanen Group's recommendation.

The majority of banks (six out of nine) and public authorities (three out of four) responding wanted no *ex ante* separation and entire or at least significant discretion for bank supervisors on structural reform. If structural reform were to happen, the majority of large banks/banking associations responding were willing to accept the ringfencing of only proprietary trading. Sixteen out of the eighteen banks/banking associations responding thought that the deposit entity should be able to provide risk management products, and they were supported by five of the six public authorities responding.

The consultation document highlighted different forms of separation and asked respondents for their views on the pros and cons of stricter legal and economic separation, as well as views on full ownership separation. Of the twenty 'standard' banks/banking associations responding, sixteen opposed a stricter legal separation and fifteen opposed a stricter economic separation, while two and three respectively expressed no opinion on the subjects. The large banks were supported consistently by the public authorities and all thirteen such bodies responding opposed a stricter legal and economic separation (EU Commission 2013b, p. 11; 2013c). Fourteen of eighteen large banks opposed full ownership separation while three expressed no views. Only one national public authority supported full ownership separation. Consistently, the position of public authorities aligned closely with that of large banks and the positioning of both was de-aligned or opposed to the positions of individuals and consumers' associations. Of the twenty-four standard banks/banking associations responding, ten opposed any separation, while six supported the German or French reform. Only one supported the bank structural reform recommended by the Liikanen Group, two supported the UK reform, while two supported a US Glass–Steagall-style ownership separation. Public authorities were divided on overall reform but two of eleven were against any reform, while five were in favour of French, German or weak reform. Only one was in favour of the Liikanen Group's proposals, while three wanted significant but different reforms. Of the nine cooperative and savings banks/banking associations that responded, all but one were in favour of reform but only one supported the reform recommended by the Liikanen Group. Only a small number of individual banks came out strongly in favour of the structural reform recommended in the Liikanen Report. These included two sizeable Spanish retail banking groups—Banco Popular 2013; La Caixa 2013—which supported reform, but only if restricted to proprietary trading and investment activities not related to retail services.

European banks and banking associations maintained their opposition to any significant structural reform in their largely hostile response to the Commission's draft regulation. The EBF described the Commission's draft regulation as 'an untimely proposal for banks' structural reform. ... Therefore, proposing an additional policy measure at this point in time that has such potentially far-reaching consequences on banks' structure, daily business and organisation is not prudent'

(EBF 2014; see also Interview 34; Bishop 2014). The French Banking Federation (FBF 2014) was very hostile to the Commission's draft regulation, arguing that, if adopted, it 'would constitute a considerable handicap in financing European companies', and would undermine the ability of EU banks 'to work effectively with companies on the markets'. The FBF was also angry that the Commission's draft regulation had 'not been submitted for review by any of the parties concerned' and that it came 'at an especially bad time and is sowing confusion and uncertainty' when major banks were already implementing national-level reforms, especially in France and Germany.

While its initial position on the Liikanen Report may have been cautious, the BBA came out strongly opposed to the Commission's draft regulation. Unusually, the BBA joined forces with the FBF to produce a joint letter, not to the Commissioner then responsible for the reform, but rather to the Commission Vice-President Franz Timmermans. The BBA and FBF called the Commission's draft reform unnecessary. They argued:

> The BBA and FBF feel that, given the fact that the Global Systemically Important Banks (GSIBs), are now safer than before the financial crisis, the Commission's proposal is not necessary. Adopting the proposal in its current form could have a negative impact in financing European countries, which is counter to the EU's efforts to restore growth and improve employment. The aim of the proposal, to strengthen financial stability and improve efficiency and consumer protection, is already addressed by national legislation in the UK and France. Finally, the data used to draft the Commission's impact assessment dates from 2010, and consequently does not correspond to the current situation of European banks. The BBA and the FBF hope that, given the reasons outlined, the Commission will consider whether the case for structural reform has been proven.
> (BBA–FBF 2014)

The BBA argued that better regulation would only come if the Commission reconsidered its proposals for bank structural reform (Chisnall 2014). BBA Director, Anthony Browne, warned that misconceived structural reforms could imperil market liquidity and run counter to the EU's objective to build a Capital Markets Union (Barker 2015). The BDB was similarly hostile to structural reform outlined in the Commission's draft regulation, arguing that 'the German economy needs and wants universal banks' (BDB 2014; see also DK 2014a, 2014b).

Other elements of the financial sector stood in solidarity with large European banks. Although spared from structural reform thanks to the adoption of relatively high size thresholds, smaller savings and cooperative banks largely maintained their opposition to the structural reform outlined in the Commission's draft regulation. The AFME (House of Lords 2015, p. 89) argued that the need for additional EU bank structural reform legislation at this stage was unproven, noting that there was 'a significant risk of conflicting with broader regulatory objectives'. The AFME described the Commission's structural reform proposal as 'an unnecessary duplication of existing measures and, if adopted, will have significant adverse economic consequences, including a withdrawal of EU capital market capacity'. The AFME also argued that the proposals would interfere with the provision of client-facing activities such as market-making and risk transformation services that were part of the fundamental economic role of banks. The AFME commissioned the consulting and audit firm PwC to prepare a report on the impact of the structural reform outlined in the Commission's draft regulation. The PwC (2014) authors outlined the high potential costs of the Commission's approach to structural reform for the banking industry, and the financial industry more generally, because of the reduction of market liquidity with negative effects for customers and the real economy more generally.

The pro-structural reform coalition

The Liikanen process, and the Commission consultations on the draft regulation that followed, provided significant scope for conflict expansion around the issue of bank structural reform. That the banking industry responded with a concerted collective lobbying effort is only one part of our story. The other is the significant mobilization of a pro-banking reform coalition of societal interests which was actively encouraged by EU policy makers to counter the influence of the financial lobby (Barker 2014a; Interview 33). This coalition gradually coalesced around, and was led by, a new group: Finance Watch.

Concern for the lack of strong EU-level interest groups to counter the influence of finance in EU policy making encouraged MEPs of all the major party groups to launch a petition in June 2010 to set up a new body. The petition was signed by another 140 national elected officials. Finance Watch was officially founded in Brussels in late June 2011. Its first Secretary General was Thierry Philipponnat, a former banker, and its board of directors included academic economists and officials from other finance-oriented lobbying groups. Finance Watch relied on EU funding, grants from a number of charitable foundations, and individual donations. The official mission of Finance Watch was 'to strengthen the voice of society in the reform of financial regulation by conducting advocacy and presenting public interest arguments to lawmakers and the public as a counterweight to the private interest lobbying of the financial industry' (Finance Watch website). The resources of Finance Watch were minimal in relation to the European banking associations and individual banks with a lobbying presence in Brussels, and national banking associations which separately followed EU legislative developments and sought to influence national policy making on these developments. Finance Watch later had national partners in Germany (Bürgerbewegung Finanzwende) and in

France. Finance Watch undertook the bulk of the EU-level active campaigning in favour of the Liikanen Group's version of bank structural reform, in opposition to the efforts of the EBF, other banking associations, and individual banks against both the Liikanen Report and the Commission's draft regulation. Finance Watch was supportive of those MEPs who blocked the Commission's draft regulation in the Committee on Economics and Finance (see below) on the grounds that this version of structural reform was insufficient (Interviews 28, 33). However, Finance Watch lacked the influence to bring about a shift in the position of member state governments and the Commission to support a tougher version of structural reform.

In his study of interest groups and EU financial market legislation, Montalbano (2021, p. 278) argues that the Finance Watch-led coalition in favour of the Liikanen Report's version of structural reform was unprecedented in its mobilization. This coalition lobbied in favour of the Liikanen version during the agenda-setting stage—and notably in the Commission's consultation exercises—against the Commission's draft regulation, and during the subsequent attempts to water down the legislation in the Council of Ministers and Parliament (see below). The three consultations that focused on structural reform in part (May and October 2012) or exclusively (May 2013) received a large majority of responses from individual citizens using a Finance Watch template. Approximately two-thirds of the 688 responses were from individuals, including a number of academic economists. Another 6 per cent of responses came from NGOs, unions, and consumers' rights associations. These responses easily outnumbered the 14 per cent from banking associations and 9 per cent from individual banks. This mobilization ensured the ongoing political salience of bank structural reform and, more generally, the TBTF issue. A number of these groups and individuals called for a tougher structural reform than had been proposed by the Liikanen Group, including a broader range of market-making activities to be transferred to the ringfenced entity and—while in support of introducing the Volcker principle to EU legislation—a broader definition of proprietary trading (for example, EuroFinUse 2013; Finance Watch 2013b; UNI Europa 2013; Ahlers 2015). Finance Watch argued that only a far-reaching separation of trading activities could make the EU's bank recovery and resolution regime credible and thus effectively tackle the TBTF problem (Finance Watch 2013a, 2013b).

However, there were also clear limits to this mobilization, reflecting the difficulties of diffuse interests in shaping EU-level policy outcomes (Smith 2008). One of the best-resourced groups lobbying in favour of structural reform was the consumers' affairs lobby, which had been represented in the Liikanen Group by Monique Goyens, the Director General of BEUC, the EU consumers' rights organization. This group and a number of national consumers' rights groups responded to the Commission's consultations and were solidly in favour of significant structural reform. However, as elsewhere, this lobby tended to focus upon bank services for individual clients/consumers and BEUC undertook minimal lobbying effort to counter bank influence at the EU level on structural reform. Those consumer groups in favour of structural reform were in large part focused upon protecting bank clients. However, the specific impact of structural reform on consumers was less obvious than a range of other bank-related issues.

The pro-banking reform coalition helped to sustain attention on the issue of TBTF during the long hiatus after the Liikanen Group was disbanded, and played an important role in countering the unified opposition of the EU banking industry during the lengthy consultation process. Ultimately, however, the weakness of the coalition was exposed during the legislative stage that followed. At this point the issue of structural reform shifted to existing institutional venues—the Council of Ministers and the European Parliament—where technical arguments were frequently subverted to the demands of national and supranational politics.

5. The legislative politics of EU structural reform

There were surprisingly few instances of publicly expressed divisions among member state governments on structural reform. However, the limited politicization of the issue at the intergovernmental level does not indicate government support for the Commission's draft regulation. The UK government was the only EU member state government that took a strong public stand in favour of the draft regulation. This support reflected in part concerns that UK bank structural reforms would put UK-headquartered banks at a competitive disadvantage. The UK Treasury found the draft regulation to be broadly compatible with the UK's approach to ringfencing and that it would thus facilitate the implementation of UK legislation, even though this legislation, in some respects, went beyond the draft regulation (Bishop 2014; Kern 2015). By June 2014, however, it was clear that the provisions of the draft regulation that allowed the UK to maintain its own distinctive structural reform were legally problematic (Open Europe 2014b). This could have caused major subsequent tensions in the EU Council of Ministers had the regulation been adopted without sufficient amendment.

The French and German governments expressed their profound concern that the proposed definition of activities to be ringfenced was harsher than that contained in proposed national legislation. Both governments produced a joint response to the Commission's May–July 2013 consultation which mirrored the arguments presented by their national banking associations and banks. They emphasized that it was of 'vital importance' that only those activities that did not serve the financing needs of the real economy were placed in the ringfenced entity, and that 'a broad range of capital market activities' should not be ringfenced. The German and French governments (2013) issued a joint statement emphasizing that they would only support EU legislation that ensured a 'balanced approach is reached in terms of activities' usefulness' and that provided sufficient 'supervisory flexibility'—and thus national discretion.

Following the publication of the Commission's draft regulation, the French and German governments withheld initial criticism. However, a range of statements by senior French officials were highly critical of the draft regulation. The Governor of the Bank of France, Christian Noyer, noted that he considered 'the ideas [Barnier] has proposed irresponsible and contrary to the interests of the European economy' (quoted in O'Donnell 2014; see also Barbière 2014). This was a surprising statement in that it was unusual for a member of the ECB's Governing Council to criticize a Commission member so directly. The French were concerned that the competitiveness of large US banks would benefit from a tough EU ringfence that restricted EU-headquartered banks from trading for clients (O'Donnell 2014; Interviews 23, 35). At the national level, a number of national parliamentary committees examining the Commission's draft regulation expressed concerns about its timing, content, and cost, and the potential for a clash with national legislation already adopted in Germany, France, and the UK (see, for example, House of Lords 2015).

The Commissioner responsible for the bank structural reform legislation from the autumn of 2014 was Lord Jonathan Hill from the UK. In November 2014, even prior to the stalemate in the European Parliament on the draft regulation, Hill acknowledged his scepticism about the likely adoption of legislation on structural reform in a private letter dated 18 November to Frans Timmermans, the Vice-President responsible for drawing up the Commission's 2015 work programme. Hill noted that he was considering shelving bank structural reform because of strong opposition from a number of member state governments, including the French, German, and British, in addition to many European banks (Barker 2014b). Hill noted that 'member states are pulling in different directions in opposition to [the draft regulation], so withdrawal could be an option next year if member state support does not pick up' (quoted in Barker 2014b). Hill also wanted to focus upon pushing through legislation linked to the Capital Markets Union project.

In its analysis of the Commission's draft regulation, the UK House of Lords European Union Committee (House of Lords 2015, p. 90) concluded that:

The ... proposals ... are highly contentious, particularly given that Member States ... have already brought forward structural measures at national level. This illustrates many of the failures in the [EU level] legislative process that we have highlighted, including a counter-intuitive scheduling of legislative reforms. The optimal moment for bank structural reform had passed by the time the proposal was brought in the dying days of the old European Parliament and Commission.

The House of Lords Committee (2015, p. 90) also noted that: 'the lack of consistency between the Volcker, Vickers and Liikanen models, not to mention the national reforms taken forward by Germany and France, is far from ideal. The case for seeking to create greater harmonization of bank structural rules across the EU is thus, in theory, a strong one.' Despite these concerns, the House of Lords Committee (2015, p. 90) was more sanguine about the likelihood of adoption: 'the political reality is that it will now be very difficult to reach agreement on the proposal. Whether the Commission and the co-legislators have either the commitment or the resolve to reach such an agreement is open to doubt.' The Commission's lack of commitment to major structural reform was a widely shared perception among those MEPs and national officials in favour of reform (Interviews 24 and 27).

At the EU level, both the ECB and the EBA were largely in favour of the Liikanen Group's recommendations on structural reform. However, they refrained from criticizing the Commission's draft regulation. On the Liikanen Report, the ECB (2013, p. 2) noted that:

> This separation can be supported insofar it provides an effective tool to protect depositors from being exposed to the losses from these high-risk activities, eliminate the cross-subsidisation that results from low-cost deposit funding subject to the safety net being used to fund risky activities, reduce complexity, enhance resolvability and thus limit taxpayers' exposure to potential losses originating from these high-risk trading activities. ... the Eurosystem is of the view that the activities subject to mandatory separation would need to be established on the basis of clear and reasonably enforceable criteria, taking into account that financial innovation would naturally contribute to blur the boundaries.

The ECB agreed with the Liikanen Group's proposal that national resolution authorities should be granted the power to impose a tougher ringfence and insisted on the need for tougher supervision to tackle the problem of banks trying to get around the ringfence with innovative solutions, and to adapt structural measures as necessary (ECB 2013, p. 3). The ECB (2013, p. 3) also emphasized that structural reform was not enough to resolve the TBTF problem and that the issue of size and interconnectedness also had to be addressed.

The EBA—the main EU-level body for setting bank supervisory guidelines—was similarly positive about both the Liikanen Report and the need for significant bank structural reform in an 'opinion' signed off by the EBA President, Andrea Enria (EBA 2012). However, the EBA (2012, p. 4) noted the need for caution: 'On the mandatory separation of proprietary trading activities and other significant trading activities' proposal of the Report, significant work on the calibration of the trigger for mandatory separation will need to be carried out before any translation into the EU regulatory framework'. The EBA (2012, p. 4) also noted that 'to ensure a consistent application of these thresholds in the Single Market, there should be a need for technical standards to adopt a common definition and accounting framework', and thus recommended the reduction of national discretion in the management of the ringfencing.

Supranational politics and the European Parliament

While the intergovernmental and inter-institutional debate on structural reform and the Commission's draft regulation was relatively muted, the party-political debate on bank structural reform in the European Parliament was highly politicized and polarized. Importantly, however, the debate was largely contained to the Parliament as attempts by MEPs, Finance Watch, and a number of supportive journalists and academics to increase political pressure on national governments were of limited success. Hence, although parliamentary conflict generated an initial burst of conflict expansion—by increasing the attention devoted to the TBTF issue, at least at the EU level—the resulting political stalemate ultimately served as a mechanism of conflict contraction, prolonging legislative gridlock and contributing to the draft regulation's eventual withdrawal.

The European Parliament demonstrated its support for significant bank structural reform as early as 3 July 2013 when a large majority of MEPs adopted a resolution supporting the initiative report and motion for a resolution previously agreed by the Committee on Economic and Monetary Affairs on 18 June and published on 24 June (European Parliament 2013). This report—'Reforming the Structure of the EU Banking Sector'—welcomed the Liikanen Group's analysis and recommendations as 'a useful contribution to initiate reforms' and the European Commission's intention to bring forward legislation on structural reform 'in order to tackle problems arising from banks being "too-big-to-fail"' (McCarthy 2013, p. 8). The Committee on Economic and Monetary Affairs took the view that EU action was necessary in this area to 'prevent the fragmentation of the EU's single market, while respecting the diversity of national banking models' (p. 8). The committee's motion noted the massive aid to EU banks since 2007, the large contribution of this aid to public indebtedness, and the large value of implicit government guarantees to the EU's biggest banks. However, the parliamentary committee also called upon the Commission to exercise appropriate caution and to engage in a 'thorough impact assessment of the potential separation of banks and alternatives' (p. 10). The parliamentary committee also heeded the 'warning issued by the EBA and the ECB that financial innovation can undermine the objectives of structural reforms' and insisted 'that structural reforms be subject to periodic review' (p. 9). The Committee on Economic and Monetary Affairs also emphasized that the European Commission and member states should promote greater diversification of the EU's banking sector by encouraging and facilitating more consumer-oriented banking and greater competition (p. 12).

However, as an indication of the entrenched political divisions to come in the European Parliament, the Committee on Economic and Monetary Affairs was also critical of some of the logic underlying the structural separation of banks (Interview 27). The committee's report noted that 'there is no evidence from the past that a separation model could contribute in a positive way to avoiding a future financial crisis or to diminishing the risk of it' (McCarthy 2013, p. 7). In its motion for a resolution, the committee noted that individual banks 'should never again be allowed to become so large that their failure causes systemic risks'; and that the size of a member state's banking sector should be limited in terms of 'size, complexity, and interconnectedness' (p. 6). The motion for resolution also urged the European Commission, *inter alia*, to: 'encourage a return to the partnership model' for investment banking so as to increase personal responsibility (p. 11); ensure 'that remuneration systems prioritise the use of instruments such as bonds subject to bail-in, and shares, rather than cash, commissions or value-based items' (p. 11); and rationalize the scale of the activities of banking groups.

The European Commission's January 2014 draft regulation—both its content and its timing—was met with considerable outrage by the Socialist and Democrat, and the Green party groups in Parliament (Interview 27). Sharon Bowles, the Liberal Democrat chair of the Economic and Monetary Affairs Committee argued that 'it's a bit insulting to present this now.... Barnier should have presented this much sooner before the election, or not at all. The deadline for the parliament to receive new, non-emergency proposals before the elections expired in July last year' (Brunsden 2014; see also Bishop 2014). The leader of the Socialist and Democrat party group, Hannes Swoboda, described the draft regulation as 'Too little, too late' (quoted in O'Donnell 2014). The Greens' finance spokesperson and Economic and Monetary Affairs Committee member, Philippe Lamberts, argued. 'These crucial and much-anticipated legislative proposals on the structural reform of Europe's banking sector fall short of what is needed to truly address the flaws in the sector' (Greens/EFA 2014). In particular, he criticized the very restrictive definition of proprietary trading. Another Green MEP, Sven Giegold, compared the Commission's draft regulation unfavourably, pointing out that 'the Liikanen group had put forward a simple, un-bureaucratic proposal as to how large banks could have been made much safer' (quoted in Bishop 2014). Giegold also argued that 'rather than saying certain types of business should be separated, there are loads of exceptions' (quoted in O'Donnell 2014).

The publication of Commissioner Hill's private letter to the Commission Vice-President Frans Timmermans on the possible demise of the draft regulation on structural reform elicited an outraged reaction from Socialist and Green MEPs. Lord Hill had promised during his confirmation hearings in the European Parliament to 'take forward' the draft regulation (Barker 2014a). Socialist and Green MEPs warned Hill against backtracking on his pledge to the Parliament. Philippe Lamberts, then leader of the Green party group, announced that 'this signal is utterly unacceptable' and that Hill 'seems to be bending at the slightest pressure from member states and industry' (quoted in Barker 2014a). In response, Commission officials said that Lord Hill stood by his commitment to Parliament and would work to help find 'a sensible and pragmatic compromise' (quoted in Barker 2014a; Interview 25).

A number of party groups were committed to maintaining political pressure for the EU to adopt stringent new legislation on structural reform. In the European Parliament, the division between those in favour of major reform and those opposed corresponded largely to party group and ideology, with those opposed principally liberal centrists, notably in the Alliance of Liberals and Democrats for Europe (ALDE), and on the centre-right (EPP). Those in favour of a weak structural reform—and even weaker than the reform proposed by the Commission in its draft regulation—lacked a majority of votes on the Economic and Monetary Affairs Committee that debated and considered possible amendments to the draft regulation: during the 2014–19 parliament, eighteen out of sixty-one committee members were in the EPP; five in the ALDE, and five in the more Eurosceptic European Conservatives and Reformists, which included the British Conservatives. Those strongly opposed to the Commission's draft regulation and in favour of a much stronger structural reform—the Socialists and Democrats, and the Greens—had, respectively, sixteen and four members (Barker 2015). The Eurosceptic bloc's MEPs also supported a tougher ringfence than that provided in the draft regulation.

Partisan political tensions linked to structural reform increased during the 2014 European Parliament elections. The politicization of the issue was heightened by a number of party groups that campaigned explicitly with the promise to push for a stronger ringfence following the elections. The European Greens were the most active proponents and highlighted the need for structural reform in their 2014 manifesto and were critical of the Commission's draft regulation. The Greens argued in favour of a strong ringfence for all banks, not just a ban on proprietary trading, and drew a direct link to bank lending to the real economy (Crisp 2014). The Belgian Green MEP Philippe Lamberts opposed 'a timid kind of text' and was in favour of 'a more Vickers-like reform, splitting, compartmentalizing the banking industry so as to make sure, at least, that the deposit-taking banks would have no other option but to focus on the real economy' (Crisp 2014). Some observers claimed that Green and Socialist MEPs were 'keen to act against banks after the failure to introduce an EU-wide Financial Transaction Tax' (Crisp 2014; also Interview 28).

In the European Parliament, the centre-right EPP—the largest party group in the 2014–19 parliament—was very cautious on reform. Centre-right scepticism on structural reform was associated above all with Gunnar Hökmark, a Swedish centre-right MEP. Hökmark was *rapporteur* on the draft regulation in the Economic and Monetary Affairs Committee, having led the European Parliament's work on the BRRD in 2013–14. Hökmark was an economic liberal and had previously been Managing Director of Sweden's leading free-market think tank, Timbro. In December 2014, Hökmark tabled a draft report, supported by the EPP and a number of other centrist and conservative MEPs, and which aligned closely with the demands of the banking industry (Barker 2015; Interview 28). The report challenged the assumptions of the TBTF problem and the need to target size, business models, and trading activities in order to improve financial stability. Hökmark described universal banks as being better placed to manage risks than specialized banks: 'Having more legs than one meant being more resilient to crises' (Hökmark 2014, p. 53). The report also warned against attempting to imitate the banking model of the US when the European system had developed over hundreds of years. 'Less reliance on universal banks will not mean a rapid emergence of new channels for financing, but rather a slow development of new institutions and lending, and thereby a decline in investment' (p. 53). Hökmark added that 'It is important to state that there is nothing telling us that trading is more risky than lending, rather the opposite' (p. 53).

The draft report presented ninety amendments to the draft regulation, representing a substantial weakening of the Commission's proposals. It recommended a different risk-based model to ensure that a bank could be resolved if it was failing or likely to fail. In particular, the report presented the separation of trading and deposit-taking activities as a last resort option available to the supervisory and resolution authorities, which would have to resort first to 'enhanced supervision or higher capital requirements' (Hökmark 2014, pp. 16, 27–30, amendment 19, 44, 47). The report recommended additional possibilities for derogation from the regulation without Commission approval, thus creating broad national discretion (pp. 7–8, amendment 4). Hökmark also advocated that the significant restriction in the scope of trading activities should eventually be separated, exempting a broad range of derivatives and hedge-fund transactions (pp. 22, 32–3, amendment 31, 52).

The main national and EU banking associations came out forcefully in support of Hökmark's draft report. The EBF acknowledged that the report presented the key concerns shared by banks, and thus offered the best basis for further discussions among co-legislators (EBF 2015; Interview 34). Significantly, powerful banking groups also demonstrated their ability to leverage alliances with the wider business community in opposition to the draft regulation. In a particularly significant intervention, the BDB produced a joint paper with the Chamber of Industry and Commerce backing Hökmark's proposed amendments. Business was at pains to highlight the dangers of stifling bank corporate financing and risk management services for internationally active enterprises (BDI–DIHK–BDB 2015). Similarly, the FBF (2015, p. 3) used the Commission's consultation on the Capital Markets Union in 2015 as another opportunity both to support the Hökmark draft report and to challenge bank structural reform, which was presented as directly contradicting the rationale and objectives of the Union. By contrast, Finance Watch, and a number of consumers' associations, denounced the proposed amendments in Hökmark's draft report. They argued that the amendments would make bank structural reform 'an ineffective shell regulation' (Finance Watch 2015a) by reducing the number of affected banks to below ten (Hirst 2015b). Christophe Nijdam, Secretary General of Finance Watch, insisted that 'Effective structural reform would free megabanks' lending operations to focus on serving the real economy' (quoted in Hirst 2015b).

The *rapporteur*'s draft report—finalized in May 2015—fuelled further politicization and exposed the increasingly partisan and polarized nature of the debate over structural reform in the European Parliament. The Liberals (ALDE) adopted a similarly cautious position to the EPP and supported Hökmark's proposed amendments (Hirst 2015a). Sylvie Goulard, the French MEP who coordinated the Liberals' response to the report, noted that she admired Hökmark's 'pragmatic' approach and that MEPs' first priority should be to ensure investment and growth for the real economy (Hirst 2015a). She added—without elaboration—that the landscape of the banking sector had changed considerably since publication of the Liikanen Report, thus making a major structural reform unnecessary. By contrast, the Socialist and Green members of the Economic and Monetary Affairs Committee accused centre-right members of being unwilling to take on banks that they described as 'too-big-to-fail, too big to save and too big to resolve' (Hirst 2015b; also Interview 28). They claimed that the proposed amendments ignored the lesson of the financial crisis: namely, that risk-taking universal banks posed a systemic risk to European economies (Hirst 2015b; Interview 26). Jakob von Weizsäcker, a German MEP who led negotiations on the draft regulation for the Socialists, said: 'We need to be very careful that this in the end does not turn into a figleaf piece of legislation' (quoted in Barker 2015).

In the end, these partisan tensions proved insurmountable. On 26 May 2015, the Economic and Monetary Affairs Committee voted narrowly to reject the Hökmark draft report, by thirty votes to twenty-nine (EU Parliament 2015). Committee members failed to agree compromises on a number of issues in the draft regulation, including those on the negative scope of the ringfence (Art. 4), the metrics to decide when to ringfence activities (Art. 5), the ban on proprietary trading (Art. 6), and the modalities of bank separation (Art. 10). Green MEP Philippe Lamberts described the resulting political stalemate in the committee as follows:

> Today's chaotic vote has left this crucial and much-anticipated structural reform of Europe's banking sector in limbo. The final draft legislative report would have failed to provide meaningful separation of retail and investment banking activities. This would have robbed the reform of the core element it was intended to achieve and, as such, the fact it was rejected is a good thing. However, it reflects badly on the rapporteur and the parliament's credibility. We now need to go back

to the drawing board and ensure a proper reform. There is resounding expert advice on the problems with banks combining essential day-to-day banking activities and risky investment activities, and the need to therefore separate these activities. There is a glaring need to clearly separate essential day-to-day banking activities relating to households and businesses (saving and lending) and banking activities relating to financial markets (inherently more unstable). This is essential for ending the existence of 'too big to fail' banks as well as the massive implicit public subsidies they receive. Taxpayers' money should no longer be used to bail out failed speculative activities by risky banking arms. We hope today's vote will now provide the opportunity for a rethink to ensure we deliver this.

(quoted in Greens/EFA 2015)

The intensity of the political divisions in the committee and in the European Parliament on bank structural reform, which worked to block legislation, must be emphasized (BEUC 2015). While it was common for the Parliament to adopt major amendments on EU legislation in a range of policy areas, it was rare for it to prevent the adoption of a piece of legislation as it effectively did on bank structural reform (Interview 51).

On 19 June 2015, the Council of Ministers published its agreed negotiating stance on the draft regulation (Council of the EU 2015). The Council's position was considerably less tough than the Commission's draft regulation (Verma 2015). It reflected the demands of the French and German governments that the EU regulation better align with French and German laws, the banking industry, and the position of the centre-right in the European Parliament. The Council's revised draft bill proposed full separation of only proprietary trading activities. It also explicitly excluded a larger range of investment activities from the separation requirements, based on their alleged critical relevance for corporate financing, including investments in alternative investment funds and other funds 'not substantially leveraged' (Council of the EU 2015, p. 12). Significantly, the Council raised the threshold for structural separation, proposing that this would only apply to larger retail deposit-taking banking groups if they engaged in proprietary trading—with a proposed exemption for banks holding total retail deposits of less than €35bn—or to banks with total trading activities worth at least €70bn, or 10 per cent of total assets. However, in the latter case, enhanced supervision or higher capital requirements could be imposed by the ECB instead of structural reform. The Council's revised regulation appeared to move away from automaticity of separation based on threshold and granted significant national supervisory discretion in any separation decision (Verma 2015). National governments remained concerned above all that EU regulation would force governments to modify existing national legislation on structural reform, and sought to circumvent the potential legal problems that this would generate. The Council thus agreed that national governments should be able to choose between two options for separation: the first corresponding to the UK ringfencing of core retail services; and the second in line with the German and French version of structural reform, thus separating proprietary trading and other risky activities (Council of the EU 2015, pp. 6–7).

In response to the publication of the Council's negotiated position, Sharon Bowles, the former Liberal Democrat MEP and Chair of the Economic and Monetary Affairs Committee, summed up the intractability of the political stalemate, arguing that her:

> instinctive response is that it may be hard to assuage the concerns of the left/centre-left but returning to Liikanen is a logical position for the Council. It is worth noting that if it goes to a second reading then the Parliament has to muster an overall majority [of those present at a given vote] to amend the Council position. In the past, threats of second reading have been used against the Council, but in circumstances like this they may act in Council's favour. The left may have to face a choice between something or nothing.
>
> (quoted in Verma 2015)

Following the rejection of the Hökmark report, the European Parliament remained implacably divided into two opposing groups of roughly equal numbers of MEPs (Weber 2016). The Parliament planned to resume negotiations on structural reform in September 2015, but this plan was quickly pushed aside in recognition of the entrenched differences (Interviews 26 and 27). Although the Parliament's annual report on Banking Union in 2015 renewed the call for rapid legislative agreement on the draft regulation (EU Parliament 2016, p. 6), its 2016 report made no mention of structural reform. In September 2016, the Commission Vice-President responsible for financial services, Valdis Dombrovkis, met with a negotiating team from the Parliament with the aim of relaunching the stalled legislative process and helping to broker agreement among MEPs (Weber 2016). But these efforts failed to overcome what Hökmark described as 'sharp divisions' (Weber and Jennen 2016) and the legislation was finally abandoned by the Commission a year later.

In the end, EU-level bank structural reform was defeated by three factors: first, the opposition of leading member states in the Council of Ministers, allied with powerful national and European banking associations, to the Liikanen Group's recommendations; second, the European Commission's attempt to accommodate these demands by substantially weakening structural reform in the draft regulation; and third, political stalemate in the European Parliament stemming from the opposition of Socialist and Green MEPs to the Commission's revised regulation and their refusal to support the EPP *rapporteur*'s proposed amendments. Conceivably, had MEPs reached agreement on a significantly amended version of the draft regulation, EU legislation most likely would eventually have been approved— albeit involving a substantially weaker version of structural reform than had been proposed by the Liikanen Group. Crucially, however, the Parliament's failure to reach agreement meant that the institutional trialogues—the negotiations among the Commission, the Council of Ministers, and the Parliament to resolve differences on draft legislation and agree a compromise text—were never launched. National governments could in theory have stepped in to try to resolve the parliamentary stalemate by indicating their willingness to support EU rules closer to the original Liikanen Group's recommendations. However, with national ringfencing legislation either already agreed—as in the UK, France, and Germany—or having been rejected—as in the Netherlands—the governments of the largest EU member states had little incentive to do so.

6. Conclusion

In January 2014, Michel Barnier insisted that the criticisms generated by the European Commission's draft regulation were an indication that it was pitched just right, hitting the perfect 'point of balance' between US, UK, French, and German initiatives on bank structural reform (quoted in Bishop 2014). 'I'm not surprised by the reactions', Barnier claimed:

> Have you ever seen any of my proposals welcomed with enthusiasm by the financial sector? These banks continue to engage in risky market activity that turns a profit but does not serve their customers. Is that proper? I say no.
> (quoted in Bishop 2014)

Barnier's claims of a right 'balance' were arguably supported by subsequent developments, during which it became clear that French and German opposition remained entrenched, and the UK government remained cautious despite initially positive comments. Financial industry opposition persisted, and both the right and left in the European Parliament were entrenched in their opposition to the Commission's draft regulation.

Following more than two years without progress, the European Commission formally announced its withdrawal of the draft regulation in its Work Programme for 2018 (EU Commission 2017, p. 2). In its very brief explanation of the withdrawal, the Commission noted the following:

> No foreseeable agreement. The file has not progressed since 2015. In addition, the main financial stability rationale of the proposal has in the meantime been addressed by other regulatory measures in the banking sector and most notably the entry into force of the Banking Union's supervisory and resolution arms.

In addition to noting the political obstacles to adoption, the Commission claimed—with no evidence offered—that bank structural reform was no longer necessary. The Commission thus directly contradicted what it had emphasized was a crucial reason for adopting structural reform, as noted in the explanatory memorandum to its 2014 draft regulation—that it was to ensure the effective operation of the SSM and the EU bank resolution regime (EU Commission 2014a, p. 5). Unsurprisingly, those banks and associations that commented on the withdrawal of the legislation warmly welcomed the Commission's decision (see, for example, BBVA 2017). By contrast, Finance Watch responded by claiming that the failure of EU reform demonstrated that the banking industry was simply 'too-big-to-regulate' (Pieper 2017). Tellingly, Christian Stiefmueller, a senior policy analyst at Finance Watch, argued that the demise of the Commission's draft regulation was 'testimony to the iron grip the financial industry's lobby still exerts on governments and legislators' (quoted in Pieper 2017).

Although the blocked structural reform in the EU represents a hybrid case for our explanatory framework, it nonetheless provides further confirmation of our main theoretical claims. First, a specific form of venue shifting at the EU level—the creation of the Liikanen Group—served to depoliticize the issue and supported the development of substantive reform proposals by insulating the process from industry lobbying. It did so by bringing together a group of highly respected 'experts' on banking issues, and facilitating conflict expansion by encouraging the mobilization of a vocal pro-reform coalition, led energetically by Finance Watch. Second, once the structural reform agenda was handed back to existing institutional venues—in the Council of Ministers and Parliament—the importance of financial industry lobbying became more pronounced. In particular, we argue that banks leveraged cooperative financial power at the legislative stage to reduce momentum for reform: through powerful national banking associations working closely with reform-sceptic governments—including the French, German, and Dutch in the Council; and through influential European banking associations with close ties to the European Commission and Parliament. There were proposals to weaken the Commission's draft legislation that many already argued fell unacceptably short of the structural reform recommended by the Liikanen Group. These proposals fatally provoked the fierce opposition of Socialist and Green MEPs, contributing to stalemate in the Parliament and eventual defeat.

10
Conclusion

Contribution and Future Research

This concluding chapter begins by recalling the main puzzle and research questions that guide the book, and then assesses the limits of existing political economy and public policy scholarship in financial regulation in section 2. The third section reviews our key findings and details the book's wider empirical and theoretical contribution to research in the political economy and public policy of finance. In particular, we set out how the development and application of the comparative financial power framework advances theoretical and empirical scholarship with respect to business power, as well as international and comparative political economy perspectives on financial regulation. The final section provides a guide to future research by considering the wider application of our analytical approach to other regulatory issues and country cases.

1. The puzzle

The global financial crisis generated a raft of regulatory reforms aimed at making the financial system safer and more robust. The most persistent issue, and arguably the most difficult to solve, was how to address the problem of TBTF: namely, the fact that some banks had simply become too important economically and politically to fail. Critics warned that this TBTF status effectively amounted to an implicit state subsidy that exacerbated risk-taking behaviour through moral hazard (Alessandri and Haldane 2009; Haldane 2012; Hardie and Howarth 2013a; Bell and Hindmoor 2015a). The need to protect ordinary taxpayers and depositors from the high-risk speculative activities of investment banks was a central theme of international negotiations at the height of the crisis (G20 2009). Despite this, however, few global coordination efforts to tackle TBTF banks resulted in clear policy guidelines—capital requirements, to the extent that they made large banks safer in the event of crisis, were one exception. At the EU level, member state governments collectively adopted a range of rules to make finance, and specifically banking, safer. To mitigate the problem of TBTF specifically, the EU member states adopted new EU resolution rules and funds to facilitate shutting down banks without recourse to government bail-out funds. The potential effectiveness of these rules and funds remained to be tested through the resolution of a TBTF bank. However, there are important reasons to be sceptical (see Asimakopoulos and Howarth 2021). On structural reform—potentially the most direct way to tackle the TBTF problem—there was no international coordination and EU-level policy making failed. National governments opted to pursue their own reform trajectories. The central aim of this book is to understand why.

Our analysis focuses on six major jurisdictions—the US, UK, France, Germany, the Netherlands, and the EU—which shared a number of important features. In the decades prior to the global financial crisis, all six cases had witnessed the growth of large, universal banks engaged in 'market-based banking' (Hardie and Howarth 2013a). As such, many banks had undergone a rapid expansion of trading assets on their balance sheets, and had become increasingly dependent on short-term wholesale finance to fund lending (Hardie and Howarth 2013a). While hugely profitable, market-based banking brought greater vulnerability to disruption in financial markets, meaning that relatively small losses were amplified by the banks' large trading books (Bell and Hindmoor 2015b). As a result, all the banking systems were hit hard by the financial crisis, resulting in plummeting share prices and credit rating downgrades for the largest banks, and debt write-downs for many. Moreover, governments were forced to rescue their banks by providing unprecedented state support in the form of liquidity injections, government bail-outs, and credit guarantees (Woll 2014).

In the years that followed, politicians in all six jurisdictions came under mounting political pressure to deal directly with the problem of TBTF banks. In particular, attention shifted to regulatory measures designed to separate retail banks structurally from higher-risk speculative activities—either through tighter restrictions on trading and/or ringfencing rules. The impetus for this bank structural reform frequently came from electoral dynamics which led prominent political figures to make early commitments to pursue bank structural reform. In the US, President Obama decided to support new trading restrictions on large Wall Street banks. In the UK, the coalition government established the ICB to consider options for structural separation. In France, President Hollande was elected in 2012 having pledged to implement a full split between retail and investment banks. In Germany, Chancellor Merkel responded to pressure from the opposition SPD for tough new bank 'ringfencing' rules by developing her own proposals. In the Netherlands, Finance Minister Wouter Bos spoke positively about the need for new restrictions on proprietary trading at the height of the crisis; while in the EU, Internal Market Commissioner, Michel Barnier, announced the creation of a High-Level Expert Group to consider EU regulation on structural reform.

Here, however, the similarity among our six cases ends. In the US, the Obama administration mobilized sufficient political support in Congress to secure legislative approval for a stringent ban on proprietary trading (the 'Volcker Rule'). Likewise, in the UK, the Conservative–Liberal Democrat government moved quickly to endorse the recommendations of the 'Vickers' Commission to ringfence retail banks, prohibiting them from trading in a range of financial instruments. In contrast, the French government soon backtracked on its earlier commitment to major structural reform, while the German government moved to sideline SPD leader Peer Steinbrück's ambitious reform proposals. Instead, both governments opted to implement much weaker measures requiring banks to ringfence only a narrow set of proprietary trading activities. In the Netherlands, the possibility of far-reaching structural reform was ruled out by the two commissions that examined the topic. Instead, senior politicians focused their reform efforts on enhancing bank supervision and capping banker bonus levels. Finally, in an effort to foster greater coordination across Europe, the EU Commission developed its own ringfencing proposals—a watered-down version of the recommendations of the High-Level Expert Group chaired by Erkki Liikanen. However, its proposal stalled in the legislative process and was finally abandoned in October 2017.

Given that TBTF banking was a highly salient political issue in the wake of the crisis, and that senior politicians and other policy makers in all five national jurisdictions made clear commitments to structural reform, and that the influential Liikanen Group was so supportive, how can we explain such wide divergence in regulatory outcomes? The following section summarizes why we believe that existing political-economy scholarship fails to provide an adequate answer to this puzzle.

2. The limits of political-economy scholarship

In Chapter 2, we outline why existing international and comparative political economy scholarship on financial regulation fails to explain bank structural reform. For example, we note that theoretical perspectives in IPE emphasizing the 'market power' (Simmons 2001; Drezner 2007) and/or 'regulatory capacity' of large jurisdictions (Bach and Newman 2007; Posner 2009; Büthe and Mattli 2011) struggle to account for post-crisis developments in this area. At the height of the global financial crisis, several countries—notably the US and the UK—moved quickly to introduce reforms aimed at curbing the speculative activities of their largest banks. Yet despite constituting amongst the largest financial jurisdictions, with considerable market power and regulatory capacity, and the potential to exploit first-mover advantage, there was almost no serious attempt to coordinate these important regulatory initiatives at the international level. A similar pattern characterizes developments in the EU. Although by late 2013 the largest member states—the UK, France, and Germany—had decided to implement varying forms of bank ringfencing, the EU authorities were ultimately unable to forge an agreement on EU-wide structural reform.

We also argue that bank structural reform challenges 'new interdependence' approaches in IPE focused on the role of powerful transnational coalitions of financial interests (Cerny 2010; Djelic and Quack 2010; Farrell and Newman 2014a, 2016; Newman and Posner 2016a, 2016b) and transgovernmental networks of financial regulators (Porter 2014; Seabrooke and Nilsson 2015; Tsingou 2015; Henriksen and Seabrooke 2016). It is self-evident that accounts focused on transnational causality are not well placed to explain significant variation in banking reforms across different national jurisdictions. Moreover, alternative explanations based on the power of global finance to pressure the governments of countries with large numbers of internationally oriented banks also perform poorly against the empirical record. Hence, those countries that were home to the largest number of G-SIBs at the height of the crisis—the US (8) and the UK (5)—implemented the most far-reaching bank structural reforms since the crisis. By contrast, the other three countries we examine hosted fewer G-SIBs—France (4), Germany (2), and the Netherlands (1)—but rowed back on their commitment to tougher regulation.

The explanatory power of CPE approaches, notably the VoC literature (Hall and Soskice 2001), is similarly limited (see also Zysman 1983; Story and Walter 1997). From a VoC perspective, one would expect the US and UK governments to have resisted substantive structural reforms to banking in order to preserve the competitiveness of their lightly regulated banking systems; by contrast, the French and German governments should have supported the imposition of tighter restrictions on the sort of speculative financial activities associated with 'Anglo-Saxon' capitalism in order to create a more level playing field. It is difficult to reconcile these expectations, however, with national patterns of post-crisis reform. Paradoxically, it was the US administration and the UK government that intervened decisively to restrict the trading activities of their largest banks, while the French and German governments sought to defend the traditional model of universal banking. Moreover, it is unclear from a VoC perspective what position to expect the Netherlands—which combines features of coordinated markets with liberal financial regulation—to take on structural reform.

Later iterations of this comparativist perspective, pointing to the need to examine VoFC and the growth of 'market-based banking' (Hardie and Howarth 2013a), provide a partial explanation of variation on the adoption of structural reform. A VoFC analytical framework goes some way to explaining why a number of European national governments were reluctant to impose new regulatory restrictions on universal banks that had become increasingly reliant on short-term wholesale funding (for example, see Hardie and Macartney 2016). But a VoFC framework still fails to explain why French and German leaders made political commitments to introduce structural separation in the first place. More importantly, it also offers no explanation for why the US and UK governments would potentially undermine the competitive position of their largest SIBs given their dependence on market-based banking.

We also review CPE explanations citing the importance of exposure to internationally focused banks (see Mügge 2006; Engelen and Konings 2010; Epstein

2017) as a possible reason for supporting structural reform to minimize financial instability. However, we argue that these explanations fail to provide a firm basis upon which to derive unambiguous empirical expectations. In the UK case, for example, structural separation would have a negligible impact on foreign bank operations, while potentially placing three of the largest UK-headquartered banks at a significant competitive disadvantage. In our other four country cases, patterns of internationalization did not neatly correlate with industry or government preferences on structural reform. While the UK and US had high levels of foreign bank assets as a proportion of total bank assets prior to the crisis, these fell sharply in the US after 2008 (Hardie and Maxfield 2013). Moreover, although foreign bank exposure in France and the Netherlands was consistently lower, levels in Germany were significantly higher and similar to that found in the UK by 2013. Many European banks also had significant non-domestic holdings—notably in France and the Netherlands—and yet this did not translate into government support for structural reform. In the German case, both large global banks and domestically focused savings, cooperative, and regional banks unified in opposition to major structural reform, contrary to what their business models would lead us to expect.

In short, we argue that there was a significant gap in the existing scholarship with respect to explaining a crucial set of post-crisis regulatory reforms. In particular, we argue that there was a need for a better understanding of how the power and influence of the financial industry is mediated by the relational and institutional context within which it is located. To address these limitations, Chapter 2 integrates insights from public policy and political economy scholarship to provide a more granular analysis of bank influence in different countries. The following section outlines how the *comparative financial power* framework that we develop in the book, and the empirical findings derived from its application to six jurisdictions, contributes to the wider literature on theories of business power and the political economy of finance.

3. Contribution to the literature

In this section we detail the book's wider empirical and theoretical contribution to research in three areas: theories of business power, the political economy of finance, and typologies of regulatory reform.

Theories of business power

Business power perspectives start from the proposition that private firms wield two forms of power: instrumental power, concerned with lobbying activities, access to policy makers, public campaigning, and political contributions; and structural power, related to the idea that policy makers anticipate and respond to business preferences on account of their dependence on business for investment, growth, and job creation (Lindblom 1977; Block 1980; Swank 1992; Przeworski and Wallerstein 1988). We argue that theories of business power are problematic when applied to our cross-section of cases. It is self-evident that structural and instrumental power alone cannot explain patterns of cross-national variation. The capacity of large banks to threaten disinvestment (structural power) or to mobilize lobbying resources (instrumental power) has remained largely constant over time, and so cannot explain the sudden shift to more stringent regulation in certain jurisdictions since the crisis, but not in others. In particular, our case study countries with large financial sectors both in real terms and relative to the size of the national economy (the UK), and formidable financial lobbying resources (such as Wall Street in the US), are—paradoxically—those that went the furthest in cracking down on the activities of their own banks. Even if we follow Culpepper and Reinke (2014) in discounting the structural power of US banks on account of their dependence on the US internal market, business power still fails to explain the tough response of the UK authorities—even in the face of explicit threats to leave by some of the UK's largest global banks.

Our findings contribute to the further specification of business power in at least three ways. First, our analysis advances the theory by disaggregating the nature of the 'state' and 'business', rather than presenting them as unified, monolithic interests. In particular, we highlight the extent of political competition over financial power within and between state actors, rooted in contestation over the desirability of different policy outcomes and uncertainty over the impact of policy change. Most of the cases we examine in the book highlight important examples of intra-state divisions over structural reform: in France and Germany, for example, opposition parties—the French Socialists and German SPD—championed the cause of tougher restrictions in the context of upcoming national elections, in contrast to incumbent parties. Regulators and legislators in the UK—notably, the Prime Minister, Bank of England, HM Treasury, and parliament—and the US—the White House, US Treasury, Federal Reserve, and Congress—also had divergent preferences and battled to shape the final outcome of structural reform.

Similarly, we avoid treating business as a 'black box' with unified preferences for less government interference. Our analysis certainly reveals that the preferences of large and small banks are frequently aligned, and that the financial industry often co-opts the wider business community to lobby on its behalf—as in France, Germany, and the Netherlands. Yet other countries reveal a more fragmented pattern of business lobbying. In the UK, for example, the divergent costs of bank ringfencing encouraged banks to compete with one another to secure firm-specific concessions from UK regulators, while significant divisions emerged between different sections of the business community. Similarly in the US, the large Wall Street banks did not entirely 'sing from the same hymn sheet' when engaging with the Volcker Rule, not least because its impact upon different banks varied. More importantly, the big five US banks faced concerted opposition from a sizeable community bank sector whose support the Obama administration and senior Democrats in Congress carefully cultivated.

Second, the book endogenizes our understanding of political salience by unpacking dynamics of agenda setting in the banking reform process. As Culpepper (2016, p. 462) reminds us, heightened political salience is a necessary, but not sufficient, condition for constraining business power: it must be transformed into political effect by the mobilization of interest groups and/or through the action of policy makers. Our framework draws on theories of agenda setting to illuminate the causal mechanisms through which political salience and government attention to a specific policy issue increase *and* decrease over time. These dynamics of conflict expansion and contraction help to unpack regulatory reform agendas by mapping the mobilization of organized interests around them, and revealing how these coalitions are (re)configured by the policy process. Chapter 9 on the EU provides a particularly good illustration of how interest mobilization is structured over the policy cycle: while the Commission used the agenda-setting stage to facilitate engagement with a range of societal groups by delegating structural reform to the High-Level Expert Group, the legislative phase gave way to more traditional forms of financial and business mobilization through the Council of Ministers (via national governments) and the European Parliament (through European trade associations).

Typically, from a business power perspective, as policy issues become increasingly salient, non-business groups are organized, and decision making is escalated to more visible political arenas (conflict expansion). Yet there have been few accounts of the reverse process: how opportunities which appear ripe for policy change may be deliberately closed down (conflict contraction). Specifically, we know little about how issues become less salient over time, when non-business groups demobilize, or why issues are moved from 'noisy' public to 'quiet' private institutional venues. Here the influence of business may be more pernicious as it relates to the second face of power and 'non-decision making' (Bachrach and Baratz 1962): the ability of business to keep issues off the policy agenda or—more intriguingly—to have them downplayed or removed.

Importantly, however, our case studies provide contrasting examples of how and why financial firms mobilize in an attempt to manipulate political salience. In the Netherlands and France—and, to a lesser extent, in Germany—banks worked with policy makers to reduce the salience of banking reform through processes of conflict contraction, thereby minimizing the scope of new rules on bank structure. By contrast, banks in the UK and US faced opposition from highly vocal pro-reform groups, such as consumer activists, senior regulators, and legislators. In this context of conflict expansion, banks therefore had little choice but to build 'noisy' alliances with like-minded firms and groups, and frequently engaged in 'organized combat'—to use Hacker and Pierson's (2010) terminology—to try to resist pressure for stringent new rules.

Third, the book unpacks the contingency of business power by focusing on the agency and agenda-setting role of policy makers. Rather than viewing policy makers as the passive recipients of business demands through lobbying or threats of disinvestment, we emphasize the capacity of policy makers to manipulate political salience actively by changing the institutional context for decision making. Specifically, we contextualize the analysis of financial power by developing an agent-centred account of how policy makers manipulate institutional structures and processes to further their policy goals. Institutional 'venues' are central to our understanding of dynamics of conflict expansion and contraction. This is because venues constitute institutional opportunity structures that determine the visibility, mobilization, and accessibility of outside interests in the policy process. Venues also embody distinct epistemic and normative lenses which structure how political actors understand, interpret, and 'frame' policy issues.

Importantly, these venues can be manipulated by policy makers—through the creation of new or reconfigured venues—to further their interests. We emphasize the importance of venue 'shifting' to ad hoc, specialist groups as a means of depoliticizing salient policy issues. This is because delegation to external 'experts' provides policy makers with a powerful tool to insulate policy making from day-to-day politics: encouraging deliberative decision making by drawing on external knowledge and technical expertise; signalling credibility and legitimacy about policy choices to voters; and building consensus and securing 'buy in' from relevant stakeholders. Importantly, reducing politicization through venue shifting can take the form of either conflict contraction—that is, deliberately limiting the number and range of actors involved in the process in order to facilitate agreement—or conflict expansion—that is, expanding the scope of participants involved in order to secure 'buy in' from a broader range of societal interests.

Venue shifting plays a critical part in our explanation of interest group mobilization around structural reform, and how policy makers manipulated the process to further their policy goals. Hence, in the UK and the Netherlands, political leaders sought to depoliticize the issue of bank structural reform by delegating it to a series of notionally 'independent' committees, leveraging the technical expertise and authority of their membership to develop detailed policy recommendations. But doing so in the context of very different patterns of financial interest representation gave rise to widely divergent processes. Hence, venue shifting in a context of fragmented and decentralized financial lobbying—as in the UK—constrained the influence of TBTF banks and facilitated engagement with a range of societal groups: that is, conflict expansion. Venue shifting at the EU level also resembled the UK experience, albeit at the pre-proposal stage. By contrast, venue shifting in a context of unified and centralized financial lobbying—as in the Netherlands—left the process more vulnerable to industry capture, with the result that 'expert' commissions limited involvement to a narrow range of participants with close ties to industry: that is, conflict contraction.

By contrast, in the absence of venue shifting, policy makers in our other cases had to manage the issue through conventional political channels. In this context, banking reform was generally subject to higher politicization and the outcome reflected the (shifting) balance of power between competing political and economic interests. Hence, in France and Germany, governments were able to engage in conflict contraction by carefully steering the agenda through parliament, and ameliorating political demands to crack down on TBTF banks by proposing largely symbolic ringfencing reforms. By contrast, structural reform in the US remained uniquely vulnerable to conflict expansion rooted in deeply polarized congressional politics. In this sense, the outcome of the legislative process never secured broad agreement and was forever subject to the vagaries of future electoral outcomes.

In sum, our findings provide an interesting twist on the business power debate. Specifically, we demonstrate that there is no simple, linear relationship between business power and political salience. Rather, heightened salience can serve either to constrain *or* empower private firms at different times and in different ways. Crucially, this depends on the extent to which other societal groups are mobilized around an issue, and on the particular political-institutional venue of decision making. On the one hand, when non-financial interest groups are highly mobilized—as in the US—maintaining issue salience through aggressive lobbying may be the most effective option for industry to assert influence; by contrast, where there is limited societal mobilization—as in France and Germany—it makes more sense for industry to work with sympathetic policy makers to reduce salience and de-escalate policy conflict. On the other hand, the decision of policy makers to depoliticize salient regulatory issues by delegating them to ad hoc specialist groups can serve the interests of business where these venues are effectively captured by industry—as in the Netherlands; paradoxically, however, delegation can also have the effect of insulating policy makers from industry lobbying and facilitating the mobilization of wider policy stakeholders—as in the UK and in the EU at the pre-proposal stage. Future research on business power must therefore pay greater attention to the wider societal and political-institutional context of regulatory reform to avoid systematically mis-specifying the influence of business in the policy process.

Political economy of finance

Our book makes an important contribution to scholarship on the political economy of finance from a comparative perspective. Drawing on studies of financial interest lobbying (Kastner 2014, 2018; Pagliari and Young 2014, 2016; Chalmers

2015, 2017, 2020; Winecoff 2015; Young and Pagliari 2017; James et al. 2020), we aim to unpack how and why financial power varies across different jurisdictions. Our central claim is that financial power is mediated by the relational context within which it is embedded: that is, the ability of financial firms to leverage influence by mobilizing and alliance building with like-minded firms and associations. This leads us to predict that, under conditions of heightened political salience about TBTF banks, the financial industry will be more influential in shaping regulatory outcomes when it is unified. We refer to this as *cooperative financial power*. This unity of voice will be reflected in the financial industry's ability to leverage broad sectoral and business alliances. These interconnections not only serve to coordinate and legitimize the preferences of financial firms, but also ensure that these firms are less likely to be challenged by the mobilization of countervailing groups. Conversely, we expect the financial industry to be less influential when it is divided because the fragmentation of its voice will inhibit the articulation of coherent regulatory preferences. In the absence of broad business alliances, this *competitive financial power* will be characterized by firms lobbying individually, or through (sub-) sectoral associations, and thus facing greater competition from countervailing groups to access and influence policy makers.

To provide a firmer theoretical grounding for our empirical expectations, we turn to the literature on interest intermediation (Katzenstein 1978; Hall 1986; Lehmbruch 1991; Hall and Soskice 2001; Schmidt 2002; Eising 2009). Specifically, we predict that long-standing organizational features or 'modes' of interest representation—namely, *pluralism, neo-corporatism*, and *statism*—structure the capacity of the financial sector to centralize and coordinate lobbying with other economic actors. In other words, these modes are a key determinant of whether financial power is predominantly competitive or cooperative in different national contexts. Hence, we expect countries with pluralist modes of interest representation—typified by the US and UK—to be characterized by competitive financial power. That is, financial industry lobbying will tend to be fragmented with minimal coordination; industry preferences will be more heterogeneous; and the sector will face significant competition from countervailing groups. By contrast, we argue that cooperative financial power is more characteristic of countries with a legacy of neo-corporatism, such as Germany and the Netherlands, and statist modes of intermediation, as in France. Here financial interest representation is traditionally more hierarchical and centralized; lobbying activity is more tightly coordinated; and industry preferences tend to be more homogeneous. Finally, as a hybrid case of 'elite pluralism' (Coen 1997, pp. 98–9; Broscheid and Coen 2007; Grossman 2004; Mahoney 2008; Coen et al. 2021), the EU combines important features of both competitive financial power—reflecting the fragmented and multi-level institutional landscape—and cooperative financial power—due to the access and influence granted to powerful national and European business groups.

Applying this *comparative financial power* framework to our six case studies generates three important insights. The first is the extent to which financial power is path dependent: that is, remains rooted in the institutional legacies of historic modes of interest intermediation. Recent empirical studies have hinted at the fact that financial industry lobbying displays distinctive patterns of coordination and alliance building in different countries (James et al. 2020). Our study provides important confirmation of this thesis. Indeed, we find that the nature of financial power in a jurisdiction—whether competitive or cooperative—is a key determinant of the capacity of TBTF banks to shape the outcome of structural reform. In particular, we demonstrate that the ability of banks in France, Germany, and the Netherlands to unite in opposition to ringfencing, and to call on the support of other financial firms and important economic actors in the 'real' economy, was essential to their resisting politically driven commitments to reform. By contrast, the comparatively fragmented nature of financial interest lobbying in the US and UK—characterized by TBTF banks that preferred to lobby 'alone', relatively weak sectoral and business associations, and powerful countervailing voices from within the financial industry (notably, US community banks)—fatally weakened the power of finance to dilute stringent new regulatory restrictions.

These durable features of national-level lobbying are all the more striking given the profound changes to national varieties of capitalism and the erosion of distinctive modes of interest intermediation in recent decades (Deeg 1999, 2001; Woldendorp and Delsen 2008; Streeck 2009; Clift 2012, 2014). Indeed, despite the well-documented dismantling of neo-corporatist and statist arrangements in continental Europe since the 1980s, in response to successive rounds of economic liberalization and EU market integration, it is clear that the organization and representation of powerful economic interests retain important characteristics of the post-war period—namely, that they remain relatively coordinated and centralized.

Tellingly, the framework also forces us to avoid viewing 'Wall Street' and the 'City of London' as monolithic and all-powerful economic interests. On the contrary, our analysis of the US and UK cases demonstrates that financial interest representation is surprisingly fragmented and competitive, contrary to the lazy stereotypes that are often portrayed. Indeed, our study hints at the fact that the sheer scale and diversity of the financial sector in the US and UK is as much a source of weakness as strength: namely, that the heterogeneity of distinct sectoral and sub-sectoral financial interests inhibits collective action, resulting in a highly pluralistic interest ecology. The analysis of financial power at the EU level does not of course demonstrate the same historically embedded qualities, given the relatively recent foundation of the polity. Nonetheless, the important role of domestic banking associations—notably from France, Germany, and the Netherlands—in lobbying against the Liikanen Group's proposals through their respective home governments points to the continued relevance of national interest representation. Moreover, the influence wielded by pan-European financial and business groups in relation to the European Commission and European Parliament also provides evidence of how this cooperative financial power has been extended to the EU level.

More generally, the importance of nationally embedded patterns of financial interest lobbying provides an important qualifier to IPE theories which emphasize the significance of transnational financial interests and alliances (Cerny 2010; Farrell and Newman 2014a, 2016; Newman and Posner 2016a, 2016b). In one respect, given that there was almost no attempt to coordinate bank structural reform at the global level, this is perhaps not all that surprising. However, what is more striking is the fact that the two countries that imposed the toughest restrictions on speculative activities are host to two of the world's largest global financial centres—New York and London—and are home to a number of the largest G-SIBs. This should at least give us considerable pause to reflect upon the limits of global financial power and multinational financial institutions. That the structural and instrumental power of global banks remains formidable is beyond question. But the nationally embedded character of statutory financial regulation—as opposed to non-binding global standards—and the accountability of elected officials to national voters still constitute the most important constraints that states and governments wield over the power of capital. This national embeddedness also speaks to the continued relevance of the 'dilemma' facing financial regulators in balancing the interests of industry for competitiveness with voters' demands for financial stability (Kapstein 1989)—and the wider 'hierarchy of needs' that also confronts governments with the need to fund the real economy (Howarth and Quaglia 2016a).

Our analysis also builds on existing CPE perspectives on financial regulation (Story and Walter 1997; Hardie and Howarth 2013a; Howarth and Quaglia 2016b). In particular, we stress the fact that regulatory outcomes do not automatically reflect the preferences of the strategically most important economic interests in a country, nor the desire of governments to defend their international competitiveness. Crucially, regulatory outcomes depend on how those interests are organized, coordinated, and represented through political institutions and in the policy process.

Our comparison of six cases also provides a more systematic analysis of variation in financial power between most similar cases. For example, while the power of TBTF banks in the Netherlands was rooted in centralized interest representation, the picture in Germany is more fragmented by comparison: with multiple bank associations representing different bank types, but nonetheless speaking entirely in unison. By contrast, we show how the power of the concentrated French banking system is complemented by the interpersonal connections between banks and the state, reinforced by the important presence of former high-ranking Ministry of Finance officials in the country's biggest banks. The US, UK, and even the EU cases display similar variation, reinforcing the point that there is no simple relationship between bank concentration and centralized representation. Hence, while the efforts of the largest Wall Street banks to resist the Volcker Rule were thwarted in large part by the highly vocal opposition of thousands of 'Main Street' banks, even the relatively concentrated UK banking sector struggled to forge a coherent position in response to retail bank ringfencing. At the EU level, a highly fragmented and diverse financial sector—encompassing the interests of multiple TBTF banks—nonetheless demonstrated a remarkable degree of unity, enabling them to coalesce around powerful European industry associations to channel their influence over EU policy makers.

Another important contribution of our book is to the broader scholarship on collective action and lobbying networks (see Stokman and Zeggelink 1996; Hojnacki 1997; Henry et al. 2011; Leifeld and Schneider 2012; Fischer and Sciarini 2016; Ingold and Leifeld 2016). Although distinct national patterns of financial lobbying have recently been mapped systematically through quantitative network analysis (see James et al. 2020), there are surprisingly few qualitative comparative studies devoted to this important task. Our main contribution is to show that both macro-level features of interest representation—that is, competitive versus cooperative power—and meso-level characteristics of the policy process—that is, the opportunity for venue shifting—serve as potential sources of cross-national variation in lobbying networks. Delineating these factors is not only relevant in an examination of the influence of the financial sector upon government policy making, but potentially helps to illuminate the underlying structures, processes, and conditions of network formation and evolution. Not only do our results demonstrate that the resources that large firms leverage through relational ties to others are often more important than their individual attributes. Our results also suggest that durable, institutionalized ties—typical of centralized representation through trade associations in former neo-corporatist systems, or elite interconnections between corporate leaders and the state, as in traditionally statist systems—are more important (in causal terms) than ad hoc, informal ones—characteristic of issue-specific coalition building in systems associated with pluralism. This perhaps reflects the importance of mutual trust, reciprocity, and shared beliefs in overcoming barriers to collective action, promoting resource exchange, and facilitating coordination between organizations (see Sabatier and Jenkins-Smith 1993; Weible and Sabatier 2005; Henry et al. 2011; Calanni et al. 2014).

Our findings also speak to older debates on the organization of concentrated versus diffuse interests (Olson 1965; Stigler 1971; Wilson 1980). It is evident from our findings that where the financial industry is divided and fragmented, a window of opportunity exists for a wider spectrum of political and societal interests to mobilize and shape the regulatory agenda. Here our argument broadly accords with recent studies of collective action which show that diffuse interests—such as taxpayers and consumer groups—can be highly organized and politically powerful (Baumgartner et al. 2009; Godwin et al. 2012; Trumbull 2012). This is particularly true when they ally with like-minded groups and prominent actors, like senior regulators and influential legislators. However, the US and UK provide contrasting examples of how these pro-reform coalitions emerge and exert influence. The US example is a 'bottom up' pluralist story about the mobilization of outsider interests—namely, grassroots campaigns, activists, and progressive think tanks—which gradually coalesce and are carefully cultivated by the White House and congressional backers. By contrast, the formation of the pro-reform coalition in the UK is a predominantly 'top down' process led by insider actors—senior regulators, prominent parliamentarians, and a handful of academics—who actively seek to facilitate engagement with civil society. Again, the political and institutional context—in this case, the contrast between the fragmented political landscape of Washington and the centralized Westminster–Whitehall model of government—is critical to explaining the distinct mobilization of countervailing groups in favour of bank structural reform.

Typologies of regulatory reform

The final contribution we make is to propose a typology of banking reform. It is our intention to demonstrate how typologies can be used as a valuable heuristic device and analytical tool for explaining complex regulatory processes. Distinguishing 'types' of banking reform helps to clarify and refine our concepts, delineates the underlying causal processes, and creates categories for classification and measurement (Bennett and Elman 2006). The typology we develop posits two explanatory variables: whether financial power is competitive or cooperative, as a determinant of the stringency of regulatory reform; and the opportunity for policy makers to use venue shifting, which shapes the degree to which regulatory reform is (de)politicized. Combining these variables provides a theoretically grounded basis for categorizing distinct reforms in conceptual terms, and for generating empirical expectations about the outcome of regulatory processes in different national contexts. One added value of this approach is to move away from accounts of financial regulatory reform which tend to posit a dichotomous outcome of reform or no reform. Instead, our typology allows for a more nuanced approach, recognizing that cross-national variation is multi-dimensional: in our case, varying not just in terms of substance—that is, the scope of new regulatory restrictions put in place—but also in terms of process—that is, the institutional venues used to agree rule changes.

We argue that the resulting designation of four types of bank structural reform—durable, contested, symbolic, and no reform—sheds valuable light on how similar policy processes can generate very different regulatory outcomes, depending on how they interact with patterns of interest representation. For example, venue shifting to ad hoc specialist committees in two of our cases—the UK and the Netherlands—produced highly divergent outcomes—durable reform versus no reform. In our book we show that this cannot be reduced to prior political commitments, not least because leading UK politicians demonstrated no more enthusiasm for structural reform in early 2010 than Dutch politicians at the same time. Rather, the divergent outcomes have more to do with the nature of financial power in the two countries, and the extent to which the new institutional venues could thus be insulated from industry influence. Hence, while the relatively uncoordinated nature of UK bank lobbying helped the ICB to exploit industry divisions and expose bank claims to greater scrutiny, the unity of the Dutch banking industry was pivotal in enabling it to shape the agenda at a very early stage through the Maas Commission.

Similarly, regulatory reform in the absence of venue shifting can also produce significant variation. In three of the cases we examine—the US, France, and Germany—structural reform was generally subject to higher levels of politicization. But, here again, the representation of financial interests played a critical role in steering these party-political pressures over time. In the US, for example, powerful countervailing voices from within and outside the financial industry enabled the Obama administration to exploit conflict expansion and maintain pressure on Congress. In doing so, US policy makers were eventually able to build sufficient political support to push surprisingly stringent regulatory reform—the Volcker Rule—through a deeply polarized Congress. Subsequently, however, the alignment of Wall Street interests with the Republicans opened up a highly effective institutional channel through which the banks could maintain the salience of the issue, apply pressure on regulators, and gradually chip away at the legislation. By contrast, in France and Germany, the hierarchical and disciplined character of financial lobbying enabled TBTF banks to leverage influence through conventional political institutions and policy processes. This 'quiet politics' of influence proved to be brutally effective in facilitating conflict contraction: limiting the mobilization of countervailing groups around structural reform, forcing politicians to confront the economic implications of earlier election pledges, and giving governments the political 'cover' to reverse—although not completely abandon—plans for structural reform.

We end by encouraging scholars to make greater use of explanatory typologies in political-economy scholarship on financial regulation. In short, these typologies provide a valuable theoretically grounded basis for contextualizing regulatory reform. They promote a richer empirical investigation of causal processes and mechanisms, and they facilitate the systematic comparative analysis of multiple cases.

4. Beyond banking: a guide to future research

The theoretical framework we develop in this book has significant potential to advance the comparative analysis of financial—and business—power more widely. As a guide to future research, we suggest a number of important factors to consider when applying it to other issue areas. First, the utility of our framework depends on the timing and sequencing of cross-border financial rules, at either the international or EU level. Logically, the comparative framework developed in the book works best where there is substantial variation in the dependent variable to be explained: namely, divergence in national-level financial regulation. We would most likely expect this to be the case either where cross-border rules are largely absent—for example, recent proposals regarding intermediate bank holding companies—or when these develop *after* the adoption of national-level regulations—for example, post-crisis bank resolution rules (Quaglia and Spendzharova 2017a, 2019; James and Quaglia 2020). Hence, even when detailed cross-border rules emerge in order to harmonize domestic regulations, the framework will still be very useful in explaining the prior stage of regulatory development at the national level, the extent of any divergence between jurisdictions, and, subsequently, the preferences of national regulators in EU/international-level negotiations.

On the other hand, the framework will be less useful where international-level standards, or EU-level legislation, emerge prior to domestic reforms, as this is likely to result in far less divergence between countries. Nonetheless, the framework still has the potential to offer important insights into subsequent sources of national-level variation away from international standards. This potential remains because international agreements are non-binding and EU directives must be transposed into national legislation prior to implementation. Both generally permit national competent authorities substantial discretion over implementation, giving rise to significant cross-border divergence—as we have seen with respect to post-crisis bank capital and liquidity requirements (Howarth and Quaglia 2013a; Bell and Hindmoor 2018).

Second, our framework was developed for the purpose of investigating the influence of the banking industry in different national contexts. We are confident that it could be applied to other areas of financial regulation, although we might expect the causal assumptions to be more problematic in some financial sub-sectors. The framework relies on our ability to draw a fundamental distinction between competitive and cooperative financial power—which itself rests on the assumption that industry representation is centralized and unified in some countries, and more fragmented and divided in others. We would expect these conditions to hold in several other areas of finance, such as asset management and insurance. Here we find evidence in many (European) countries of the sectors dominated by a small number of large firms, centralized trade associations, and/or close connections to policy makers (see Ban and Gabor 2016, Braun 2021; Thiemann 2018; Thiemann et al. 2018; James and Quaglia 2022). Conversely, we would expect the non-banking financial sector to be more diverse and fragmented in other jurisdictions—notably the US and at the EU level—which have deeper and/or more segmented capital markets (Dietl 1998; Becker 2007; Mattli 2019).

Moreover, there is no reason why the framework developed here might not also be applied to other economic sectors characterized by important differences in modes of interest representation across countries—for example, car manufacturing, pharmaceuticals, and agriculture. In these economic sectors, we might reasonably hypothesize that path-dependent patterns of interest representation—themselves rooted in the legacy of pluralist, neo-corporatist or statist modes of intermediation—will continue to exert a causal effect on the capacity of those sectors to shape regulatory outcomes. Hence, the typology might provide additional explanatory leverage into how business power operates in these sectors, and sources of regulatory divergence among states.

However, we also recognize that these conditions are unlikely to hold for other financial sub-sectors, notably alternative investment funds and securities markets, where the diversity of interests and the fragmentation of organization is a more general feature of the industry (Woll 2013, 2014; Quaglia and Spendzharova 2020; Quaglia 2021). Given that financial power in these areas is likely to be primarily competitive in nature across different national jurisdictions, we would expect our framework to be less useful in explaining cross-national regulatory variation. Equally, the typology will be less applicable to those economic sectors where we have a weaker theoretical basis for deriving empirical expectations about distinct modes of interest intermediation in different national contexts—for example, the retail service sector and the information technology industry. In both cases, the largely pluralist character of interest group lobbying is likely to militate against comparative analysis at a macro level.

Third, an important advance in the application of our framework would be systemically to map and measure financial interest representation. Modern network analysis tools are ideally suited to this task, and can be used to measure levels of financial interest mobilization around an issue (Young 2012; Pagliari and Young 2016), coordination of lobbying (James et al. 2021), alliance building with non-financial interests (Pagliari and Young 2014; Young and Pagliari 2017), and leadership and power in networks (Winecoff 2015; James and Christopoulos 2018). Social network analysis has also been employed to capture the policy preferences, beliefs, and values of organizational actors (Weible and Sabatier 2005; Lubell 2007; Henry et al. 2011; James and Christopoulos 2018)—and thus the existence of normative, rather than narrowly functional, ties to others. A range of quantitative techniques could therefore be used systematically to map and compare the centralization of financial interest representation, and/or the density of financial and other business lobbying networks, across a range of countries. This would permit the development of more precise indices of financial interest centralization/fragmentation and, in theory at least, the testing of a range of hypotheses about the stringency of regulatory outcomes using regression analysis.

A fourth consideration concerns our book's contribution to the comparative public policy literature (Kingdon 1995; Jones and Baumgartner 2005;

Baumgartner et al. 2006; Dodds 2012). We recognize that the parsimony of the framework is less well suited to explaining regulatory divergence where we would expect to find less variation in macro-level features of interest intermediation. Nonetheless, in this situation, the framework still provides significant explanatory power by directing our attention to the importance of meso-level features, such as agenda-setting dynamics. Indeed, we argue that focusing on policy and decision-making processes can yield important and separate comparative insights into regulatory outcomes. In particular, future studies could examine the extent to which our second independent variable—the opportunity (or not) for venue shifting—serves as a critical source of regulatory divergence between jurisdictions. Indeed, comparing countries where financial (or business) power is held constant would in theory provide a more robust test of the independent causal effect of political institutions and policy processes on regulatory outcomes. In addition, there is substantial scope to provide a more fine-grained analysis of the role of venue shifting to specialist groups and expert committees—notably with respect to their particular design, membership, consultation processes, information gathering, and decision-making rules (see Flinders and Buller 2006; Princen 2007, 2011; Flinders 2009; Dunlop 2010). Even where venue shifting does not take place, there are huge sources of variation in policy processes across jurisdictions—shaped by the design of political institutions, the distribution of political power, national 'policy styles', and/or the role of political culture (see Richardson 1982; Jackman and Miller 1996; Crothers and Lockhart 2000). In both cases, greater differentiation in national-level features of the policy process constitutes an expansive future research agenda.

Finally, we end with an appeal to broaden the selection of cases beyond the comparatively large and advanced economies considered in this book. Selecting countries for comparison outside of western Europe and North America will undoubtedly pose additional challenges with respect to determining particular modes of interest intermediation, as the scholarly literature on such cases is less well developed. Investigating a wider selection of cases will also inevitably meet significant methodological barriers in terms of data collection, access, and comparability. Nonetheless, the development of new quantitative measures and country rankings regarding the main features of corporatism provides a stronger empirical basis for undertaking meaningful comparisons (in particular, see Jahn 2016). Moreover, there is an abundance of exciting new research on financial power, bank lobbying, state–bank interaction, and financial regulation in developing economies and emerging markets (for example, Dafe 2017; Jones 2020; Naqvi 2021). Hence, there is no reason why scholars could not undertake rich comparisons—or even develop new typologies—beyond the 'usual suspects' of Europe and America, based on a deep historical analysis of patterns of lobbying, interest groups, and the policy process in selected countries. We hope that this book has played a part—if only a modest one—in encouraging other researchers to undertake just such a worthwhile endeavour.

References

Secondary Sources

Abdelal, R. 2007. *Capital Rules: The Construction of Global Finance*. Cambridge, MA: Harvard University Press.

Acharya, V., T. F. Cooley, M. Richardson, and I. Walter. 2011. *Dodd–Frank: One Year On*. London: CEPR e-book.

Admati, A., and M. Hellwig. 2014. *Bankers' New Clothes: What's Wrong with Banking and What to Do about It*. Princeton, NJ: Princeton University Press.

Albæk, E., C. Green-Pedersen, and L. Beer Nielsen. 2007. 'Making Tobacco Consumption a Political Issue in the United States and Denmark: The Dynamics of Issue Expansion in Comparative Perspective'. *Journal of Comparative Policy Analysis: Research and Practice* 9 (1): 1–20.

Alessandri, P., and A. Haldane. 2009. 'Banking on the State'. Based on a presentation delivered at the Federal Reserve Bank of Chicago 12th Annual International Banking Conference, 25 September. *BIS Review* 139.

Alter, J. 2010. *The Promise: President Obama, Year One*. New York: Simon and Schuster.

Andeweg, R. B., G. A. Irwin, and T. Louwerse. 2020. *Governance and Politics of the Netherlands*, 5th edn, London: Bloomsbury.

Asimakopoulos, I. 2019. 'Making Retail Banks Resolvable'. *European Banking Institute Working Paper Series*. DOI: 10.2139/ssrn.3471187.

Asimakopoulos, I., and D. Howarth. 2022. 'Stillborn Banking Union: Explaining Ineffective European Union Banking Resolution Rules'. *Journal of Common Market Studies* 60 (2): 264–282.

Attac and Basta. 2015. *Le Livre Noir des Banques*. Paris: Liens qui Libèrent.

Ayadi, R. 2019. *Banking Business Models: Definition, Analytical Framework and Financial Stability Assessment*. Studies in Banking and Financial Institutions. Basingstoke: Palgrave Macmillan.

Bach, D., and A. Newman. 2007. 'The European Regulatory State and Global Public Policy: Micro-institutions, Macro-influence'. *Journal of European Public Policy* 14 (6): 1–20.

Bachrach, P., and M. S. Baratz. 1962. 'Two Faces of Power'. *American Political Science Review* 56 (4): 947–952.

Baker, A. 1999. 'Nebuleuse and the "Internalization of the State" in the UK? The Case of HM Treasury and the Bank of England'. *Review of International Political Economy* 6 (1): 79–100.

Baker, A. 2006. *The Group of Seven: Finance Ministries, Central Banks and Global Finance Governance*. London: Routledge.

Baker, A. 2010. 'Restraining Regulatory Capture? Anglo America, Crisis Politics and Trajectories of Change in Global Financial Governance'. *International Affairs* 86 (3): 647–664.

Baker, A. 2013a. 'The New Political Economy of the Macroprudential Ideational Shift'. *New Political Economy* 18 (1): 112–139.

Baker, A. 2013b. 'The Gradual Transformation? The Incremental Dynamics of Macroprudential Regulation'. *Regulation and Governance* 7 (4): 417–434.

Baker, A., and D. Wigan. 2017. 'Constructing and Contesting City of London Power: NGOs and the Emergence of Noisier Financial Politics'. *Economy and Society* 46 (2): 185–210.

Ban, C., and D. Gabor. 2016. 'The Political Economy of Shadow Banking'. *Review of International Political Economy* 23 (6): 901–914.

Ban, C., L. Seabrooke, and S. Freitas. 2016. 'Grey Matter in Shadow Banking: International Organizations and Expert Strategies in Global Financial Governance'. *Review of International Political Economy* 23 (6): 1001–1033.

Bao, J., M. O'Hara, and A. Zhou. 2016. 'The Volcker Rule and Market-Making in Times of Stress'. Finance and Economics Discussion Series 2016-102. Washington: Board of Governors of the Federal Reserve System.

Bartels, L. 2010. *Unequal Democracy: The Political Economy of the New Gilded Age*. Princeton, NJ: Princeton University Press.

Barth, J. R., G. Caprio Jr, and Levine, R. 2012. *Guardians of Finance: Making Regulators Work for Us*. Cambridge, MA: MIT Press.

Baumgartner, F. R., and B. D. Jones. 1993. *Agendas and Instability in American Politics*. Chicago, IL: University of Chicago Press.

Baumgartner, F., and B. Leech. 1998. *Basic Interests: The Importance of Groups in Politics and Political Science*. Princeton, NJ: Princeton University Press.

Baumgartner, F. R., J. M. Berry, M. Hojnacki, D. C. Kimball, and B. Lebon. 2009. *Lobbying and Policy Change: Who Wins, Who Loses, and Why*. Chicago, IL: University of Chicago Press.

Baumgartner, F. R., C. Green-Pedersen, and B. D. Jones. 2006. 'Comparative Studies of Policy Agendas'. *Journal of European Public Policy* 13 (7): 959–974.

Bebchuk, L., and J. Fried. 2004. *Pay Without Performance: The Unfulfilled Promise of Executive Compensation*. Cambridge, MA: Harvard University Press.

Becker, B. 2007. 'Geographical Segmentation of US Capital Markets'. *Journal of Financial Economics* 85 (1): 151–178.

Bell, S. 2012. 'The Power of Ideas: The Ideational Shaping of the Structural Power of Business'. *International Studies Quarterly* 56: 661–673.

Bell, S., and A. Hindmoor. 2015a. *Masters of the Universe, Slaves of the Market*. Cambridge, MA: Harvard University Press.

Bell, S., and A. Hindmoor. 2015b. 'Taming the City? Ideas, Structural Power and the Evolution of British Banking Policy Amidst the Great Financial Meltdown'. *New Political Economy* 20 (3): 454–474.

Bell, S., and A. Hindmoor. 2016. 'Structural Power and the Politics of Bank Capital Regulation in the United Kingdom'. *Political Studies* 65 (1): 103–121.

Bell, S., and A. Hindmoor. 2018. 'Are the Major Global Banks Now Safer? Structural Continuities and Change in Banking and Finance since the 2008 Crisis'. *Review of International Political Economy* 25 (1): 1–27.

Bennett, A., and C. Elman. 2006. 'Qualitative Research: Recent Developments in Case Study Methods'. *Annual Review of Political Science* 9: 455–476.

Bernhagen, P. 2007. *The Political Power of Business: Structure and Information in Public Policymaking*. London: Routledge.

Beyers J., and C. Braun. 2014. 'Ties that Count: Explaining Interest Group Access to Policymakers'. *Journal of Public Policy* 34: 93–121.

Beyers, J., and B. Kerremans. 2007. 'Critical Resource Dependencies and the Europeanization of Domestic Interest Groups'. *Journal of European Public Policy* 13 (3): 460–81.

Block, F. 1980. 'Beyond Relative Autonomy: State Managers as Historical Subjects'. *Socialist Register* 17: 227–241.

Brandi, T. O., and K. Gieseler. 2013. 'Entwurf des Trennenbankengesetzes: Sanierungs- und Abwick-lungsplanung, Risikoabschirmung des Kundengeschäfts, Vershärfung von Geschäftsleiterpflicten', *Der Betrieb* 14: 741–747.

Braun, B. 2021. 'Asset Manager Capitalism as a Corporate Governance Regime'. In J. S. Hacke, A. Hertel-Fernandez, P. Pierson, K. Thelen (eds.), *The American Political Economy: Politics, Markets and Power.* pp. 270–294. Cambridge: Cambridge University Press.

Braun, M., and C. Raddatz. 2010. 'Banking on Politics: When Former High-Ranking Politicians Become Bank Directors. *World Bank Economic Review* 24 (2): 234–279.

Broome, A., and L. Seabrooke. 2015. 'Shaping Policy Curves: Cognitive Authority in Transnational Capacity Building'. *Public Administration* 93: 956–972.

Broscheid, A., and D. Coen. 2003. 'Insider and outsider lobbying of the European Commission: an informational model of forum politics'. *European Union Politics* 4 (2): 165–91.

Broscheid, A., and D. Coen. 2007. 'Lobbying Activity and Fora Creation in the EU: Empirically Exploring the Nature of the Policy Good'. *Journal of European Public Policy* 14: 346–365.

Broz, J. L. 1999. 'Origins of the Federal Reserve System: International Incentives and the Domestic Free-Rider Problem'. *International Organization* 53: 39–70.

Buckely, J., and D. Howarth. 2010. 'Gesture Politics? Explaining Financial Regulatory Reform in the European Union'. *Journal of Common Market Studies* 48 (1): 119–141.

Bunea, A. 2015. 'Sharing Ties and Preferences: Stakeholders' Position Alignments in the European Commission's Open Consultations'. *European Union Politics* 16: 281–299.

Busch, A. 2004. 'National Filters: Europeanization, Institutions and Discourse in the Case of Banking Regulations'. *West European Politics* 27 (2): 310–333.

Busch, A. 2008. *Banking Regulations and Globalization.* Oxford: Oxford University Press.

Büthe, T., and W. Mattli. 2011. *The New Global Rulers: The Privatization of Regulation in the World Economy.* Princeton, NJ: Princeton University Press.

Calanni, J. C., S. N. Siddiki, C. M. Weible, and W. D. Leach. 2014. 'Explaining Coordination in Collaborative Partnerships and Clarifying the Scope of the Belief Homophily Hypothesis'. *Journal of Public Administration Research and Theory* 25 (3): 901–927.

Calomiris, C. W., and S. H. Haber. 2014. *Fragile by Design: The Political Origins of Banking Crises and Scarce Credit.* Princeton, NJ: Princeton University Press.

Carpenter, D. 2010. 'Institutional Strangulation: Bureaucratic Politics and Financial Reform in the Obama Administration'. *Perspectives in Politics* 8 (3): 825–846.

Carpenter, D., and D. A. Moss. 2014. 'Introduction'. In D. Carpenter and D. A. Moss (eds), *Preventing Regulatory Capture: Special Interest Influence and How to Limit It*, pp. 1–23. New York: Cambridge University Press.

Cassell, M. 2021. *Banking on the State: The Political Economy of Public Savings Banks.* New York: Columbia University Press; Newcastle-upon-Tyne: Agenda.

Cerny, P. 1994. 'The Dynamics of Financial Globalization: Technology, Market Structure, and Policy Response'. *Policy Sciences* 27: 317–342.

Cerny, P. 2010. *Rethinking World Politics: A Theory of Transnational Pluralism.* Oxford: Oxford University Press.

Chabanet, D., and A. Lacharet. 2016. 'The Occupy Movement in France: Why Protests Have Not Taken Off'. In M. Ancelovici, P. Dufour, H. Nez, J. W. Duyvendak, and J. M. Jasper (eds), *Street Politics in the Age of Austerity: From the Indignados to Occupy*, pp. 279–294. Amsterdam: Amsterdam University Press.

Chalmers, A. W. 2015. 'Financial Industry Mobilisation and Securities Markets Regulation in Europe'. *European Journal of Political Research* 54: 482–501.

Chalmers, A. W. 2017. 'When Banks Lobby: The Effects of Organizational Characteristics and Banking Regulations on International Bank Lobbying'. *Business and Politics* 19: 107–134.

Chalmers, A. W. 2020. 'Unity and Conflict: Explaining Financial Industry Lobbying Success in European Union Public Consultations'. *Regulation and Governance* 14 (3): 391–408.

Chang, M., and E. Jones. 2013. 'Belgium and the Netherlands: Impatient Capital'. In I. Hardie and D. Howarth (eds), *Market-Based Banking and the International Financial Crisis*, pp. 79–102. Oxford: Oxford University Press.

Clapp, J. 2003. 'Transnational Corporate Interests and Global Environmental Governance: Negotiating Rules for Agricultural Biotechnology and Chemicals'. *Environmental Politics* 12 (4): 1–23.

Clapp, J., and E. Helleiner. 2012. 'Troubled Futures? The Global Food Crisis and the Politics of Agricultural Derivatives Regulation'. *Review of International Political Economy* 19 (2): 181–207.

Clift, B. 2004. 'The French Model of Capitalism: still exceptional?'. In J. Perraton and B. Clift (eds), *Where are National Capitalisms Now*, pp. 91–110. Basingstoke: Palgrave.

Clift, B. 2012. 'Comparative Capitalism, Ideational Political Economy and French Post-Dirigiste Responses to the Global Financial Crisis'. *New Political Economy* 17 (5): 565–590.

Clift, B. 2014. *Comparative Political Economy: States, Markets and Global Capitalism*. Basingstoke: Palgrave Macmillan.

Coates, D., and C. Hay. 2001. 'The Internal and External Face of New Labour's Political Economy'. *Government and Opposition* 36 (4): 447–471.

Cobb, R. W., and C. D. Elder. 1972. *Participation in American Politics: The Dynamics of Agenda-Building*. Baltimore, MD: John Hopkins University Press.

Coen, D. 1997. 'The Evolution of the Large Firm as a Political Actor in the European Union'. *Journal of European Public Policy* 4 (1): 91–108.

Coen, D., and J. Richardson. 2009. 'Institutionalizing and Managing Intermediation in the EU'. In J. Richardson and D. Coen (eds.), *Lobbying the European Union*, pp. 337–350. New York: Oxford University Press.

Coen, D., and J. P. Salter. 2020. 'Multilevel Regulatory Governance: Establishing Bank–Regulator Relationships at the European Banking Authority'. *Business and Politics* 22 (1): 113–134.

Coen, D., A. Katsaitis, and M. Vannoni. 2021. *Business Lobbying in the European Union* Oxford: Oxford University Press

Colonnello, S., M. Koetter, and K. Wagner. 2018. 'Effectiveness and (In)Efficiencies of a Compensation Regulation: Evidence from the EU Banker Bonus Cap'. *IWH Discussion Papers* 7. https://www.econstor.eu/bitstream/10419/227086/1/iwh-dp2018-07rev.pdf.

Connaughton, J. 2012. *The Payoff: Why Wall Street Always Wins*. Prospecta Press.

Considine, M. 1998. 'Making Up the Government's Mind: Agenda Setting in a Parliamentary System'. *Governance* 11 (3): 297–317.

Conti-Brown, P. 2017. 'The Presidency, Congressional Republicans and the Future of Financial Reform'. *Penn Wharton Public Policy Initiative* 42.

Couppey-Soubeyran, J. 2015. *Blablabanque: Le discours de l'inaction*. Paris: Michalon.

Couppey-Soubeyran, J., and L. Scialom. 2013. 'Faut il Séparer les Banques?'. *Economie Politique* 1 (57): 6–13.

Crabb, J. 2017. 'PRIMER: Dodd–Frank and Stress Testing'. *International Financial Law Review*, 22 September. https://www.iflr.com/article/b1lv056xw39r7f/primer-dodd-frank-and-stress-testing

Crabb, J. 2018. 'PRIMER: A Comparison of EU and US Bank Resolution Regimes'. *International Financial Law Review*, 20 November. https://www.iflr.com/article/b1lp1y1ksc0njt/primer-a-comparison-of-eu-and-us-bank-resolution-regimes

Cram, L. 2001. 'Whither the Commission? Reform, Renewal and the Issue-Attention Cycle', *Journal of European Public Policy* 8 (5): 770–786.

Crothers, L., and C. Lockhart. 2000. *Culture and Politics*. New York: Palgrave Macmillan.

Crotty, J. 2008. 'If Financial Market Competition Is Intense, Why Are Financial Firm Profits So High? Reflections on the Current "Golden Age" of Finance'. *Competition and Change* 12 (2): 167–183.

Crouch, C., and W. Streeck. 1997. *Political Economy of Modern Capitalism: Mapping Convergence and Diversity*. London: Sage.

Culpepper, P. D. 2011. *Quiet Politics and Business Power*. New York: Cambridge University Press.

Culpepper, P. D. 2016. 'Capitalism, Institutions and Power in the Study of Business'. In O. Fioretos, T. Falleti, and A. Sheingate (eds), *The Oxford Handbook of Historical Institutionalism*, pp. 453–466. Oxford: Oxford University Press.

Culpepper, P. D., and R. Reinke. 2014. 'Structural Power and Bank Bailouts in the United Kingdom and the United States. *Politics and Society* 42 (4): 427–454.

Cusack, T., T. Iversen, and D. Soskice. 2010. 'Coevolution of Capitalism and Political Representation: The Choice of Electoral Systems'. *American Political Science Review* 104 (2): 393–403.

Dafe, F. 2017. 'The Politics of Finance: How Capital Sways African Central Banks'. *Journal of Development Studies* 55 (2): 311–327.

Daviter, F. 2007. 'Policy Framing in the European Union'. *Journal of European Public Policy* 14 (4): 654–666.

De Andrés, P., R. Reig, and E. Vallelado. 2019. 'European Banks' Executive Remuneration Under the New European Union Regulation'. *Journal of Economic Policy Reform* 22 (3): 208–225.

De Tricornot, A., M. Thépot, and F. Dedieu. 2014. *Mon Ami C'est la Finance*. Paris: Éditions Bayard.

Deeg, R. 1999. *Finance Capitalism Unveiled: Banks and the German Political Economy*. Ann Arbor, MI: University of Michigan Press.

Deeg, R. 2001. 'Institutional Change and the Uses and Limits of Path Dependency: The Case of German Finance'. *Max Planck Institute Discussion Papers* 01/06.

Devereux, M., N. Johannesen, and J. Vella. 2019. 'Can Taxes Tame the Banks? Evidence from the European Bank Levies'. *Working Papers* 1325. Oxford University Centre for Business Taxation. 14 March. https://www.nielsjohannesen.net/wp-content/uploads/bank-levies-FULL-EJ-resubmission2-FINAL-with-tables-and-figures.pdf.

Dietl, H. 1998. *Capital Markets and Corporate Governance in Japan, Germany and the United States: Organizational Responses to Market Inefficiencies*. London: Routledge.

Djelic, M. L., and S. Quack. 2010. *Transnational Communities: Shaping Global Economic Governance*. Cambridge: Cambridge University Press.

Dodds, A. 2012. *Comparative Public Policy*. Basingstoke: Palgrave.

Donges, J., J. Eekhoff, and W. Möschel. 2001. *Privatisierung von Landesbanken un Sparkassen*. Frankfurt-am-Mein: Frankfurt Institute.

Donnelly, S., and I. Asimakopoulos. 2020. 'Bending and Breaking the Single Resolution Mechanism: The Case of Italy'. *Journal of Common Market Studies* 58 (4): 856–871.

Drezner, D. 2007. *All Politics Is Global: Explaining International Regulatory Regimes.* Princeton, NJ: Princeton University Press.

Drutman, L. 2015. *The Business of America Is Lobbying: How Corporations Became Politicized and Politics Became More Corporate.* Oxford: Oxford University Press.

Dudouet, F. X., and E. Grémont. 2010. *Les Grands Patrons En France: Du Capitalisme D'état à la Financiarisation.* Paris: Lignes de Repères.

Dunlop, C. 2010. 'Epistemic Communities and Two Goals of Delegation: Hormone Growth Promoters in the European Union'. *Science and Public Policy* 37 (3): 205–217.

Dunlop, C. A., and C. M. Radaelli. 2013. 'Systematizing Policy Learning: From Monolith to Dimensions'. *Political Studies* 61 (3): 599–619.

Dunlop, C. A., and C. M. Radaelli. 2018. 'The Lessons of Policy Learning: Types, Triggers, Hindrances and Pathologies'. *Policy and Politics* 46 (2): 255–272.

Dür, A. 2008. 'Interest Groups in the European Union: How Powerful Are They?' *West European Politics* 31 (6): 1212–1230.

Dür, A., and G. Mateo. 2012. 'Who Lobbies the European Union? National Interest Groups in a Multilevel Polity'. *Journal of European Public Policy* 19 (7): 969–987.

Dür, A., and G. Mateo. 2014. 'Public Opinion and Interest Group Influence: How Citizen Groups Derailed the Anti-counterfeiting Trade Agreement'. *Journal of European Public Policy* 21 (8): 1199–1217.

Eising, R. 2007. 'The Access of Business Interest to EU Institutions: Towards Élite Pluralism?' *Journal of European Public Policy* 14 (3): 384–403.

Eising, R. 2009. *The Political Economy of State–Business Relations in Europe: Interest Mediation, Capitalism and EU Policymaking.* London: Routledge.

Eising, R., and B. Kohler-Koch. 1999. 'Governance in the European Union: A Comparative Assessment'. In B. Kohler-Koch and R. Eising (eds), *The Transformation of Governance in the European Union*, pp. 267–285. London: Routledge.

Elayan, F. A., R. Aktas, K. Brown, and P. Pacharn. 2018. 'The Impact of the Volcker Rule on Targeted Banks, Systemic Risk, Liquidity and Financial Reporting Quality'. *Journal of Economics and Business* 96: 68–89.

Endrejat, V., and M. Thiemann. 2019. 'Balancing Market Liquidity: Banking Structural Reform Caught Between Growth and Stability'. *Journal of Economic Policy Reform* 22 (3): 226–241.

Engelen, E., and M. Konings. 2010. 'Financial Capitalism Resurgent: Comparative Institutionalism and the Challenges of Financialization'. In G. Morgan, J. L. Campbell, C. Crouch, O. K. Pedersen, and R. Whitley (eds), *The Oxford Handbook of Comparative Institutional Analysis*, pp. 601–624. Oxford: Oxford University Press.

Epstein, R. 2017. *Banking on Markets: The Transformation of Bank–State Ties in Europe and Beyond.* Oxford: Oxford University Press.

Esterling, K. 2005. *The Political Economy of Expertise: Information and Efficiency in American National Politics.* Ann Arbor, MI: University of Michigan Press.

Falkner R. 2007. *Business Power and Conflict in International Environmental Politics.* London: Palgrave Macmillan.

Farrell, H., and A. Newman. 2014. 'Domestic Institutions Beyond the Nation State: Charting the New Interdependence Approach'. *World Politics* 66 (2): 331–366.

Farrell, H., and A. Newman. 2015. 'Structuring Power: Business and Authority Beyond the Nation State'. *Business and Politics* 17 (3): 527–552.

Farrell, H., and A. Newman. 2016. 'The New Interdependence Approach: Theoretical Development and Empirical Demonstration'. *Review of International Political Economy* 23 (5): 713–736.

Fioretos, K. O. 2010. 'Capitalist Diversity and the International Regulation of Hedge Funds'. *Review of International Political Economy* 17 (3): 696–723.

Fioretos, K. O. 2011. *Creative Reconstructions: Multilateralism and European Varieties of Capitalism After 1950*. Ithaca, NY: Cornell University Press.

Fischer, M., and P. Sciarini. 2016. 'Drivers of Collaboration in Political Decision Making: A Cross-Sector Perspective'. *Journal of Politics* 78 (1): 63–74.

Fligstein, Neil, and Shin Taekjin. 2007. 'Shareholder Value and the Transformation of the US Economy, 1984–2000'. *Sociological Forum* 22 (4): 399–424.

Flinders, M. 2009. 'Review Article: Theory and Method in the Study of Delegation: Three Dominant Traditions'. *Public Administration* 87 (4): 955–971.

Flinders, M., and J. Buller. 2006. 'Depoliticisation: Principles, Tactics and Tools'. *British Politics* 1 (3): 293–318.

Franke, M. 2020. *Regierungspolitik in der Weltfinanzkrise: Der Einfluss von Interessen, Ideen und Institutionen in Deutschland und Großbritannien am Beispiel des Bankensektors und der Automobilindustrie*. Baden-Baden: Nomos.

Frieden, J. A. 1988. 'Sectoral Conflict and Foreign Economic Policy, 1914–1940'. *International Organization* 42: 59–90.

Fuchs, D. 2007. *Business Power in Global Governance*. Boulder, CO: Lynn Rienner.

Gabor, D. 2016. 'The (Impossible) Repo Trinity: The Political Economy of Repo Markets'. *Review of International Political Economy* 23 (6): 967–1000.

Gambacorta, L., and A. van Rixtel. 2013. 'Structural Bank Regulation Initiatives: Approaches and Implications'. *Bank for International Settlements (BIS) Working Papers* 412. 26 April.

Ganderson, J. 2020a. 'To Change Banks or Bankers? Systemic Political (In)action and Post-Crisis Banking Reform in the UK and the Netherlands'. *Business and Politics* 22 (1): 196–223.

Ganderson, J. 2020b. 'Politics by Association: Party Competition and Post-Crisis Bank Structural Reform in the UK, the Netherlands and Germany'. Ph.D. thesis, European University Institute, Florence, Italy.

García Alcubilla, R., and J. Ruiz del Pozo. 2012. *Credit Rating Agencies on the Watch List: Analysis of European Regulation*. Oxford. Oxford University Press.

Giraud, P. N. 2009. *Le Commerce des Promesses: Petit Traité sur la Finance Moderne*. Paris: Points Seuil.

Godwin, K., S. H. Ainsworth, and E. Godwin. 2012. *Lobbying and Policymaking: The Public Pursuit of Private Interests*. Thousand Oaks, CA: CQ Press.

Goldbach, R. 2015a. *Global Governance and Regulatory Failures*. Basingstoke: Palgrave.

Goldbach, R. 2015b. 'Asymmetric Influence in Global Banking Regulation, Transnational Marmonization, the Competition State, and the Roots of Regulatory Failure'. *Review of International Political Economy* 22 (6): 1087–1127.

Goldstein, M. 2012. 'The EU's Implementation of Basel III: Deeply Flawed Compromise'. *VoxEU*, CEPR. 27 May. https://voxeu.org/article/eu-s-implementation-basel-iii-deeply-flawed-compromise.

Gray, V., and D. Lowery. 1996. *The Population Ecology of Interest Representation*. Ann Arbor, MI: University of Michigan Press.

Graz, J. C., and A. Nölke. 2008. *Transnational Private Governance and its Limits*. London: Routledge.

Green-Pedersen, C. 2007. 'The Conflict of Conflicts in Comparative Perspective: Euthanasia as a Political Issue in Denmark, Belgium and the Netherlands'. *Comparative Politics* 39 (3): 273–291.

Greenwood, J. 2017. *Interest Representation in the European Union*, 4th edn. London: Palgrave.

Gren, J., D. Howarth, and L. Quaglia. 2015. 'Supranational Banking Supervision in Europe: The Construction of a Credible Watchdog'. *Journal of Common Market Studies* 53 (1): 181–199.

Grossman, E. 2004. 'Bringing Politics Back In: Rethinking the Role of Economic Interest Groups in European Integration'. *Journal of European Public Policy* 11 (4): 637–654.

Haas, P. M. 1992. 'Introduction: Epistemic Communities and International Policy Coordination'. *International Organization* 46 (1): 1–36.

Hacker, J. S., and P. Pierson. 2002. 'Business Power and Social Policy: Employers and the Formation of the American Welfare State'. *Politics and Society* 30 (2): 277–325.

Hacker, J. S., and P. Pierson. 2010. *Winner-Take-All Politics: How Washington Made the Rich Richer—And Turned Its Back on the Middle Class*. New York: Simon & Schuster.

Hackethal, A., R. H Schmidt, and M. Tyrell. 2005. 'Banks and German Corporate Governance: On the Way to a Capital Market-Based System?' *Corporate Governance* 13 (3): 397–407.

Haldane, A. 2012. Speech 'On Being the Right Size'. Institute of Economic Affairs 22nd Annual Series and the 2012 Beesley Lectures, Institute of Directors, London, 25 October.

Hall, P. A. 1986. *Governing the Economy: The Politics of State Intervention in Britain and France*. Oxford: Oxford University Press.

Hall, P. A., and D. Soskice. 2001. *Varieties of Capitalism: The Institutional Foundations of Comparative Advantage*. Oxford: Oxford University Press.

Hardie, I., and D. Howarth. 2009. 'Die Krise but Not La Crise? The Financial Crisis and the Transformation of German and French Banking Systems'. *Journal of Common Market Studies* 47 (5): 1019–1039.

Hardie, I., and D. Howarth. 2013. 'Market-Based Banking as the Worst of All Worlds: Illustrations from the United States and United Kingdom'. In I. Hardie and D. Howarth (eds.), *Market Based Banking and the International Financial Crisis*. pp. 56–78. Oxford: Oxford University Press.

Hardie, I., and D. Howarth. 2013a. *Market-Based Banking and the International Financial Crisis*. Oxford: Oxford University Press.

Hardie, I., and D. Howarth. 2013b. 'A Peculiar Kind of Devastation: German Market-Based Banking'. In I. Hardie and D. Howarth (eds), *Market-Based Banking and the International Financial Crisis*, pp. 103–127. Oxford: Oxford University Press.

Hardie, I., and H. Macartney. 2016. 'Too Big to Separate? EU Ring-Fencing and the Defence of Too-Big-To-Fail Banks'. *West European Politics* 39 (3): 503–525.

Hardie, I., and S. Maxfield. 2013. 'Market-Based Banking as the Worst of All Worlds: Illustrations from the United States and United Kingdom'. In I. Hardie and D. Howarth (eds.), *Market Based Banking and the International Financial Crisis*. pp. 56–78. Oxford: Oxford University Press.

Hardie, I., D. Howarth, S. Maxfield, and A. Verdun. 2013. 'Banks and the False Dichotomy in the Comparative Political Economy of Finance'. *World Politics* 65 (4): 691–728.

Harvey, C., and M. Maclean. 2008. 'Capital Theory and the Dynamics of Elite Business Networks in Britain and France'. In M. Savage and K. Williams (eds), *Remembering Elites*, pp. 105–120. Oxford: Blackwell.

Hay, C., and B. Rosamond. 2002. 'Globalisation, European Integration and the Discursive Construction of Economic Imperatives'. *Journal of European Public Policy* 9: 147–167.

Heinz, J., E. Laumann, R. Nelson, and R. Salisbury. 1993. *The Hollow Core: Private Interests in National Policy Making*. Cambridge, MA: Harvard University Press.

Helleiner, E. 2010. 'A Bretton Woods Moment? The 2007-2008 Crisis and the Future of Global Finance'. *International Affairs* 86: 619-636.

Helleiner, E. 2014. *The Status Quo Crisis: Global Financial Governance After the 2008 Meltdown*. Oxford: Oxford University Press.

Helleiner, E., and J. Thistlethwaite. 2013. 'Subprime Catalyst: Financial Regulatory Reform and the Strengthening of US Carbon Market Governance'. *Regulation and Governance* 7: 496-511.

Helleiner, E., S. Pagliari, and I. Spagna. 2018. *Governing the World's Biggest Market: The Politics of Derivatives Regulation After the 2008 Crisis*. Oxford: Oxford University Press.

Hellwig, M. 2018. 'Germany and the Financial Crises 2007-2017'. Max Planck Institute for Research on Collective Goods. *Working Papers*. Cologne: Max Planck Institute.

Henriksen, L. F., and L. Seabrooke. 2016. 'Transnational Organizing: Issue Professionals in Environmental Sustainability Networks'. *Organization* 23 (5): 722-741.

Henry, A. D., M. Lubell, and M. McCoy. 2011. 'Belief Systems and Social Capital as Drivers of Policy Network Structure: The Case of California Regional Planning'. *Journal of Public Administration Research and Theory* 21 (3): 419-444.

Hicks, A. M., and L. Kenworthy. 1998. 'Cooperation and Political Economic Performance in Affluent Democratic Capitalism'. *American Journal of Sociology* 103: 1631-1672.

Hodson, D., and D. Mabbett. 2009. 'UK Economic Policy and the Global Financial Crisis: Paradigm Lost?'. *Journal of Common Market Studies* 47 (5): 1041-1061.

Hojnacki, M. 1997. 'Interest Groups' Decisions to Join Alliances or Work Alone'. *American Journal of Political Science* 41 (1): 61-87.

Hollman, M. 2018. *Interest Group Organisation in the European Union: How Internal Organisational Structures Shape Interest Group Agency*. London: Routledge.

Holmes, C. 2009. 'Seeking Alpha or Creating Beta? Charting the Rise of Hedge Fund-Based Financial Ecosystems', *New Political Economy* 14: 431-450.

Hopkin, J., and K. A. Shaw. 2016. 'Organized Combat or Structural Advantage? The Politics of Inequality and the Winner-Take-All Economy in the United Kingdom'. *Politics and Society* 44 (3): 345-371.

Howarth, D. 2013. 'France and the International Financial Crisis: The Legacy of State-Led Finance'. *Governance* 26 (3): 369-395.

Howarth, D. 2021. 'Comment Expliquer les Réformes du Secteur Financier en Europe: Acteurs, Idées ou Institutions?' In S. Saurruger and P. Hassenteufel (eds), *Les Politiques Publiques dans la Crise: 2008 et ses Suites*, pp. 111-43. Paris: Presses de Sciences Po.

Howarth, D., and S. James. 2020. 'The Politics of Bank Structural Reform: Business Power and Agenda Setting in the UK, France and Germany'. *Business and Politics* 22 (S1): 25-51.

Howarth, D., and L. Quaglia. 2013a. 'Banking on Stability: The Political Economy of New Capital Requirements in the European Union'. *Journal of European Integration* 35 (3): 333-346.

Howarth, D., and L. Quaglia. 2013b. 'Banking Union as Holy Grail: Rebuilding the Single Market in Financial Services, Stabilizing Europe's Banks and "Completing" Economic and Monetary Union'. *Journal of Common Market Studies* 51 (1): 103-123.

Howarth, D., and L. Quaglia. 2014. 'The Steep Road to Banking Union: The Setting Up of the Single Resolution Mechanism'. *Journal of Common Market Studies Annual Review* 50 (1): 125-140.

Howarth, D., and L. Quaglia. 2016a. *The Political Economy of Banking Union*. Oxford: Oxford University Press.

Howarth, D., and L. Quaglia. 2016b. 'Internationalised Banking, Alternative Banks and the Single Supervisory Mechanism'. *West European Politics* 39 (3): 438–461.

Howarth, D., and L. Quaglia. 2016c. 'The Comparative Political Economy of Basel III in Europe'. *Policy and Society* 35 (3): 205–214.

Howarth, D., and L. Quaglia. 2018a. 'The Difficult Construction of a European Deposit Insurance Scheme: A Step Too Far in Banking Union?'. *Journal of Economic Policy Reform* 21 (3): 190–209.

Howarth, D. and L. Quaglia. 2018b. 'Brexit and the Battle for Financial Services'. *Journal of European Public Policy* 25 (8): 1118–1136.

Howarth, D., and T. Sadeh. 2008. 'Economic Interests and the European Union'. Special edition of *British Journal of Politics and International Relations* 10 (1): 1–8.

Huber, E., and J. D. Stephens. 2001. *Development and Crisis of the Welfare State: Parties and Policies in Global Markets*. Chicago, IL: University of Chicago Press.

Hula, K. 1999. *Lobbying Together*. Washington, DC: Georgetown University Press.

Hungin, H. 2016a. 'Transcript of Interview with New York Federal Reserve Official'. 1 March 2016. New York. On file with the authors. Interview conducted for Hungin (2020).

Hungin, H. 2016b. 'Transcript of Interview with Congressional Advisor'. 22 March 2016. Washington. On file with the authors. Interview conducted for Hungin (2020).

Hungin, H. 2016c. 'Transcript of Interview with US Treasury Official'. 6 May 2016. Washington. On file with the authors. Interview conducted for Hungin (2020).

Hungin, H. 2016d. 'Transcript of Interview with Federal Reserve Official'. 16 May 2016. Washington. On file with the authors. Interview conducted for Hungin (2020).

Hungin, H. 2020. 'The Politics of Central Bank Reform: Post-Financial Crisis Institutional Reform in the USA and UK'. Ph.D. thesis, Department of Political and Social Sciences, European University Institute, Florence, Italy.

Hungin, H., and S. James. 2017. 'Contested Interests: The Domestic Politics of Central Bank Reform in the US and UK'. Public Administration Symposium Workshop, 30 March, Florence, Italy.

Hungin, H., and S. James. 2018. 'Central Bank Reform and the Politics of Blame Avoidance in the UK'. *New Political Economy* 24 (3): 334–349.

Igan, D., P. Mishra, and T. Tressel. 2009. 'A Fistful of Dollars: Lobbying and the Financial Crisis', *IMF Working Papers* WP/09/287,Washington, DC: IMF.

Ingold, K., and P. Leifeld. 2016. 'Structural and Institutional Determinants of Influence Reputation: A Comparison of Collaborative and Adversarial Policy Networks in Decision Making and Implementation'. *Journal of Public Administration Research and Theory* 26 (1): 1–18.

Jabko, N., and E. Massoc. 2012. 'French Capitalism Under Stress: How Nicolas Sarkozy Rescued the Banks'. *Review of International Political Economy* 19 (4): 562–585.

Jackman, R. W., and R. A. Miller. 1996. 'A Renaissance of Political Culture?' *American Journal of Political Science* 40 (3): 632–659.

Jacobs, L., and D. King. 2016. *Fed Power: How Finance Wins*. Oxford: Oxford University Press.

Jahn, D. 2016. 'Changing of the Guard: Trends in Corporatist Arrangements in 42 Highly Industrialized Societies from 1960 to 2010'. *Socio-Economic Review* 14 (1): 47–71.

James, S. 2016. 'The Domestic Politics of Financial Regulation: Informal Ratification Games and the EU Capital Requirement Negotiations'. *New Political Economy* 21 (2): 187–203.

James, S. 2018. 'The Structural-Informational Power of Business: Credibility, Signaling and the UK Banking Reform Process'. *Journal of European Public Policy* 25 (11): 1629–1647.

James, S., and D. Christopoulos. 2018. 'Reputational Leadership and Preference Similarity: Explaining Organisational Collaboration in Bank Policy Networks'. *European Journal of Political Research* 57 (2): 518–538.

James, S., and L. Quaglia. 2019. 'Why Does the UK Have Inconsistent Preferences on Financial Regulation? The Case of Banking and Capital Markets'. *Journal of Public Policy* 39 (1): 177–200.

James, S., and L. Quaglia. 2020. *The UK and Multi-level Financial Regulation: From Post-Crisis Reform to Brexit*. Oxford: Oxford University Press.

James, S. and L. Quaglia. 2022. 'Epistemic Contestation and Interagency Conflict: The Challenge of Regulating Investment Funds'. *Regulation and Governance*. doi.org/10.1111/rego.12457.

James, S., H. Kassim, and T. Warren. 2021. 'From Big Bang to Brexit: The City of London and the Discursive Power of Finance'. *Political Studies*. DOI: 10.1177/0032321720985714.

James, S., S. Pagliari, and K. Young. 2021. 'The Internationalization of European Financial Networks: A Quantitative Text Analysis of EU Consultation Responses'. *Review of International Political Economy* 28 (4): 898–925.

Johal, S., M. Moran, and K. Williams. 2014. 'Power, Politics and the City of London after the Great Financial Crisis'. *Government and Opposition* 49 (3): 400–425.

John, P. 2017. 'Theories of Policy Change and Variation Reconsidered: A Prospectus for the Political Economy of Public Policy'. *Policy Sciences* 51 (1): 1–16.

Johnson, S., and J. Kwak. 2010. *13 Bankers: The Wall Street Takeover and the Next Financial Meltdown*. New York: Pantheon.

Jones, B. D., and F. R. Baumgartner. 2005. *The Politics of Attention: How Government Prioritizes Problems*. Chicago, IL: University of Chicago Press.

Jones, E. 2020. *The Political Economy of Bank Regulation in Developing Countries: Risk and Regulation*. Oxford: Oxford University Press.

Kaiser, R. 2013. *Act of Congress: How America's Essential Institution Works, and How It Doesn't*. New York: Vintage.

Kapstein E. 1989. 'Resolving the Regulator's Dilemma: International Coordination of Banking Regulations'. *International Organization* 43 (2): 323–347.

Kastner, L. 2014. '"Much Ado About Nothing?" Transnational Civil Society, Consumer Protection and Financial Regulatory Reform'. *Review of International Political Economy* 21 (6): 1313–1345.

Kastner, L. 2018. 'Business Lobbying Under Salience: Financial Industry Mobilization Against the European Financial Transaction Tax'. *Journal of European Public Policy* 25 (11): 1648–1666.

Katzenstein, P. J. 1978. *Between Power and Plenty: Foreign Economic Policies of Advanced Industrial States*. Madison, WI: University of Wisconsin Press.

Keller, E. 2018. 'Noisy Business Politics: Lobbying Strategies and Business Influence After the Financial Crisis'. *Journal of European Public Policy* 25 (3): 287–306.

Kern, A. 2015. 'Regulating the Structure of the EU Banking Sector'. *European Business Organization Law Review* 16: 227–253.

Kingdon, J. 1995. *Agendas, Alternatives, and Public Policies*. New York: Longman Classics.

Klüver, H. 2013. *Lobbying in the European Union: Interest Groups, Lobbying Coalitions, and Policy Change*. Oxford: Oxford University Press.

Knaack, P. 2015. 'Innovation and Deadlock in Global Financial Governance: Transatlantic Coordination Failure in OTC Derivatives Regulation'. *Review of International Political Economy* 22 (6): 1217–1248.

Krahnen, J. P. 2013. 'Rescue by Regulation? Key Points of the Liikanen Report'. *SAFE White Paper Series* 9. Goethe University. https://safe-frankfurt.de/fileadmin/user_upload/editor_common/Policy_Center/Krahnen_Rescue_by_Regulation.pdf.

Krawiec, K. D. 2013. 'Don't "Screw Joe the Plumber": The Sausage-Making of Financial Reform'. *Arizona Law Review* 55: 53–82.
Krawiec, K. D., and G. Liu. 2015. 'The Volcker Rule: A Brief Political History'. *Capital Markets Law Review* 10 (4): 507–522.
Krippner, Greta R. 2011. *Capitalizing on Crisis: The Political Origins of the Rise of Finance*. Cambridge, MA: Harvard University Press.
Kumpan, C. 2014. 'Das Verbot von Eigengeschäften für Banken: Eine Rechtsvergleichende Analyse'. *ZBB/JBB* 4 (14): 201–211.
Kydland, F., and E. Prescott. 1977. 'Rules Rather than Discretion: The Inconsistency of Optimal Plans'. *Journal of Political Economy* 85: 473–491.
Lall, R. 2012. 'From Failure to Failure: The Politics of International Banking Regulation'. *Review of International Political Economy* 19 (4): 609–638.
Lall, R. 2015. 'Timing as a Source of Regulatory Influence: A Technical Elite Network Analysis of Global Finance'. *Regulation & Governance* 9(2): 125–143.
Lascelles, D., and M. Boleat. 2002. *Who Speaks for the City? Trade Associations Galore*. London: Centre for the Study of Financial Innovation.
Lazonick, W., and M. O'Sullivan. 2000. 'Maximizing Shareholder Value: A New Ideology for Corporate Governance'. *Economy and Society* 29: 13–35.
Lehmann, M., and J. Rehahn. 2014. 'Trennbanken nach Brüsseler Art: Der Kommissionsvorschlag vor dem Hintergrund nationaler Modelle'. *WM Wertpapiermitteilungen: Zeitschrift für Wirtschafts- und Bankrecht* 68: 1793–1803.
Lehmbruch, G. 1984. 'Concertation and the Structure of Corporatist Networks'. In J. H. Goldthorpe (ed.), *Order and Conflict in Contemporary Capitalism*, pp. 60–80. Oxford: Oxford University Press.
Lehmbruch, G. 1991. 'The Organization of Society, Administrative Strategies, and Policy Networks: Elements of a Developmental Theory of Interest Systems'. In R. M. Czada and A. Windhoff-Heritier (eds), *Political Choice: Institutions, Rules and the Limits of Rationality*, pp. 121–158. London: Routledge.
Lehmbruch, G., and P. C. Schmitter. 1982. *Patterns of Corporatist Policy-Making*. London: Sage.
Leifeld, P., and V. Schneider. 2012. 'Information Exchange in Policy Networks'. *American Journal of Political Science* 56 (3): 731–744.
Lijphart, A. 1999. *Patterns of Democracy: Government Forms and Performance in Thirty-Six Countries*. New Haven, CT: Yale University Press.
Lijphart, A. 2012. *Patterns of Democracy: Government Forms and Performance in Thirty-Six Countries*. Second Edition. New Haven: Yale University Press.
Lijphart, A., and M. M. L. Crepaz. 1991. 'Corporatism and Consensus Democracy in Eighteen Countries: Conceptual and Empirical Linkages'. *British Journal of Political Science* 21: 235–256.
Lindblom, C. E. 1977. *Politics and Markets*. New York: Basic Books.
Lindvall, J. 2009. 'The Real but Limited Influence of Expert Ideas'. *World Politics* 61 (4): 703–730.
Lombardi, D., and M. Moschella. 2017. 'The Symbolic Politics of Delegation: Macroprudential Policy and Independent Regulatory Authorities'. *New Political Economy* 22 (1): 92–108.
Loonen, T., and M. Rutgers. 2017. 'Swearing to Be a Good Banker: Perceptions of the Obligatory Banker's Oath in the Netherlands'. *Journal of Banking Regulation* 18 (1): 28–47.

Lubell, M. 2007. 'Familiarity Breeds Trust: Collective Action in a Policy Domain'. *Journal of Politics* 69: 237–250.

Lutz, S. 2000. 'From Managed to Market Capitalism? German Finance in Transition'. *German Politics* 9 (2): 149–171.

Macartney, H. 2010. *Variegated Neoliberalism: EU Varieties of Capitalism and International Political Economy*. London: Routledge.

Macartney, H. 2014a. 'From Merlin to Oz: The Strange Case of Failed SME Lending Targets in the UK'. *Review of International Political Economy* 21 (4): 820–846.

Macartney, H. 2019. *The Bank Culture Debate: Ethics, Values and Financialisation in Anglo-America*. Oxford: Oxford University Press.

Macartney, H., D. Howarth, and S. James. 2020. 'Bank Power and Public Policy Since the Financial Crisis'. *Business and Politics* 22 (1): 1–24.

Macdonald, A. 2001. *The Business of Representation: The Modern Trade Association*. London: Trade Association Forum.

Maclean, M., C. Harvey, and J. Press. 2006. *Business Elites and Corporate Governance in France and the UK*. Basingstoke: Palgrave Macmillan.

Magone, J. M. 2011. *Contemporary European Politics: A Comparative Introduction*. Abingdon: Routledge.

Mahoney, C. 2008. *Brussels versus the Beltway: Advocacy in the United States and the European Union*. Washington, DC: Georgetown University Press.

Mahoney, C., and F. R. Baumgartner. 2015. 'Partners in Advocacy: Lobbyists and Government Officials in Washington'. *Journal of Politics* 77: 202–215.

Mahoney, C., and M. J. Beckstrand. 2011. 'Following the Money: European Union Funding of Civil Society Organization'. *Journal of Common Market Studies* 49 (6): 1339–1361.

Majone, G. 1997. 'From the Positive to the Regulatory State: Causes and Consequences of Changes in the Mode of Governance'. *Journal of Public Policy* 17 (2): 139–167.

Majone, G. 2001. 'Two Logics of Delegation: Agency and Fiduciary Relations in the EU'. *European Union Politics* 2 (1): 103–122.

Majone, G. 2005. *Dilemmas of European Integration*. Oxford: Oxford University Press.

Marks, G., and L. Hooghe. 2001. *Multi-level Governance and European Integration*. Lanham, MD: Rowman and Littlefield.

Martin, C. 2000. *Stuck in Neutral: Business and the Politics of Human Capital Investment Policy*. Princeton, NJ: Princeton University Press.

Masciandaro, D., and M. Suardi. 2014. 'Public Interest and Lobbies in Reforming Banking Regulation: Three Tales of Ring Fencing'. *International Review of Economics* 61: 305–328.

Massoc, E. 2020. 'Banks, Power and Political Institutions: The Divergent Priorities of European States Towards "Too-Big-To-Fail" Banks: The Cases of Competition in Retail Banking and the Banking Structural Reform'. *Business and Politics* 22 (1): 135–160.

Mattli, W. 2019. *Darkness by Design: The Hidden Power in Global Capital Markets*. Princeton, NJ: Princeton University Press.

Mattli, W., and N. Woods. 2009. *The Politics of Global Regulation*. Princeton, NJ: Princeton University Press.

Mauduit, L. 2013. *L'étrange Capitulation*. Paris: Jean-Claude Gawsewitch.

May, T., J. McHugh, and T. Taylor. 1998. 'Business Representation in the UK Since 1979: The Case of Trade Associations'. *Political Studies* 46 (2): 260–275.

McCarty, N., K. T. Poole, and H. Rosenthal. 2015. *Political Bubbles: Financial Crises and the Failure of American Democracy*. Princeton, NJ: Princeton University Press.

McCubbins, M. D., and T. Schwartz. 1984. 'Congressional Oversight Overlooked: Police Patrols Versus Fire Alarms'. *American Journal of Political Science* 28 (1): 165–179.

McGrath, C. 2005. *Lobbying in Washington, London and Brussels: The Persuasive Communication of Political Issues*. Lampeter: Edwin Mellen Press.

McKeen-Edwards, H., and T. Porter. 2013. *Transnational Financial Associations and the Governance of Global Finance: Assembling Wealth and Power*. London: Routledge.

McPhilemy, S. 2013. 'Formal Rules Versus Informal Relationships: Prudential Banking Supervision at the FSA Before the Crash'. *New Political Economy* 18 (5): 748–767.

Miller, G. J., and A. B. Whitford. 2016. *Above Politics: Bureaucratic Discretion and Credible Commitment*. Cambridge: Cambridge University Press.

Mitchell, N. J. 1997. *The Conspicuous Corporation: Business, Public Policy, and Representative Democracy*. Ann Arbor, MI: University of Michigan Press.

Mizruchi, M. S. 2013. *The Fracturing of the American Corporate Elite*. Cambridge, MA: Harvard University Press.

Montalbano, G. 2020. 'Policy Entrepreneurship and the Influence of the Transnational Financial Industry in the EU Reform of Securitization'. *Business and Politics* 22 (1): 85–112.

Montalbano, G. 2021. *Competing Interest Groups and Lobbying in the Construction of the European Bank Union*. Basingstoke: Palgrave Macmillan.

Moran, M. 1991. *The Politics of the Financial Services Revolution: The USA, UK and Japan*. Basingstoke: Macmillan.

Moran, M. 2009. *Business, Politics and Society: An Anglo-American Comparison*. Oxford: Oxford University Press.

Morin, F. 2015. *L'Hydre Mondiale: L'Oligopole Bancaire*. Montréal: Lux.

Möslein, F. 2013a. 'Grundsatz- und Anwendungsfragen zur Spartentrennung nach dem Sog. Trennbankengesetz'. *Afusatz BKR*: 397–405.

Möslein, F. 2013b. 'Die Trennung von Wertpapier- und Sonstigem Bankgeschäft: Trennbankensystem, Ring-Fencing und Volcker-Rule als Mittel zur Eindämmung systemischer Gefahren für das Finanzsystem'. *ORDO: Jahrbuch für die Ordnung von Wirtschaft und Gesellschaft* 64: 349–376.

Mügge, D. 2006. 'Reordering the Marketplace: Competition Politics in European Finance'. *Journal of Common Market Studies* 44 (5): 991–1022.

Mügge, D. 2010. *Widen the Market, Narrow the Competition: Banker Interests and the Making of a European Capital Market*. Colchester: ECPR.

Mügge, D. 2011. 'The Limits of Legitimacy and the Primacy of Politics in Financial Governance'. *Review of International Political Economy* 18 (1): 52–74.

Mügge, D. 2012. 'From Pragmatism to Dogmatism: EU Governance, Policy Paradigms, and Financial Meltdown'. *New Political Economy* 16 (2): 185–206.

Mügge, D. 2014. *Europe and the Governance of Global Finance*. Oxford: Oxford University Press.

Mügge, D., and B. Stellinga. 2015. 'The Unstable Core of Global Finance: Contingent Valuation and Governance of International Accounting Standards'. *Regulation and Governance* 9 (1): 47–62.

Mullineux, A., and E. Terberger. 2006. *The British Banking System: A good role model for Germany?* Anglo-German Foundation Report. London: Anglo-German Foundation.

Naqvi, N. 2021. 'Renationalizing Finance for Development: Policy Space and Public Economic Control in Bolivia'. *Review of International Political Economy* 28 (3): 447–478.

Newman, A., and E. Posner. 2011. 'International Interdependence and Regulatory Power: Authority, Mobility, and Markets'. *European Journal of International Relations* 17 (4): 589–610.
Newman, A., and E. Posner. 2016a. 'Transnational Feedback, Soft Law, and Preferences in Global Financial Regulation'. *Review of International Political Economy* 23 (1): 123–152.
Newman, A., and E. Posner. 2016b. 'Structuring Transnational Interests: The Second-Order Effects of Soft Law in the Politics of Global Finance'. *Review of International Political Economy* 23 (5): 768–798.
Newman, A., and E. Posner. 2018. *Voluntary Disruptions: International Soft Law, Finance, and Power*. Oxford: Oxford University Press.
Oatley, T., and R. Nabors. 1998. 'Redistributive Cooperation: Market Failure, Wealth Transfers, and the Basle Accord'. *International Organization* 52 (1): 35–54.
Oatley, T., W. Winecoff, A. Pennock, and S. Danzman. 2013. 'The Political Economy of Global Finance: A Network Model'. *Perspectives on Politics* 11 (1), 133–153.
Offerlé, M. 2009. *Sociologie des Organisations Patronales*. Paris: La Découverte.
Olson, M. 1965. *The Logic of Collective Action: Public Goods and the Theory of Groups*. Cambridge, MA: Harvard University Press.
Oppolzer, K. 2019. *Ring-Fencing in Europe: The EU's Bank Structural Reform and a Legal Comparative Look at National Legislation in Europe's Three Financial Capitals*. Baden-Baden: Nomos.
Pagliari, S. 2011. 'Who Governs Finance? The Shifting Public–Private Divide in the Regulation of Derivatives, Rating Agencies and Hedge Funds'. *European Law Journal* 18 (1): 44–61.
Pagliari, S. 2013a. 'Public Salience and International Financial Regulation: Explaining the International Regulation of OTC Derivatives, Rating Agencies, and Hedge Funds'. Ph.D. thesis, University of Waterloo, Ontario.
Pagliari, S. 2013b. 'A Wall Around Europe? The European Regulatory Response to the Global Financial Crisis and the Turn in Transatlantic Relations'. *Journal of European Integration* 35 (4): 391–408.
Pagliari, S., and K. L. Young. 2014. 'Leveraged Interests: Financial Industry Power and the Role of Private Sector Coalitions'. *Review of International Political Economy* 21 (3): 575–610.
Pagliari, S., and K. L. Young. 2016. 'The Interest Ecology of Financial Regulation: Interest Group Plurality in the Design of Financial Regulatory Policies'. *Socio-Economic Review* 14 (2): 309–337.
Pauly, L. W. 1997. *Who Elected the Bankers? Surveillance and Control in the World Economy*. Ithaca, NY: Cornell University Press.
Perry, J., and A. Nölke. 2006. 'The Political Economy of International Accounting Standards'. *Review of International Political Economy* 13 (4): 559–586.
Peters, B. G. 2001. 'Agenda-Setting in the European Union'. In J. Richardson (ed.), *European Union: Power and Policy-Making*, 2nd edn, pp. 77–94. London and New York: Routledge.
Philippon, T. 2007. *Le Capitalisme D'Héritiers: La Crise Française du Travail*. Paris: Seuil.
Pollack, M. A. 1997. 'Delegation, Agency, and Agenda Setting in the European Community'. *International Organization* 51 (1): 99–134.
Pollack, M. A. 2002. 'Learning from the Americanists (Again): Theory and Method in the Study of Delegation'. *West European Politics* 25 (1): 200–219.
Porter, T. 2014. 'Technical Systems and the Architecture of Transnational Business Governance Interactions'. *Regulation and Governance* 8 (1): 110–125.

Posner, E. 2009. 'Making Rules for Global Finance: Transatlantic Regulatory Cooperation at the Turn of the Millennium'. *International Organization* 63 (4): 665-699.
Posner, E. 2010. 'Sequence as Explanation: The International Politics of Accounting Standards'. *Review of International Political Economy* 14 (4): 639-664.
Posner, E., and N. Véron. 2010. 'The EU and Financial Regulation: Power Without Purpose?' *Journal of European Public Policy* 17 (3): 400-415.
Powell, G. B. 2000. *Elections as Instruments of Democracy: Majoritarian and Proportional Visions*. New Haven, CT: Yale University Press.
Princen, S. 2007. 'Agenda-Setting in the European Union: A Theoretical Exploration and Agenda for Research'. *Journal of European Public Policy* 14 (1): 21-38.
Princen, S. 2011. 'Agenda-Setting Strategies in EU Policy Processes'. *Journal of European Public Policy* 18 (7): 927-943.
Przeworski, A., and M. Wallerstein. 1988. 'Structural Dependence of the State on Capital'. *American Political Science Review* 82 (1): 11-29.
Quaglia, L. 2008. 'Setting the Pace? Private Financial Interests and European Financial Market Integration'. *British Journal of Politics and International Relations* 10 (1): 46-63.
Quaglia, L. 2009. 'The 'British Plan' as a Pace-Setter: The Europeanization of Banking Rescue Plans in the EU?'. *Journal of Common Market Studies* 47 (5): 1063-83.
Quaglia, L. 2010a. *Governing Financial Services in the European Union*. London: Routledge.
Quaglia, L. 2010b. 'Completing the Single Market in Financial Services: The Politics of Competing Advocacy Coalitions'. *Journal of European Public Policy* 17 (7): 1007-1022.
Quaglia, L. 2011. 'The "Old" and "New" Political Economy of Hedge Funds Regulation in the European Union'. *West European Politics* 34 (4): 665-682.
Quaglia, L. 2012. 'The "Old" and "New" Politics of Financial Services Regulation in the European Union'. *New Political Economy* 17 (4): 515-535.
Quaglia, L. 2014a. *The European Union and Global Financial Regulation*. Oxford: Oxford University Press.
Quaglia, L. 2014b. 'The European Union, the USA and International Standard-Setting in Finance'. *New Political Economy* 19 (3): 427-444.
Quaglia, L. 2017. 'The Political Economy of Post-Crisis International Standards for Resolving Financial Institution'. *New Political Economy* 22 (5): 595-609.
Quaglia, L. 2019. 'The Politics of State Compliance with International Financial Standards'. *Governance* 32 (1): 45-62.
Quaglia, L. 2021. 'It Takes Two to Tango: The European Union and the International Governance of Securitization in Finance'. *Journal of Common Market Studies*. DOI: 10.1111/jcms.13227.
Quaglia, L., and A. Spendzharova. 2017a. 'Post-Crisis Reforms in Banking: Regulators at the Interface Between Domestic and International Governance'. *Regulation and Governance* 11 (4): 422-437.
Quaglia, L., and A. Spendzharova. 2017b. 'The Conundrum of Solving 'Too Big to Fail' in the European Union: Supranationalization at Different Speeds'. *Journal of Common Market Studies* 55 (5): 1110-1126.
Quaglia, L., and A. Spendzharova. 2019. 'Regulators and the Quest for Coherence in Finance: The Case of Loss Absorbing Capacity for Banks'. *Public Administration*. DOI: 10.1111/padm.12549.
Quaglia, L., and A. Spendzharova. 2020. 'Regime Complexity and Managing Financial Data Streams: The Orchestration of Trade Reporting for Derivatives'. *Regulation and Governance*. DOI: 10.1111/rego.12377.

Quaglia, L., D. Howarth, and M. Liebe. 2016. 'The Political Economy of European Capital Markets Union'. *Journal of Common Market Studies* 54 (1): 185–203.

Quinn, D. P., and R. Y. Shapiro. 1991. 'Business Political Power: The Case of Taxation'. *American Political Science Review* 85 (3): 851–874.

Radaelli, C. M. 1995. 'The Role of Knowledge in the Policy Process'. *Journal of European Public Policy* 2 (2):159–183.

Rasmussen, A., and B. J. Carroll. 2013. 'Determinants of Upper-Class Dominance in the Heavenly Chorus: Lessons from European Union Online Consultations'. *British Journal of Political Science* 44: 445–459.

Rasmussen, M. K. 2015. 'The Battle for Influence: The Politics of Business Lobbying in the European Parliament'. *Journal of Common Market Studies* 53 (2): 365–382.

Reinicke, W. H. 1995. *Banking, Politics and Global Finance: American Commercial Banks and Regulatory Change, 1980–1990*. Brookfield, VT: Edward Elgar.

Rhinard, M. 2010. *Framing Europe: The Policy Shaping Strategies of the European Commission*. Boston, MA: Republic of Letters.

Richardson, J. 1982. *Policy Styles in Western Europe*. Winchester, MA: Allen and Unwin.

Rixen, T. 2013. 'Why Reregulation After the Crisis is Feeble: Shadow Banking, Offshore Financial Centers, and Jurisdictional Competition'. *Regulation and Governance* 7 (4): 435–459.

Rixen, T. 2015. 'Offshore Financial Centers, Shadow Banking and Jurisdictional Competition: Incrementalism and Feeble Re-regulation'. In M. Moschella and E. Tsingou (eds), *Change Agents and Veto Players: Explaining Incremental Change in Global Financial Governance Post-Crisis*, pp. 95–123. Colchester: ECPR Press.

Rochefort, D. A., and R. W. Cobb. 1994. *The Politics of Problem Definition: Shaping the Policy Agenda*. Lawrence, KS: University Press of Kansas.

Roemer-Mahler, A. 2013. 'Business Conflict and Global Politics: The Pharmaceutical Industry and the Global Protection of Intellectual Property Rights'. *Review of International Political Economy* 20: 121–152.

Rogowski, R. 1990. *Commerce and Coalitions: How Trade Affectrs Domestic Political Alignments*. Princeton: Princeton University Press.

Rogowski, R., and M. A. Kayser. 2002. 'Majoritarian Electoral Systems and Consumer Power: Price-Level Evidence from the OECD Countries'. *American Political Science Review* 46 (3): 526–539.

Rothkopf, D. 2012. *Power, Inc.: The Epic Rivalry Between Big Business and Government—And the Reckoning that Lies Ahead*. Basingstoke: Macmillan.

Ryan, P., and N. Zeigler. 2016. 'Patchwork Pacesetter: The United States in the Multilevel Process of Financial Market Regulation'. In R. Mayntz (ed.), *Negotiated Reform: The Multilevel Governance of Financial Regulation*, pp. 65–96. Frankfurt-on-Main: Deutsche Nationalbibliothek.

Sabatier, P. 1988. 'An Advocacy Coalition Framework of Policy Change and the Role of Policy-Oriented Learning Therein'. *Policy Sciences* 21: 129–168.

Sabatier, P., and H. Jenkins-Smith. 1993. *Policy Change and Learning: An Advocacy Coalition Approach*. Boulder, CO: Westview Press.

Scharpf, F. W. 1997. *Games Real Actors Play: Actor-Centered Institutionalism in Policy Research*. Boulder, CO: Westview.

Schattschneider, E. E. 1960. *The Semi-sovereign People*. New York: Holt, Rinehart, and Winston.

Schelo, S., and A. Steck. 2013. 'Das Trennbankengesetz: Prävention durch Bankentestamente und Risikoabschirmung'. *ZBB/JBB* 4 (13): 227–244.

Schmidt, V. 1996. *From the State to Market? The Transformation of French Business and Government.* Cambridge: Cambridge University Press.

Schmidt, V. A. 2002. *The Futures of European Capitalism.* Oxford: Oxford University Press.

Schmitter, P. C., and G. Lehmbruch. 1979. *Trends Towards Corporatist Intermediation.* Beverley Hills, CA: Sage.

Schneider, G., D. Finke, and K. Baltz 2007. 'With a Little Help from the State: Interest Intermediation in the Domestic Pre-negotiations of EU Legislation', *Journal of European Public Policy* 14 (3): 444–459.

Scholte, J. A. 2013. 'Civil Society and Financial Markets: What Is Not Happening and Why', *Journal of Civil Society* 9(2): 129–147.

Schulz, A. 2010. 'Wir Brauchen einen Besseren Staat und Zugleich Gesunde Banken und Marktstrukturen'. *Zeitschrift für das Gesamte Kreditwesen.*

Schwartz, H. 2008. 'Housing, global finance, and American hegemony: Building conservative politics one brick at a time', *Comparative European Politics*, 6 (3): 262-284.

Schwartz, H., and Seabrook, L. 2008. 'Varieties of Residential Capitalism in the International Political Economy: Old Welfare States and the New Politics of Housing', *Comparative European Politics,* 6: 237–261.

Seabrooke, L. 2014. 'Epistemic Arbitrage: Transnational Professional Knowledge in Action', *Journal of Professions and Organization* 1 (1): 49–64.

Seabrooke, L., and E. R. Nilsson. 2015. 'Professional Skills in International Financial Surveillance: Assessing Change in IMF Policy Teams'. *Governance: An International Journal of Policy, Administration and Institutions* 28 (2): 237–254.

Seabrooke, L., and E. Tsingou. 2009. 'Power Elites and Everyday Politics in International Financial Reform'. *International Political Sociology* 3 (4): 457–461.

Seabrooke, L., and E. Tsingou. 2014. 'Distinctions, Affiliations, and Professional Knowledge in Financial Reform Expert Groups'. *Journal of European Public Policy* 21 (3): 389–407.

Selmier, W. T. 2013. 'Stand by Me: Friends, Relationship Banking, and Financial Governance in Asia'. *Business Horizons* 56 (6): 733–741.

Shonfield, A. 1965. *Modern Capitalism: The Changing Balance of Public and Private Power.* Oxford: Oxford University Press.

Siaroff, A. 1999. 'Corporatism in 24 Industrial Democracies: Meaning and Measurement'. *European Journal of Political Research* 36 (2): 175–205.

Simmons, B. A. 2001. 'The International Politics of Harmonization: The Case of Capital Market Regulation'. *International Organization* 55 (3): 589–620.

Sinclair, T. 2005. *The New Masters of Capital: American Bond Rating Agencies and the Politics of Creditworthiness.* Ithaca, NY: Cornell University Press.

Singer, D. 2004. 'Capital Rules: The Domestic Politics of International Regulatory Harmonization'. *International Organization* 58 (3): 531–565.

Singer, D. 2007. *Regulating Capital: Setting Standards for the International Financial System.* Ithaca, NY: Cornell University Press.

Skeel, D. A. 2010. *The New Financial Deal: Understanding the Dodd–Frank Act and Its (Unintended) Consequences.* New York: Wiley

Smith, M. A. 2000. *American Business and Political Power: Public Opinion, Elections, and Democracy.* Chicago, IL: University of Chicago Press.

Smith, M. 2008. 'All Access Points Are Not Created Equal: Explaining the Fate of Diffuse Interests in the EU'. *British Journal of Politics and International Relations* 10 (1): 64–83.

Soroka, S. N. 2002. *Agenda-Setting Dynamics in Canada.* Vancouver and Toronto: UBC Press.

Spendzharova, A. 2016. 'Regulatory Cascading: Limitations of Policy Design in European Banking Structural Reforms'. *Policy and Society* 35 (3): 227–237.

Spillman, L. 2012. *Solidarity in Strategy: Making Business Meaningful in American Trade Associations*. Chicago, IL: University of Chicago Press.

Stellinga, B., and D. Mügge. 2017. 'The Regulator's Conundrum: How Market Reflexivity Limits Fundamental Financial Reform'. *Review of International Political Economy* 24 (3): 393–423.

Stigler, G. 1971. 'The Theory of Economic Regulation'. *Bell Journal of Economics and Management Science* 2 (1): 3–21.

Stockhammer, E. 2004. 'Financialization and the Slowdown of Accumulation'. *Cambridge Journal of Economics* 28: 719–741.

Stokman, F. N., and E. P. H. Zeggelink, 1996. 'Is Politics Power or Policy Oriented? A Comparative Analysis of Dynamic Access Models in Policy Networks'. *Journal of Mathematical Sociology* 21 (1–2): 77–111.

Story, J., and I. Walter. 1997. *Political Economy of Financial Integration in Europe: The Battle of the System*. Manchester: Manchester University Press.

Streeck, W. 2009. *Re-forming Capitalism: Institutional Change in the German Political Economy*. Oxford: Oxford University Press.

Swank, D. 1992. 'Politics and the Structural Dependence of the State in Democratic Capitalist Nations'. *American Political Science Review* 86 (1): 38–54.

Tallberg, J. 2003. 'The Agenda-Shaping Powers of EU Council Presidency'. *Journal of European Public Policy* 10 (1): 1–19.

Thiemann, M. 2014. 'In the Shadow of Basel: How Competitive Politics Bred the Crisis'. *Review of International Political Economy* 21 (6): 1203–1239.

Thiemann, M. 2018. *The Growth of Shadow Banking: A Comparative Institutional Analysis*. Cambridge: Cambridge University Press.

Thiemann, M., M. Birk, and J. Friedrich. 2018. 'Much Ado About Nothing? Macro-Prudential Ideas and the Post-Crisis Regulation of Shadow Banking'. *Kölner Zeitschrift für Soziologie und Sozialpsychologie* 70 (1), 256–286.

Thompson, H. 2017. 'How the City of London Lost at Brexit: A Historical Perspective'. *Economy and Society* 46 (2): 211–228.

Trumbull, G. 2006. *Consumer Capitalism: Politics, Product Markets and Firm Strategy in France and Germany*. Ithaca, NY: Cornell University Press.

Trumbull, G. 2012. *Strength in Numbers: The Political Power of Weak Interests*. Cambridge, MA: Harvard University Press.

Tsingou, E. 2003. 'Transnational Policy Communities and Financial Governance: The Role of Private Actors in Derivatives Regulation'. *CSGR Working Papers* 111 (3).

Tsingou, E. 2008. 'Transnational Private Governance and the Basel Process: Banking Regulation, Private Interests and Basel II'. In J. C. Graz and A. Nölke (eds), *Transnational Private Governance and Its Limits*, pp. 58–68. London: Routledge.

Tsingou, E. 2014. 'The Club Rules in Global Financial Governance'. *Political Quarterly* 85 (4): 417–419.

Tsingou, E. 2015. 'Club Governance and the Making of Global Financial Rules'. *Review of International Political Economy* 22 (2): 225–256.

Underhill, G. R. D., and T. Zhang. 2008. 'Setting the Rules: Private Power, Political Underpinnings, and Legitimacy in Global Monetary and Financial Governance'. *International Affairs* 84 (3): 535–554.

Veltrop, D., and J. de Haan. 2014. 'I Just Cannot Get You Out of My Head: Regulatory Capture of Financial Sector Supervisors'. *De Nederlandsche Bank Working Papers* 410.

Veronesi, P., and L. Zingales. 2010. 'Paulson's Gift'. *Journal of Financial Economics* 97 (3): 339–368.

Vickers, J. 2016. 'Banking Reform in the UK'. Presentation at Griswold Center for Economic Policy Studies and Julis-Rabinowitz Center for Public Policy and Finance, Princeton University. 22 September.

Vidal, J. B. I., M. Draca, and C. Fons-Rosen. 2012. 'Revolving Door Lobbyists'. *American Economic Review* 102 (7): 3731–3748.

Visser, J., and A. Hemerijck. 1997. *A Dutch Miracle: Job Growth, Welfare Reform and Corporatism in the Netherlands*. Amsterdam: Amsterdam University Press.

Watson, M. 2008. 'Constituting Monetary Conservatives via the "Savings Habit": New Labour and the British Housing Market Bubble', *Comparative European Politics*, 6: 285–304.

Weible, C. M., and P. A. Sabatier. 2005. 'Comparing Policy Networks: Marine Protected Areas in California. *Policy Studies Journal* 33 (2): 181–202.

Wilmarth, A. E., Jr. 2013. 'Turning a Blind Eye: Why Washington Keeps Giving In to Wall Street'. *University of Cincinnati Law Review* 81 (4): 1283–1444.

Wilson, J. 1980. *The Politics of Regulation*. New York: Basic Books.

Winecoff, K. 2015. 'Structural Power and the Global Financial Crisis: A Network Analytical Approach'. *Business and Politics* 17 (3): 495–525.

Witko, C. 2016. 'The Politics of Financialization in the United States, 1949–2005'. *British Journal of Political Science* 46 (2): 349–370.

Wittenberg, T. 2015. 'Regulatory Evolution of the EU Credit Rating Agency Framework'. *European Business Organization Law Review* 16 (4): 669–709.

Woldendorp, J., and L. Delsen. 2008. 'Dutch Corporatism: Does It Still Work? Policy Formation and Macroeconomic Performance 1980–2005'. *Acta Politica* 43: 308–332.

Wolffe, R. 2011. *Revival: The Struggle for Survival in the Obama White House*. New York: Broadway Books.

Woll, C. 2013. 'Lobbying Under Pressure: The Effect of Salience on European Hedge Fund Regulation'. *Journal of Common Market Studies* 51 (3): 555–572.

Woll, C. 2014. *The Power of Inaction*. Ithaca, NY: Cornell University Press.

Woolley, J. T., and J. N. Zeigler. 2011. 'The Two-Tiered Politics of Financial Reform in the United States'. *Working Papers*, Institute for Research on Labor and Employment, UC Berkeley.

Young, K. 2012. 'Transnational Regulatory Capture? An Empirical Examination of the Transnational Lobbying of the Basel Committee on Banking Supervision'. *Review of International Political Economy* 19 (4): 663–688.

Young, K. 2014. 'Losing Abroad but Winning at Home: European Financial Industry Groups in Global Financial Governance Since the Crisis'. *Journal of European Public Policy* 21 (3): 367–388.

Young, K. 2015. 'Not by Structure Alone: Power, Prominence, and Agency in American Finance'. *Business and Politics* 17 (3): 443–472.

Young, K., and S. Pagliari. 2017. 'Capital United? Business Unity in Regulatory Politics and the Special Place of Finance'. *Regulation and Governance* 11 (1): 3–23.

Zeigler, J. N., and J. T. Woolley. 2016. 'After Dodd–Frank: Ideas and the Post-Enactment Politics of Financial Reform in the United States'. *Politics and Society* 44 (2): 249–280.

Zimmerman, H. 2010. 'Varieties of Global Financial Governance? British and German Approaches to Financial Market Regulation'. In E. Helleiner, S. Pagliari and H. Zimmerman (eds), *Global Finance in Crisis: The Politics of International Regulatory Change*, pp. 121–136. Abingdon: Routledge.

Zysman, J. 1983. *Government, Markets and Growth: Financial Systems and the Politics of Industrial Change*. Ithaca, NY: Cornell University Press.

Primary News Sources

Aartrijk, P. van 2009. 'Consumentenbond wil Grote Hervorming Banken'. *Algemeen Nederlands Persbureau ANP*. 18 November. https://advance-lexis-com.ezproxy.ub.unimaas.nl/api/document?collection=news&id=urn:contentItem:7X4B-NRN0-YB5C-12M8-00000-00&context=1516831.
Adler, J. 2012. 'Blair's Systemic Risk Council to Highlight "What's Not Happening"'. *American Banker*. 18 June. https://www.americanbanker.com/news/bairs-systemic-risk-council-to-highlight-whats-not-happening.
Ahlers, C. 2015. 'Just a Little Bit of Banking Separation'. *Finance Watch*. 26 February. https://www.finance-watch.org/just-a-little-bit-of-banking-separation/.
Alberts, J., and M. Oberndorff. 2013. 'Business as Usual in de Bankensector'. *Vrij Nederland*. 14 December. https://www.vn.nl/business-as-usual-in-de-bankensector-2/.
American Banker. 2012. 'So Long as Big-Banks Can't Fails, Small Banks Need TAG'. *American Banker*. 24 February. https://www.americanbanker.com/opinion/so-long-as-big-banks-cant-fail-small-banks-need-tag.
ANP (Algemeen Nederlands Persbureau). 2011. 'Veel Nedrlandeers Willen Banken Splitsen'. IEX.nl. 23 November. https://www.iex.nl/Nieuws/528745/Veel-Nederlanders-willen-banken-splitsen.aspx.
ANP (Algemeen Nederlands Persbureau). 2013. 'Rabo-Topman: Splitsen Banken Niet Veiliger'. *BNDeStem*. 22 April. https://www.bndestem.nl/overig/rabo-topman-splitsen-banken-niet-veiliger~a4a5fb76/.
Armstrong, R. 2020. 'US Banks Cleared to Invest in Venture Capital and Loan Funds'. *Financial Times*. 30 January. https://www.ft.com/content/e4565f3a-4388-11ea-abea-0c7a29cd66fe.
Arnold, M., E. Dunkley, and C. Binham. 2015. 'UK Banks Quietly Confident They Can Cope with Ringfencing'. *Financial Times*. 17 September. https://www.ft.com/content/53cd87be-5d2c-11e5-a28b-50226830d644.
Baer, J. 2011a. 'Morgan Stanley to Spin Off Prop Trading Desk'. *Financial Times*. 10 January. https://www.ft.com/content/6c285214-1cfc-11e0-8c86-00144feab49a.
Baer, J. 2011b. 'Goldman Winds Down Proprietary Trading Arm'. *Financial Times*. 16 February. https://www.ft.com/content/bd4d2d2a-3964-11e0-97ca-00144feabdc0.
Banking Strategist. 2021. 'Community Banks: Numbers by State and Asset Size'. Bankingstrategist.com. https://www.bankingstrategist.com/community-banks-number-by-state-and-asset-size.
Barbière, C. 2014. 'Le Projet Européen de Réforme Bancaire Jugé Irresponsable en France'. Euractiv.fr. 30 January. https://www.euractiv.fr/section/euro-finances/news/le-projet-europeen-de-reforme-bancaire-juge-irresponsable-en-france/.
Barker, A. 2012. 'UK in Furious Rejection of EU Bank Plan'. *Financial Times*. 3 May. https://www.ft.com/content/82eab320-949c-11e1-bb0d-00144feab49a.
Barker, A. 2014a. 'EU Bank Overhaul Pleases Few in Search for Middle Way'. *Financial Times*. 29 January. https://www.ft.com/content/3cb5bd5c-8903-11e3-bb5f-00144feab7de.
Barker, A. 2014b. 'EU's Hill Considers Shelving Bank Structural Reforms'. *Financial Times*. 4 December. https://www.ft.com/content/9fe30148-7bd1-11e4-a7b8-00144feabdc0.
Barker, A. 2015. 'EU reforms to break up banks at risk'. *Financial Times*. 29 January. https://www.ft.com/content/09025d06-a7d1-11e4-97a6-00144feab7de
Becker, A. 2012. 'Zerschlagung von Banken als Schutz vor Krisen?'. DW.com. 26 September. https://www.dw.com/de/zerschlagung-von-banken-als-schutz-vor-krisen/a-16153230.

REFERENCES 313

Barker, A. and B. Masters. 2012. 'Britain stands alone on EU financial reform'. *Financial Times*. 3 May. https://www.ft.com/content/8e6d8dfe-953b-11e1-8faf-00144feab49a

Berensten, L. 2012a. 'Kabinet Legt Banken via Britse én Amerikaanse Regel Aan Banden'. *Financieele Dagblad*. 1 March. https://fd.nl/frontpage/Print/krant/Pagina/Economie__ _Politiek/799605/kabinet-legt-banken-via-britse-en-amerikaanse-regel-aan-banden.

Berensten, L. 2012b. 'De Jager: Voorzichtig met Splitsen van Banken: DNB Tegen Verstrekkende Ingreep'. *Financieele Dagblad*. 7 March. https://fd.nl/frontpage/economie-politiek/798992/de-jager-voorzichtig-met-splitsen-van-banken.

Berkowitz, B., and H. Ten Wolde. 2010. 'Dutch Central Bank to be Overhauled After DSB Report'. *Reuters*. 29 June. https://www.reuters.com/article/dsb-idUKLDE65S0 TG20100629.

Better Markets. 2021. 'John Reed, Citibank & Financial Reform'. Bettermarkets.com. 23 May. https://bettermarkets.com/resources/john-reed-citibank-financial-reform/.

Biegelsen, A. 2011. 'Goldman Lobbyists Have Met with Dodd–Frank Regulators Nearly 100 Times'. Publicintegrity.org. 19 July. https://publicintegrity.org/inequality-poverty-opportunity/goldman-lobbyists-have-met-with-dodd-frank-regulators-nearly-100-times/.

Bimbaum, J. 2005. 'The Road to Riches is Called K Street: Lobbying Firms Hire More, Pay More, Charge More to Influence Government'. *Washington Post*. 22 June. https:// www.washingtonpost.com/archive/politics/2005/06/22/the-road-to-riches-is-called-k-street/6e9e2ca1-f2f6-4b81-ade8-9098550c45b8/.

Binham, C. 2019. 'Ringfencing Rules Could Leave British Banks at a Disadvantage'. *Financial Times*. 1 January. https://www.ft.com/content/489798c4-0db6-11e9-a3aa-118c761d2745.

Binham, C., and E. Dunkley. 2017. 'Regulators Get Ready to Authorise "Ringfenced" UK Banks'. *Financial Times*. 19 August. https://www.ft.com/content/5ca81a48-8372-11e7-a4ce-15b2513cb3ff.

Bishop, G. 2014. 'Too Little, Too Late, Too Light'. *Encompass*. March. https://encompass-europe.com/comment/too-little-too-late-too-light.

Blitz, J. 2005. 'Blair Accentuates the Positive After Opening Attacks'. *Financial Times*. 14 April. https://www.ft.com/content/c88e6998-ad14-11d9-ad92-00000e2511c8

Bonnefous, B. 2013. 'Loi Bancaire: Des Élus PS Espèrent "Muscler" un Texte "Inachevé"'. *Le Monde*. 31 January. https://www.lemonde.fr/politique/article/2013/01/31/loi-bancaire-des-elus-ps-espere-muscler-un-texte-inacheve_1825707_823448.html.

Boonstra, W. 2011. 'Banken Splitsen is Geen Goed Idee'. *Financieele Dagblad*. 16 June. https://fd.nl/frontpage/economie-politiek/columns/wim-boonstra/718447/banken-splitsen-is-geen-goed-idee.

Brandi, T. O. 2013. 'Trennbankengesetz Durch Bundestag Verabschiedet'. *Handelsblatt*. 27 May. https://blog.handelsblatt.com/rechtsboard/2013/05/27/trennbankengesetz-durch-bundestag-verabschiedet/.

Brandão de Brito, J. M. 2009. 'New Rules on Liquidity Could Do More Harm than Good'. *Financial Times*. 2 December. https://www.ft.com/content/272a4302-df77-11de-98ca-00144feab49a

Braun, M. 2012. 'Der Libor-Skandal un die Deautsche Bank'. *Deutschelandfunk*. 28 November. https://www.deutschlandfunk.de/der-libor-skandal-und-die-deutsche-bank.769.de.html?dram:article_id=229206.

Broekhuizen, K. 2011. 'Kamer Blijft Cultuurverandering Banken Goed Volgen'. *Financieele Dagblad*. 8 March. https://fd.nl/frontpage/Print/krant/Pagina/Economie___Politiek/ 780364/kamer-blijft-cultuurverandering-banken-goed-volgen.

Broekhuizen, K., and J. Piersma. 2011. 'Crisis Splijt en Verzwakt Bankenlobby', *Financieele Dagblad*, 16 April. https://fd.nl/frontpage/Print/krant/Pagina/Ondernemen/782732/crisis-splijt-en-verzwakt-bankenlobby.

Brunsden, J. 2014. 'EU's Too-Big-to-Fail Plan Seen as Too Late to Win Approval'. *Bloomberg*. 29 January. https://www.bloomberg.com/news/articles/2014-01-28/too-big-to-fail-plan-for-eu-banks-seen-too-late-to-win-approval.

Brush, S. 2010. 'Wall Street Bill Tests Scott Brown's Clout'. *The Hill*. 22 June. https://thehill.com/homenews/senate/104631-wall-street-bill-tests-scott-browns-clout.

Burgis, T. 2012. 'The Liikanen Report Decoded'. *Financial Times*. 2 October. https://www.ft.com/content/0ff0b3a4-0c8a-11e2-a73c-00144feabdc0.

Burns, J. F., and L. Thomas. 2009. 'Anglo-American Capitalism on Trial'. *New York Times*. 28 March. https://www.nytimes.com/2009/03/29/weekinreview/29burns.html.

Cassidy, J. 2010. 'The Volcker Rule: Obama's Economic Adviser and His Battles Over the Financial-Reform Bill'. *New Yorker*. 19 July. https://www.newyorker.com/magazine/2010/07/26/the-volcker-rule.

Castle, T. 2010. 'Update 2-Boe's King Calls for Radical reform of Banks'. *Reuters*. 26 January. https://www.reuters.com/article/britain-banks-idUSLDE60P13F20100126.

CNBC. 2010. 'Camden Fine—Supporting Volcker'. CNBC. 26 February. https://www.cnbc.com/video/2010/02/26/supporting-volcker.html.

CNN. 2010. 'Poll: Americans Split on Two Top Obama Initiatives'. June 2.

Couwenbergh, P. 2011. 'Debat Over Extra Slot bij Nederlandse Banken'. *Financieele Dagblad*. 13 December. https://fd.nl/frontpage/beleggen/723252/debat-over-extra-slot-bij-nederlandse-banken.

Crabb, J. 2018. 'PRIMER: A Comparison of EU and US Bank Resolution Regimes'. *IFLR*. 20 November. https://www.iflr.com/article/b1lp1y1ksc0njt/primer-a-comparison-of-eu-and-us-bank-resolution-regimes.

Crabtree, S. 2013. 'European Countries Lead World in Distrust of Banks: Lack of Confidence in Financial Institutions May Impede Region's Recovery'. Gallup.Com. 20 May. http://news.gallup.com/poll/162602/european-countries-lead-world-distrust-banks.aspx.

Crisp, J. 2014. 'Greens Vow to Push for a Bank Ring-Fence After EU Elections'. *Euractiv*. 16 May. https://www.euractiv.com/section/euro-finance/news/greens-vow-to-push-for-bank-ring-fence-after-eu-elections/.

Crittenden, M. R., and V. McGrane. 2010. 'How the CFTC Got Power'. *Wall Street Journal*. 15 July. https://www.wsj.com/articles/SB10001424052748704746804575367242923030332.

Curtis, P. 2011. 'Bankers Say Put Reforms on Hold Until Markets and Economy Recover'. *The Guardian*. 29 August. https://www.theguardian.com/business/2011/aug/29/banking-reforms-john-vickers.

Daan van Lent, J. 2009. 'Banken moeten tempo maken Banken doen wat vroeger uit den Boze was; Minister Bos: het moet bij de Bankiers niet bij mooie Woorden blijven'. *NRC Handelsblad*. 8 April. https://advance-lexis-com.ezproxy.ub.unimaas.nl/api/document?collection=news&id=urn:contentItem:7WG1-2SD1-2RM0-C0HV-00000-00&context=1516831.

Daneshkhu, S. 2012. 'France to Unveil Flagship Bank Reform'. *Financial Times*. 18 December. https://www.ft.com/content/8b8fa042-4907-11e2-b94d-00144feab49a.

Daneshkhu, S., and A. Barker. 2012. 'French Banks Lobby Against Reform'. *Financial Times*. 23 October. https://www.ft.com/content/f3b85fbe-1c76-11e2-a63b-00144feabdc0.

Daneshkhu, S., and H. Carnegy. 2012. 'France Unveils Bank Reforms'. *Financial Times*. 19 December. https://www.ft.com/content/1463dd22-49d8-11e2-a7b1-00144feab49a

Dealbook. 2010. 'Fidelity and State Street Win in Brown Deal'. *New York Times Dealbook*. 14 July. https://dealbook.nytimes.com/2010/07/14/fidelity-and-state-street-win-in-brown-deal/?mtrref=www.google.com&gwh=3B76E2D0EDD9F1C813E0397C3AB C0B44&gwt=pay&assetType=PAYWALL.

Dealbook. 2017. 'Bill to Erase Some Dodd–Frank Banking Rules Passes in House'. *New York Times*. 8 June. https://www.nytimes.com/2017/06/08/business/dealbook/house-financial-regulations-dodd-frank.html.

Degenkamp, J. Th., and Emeritus Hoogleraar Rechtswetenschap Rug. 2013. 'Hoogste Tijd om Banken te Splitsen'. *Trouw*. 5 February. https://www.trouw.nl/nieuws/hoogste-tijd-om-banken-te-splitsen~b9fd682b/?referrer=https%3A%2F%2Fwww.google.com%2F.

Demling, A. 2012. 'Abgeordnete Scheitern an den Mauer-Banken'. Spiegel.de. 28 November. http://www.spiegel.de/wirtschaft/unternehmen/libor-anhoerung-im-bundestag-die-deutsche-bank-schweigt-und-siegt-a-869840.html.

Dexheimer, E. 2018. '"Big Number" on Dodd–Frank Isn't as Big as Republicans Wanted'. *Bloomberg*. 22 May. https://www.bloomberg.com/news/articles/2018-05-22/-big-number-on-dodd-frank-isn-t-as-big-as-republicans-wanted.

Douglas, D. 2013. 'Brown–Vitter Bill Seeks to End "Too-Big-To-Fail"'. *Washington Post*. 24 April. https://www.washingtonpost.com/business/economy/brown-vitter-bill-seeks-to-end-too-big-to-fail/2013/04/24/79998784-aba6-11e2-a198-99893f10d6dd_story.html.

Douwes, D. 2010. 'Parlementaire Enquête Crisis'. *De Volkskrant*. 15 September. https://www.volkskrant.nl/nieuws-achtergrond/parlementaire-enquete-crisis~b592e90e/.

Douwes, D., and R. Giebels. 2010a. 'Voor Deel 2 mag Jan de Wit zijn Tanden Meer Laten Zien'. *De Volkskrant*. 12 May. https://www.volkskrant.nl/nieuws-achtergrond/voor-deel-2-mag-jan-de-wit-zijn-tanden-meer-laten-zien~b2c304cd/.

Douwes, D., and R. Giebels. 2010b. 'Iemand Moet Schuldig Zijn'. *De Volkskrant*. 6 February. https://www.volkskrant.nl/economie/iemand-moet-schuldig-zijn~b52bf8af/.

Drawbaugh, K. 2012. 'Analysis: Wall St. Cash Flows to Romney Over Obama'. *Reuters*. 2 February. https://www.reuters.com/article/us-usa-campaign-wall-street-idUSTRE81100Y20120202.

Drif, A. 2012. 'Pour Christian Noyer, la Scission des Banques Pourrait Nuire à L'économie'. *Les Echos*. 15 May. https://www.lesechos.fr/2012/05/pour-christian-noyer-la-scission-des-banques-pourrait-nuire-a-leconomie–356740.

Drutman, L., and B. Chartoff. 2013. 'What the Banks' Three-Year War on Dodd–Frank Looks Like'. Sunlight Foundation. 22 July. https://sunlightfoundation.com/2013/07/22/dodd-frank-3-year/.

Dunkley, E., and C. Binham. 2015. 'Banks Hail Concession on Ringfencing'. *Financial Times*. 15 October. https://www.ft.com/content/c76faf72-734c-11e5-bdb1-e6e47 67162cc.

Eavis, P. 2014. 'Fed's Delay of Parts of Volcker Rule is Another Victory for Banks'. *New York Times Dealbook*. 19 December. https://dealbook.nytimes.com/2014/12/19/feds-delay-of-parts-of-volcker-rule-is-another-victory-for-banks/?mtrref=www.google.com&gwh=64DF8709D31F68DD6346479E6EF406AA&gwt=pay&assetType=PAYWALL.

The Economist. 2010. 'When the River Runs Dry: The perils of a Sudden Evaporation of Liquidity'. 13 February. https://www.economist.com/special-report/2010/02/13/when-the-river-runs-dry.

Edinger, A. 2013. 'Bafin–Chefin: "Eine strukturelle Trennung allein reicht nicht"'. *Wall Street Journal.* 22 January. https://www.wsj.com/articles/SB10001424127887324624404578258020075943376.

Eichelberger, E. 2012. 'Will Obama Beat Back a "Nuclear" Attack' by the Big Banks?' *Mother Jones.* 6 December. https://www.motherjones.com/politics/2012/12/financial-reform-dodd-frank-volker-rule-obama/.

Eichler, A. 2012. 'Ex-Wall Street Banker: Volcker Rule Will Correct a Dangerous Mistake'. *Huffington Post.* 18 April. https://www.huffingtonpost.co.uk/entry/roger-vasey-merrill-lynch-banker-volcker-rule_n_1434225?ri18n=true.

Eisinger, J. 2012. 'The Volcker Rule Made Bloated and Weak'. *New York Times Dealbook.* 22 February. https://dealbook.nytimes.com/2012/02/22/the-volcker-rule-made-bloated-and-weak/?mtrref=www.google.com&gwh=CC0A1A1BA816208114A8D642BEF9088E&gwt=pay&assetType=PAYWALL.

Erasmus. 2017. 'La Séparation Bancaire en France, Éléments Historiques et Arguments'. *Médiapart.* 20 October. https://blogs.mediapart.fr/erasmus/blog/201017/la-separation-bancaire-en-france-elements-historiques-et-arguments.

Ewing, J., and M. Eddy. 2019. 'Merger Talks of Deutsche Bank and Commerzbank Roil Emotions'. *New York Times.* 19 April. https://www.nytimes.com/2019/04/19/business/deutsche-bank-commerzbank-merger.html?searchResultPosition=2.

Faure-Dauphin, F., and H. Atthenout. 2013. 'CRA III and the Over-Reliance on Rating in Question'. *Allen & Overy.* 15 July. https://www.allenovery.com/en-gb/global/news-and-insights/publications/cra-iii-and-the-over-reliance-on-rating-in-question.

Fedor, L. 2015. 'Andrew Tyrie tells regulators "not give in to special pleading from banks" over post-crisis regulations'. City AM, 16 November. https://www.cityam.com/andrew-tyrie-tells-regulators-not-give-in-to-special-pleading-from-banks-over-post-crisis-regulations/

Fleming, S. 2014. 'Business Hits "Brick Wall" in Talks on UK Banking Ring Fence'. *Financial Times.* 15 April. https://www.ft.com/content/d7904898-c4bc-11e3-9aeb-00144feabdc0.

Flitter, E., and A. Rappeport. 2018. 'Bankers Hate the Volcker Rule. Now, It Could Be Watered Down'. *New York Times.* 21 May. https://www.nytimes.com/2018/05/21/business/volcker-rule-fed-banks-regulation.html.

Fifield, A. 2010. 'G7 Warms to Idea of Bank Levy'. *Financial Times.* 6 February. https://www.ft.com/content/f64999e2-134a-11df-9f5f-00144feab49a.

Financial Times. 2010. 'Fears for German Banks Under New Rules'. 9 September. https://www.ft.com/content/63677394-bc35-11df-8c02-00144feab49a.

Financial Times. 2016. 'Stress Tests Do Little to Restore Faith in European Banks'. 30 July. https://www.ft.com/content/b5c21178-557f-11e6-befd-2fc0c26b3c60.

Financieel Management. 2004. 'Code-Tabaksblat Beter dan Sarbanes Oxley'. 19 October. https://financieel-management.nl/artikelen/code-tabaksblat-beter-dan-sarbanes-oxley/.

Financieele Dagblad. 2010. 'Bos Steunt Plan Obama om Banken te Splitsen'. 26 January. https://fd.nl/frontpage/Archief/650740/bos-steunt-plan-obama-om-banken-te-splitsen.

Finch, J. 2009. 'Walker Report a "Crashing Disappointment"'. *The Guardian.* 26 November. https://www.theguardian.com/business/2009/nov/26/walker-report-banking-comment?mobile-redirect=false.

Fox Business. 2012. 'Interview: JPMorgan CEO Jamie Dimon on Regulation, Volcker Rule; Some of the Global Regulations Are "Un-American"'. Gurufocus.com. 24 January. https://www.gurufocus.com/news/159099/interview-jpmorgan-ceo-jamie-dimon-on-regulation-volcker-rule-some-of-the-global-regulations-are-unamerican.

Giebels, R. 2011. '"Mond dicht" en "zeg alles" voor de commissie-De Wit; Tegenstelling'. *De Volkskrant.* https://advance-lexis-com.ezproxy.ub.unimaas.nl/api/document?collection=news&id=urn:contentItem:5489-X8R1-JC8W-Y0CD-00000-00&context=1516831.

Giraud, G. 2013a. 'Le Projet Moscovici Enterre la Séparation des Banques'. *Revue Projet.* 21 January. https://www.revue-projet.com/articles/le-projet-moscovici-enterre-la-separation-des-banques.

Giraud, G. 2013b. 'Pourquoi les Banques Refusent d'être Scindées'. *Revue Projet.* 9 January. https://www.revue-projet.com/articles/pourquoi-les-banques-refusent-d-etre-scindees/

Giraud, P.N. 2012. 'Faut-il Séparer les Banques de Dépôt et les Banques d'Investissement?' Lafinancepourtous.com. 17 June. https://www.lafinancepourtous.com/decryptages/crises-economiques/crise-des-subprimes/faut-il-separer-les-banques-de-depot-et-les-banques-dinvestissement/.

Goff, S. 2011. 'The Price of Protection'. *Financial Times.* 11 September. https://www.ft.com/content/02106668-d96d-11e0-b52f-00144feabdc0

Goff, S., and P. Jenkins. 2011. 'UK Banks Divided Over Ringfencing'. *Financial Times.* 8 June. https://www.ft.com/content/fdeb2bb2-91e2-11e0-b8c1-00144feab49a.

Göhner, R., G. Hofmann, M. Kerber, K. P. Schackmann-Fallis, M. Wansleben, J. Tolckmitt, H. Schwannecke, H. Reckers, and M. Kemmer. 2013. 'Universalbanken Stärken Finanzmarktstabilität und Sichern Unternehmensfinanzierun'. *Bankenverband.* 17 January. https://bankenverband.de/newsroom/presse-infos/universalbanken-staerken-finanzmarktstabilitaet-und-sichern-unternehmensfinanzierung/.

Golla, M. 2012. 'Scandale du Libor: Deux Banques Françaises Suspectées'. *Le Figaro.* 19 July. https://www.lefigaro.fr/societes/2012/07/19/20005-20120719ARTFIG00248-scandale-du-libor-deux-banques-francaises-suspectees.php.

Graaf, H. de 2009. 'Triodos Pleit Voor Splitsen Banken'. *NRC Handelsblad.* 12 February. https://www.nrc.nl/nieuws/2009/02/12/triodos-pleit-voor-splitsen-banken–11682775-a335388.

Groot, C. de 2013. 'The Report of the Commission on the Structure of Dutch Banks'. *Leiden Law Blog.* 5 July. https://leidenlawblog.nl/articles/the-report-of-the-commission-on-the-structure-of-dutch-banks.

Guerrera, F., and D. Pimlott. 2010. 'Pandit and King Clash over Basel III'. *Financial Times.* 26 October. https://www.ft.com/content/1d392ba0-e071-11df-99a3-00144feabdc0.

Hamilton, J. 2013. 'Fed Liquidity Proposal Seen Trading Safety for Costlier Credit'. *Bloomberg.* 25 October. https://www.bloomberg.com/news/articles/2013-10-24/fed-weighs-liquidity-demands-aimed-to-keep-biggest-banks-safe.

Hamilton, J. 2017. 'Mnuchin Puts Pressure on Banks Over Volcker Rule, Glass–Steagall'. *Bloomberg.* 19 January. https://www.bloomberg.com/news/articles/2017-01-19/mnuchin-backs-volcker-rule-while-raising-liquidity-concerns.

Handelsblatt. 2012. 'Steinbrücks Plan für die Banken'. 25 September. https://www.handelsblatt.com/politik/deutschland/finanzmarktregulierung-steinbruecks-plan-fuer-die-banken/7176450.html?ticket=ST-4465556-eZwCphf3k9BtbVDbV4AC-ap2.

Harskamp, G. van 2009. 'We kenden de risico's toen nog niet' 'Mentaliteitsverandering is hard nodig' 'Schaf depositogarantie af'; Voormalig ING-topman Cees Maas wil dat banken leren van hun fouten. *Nederlands Dagblad.* 8 April. https://advance-lexis-com.ezproxy.ub.unimaas.nl/api/document?collection=news&id=urn:contentItem:7VDC-30B0-YB4F-K51M-00000-00&context=1516831.

Heilmann, J. 2010. 'Obama Is From Mars, Wall Street Is From Venus'. *New York Magazine.* 21 May. https://nymag.com/news/politics/66188/.

Heltman, J. 2017. 'Nine Banks that Have Fallen Short on the Fed's Stress Tests'. *American Banker.* 19 June. https://www.americanbanker.com/slideshow/nine-banks-that-have-fallen-short-on-the-feds-stress-tests.

Herszenhorn, D. 2009. 'Obama Uneasy about Taks on Bonuses'. *New York Times.* 19 March. https://www.nytimes.com/2009/03/21/us/politics/21bailout.html.

Hirst, N. 2015a. 'Centre-Right Backs Universal Banks'. *Politico.* 8 January. https://www.politico.eu/article/centre-right-backs-universal-banks/.

Hirst, N. 2015b. 'MEPs to Debate Breaking Up the Eurozone's Biggest Banks'. *Politico.* 20 January. https://www.politico.eu/article/meps-to-debate-breaking-up-the-eurozones-biggest-banks/.

Hofs, Y. 2013. 'Niet Allen Banken Zochten de Grens'. *De Volkskrant.* 15 January. https://www.volkskrant.nl/nieuws-achtergrond/niet-alleen-banken-zochten-de-grens~ba8a91a2/.

Hollinger, P., B. Hall, R. Atkins, and L. Barber. 2009. 'France Urges Inquiry into Competition Abuse'. *Financial Times.* 17 November. https://www.ft.com/content/db557044-d2fd-11de-af63-00144feabdc0.

Horde, C. de, and L. Willems. 2012. 'Er was Zelfs bij Banken Draagvlak Voor een Radicale Aanpak: Dat is Snel Verdwenen'. *Financieele Dagblad.* 14 April. https://fd.nl/frontpage/economie-politiek/799983/er-was-zelfs-bij-banken-draagvlak-voor-een-radicale-aanpak-dat-is-snel-verdwenen.

Hulse, C., and D. Herszenhorn. 2009. 'House Approves 90% Tax on Bonuses After Bailouts'. *New York Times.* 19 March. https://www.nytimes.com/2009/03/20/business/20bailout.html.

Jakobs, H. J. 2012. 'Wer Großbanken Zerschlägt, Schadet der Wirtschaft'. *Süddeutsche Zeitung.* 26 July. https://www.sueddeutsche.de/wirtschaft/forderung-nach-bankenkontrolle-wer-grossbanken-zerschlaegt-schadet-der-wirtschaft-1.1422536.

Janssen, H. 2013. 'Steinbrück und die Kriegserklärung an die Banken'. Spiegel.de. 12 February. https://www.spiegel.de/politik/deutschland/faktencheck-peer-steinbrueck-und-das-bankensystem-a-882586.html.

Jenkins, P. 2013a. 'Vicker Calls for Doubling of Bank Capital Levels'. *Financial Times.* 8 September. https://www.ft.com/content/8eaf8538-1893-11e3-83b9-00144feab7de.

Jenkins, P. 2013b. 'Brussels Softens Line on Bank Ringfences'. *Financial Times.* 29 January. https://www.ft.com/content/87c6c5f0-6a3e-11e2-a3db-00144feab49a.

Jenkins, P., and C. Jones. 2012. 'Tucker Backs Government Bank Reforms'. *Financial Times.* 23 November. https://www.ft.com/content/60bcc45a-34ab-11e2-8b86-00144feabdc0.

Jenkins, P., B. Masters, and C. Giles. 2011a. 'City Reels After King Demands Break-Up'. *Financial Times.* 7 March. https://www.ft.com/content/e357d2ba-48fd-11e0-af8c-00144feab49a.

Jenkins, P., B. Masters, T. Alloway, S. Goff, and G. Parker. 2011b. 'Vickers Plan Shakes up City'. *Financial Times.* 12 September. https://www.ft.com/content/68870a5c-dd03-11e0-b4f2-00144feabdc0#axzz2QA0urxKB.

Jenkins, P., S. Goff, and M. Murphy. 2011c. 'Finance: Flight Delayed'. *Financial Times.* 14 April. https://www.ft.com/content/d85fbb0c-66cb-11e0-8d88-00144feab49a.

Joanny, M. 2012. 'Paris Risquerait de Préempter la Réforme Bancaire de l'UE'. Challenges.fr. 22 November. https://www.challenges.fr/entreprise/paris-risquerait-de-preempter-la-reforme-bancaire-de-l-ue_243924.

Johnson, S. 2009. 'The Quiet Coup'. *The Atlantic*. May. https://www.theatlantic.com/magazine/archive/2009/05/the-quiet-coup/307364/
Jonker, U. 2012. 'De Wit Laat Onderste Steen in Brussel Rustig Liggen'. *Financieele Dagblad*. 14 April. https://fd.nl/frontpage/Print/krant/Rubriek/Brussel/855317/de-wit-laat-onderste-steen-in-brussel-rustig-liggen.
Jopson, B. 2017a. 'Donald Trump Still Open to Bank Break-Up Proposals'. *Financial Times*. 7 April. https://www.ft.com/content/6e6c7baa-1b14-11e7-bcac-6d03d067f81f.
Jopson, B. 2017b. 'With Alumni in the White House, Goldman Sees an Opening'. *Financial Times*. 22 August. https://www.ft.com/content/39db4fd0-49e8-11e7-919a-1e14ce4af89b.
Jopson, B. 2018. 'US Congress Rolls Back Parts of Post-Crisis Bank Rules'. *Financial Times*. 22 May. https://www.ft.com/content/649e6d66-5deb-11e8-ad91-e01af256df68.
Kaiser, S. 2012. 'Fight Looms Over EU Plans for Bank Reform'. *Spiegel International*. 3 October. http://www.spiegel.de/intenational/europe/analysis-of-eu-report-recommending-big-banks-be-split-up-a-859297.html.
Kalse, E., and D. van Lent. 2009. 'Verder dan "Betreuren" Komen de Banken Niet: Kredietcrisis Commissie van Bankiers Probeert Wettelijke Maatregelen Tegen Financiële Sector te Voorkomen'. *NRC Handelsblad*. 7 April. https://www.nrc.nl/nieuws/2009/04/07/verder-dan-betreuren-komen-de-banken-niet-11709567-a1268030.
Kalse, E., and D. van Lent. 2010. 'Collectief Blind, en Collectief Schuldig: Commissie-DeWit Ziet Geen Hoofdschuldige; Oud-Minister Bos Liet te Veel aan Toezichthouder Over. *NRC Handelsbald*. 10 May. https://www.nrc.nl/nieuws/2010/05/10/collectief-blind-en-collectief-schuldig-11887554-a1148906.
Kalse, E., and J. Wester. 2010a. 'Moeizame Strijd om Meer Toezicht: Commissie-DeWit'. *NRC Handelsblad*. 21 January. https://www.nrc.nl/nieuws/2010/01/21/moeizame-strijd-om-meer-toezicht-11840272-a1269978.
Kalse E., and J. Wester. 2010b. 'Parlementariërs Begrijpen Bankiers Niet—en Andersom; Commissie-De Wit'. *NRC Handelsblad*. 30 January. https://www.nrc.nl/nieuws/2010/01/30/parlementariers-begrijpen-bankiers-niet-en-andersom-11844449-a1334760.
Kapoor, S. 2013. 'Reset EU Bank Rules to Restore Faith'. *Financial Times*. 13 February. https://www.ft.com/content/3ec5eb9a-6ad1-11e2-9670-00144feab49a.
Kissler, A. 2013. 'Trennbankengesetz Soll ein Jahr Später Kommen'. *Wall Street Journal*. 15 May. https://www.wsj.com/articles/SB10001424127887324767004578485051479408158.
Klein, A. 2017. 'A Primer on Dodd–Frank's Orderly Liquidation Authority'. *Brookings*. 5 June. https://www.brookings.edu/blog/up-front/2017/06/05/a-primer-on-dodd-franks-orderly-liquidation-authority/.
Kockelmans, F. 2012. 'Banken nemen kritiek De Wit ter harte (2)'. ANP (Algemeen Nederlands Persbureau). 11 April.
Köhler, P. 2004. 'Oppositionsparteien Planen Privatisierung der Öffentlich-Rechtlichen Kreditinstitute: CDU und FDP greifen Sparkassen an'. *Handelsblatt*. 27 September. https://www.handelsblatt.com/finanzen/banken-versicherungen/oppositionsparteien-planen-privatisierung-der-oeffentlich-rechtlichen-kreditinstitute-cdu-und-fdp-greifen-sparkassen-an-seite-2/2407304-2.html.
Kosman, J. 2010. 'Volcker Fooled'. *New York Post*. 23 February. https://nypost.com/2010/02/23/volcker-fooled/.
Kosterman, R. 2010. 'Wellink in de Touwen: Nout Wellink Krijgt bij de Commissie-De Wit de ene na de Andere Veeg uit de Pan'. *Elsevier Weekblad*. 10 January, 44, 66, 4.

Kreling, T., and E. van der Walle. 2012. 'Commissie-De Wit Oordeelt Grimmig Over Aanpak Bankencrisis'. *NRC Handelsblad*. 11 April. https://www.nrc.nl/nieuws/2012/04/11/commissie-de-wit-oordeelt-grimmig-over-aanpak-bankencrisis-1093634-a971844.

LaCapra, L. T. 2011. 'Goldman Lobbying Hard to Weaken Volcker Rule'. *Reuters*. 4 May. https://www.reuters.com/article/us-goldman-volcker-idUSTRE7434PZ20110504.

Lalkens, P. 2012a. 'De Jager Belooft Bankencommissie'. *Financieele Dagblad*. 28 March. https://fd.nl/frontpage/Print/krant/Pagina/Economie___Politiek/854358/de-jager-belooft-bankencommissie.

Lalkens, P. 2012b. 'Weer een Commissie'. *Financieele Dagblad*. 30 March. https://fd.nl/frontpage/Print/krant/Rubriek/Economie/854423/weer-een-commissie.

Lambert. L. 2016. 'US Regulators Fail "Living Wills" at Five of Eight Big Banks'. *Reuters*. 13 April. https://www.reuters.com/article/us-usa-banks-idUSKCN0XA1B4.

Larosière, J. de 2010. 'Financial Regulators Must Take Care Over Capital'. *Financial Times*. 16 October. https://www.ft.com/content/55c69966-b9cc-11de-a747-00144feab49a.

Larosière, J. de 2011. 'Don't Punish the Banks that Performed Best: Basel III May Create New Risks'. *Financial Times*. 4 March. https://www.ft.com/content/1b085c0e-45e1-11e0-acd8-00144feab49a.

Larosière, J. de 2012. 'Seductive Simplicity of Ringfencing'. *Financial Times*. 26 September. https://www.ft.com/content/28196dde-0705-11e2-92b5-00144feabdc0.

Laurent, S. 2013. 'Ce qu'il Reste de la Réforme Bancaire de François Hollande'. *Le Monde*. 6 February. https://www.lemonde.fr/politique/article/2013/02/06/ce-qu-il-reste-de-la-reforme-bancaire-de-francois-hollande_1827317_823448.html.

Le Guernigou, Y. 2010. 'UPDATE 1—France, Germany Renew Call for Tougher Regulation. *Reuters*. 21 June. https://www.reuters.com/article/france-germany-regulation-idUSLDE65K27X20100621.

Lejoux, C. 2013. 'Karine Berger: "la loi bancaire, un cessez-le-feu avec la finance folle, mais pas la fin de la guerre"'. *La Tribune*. 17 July. https://www.latribune.fr/entreprises-finance/banques-finance/industrie-financiere/20130717trib000776237/karine-berger-la-loi-bancaire-un-cessez-le-feu-avec-la-finance-folle-mais-pas-la-fin-de-la-guerre.html.

Leonhardt, D. 2010. 'Heading Off the Next Financial Crisis'. *New York Times Magazine*. 25 March. https://www.nytimes.com/2010/03/28/magazine/28Reform-t.html

Leroy, P. H. 2012. 'En Finir avec le Mythe de la Banque Universelle'. *Le Monde*. 19 November. https://www.lemonde.fr/idees/article/2012/11/19/en-finir-avec-le-mythe-de-la-banque-universelle_1792120_3232.html.

Libération. 2013. 'Les Députés Adoptent Définitivement le Projet de Réforme Bancaire'. Libération. 17 July. https://www.liberation.fr/futurs/2013/07/17/les-deputes-adoptent-definitivement-le-projet-de-reforme-bancaire_918971/.

Lofchie, S. 2014. 'Better Markets Amicus Brief Supports CFTC's Cross-Border Guidance'. Center for Financial Stability. 21 March. http://centerforfinancialstability.org/wp/2014/03/21/better-markets-amicus-brief-supports-cftcs-cross-border-guidance/.

Lyster, L. 2013. 'Big Banks Still Write the Rules: Fmr Inspector General of Bank Bailout'. Yahoo!Finance. 29 May. https://finance.yahoo.com/blogs/daily-ticker/big-banks-still-write-rules-fmr-inspector-general-131105952.html?guccounter=1.

Mabille, P. 2012. 'Le Projet de loi Bancaire est une Réforme Canada Dry: Renforçons Plutôt nos Banques!'. *La Tribune*. 19 December. https://www.latribune.fr/opinions/tribunes/20121218trib000737994/le-projet-de-loi-bancaire-est-une-reforme-canada-dry.-renforcons-plutot-nos-banques-.html.

McKenna, F. 2017. 'Biggest Banks Prefer Full Volcker Rule Repeal, But a Rewrite Would Do'. *Market Watch*. 19 August. https://www.marketwatch.com/story/biggest-banks-prefer-full-volcker-rule-repeal-but-a-rewrite-would-do-2017-08-11.

McLannahan, B. 2018a. 'US Has More Than 5,600 Banks: Consolidation Is Coming'. *Financial Times*. 23 May. https://www.ft.com/content/41af5986-5e05-11e8-9334-2218e7146b04.

McLannahan, B. 2018b. 'US Banks Can Now Expect a Streamlined Volcker Rule 2.0'. *Financial Times*. 25 May. https://www.ft.com/content/25ef17c2-5fd6-11e8-9334-2218e7146b04.

McLannahan, B., and S. Fleming. 2017. 'US Treasury Department Seeks to Revamp Obama-Era Regulations'. *Financial Times*. 13 June. https://www.ft.com/content/3ad08c46-4fcb-11e7-bfb8-997009366969.

Masters, B. 2012. 'Strasbourg Hears Call for Tougher Rules for Banks'. *Financial Times*. 2 February. https://www.ft.com/content/f1e4cdd8-4d8e-11e1-b96c-00144feabdc0.

Masters, B., and S. Goff. 2011. 'Banks Accused of "Dishonesty" on Reform'. *Financial Times*. 23 November. https://www.ft.com/content/e33fee66-1526-11e1-b9b8-00144feabdc0.

Masters, B., K. Burgess, and S. Goff. 2011. 'Osborne Grants Big Banks a Concession'. *Financial Times*. 19 December. https://www.ft.com/content/8e31d670-2a5f-11e1-8f04-00144feabdc0.

Mattingly, P. 2012. 'Why Romney Won't Kill Dodd–Frank'. *Bloomberg*. 7 September. https://www.bloomberg.com/news/articles/2012-09-06/why-romney-wont-kill-dodd-frank.

Miedema, D. 2014. 'US Regulator Estimates Volcker Rule's Cost for Banks'. *Reuters*. 20 March. https://www.reuters.com/article/us-banks-volcker-costs-idUSBREA2J2 5O20140320.

Moore, M. J., and D. Campbell. 2013. 'Wall Street Sweats Out Volcker Rule with 18 of Revenue in Play'. *Bloomberg*. 4 December. https://www.bloomberg.com/news/articles/2013-12-04/wall-street-sweats-out-volcker-rule-with-18-of-revenue-in-play.

Moules, J. 2011. 'Business Skeptical Over Vickers Report. *Financial Times*. 12 September. https://www.ft.com/content/dd9a81f2-da10-11e0-b199-00144feabdc0?siteedition=uk#axzz2jh3739nb.

Mustoe, H. 2013. 'UK Should Shun "Difficult" Volcker Rule, Says John Vickers'. *Bloomberg*. 16 January. https://www.bloomberg.com/news/articles/2013-01-16/u-k-should-shun-difficult-volcker-rule-says-john-vickers.

Nathan, H. 2012. 'La Capitulation Bancaire de Pierre Moscovici'. *Marianne*. 23 December. https://www.marianne.net/politique/la-capitulation-bancaire-de-pierre-moscovici.

Neuerer, D. 2013. 'Steinbrück ist Schäubles Lex Deutsche Bank Glass–Steagall Banking Law'. *Reuters*. 26 October.

New York Times. 2009. 'Opinion—Letter—Volcker's Advice'. 22 October. https://www.nytimes.com/2009/10/23/opinion/l23volcker.html.

Nods, R. 2012. 'Toch Maar Samen Verder; Alleen SP en PVV Willen Banken Rigoureus in Tweeën Splitsen, Zoals de Commissie-De Wit Aanbeval'. *Elsevier Weekblad*. 11 February. https://www.ewmagazine.nl/auteur/remko-nods/.

NRC Handelsblad. 2010. 'Wellink Deelt Conclusies Commissie-De Wit Niet Volledig'. 28 December. https://advance-lexis-com.ezproxy.ub.unimaas.nl/api/document?collection=news&id=urn:contentItem:51TH-B811-DYRY-N1KJ-00000-00&context=1516831.

NRC Handelsblad. 2012. 'Bankiers Waarschuwen: Splitsen van Banken is Slecht'. 1 February. https://www.nrc.nl/nieuws/2012/02/01/bankiers-waarschuwen-splitsen-van-banken-is-slecht-1066060-a1004934.

L'Obs. 2013. 'La Réforme Bancaire Définitivement Adoptée par le Parlement'. 18 July. https://www.nouvelobs.com/societe/20130718.AFP9886/la-reforme-bancaire-definitivement-adoptee-par-le-parlement.html.

O'Donnell, J. 2014. 'Update 3-Europe's Bid to Reform Mega-Banks Hits Resistance in France'. *Reuters.* 29 January. https://www.reuters.com/article/eu-banks-idUSL5N0L31P120140129.

Onaran, Y. 2012. 'Bank Lobby Widened Volcker Rule, Inciting Foreign Outrage'. *Bloomberg.* 23 February. https://www.bloomberg.com/news/articles/2012-02-23/banks-lobbied-to-widen-volcker-rule-before-inciting-foreigners-against-law.

Open Europe. 2014a. 'The Long Lost Liikanen Report Returns—But It Looks Pretty Different'. 29 January. http://openeuropeblog.blogspot.com/2014/01/the-long-lost-liikanen-report-returns.html.

Open Europe 2014b. 'When It Rains, It Pours: EU legal Opinion Puts UK on Backfoot Over Revamped Liikanen Rules'. 17 June. http://openeuropeblog.blogspot.com/2014/06/when-it-rains-its-pours-eu-legal.html.

Oudéa, F. 2015. 'Europe Needs Homegrown Bulge Bracket Banks'. *Financial Times.* 11 October. https://www.ft.com/content/b911380e-6e8a-11e5-8171-ba1968cf791a.

Palmer, A. 2012. 'JPMorgan Prepares for DC's Worst'. *Politico.* 14 May. https://www.politico.com/story/2012/05/jpmorgan-prepares-for-dcs-worst-076290.

Le Parisien. 2012. 'Une Loi en Chantier pour Mieux Encadrer les Banques'. 19 December. https://www.leparisien.fr/economie/votre-argent/conseil-des-ministres-une-loi-en-chantier-pour-mieux-encadrer-les-banques-19-12-2012-2420007.php.

Parker, G. 2013. 'Lawson Urges Full Nationalisation of RBS'. *Financial Times.* 31 January. https://www.ft.com/content/c4a72ba8-6bc5-11e2-a700-00144feab49a#axzz2JuzjidpI.

Parker, G., and S. Goff. 2014. 'Miliband Outlines Plans to Go Further than Coalition on Bank Reform'. *Financial Times.* 17 January. https://www.ft.com/content/62812814-7f7b-11e3-b6a7-00144feabdc0.

Parker, G., S. Goff, and E. Rigby. 2013. 'Vince Cable Attacks Bank of England's Capital Taliban'. *Financial Times.* 23 July. https://www.ft.com/content/a6367d06-f377-11e2-942f-00144feabdc0.

Het Parool. 2010. 'De Commissie Is Klaar. En nu?' 8 May. https.//advance-lexis.com.ezproxy.ub.unimaas.nl/api/document?collection=news&id=urn:contentItem:7YDM-S040-Y9M6-H06J-00000-00&context=1516831.

Patterson, S., and V. McGrane. 2012. 'JP Morgan May Lose Sway in DC'. *Wall Street Journal.* 13 May. https://www.wsj.com/articles/SB10001424052702303550550457740242281 5972562.

Pieper, J. 2017. 'Too-Big-To-Regulate: The EU's Bank Structural Reform Proposal Fails'. *Finance Watch.* 25 October. https://www.finance-watch.org/press-release/too-big-to-regulate-the-eus-bank-structural-reform-proposal-failed/.

Pignal, S., and A. Barker. 2011a. 'Barnier Panel to Study Break-Up of EU banks'. *Financial Times.* 22 November. https://www.ft.com/content/ec184d06-1537-11e1-855a-00144feabdc0.

Pignal, S., and P. Jenkins. 2011b. 'Dexia Poses Setback for EBA Stress Tests'. *Financial Times.* 5 October. https://www.ft.com/content/0f638a80-ef6a-11e0-bc88-00144feab49a.

Pike, K. 2013. 'Too Big to Regulate'. *Independent Banker.* 1 May. https://independentbanker.org/2013/05/too-big-to-regulate/.

Pompa, F., and D. Gainer. 2013. 'Who Killed Financial Reform: After Three Years, Key Parts of the Plan to Avert Another Wall Street Crisis Remain Undone'. *USA Today.* 4 June.

Pouzin, G. 2014a. 'Les Secrets Inavouables de la Fausse loi de Séparation Bancaire'. Deontofi.com. 5 May. https://deontofi.com/les-secrets-inavouables-de-la-fausse-loi-de-separation-bancaire/.
Pouzin, G. 2014b. 'Le Complot des Banques Contre la Séparation de Leurs Activités Spéculatives'. Deontofi.com. 5 May. https://deontofi.com/le-complot-des-banques-contre-la-separation-de-leurs-activites-speculatives/.
Price, M., and P. Schroeder. 2018. 'Small Banks Trump Wall Street on Dodd–Frank Rewrite'. *Reuters*. 23 May. https://www.reuters.com/article/us-usa-house-banks-lobbying-idUSKCN1IN328.
Protess, B. 2012. 'Regulators to Ease a Role on Derivatives Dealers'. *New York Times Dealbook*. 17 April. https://dealbook.nytimes.com/2012/04/17/regulators-to-ease-a-rule-on-derivatives-dealers/?mtrref=www.google.com&gwh=76538966BDC4C6A93F797C6BE3C80D09&gwt=pay&assetType=PAYWALL.
Puzzanghera, J. 2010. 'Bernanke Urges Lawmakers Not to Slash Fed's Regulatory Authority'. *Los Angeles Times*. 18 March. https://www.latimes.com/archives/la-xpm-2010-mar-18-la-fi-bernanke18-2010mar18-story.html.
Rathee, A. 2012. 'Has JPMorgan Shot Itself in the Foot on Volcker'. CheatSheet.com. 11 May. https://www.cheatsheet.com/money-career/has-jpmorgan-shot-itself-in-the-foot-on-volcker.html/.
Raymond, G. 2013. 'Interview. Gilles Carrez sur la réforme bancaire: "Je crains l'inventivité des banquiers"'. *Le HuffPost*, 12 février. https://www.huffingtonpost.fr/2013/02/11/gilles-carrez-reforme-bancaire-speculation-hollande-banques_n_2665648.html.
Reformatorisch Dagblad. 2012. 'Kamer en Banken Acter Conclusies Commissie-De Wit'. 12 April. https://advance-lexis-com.ezproxy.ub.unimaas.nl/api/document?collection=news&id=urn:contentItem:55CY-44Y1-JC8W-Y3T8-00000-00&context=1516831.
Reuters Staff. 2010. 'Goldman's Blankfein Says Could Support Volcker Rule: Report'. *Reuters*. 2 May. https://www.reuters.com/article/us-goldman-blankfein-idUSTRE6412U320100502.
Reuters Staff. 2016. 'Trump Calls for "21st Century" Glass–Steagall Banking Law'. *Reuters*. 26 October. https://www.reuters.com/article/us-usa-election-trump-banks-idUSKCN12Q2WA.
Rivlin, G. 2013. 'How Wall Street Defanged Dodd–Frank'. *The Nation*. 30 April. https://www.thenation.com/article/archive/how-wall-street-defanged-dodd-frank/.
Robinson, G. 2009. 'Berlin to Urge G20 on Bank Rules'. *Financial Times*. 1 September. https://www.ft.com/content/61ea7128-7443-34eb-874f-dffd271e4ed9.
Robinson, G. 2010. 'FSA Extends Scrutiny'. *Financial Times*. 29 January. https://www.ft.com/content/f3404c38-f772-3f0d-80a6-8819bb5fe4e2.
Roest, A. 2011. 'Creëer een Servicebank en een Handelsbank'. *De Volkskrant*. 2 April. https://advance-lexis-com.ezproxy.ub.unimaas.nl/api/document?collection=news&id=urn:contentItem:52J5-YDB1-JC8W-Y1SJ-00000-00&context=1516831.
Roger, P. 2013. 'Karine Berger Gagne ses Galons sur la Loi Bancaire'. *Le Monde*. 19 February. https://www.lemonde.fr/politique/article/2013/02/19/karine-berger-gagne-ses-galons-sur-la-loi-bancaire_1834836_823448.html.
Rooij, A. de 2019. 'Pleidooi Voor Terugkeer Spaar- en Betaalbank'. *Reformatorisch Dagblad*. 18 January. https://www.digibron.nl/pdfviewer/collectie/Digibron/page/16/id/tag:RD.nl,20190118:newsml_dca72a8fe613f18318be17f8ecba2d65.
Rush, L. 2007. 'Influence: A Booming Business—Record $1.3 Billion Spent to Lobby State Government'. Center for Public Integrity. 20 December. https://publicintegrity.org/politics/state-politics/influence/hired-guns/influence-a-booming-business/.

Scaggs, A. 2017. 'A Summary of Significant Treasury Proposals that Don't Require Congress'. *Financial Times*. 13 June. https://www.ft.com/content/f854991b-86dd-3d9d-a9d4-81a395efde20.

Scannell, K. 2009. 'Big Companies Go to Washington to Fight Regulations on Fancy Derivates'. *Wall Street Journal*. 10 July. https://www.wsj.com/articles/SB124718445317920379.

Schouten, F., K. Dilanian, and M. Kelley. 2008. 'Lobbyists in "Feeding Frenzy" Over Crisis'. *USA Today*. 30 September. https://www.usatoday.com/news/politics/election2008/2008-09-24-lobbying_N.htm.

Solomon, D. 2010. 'Bachus Urges Regulators Not to rigidly Implement Volcker Rule. *Wall Street Journal*. 4 November. https://www.wsj.com/articles/SB10001424052748703805704575594473849188154.

Spiegel International. 2012. 'A Reputation in Ruin: Deutsche Bank Slides into a Swamp of Scandal'. 19 December. https://www.spiegel.de/international/business/deutsche-bank-reputation-at-stake-amid-a-multitude-of-scandals-a-873544.html.

Spiegel.de. 2012. 'Deutsche-Bank-Chef Jain Düpiert Bundestag'. 22 November. https://www.spiegel.de/politik/deutschland/deutsche-bank-chef-jain-duepiert-bundestag-a-868740.html.

Stacey, K. 2012. 'MPs Back Forced Separation of Banks'. *Financial Times*. 26 December. https://www.ft.com/content/57e63c4e-4f72-11e2-a744-00144feab49a?siteedition=uk#axzz2QA0urxKB.

Stacey, K. 2019. 'US Regulators Unveil Final Rewrite of Volcker Rule'. *Financial Times*. 20 August. https://www.ft.com/content/05673218-c35e-11e9-a8e9-296ca66511c9.

Stam, S. 2010. 'Constanter 'Zelfonderzoek Banken Gebrekkig: Conclusies en Aanbevelingen van cie. De Wit NVB: Banken Hebben hun les Geleerd'. *Nederlands Dagblad*. 11 May. https://advance-lexis-com.ezproxy.ub.unimaas.nl/api/document?collection=news&id=urn:contentItem:7YF7-G8C1-2RNC-W187-00000-00&context=1516831.

Stewart, J. B. 2011. 'Volcker Rule, Once Simple, Now Boggles'. *New York Times*. 21 October. https://www.nytimes.com/2011/10/22/business/volcker-rule-grows-from-simple-to-complex.html.

Stubbe, A. 2016. 'Trennbanken: Auslegungshilfe zum Abschirmungsgesetz'. BaFin. 15 February. https://www.bafin.de/SharedDocs/Veroeffentlichungen/DE/Fachartikel/2016/fa_bj_1602_trennbanken.html.

Sustainable Finance Lab. 2011. 'Maak Financiële Sector Weer Veilig en Simpel'. *De Volkskrant*. 26 November. https://www.volkskrant.nl/nieuws-achtergrond/maak-financiele-sector-weer-veilig-en-simpel~b6e81095/.

Sweetland-Edwards, H. 2013. 'He Who Makes the Rules'. *Washington Monthly*. March/April. https://washingtonmonthly.com/magazine/marchapril-2013/he-who-makes-the-rules/.

Tagesschau.de. 2013. 'Bundesrat Stimmt Trennbankengesetz Zu'. 7 June. https://web.archive.org/web/20130609022258/http://www.tagesschau.de/wirtschaft/bundesrat-stimmt-trennbankengesetz-zu100.html.

Tang, P., and K. Vendrik. 2012. 'Banken Houden in Nederland en Europa de Overheden nog Steeds Onder Schot: Commissie-De Wit Gaat Voorbij aan Belangrijkste Probleem dat Overheden Toen en nu Geen Keus Hadden'. *Financieele Dagblad*. 30 June. https://advance-lexis-com.ezproxy.ub.unimaas.nl/api/document?collection=news&id=urn:contentItem:560R-PDP1-DYRY-N2MD-00000-00&context=1516831.

De Telegraaf. 2011. 'Banken Splitsen bij Nieuwe Crisis'. 9 July.

Tett, G. 2009. 'Global Insight: Germans Open Can of Worms'. *Financial Times*. 8 July. https://www.ft.com/content/18b2128c-6be6-11de-9320-00144feabdc0.

Tilburg, R. van 2011. 'Waar Blijft de Hellehond van de Zuidas?'. *Groene Amsterdammer*. 12 October. https://www.groene.nl/artikel/waar-blijft-de-hellehond-van-de-zuidas.

Tilburg, R. van 2012. 'Minister Moet nu Ingrijpen Bij Banken'. *De Volkskrant*. 7 February. https://www.volkskrant.nl/nieuws-achtergrond/minister-moet-nu-ingrijpen-bij-banken~bda59847/.

Torello, A., and W. Horobin. 2011. 'ECOFIN: EU Finance Ministers Clash on Financial Transaction Tax'. *Wall Street Journal*. 8 November. https://www.wsj.com/articles/SB10001424052970204554204577025750960668474.

Touryalai, H. 2012. 'Volcker Rule Refugees', *Forbes*. 21 March. https://www.forbes.com/sites/halahtouryalai/2012/03/21/volcker-rule-refugees/?sh=b72579851a3c.

Treanor, J. 2011. 'Banks Put Yearly Bill for Radical Reforms at £15bn'. *The Guardian*. 20 March. https://www.theguardian.com/business/2011/mar/20/banking-reform-john-vickers-report.

Tyrie, A. 2013. 'Electrify the Banking Ringfence'. *Financial Times*. 27 January. https://www.ft.com/content/a6ff40a6-5fd9-11e2-8d8d-00144feab49a#axzz2QA0urxKB.

Uchitelle, L. 2009. 'Volcker Fails to Sell a Bank Strategy'. *New York Times*. 20 October. https://www.nytimes.com/2009/10/21/business/21volcker.html.

Vanheste, T., and M. Oberndorff. 2011. 'Gegijzeld Door de Banken; Reportage/Waar Blijft de Financiële Hervorming?' *Vrij Nederland*. 16 July. https://www.vn.nl/gegijzeld-door-de-banken/.

Verdieping Trouw. 2010. 'Veel Banken Leven Eigen Regels Niet na: Commissie Ziet Weinig Vooruitgang Banken wacht Botsing met Parlement. 3 December. https://www.trouw.nl/nieuws/veel-banken-leven-eigen-regels-niet-na~b5d70915/.

Verma, S. 2015. 'EU reforms run into regulatory conflict'. *Euromoney*, 27 July. https://www.euromoney.com/article/b12km9nskjdg3s/eu-reforms-run-into-regulatory-conflict.

Visser, M. 2012. 'Iedereen Spekkoper bij Grotere Banken'. *Trouw*. 24 April. https://www.trouw.nl/nieuws/iedereen-spekkoper-bij-grotere-banken~bdb5c27d/.

Waard, P. de 2012. 'Moeten Banken Worden Opgeknipt?'. *De Volkskrant*. 11 September. https://www.volkskrant.nl/nieuws-achtergrond/moeten-banken-worden-opgeknipt~bcf0fb43/.

Walle, E. van der 2011. 'Bij de Volgende Crisis Doen ze het Beter: De Commissie-De Wit Hoort de Komende Weken de Hoofdrolspelers in de Bankencrisis van 2008'. *NRC Handelsblad*. 29 November. https://www.nrc.nl/nieuws/2011/11/29/bij-de-volgende-crisis-doen-ze-het-beter-12117005-a1094963.

Walle, E. van der, and J. Wester. 2011. 'Het Gaat De Wit om de Waarheid'. *NRC Handelsblad*. 7 November. https://www.nrc.nl/nieuws/2011/11/07/het-gaat-de-wit-om-de-waarheid-12043896-a457195.

Washington Post. 2017. '"We Expect to be Cutting a Lot Out of Dodd–Frank" Trump Promises'. *Washington Post*. 3 February. https://www.washingtonpost.com/videopolitics/we-expect-to-be-cutting-a-lot-out-of-dodd-frank-trump-promises/2017/02/03/dea4e7e4-ea28-11e6-903d-9b11ed7d8d2a_video.html.

Wawoe, K. W. 2010. 'Commissie-De Wit Laat Soms de Tanden Zien, Maar Bijt Niet'. *De Volkskrant*. 12 May. https://www.volkskrant.nl/economie/commissie-de-wit-laat-soms-de-tanden-zien-maar-bijt-niet~b6289e13/.

Webb, S., and K. Bart. 2013. 'European Banks Pay Heavy Price for Scandals'. *Reuters*. 29 October. https://www.reuters.com/article/us-european-banks-idUSBRE99S0D720131029.

Weber, A. 2016. 'EU Bank-Breakup Push Still "Locked" After Dombrovskis Effort'. *Bloomberg.* 25 October. https://www.bloomberg.com/news/articles/2016-10-25/eu-bank-separation-push-still-locked-after-dombrovskis-effort.

Weber, A., and B. Jennen. 2016. 'Dobrovskis Won't Budget EU Bank-Separation Bill, Hoekmark Says'. *Bloomberg.* 15 September. https://www.bloomberg.com/news/articles/2016-09-15/dombrovskis-won-t-budge-eu-bank-separation-bill-hoekmark-says.

Wefers, A. 2012. 'Reguliere—Aber Rede auch Drüber'. *Börsen-Zeitung.* 29 September. https://www.boersen-zeitung.de/konjunktur-politik/reguliere—aber-rede-auch-drueber-89c54069-6501-4f9e-a34f-28128a314f35.

Willems, L. 2010. 'Kamer Omarmt Advies Commissie-De Wit Maar is Bezorgd Over Aantal Maatregelen'. *Financieele Dagblad.* 15 September. https://fd.nl/frontpage/Print/krant/Pagina/Economie___Politiek/710605/kamer-omarmt-advies-commissie-de-wit-maar-is-bezorgd-over-aantal-maatregelen.

Willems, L. 2011. 'Commissievoorzitter Jan de Wit Moet na Aftocht Dion Graus nóg Neutraler Ogen'. *Financieele Dagblad.* 12 November. https://fd.nl/frontpage/economie-politiek/columns/den-haag/722366/commissievoorzitter-jan-de-wit-moet-na-aftocht-dion-graus-nog-neutraler-ogen.

Willems, L. 2012. 'Banken Waarschuwen: Splitsen Schaadt Economie én Ons'. *Financieele Dagblad.* 1 February. https://fd.nl/frontpage/Print/krant/Pagina/Economie___Politiek/834344/banken-waarschuwen-splitsen-schaadt-economie-en-ons.

Willems, L., and E. Hermanides. 2011. 'Banken Danken Kabinet: Niet Scheiden Maar Scheidbaar Zijn'. *Financieele Dagblad.* 9 July. https://fd.nl/frontpage/Print/krant/Pagina/Economie___Politiek/785762/banken-danken-kabinet-niet-scheiden-maar-scheidbaar-zijn.

Willems, P. 2013. 'Net Tegen Bankenlobby: Banekn SNbS'. *Elsevier Weekblad.* 14 December. https://advance-lexis-com.ezproxy.ub.unimaas.nl/api/document?collection=news&id=urn:contentItem:5B1M-67K1-DXG5-Y206-00000-00&context=1516831.

Williams, B. 2013. 'Volcker Overruled?'. *Harvard University Blog.* 18 November. https://ethics.harvard.edu/blog/volcker-overruled.

Wilson, J. 2013. 'Germany Rejects Whole-Bank Ringfencing'. *Financial Times.* 30 January. https://www.ft.com/content/593458ce-6ae8-11e2-9871-00144feab49a.

Wit, J. de 2012. 'Endrapport van de Parlementaire Enquête Financieel Stelsel'. *PDC.* Den Haag: *Tweede Kamer.* Accessed 1 March 2019. https://www.parlementairemonitor.nl/9353000/1/j9vvij5epmj1ey0/viykic4m8azk.

Official Sources (Official Public and Private Sector Sources)

Assemblée Nationale. 2013a. 'Rapport Fait au nom de la Commission des Finances, de L'économie Générale et du Contrôle Budgétaire sur le Projet de loi de Séparation et de Régulation des Activités Bancaires' 566. Karine Berger Rapporteur. 7 February. https://www.assemblee-nationale.fr/14/rapports/r0707.asp.

Assemblée Nationale. 2013b. 'Assemblée Nationale XIVe Législature, Session Ordinaire de 2012–2013, Compte Rendu Intégral, Deuxième Séance'. 12 February. https://www.assemblee-nationale.fr/14/cri/2012-2013/20130145.asp.

Beck, T., A. Demirgüç-Kunt, R. Levine, M. Cihak, and E. H. B. Feyen. 2018. 'Financial Structure Database'. World Bank. http://www.worldbank.org/en/publication/gfdr/data/financial-structure-database.

Board of Governors of the Federal Reserve System. 2014. *Order Approving Extension of Conformance Period Under Section 13 of the Bank Holding Company Act*. 18 December. https://www.federalreserve.gov/newsevents/pressreleases/files/bcreg20141218a1.pdf.

Bundesregierung. 2008–2010. *Neue Globale Finanzmarktarchitektur*. https://www.bundesregierung.de/breg-de/themen/g7-g20/neue-globale-finanzmarktarchitektur-360344.

Bündnis 90/Die Grünen-Fraktion im Deutschen Bundestag. 2011. 'Einsetzung einer Kommission des Deutschen Bundestages zur Regulierung der Großbanken'. Bundestagdrucksache 17/7359. 19 October, Berlin: Deautscher Bundestag.

CCSF (Comité Consultatif du Secteur Financier). 2014. *Rapport Annuel du Comité Consultatif du Secteur Financier 2013*. 16 December. Accessed 19 March 2021. https://www.banque-france.fr/sites/default/files/medias/documents/ccsf_rapport_annuel_2013-integral.pdf.

CDA (Christen-Democratisch Appèl). 2012. 'Concept Verkiezingsprogram 2012–2017: Iedereen'. https://d14uo0i7wmc99w.cloudfront.net/Afdelingen/Zuid_Holland/Kaag_en_Braassem/Iedereen_verkiezingsprogram_2012_2017_digitaal.pdf.

CDA (Christen-Democratisch Appèl). 2014. 'Naar een Slagvaardig Europa: Verkiezingsprogramma: Europees Parlement 2014–2019'. https://ep2014.bof.nl/verkiezingsprogramma/CDA_EP2014.pdf.

CDA (Christen-Democratisch Appèl). 2017. 'Keuzes voor een Beter Nederland: Verkiezingsprogramma 2017–2021'. https://d14uo0i7wmc99w.cloudfront.net/Afdelingen/Friesland/Weststellingwerf/documenten/CDAlandelijkverkiezingsprogramma2017-2021.pdf.

Competition and Markets Authority. 2014. *Personal Current Accounts and Banking Services to Small and Medium-Sized Enterprises*. 6 November. Accessed 19 March 2021. https://assets.publishing.service.gov.uk/government/uploads/system/uploads/attachment_data/file/371407/Decision-MIR-Final_14.pdf.

Conservative Party. 2010. *Invitation to Join the Government of Britain: The Conservative Manifesto*. London: Conservative Research Department.

Council of the EU. 2013. 'Opinion of the Legal Service: Proposal for a Council Directive Implementing Enhanced Cooperation in the Area of Financial Transaction Tax (FTT)'. 2013/0045 (CNS). 6 September. https://data.consilium.europa.eu/doc/document/ST-6013-2016-INIT/en/pdf.

Council of the EU. 2015. 'Proposal for a Regulation of the European Parliament and of the Council on Structural Measures Improving the Resilience of EU Credit Institutions'. General Approach. 10150/15. 2014/0020 (COD). 19 June. https://data.consilium.europa.eu/doc/document/ST-10150-2015-INIT/en/pdf.

CU (ChristenUnie). 2010. 'Vooruitzien: Christelijk-Sociaal Perspectief'. https://www.christenunie.nl/l/library/download/urn:uuid:7ab581e7-0218-4c5b-a451-29a6cd9b6839/christenunie+verkiezingsprogramma+tweede+kamer+2010.pdf?redirected=1'.

CU (ChristenUnie). 2012. 'Verkiezingsprogramma ChristenUnie 2013–2017 Voor de Verandering: 7 Christelijke-Sociale Hervorming'. https://www.christenunie.nl/l/library/download/10136013/printversie+verkiezingsprogramma+christenunie+2013-2017.pdf?redirected=1.

CU (ChristenUnie). 2017. 'Hoopvol Realistisch: Voorstellen voor een Samenleving met Toekomst—Verkiezingsprogramma 2017–2021'. https://www.christenunie.nl/l/library/download/10071522/verkiezingsprogramma+2017-2021+christenunie.pdf?redirected=1.

CU (ChristenUnie) and SGP. 2014. 'Samenwerking JA, Superstaat NEE: Verkizeingsprogramma ChristenUnie en SGP 2014-2019'. https://www.christenunie.nl/l/library/download/urn:uuid:9ca31528-1695-4bea-b25e-d2d63943a871/verkiezingsprogramma+christenunie-sgp+europees+parlement+2014.pdf?redirected=1.

D66 (Democraten 66). 2010. 'We willen het anders: Verkiezingsprogramma D66 voor de Tweede Kamer 2010-2014'. https://dnpprepo.ub.rug.nl/19/13/D66conceptverkiezingsprogramma2010.pdf.

D66 (Democraten 66). 2012. 'En nu vooruit D66: Op weg naar een welvarende, duurzame toekomst: Verkiezinggsprogramma D66 voor de Tweede Kamer 2012/2017'. https://dnpprepo.ub.rug.nl/545/19/D66Verkiezingsprogramma2012.pdf.

D66 (Democraten 66). 2014. 'Nu vooruit D66: Europa verdient beter: Verkiezingsprogramma Europees Parlement 2014'. https://wiki.piratenpartij.nl/_media/pdf:concurrentie:eu:d66_2014_eu.pdf.

D66 (Democraten 66). 2016. 'D66 Verkiezingsprogramma 2017-2021'. https://dnpprepo.ub.rug.nl/10864/1/D66_vp_TK2017_def.pdf.

De Wit. 2010. 'Eindrapport van het Parlementair Onderzoek van het Financieel Stelsel 31980'. Vergaderjaar 2009-10, 10 May. Den Haag: Tweede Kamer der Staten-Generaal. https://www.tweedekamer.nl/kamerstukken/detail?id=2010Z07920&did=2010D21587.

De Wit. 2012. 'Eindrapport van de Parlementaire Enquête Financieel Stelsel 31980'. Vergadergaar 2011-12, 11 April. Den Haag. https://www.parlementairemonitor.nl/9353000/1/j9vvij5epmj1ey0/viykic4m8azk.

Deutscher Bundesrat. 2013.'Plenarprotokoll 910: Punkt 11 Gesetz zur Abschirmung von Risiken und zur Planung der Sanierung und Abwicklung von Kreditinstituten und Finanzgruppen'. 7 June, p. 307c. https://www.bundesrat.de/SharedDocs/downloads/DE/plenarprotokolle/2013/Plenarprotokoll-910.pdf?__blob=publicationFile&v=4#page=307.

Deutscher Bundesrat. 2014. 'Vorschlag für eine Verordnung des Europäischen Parlaments und des Rates über strukturelle Maßnahmen zur Erhöhung der Widerstandsfähigkeit von Kreditinstituten in der Union COM(2014) 43 final'. Ratsdok. 6022/14. Drucksache 45/14 (Beschluss). 11 April. https://www.umwelt-online.de/PDFBR/2014/0045_2D14B.pdf.

Deutscher Bundestag. 2013a. 'Finanzausschuss Wortprotokoll'. Finance Committee, Session 62, Protokoll 17/138. 22 April. Berlin: Deutscher Bundestag.

Deutscher Bundestag. 2013b. 'Stenografischer Bericht'. Plenarprotokoll 17/229. 15 March. Berlin: Deutscher Bundestag.

Deutscher Bundestag. 2013c. 'Schäuble für Vorreiterrolle bei der Bankenregulierung'. Dokumente. 15 March. Berlin: Deutscher Bundestag. https://www.bundestag.de/dokumente/textarchiv/2013/43384773_kw11_de_banken-211540.

Deutscher Bundestag. 2013d. 'Stenografischer Bericht'. Plenarprotokoll 17/241. 17 May. Berlin: Deutscher Bundestag.

Deutscher Bundestag. 2013e. 'Die Bankenaufsicht soll europäisch werden'. Dokumente. 17 May. Berlin: Deutscher Bundestag. https://www.bundestag.de/dokumente/textarchiv/2013/44775441_kw20_de_bankenunion-212400.

Deutschlandradio.de. 2013. 'Bundestag will Sparer Besser schützen: Großbanken Müssen ab 2016 Risikogeschäfte separieren'. 17 May. https://www.deutschlandradio.de/bundestag-will-sparer-besser-schuetzen.331.de.html?dram:article_id=247066.

EU Commission. 2009. 'DG Competition's Review of Guarantee and Recapitalisation Schemes in the Financial Sector in the Current Crisis'. 7 August. https://ec.europa.eu/competition/state_aid/legislation/review_of_schemes_en.pdf.

EU Commission. 2011. 'Proposal for a Council Directive on a Common System of Financial Transaction Tax and Amending Directive'. 2008/7/EC. 28 September. https://eur-lex.europa.eu/legal-content/EN/ALL/?uri=CELEX:52011PC0594.

EU Commission. 2012. 'High Level Expert Group on Reforming the Structure of the EU Banking Sector—Mandate'. 2 October. Brussels. https://ec.europa.eu/commission/presscorner/detail/en/IP_12_1048.

EU Commission. 2013a. 'Commission Staff Working Document: Impact Assessment Accompanying the Document Proposal for a Council Directive Implementing Enhanced Cooperation in the Area of Financial Transaction Tax Analysis of Policy Options and Impacts'. 14 February. https://eur-lex.europa.eu/legal-content/EN/ALL/?uri=CELEX:52013SC0028.

EU Commission. 2013b. 'Summary of Replies to the Stakeholder Consultation Reform of the Banking Sector'. https://ec.europa.eu/finance/consultations/2013/banking-structural-reform/docs/summary-of-responses_en.pdf.

EU Commission. 2013c. Contributions: Consultation on the Structural Reform of the Banking Sector'. https://ec.europa.eu/finance/consultations/2013/banking-structural-reform/contributions_en.htm.

EU Commission. 2014a. 'Proposal for a Regulation of the European Parliament and of the Council, on Structural Measures Improving the Resilience of EU Credit Institutions'. 2014/0020 (COD). 29 January. https://eur-lex.europa.eu/legal-content/EN/TXT/PDF/?uri=CELEX:52014PC0043&from=EN.

EU Commission. 2014b. 'Commission Staff Working Document: Executive Summary of the Impact Assessment, Accompanying the Proposal for a Regulation of the European Parliament and of the Council, on Structural Measures Improving the Resilience of EU Credit Institutions'. 29 January. https://eur-lex.europa.eu/legal-content/EN/TXT/PDF/?uri=CELEX:52014SC0031&from=EN.

EU Commission. 2017. '2018 Commission Work Programme—Annex IV: Withdrawals'. COM(2017) 650 Final. 27 October. Brussels. https://ec.europa.eu/info/publications/2018-commission-work-programme-key-documents_en.

EU Parliament (EP). 2010. 'Resolution on Basel II and Revision of the Capital Requirements Directives (CRD 4)'. 21 September. Brussels: Committee of Economic and Monetary Affairs.

EU Parliament. 2011. 'Draft Report on the Proposal for a Regulation of the European Parliament and of the Council on Prudential Requirements for Credit Institutions and Investment Firms'. Brussels: Committee on Economic and Monetary Affairs.

EU Parliament (Committee on Economic and Monetary Affairs). 2013. 'Draft Report on Reforming the Structure of the EU's Banking Sector'. Brussels: Committee on Economic and Monetary Affairs.

EU Parliament (Committee on Economic and Monetary Affairs). 2015. Minutes. Meeting of 26 May 2015, 15.00–18.30. Brussels. https://www.europarl.europa.eu/doceo/document/ECON-PV-2015-05-26-1_EN.pdf?redirect.

EU Parliament (Committee on Economic and Monetary Affairs). 2016. 'Report on the Banking Union: Annual Report 2015'. A8-0033/2016, 2015/2221(INI), 19 February, Brussels. https://www.europarl.europa.eu/doceo/document/A-8-2016-0033_EN.html.

FBC (Future of Banking Commission). 2009. 'Future of Banking Commission Final Report'. London: FBC.

Finance Watch. 2012. 'The French President, François Hollande, Is On Track to Miss His Election Pledge to Reform France's Largest Banks, According to Public Interest Association'. 12 December. https://www.finance-watch.org/press-release/french-president-set-to-miss-his-pledge-on-bank-reform-finance-watch-warns-in-open-letter/.

Finance Watch. 2013a. 'Europe's Banking Trilemma: Why Banking Reform is Essential for a Successful Banking Union'. 5 September. https://www.finance-watch.org/press-release/europes-banking-trilemma-finance-watch-releases-report-on-banking-union-and-bank-structure-reform/.

Finance Watch 2013b. 'Response to the Public Consultation from the European Commission on a Reform of the Structure of the EU Banking Sector'. 11 July. https://www.finance-watch.org/publication/finance-watch-response-to-ec-consultation-on-banking-structure/.

Finance Watch. 2013c. 'Loi de Séparation et de Régulation des Activités Bancaires: Analyse du Projet Remis par le Gouvernement Français et Propositions d'Amendements Janvier 2013'. https://www.finance-watch.org/wp-content/uploads/2018/08/20130129-Analyse_et_amendements_loi_bancaire_Finance_Watch.pdf.

Finance Watch. 2015a. 'Draft ECON Report Would Make Bank Structure Reform Ineffective'. Press release. 8 January. https://www.finance-watch.org/press-release/draft-econ-report-would-make-bank-structure-reform-ineffective-says-finance-watch/.

French Government. 2012. 'Projet de Loi de Separation et de Regulation des Activités Bancaires'. NOR: EFIX1239994L. 18 December. https://www.assemblee-nationale.fr/14/projets/pl0566-ei.asp.

FSA (Financial Services Authority). 2009. 'Strengthening Liquidity Standards Including Feedback on CP08/22, CP09/13, CP09/14'. October. http://www.centerforfinancialstability.org/forum/fsa_liquidity_standards_transitional_measures_200906.pdf.

FSB (Financial Stability Board). 2018. 'Implementation and Effects of the G20 Financial Regulatory Reforms Fourth Annual Report'. 28 November. Washington, DC: FSB. https://www.fsb.org/wp-content/uploads/P281118-1.pdf.

FSB (Financial Stability Board). 2020. 'Implementation and Effects of the G20 Financial Regulatory Reforms Sixth Annual Report'. 13 November. Washington, DC: FSB. https://www.fsb.org/2020/11/implementation-and-effects-of-the-g20-financial-regulatory-reforms-2020-annual-report/.

G20. 2009. 'G20 Leaders Statement: The Pittsburg Summit'. 24–5 September. http://www.g20.utoronto.ca/2009/2009communique0925.html.

German and French governments. 2013. 'Consultation on Reforming the Structure of the EU Banking Sector'. Joint German and French Response. Berlin/Paris. https://ec.europa.eu/finance/consultations/2013/banking-structural-reform/docs/contributions/public-authorities/germany-and-france-joint-response_en.pdf.

German Ministry of Finance. 2013. 'Gesetz zur Abschirmung von Risiken und zur Planung der Sanierung und Abwicklung von Kreditinstituten und Finanzgruppen' [*Trennbankengesetz*]. *Bundesgesetzblatt Jahrgang 47*. 12 August, Bonn. https://www.bgbl.de/xaver/bgbl/start.xav#__bgbl__%2F%2F*%5B%40attr_id%3D%27bgbl113s3090.pdf%27%5D__1616501900172.

GroenLinks. 2010. 'Klaar voor de Toekomst: Verkizingsprogramma 2010'. https://www.parlement.com/9291000/d/2010_groenlinks_verkiezingsprogramma.pdf.

GroenLinks. 2012. 'Groene Kansen voor Nederland'. https://groenlinks.nl/sites/groenlinks/files/Verkiezingsprogramma_GroenLinks_Groene_kansen_voor%20Nederland.pdf.pdf.

GroenLinks. 2014. 'Ons Europa: Europese Verkiezingen 2014'. https://ep2014.bof.nl/verkiezingsprogramma/GL_EP2014.pdf.

GroenLinks. 2017. 'Tijd voor Verdandering: Verkiezingsprogramma GroenLinks 2017–2021'. https://deformatiewijzer.nl/wp-content/uploads/2017/02/Verkiezingsprogramma-GroenLinks-2017-20213.pdf.

Group of Thirty. 2009. 'Financial Reform: A Framework for Financial Stability'. Washington, DC.
Guebert, J. 2010. 'Plans for the Fourth G20 Summit: Co-chaired by Canada and Korea in Toronto, June 26–27, 2010'. 25 May. http://www.g20.utoronto.ca/g20plans/g20plans100525.pdf.
HBOS (Halifax Bank of Scotland). 2009. 'Annual Report and Accounts 2008'. https://www.lloydsbankinggroup.com/assets/pdfs/investors/financial-performance/hbos-plc/archive/2008/2008-hbos-ra.pdf.
HM Government. 2013. *Financial Services (Banking Reform) Act 2013*, December, London.
HM Treasury. 2008. 'Government Statement on Financial Support'. 8 October, London: Stationery Office.
HM Treasury. 2013. 'Financial Services (Banking Reform) Bill, Impact Assessment No. HMT 1302'. 9 January. https://www.parliament.uk/globalassets/documents/impact-assessments/IA13-005.pdf.
HM Treasury. 2014. 'Banking Reform: Draft Pensions Regulation Impact Assessment'. 5 July. https://assets.publishing.service.gov.uk/government/uploads/system/uploads/attachment_data/file/336121/banking_reform_impact_assessment_05072014.pdf.
House of Commons. 2018. *Financial Services' Contribution to the UK Economy: Research Briefing*. London: House of Commons Library.
House of Lords (European Union Committee). 2015. 'The Post-Crisis Financial Regulatory Framework: Do the Pieces Fit?'. *HL Papers* 103. 2 February. https://publications.parliament.uk/pa/ld201415/ldselect/ldeucom/103/10311.htm.
ICB (Independent Commission on Banking). 2011a. 'Interim Report: Consultation on Reform Options'. April. London: Crown. https://bankwatch.files.wordpress.com/2011/04/icbinterimreportexecutivesummary.pdf.
ICB (Independent Commission on Banking). 2011b. 'Independent Commission on Banking: Final Report'. September. London: Crown. https://bankingcommission.s3.amazonaws.com/wp-content/uploads/2010/07/ICB-Final-Report.pdf.
IMF (International Monetary Fund). 2009. 'Germany: 2008 Article IV Consultation—Staff Report; Staff Supplement; Public Information Notice on the Executive Board Discussion; and Statement by the Executive Director for Germany'. January. *IMF Country Reports* 09/15. https://www.imf.org/-/media/Websites/IMF/imported-flagship-issues/external/pubs/ft/GFSR/2009/01/pdf/_textpdf.ashx.
IMF. (International Monetary Fund). 2011. 'United Kingdom: Staff Report for the 2011 Article IV Consultation—Supplementary Informatio'. July. *IMF Country Report*, No. 11/220, Supplementary Report.
IMF (International Monetary Fund). 2013. 'Creating a Safer Financial System: Will the Volcker, Vickers and Liikanen Structural Measures Help?'. *IMF Staff Discussion Note*, May 2013. https://www.elibrary.imf.org/view/journals/006/2013/004/006.2013.issue-004-en.xml.
IMF (International Monetary Fund). 2014. 'Fiscal Monitor'. 8 October. https://www.imf.org/en/Publications/FM/Issues/2016/12/31/Back-to-Work-How-Fiscal-Policy-Can-Help-41629.
Moody's Investors Service. 2017. 'Banking System Profile—France', Sector Profile, November.
National Bank of Belgium. 2013. 'Structural Banking Reforms in Belgium: Final Report'. Brussels: NBB. Available at http://www.nbb.be/doc/ts/publications/NBBReport/2013/StructuralBankingReformsEN.pdf. Jul 2013.

National Commission on the Causes of the Financial and Economic Crisis in the United States. 2011. 'The Financial Crisis Inquiry Report'. Washington, DC: US Government Printing Office. https://www.govinfo.gov/content/pkg/GPO-FCIC/pdf/GPO-FCIC.pdf.
OBR (UK Office for Budget Responsibility). 2019. 'Bank Levy'. 16 April. https://obr.uk/forecasts-in-depth/tax-by-tax-spend-by-spend/bank-levy/.
OCC (Office of the Comptroller of the Currency). 2017. 'OCC Solicits Public Comments on Revising the Volcker Rule'. 2 August. https://www.occ.gov/news-issuances/news-releases/2017/nr-occ-2017-89.html.
PCBS (Parliamentary Commission on Banking Standards). 2012. 'First Report of Session 2012–13'. *HL Papers* 98, *HC Papers* 848. London: Stationery Office.
PCBS (Parliamentary Commission on Banking Standards). 2013a. 'Changing Banking for Good: First Report of Session 2013–14 IX'. 21 January.
PCBS (Parliamentary Commission on Banking Standards). 2013b. 'Minutes of Evidence'. *HL Papers* 27-III, *HC Papers* 175-III. https://publications.parliament.uk/pa/jt201314/jtselect/jtpcbs/27/130306.htm.
PwC (PricewaterhouseCoopers). 2011. 'PwC Newsflash: Dutch Bank Levy'. https://www.pwc.com/gr/en/news/assets/tax-dutch-bank-levy.pdf.
PwC (PricewaterhouseCoopers). 2014. 'Impact of Bank Structural Reform in Europe Report for AFME'. AFME.eu. 27 November. https://www.afme.eu/Publications/Reports/Details/pwc-report-onimpact-of-bank-structural-reforms-in-Europe.
PwC (PricewaterhouseCoopers). 2017. 'The Dutch Disadvantage'. September. https://www.pwc.nl/nl/assets/documents/pwc-the-dutch-disadvantage.pdf.
PvdA (Partij van de Arbeid). 2010. 'Verkiezingsprogramma Tweede-Kamer Verkiezingen 2010: Iedereen telt mee: De kracht van Nederland'. https://www.parlement.com/9291000/d/2010_pvda_verkiezingsprogramma.pdf.
PvdA (Partij van de Arbeid). 2012. 'Nederland sterker & socialer: Verkiezingsprogramma Tweede Kamerverkiezingen 2012: PvdA'. https://dnpprepo.ub.rug.nl/492/7/PvdATK2012def.pdf.
PvdA (Partij van de Arbeid). 2014. 'PvdA: Voor een Europa dat Werkt: Verkiezingsprogramma'. https://ep2014.bof.nl/verkiezingsprogramma/PvdA_EP2014.pdf.
PvdA (Partij van de Arbeid). 2017. 'PvdA: Een Verbonden Samenleving: Verkizeingsprogramma 2017'. https://dnpprepo.ub.rug.nl/10867/19/PvdA-Verkiezingsprogramma-2017.pdf.
Sénat. 2013. 'Rapport Fait au nom de la Commission des Finances (1) sur le Projet de loi Adopté par l'Assemblée Nationale, de Séparation et de Régulation des Activités Bancaires', 422, 12 March, rapporteur Richard Yung.
SP (Socialistische Partij). 2010. 'Een Beter Nederland voor Minder Geld: Verkizeingsprogramma SP 2011–2015'. https://www.sp.nl/sites/default/files/sp-verkiezingsprogramma-2010.pdf.
SP (Socialistische Partij). 2013. 'Nieuw Vertrouwen: Verkiezingsprogramma SP 2013–2017'. https://www.sp.nl/sites/default/files/sp-verkiezingsprogramma-nieuw-vertrouwen_0.pdf.
SP (Socialistische Partij). 2014. 'Superstaat Nee, Samenwerken Ja: Nee Tegen deze EU: Europese Verkiezingen'. https://www.sp.nl/sites/default/files/europees-verkiezingsprogramma-sp.pdf.
SP (Socialistische Partij). 2017. 'Programma voor een Sociaal Nederland voor de Verkiezingen van 15 maart 2017'. https://www.sp.nl/sites/default/files/pak_de_macht.pdf.

SPD (Sozialdemokratische Partei Deutschlands) and Bündnis 90/Die Grünen. 2013. 'Ein neuer Anlauf zur Bändigung der Finanzmärkte: Erpressungspotenzial Verringern—Geschäfts- und Investmentbanking trennen'. *Drucksachen* 17/12687. 12 March. Deutscher Bundestag. https://dserver.bundestag.de/btd/17/126/1712687.pdf.

Treasury Select Committee. 2011. 'Independent Commission on Banking: Final Report, Oral and Written Evidence'. HC680, HC1534. Session 2010–12. London: Stationery Office.

US Chamber of Commerce. 2011. 'US Chamber Calls for Re-proposal and Delay of Volcker Rule'. Press release. *uschamber.com*. 16 November. https://www.uschamber.com/press-release/us-chamber-calls-re-proposal-and-delay-volcker-rule.

US Senate Permanent Subcommittee on Investigations. 2011. 'Wall Street and the Financial Crisis: Anatomy of a Financial Collapse'. Majority and Minority Staff Report. 13 April. Washington, DC. https://www.hsgac.senate.gov/imo/media/doc/PSI%20REPORT%20-%20Wall%20Street%20&%20the%20Financial%20Crisis-Anatomy%20of%20a%20Financial%20Collapse%20(FINAL%205-10-11).pdf.

US Treasury Department. 2009. 'Financial Regulatory Reform, A New Foundation: Rebuilding Financial Supervision and Regulation'. Washington, DC.

US Treasury Department. 2012. 'Troubled Asset Relief Program—Transaction Report'. 10 September. Washington, DC. https://www.treasury.gov/initiatives/financial-stability/reports/Documents/August%202012%20Monthly%20Report.pdf.

Veltrop, D., and J. de Haan. 2014. 'I Just Cannot Get You Out of My Head: Regulatory Capture of Financial Sector Supervisors'. *De Nederlandsche Bank Working Papers* 410. https://papers.ssrn.com/sol3/papers.cfm?abstractid=2391123.

VVD (Volkspartij voor de Vrijheid en Democratie). 2010. 'Orde op Zaken: Conceptverkiezingsprogramma 2010'. https://dnpprepo.ub.rug.nl/3/2/VVD-VerkProg-TK-2010-concept.pdf.

VVD (Volkspartij voor de Vrijheid en Democratie). 2012. 'Niet Doorschuiven maar Aanpakken: Verkiezingsprogramma VVD 2012–2017: Tweede Kamerverkiezingen 12 September 2012'. https://www.vvd.nl/content/uploads/2016/11/verkprog2012.pdf.

VVD (Volkspartij voor de Vrijheid en Democratie). 2014. 'Europa Waar Nodig: Verkiezingsprogramma VVD: Europees Parlement 2014'. https://www.vvd.nl/content/uploads/2016/11/verkprogeuropa2014.pdf.

VVD (Volkspartij voor de vrijheid en democratie). 2016. 'Zeker Nederland: VVD Verkizeingsprogramma 2017–2021'. https://storage.googleapis.com/caramel-binder-207612.appspot.com/uploaded/hofvantwente.vvd.nl/files/58d3d3e344522/het-verkiezingsprogramma-volledig.pdf.

Walker, D. (2009). 'A Review of Corporate Governance in UK Banks and Other Financial Industry Entities'. 26 November. https://webarchive.nationalarchives.gov.uk/ukgwa/20100407204218/http://www.hm-treasury.gov.uk/d/walker_review_261109.pdf.

WRR (Wetenschappelijke Raad voor het Regeringsbeleid). 2019. 'Geld en Schuld, de Publieke Rol van Banken'. 17 January. https://www.wrr.nl/publicaties/rapporten/2019/01/17/geld-en-schuld—de-publieke-rol-van-banken.

Legislation

Dodd–Frank Wall Street Reform and Consumer Protection Act H.R. 4173. 2010. Washington, DC. https://www.cftc.gov/sites/default/files/idc/groups/public/@swaps/documents/file/hr4173_enrolledbill.pdf.

Dutch Government. 2012. 'Wet bijzondere maatregelen financiële ondernemingen' [Intervention Act]. *Staatsblad van het Koninkrijk der Nederlanden*. 12 June. https://zoek.officielebekendmakingen.nl/stb-2012-241.html.

European Parliament and the Council. 2009. 'Regulation (EC) No. 1060/2009 of the European Parliament and of the Council on Credit Rating Agencies', 16 September. https://eur-lex.europa.eu/legal-content/EN/TXT/?uri=uriserv:OJ.L_.2009.302.01.0001.01.ENG&toc=OJ:L:2009:302:TOC.

European Parliament and the Council. 2013. *Capital Requirements Directive IV*. Directive 2013/36/EU. 26 June. https://eur-lex.europa.eu/legal-content/EN/ALL/?uri=CELEX%3A32013L0036.

European Parliament and the Council. 2014. Bank Recovery and Resolution Directive (BRRD). Directive 2014/59/EU. 15 May. https://eur-lex.europa.eu/legal-content/EN/TXT/?uri=uriserv:OJ.L_.2014.173.01.0190.01.ENG.

Financial Choice Act H.R. 10. 2017. Washington, DC. https://www.congress.gov/bill/115th-congress/house-bill/10.

French Government. 2009. 'Arrêté du 5 mai 2009 relatif à l'identification, la mesure, la gestion et le contrôle du risque de liquidité'. NOR: ECET0908654A. 20 May. https://www.legifrance.gouv.fr/jorf/id/JORFTEXT000020635107.

French Government. 2013. 'Loi de Separation et de Regulation des Activités Bancaires'. NOR: EFIX1239994L. 26 July. https://www.legifrance.gouv.fr/jorf/id/JORFTEXT000027754539?r=SWaVINHLiJ.

HM Treasury. 2009. Banking Act 2009. London: Stationery Office. https://www.legislation.gov.uk/ukpga/2009/1

Single Resolution Mechanism Regulation (SRMR). 2014. 'Regulation (EU) No. 806/2014 of the European Parliament and of the Council of 15 July 2014 Establishing Uniform Rules and a Uniform Procedure for the Resolution of Credit Institutions and Certain Investment Firms in the Framework of a Single Resolution Mechanism and a Single Resolution Fund'.

US Senate. 2010. 'Prohibiting Certain High-Risk Investment Activities by Banks and Bank Holding Companies'. Testimony before the US Senate Committee on Banking, Housing and Urban Affairs, 111th Congress, 5–8, 49–51. 2 February 2010.

Position Papers

ABI (Italian Banking Association). 2013. 'ABI Response to the DG Internal Market and Services Consultation Paper—'Reforming the Structure of the EU Banking Sector'. Rome. https://ec.europa.eu/info/departments/financial-stability-financial-services-and-capital-markets-union/consultations-banking-and-finance_en.

AFEP (French Association of Private Enterprises). 2013. 'Response of AFEP to the Consultation of the European Commission on the Reform of the Structure of the Banking Sector in the European Union'. https://ec.europa.eu/finance/consultations/2013/banking-structural-reform/contributions_en.htm.

AFME–ISDA (Association for Financial Markets in Europe–International Swaps and Derivatives Association). 2013. 'Response Submission from AFME and ISDA to the Consultation by the Commission on the Structural Reform of the Banking Sector'. 11 July. https://ec.europa.eu/finance/consultations/2013/banking-structural-reform/docs/contributions/registered-organisations/afme-isda-joint-response_en.pdf.

AFR (Americans for Financial Reform). 2017. 'The Trump Treasury and the Big Bank Agenda'. Ourfinancialsecurity.org. https://ourfinancialsecurity.org/wp-content/uploads/2017/06/The-Trump-Treasury-And-The-Big-Bank-Agenda.pdf.

Bachus, S. 2010. Letter to Members of the Financial Services Oversight Council. 3 November, Washington, DC. http://media.ft.com/cms/d983eaa6-e793-11df-8ade-00144feab49a.pdf.

BaFin. 2009. 'Mindestanforderungen an das Risikomanagement—MaRisk'. 14 August. https://www.caplaw.eu/file_download.php?l=de&sect=ov&mod=Kapitalmarktrecht&type=grundlagen&c=36&q=&d=bafin_rundschreiben_marisk_090814.pdf.

BaFin. 2016. 'Interpretive Guidance on Article 2 of the German Act on Ring-Fencing Risk and the Recovery and Resolution Planning for Credit Institutions and Financial Groups dated 7 August, Official Journal I p. 3090 Bank Separation Act (*Abschirmungsgesetz*)'. https://www.bundesbank.de/resource/blob/623090/eb1ea4ea75aa2abbf56049d349aca6e2/mL/interpretative-guidance-bafin-data.pdf.

Banco Popular. 2013. 'Response to EC Consultation on the Reforming the Structure of the EU Banking Sector'. 11 July. https://ec.europa.eu/finance/consultations/2013/banking-structural-reform/docs/contributions/non-registered-organisations/banco-popular_en.pdf.

Bank of England. 2011. 'News Release—Financial Policy Committee Statement from its Policy Meeting, 20 September'. Press Office. Accessed 12 January 2014. https://www.bankofengland.co.uk/-/media/boe/files/statement/fpc/2011/financial-policy-committee-statement-september-2011.pdf.

Barclays. 2013. 'Barclays Response to the European Commission's Consultation on Reform of the EU Banking Sector'. 11 July. https://ec.europa.eu/finance/consultations/2013/banking-structural-reform/docs/contributions/registered-organisations/barclays_en.pdf.

BBA (British Bankers' Association). 2012. 'BBA Statement on European Commission Liikanen Review of EU Banking Sector', 2 October. https://www.bba.org.uk/news/press-releases/bba-statement-on-european-commission-liikanen-review-of-eu-banking-sector/#.YLU0Oy0RpNg.

BBA (British Bankers' Association). 2013. 'Reforming the Structure of the EU Banking Sector'. https://ec.europa.eu/finance/consultations/2013/banking-structural-.

BBA–FBF (British Bankers' Association–French Banking Federation). 2014. 'EU Structural Reform: Better Regulation', 24 November. https://www.bba.org.uk/policy/financial-and-risk-policy/bank-reform/european-and-international/eu-structural-reform-better-regulation/.

BBVA (Banco Bilbao Vizcaya Argentaria). 2017. 'European Commission Withdraws Banking Structural Reform Proposal'. BBVA Research. 27 October. https://www.bbvaresearch.com/wp-content/uploads/2017/10/Regulation-Watch-EC-withdraws-Banking-Structural-Reform.pdf.

BCBS (Basel Committee on Banking Supervision). 2010a. 'Group of Governors and Heads of Supervision Announces Higher Global Minimum Capital Standards'. Press release. BIS.org. 12 September. https://www.bis.org/press/p100912.htm.

BCBS (Basel Committee on Banking Supervision). 2010b. 'Assessing the Macroeconomic Impact of the Transition to Stronger Capital and Liquidity Requirements'. *Final Report*. BIS.org. 17 December. https://www.bis.org/publ/othp12.htm.

BDB (Bundesverband deutscher Banken). 2012a. 'Positionspapier Verbessert eine Bankenstrukturreform in Europa die Finanzstabilität?' 23 May. https://bankenverband.de/media/files/BdB-PP_23052012.pdf.

REFERENCES

BDB (Bundesverband deutscher Banken). 2012b. 'Trennbanken Kein Geeigneter Weg zur Erhöhung der Finanzstabilität in Deutschland'. 2 October. https://www.bvr.de/Presse/Deutsche_Kreditwirtschaft/Deutsche_Kreditwirtschaft_Trennbanken_kein_geeigneter_Weg_zur_Erhoehung_der_Finanzstabilitaet_in_Deutschland_Wirtschaftsstandort_wuerde_geschwaecht.

BDB (Bundesverband deutscher Banken). 2012c. 'Comments of the Association of German Banks on the Final Report of the High-Level Expert Group on Reforming the Structure of the EU Banking Sector'. 8 November. https://bankenverband.de/media/files/BdB-StN_08112012_en.pdf.

BDB (Bundesverband deutscher Banken). 2014. 'Bankenverband zur Veröffentlichung eines Vorschlags der EU-Kommission zur Bankenstrukturreform'. 29 January. Berlin. https://bankenverband.de/newsroom/presse-infos/bankenverband-zur-veroeffentlichung-eines-vorschlags-der-eu-kommission-zur-bankenstrukturreform/.

BDI–DA (Federation of German Industries–German Institute for Share Promotion). 2013. 'EU Commission's Consultation Paper on Reforming the Structure of the EU Banking Sector'. Berlin/Frankfurt am Main. https://ec.europa.eu/finance/consultations/2013/banking-structural-reform/contributions_en.htm.

BDI–DIHK–BDB (Federation of German Industries–German Chamber of Commerce and Industry–Association of German Banks). 2015. 'Banking Structural Reform Puts Corporate Financing at Risk'. 29 January. Berlin. https://bankenverband.de/media/files/2015-01-28-BSR-Position-Paper-BDI-DIHK-BdB_final_OX3qhwT.pdf.

BEUC. 2015. 'Structural Banking Reform: MEPs Block Weakened Rules on Bank Separation'. 4 June. Brussels. https://www.beuc.eu/press-media/news-events/structural-banking-reform-mepsblock-weakened-rules-bank-separation.

BIS (Bank for International Settlements). 2018. 'FSB, Gloval Shadow Banking Monitoring Report 2016'. May.

Bos, W. 2010. 'Letter to Timothy F. Geithner'. FM/2009/188 M. 25 January.

Bundesbank. 2007. '2007 Financial Stability Review'. November. https://www.bundesbank.de/resource/blob/704384/292727e0ea95bcb2aee69f74eac5ebf1/mL/2007-finanzstabilitaetsbericht-data.pdf.

CBI (Confederation of British Industry). 2013. 'Structural Reform of the Banking Sector: CBI Submission to the European Commission'. July. https://ec.europa.eu/finance/consultations/2013/banking-structural-reform/docs/contributions/registered-organisations/confederation-of-british-industry-cbi-_en.pdf.

Chisnall, P. 2014. 'Better Regulation Will Only Come if the European Commission. Reconsiders its Proposals for Banking Structural Reform'. British Bankers' Association, London. 24 November.

Crédit Agricole. 2013. 'European Commission Consultation on Reforming the Structure of the EU Banking Sector—Response of the Crédit Agricole Group'. 11 July. https://ec.europa.eu/finance/consultations/2013/banking-structural-reform/docs/contributions/registered-organisations/credit-agricole-group_en.pdf.

De Larosière Group. 2009. 'The High-Level Group on Financial Supervision in the EU'. Report. 25 February. https://ec.europa.eu/economy_finance/publications/pages/publication14527_en.pdf.

Deutsche Bank. 2013. 'Reforming the Structure of the EU Banking Sector'. 11 July. London. https://ec.europa.eu/finance/consultations/2013/banking-structural-reform/docs/contributions/registered-organisations/deutsche-bank_en.pdf.

Djankov, S., J. Ligi, I. Simonyte, I. Miklos, E. Salgado, A. Borg, P. Norman, and G. Osborne. 2011. 'Letter to Commissioners Michel Barnier and Ollie Rehn'. 19 May. http://online.wsj.com/public/resources/documents/BASEL-Letter-20110519.pdf.

DK (Deutsche Kreditwirtschaft). 2013a. 'Deutsche Kreditwirtschaft Warnt vor zu Großer Eile bei Gesetzesplänen zur Abspaltung des Eigenhandels von Kreditinstituten'. 31 January. Berlin. https://die-dk.de/themen/pressemitteilungen/deutsche-kreditwirtschaft-warnt-vor-zu-groer-eile-bei-gesetzesplanen-zur-abspaltung-des-eigenhandels-von-kreditinstituten-f91d9e/.

DK (Deutsche Kreditwirtschaft). 2013b. 'Opinion to Directorate General Internal Market and Services: Consultation Paper on Reforming the Structure of the EU Banking Sector'. 13 July. https://bankenverband.de/media/files/DK-StN_10072013_en.pdf.

DK (Deutsche Kreditwirtschaft). 2014a. 'Comments on the Proposal for a Regulation of the European Parliament and of the Council on structural measures improving the resilience of EU credit institutions dated 29 January 2014'. COM (2014) 43. 14 July. https://www.bvr.de/p.nsf/0/EF155A0A59D3A70DC1257DC700489D07/$file/ENG_DK%20Stellungnahme%20TrennbankenVO%2014072014.pdf.

DK (Deutsche Kreditwirtschaft). 2014b. 'Stellungnahme DK zum EU-Trennbankenvorschlag'. 14 March. Berlin. https://bankenverband.de/themen/eu-trennbankenvorschlag/.

EACB (European Association of Co-operative Banks). 2012. 'EACB Contribution to the Consultation by the High Level Expert Group on Reforming the Structure of the EU Banking Sector'. 1 June. http://www.eacb.coop/en/news/eacb-news/eacb-contribution-to-the-consultation-by-the-high-level-expert-group-on-reforming-the-structure-of-the-eu-banking-sector.html.

EACB (European Association of Co-operative Banks). 2013. 'Draft EACB Response to the Commission Consultation on Reforming the Structure of EU Banking Sector'. 11 July. https://ec.europa.eu/finance/consultations/2013/banking-structural-reform/contributions_en.htm. https://ec.europa.eu/finance/consultations/2013/banking-structural-reform/docs/contributions/registered-organisations/european-association-of-co-operative-banks_en.pdf.

EAPB (European Association of Public Banks). 2013. 'EAPB Comments on the Consultation of the European Commission. Reforming the Structure of the Banking Sector'. 11 July. https://ec.europa.eu/finance/consultations/2013/banking-structural-reform/docs/contributions/registered-organisations/european-association-of-public-banks_en.pdf.

EBA (European Banking Authority). 2012. 'Opinion of the European Banking Authority on the Recommendations of the High-Level Expert Group on Reforming the Structure of the EU Banking Sector'. EBA BS 2012 219. 11 December. https://www.eba.europa.eu/sites/default/documents/files/documents/10180/16103/ee9e65a6-9dac-4777-898a-1e1bd57f7c64/EBA-BS-2012-219—opinion-on-HLG-Liikanen-report—2-.pdf.

EBA (European Banking Authority). 2015. 'Guidelines on Methods for Calculating Contributions to Deposit Guarantee Schemes'. EBA/GL/2015/10. May. London: EBA.

EBF (European Banking Federation). 2012a. 'Response from the European Banking Federation on the Final Report from the High-Level Expert Group on Reforming the Structure of the EU Banking Sector, Chaired by Erkki Liikanen'. 13 November. Brussels. http://www.ebf-fbe.eu/uploads/D1994D-2012-Final%20EBF%20consultation%20response%20for%20the%20final%20report%20from%20the%20Liikanen%20HLEG.pdf.

EBF (European Banking Federation). 2012b. 'EBF Key Information Documents: The Liikanen Report Mandatory Separation of High-Risk Trading Activities'. Brussels. https://www.ebf.eu/wp-content/uploads/2017/01/KID-final-Likkanen.pdf.

EBF (European Banking Federation). 2013. 'EBF Response to the European Commission Consultation on the Structural Reform of the Banking Sector'. 10 July. https://ec.

europa.eu/finance/consultations/2013/banking-structural-reform/docs/contributions/registered-organisations/european-banking-federation_en.pdf.

EBF (European Banking Federation). 2014. 'The European Commission's Proposal for a Regulation on Structural Measures Improving the Resilience of EU Credit Institutions: A Critical Assessment of the EBF Banking Structural Reform Expert Group'. 11 November. https://www.ebf.eu/wp-content/uploads/2017/01/EBF_009834-Final-report-BSR-expert-group.pdf.

EBF (European Banking Federation). 2015. 'Statement European Banks Take Note of European Parliament Report on Bank Separation'. 8 January. https://www.ebf.eu/wp-content/uploads/2017/01/EBF_012607-Statement-on-ECON-BSR-Report.pdf.

ECB (European Central Bank). 2008. *Banking Structures Report.*

ECB (European Central Bank). 2013. 'Bank Structural Reform—Position of the Eurosystem on the Commission's Consultation Document'. 24 January. https://www.ecb.europa.eu/pub/pdf/other/120128_eurosystem_contributionen.pdf.

ECB (European Central Bank). 2014. *EU Banking Structures Report.* October. https://www.ecb.europa.eu/pub/pdf/other/bankingstructuresreport201410.en.pdf.

ECB (European Central Bank). 2015. 'The fiscal impact of financial sector support during the crisis', ECB Economic Bulletin, Issue 6, pp. 74–87. https://www.ecb.europa.eu/pub/pdf/other/eb201506_article02.en.pdf.

EELV (Europe Écologie Les Verts). 2013. 'Libérer L'économie du Modèle de la Banque Universelle et du Poids des Paradis Juridiques et Fiscaux'. 23 January. https://www.eelv.fr/liberer-leconomie-du-modele-de-la-banque-universelle-et-du-poids-des-paradis-juridiques-et-fiscau/.

EFR (European Financial Services Round Table). 2013a. 'EFR Response to the Commission Consultation on Reforming the Structure of EU Banking Sector'. On file with the authors.

EFR (European Financial Services Round Table). 2013b. 'EFR Answers to the Green Paper Questions: Green Paper on Long-Term Financing of the European Economy', 25 June. Brussels. https://ec.europa.eu/finance/consultations/2013/long-term-financing/docs/contributions/registered-organisations/european-financial-services-round-table1_en.pdf.

ESBG (European Savings Banks Group). 2013. 'ESBG Response to the European Commission Consultation on the Structural Reform of the Banking Sector'. July. https://www.wsbi-esbg.org/SiteCollectionDocuments/ESBG%20common%20response%20to%20the%20European%20Commission%20consultation%20on%20the%20Structural%20Reform%20of%20the%20Banking%20Sector.pdf.

EuroFinUse. 2013. EuroFinUse's Response to the European Commission Consultation Document on 'Reforming the Structure of the EU Banking Sector'. 11 July. https://ec.europa.eu/finance/consultations/2013/banking-structural-reform/docs/contributions/registered-organisations/eurofinuse_en.pdf.

FBF (French Banking Federation). 2013a. 'Réforme Bancaire: Rôle de la Banque de Marché et Comparaisons Internationales. January. http://mobile.fbf.fr/fr/files/94MJYC/Reforme-bancaire-role-bqe-de-marche-janvier2013.pdf.

FBF (French Banking Federation). 2013b. 'French Banking Federation Response on the European Commission Consultative Document Reforming the Structure of the EU Banking Sector'. https://ec.europa.eu/finance/consultations/2013/banking-structural-reform/contributions_en.htm. https://ec.europa.eu/finance/consultations/2013/banking-structural-reform/docs/contributions/registered-organisations/federation-bancaire-francaise_en.pdf.

FBF (French Banking Federation). 2013c. 'Réforme Bancaire: Mythes ou Réalité—Des Réponses aux Idées Reçues sur les Activités Bancaires'. Paris: Direction Information et Relations Extérieures. http://www.banques.fr/fr/files/94FKPM/Reforme-bancaire-mythes-ou-realites-janvier2013.pdf.

FBF (French Banking Federation). 2014. 'The Draft Regulation on Structural Reform in European Banking Would Undermine Corporate Financing'. 29 January. http://www.fbf.fr/web/Internet2010/Content_EN.nsf/DocumentsByIDWeb/9FTJ6C?OpenDocument.

FBF (French Banking Federation). 2015. 'FBF Response to the Consultation on the Commission Green Paper for Capital Markets Union'. http://www.fbf.fr/fr//files/9WNJDC/FBF-response-CMU-Green-paper-13052015.pdf.

Forrester, J. P., C. A. Hitselberger, J. P. Taft, T. J. Delaney, and M. Bisanz. 2020. 'US Bank Regulators Finalize Net Stable Funding Ratio Rule'. Mayerbrown.com. 30 October. https://www.mayerbrown.com/en/perspectives-events/publications/2020/10/us-bank-regulators-finalize-net-stable-funding-ratio-rule.

Frontline. 2012. 'The Financial Crisis—The Frontline Interviews—Obama and Wall Street'. pbs.org. https://www.pbs.org/wgbh/pages/frontline/oral-history/financial-crisis/tags/obama-and-wall-street/.

Gensler, G. 2009. 'Testimony Before the House Financial Services Committee'. Commodity Futures Trading Commission. 7 October. https://www.cftc.gov/PressRoom/SpeechesTestimony/opagensler-13.

Giegold, S. 2011. 'Britische Vorschläge zur Reform des Bankensektors Sind Schritt in die Richtige Richtung—Nun Sind Deutschland und Frankreich Gefordert'. The Greens/EFA in the European Parliament. 12 September. https://sven-giegold.de/britische-vorschlage-zur-reform-des-bankensektors-sind-schritt-in-die-richtige-richtung-nun-sind-deutschland-und-frankreich-gefordert/.

Gonon, F. R., D. R. Sahr, A. Lange, M. Compton, and C. A. Hellepute. 2014. 'Does Volcker + Vickers = Liikanen? EU proposal for a Regulation on Structural Measures Improving the Resilience of EU Credit Institutions'. Mayer Brown Legal Update, February. https://www.mayerbrown.com/files/Publication/f6722a7a-b666-4384-931f-0f77d6424e37/Presentation/PublicationAttachment/1a249a85-3015-43eb-8389-26237a62e419/update_volcker_vickers_feb14.pdf.

Greens/EFA (European Free Alliance). 2014. 'Banking Sector Reform: Proposals on Separation Fall Short of What Is Needed to Repair Banking Sector'. 29 January. https://www.greens-efa.eu/en/article/press/banking-sector-reform-4468.

Greens/EFA (European Free Alliance). 2015. 'Chaotic Vote Leaves Crucial Banking Structure Reform in Limbo'. Press release. 26 May. https://www.greens-efa.eu/en/article/press/banking-sector-reform.

Haag, H., and J. L. Steffen. 2020. 'Banking Regulation in Germany: Overview'. Thomson Reuters Practical Law. https://uk.practicallaw.thomsonreuters.com/w-007-4084?transitionType=Default&contextData=(sc.Default)&firstPage=true.

Hökmark, G. (Rapporteur, Economic and Monetary Affairs Committee). 2014. 'Draft Report on the Proposal for a Regulation of the European Parliament and of the Council on Structural Measures Improving the Resilience of EU Credit Institutions'. COM(2014)0043–C7-0024/2014–2014/0020(COD). Committee on Economic and Monetary Affairs. 22 December. https://www.europarl.europa.eu/doceo/document/ECON-PR-546551_EN.pdf.

Hollande, F. 2012a. 'Les 60 Engagements'. Luipresident.fr. https://www.luipresident.fr/francois-hollande/60-engagements.

Hollande, F. 2012b. 'Bourget Discourse'. 22 January. https://www.nouvelobs.com/election-presidentielle-2012/sources-brutes/20120122.OBS9488/l-integralite-du-discours-de-francois-hollande-au-bourget.html.

HypoVereinsbank. 2010. *HypoVereinsbank Annual Report.* Munich: Unicredit Bank AG Head Office.

Issing, O., J. Asmussen, P. Krahnen, K. Regling, J. Weidmann, and W. White. 2009. 'New Financial Order Recommendations by the Issing Committee Part II'. Centre for Financial Studies. March. https://www.ifk-cfs.de/research/years/archive/2009/publication-storage/white-paper-no-2.html.

Johnson, R. 2009. 'Testimony Before the US House of Representatives Committee on Financial Services Hearing on Reform of the Over-the-Counter Derivative Market: Limiting Risk and Ensuring Fairness'. Economists' Committee for Stable, Accountable, Fair and Efficient Financial Reform. 7 October. Amherst, MA. https://www.peri.umass.edu/images/Johnson_testimony.pdf.

King, M. 2009. 'Monetary Policy Developments'. Speech delivered 20 October, Edinburgh.

La Caixa. 2013. 'Consultation by the Commission on the Structural Reform of the Banking Sector, Response by "la Caixa" Group'. https://ec.europa.eu/finance/consultations/2013/banking-structural-reform/contributions_en.htm. https://ec.europa.eu/finance/consultations/2013/banking-structural-reform/docs/contributions/non-registered-organisations/la-caixa-group_en.pdf.

Lauermann, H. U., and K. Struve. 2015. 'Bank Levies: A Step Towards Harmonisation'. *International Tax Review.* 16 June. https://www.internationaltaxreview.com/article/b1f9jyt9m1zyxp/bank-levies-a-step-toward-harmonisation.

Lepetit, J. F. 2010. *Rapport sur le Risque Systémique.* Paris: Ministère de l'Economie, de l'Industrie et de l'Emploi. https://www.vie-publique.fr/rapport/31038-rapport-sur-le-risque-systemique.

Liikanen Group (High-Level Expert Group on Reforming the Structure of the EU Banking Sector). 2012. 'Final Report'. 2 October, Brussels: Financial Stability, Financial Services and Capital Markets Union. https://ec.europa.eu/commission/presscorner/detail/en/IP_12_1048.

Lobbypedia.de. 2011. 'Expertengruppe Neue Finanzmarktarchitektur'. https://lobbypedia.de/wiki/Expertengruppe_Neue_Finanzmarktarchitektur.

Maas, C., S. Eijffinger, W. van den Goorbergh, and T. de Swann. 2009. *Naar Herstel van Vertrouwen.* The Hague: Adviescommissie Toekomst Banken. https://www.dekamer.be/kvvcr/pdf_sections/comm/common/asset.pdf.

McCarthy, A. 2013. 'Report on Reforming the Structure of the EU Banking Sector'. European Parliament, Committee on Economic and Monetary Affairs, A7-0231/2013, 2013/2021(INI), 24 June. https://www.europarl.europa.eu/doceo/document/A-7-2013-0231_EN.pdf?redirect.

Merkley.senate.gov. 2010. 'Merkley–Levin Amendments to Crack Down on High-Risk Proprietary Trading'. 10 May. https://www.merkley.senate.gov/news/press-releases/merkley-levin-amendment-to-crack-down-on-high-risk-proprietary-trading.

Mesnard, B., A. Margerit, and M. Magnus. 2017. 'The Resolution of Banco Popular'. European Parliament Briefing. Economic Governance Support Unit. https://www.europarl.europa.eu/RegData/etudes/BRIE/2017/602093/IPOL_BRI(2017)602093_EN.pdf.

Nederlandse Vereniging van Banken. 2010. 'NVB-Reactie Rapport Commissie De Wit'. 10 May. http://old.findinet.nl/bedrijfsvoering/crisis/nvb_de_wit100510.htm.

Obama, B. 2008. 'Campaign Speech'. 15 September. Grand Junction, CO.

Obama, B. 2009a. 'Remarks on Financial Regulatory Reform'. *The American Presidency Project*. 17 June. https://www.presidency.ucsb.edu/documents/remarks-financial-regulatory-reform.

Obama, B. 2009b. 'Address at Federal Regulatory Reform'. *The American Presidency Project*. 14 September. https://www.presidency.ucsb.edu/documents/remarks-new-york-city.

Obama, B. 2009c. 'Interview with Steve Kroft on CBS'. *60 Minutes*. 13 December.

Occupy the SEC. 2012. 'Comment Letter'. Occupythesec.org. 13 January. https://www.sec.gov/comments/s7-41-11/s74111-230.pdf.

OpenSecrets. 2022a. 'Client Profile: American Bankers Assn'. OpenSecrets.org. https://www.opensecrets.org/federal-lobbying/clients/summary?cycle=2021&id=D000000087.

OpenSecrets. 2022b 'Client Profile: JPMorgan Chase & Co'. OpenSecrets.org. https://www.opensecrets.org/federal-lobbying/clients/summary?id=D000000103.

Osborne, G. 2015. 'Mansion House 2015: Speech by the Chancellor of the Exchequer'. HM Treasury. Gov.uk. 10 June. https://www.gov.uk/government/speeches/mansion-house-2015-speech-by-the-chancellor-of-the-exchequer.

Paulis, E. 2012. Deputy Director General, DGMARKT. Presentation and After Dinner Discussion at the University of Edinburgh. 14 March.

Pisani-Ferry, J. 2015. 'Central Bank Advocacy of Structural Reform: Why and How?' France Stratégie. August. https://www.strategie.gouv.fr/sites/strategie.gouv.fr/files/atoms/files/pisani-ferry_jean_sintra_rev.pdf.

Samsom, D. 2012. *Beter Bankieren*. Amsterdam: PvdA.

Schmidt, A. 2012. 'Pressekonferenz zur Vorstandssitzung des Bundesverbandes deutscher Banken'. Berlin: Bundesverbandes Deutscher Banken.

Schröder, M., G. Lang, L. Jaroszek, and C. Dick. 2013. *Trennbanken: Eine Analytische Bewertung von Trennbankelementen und Trennbankensystemen im Hinblick auf Finanzmarktstabilität Abschlussbericht für den Bundesverband Öffentlicher Banken Deutschlands (VÖB), Berlin*. Mannheim: Centre for European Economic Research. http://ftp.zew.de/pub/zew-docs/gutachten/Trennbanken2013.pdf.

Smolders, N. 2012. 'Lijkanen Committee to Overhaul European Banking Industry'. *Rabobank Special Report 2012/19*. December. https://economics.rabobank.com/contentassets/165946a7c1d545bb9b4892698394ff02/sr1219nsm_liikanen_committee_to_overhaul_european_banking_industry_eng.pdf.

SOMO (Stichting Onderzoek Multinationale Ondernemingen). 2013. 'Taking Lobbying Public: The Transparency of Dutch Banks' Lobbying Activities'. SOMO. http://lobbywatch.nl/wp-content/uploads/2016/12/SOMO-2013-Taking-Lobbying-Public.pdf.

Steinbrück, P. 2012. 'Vertrauen Zurückgewinnen: Ein neuer Anlauf zur Bändigung der Finanzmärkte'. SPD Bundestags Fraktion. 25 September. https://www.spdfraktion.de/system/files/documents/konzept_aufsicht_und_regulierung_finanzmaerkte.pdf.

Treur, L. 2012. 'Retail and Investment Banking: The Trials of Separation'. *Rabobank Special Report 2012/10*. July. https://economics.rabobank.com/contentassets/d5bc0858eb5b436c8d4c48ee6bc0c694/sr1210ltr_retail_and_investment_banking.pdf.

Turner, A. 2009. *The Turner Review: A Regulatory Response to the Global Banking Crisis*. London: Financial Services Authority. http://www.actuaries.org/CTTEES_TFRISKCRISIS/Documents/turner_review.pdf.

UNI Europa Finance. 2013. 'UNI Europa Finance Response to the Consultation on Reforming the Structure of the EU Banking Sector'. 11 July. https://ec.europa.eu/

finance/consultations/2013/banking-structural-reform/docs/contributions/registered-organisations/uni-europa-finance-sector-_en.pdf.

UniCredit. 2013. 'UniCredit Reply to the European Commission's Consultation on the Structural Reform of the Banking Sector'. 11 July. https://ec.europa.eu/finance/consultations/2013/banking-structural-reform/docs/contributions/registered-organisations/unicredit_en.pdf.

Vander Stichele, M. 2016. *A Structural Problem in the Shadows: Lobbying by Banks in the Netherlands*. Amsterdam: Drukkerij Raddraaier. https://www.somo.nl/nl/wp-content/uploads/sites/2/2016/11/A-structural-problem.pdf.

Warren, E., J. McCain, M. Cantwell, and A. King. 2017. 'Senators Warren, McCain, Cantwell and King Introduce 21st Century Glass–Steagall Act'. Press release. Warren.senate.gov. 6 April. https://www.warren.senate.gov/newsroom/press-releases/senators-warren-mccain-cantwell-and-king-introduce-21st-century-glass-steagall-act.

Weidmann, J. 2014. 'Stable Banks for a Stable Europe'. Speech delivered to the 20th German Banking Congress, Berlin. 7 April. https://www.bis.org/review/r140415b.htm.

Wijffels, H. 2013. *Naar een Dienstbaar en Stabiel Bankwezen*. Den Haag: Rijksoverheid. Accessed 1 March 2019. https://www.vno-ncw.nl/sites/default/files/downloadables_vno/Rapport_Commissie_Structuur_Nederlandse_Banken_0.pdf.

WSBI-ESBG (The World Savings Banks Institute's European Savings Banks Group). 2012. 'ESBG Common Response to the European Commission Consultation on the Liikanen Report Recommendations'. November. https://ec.europa.eu/finance/consultations/2012/hleg-banking/docs/contributions/registered-organisations/european-savings-bank-group_en.pdf.

Interviews (Chronological Order)

Interview 1, US regulatory official, Washington, 1 December 2011
Interview 2, senior Bank of England official, London, 12 April 2013
Interview 3, US bank lobbyist, Washington, DC, 9 May 2013
Interview 4, financial regulation legal advisor, London, 10 May 2013
Interview 5, ICB official, London, 3 June 2013
Interview 6, UK bank lobbyist, London, 6 June 2013
Interview 7, FBF official, Paris, 6 June 2013
Interview 8, UK bank lobbyist, London, 24 July 2013
Interview 9, ICB official, London, 8 August 2013
Interview 10, UK financial lobbyist, London, 16 August 2013
Interview 11, UK bank lobbyist, London, 18 September 2013
Interview 12, UK bank lobbyist, London, 25 September 2013
Interview 13, UK bank lobbyist, London, 2 October 2013
Interview 14, UK bank lobbyist, London 15 October 2013
Interview 15, UK bank lobbyist, London, 22 May 2014
Interview 16, UK Treasury official, London, 23 June 2014
Interview 17, Socialist National Assembly finance committee member, Paris, 10 February 2016
Interview 18, UMP Senate finance committee member, Paris, 10 February 2016
Interview 19, high-ranking French banker, Paris, 11 February 2016
Interview 20, UMP National Assembly financial committee member, Paris, 12 February 2016

Interview 21, French economics expert, Paris, December 2016
Interview 22, Issing Commission member, Frankfurt, 20 January 2017
Interview 23, Belgian permanent representation to the EU, official, Brussels, 17 May 2017
Interview 24, Finnish permanent representation to the EU official, Brussels, 18 May 2017
Interview 25, EU Commission official, Directorate-General Internal Market, Brussels, 18 May 2017
Interview 26, former MEP on the Committee on Economic and Monetary Affairs during the 2009–14 and 2014–19 parliaments, Brussels, 19 May 2017
Interview 27, former MEP on the Committee on Economic and Monetary Affairs during the 2009–14 parliament, Brussels, 12 October 2017
Interview 28, former MEP on the Committee on Economic and Monetary Affairs during the 2014–19 parliament, Brussels, 13 October 2017
Interview 29, former Bundestag finance committee member and staff member, Berlin, by Skype, 13 October 2017
Interview 30, Finance Watch official, Brussels, 11 May 2018
Interview 31, WSBI-ESBG official, Brussels, 2 March 2019
Interview 32, WSBI-ESBG official, Brussels, 6 March 2019
Interview 33, Finance Watch official, Brussels, 6 March 2019
Interview 34, EBF official, Brussels, 7 March 2019
Interview 35, EACB official, Brussels, 8 March 2019
Interview 36, Liikanen Group member 1, Brussels, 8 March 2019
Interview 37, EBF policy officer, Brussels, 28 October 2019
Interview 38, Liikanen Group member 2, by email, 15 November 2019
Interview 39, DSGV official, Berlin, 21 November 2019
Interview 40, BDB official, Berlin, 22 November 2019
Interview 41, Wijffels Commission member, by e-mail, 16 April 2020
Interview 42, Maas Commission member, 5 May 2020
Interview 43, Socialist National Assembly members, Paris, 15 May 2020
Interview 44, CDA politician, 19 May 2020
Interview 45, Wijffels Commission members, by email, 25 May 2020
Interview 46, De Wit Commission member, 27 May 2020
Interview 47, NVB official, 2 June 2020
Interview 48, French Ministry of Finance official, Paris, 13 June 2020
Interview 49, Socialist National Assembly members, Paris, 26 June 2020
Interview 50, former bank lobbyist, Brussels, by email, 2 June 2021
Interview 51, European Parliament Secretariat official, Luxembourg, 23 September 2021

Index

ABLV Luxembourg 97
ABN-AMRO (Netherlands) 71t, 215, 219, 223–4, 230, 237
   Antonveneta takeover 233
acute stress scenario 90
   see also stress tests
adequacy threshold 85
ad hoc specialist groups 20–1, 30, 58–63, 281–2, 287, 291
   European Union 241, 242–3
   Netherlands 53, 216, 217, 238
   United Kingdom 147, 149, 150, 169
   United States 143
Admati, A. 181
adversarial politics 7–8, 17
Advisory Commission on the Future of Banks see Maas Commission
Advisory Scientific Committee 106
Advisory Technical Committee 106
Aegon (Netherlands) 71t, 215, 223
agenda-setting 19, 27, 31, 56–60, 242, 261, 280–1
AIG 83, 95, 110
Algebris 152
Allais, M. 208
alliance building 18, 21–2, 29, 280, 283–5, 290
   comparative financial power approach 32–3, 40, 42–5, 48, 50, 60, 62
   EU 268
   France 200
   Netherlands 216
   United Kingdom 159
   United States 123
Alliance of Liberals and Democrats for Europe (ALDE) 169, 267
alternative investment funds and securities markets 4t, 112, 116, 173–4, 184, 251, 270, 290
American Banking Association (ABA) 47, 116, 119, 132, 138
American Bridge 138
Americans for Financial Reform (AFR) 48, 122–3, 130, 138
Angelides, P. 124
Anglo-Saxon capitalism 35, 67, 142, 200, 210, 277

anti-capitalism/anti-globalization movement (ATTAC) (France) 207
anti-finance coalitions and factions 8
anti-terrorism legislation 145
Asmussen, J. 182–3
ASN Bank (Netherlands) 232
Asset-Backed Commercial Paper (ABCP) 93, 105
Asset Backed Securities (ABS) 80t, 90
asset management 116, 133, 196, 289
Asset Protection Scheme (UK) 145
Association for Financial Markets in Europe (AFME) 49, 56, 161, 259–60
Austria 45
Ayrault, J.-M. 198, 209, 210

Bachmann, M. 130
Bachus, S. 129
Bailey, A. 164, 168
bail-ins 80t, 96–7, 98, 157, 236, 245–6, 266
bail-outs 1–3, 13–14, 26, 29, 50, 95, 97, 274–5
   European Union 247
   France 194
   Germany 170, 176, 187, 188
   Netherlands 215, 222, 224, 230–1
   United Kingdom 145, 146, 152, 154
   United States 110, 113, 118, 121
Bair, S. 122, 127, 134
Balkenende, J.P. 223
Banco Populare di Vicenza 97
Banco Popular Español (Popular) 97, 258
Bank of America 101, 115, 117, 133, 134
   Merrill Lynch takeover 72, 110
Bank of Credit and Commerce International (BCCI) 144
Bank of England 48–9, 96, 104, 106, 145, 148, 150–1, 154–7, 163, 165–6, 168
   Court of Directors 103t
   Financial Policy Committee (FPC) 101
   Financial Stability Committee 103t
   Governor 88
Bankers' Oath (Netherlands) 218, 220, 227
Bank of France 198–200, 212
bank funding gap 9, 9t
Banking Act 2009 (UK) 146

INDEX 345

Banking Act (Germany) 22–3, 170, 173–4, 182, 185
Banking Association (ABI) (Italy) 257
Banking Association (BDB) (Germany) 175, 179, 180, 256, 259, 268
Banking Code (Netherlands) 218, 220, 222, 226, 227, 234, 236
Banking Commission (France) 92
Banking Industry Committee (DK) (Germany) 52
banking law (Germany) 105
Banking Reform Act (UK) 5t, 142, 157–62, 164–5, 167, 168
banking scandals
  France 193, 207
  Germany 189
  Netherlands 218, 221–2
  United Kingdom 144, 154, 162
  United States 134
banking system assets 13t
banking system concentration 14t
Bank for International Settlements (BIS) 24, 66, 81
Bank Recapitalisation Fund (UK) 145
Bank Recovery and Resolution Directive (BRRD) (EU) 15, 76–7, 80t, 96, 99, 174, 196, 204, 230, 255, 268
Bank of Scotland 145
Bank Separation Law (*Trennbankengesetz*) (Germany) 4t, 28, 170, 173, 178, 184, 188, 190
bank supervision, reinforcing 102–7, 103t
Bannon, S. 137
Banques Populaires 71t, 72, 193
Banques Populaires, Caisses d'Epargne (BPCE) (France) 71t, 72, 193–4, 196, 203
Bänziger, H. 244
Barclays (UK) 24, 36, 71t, 101, 134, 152–3, 159–62, 166, 207
Barings Bank 144
Barnier, M. 2, 201, 240, 243, 250, 263, 266, 272, 275
Barr, M. 123
Barroso, J.-M. 240
Basel Committee on Banking Supervision (BCBS) 26, 90
  Netherlands 66, 84–5, 86–7, 89, 91–2, 234
  United Kingdom 154
  United States 108
Basel I 84, 87
Basel II 84–5, 87, 88, 92
Basel III 66, 79t, 85, 89–93, 107
  capital requirements 77, 86–7, 88

Final Rule 85
Germany 180
Netherlands 224, 232, 233
United Kingdom 151, 155, 167
Baumel, L. 206
Bear Stearns 95
Belgium 216
Bell, S. 7, 38
Berger, K. 195, 206, 210–11
Bernanke, B. 110
Berruyer, O. 206
Better Markets 122, 134, 139
Bierman, M. 231–2
'Big Bang' deregulation (UK) 49–50, 144
Bipartisan Policy Center (USA) 118, 122
Blankfein, L. 117, 126
Block, F. 37
BNP-Paribas (France) 71t, 193–4, 196, 214
  banque de financement et d'investissement (BFI) 195
  Dexia takeover 212
  Fortis takeover 212
Boeing Aerospace 117
bonuses and bonus caps 3, 66, 70, 71t, 72, 74t, 78t, 82, 83, 84, 276
  Netherlands 218, 220–1, 222, 232
  United Kingdom 154
  United States 114, 116
Born, B. 132
Bos, W. 2, 29, 215, 218–20, 223–5, 233, 238, 275
Bowles, S. 266, 271
BP 133
Bradford and Bingley (UK) 145, 150
Bradley, B. 122
Briatta, G. 199
bright-line rules 139
British Bankers' Association (BBA) 150, 153, 161, 254, 259
  see also UK Finance257
British Chambers of Commerce (BCC) 153
Browne, A. 259
Brown, G. 50, 72, 73t, 145
Brown, S. 114–15, 123, 126, 127–8, 135
Building Societies Act (UK) 161
Bundesbank (Germany) 103t, 105, 185
Bundesrat (Germany) 184–6, 188
Bundestag (Germany) 170, 182–9
Burgmans Commission 222
Bush, G. 17, 110
Business Council (USA) 126
business power theories 7, 30, 31, 37–41, 44, 278–82

Business Roundtable and National Association of Manufacturers (USA) 117
Busiris, S. 208
buy-ins 20, 59–60, 143, 147, 165, 169, 281

Cable, V. 146, 151, 154, 155, 160, 162
Cahuzac, J. 194
Cameron, D. 2, 151
Campa, J.M. 245
Cantwell, M. 123, 135
capital adequacy 84–5
capital buffers 85, 88
   European Union 240, 246
   Netherlands 232, 234
   United Kingdom 157–8
capitalism
   Anglo-Saxon 35, 67, 142, 200, 210, 277
   comparative 54
   liberal market 7
   Varieties of Capitalism (VoC) 277, 284
   Varieties of Financial Capitalism (VoFC) 34–5
Capital Markets Union (EU) 98, 259, 263, 268
capital requirements 5t, 14–16, 24–6, 28, 33, 35, 66, 98–9, 107, 274
   European Union 84–8, 250, 268, 270
   France 86, 88–9, 212
   Germany 86, 88–9, 185
   Netherlands 86, 88–9, 218, 224–5, 230, 233
   reinforced 84–9
   United Kingdom 86–9, 142, 146, 148, 151, 155, 167, 168
   United States 84–9, 114, 136, 138
Capital Requirements Directive (CRD) (EU) 84, 85, 233
Capital Requirements Directive IV (CRD-IV) (EU) 78t, 79t, 80t, 83, 86–8, 90, 92, 94, 252
Capital Requirements Regulation (CRR) 92
capital strengthening 79t
Carrez, G. 211–12
case selection and alternative explanations 8–18
Caterpillar 117
Cazes, J. 203
central counterparties (CCPs) 112
centralized associations 29
Chabanet, D. 208
Chamber of Industry and Commerce (EU) 268
Chambers of Commerce and Industry (DIHK) (Germany) 180
Chifflet, J.-P. 196–7
Chilton, B. 132
Christian Democratic Party (CDA) (Netherlands) 17, 52, 215, 218, 224, 226–7, 229, 234

Christian Democratic Union (CDU) (Germany) 17, 105, 171, 175–6, 177–8, 188, 190
Christian Social Union (CSU) (Germany) 17, 175–6, 177
Christian Union (CU) (Netherlands) 17, 229
Citigroup 101, 110, 115, 117–18, 134
CityUK 50
clawback rule 78t, 83, 84
Clayton, J. 137
Clearing House, The (USA) 138
Clegg, N. 151, 162
Clinton, H. 135–6
club governance 48, 59
Coalition Agreement (UK) 147, 149
Coalition for Derivatives End-Users (USA) 117, 119
Coalition of Physical Energy Companies (USA) 133
Coburn, T. 124
Coface (France) 203
Cohn, G. 137
Cohrs, M. 163
Cole, C. 122
College of Commissioners (EU) 243, 251
Collins Amendment (USA) 5t
Combée, B. 236
commercial banking 95
   European Union 247
   France 54, 204
   Germany 51, 88, 175, 178–80, 181, 182, 256
   Netherlands 228
   United States 112, 132, 135
Commerzbank (Germany) 71t, 72, 188
Commission on the Structure of Dutch Banks *see* Wijffels Commission
Committee on Economic and Monetary Affairs (EU) 240–1, 265–7
   'Reforming the Structure of the EU Banking Sector' 265
Committee on Economics and Finance (EU) 261
Committee of European Banking Supervisors (CEBS) 56
Commodity Futures Trading Commission (CFTC) (USA) 104, 106, 112, 119, 130, 131, 133–4
Commodity Markets Oversight Coalition (CMOC) (USA) 119
Common Deposit Guarantee Scheme (DSG) Directive (EU) 77
Common Equity Tier 1 (CET1) capital 4t, 5t, 85, 157
Communist Party (France) 208

INDEX 347

community banking 21–2, 47, 120–2, 138, 140, 280, 284
comparative capitalism 54
comparative democracy 7
comparative financial power 18, 27, 30, 31–64, 274, 278, 284
 agenda-setting and venue shifting 56–60
 case study selection 62–3
 financial interest lobbying 41–4
 interest representation, modes of 44–56
  competitive financial power 46–50
  cooperative financial power 50–6
 political economy 31–41
  business power theories 37–41
  comparative political economy (CPE) 34–7
  international political economy (IPE) 32–4
comparative political economy (CPE) 7–8, 30, 31, 34–7, 277, 285
Competition and Markets Authority (UK) 165
competitive financial power 18–20, 27–8, 31, 46–50, 61t, 63, 289
 financial interest lobbying 44, 60
 France 191
 political economy of finance 283–4, 286
 regulatory reform typologies 287
 United Kingdom 46, 48–9, 150–7, 169
 United States 46–8, 115–24, 140
comply or explain principle 106, 107, 218
Comprehensive Capital Analysis and Review (CCAR) (USA) 101
Confederation of British Industry (CBI) 153, 159, 161, 166
Confederation of Skilled Crafts (ZDH) (Germany) 180
Conference Committee (USA) 127
conflict contraction 22, 23, 29
 agenda setting and venue shifting 57–60
 business power theories 280–2
 European Union 242
 financial interest group lobbying 61
 France 192, 193, 201–7
 Germany 171, 182, 185–9
 Netherlands 216, 217, 238
 no reform 62
 regulatory reform typologies 288
conflict expansion 19–20, 22
 agenda-setting and venue shifting 57–60
 business power theories 280–2
 durable reform 62
 European Union 241–2, 244, 248, 250, 260–1, 265, 273
 financial interest group lobbying 61
 France 205
 Netherlands 217, 222, 227

 regulatory reform typologies 288
 United Kingdom 143, 147, 149, 163, 169
 United States 109, 114, 128, 134, 140
congressional committees (USA) 129
consensus building/consensual politics 7, 8, 17, 59–60, 227, 231, 281
Conservative-Liberal-Democrat coalition (UK) 2–3, 73t, 87, 104, 142, 147, 275
Conservative Party (UK) 17, 142, 144, 146, 154–5, 158, 167, 267
Consultative Committee on the Financial Sector (CCSF) (France) 202
Consumentenbon (Netherlands) 220
consumer affairs lobby 261–2
consumer associations 43, 236, 249
Consumer Federation of America 122
Consumer Financial Protection Bureau (CFPB) (USA) 104, 105, 106, 112, 113, 121, 129, 136–7
consumer rights associations (France) 207
contested reform 21–2, 31, 61t, 62, 287
 see also in particular United States
cooperative banks 9, 22, 88, 203, 278
 European Union 251, 254, 255–9
 France 194
 Germany 51–2, 179–80, 184, 256
 see also public law cooperative and savings banks (Germany)
cooperative financial power 18–23, 27, 29–31, 50–6, 61t, 63, 289
 European Union 55–6, 241, 253–62, 273
 financial interest lobbying 44, 60
 France 53–5, 192, 193, 196, 198, 213, 254, 256–9, 261
 Germany 51–2, 54, 171–2, 178–81, 190, 254, 256–9, 260
 Netherlands 52–3, 54, 216, 217, 231–5, 238, 254
 no reform 62
 political economy of finance 283–5, 286
 regulatory reform typologies 287
 TBTF banks 65
 United Kingdom 55, 257–8
 United States 55
corporate governance reforms (EU) 246
corporatism 54, 291
 see also neo-corporatism
Council of Central Business Organization (RCO) (Netherlands) 52
Council of Financial Regulation and Systemic Risk (CORE-FRIS) (France) 200, 202–4, 213
Council on Financial Stability (HCSF) (France) 202

countervailing groups 18–21, 28, 43–4, 46, 61–2, 283–4, 287–8
Couppey-Soubeyran, J. 207–8
covered funds 109, 112, 133, 138–9
Crapo, M. 137
Crédit Agricole 134, 193, 196, 207
credit banking (France) 197
credit guarantees 2, 65, 70, 145, 194, 215, 275
Crédit Mutuel 194, 196
credit rating agencies (CRAs) 66, 78t, 81–2
Cridland, J. 153
Culpepper, P.D. 39–40, 279–80

Darling, A. 145, 155
decentralization 51, 281
Dedieu, F. 209
Dekabank (Germany) 172, 178, 180
De Larosière Group 106
delegation theories 58–9
deleveraging 27
Deloitte 151
de minimis exception 4t, 128
Democrats (EU) 266–7
Democrats (USA) 22, 108, 111, 113–15, 122–3, 125, 127, 129, 136, 138, 140, 280
demonstration effect 43
Demos (USA) 122
Department of Trade and Industry (DTI) (UK) 49
depoliticization 19–21, 27–9, 31
  agenda setting and venue shifting 58–60
  business power theories 281, 282
  durable reform 62
  European Union 241–2, 273
  interest group lobbying 61
  Netherlands 216, 238
  regulatory reform typologies 287
  United Kingdom 143, 147, 150, 165, 169, 191
deposit banking (France) 193, 197
deposit guarantee schemes 75–7, 98, 252
Deposit Insurance Fund (DIF) (USA) 95
deposit-taking banks 174, 247, 252, 253, 267–8, 270–1
deregulation 7, 45, 49, 111, 144
derivatives trading 68, 113
  European Union 251, 268
  United States 116, 119, 122, 127, 133–4
Deutsche Bank 36, 52, 101, 134, 172, 177, 179, 181, 187, 189
  Commerzbank merger 181
De Wit Commission 21, 30, 63, 216–17, 223, 234–5, 236
  final report 220–1
Dexi 102

Diamond, B. 160
Die Linke (Germany) 176, 187, 189
Dijsselbloem, J. 226
Dimon, J. 117–18, 120
Directorate-General Internal Market (DG MARKT) 243
Dodd, C. 125
Dodd-Frank Act stress tests (DFAST) 101
Dodd-Frank Act (USA) 4t, 5t, 109, 115–17, 119, 122–4, 126–33, 135–8, 140–1, 146
  TBTF banks 78t, 80t, 81, 84–5, 95–6, 98–9, 100t, 101
  see also Volcker Rule
Dombrovkis, V. 271
Döring, P. 177
double counting of insurance subsidiary capital 79t
draft law (France) 194–6, 198–211
Draghi, M. 209
Dresdner Bank (Germany) 72, 183
Drezner, D. 32
DSB Bank (Netherlands) 222
durable reform 20, 31, 61–2, 61t, 142–3, 169, 191, 287
Dutch Banking Association (NVB) 21, 52, 53, 217, 218, 231, 234–5
Dutch National Bank (DNB) 103t, 219, 222, 223, 225, 226, 229–30, 233
DZ Bank (Germany) 172, 178, 180, 184

Ecole Nationale d'Administration (ENA) 199
Economic Growth, Regulatory Relief and Consumer Protection Act (2018) (USA) 96, 137
Economic and Monetary Affairs Committee (EU) 269
Economic and Monetary Union (EMU) (EU) 144
Economic Recovery Advisory Board (USA) 112
Eijffinger, S. 217, 236
elite pluralism 19, 56, 241, 283
Endrejat, V. 253
Enhanced Cooperation 76
Enria, A. 264
equity capital 167
equity purchases 145
European Association of Cooperative Banks (EACB) 56, 256
European Association of Public Banks (EAPB) 256
European Banking Authority (EBA) 56, 77, 78t, 83, 102, 104, 251–2, 264–5
European Banking Federation (EBF) 56, 254–5, 258, 261, 268

European Banking Union 34, 56, 77, 96, 103t, 226, 236, 250, 271
European Central Bank (ECB) 66, 88, 106, 227, 264–5, 270
  Governing Council 263
European Commission 3, 6, 16, 23, 30, 66, 243–4, 252–3, 256
  bank supervision reinforcement 106
  business power theories 280
  capital requirements 86–7, 88
  consultation document (2013) 248–9, 258–9, 261, 262
  cooperative financial power 55–6, 254
  credit rating agencies (CRAs) 81
  draft regulation (2014) 240–2, 250–4, 259–66, 267–8, 270–3
  draft regulation on structural reform 188
  Germany 175, 189
  legislative politics 264, 265–6
  political economy of finance 285
  revenue-raising regulation and fiscal policy 76
  structural reform proposals 260, 276
  United Kingdom 162, 168
European Conservatives and Reformists 267
European Consumer Organization (BEUC) 261–2
European Council of Ministers 55, 216, 240–2, 243, 261, 262, 270–2, 280
European Parliament 3, 23, 30, 240–3, 250–1, 261–3
  business power theories 280
  capital requirements 86
  cooperative financial power 55
  political economy of finance 285
European People's Party (EPP) 243–4, 267–9
European Supervisory Agencies (ESAs) 56, 106
European Systemic Risk Board (ESRB) 103t, 250, 255
  General Board 106
European Union 1, 7–9, 14–17, 19, 23, 26–7, 30, 240–73, 274–6, 289
  bank supervision reinforcement 104
  business power theories 280, 281–2
  capital requirements 84–8, 250, 268, 270
  comparative financial power approach 63
  comparative political economy (CPE) 34
  consultation process and draft regulation 248–53
  cooperative financial power 55–6, 253–62
  credit rating agencies (CRAs) 81
  fiscal cost of public support to financial sector 15f

foreign banks and foreign subsidiaries 252
  and France 212
  and Germany 183
  international political economy (IPE) 32, 33
  legislative politics of structural reform 262–82
  liquidity rules 92, 93, 94
  minimum capital standards 246
  political economy of finance 283, 284–6
  pro-structural reform coalition 260–2
  resolution rules 96–8
  supranational politics and European Parliament 265–72
  TBTF banks 65, 67, 69, 107
  US banks 252
  venue shifting: Liikanen Group 242–8
executive power 7
existing scholarship, limits of 3–8

Fahrenschon, G. 1880
failed or stalled reform 8
Fannie May (USA) 110
FB 84
Feber, M. 176
Federal Association of German Cooperative Banks (BVR) 179
Federal Association of German Public Sector Banks (VÖB) 179
Federal Deposit Insurance Act 1950 (FDIC) (USA) 95–6
Federal Deposit Insurance Corporation (FDIC) (USA) 71t, 85, 99, 104, 106, 121, 131, 135, 137
Federal Financial Supervisory Authority (BaFin) (Germany) 78t, 82, 105, 184
  Interpretive Guidance of the Bank Separation Law 173–4
Federal Housing Finance Agency (FHFA) (USA) 106
Federal Reserve (USA) 111–15, 119, 122, 125, 127, 130–1, 133, 136, 139
  comparative financial power approach 63
  TBTF banks 85, 91, 95–6, 99, 101, 103t, 104–5, 106
Federation of German Consumer Organizations 189
Federation of German Industries (BDI) 180
Federation of Small Business (FSB) (UK) 153
Federation of Trade Unions (DGB) (Germany) 189
Fernandez, R. 201
Fidelity (USA) 128, 152
Fillon, F. 202, 212
final law (2013) (France) 194, 198, 209
finance capital unity thesis 42

350 INDEX

finance committees
   France 192, 194, 200–1, 204–6, 208, 210–12
   Germany 170, 182, 184–9
Finance Market law (Germany) 92, 102
'finance pour tous, La' 208
Finance Watch 23
   European Union 241, 260–1, 265, 269, 273
   France 194, 195–6, 203–4, 207, 209
Financial Accounting Standards Board (USA) 102
Financial CHOICE Act (2017) (USA) 109, 136–8
Financial Conduct Authority (FCA) (United Kingdom) 104, 106
Financial Crisis Inquiry Commission (USA) 124
Financial Crisis Responsibility Fee (USA) 73t, 114
financial interest group literature 18
financial interest lobbying 19–20, 27, 30, 31, 41–4, 60–1, 61t, 290
   business power theories 282
   competitive financial power 46–7, 48, 49
   cooperative financial power 55–6
   European Union 253, 254, 260–2
   France 192, 198
   Germany 171, 178–9, 180
   international political economy (IPE) 33
   Netherlands 231, 233, 238
   no reform 62
   political economy of finance 282–6
   regulatory reform typologies 288
   United Kingdom 143, 150–1, 156, 158–9, 161, 164, 165, 167, 169
   United States 108, 115–17, 118, 122, 123, 132, 133
Financial Market Authority (AFM) 225
financial market law (2009) (Germany) 105
Financial Policy Committee (FPC) (UK) 106, 156, 161, 165, 167
financial power 283–4, 285
   see also comparative financial power; competitive financial power; cooperative financial power
Financial Services Authority (FSA) (UK) 90, 101, 104, 144, 150, 154
Financial Services (Banking Reform) Act (UK) 4t
Financial Services Global Competitiveness Group 50
Financial Services Roundtable (FSR) (USA) 47, 116
Financial Stability Board (FSB) (UK) 82, 86, 97, 105, 168, 186

Financial Stability Oversight Council (FSOC) (USA) 91, 101, 103t, 105–7, 111–13, 125, 129–31, 134, 136
Financial System Inquiry Commission *see* De Wit Commission
Financial Transactions Tax (FTT) 73t, 76, 204, 267
financial unity 18, 27, 31, 43, 44
Fine, C. 119–21
first-mover advantage 7, 32, 108, 276
fiscal cost of public support 15f
Fisher, R. 134
Fitch 81
Flint, D. 165
Flosbach, K.P. 178
Force Ouvrière (FO) (France) 208
Fortis Bank (Netherlands) 70, 71t, 215, 221, 223
fragmentation 46, 48–9, 98, 281, 283–7
   European Union 241
   France 191
   United States 108, 115, 116, 126, 128, 131
France 1–3, 4–5t, 6–10, 13–17, 19, 23, 26, 29, 140, 171, 191–214, 216, 275–8
   bankers and bureaucrats 198–201
   bank financial liabilities held for trading 95t
   bank funding gap 9t
   bank governance and transparency 100t, 101, 102
   banking system assets 13t
   banking system concentration 14t
   bank leverage 87t
   bank supervision reinforcement 102, 103t, 104, 105–6
   business power theories 279–80, 282
   capital requirements 86, 88–9, 212
   comparative financial power approach 63
   comparative political economy (CPE) 34, 35, 36
   consultation process and draft regulation 252–3
   draft law, limited parliamentary control over 204–7
   and European Union 241–2, 272–3
   financial inspectorate 198–9
   fiscal cost of public support to financial sector 15f
   government financial support 70, 71t, 72
   grandes écoles 53–4
   grands corps 54
   institutional channels 192
   institutional venues 201
   interest representation 45
   law of 1945 193
   law of 1984 193

law of 2013 195
Law on the Separation and Regulation of Banking Activities 4t
legislative politics 262-4, 270-2
liquid assets 93t
liquidity rules 91-2, 93
National Assembly 192
  finance committee 194, 200-1, 204, 205-8, 210, 211, 212-13
political economy of finance 283, 284
politicization of structural reform 175
pro-structural reform coalition, weak 207-12
  civil society, disparate forces in 207-9
  political champions of symbolic reform 209-12
regulatory measures 78-80t, 288
remuneration practices 82-3
revenue-raising regulation and fiscal policy 72, 73-4t, 75
Senate 192
  finance committee 200, 204, 205-7, 211, 212-13
share of borrowing in total bank funding 94t
share of deposits in total funding 94t
structural reform, weak 193-6
tier-1 capital 86t
Treasury 198-200, 212
venue shifting, absence of and conflict contraction 201-7
France Stratégie 209
Frank, B. 121, 123, 125, 128
Freddie Mac (USA) 110
Free Democratic Party (FDP) (Germany) 17, 105, 175, 188
Free Democratic Party (FPD) (Germany) 178
French Banking Federation (FBF) 54, 196, 198, 200, 203, 206, 259, 268
Banking Reform: Myth or Reality 197
Front de gauche 212
future research 288-91

Gabbard, T. 135
Gabriel, S. 176
Gambke, T. 187
Ganderson, J. 7, 16, 226
Geithner, T. 16, 84, 110, 114, 120, 126, 219
General Confederation of Labour (CGT) (France) 208
Gensler, G. 123, 134
Germany 1-3, 4-5t, 6-8, 10, 13-17, 19, 22-3, 26, 170-90, 216, 275-8
  Allfinanz approach 51
  bank financial liabilities held for trading 95t
  bank funding gap 9t

bank governance and transparency 99, 100t, 102
banking associations 52
banking system assets 13t
banking system concentration 14t
bank leverage 87t
bank supervision reinforcement 102, 103t, 105
business power theories 279-80, 282
capital requirements 86, 88-9, 185
comparative financial power approach 63
comparative political economy (CPE) 34, 35, 36-7
consultation process and draft regulation 252-3
and European Union 241-2, 272-3
fiscal cost of public support to financial sector 15f
government financial support 70, 71t, 72
Grand Coalition government 105
interest representation 45
legislative politics 262-4, 270-2
liquid assets 93t
local and regional banks 51
patient capital 51
political economy of finance 283, 284, 285
politicization of structural reform 175-8
regional public law *Landesbanken* 51
regulatory measures 78-80t, 288
remuneration practices 82-3
revenue-raising regulation and fiscal policy 72, 73-4t, 75-6
sectoral associations 52
share of borrowing in total bank funding 94t
share of deposits in total funding 94t
stabilization fund 71t
structural reform, weak 172-8
tier-1 capital 86t
trade associations 51
Giancarlo, C. 137
Giegold, S. 266
Giraud, G. 206
Giraud, P.-N. 208
Glass-Steagall Act 1933 (USA) 112, 119, 135, 136-7, 155, 164, 258
global systemically important banks/institutions (G-SIBs/G-SIFIs) 33, 35, 80t, 88, 95, 158, 167, 259, 277, 285
Goldman Sachs 83, 101, 110, 114, 115, 117-18, 120, 126, 133
Goulard, S. 269
governance, reinforcing 99-102, 100t
Government Accountability Office (GAO) (USA) 130

government committees 29, 192
government financial support 27, 69, 70–2, 71t
Goyens, M. 245, 261–2
Green-Left (GroenLinks) Party (Netherlands) 224, 228
Green Party 24, 30
Green Party (EELV) (France) 205
Green Party (EU) 266–7, 269, 271, 273
Green Party (Germany) 175, 183, 186–7, 189, 190
Gröhne, H. 177

Hacker, J.S. 38, 281
Haldane, A. 155, 156
Halifax Bank of Scotland (HBOS) 72, 90, 145, 150
Hardie, I. 35
Hausbank (Germany) 51
hedge fund transactions 4t, 33, 66
  European Union 247, 248, 251, 253, 268
  France 196
  Germany 174
  United States 109, 112–13, 119, 128, 135, 139
Hellwig, M. 181
Hensarling, J. 129, 136
Hickel, R. 188
high-frequency trading 4t, 23, 173, 177–8, 195
High-Level Expert Group *see* Liikanen Group
high-quality liquid assets (HQLAs) 91
high-risk investment banking 68–9
Hill, Lord J. 263, 266–7
Hindmoor, A. 7, 38
Hines, J. 129
Hoenig, T. 134, 137
Hökmark draft report 268–9, 271
Hökmark, G. 267–9
Hollande, F. 2, 17, 23, 29, 35, 175–6, 191–2, 194, 196, 200, 202, 205, 209–11, 213, 216, 243, 275
Holland Financial Group 53
House Financial Services Committee (USA) 125, 129
House of Lords European Union Committee (UK) 263–4
HSBC (UK) 24, 36, 134, 152–3, 159–60, 165–6
Huber, J. 188
hybrid capital 79t, 84–5, 88
Hypo Real Estate (HRE) (Germany) 71t, 183, 188

IBM 117
Icesave (Iceland) 223–4
IKB 105

Independent Commission on Banking (ICB) (UK) 2, 20, 28, 63, 88, 142–3, 146–53, 155, 158–63, 167–9, 243, 275, 288
  Final Report (2011) (UK) 151, 156, 157
  'ICB Issues' Paper (2010) 150
  Interim Report (2011) (UK) 150, 155, 156
Independent Community Bankers of America (ICBA) 48, 120–2, 138
industry associations 22, 42, 47–8, 53, 120, 161, 286
ING (Netherlands) 10, 71t, 215, 222, 223, 230, 231–2, 233, 237, 239
Institute of Directors (UK) 49, 153
Institute of International Bankers 139
institutional factors 17, 19, 27, 31, 34, 39, 41, 286
instrumental power 38–9, 278–9, 285
insurance companies 181, 289
insured depositary institutions (IDIs) (USA) 99
interest intermediation 19, 44–5, 54–5, 283–4, 290–1
interest rate and foreign currency swaps 4t, 128
interest representation, modes of 31, 44–56
  competitive financial power 46–50
  cooperative financial power 50–6
International Accounting Standards Board 102
International Centre for Financial Regulation (ICFR) 50
International Financial Services London 50
International Institute of Finance (IIF) 116
International Monetary Fund (IMF) 73t, 75, 87, 102
international political economy (IPE) 7, 30, 31, 32–4, 36, 276, 285
International Regulatory Strategy Group (IRSG) 50
International Swaps and Derivatives Association (ISDA) (USA) 49, 116, 133
Intervention Act (Netherlands) 226, 229, 230, 237
Investec 152
investment banking 2, 9, 25, 274, 275
  capital requirements 85, 87
  comparative political economy (CPE) 35
  competitive financial power 47, 50
  European Union 247, 266
  France 193, 197, 203, 204
  Germany 172, 176–7, 180
  government financial support 70
  Netherlands 220, 228, 230, 232, 233
  obligatory resolution plans 99
  revenue-raising regulation and fiscal policy 75, 77
  TBTF banks 67, 69
  United Kingdom 149, 150, 152, 155, 157, 158
  United States 112, 117, 118, 119, 132, 133, 135

IOSCO 81
Issing Commission (Germany) 182-3
Issing, O. 182
issuance procedure 76
Italy 97

Jacobs, B. 221
Jager, J.C. de 229-30, 234, 236-7
Jager, K.-J. de 218
Jahn, D. 54
Jain, A. 178, 189
Jenkins, R. 156, 167
Jérôme Kerviel/Société Générale 101
Johnson, S. 113, 122, 123
Jones, W. 135
JP Morgan 101, 115, 117-18, 134
  Bear Stearns takeover 72, 110

Kapoor, S. 250
Kapstein, E. 37
Kaptur, M. 135
Kastner, L. 48
Kaufman, T. 126
Kaupthing (Iceland) 145
Keller, E. 40
Kemmer, M. 179
Kennedy, E. 114
King, A. 135
King, M. 16, 75, 154, 155, 156, 164, 185, 187, 201
Knot, K. 230, 234
König, E. 185-6
KPMG 25
Krahnen, J.P. 183, 188, 245
Kwak, J. 123

Labour Party (PvdA) (Netherlands) 17, 215, 218, 220, 224, 228
Labour Party (UK) 17, 144, 145-6, 154
  White Paper (2009) 104
La Caixa (Spain) 258
Lacharet, A. 208
Lagarde, C. 212
Lagarde Report 99, 100t
Lallois, L. 245
Lamberts, P. 266-7, 269-70
Lamfalussy committees 56
Landesbanken (Germany) 67, 88, 102, 172, 181, 182, 184
Landsbanki (Iceland) 145
Landsdowne 152
Larosière, J. de 87, 203, 214
Lawson, Lord N. 163
Legal and General 152
legislative phase 124, 132, 242, 280

legislative politics of the EU 262-72
  supranational politics and the EU
    Parliament 265-72
legitimacy coalitions 48
Lehman Brothers 95, 109-10
Lellouche, P. 200-1
Lepetit, J.-F. 203
Leroy, P.-H. 198
leverage ratio 5t, 80t, 84-5, 86, 87t, 88-9, 102
  Netherlands 87t, 226
  United Kingdom 87t, 155, 158, 161, 165, 167
  United States 167
levies 75-6
Levin, C. 123, 124, 126, 127
Liberal Democrats (D66) (Netherlands) 228, 234
Liberal Democrats (United Kingdom) 146, 154, 162
liberalization 33, 45, 47, 49, 53, 54, 284
liberal market capitalism 7
Liberals (EU) 169
Libor rate-rigging scandal 134, 160, 161-2, 189, 207, 222
light touch regulatory regime 50, 66-7, 104, 142, 144
Liikanen, E. 3, 23, 30, 63, 206, 214, 240, 243, 244, 253, 276
Liikanen Group/Liikanen Report 2, 4t, 6, 22-4, 30, 63, 130, 273, 275-6
  business power theories 280
  comparative political economy (CPE) 35
  cooperative financial power 255-6, 257-8, 259, 260-2
  European Union 240-2, 249-55
  France 194, 196, 201, 203, 213-14
  Germany 171-7, 179, 185-90
  legislative politics 263-6, 269, 271-2
  Netherlands 215-16, 226, 229, 232, 235-7
  political economy of finance 284
  United Kingdom 158
Lincoln Amendment (USA) 128
Lincoln, B. 127
Lindblom, C.E. 37
Liquidity Coverage Ratio (LCR) 79t, 86, 90-2
liquidity injections 2, 275
liquidity requirements 14-16, 24-6, 28, 33, 35, 79t, 107
  United Kingdom 145, 146
  United States 136, 138
liquidity reserves 9, 92, 144, 173
liquidity rules 85, 89-95
living wills/resolution plans 80t, 98, 99, 138, 229
Lloyds Bank 145, 148, 152-3, 159-61, 165-6

Lloyds Bank (*Continued*)
  HBOS merger 70, 71*t*, 151
Lloyds TSB 72, 102
'London Whale' trading scandal 118, 134

Maas, C. 29, 217
Maas Commission 21, 63, 99, 218, 224, 225, 227, 234–5, 288
Macartney, H. 35, 99
McCain, J. 111, 135
McConnell, M. 126
Macron, E. 199
macroprudential supervision 103*t*
macroprudential tools 146
majoritarian systems 7, 16–17
market-based banking 2, 9, 35, 51, 172, 275, 277
market-making activities 34
  European Union 247, 253, 254, 260, 261
  France 204
  Germany 173, 175
  United Kingdom 144, 158
  United States 130, 139
market power 7, 32, 276
market shaping approach 34
mark to market accounting 42, 100*t*, 102
Mascolo, G. 180
MassMutual (USA) 128
Massoc, E. 7, 211
Mazzucchelli, M. 245
MEDEF (France) 54, 197, 203
Meister, M. 178
Merkel, A. 2, 17, 28, 171, 176, 178, 182, 183, 275
Merkley, J. 123, 127
Merkley-Levin Amendment (USA) 126, 128
MFGlobal 134
microprudential supervision 103*t*
Miliband, E. 154
minimum requirements for own funds and eligible liabilities (MREL) 98
'Minimum requirements for risk management' 92
Ministry of Finance
  France 198, 202, 210, 214, 285
  Germany 78*t*, 181–2
  Netherlands 53, 225–6, 233–4
Mnuchin, S. 137
Moerland, P. 232
Montalbano, G. 261
Monte Paschi di Siena 97
Moody's Investors Services 81
moral hazard 1, 25, 75, 112, 219, 274
Morgan Stanley 110, 115, 117–18, 133
Morin, F. 208–9
Moscovici, P. 194, 196, 201, 206, 209–10, 212

Musca, X. 199
mutual banks (France) 54

Namias, N. 203
narrow banking 148, 155–6
Nathan 214
national bank associations 23, 30
National Bank of Belgium 190
national bank champions 1, 9, 23, 35
  France 54, 193, 201, 210, 213
  Germany 52, 181
  Netherlands 233
National Credit Union Administration Board (NCUA) agenda setting 106
Nationwide 151, 153, 161
Natixis (France) 203
neo-corporatism 19, 45–6, 50, 51–2, 283–4, 286, 290
Netherlands 1–3, 6–9, 13–17, 19, 21, 23, 26, 29–30, 53, 215–39, 275–8
  advisory councils 53
  bank financial liabilities held for trading 95*t*
  bank funding gap 9*t*
  bank governance and transparency 100*t*, 102
  Banking Code 83, 99, 100*t*
  banking system assets 13*t*
  banking system concentration 14*t*
  bank supervision reinforcement 102, 103*t*, 105
  business power theories 279–82
  business and trade unions 52
  capital requirements 86, 88–9, 218, 224–5, 230, 233
  central bank 53
  comparative financial power approach 63
  comparative political economy (CPE) 36
  and European Union 241, 272–3
  fiscal cost of public support to financial sector 15*f*
  government financial support 71*t*
  House of Representatives 223, 226
  industry associations 53
  international political economy (IPE) 33
  Intervention Act (2012) 80*t*, 99, 105
  leverage ratio 87*t*, 226
  liquid assets 93*t*
  liquidity rules 91–2, 93, 94
  mandatory deposit insurance 218
  political economy of finance 283, 284, 285
  regulatory measures 78–80*t*
  regulatory reform typologies 287–8
  revenue-raising regulation and fiscal policy 72, 73–4*t*, 75–6
  share of borrowing in total bank funding 94*t*

share of deposits in total funding 94t
tier-1 capital 86t
Treasury 219
venue shifting 213, 216, 238
venue shifting: De Wit Commission 222–31
    politics of structural reform 225–31
venue shifting: Maas Commission 217–22
    conflict expansion 218–22
venue shifting: Wijffels Commission 235–7
Net Stable Funding Ratio (NSFR) 79t, 86, 90–2, 93, 94, 107
Neuville, C. 206
New Deal 46, 135
New Democrat Coalition (USA) 127
New Labour (United Kingdom) 144
Nijdam, C. 195, 214, 269
NordLB 97
no reform 20–1, 25, 27, 29–30, 31, 61, 62, 287
Northern Rock (UK) 71t, 144, 150
Noyer, C. 185, 200–1, 263

Obama, B. 17, 63, 108–9, 219, 275, 280, 288
    bank regulation reinforcement, limited and varied 81, 83–4
    bank supervision, reinforcing 104–6
    competitive financial power 115–17, 119–20, 122–4
    Economic Recovery Advisory Board 112
    Financial Accounting Standards Board 102
    financial reform bill 2
    implementation obstacles 129–30
    institutional venues 125–6
    market-based banking 35–6
    politics of structural reform 111, 113–14
    revenue-raising regulation and fiscal policy 72, 73t, 74t, 75
    Volcker Rule 26, 28, 136, 140
Obama, B. proprietary trading 21–2
Occupy movement (France) 208
Occupy the SEC (USA) 134
off-balance-sheet activities 80t, 91
Office of the Comptroller of the Currency (OCC) (USA) 85, 104, 106, 131, 139
Office of Thrift Supervision (OTS) (USA) 104, 131
Orderly Liquidation Authority (OLA) (USA) 96
Organization for Economic Cooperation and Development (OECD) 199
Osborne, G. 146, 151, 155, 167
Otting, J. 137
Oudéa, F. 195
'Our Money' (Netherlands) 238
over-the counter derivatives (OTCDs) 112
overview of structural reforms 4–5t

pantouflage (France) 23, 54
Papiasse, A. 195
Parliamentary Commission on Banking Standards (PCBS) (UK) 20, 28, 63, 143, 162–8, 169
parliamentary committees 22, 23, 29, 184, 201, 204–5, 263, 265
Party for Freedom (PVV) (Netherlands) 227
Paulson, H. 110
'peak' business associations 42, 45, 49, 50, 51
Pébereau, M. 199
Pelosi, N. 136
People's Party for Freedom and Democracy (VVD) (Netherlands) 17, 218, 224, 226–7, 229, 234
Pew Memorial Trust 122
Pfandbriefe (Germany) 92, 94
Philliponat, T. 188–9, 206, 209, 260
Pierson, P. 38, 281
Pisani-Ferry, J. 209
Plasterk, R. 228
Plihon, D. 207
pluralism 19, 45–6, 48, 283, 286–7, 290
    elite 19, 56, 283
Poβ, J. 187
polarization 130, 265, 269, 282
Polder model of tripartite cooperation (Netherlands) 52, 227
Political Action Committees (PACs) 47
political economy of financial regulation 31–41, 282–7
    business power theories 37–41
    see also comparative political economy (CPE); international political economy (IPE)
political economy scholarship, limits of 276–8
political and institutional structures 16–17
political partisanship 17
political and party systems 8
political power 39
political salience 18, 39–41, 43, 44, 189, 193, 210, 237, 254, 261, 280–3
politicization 22, 282, 288
    European Union 241, 262, 265
    France 192, 201, 211
    Germany 171, 185, 188, 190
    Netherlands 220
    United States 109, 128, 133, 191
politics of banking reform 16–17, 24–5
Pompidou, G. 199
Post-bank (Netherlands) 239
Postcheque and Giro Service (PCGD) (Netherlands) 239
Powell, D. 137
power sharing 7

Price Waterhouse Coopers (PwC) 'Project
    Oak' 150, 260
private banks 51, 54, 161, 228
private equity funds (United States) 109, 119,
    128, 139
Project Merlin (UK) 71t
proprietary trading restrictions 2, 22, 23, 29,
    275, 276
  European Union 240, 247, 250-1, 253, 255,
    258, 261, 264, 266-7, 269-71
  France 195
  Germany 175, 177, 186-8, 190
  Netherlands 221, 228, 236
  United Kingdom 146, 148, 150, 158
  United States 109, 112-14, 116-19, 122,
    124-6, 131, 133, 135-40
pro-reform factions 7
Prudential Regulation Authority (PRA)
    (UK) 104, 165-7
Prudential Regulation Committee (PRC)
    (UK) 101
Public Citizen (USA) 130
Public Interest Research Group (PIRG)
    (USA) 122, 130
public law cooperative and savings banks
    (Germany) 51, 170, 172, 178-81, 256

Quarles, R. 137

Rabobank (Netherlands) 134, 219, 222, 230,
    231-2
Radical Party of the Left (PRG) (France) 205
recovery plans *see* resolution and recovery plans
Recovery and Resolution Directive (EU) 182
Reed, J. 119, 122
'Regaining Trust: A New Approach to Taming
    the Financial Markets' (Germany) 176-7
regional banks 22, 51, 102, 278
Regling, K. 182
regulatory agencies 22, 38, 41, 47, 55, 91, 107,
    109, 111, 113, 128-35, 141
regulatory arbitrage 7, 26
regulatory capacity 7, 32, 276
regulatory capture 59
regulatory convergence 7, 26
regulatory outcomes 3, 8, 13, 18, 20-1, 37, 41,
    44, 276, 283, 285, 287, 290-1
Regulatory Requirements for Compensation
    Systems in Financial Institutions
    Regulation (Germany) 82
regulatory standards 34, 112
Reinke, R. 39, 279
remuneration practices, limited restrictions
    of 82-4

remuneration rules 78t
Républicains (France) 205
Republicans (USA) 22, 28, 96, 108-9, 111, 113,
    126, 129, 136-8, 140-1, 288
resolution and recovery plans 14-16, 24-6, 33,
    76, 274, 289
  European Union 240, 246, 250, 252, 255, 261,
    273
  France 196, 204
  Germany 98, 174
  Netherlands 230-1, 237
  obligatory 98-9
  United Kingdom 146
resolution rules 95-8
retail banking 2, 28, 88, 97, 275, 276, 286
  European Union 240, 247-8, 249, 251, 255
  Germany 176-7, 179
  Netherlands 220, 228, 229-30, 232, 238
  TBTF banks 68, 69, 107
  United Kingdom 144, 149, 150, 153, 155,
    156-7, 165-6
revenue-raising regulation and fiscal policy 27,
    72-7, 73-4t
'revolving' doors' 41, 53, 54
Rijkspostpaarbank (RPS) (Netherlands) 239
ringfencing 2-3, 7, 14, 21, 23-5, 28-30, 275-7
  business power theories 279, 282
  comparative political economy (CPE) 35
  European Union 240-2, 246-7, 251-8, 261-5,
    267, 269, 271-2
  France 192, 195-8, 201, 204, 206, 208, 214
  Germany 170, 172-7, 184, 187, 190
  Netherlands 215-17, 219-20, 222, 225,
    228-9, 232-3, 234-7
  political economy of finance 284, 286
  TBTF banks 65, 67
  United Kingdom 137, 148-53, 156-7, 160-8
  United States 135, 142-3
risk-taking and speculative activities 1, 2
risk-weighted assets (RWAs) (UK) 5t, 166, 168
Rocholl, J. 181
Rolls-Royce 161
Romney, M. 129
Roosevelt Institute 122
Rösler, P. 177, 184
Roubini, N. 113
Royal Bank of Scotland (RBS) 36, 70, 134, 145,
    148, 152, 159-60, 165-6
Rubin, R. 126
Ryan, P. 136
Ryan, T. 135

S&P Global Ratings 81
Sachsen Landesbank 105

SAFE Banking Amendment (USA) 126
Samenwekended Nederlandse Spaarbanken (SNS) 215
Sands, P. 161
Santander 36, 97, 101, 145, 153, 159–60, 165–6
Sapin, M. 194
Sarbanes-Oxley Act (USA) 67
Sarkozy, N. 17, 82, 194, 201, 212
savings banks 9, 22, 88, 278
  European Union 251, 254, 255–9
  France 194, 203
  Germany 52, 179–80
  Netherlands 221
  see also public law cooperative and savings banks (Germany)
Savings Banks Finance Group (Germany) 256
Savings Banks and Giro Association (DSGV) (Germany) 179
savings and loans bank (Netherlands) 239
Savings and Loans crisis (USA) 197
Schattschneider, E.E. 57
Schäuble, W. 171, 176–8, 186
Scheltema, M. 222
Schick, G. 187–8
Schmittmann, J.P. 222
Schoenmaker, D. 236
Scholz, O. 181
Schroders 152
Schwartz, H. 69
Scialmom, L. 206–7
Scientific Council for Government Policy (WRR) (Netherlands) 238–9
Seabrooke, L. 69
Securities and Exchange Commission (SEC) (USA) 78*t*, 104, 106, 112, 126, 131, 133–4
  Office of Credit Ratings 81
  White Paper 112–13
Securities Industry and Financial Markets Association (SIFMA) (USA) 47, 116, 118, 119, 133, 139
securitization 9, 35, 65, 69, 80*t*, 81, 89, 112, 139, 175, 247
Separation Proposal (EU) 246
Sergeant, C. 245–6
shadow banking sector 136, 158, 186, 253
Shell 133
short-term wholesale market funding 35, 68–70, 72, 89–94, 99, 275, 277
  European Union 249
  Netherlands 233
  United Kingdom 144
Sieling, C. 187
Single Point of Entry (SPOE) method 96

Single Resolution Board (SRB) 97
Single Resolution Fund (SRF) 77
Single Resolution Mechanism Regulation (SRMR) 15, 77, 96
Single Resolution Mechanism (SRM) 56, 250
Single Supervisory Mechanism (SSM) 104, 226, 250, 255, 273
small and medium-sized enterprises (SMEs) 22, 29
  Germany 51, 170, 178, 180, 181
  United Kingdom 153, 157, 166
SNS Bank (Netherlands) 71*t*, 223
SNS Reaal (Netherlands) 222, 230
Social Democratic Party (SPD) (Germany) 2, 22, 28, 171, 175–6, 177–8, 186–7, 190, 275, 276, 279
Social and Economic Council (SER) (Netherlands) 52
Socialist Party (EU) 266–7, 269, 271, 273
Socialist Party (France) 23, 29, 191–5, 196, 198, 200, 201–2, 204–7, 209–11, 213, 279
Socialist Party (SP) (Netherlands) 220, 228
Société Générale 134, 193, 196
  Libor rate scandal 207
Society of Financial Analysts (AFG) (France) 196
Söder, M. 177
sovereign-bank debt loop 97
specialist banks 184
specialist committees 63, 216, 227, 287
Spottiswoode, C. 147
stabilization fund 71*t*, 72, 75
Standard Chartered (UK) 24, 102, 134, 145, 151, 152, 160–1
Standard Life (UK) 152
State Street (USA) 128
state subsidy 1, 148
statism 19, 45–6, 50, 54, 283–4, 286, 290
Steinbrück, P. 172, 175–80, 184, 186, 189–90, 276
Stiefmueller, C. 273
Stiglitz, J. 113
stress tests 27, 92, 100*t*, 101–2, 104, 137–9, 245
structural power 38–9, 159, 246, 278–9
structural separation 4*t*, 6, 16, 23–5, 28, 34–7, 275, 277–8
  EU 266, 270
  Germany 180
  United Kingdom 146, 148, 150, 154, 157, 164
structured credit products 112
subprime mortgage market 108, 140
Summers, L. 114, 126
Sustainable Finance Lab (Netherlands) 220, 232
Sweden 87

358 INDEX

Swoboda, H. 266
symbolic reform 22–4, 29, 31, 61*t*, 62, 287
  France 192, 196, 198, 201, 207, 209, 213
  Germany 172, 185–9, 190
systemically important financial institutions/banks (SIFIs/SIBs) 13, 14*t*, 80*t*, 85, 95, 97–9, 105, 277
  European Union 253
  France 14*t*
  Germany 14*t*, 174, 185
  Netherlands 14*t*, 215
  United Kingdom 14*t*, 168
  United States 14*t*, 109, 112–13, 121, 130, 134–7
  see also global systemically important banks/institutions (G-SIBs/G-SIFIs)
systemic financial risk 144, 146
systemic risk buffers 168, 185
Systemic Risk Council (USA) 122, 134

tailoring rule 91, 96
Taylor, M. 147, 163, 167
Taylor Report 80*t*
ter Haar, B. 223
Thatcher, M. 49
TheCityUK 161
Thépot, M. 209
Thiemann, M. 253
tier-1 capital 85, 86*t*, 88, 107, 128, 158, 167
  see also Common Equity Tier 1 (CET1) capital
Timmermans, F. 259, 263, 266
Tobin tax 72, 73*t*, 75
too big to fail (TBTF) banks 1–3, 10, 14, 16, 18, 21, 23–8, 30, 64, 65–107, 274, 276
  bank resolution rules 95–8
  bank supervision 102–7, 103*t*
  business power theories 281–2
  capital requirements 84–9
  comparative political economy (CPE) 37
  continued dominance 67–70
  credit rating agencies (CRAs) 81–2
  European Union 65, 67, 69, 107, 247, 250, 257, 261–2, 264–5, 268–70
  financial interest lobbying 43–4
  France 66–7, 69, 107, 199, 201, 212–13
  Germany 66–9, 107, 170, 172, 176, 183, 185, 187, 189
  governance and transparency 99–102, 100*t*
  government financial support 70–2, 71*t*
  high risk investment banking 68–70
  interest group lobbying 60
  liquidity rules and stable bank funding 89–95
  Netherlands 66, 67, 69, 107, 216–17, 219, 222, 228–9, 235, 237

political economy of finance 283, 284, 285–6
  regulatory measures 77–99, 78–80*t*
  regulatory reform typologies 288
  remuneration practices 82–4
  resolution planning 98–9
  revenue-raising regulation and fiscal policy 72–7, 73–4*t*
  United Kingdom 66–9, 107, 143, 146–7, 150, 153–5, 157, 167, 169
  United States 65–6, 68–9, 107–8, 112–14, 119, 121–2, 126, 135–6
Total Loss Absorbency Capacity (TLAC) 80*t*
trade associations 45–6, 49–51, 280, 286, 289
  EU 254
  Germany 180
  United Kingdom 150, 153, 160–1
  United States 118, 138
trade unions 51–2, 189, 208
trading account 131
trading assets 2, 9, 35, 196, 246–7, 275
transactions tax 72, 75
  see also Financial Transactions Tax (FTT)
transparency 27, 41, 78*t*, 81, 89, 99–102, 100*t*, 112, 203–4, 226
Tricornot, A. de 209
Triodos Bank (Netherlands) 221
Troost, A. 188
Troubled Asset Relief Program (TARP) (USA) 70, 83–4, 110, 120
Trumbull, G. 48, 55
Trump, D. 22, 28, 85, 96, 109, 135–40, 141
Tucker, Sir P. 156
Tuma, Z. 246
Turnbull, Lord A. 163
Turner, Lord A. 16, 154, 155
Turner Review 104
Tyrie, A. 162–4, 167

UBS 134
UDI (France) 211–12
UK Finance 257
UK Financial Investments (UKFI) 145, 151–2
Union pour un mouvement populaire (UMP) (France) 193, 202, 205, 211–12
unit banks 47
United Kingdom 1–2, 4–5*t*, 6–10, 19–20, 25–6, 28, 140, 142–69, 275–6, 278
  bank funding gap 9*t*
  bank governance and transparency 100*t*, 101–2
  banking crisis 143–6
  banking system assets 13*t*
  banking system concentration 14*t*

INDEX 359

bank supervision reinforcement 102, 103*t*, 106
Bank-Treasury-City nexus 48
Brexit 83, 168
business power theories 38, 39, 279–82
capital requirements 86–9, 142, 146, 148, 151, 155, 167, 168
case selection and alternative explanations 13–17
City of London 48–50, 143–4, 147, 151, 153, 162, 167
comparative financial power approach 63
comparative political economy (CPE) 34, 35, 36
consultation process and draft regulation 252–3
and EU 246, 272–3
fiscal cost of public support to financial sector 15*f*
government financial support 70, 71*t*, 72
interest representation 45
international political economy (IPE) 32, 33
legislative politics 262–3, 271–2
leverage ratio 87*t*, 155, 158, 161, 165, 167
liquid assets 93*t*
liquidity rules 90–1, 93, 94
political economy of finance 283, 284, 285–6, 287
pro-banking reform coalition 154–7
regulatory measures 77, 78–80*t*
regulatory reform typologies 287–8
remuneration practices 82–3
revenue-raising regulation and fiscal policy 72, 73–4*t*, 75–6
share of borrowing in total bank funding 94*t*
share of deposits in total funding 94*t*
tier-1 capital 86*t*, 158, 167
Treasury 63, 106, 150, 151, 156, 158–62, 165–6, 262
venue shifting 143, 169, 191
venue shifting: Independent Commission on Banking (ICB) 146–50
venue shifting: Parliamentary Commission on Banking Standards (PCBS) 162–8
effective implementation 165–8
voluntary asset protection programme 71*t*
United States 1–3, 4–5*t*, 6–10, 13–15, 17, 19, 25, 28, 108–41, 272, 275, 289
bank funding gap 9*t*
bank governance and transparency 99, 100*t*
banking crisis 109–15
banking system assets 13*t*
banking system concentration 14*t*

bank leverage 87*t*
banks operating in European Union 252
bank supervision reinforcement 103*t*, 106–7
business power theories 39, 279–80, 282
capital requirements 84–9, 114, 136, 138
Chamber of Commerce 47, 122, 132
Center for Capital Markets Competitiveness 116–17
comparative financial power approach 63
comparative political economy (CPE) 34, 35, 36
Congress 288
congressional committee system 125
contested reform 21–2
equity warrants 70
fiscal cost of public support to financial sector 15*f*
golden parachute contracts 78*t*, 83–4
government financial support 71*t*
House of Representatives 72, 74*t*, 106
implementation obstacles 128–35
institutional venues 124–8
interest representation 45
international political economy (IPE) 32, 33
legislative politics 263
leverage ratio 167
liquid assets 93*t*
loan guarantees 110
obligatory resolution plans 98–9
political economy 276–8
political economy of finance 283, 284, 285–6, 287
politics of structural reform 111–15
regulatory measures 77, 78–80*t*
regulatory reform typologies 288
remuneration practices 82
revenue-raising regulation and fiscal policy 72, 73–4*t*, 76
Senate 72
Banking Committee 119, 125
Permanent Subcommittee on Investigations 124
share of borrowing in total bank funding 94*t*
share of deposits in total funding 94*t*
TBTF banks 65
think tanks 122
tier-1 capital 86*t*, 128
Treasury 70, 72, 96, 110–11, 125, 126, 130, 138
Office of Financial Research (OFR) 106
White Paper (2009) 121, 125
Wall Street 108, 133, 140, 201, 275, 288
banking crisis 110–11, 113

United States (*Continued*)
    comparative financial power approach 47–8
    competitive financial power 115–16, 118–20, 122
    implementation obstacles 129
    institutional venues 126–7
    Volcker Rule repeal 137–8
    Wall Street Reform and Consumer Protection Act 114
universal banking 1–2, 7, 9, 11–12*t*, 24, 87, 275, 277
    European Union 255, 268–9
    France 12*t*, 175, 193, 195–8, 200–1, 203–4, 208, 211, 243
    Germany 11*t*, 51, 170, 172, 174, 178–80, 188, 256, 259
    Netherlands 12*t*, 233
    resolution rules 98
    revenue-raising regulation and fiscal policy 77
    TBTF banks 107
    United Kingdom 11*t*, 144, 148, 150, 152–4, 157, 159
    United States 11*t*, 116, 119

van der Walle, E. 221
van Egmond, K. 220
Vanhevel, J. 246
van Keulen, S. 234
van Vliet, R. 228
Varieties of Capitalism (VoC) 277, 284
Varieties of Financial Capitalism (VoFC) 34–5
Vasey, R. 119
Veneto Banca 97
venue shifting 19–21, 23, 27–8, 30–1, 56–61, 63–4, 291
    business power theories 281
    durable reform 62
    European Union 241–8
    France 247
    Germany 247
    political economy of finance 286
    regulatory reform typologies 287
    TBTF banks 65
    United States 57
    see also ad hoc specialist groups; *and in particular under* Netherlands; United Kingdom
venue shifting, absence of
    France 193, 213
    Germany 172, 182–5
    United States 115, 124, 191

Vickers Commission (UK) 3, 28, 275–6
    competitive financial power 156
    and EU 243, 257, 263
    and Netherlands 229–30, 237
    Steinbrück proposals 177
    venue shifting 162–3, 165–6
Vickers, Sir J. 147, 149, 155, 158, 167–8, 188, 195, 210
Villeroy de Galau, F. 199
Vitter, D. 135
Volcker, P. 112–14, 117, 119, 122–3, 125, 127, 133, 164
Volcker Rule 2, 4*t*, 7, 22, 25–6, 28, 109, 141, 275
    banking crisis 113–14
    business power theories 280
    competitive financial power 115–19, 121
    and European Union 251, 257, 261, 263
    financial industry 132–5
    France 195
    Germany 188
    institutional venues 126–8
    Netherlands 219, 228, 229–30
    political economy of finance 286
    regulatory agencies 130–2
    repeal: Trump administration 135–40
    Republicans and Congress 129–30
Volker Wissing (Germany) 184
Voluntary Banking Code (Netherlands) 78*t*
von Bomhard, N. 181
von Weizsäcker, J. 269

Wagenknecht, S. 187–8
Walker J 153
Walker Review 99, 100*t*, 101
Walker, Sir D. 165
Wall Street Reform and Consumer Protection Act (USA) 128
Warren, E. 112, 123, 135, 136
Washington Mutual 110
Wassenaar agreement 52
Weidmann, J. 182–3, 185
Welby, J. 163, 167
Wellink, N. 223–4, 233
Wells Fargo-Wachovia takeover 72, 110
Wester, J. 221
Wheatley, M. 167
Which? – Future of Banking Commission 156
White, W. 183
Wijffels Commission 21, 30, 63, 215, 217, 238
    'Towards a Serviceable and Stable Banking Sector' 235–6
Wijffels, H. 220, 236–7, 238, 246

Wijffels Sustainable Finance Lab 221
Winters, B. 147
Wit, J. de 223
Wolf, M. 147
Woolley, J.T. 7, 25
World Economic Forum 159
World Economy, Ecology and Development (WEED) 189

World Savings Banks Institute - European Savings Banks Group 256
Wyman, O. 150

Yingling, E. 120
Young, K. 37

Zeigler, J.N. 7, 25
Zöllmer, M. 187